Lecture Notes in Computer Science

Lecture Notes in Computer Science

Vol. 23: Programming Methodology. 4th Informatik Symposium, IBM Germany Wildbad, September 25–27, 1974. Edited by C. E. Hackl. VI, 501 pages. 1975.

Vol. 24: Parallel Processing. Proceedings 1974. Edited by T. Feng. VI, 433 pages. 1975.

Vol. 25: Category Theory Applied to Computation and Control. Proceedings 1974. Edited by E. G. Manes. X, 245 pages. 1975.

Vol. 26: GI-4. Jahrestagung, Berlin, 9.–12. Oktober 1974. Herausgegeben im Auftrag der GI von D. Siefkes. IX, 748 Seiten. 1975.

Vol. 27: Optimization Techniques. IFIP Technical Conference. Novosibirsk, July 1–7, 1974. (Series: I.F.I.P. TC7 Optimization Conferences.) Edited by G. I. Marchuk. VIII, 507 pages. 1975.

Vol. 28: Mathematical Foundations of Computer Science. 3rd Symposium at Jadwisin near Warsaw, June 17–22, 1974. Edited by A. Blikle. VII, 484 pages. 1975.

Vol. 29: Interval Mathematics. Procedings 1975. Edited by K. Nickel. VI, 331 pages. 1975.

Vol. 30: Software Engineering. An Advanced Course. Edited by F. L. Bauer. (Formerly published 1973 as Lecture Notes in Economics and Mathematical Systems, Vol. 81) XII, 545 pages. 1975.

Vol. 31: S. H. Fuller, Analysis of Drum and Disk Storage Units. IX, 283 pages. 1975.

Vol. 32: Mathematical Foundations of Computer Science 1975. Proceedings 1975. Edited by J. Bečvář. X, 476 pages. 1975.

Vol. 33: Automata Theory and Formal Languages, Kaiserslautern, May 20–23, 1975. Edited by H. Brakhage on behalf of GI. VIII, 292 Seiten. 1975.

Vol. 34: GI – 5. Jahrestagung, Dortmund 8.–10. Oktober 1975. Herausgegeben im Auftrag der GI von J. Mühlbacher. X, 755 Seiten. 1975.

Vol. 35: W. Everling, Exercises in Computer Systems Analysis. (Formerly published 1972 as Lecture Notes in Economics and Mathematical Systems, Vol. 65) VIII, 184 pages. 1975.

Vol. 36: S. A. Greibach, Theory of Program Structures: Schemes, Semantics, Verification. XV, 364 pages. 1975.

Vol. 37: C. Böhm, λ-Calculus and Computer Science Theory. Proceedings 1975. XII, 370 pages. 1975.

Vol. 38: P. Branquart, J.-P. Cardinael, J. Lewi, J.-P. Delescaille, M. Vanbegin. An Optimized Translation Process and Its Application to ALGOL 68. IX, 334 pages. 1976.

Vol. 39: Data Base Systems. Proceedings 1975. Edited by H. Hasselmeier and W. Spruth. VI, 386 pages. 1976.

Vol. 40: Optimization Techniques. Modeling and Optimization in the Service of Man. Part 1. Proceedings 1975. Edited by J. Cea. XIV, 854 pages. 1976.

Vol. 41: Optimization Techniques. Modeling and Optimization in the Service of Man. Part 2. Proceedings 1975. Edited by J. Cea. XIII, 852 pages. 1976.

Vol. 42: James E. Donahue, Complementary Definitions of Programming Language Semantics. VII, 172 pages. 1976.

Vol. 43: E. Specker und V. Strassen, Komplexität von Entscheidungsproblemen. Ein Seminar. V, 217 Seiten. 1976.

Vol. 44: ECI Conference 1976. Proceedings 1976. Edited by K. Samelson. VIII, 322 pages. 1976.

Vol. 45: Mathematical Foundations of Computer Science 1976. Proceedings 1976. Edited by A. Mazurkiewicz. XI, 601 pages. 1976.

Vol. 46: Language Hierarchies and Interfaces. Edited by F. L. Bauer and K. Samelson. X, 428 pages. 1976.

Vol. 47: Methods of Algorithmic Language Implementation. Edited by A. Ershov and C. H. A. Koster. VIII, 351 pages. 1977.

Vol. 48: Theoretical Computer Science, Darmstadt, March 1977. Edited by H. Tzschach, H. Waldschmidt and H. K.-G. Walter on behalf of GI. VIII, 418 pages. 1977.

Vol. 49: Interactive Systems. Proceedings 1976. Edited by A. Blaser and C. Hackl. VI, 380 pages. 1976.

Vol. 50: A. C. Hartmann, A Concurrent Pascal Compiler for Minicomputers. VI, 119 pages. 1977.

Vol. 51: B. S. Garbow, Matrix Eigensystem Routines – Eispack Guide Extension. VIII, 343 pages. 1977.

Vol. 52: Automata, Languages and Programming. Fourth Colloquium, University of Turku, July 1977. Edited by A. Salomaa and M. Steinby. X, 569 pages. 1977.

Vol. 53: Mathematical Foundations of Computer Science. Proceedings 1977. Edited by J. Gruska. XII, 608 pages. 1977.

Vol. 54: Design and Implementation of Programming Languages. Proceedings 1976. Edited by J. H. Williams and D. A. Fisher. X, 496 pages. 1977.

Vol. 55: A. Gerbier, Mes premières constructions de programmes. XII, 256 pages. 1977.

Vol. 56: Fundamentals of Computation Theory. Proceedings 1977. Edited by M. Karpiński. XII, 542 pages. 1977.

Vol. 57: Portability of Numerical Software. Proceedings 1976. Edited by W. Cowell. VIII, 539 pages. 1977.

Vol. 58: M. J. O'Donnell, Computing in Systems Described by Equations. XIV, 111 pages. 1977.

Vol. 59: E. Hill, Jr., A Comparative Study of Very Large Data Bases. X, 140 pages. 1978.

Vol. 60: Operating Systems, An Advanced Course. Edited by R. Bayer, R. M. Graham, and G. Seegmüller. X, 593 pages. 1978.

Vol. 61: The Vienna Development Method: The Meta-Language. Edited by D. Bjørner and C. B. Jones. XVIII, 382 pages. 1978.

Vol. 62: Automata, Languages and Programming. Proceedings 1978. Edited by G. Ausiello and C. Böhm. VIII, 508 pages. 1978.

Vol. 63: Natural Language Communication with Computers. Edited by Leonard Bolc. VI, 292 pages. 1978.

Vol. 64: Mathematical Foundations of Computer Science. Proceedings 1978. Edited by J. Winkowski. X, 551 pages. 1978.

Vol. 65: Information Systems Methodology, Proceedings, 1978. Edited by G. Bracchi and P. C. Lockemann. XII, 696 pages. 1978.

Vol. 66: N. D. Jones and S. S. Muchnick, TEMPO: A Unified Treatment of Binding Time and Parameter Passing Concepts in Programming Languages. IX, 118 pages. 1978.

Vol. 67: Theoretical Computer Science, 4th GI Conference, Aachen, March 1979. Edited by K. Weihrauch. VII, 324 pages. 1979.

Vol. 68: D. Harel, First-Order Dynamic Logic. X, 133 pages. 1979.

Vol. 69: Program Construction. International Summer School. Edited by F. L. Bauer and M. Broy. VII, 651 pages. 1979.

Vol. 70: Semantics of Concurrent Computation. Proceedings 1979. Edited by G. Kahn. VI, 368 pages. 1979.

Vol. 71: Automata, Languages and Programming. Proceedings 1979. Edited by H. A. Maurer. IX, 684 pages. 1979.

Vol. 72: Symbolic and Algebraic Computation. Proceedings 1979. Edited by E. W. Ng. XV, 557 pages. 1979.

Vol. 73: Graph-Grammars and Their Application to Computer Science and Biology. Proceedings 1978. Edited by V. Claus, H. Ehrig and G. Rozenberg. VII, 477 pages. 1979.

Vol. 74: Mathematical Foundations of Computer Science. Proceedings 1979. Edited by J. Bečvář. IX, 580 pages. 1979.

Vol. 75: Mathematical Studies of Information Processing. Proceedings 1978. Edited by E. K. Blum, M. Paul and S. Takasu. VIII, 629 pages. 1979.

Vol. 76: Codes for Boundary-Value Problems in Ordinary Differential Equations. Proceedings 1978. Edited by B. Childs et al. VIII, 388 pages. 1979.

Lecture Notes in Computer Science

Edited by G. Goos and J. Hartmanis

127

Y. Wallach

Alternating Sequential/Parallel Processing

Springer-Verlag
Berlin Heidelberg New York 1982

Autor

Y. Wallach
Wayne State University, College of Engineering
Department of Electrical and Computer Engineering
Detroit, Michigan 48202, USA

CR Subject Classifications (1981): 6.2, 5.25, 5.29

ISBN 3-540-11194-8 Springer-Verlag Berlin Heidelberg New York
ISBN 0-387-11194-8 Springer-Verlag New York Heidelberg Berlin

Printed in Germany

Printing and binding: Beltz Offsetdruck, Hemsbach/Bergstr.
2145/3140-543210

FOREWORD

The fields of "parallel processing" and "complexity theory" have drawn the attention of researchers for the last 20-30 years. In essence, the idea is that speeding up computations by building ever faster computers will either stop or will not be very profitable. What can then be more natural than connecting computers in parallel? With p processors, we might get slightly less than a p-fold increase in speed, but an increase we will certainly get.

Still, after all these years and a large body of excellent results, parallel processing has not triumphed. A researcher working for a computer manufacturer even told me that "parallel processing will never work." What are the reasons for such pessimism?

(1) The first is that those systems which were built were applied to what I call "inherently parallel" problems. Thus, PEPE tracks a number of targets; each processor has a single target assigned to it on which it works independently of and concurrently with other processors. Payroll processing may be another example of an inherently parallel problem; there is no connection between my salary and that of my boss, so they can be processed independently.

Invariably, the question was asked how many such problems exist. A look at any book on numerical analysis was rather disappointing: very few algorithms were anything but purely sequential. Whether our minds work so that we do not do "B" until having finished "A", or we are taught to solve problems that way, is immaterial. The fact remains that few problems seem to be inherently parallel.

(2) Mathematicians have the habit that if they cannot have the computer they need, they define a theoretical model and leave the worry of building it to engineers. Unfortunately, the abstract system so defined suffered from not being practical. Let me give examples of what I mean.

- The model assumes that all p processors are connected to a large, common memory. Whenever two or more processors requested the same word from it, they would get if instantaneously. This is clearly not achievable and leads to strange behaviors: one system apparently slowed down with the addition of processors.

- The number of processors was to be unbounded. It had better be so, since, as shown in one example of this book, multiplying two (nxn) matrices, requires n^3 processors. A rather "lean" matrix of n=100 would thus require a million processors.

(3) One of the first parallel systems built, the Illiac, has "private memories" for the "slaves." Unfortunately, the connections are such that quite often only one of the 64 "slaves" or only the single master works - the rest are idle. This is the case of "sequentialization" and attempts to reduce it were not always crowned with success.

(4) A rather important objective of parallelization was that of reliability

and availability. The first is defined here as the ability to identify a faulty unit and amputate it, the second as the capability to proceed working despite this removal. Illiac and similar systems have neither: if a unit fails, it must be exchanged or repaired before the system can work again.

This book is going to suggest a solution to this dilemma based on a single observation:

Problems are neither inherently parallel nor completely sequential. Solutions should adapt themselves to this fact rather than fighting it.

Take it in another way. When you are walking, the mind directs the movement of your legs and hands changing from time to time the pace, direction, etc. The mind works sequentially, the legs and hands are mostly independent and you would like to minimize the movements or time. In computerese: Assemble a master/slaves systems such that the master directs sequentially the slaves which then work in parallel, rather independently on different data (stones or meadows).

The first part of the book (Chapters 1 to 4) will develop a hardware system called ASP for "Alternating Sequential/Parallel" which, as its name implies, adapts well to the central idea, is more than just a model (one system is commercially available, another is being assembled), includes "private memories" and should have high reliability/availability because of symmetry. The second part (Chapters 5 to 11) develops algorithms and programs for it. For each of these programs, the speedup was calculated; they all approach more or less the optimum.

The development of these algorithms was so easy that the thought occurred to me that something must be wrong. On second thought, I concluded that this was only natural since the following comparison, with other approaches holds: instead of trying to eliminate completely the sequential parts of a solution we try only to minimize it. The first is not always possible, but in the second case the amount of minimization reflects only the author's ingenuity; I am sure readers will improve on some or all algorithms proposed by me. They might also add to the general approaches developed: "vertical programming" and "block schemes" as well as "tearing," "chasing" and the like.

The problems chosen are all in numerical, linear algebra because, as once observed, 75% of all scientific problems lead to linear equations. Since most work on other parallel systems also centered on linear algebra, a comparison of efficiency, speedup etc. between them and the ASP-methods is possible.

This is really a research report. Therefore the work of and on other systems is only briefly sketched - as much as needed for the comparison. Additionally, since the field of numerical solutions to linear algebra problems is very well covered in literature, it also is only sketched - wherever needed for developing ASP-algorithms. The reader is referred to the book by Young [Yo 71] for iterative methods and to the books by Young and Gregory [YG] and by Stoer and Bullirsch [SB] for all the rest. Especially the last is warmly recommended and I assume that the reader knows the relevant material so that no repetition is needed.

Let me close with additional remarks:

(1) The numbering is according to sections. Thus, equation (15) in section 2 of chapter 5 is referred to as (15) throughout chapter 5, but as 5.2.15 in other chapters.

(2) The book can be used for two graduate courses. The first part on the model (architecture) of parallel systems would have to be expanded early - each section of chapters 2 and 4 could (and probably should) be expanded into a separate chapter. The second part (chapters 5 to 9) could also be expanded - especially on the use of other (non-ASP) languages and algorithms.

(3) Instead of having a motto for every chapter, I offer two here:

"Nothing will ever be attempted if all possible objections must be first overcome".

"Science seeks the truth, engineering - the compromise." The first, by Samuel Johnson explains why I have had the audacity to offer a new solution at all. The second, by me, explains why it had to be a compromise solution: I am an engineer, not a mathematician. I will also be only too happy if readers will point out to me mistakes. On the whole, I hope they find the approach to be new but correct and simple.

A large part of chapters 6, 7 and 8 is from the Ph.D. Thesis and the papers which Dr. Conrad published with me. I very much thank him for his cooperation.

Thanks go also to Dr. B.Z. Barta, Prof. K.S. Fu, Prof. W. Handler, Dr. O. Herzog, Prof. M. Schlesinger, Mr. A. Shimor, Mr. J. Tenenbaum and Mr. B. Waumans - they all read and made remarks to the manuscript. Finally, I would like to thank my students who had to endure constant changes of text throughout the last eight years. I am afraid that constant rewriting has introduced more errors than is usual - for which I ask the readers forgiveness. The main points he should gather from this book are:

- ASP is a new hardware unlike other models

- Because ASP drops the requirement of complete parallelization, it is easy to develop new and efficient algorithms. I would be glad to hear from readers who have done it in their field of work.

NOTATION

Acronyms are used frequently in the text, but may be forgotten as soon as the particular Section is completed, except for the following:

- Apps = Abstract pps
- pps = parallel processing systems (nonsingular-pp's)
- Kopps, Mopps and Topps = Korn's, Multibus and Tristate oriented pps resp.
- ASP = Alternating Sequential/Parallel system
- EPOC = Electric Power Control
- Poof = Parallel, optimally ordered factorization
- SIMD = Single-instruction, Multiple-data system
- MIMD = Multiple-instruction, Multiple-data system
- PEPE = Parallel Ensemble of Processing Elements
- SMS = Siemens' Multiprocessing System
- CU = Control unit
- PE = Processing element
- ME = Memory element

We will use capital underlined letters for matrices, lower-case underlined for vectors, lower case and Greek letters for scalars. In particular we use:

Matrices

A - general
B - optimization
C - general
D - diagonal
E - error
F - Frobenius
G - Givens'
H - Householder's
I - Iteration
J - Jacobian
L - lower (left part of A)
M - symmetric
O - zero
P - permutation
Q - orthonormal
R - right (upper part of A)
S - similarity
T - tridiagonal
$\underline{a}_{.i}$ = i-th column of $\underline{A}$; $\underline{a}_{i.}$ = i-th row of $\underline{A}$
a_{ij} = (i,j)-th element of $\underline{A}$
$\underline{a}*\underline{b}$ = scalar product
$\underline{a}^T$ = transpose of $\underline{A}$

Vectors

b - A $\underline{x}$ = $\underline{b}$
c - control
f - function
g - gradient
h - constraints
r - residual
s - state, speedup
x,z - general vectors

Scalars

c = no. of nonzero terms
d = density (c/n)
e = error
f = function
h = slice width
m = number of memories
n = dimension
p = number of slaves
q = index of slave
r = residual
t = time
w = overrelaxation factor
$\alpha,\mu,\tau,\beta,\gamma$ are times of addition/subtraction, multiplication/division, transfer, synchronization and square root taking respectively.
λ = eigenvalue
$\omega = \alpha + \mu$
Ω = number of operations
ρ = (time) ratio
η = efficiency
ν = utilization
σ = speedup

Additional letters are used, but being local (to a few pages) may be forgotten as soon as you finish reading.

Springer-Verlag would like to thank the following publishers for granting permission to quote from the following original papers:

I.E.E.E.

Barnes et al:"The Illiac-IV Computer",Trans.IEEE,Vol.C-17,No8,746-760.

Davis:"The Illiac-IV Processing Element",Trans.IEEE,Vol.C-18,No9,800-816, 1969.

Gilmore:"Matrix Computations on an Associative Processor",Proc.Sagamore Conference, 272-290, 1974.

Wallach:"Parallel Processor Systems in Power-Dispatch",IEEE-Summer Power Meeting,July 74,Papers 74334-9 and C74355-6.

Batcher:"Staran/Radcap Hardware Architecture" and "The flip-network in Staran", Sagamore Conference, 147-152 and 65-71 respectively.

Conrad,Wallach:"Parallel,Optimally Ordered Factorization",PICA-Conf. (IEEE),May 1977, 302-306.

Kuck:"Illiac-IV Software and Application Programming",Trans.IEEE, Vol. C-17,758-770,1968.

Wing,Huang:"A parallel triangularization process of sparse matrices", Proc.International Conf.on Parallel Processing,August, 1977

Conrad,Wallach:"Iterative solutions of linear equations on a parallel processing system",Trans.IEEE,Vol.C-26,No2,1977,838-847.

Conrad,Wallach:"On block-parallel methods for solving linear equations Trans.IEEE,Vol.C-29,No5,354-359,1980.

Leven,Wallach,Conrad:"Mathematical programming methods for power dispatch",PICA-Conf.(IEEE-CH1317-3/79),1979, 137-141.

Feng:"Some characteristics of Associative/Parallel Processing", Proc. Sagamore Conf,1972, 5-16.

Evensen,Troy:"Introduction to the architecture of a 288-element PEPE" Sagamore Conf,1973, 162-169.

Shimor,Wallach:"A multibus-oriented parallel processing system-Mopps" Trans.IEEE,Vol.IECI-25,No.2,1978,137-142.

North-Holland Publ.Co.

Kober,Kopp,Kuznia:"SMS 101...",EuromicroJournal,1976,56-64.

Kober:"A fast communication processor for the SMS Multimicroproc-ssor System",Euromicro-Journal,1976,183-189.

Kober,Kuznia:"SMS-A Multiprocessor Architecture for High-Speed Numerical Calculations", Euromicro-Journal,Vol.5,1979,48-52.

Nagel:"Solving Linear Equations with the SMS 201",Euromicro-Journal , 1979,Vol.5, 53-54.

Tomann,Liedl:"Reliability in Microcomputer Arrays",Euromicr-Journal , 1980.

Wallach,Leven:"Alternating Sequential/Parallel Versions of the Simplex Algorithm", Euromicro-Journal, Vol.6,1980,237-242.

Richter,Wallach:"Remarks on a real-time,master-slaves operating system Microprocessing and Microprogramming, Vol.7,1981.

Pergammon Infotech

Infotech State of the Art Report "Multiprocessor Systems", Pergamon Infotech Limited, Maidenhead UK (1976)

Simulation Councils, Inc.

Korn:"Back to Parallel Computation", Simulation, August 74.

Technical Publishing Company, A Dun&Bradsteet Company

McIntire:"An Introduction to the Illiac-IV Computer",Datamation, April,1970.

CONTENTS

1. INTRODUCTION

Aims: To define the terms throughput, speedup, availability, reliability, parallelism, pipelining, etc. To start classification of systems and introduce "Alternating Sequential/Parallel" - ASP processing. To set-up a list of topics to be discussed later.

1.1 AN OVERVIEW

This book deals with parallel hardware and software and it is only fitting to start it by mentioning the reasons for wanting to connect processors and execute programs in parallel. What we try to achieve are:

- Higher speeds
- Lower costs
- Better reliability and availability as well as
- Modularity.

Let us discuss each of these goals before proceeding to the problems of parallel systems.

The speed of computers has increased by leaps and bounds since their introduction in the 1940's. Unfortunately, it seems difficult or costly to increase the speed at the same pace much longer. A simple calculation will show that because of basic physical laws we seem to be approaching the upper limit of the speed at which a digital computer can transfer information. To this end, let us compare the (hardware) speeds in the past to those possible in the future. An addition (32 bit-words) required about 300 milliseconds in 1944 (on a relay computer), 300 microseconds in 1954 (on a tube computer) and 300 nanoseconds in 1964 (on CDC 6600). Suppose we try to build a computer with an addition time of 300 picoseconds. Since the speed at which an electrical signal travels is 0.03 cm/psec, it would propagate only 9 cm (less than 4") during the entire execution time of the instruction. It will be difficult to achieve such extremely small propagation delays or reduce so much the distances (except, maybe in VLSI). If we want to increase the speed, an attempt must be made to find other solutions rather than always reducing the circuit execution or propagation time.

One such direction is connecting processing elements in parallel. Stated simply, we hope that connecting p processors will increase the overall speed acceptably close to p times that of a single processor.

The idea is not new: In 1842 Manabrea described the lectures by Babbage [MM61] and wrote, "... the machine can...give several results at the same time, which will greatly abridge the whole amount..." of time. This amounts to parallelism, but since in modern times a number of terms were coined for parallelism, we should sort them out before we discuss parallel systems in more detail.

In general purpose (computer center) environments, the term "throughput" is used. It means simply the number of different and separate jobs that a processor is able to process in a given time. Hopefully with p processors it will be higher than with a single processor (and also correspondingly more expensive). Note though, that if we install p separate computers, the throughput will increase p-fold, but the turnaround time for any individual user will not change appreciably.

Another term used in connection with parallelism is that of "multiprogramming". The idea is to process a number of jobs in a single cpu and a number of I/O devices in an overlapped fashion. The turnaround time should be considerably lower despite the fact that only a single cpu is available.

In multiprogramming the attempt is made to decrease the time to put through a number of jobs. In contradistinction, with "speedup", the time it takes to put a single program through the system should be reduced.

In order to distinguish them even more, we might differentiate between "concurrency" and "parallelism". Concurrency should mean that unrelated events are executed at the same time, i.e., data is transferred from a disk to a line printer while the processor works on the same or some other program. Processing all bits of a word or p parts of a single program simultaneously is parallelism.

We can define space- and time-related parallelism. In the first case a number of geographically distributed processors may work on the same job, whereas, in the second case various stages of processing the same instructions are "pipelined".

To sum up: In this book we are concerned with achieving speedup (not throughput) by space parallelism at a reasonable cost and not with concurrency or pipelining.

As long as the only processors available on the market were of the "dinosaur" variety, the cost of connecting a number of them was prohibitive. Moreover, the speedup does not increase necessarily with price. Since priority arbiters will allow only a single access of a processor to a memory block at any given time, some processors will have to wait ("memory contention"). Hence, the speedup will increase less than p, the price by p and the solution may be counterproductive.

With the appearance of minicomputers, the price/performance comparison of uni/multiprocessors has changed. Minicomputers (and even more so, microprocessors) appear to be at least an order of magnitude more cost-effective than the larger machines. There are a number of apparent reasons [Fu 76] for this phenomenon.

"1. Continuing advances in semi-conductor technology favor the small processor. LSI (Large-Scale-Integration) memory, arithmetic and logic chips have been able to dramatically cut the cost of producing minicomputers. Recent LSI advances such as the Intel 3000 bit-slice processing element and the DEC LSI-11 will continue to drive down the price of minicomputers. The larger processors that rely on specialized logic to speed-up arithmetic functions, prefetch and buffer instructions, overlap instruction execution, etc. are less able to exploit the present

(LSI) technology.

2. Economics of scale. A product line that produces on the order of 10,000 minicomputers a year (or 10^5 to 10^6 microcomputers a year) will not have the overhead per computer that a product line has that produces 50 to 100 (large uniprocessor) computer systems a year.

3. Pricing policies bury the cost of software development for the large computer systems in the price of the hardware."

We might add here some remarks, mostly to account for recent developments. So, for instance INTEL commenced the iAPX432 -a 32-bit processor (thus opening the "floating point" market for microcomputers). On the other hand when discussing prices, one should not forget software; software costs more than hardware. Both hardware and software costs consist of design and implementation costs which are reduced by high volume. Even in conventional computers (say, micro) large quantities can be sold so that both hardware and software costs can be ammortized. The point is, that parallel systems use mass-produced LSI-units and may achieve it easier.

The analysis in [Fu 76] shows a multiprocessor to have a cost performance advantage of three to four over uniprocessor systems when implementations using similar technologies are considered. This comparison is shown to be very sensitive to memory prices and considerable attention should be given to normalizing memory costs between the two systems.

The above considerations apply even more now because of the rapid development and cost-decrease of microprocessors. Grosh's Law and Minsky's Conjecture (which claimed that the cost of parallel processors would not be competitive), were dispelled in [TP 73]. In particular, it is noted that a parallel "Pepe"-system with enough processing elements to provide the "Mips"-capability of a CDC7600 would cost only 10% of a CDC7600. Parallel processing nowadays would use microprocessors or VLSI units, stay in the framework of present-day technology and therefore be even more cost-effective than indicated above.

Another reason for judging a parallel processing system (to be called from now on a pps) to be more priceworthy is as follows. Up to the present, computers were bought and installed as single units. Whenever a larger or faster computer was needed, the old computer had to be abandoned and a new one bought (or leased). It seems a much better approach to use a pps and add processing power when and if needed. This may be called "incremental augmentation" or "modularity". It allows matching of a specific architecture to the needs of the customer.

The most important advantages of pps' are not their speedups or cost/effectiveness, but their availability and reliability. This applies to process-control applications with which this book is concerned.

In process control a failure can have a much more dramatic effect on the safety of the staff, the damage value (in M$) and on the loss of vital data than in a "computer center" environment. This explains why it is so important to have a system available all the time and be able to rely on its proper functioning.

A unicomputer is as reliable as the weakest of its parts. Also, when a single computer is used, its failure is catastrophic, whereas in pps the remaining processors are potentially available and could work undisturbed, yielding what is called (gracefully) degraded service. This seems to have been achieved in the case of the STAR-system [RLT 78].

It is sometimes required to remove a part of a pps either semipermanently for maintenance or because a fault was detected in one of its parts. The system should nevertheless be available and continue its service at only a slightly slower pace. Moreover, if possible, this continuity of service should be achievable without expenditure on redundant components as is done in some telephone exchanges or other "fault tolerant" systems. In these systems the hardware is duplicated or triplicated and all results are compared. Reliability is ensured by modular redundancy and majority voting (say 2 out of 3) but is expensive and thus increases the cost/ effectiveness. We will try other solutions.

The definitions we will use are as follows: Reliability is the capability to identify and remove a faulty component. Availability is the ability to provide service even after the removal of a faulty component. We discuss them in more detail later.

The reasons for parallel processing, namely speed, cost/effectiveness, reliability and availability are interrelated. For instance, it seems difficult to put a price on the increased reliability achieved through the use of parallelism in air-traffic controllers. Even the shut-down of flight reservations because of an unavailable computer has a price. The increased speed of power dispatch computers could have possibly prevented a blackout so that speed also influences price.

We have mentioned the advantages of pps, namely, availability, reliability, speed, cost/effectiveness and modularity. Still, the progress of parallelization is not impressive [En 77]. What are the reasons?

It was once stated [BS 76] that parallel processors are not being installed, despite their apparent advantages, primarily because:

"1. The basic nature of engineering is to be conservative. This is a classical deadlock situation: we cannot learn how to program multiprocessors until such systems exist; a system will not be built before programs are ready.

2. The market does not demand them. Another deadlock: how can the market demand them since the market does not even know that such a structure can exist? IBM has not yet blessed the concept."

To this inertia we would like to add the following problems attributed to pps':

- Restricted area of applications
- Unavailability of "parallel" mathematics
- Ignorance about possible problem decomposition
- Large expenditures projected for language and program development.

Let us start the discussion of these problems with a quotation [Ku 78] which could have been used as a motto: "A good computer system designer must first heed the problems of the intended system users, the technology from which the system will be built, and the people who will carry out the construction and programming of his design". In this book, we deal primarily with on-line, real-time (process-control) applications using LSI or VLSI technology and try to ease reprogramming by presenting some simple and general algorithms and extending sequential, "higher-level" languages only by very few additional constructs.

The type of applications envisaged is such that the system is under complete control of the programmer; a single program is executed at any particular time on all processors and the results should be available on short notice, i.e. so that the operator has the illusion of an immediate answer to any of his querries. In a computer-center application, there might be a number of jobs processed "simultaneously" - but they are independent e.g. student jobs, and the processor is actually working sequentially. The impression of parallelism is created by multiprogramming, i.e. switching the processor between the jobs and using I/O-channels with direct memory access. The difference between the two is essential.

The area of applications is not as restricted as it might seem. Thus [TW 75] list among others filtering, tracking, document retrieval, file manipulation, data management, weather forecasting, air-traffic control, data compression, signal processing, information retrieval, sorting, symbol manipulation, pattern recognition, picture processing, dynamic programming, differential equations and matrix operations. A particular job, that of economic control of distributing electric power will be dealt with more closely later and it will be shown that most of its programs are based on numerical, linear algebra. We may now sum up the discussion on the areas of application thus: The applications are very varied, encompassing most large processing jobs, but in this book we will deal only with real-time control and develop only parallel algorithms of linear algebra. This by itself is general enough to counter the criticism of restricted application.

Since no "parallel mathematics" was available, a lot of effort went into developing it. Most of the Foreword deals with the reasons for its lack of success and with developing a new idea - that of "Alternating Sequential/Parallel" processing. Since it is in this area that this book makes a contribution, the reader is again referred back to the Foreword. At this point, let us only mention that most algorithms are neither entirely sequential, nor completely parallel. There are always parts which must proceed sequentially, but in some of the present-day parallel systems (abstract model, pipeline and array computers) either all processors work or most of them are idle. As a first cautious step in the direction of more practical parallelism, these notes suggest the use of "Alternating Sequential/Parallel" (ASP) processing. The hardware capable of ASP-Processing is described in the first part and some particular algorithms for it are described in the second part of this book.

Let us next sketch an outline of the book.

It was already noted that the area of application is the determining factor in a computer system design. These will be reviewed in 1.3 leading us to a basic differentiation of problems into inherently parallel problems and those which are not.

Section 1.2 includes a classification of the hardware of parallel processing systems. A well-known classification [Fl 72] of parallel computers is that of SIMD-Single Instruction, Multiple Data and MIMD-Multiple Instruction, Multiple Data Systems. As already mentioned, we would also like to differentiate between process-control applications which are on-line, real-time and computer-center applications which are not. Additionally, we will distinguish associative processors and use the Erlanger Classification System [Ha 77]. Not included in it is the question of whether the system should be a centralized, master/slave system or a decentralized "multiprocessor" system. We will, therefore, review in Chapter 2 some of the existing systems. This will suggest the use of a hierarchical system with a central controller (the "master") and p "slaves" and programming it in a way in which sequential and parallel parts alternate (this is the reason for the title of the book: Alternating Sequential/Parallel Processing.)

Having settled on a pps with a master and p slaves, the next question is whether the master will be identical to the slaves (a symmetrical system) or not. For the sake of higher reliability/availability the symmetric system will be found to be better.

Every pps will include an interconnection network (the "switch") which connects the (p+1) processors (the master and its p "slaves") to the (common) "store". Section 2.3 describes the characteristics of various switches and shows that a single time-sliced bus is sufficient for the pps.

Another hardware decision will be made in Chapter 2, namely that each slave should have its own private "memory". This will enable it to work in the ASP- or Alternating Sequential/Parallel mode.

If an aggregate of hardware which includes a shared memory ("store") and a number of private "memories" is assumed, then the master must have access to all memories and should view all of them as a single address space. Even more so if, as in decentralized systems, there is only a single memory.

The review of pps' in Chapter 2 and the specifications for the bus and memory help in designing the Mopps (Multibus-oriented, Modified or if you prefer My own pps) in Chapter 3. For instance, the reasons underlying the design of one of the computers mentioned in Chapter 2 which lead to the use of "private memories" for the slaves, hold for Mopps too.

We will start the design by adoption of a pps suggested by Prof. G. Korn [Ko74] as an initial model because it is the simplest.

The Kopps (Korn's pps) as originally suggested requires certain changes and the discussion of these, as well as of the performance characteristics, lead [SW 78] to a suggested "Modified parallel processing system", the Mopps or a modification, the "Tristate Operated pps," the Topps. It should be emphasized that a similar model, the SMS, is commercially available [KKK 76, Ko 76, Ko 77, Kop 77, KK 79]. Hence, this book is not dealing with a hypothetical, but rather with an existing system.

Topps differs from Mopps in that microprocessors instead of minicomputers are used. This is not too important, since we view a pps as replacement of a computer on any level (a dinosaur by a number of minis, a mini by a number of micros). Still, it does lead to some differences in hardware which are discussed.

Having defined the basic hardware, we now turn to an implementation, and this leads to a language problem. It is shown in Chapter 4 that we need only five extensions to PL/I in order to program Mopps. Moreover, these extensions are such that programs written in it may be simulated using the multitasking facility of PL/I.

Next, we discuss the operating system (the SMS'es have an off-line; we need an on-line system) since the main problem may be how to design the pps so that it will need a simple operating system. In Chapter 4 we show the reasons why the operating system of Mopps is in fact simple.

It seems that even today one of the bottlenecks of decentralized multiprocessors is the lack of a suitable operating system for the aggregate. Since several processes must be coordinated, the overhead grows. This may complicate very much the operating system and it is possible that the addition of slaves may increase instead of decrease the (average) time per computation. If, on the other hand, the operating system resides in a separate "master" and is small enough to guarantee efficient service, then the necessary conditions for success may be achieved.

Reliability is not only a hardware, but is also a software problem. Obviously, if the operating system works incorrectly, an extremely unreliable computer system results. Remedies suggested are that the operating system should be written in a high-level instead of an assembly language, so that "structured" programming may be applied and the programs are more legible, better documented and easier to check out. Either the decomposition of the job into tasks or building it on a small kernel with multilayered extensions were also suggested in order to enhance reliability; but as a rule, little has been done on software reliability which could be used in practice - not even for simple programs. We will hardly deal with it, except that we will extend a high-level and not program in assembly language. Also, bearing in mind that the pps is a programmer-dedicated system, i.e., such that the entire program and data outlay is under complete control of the programmer, the operating system of the master may be simple enough to facilitate software reliability.

With Chapter 5 the algorithmic part of the book starts.

Most algorithms of numerical analysis are sequential. This is probably the result of the reasoning process of human beings (human beings think in a partially ordered system e.g. when they are planning). If computers have to be applied in parallel, solving simultaneously a given problem the algorithm for solving this problem must be rewritten. For some problems of linear algebra this is done starting with Chapter 5.

Linear algebra problems were chosen since they consume a large part, by one account 75% of all numerical calculations [Fo 64]. They are also the best known and we can base the second part of the book on previous knowledge. The books [SB] and [YG] describe the material nicely; in particular [SB] will be used repeatedly and the part of it which deals with linear algebra is assumed to be known.

Despite this, three topics are discussed in Chapter 5: a summary of elimination methods, complex numbers and quads, as needed for, say, power system problems and other, relatively new methods. In Chapter 6 elimination methods devised for other pp's are compared with those proposed for ASP.

New and general types of methods which lead to high speedups are then developed. One is based on processing blocks instead of single elements, the other on solving a number of subproblems and using results of these for the overall solution. Both the "chasing" method discussed in Chapter 8, as well as another general approach to ASP-solutions, "vertical programming" is the basis for iterative methods discussed in Chapter 7. The remaining chapters use these general approaches.

All algorithms are "programmed" in the PPL/I language defined in Chapter 4 and their speedups are calculated. It is shown that the algorithms developed have indeed high speedups and efficiencies. Assuming that good algorithms can also be developed for other problems, we advance the following conclusions:

(a) ASP's are simple, cost/effective, reliable systems with high availability

(b) Alternating sequential/parallel processing is natural and thus very simple. It leads to speedups approaching the ideal.

1.2 HARDWARE CLASSIFICATION

Aims: To explain the notions of asynchronous, pipeline, array and functionally parallel systems. Classification according to instruction and data streams. Associativity. Other classification schemes.

It was said [Ha 77] that language guides thought and that therefore language sometimes prevents the appropriate solution of a problem being found. In many cases not only a language (it can be referred to as a calculus or notation) but also classification schemes can be a barrier rather than an aid in solving a problem.

If such a classification scheme is applied to animals and plants, then the elements are existing objects and the scheme cannot completely fail even though the discovery of a new species can present difficulties in fitting it into an existing classification scheme. Such a scheme can be called a taxonomy, since all the species are considered to be descended from a single species. It seems more difficult to create a classification scheme, or even a taxonomy, for some areas of contemporary technology since it is necessary to be able to project future advances as well as place existing examples in it. We will try to do it anyway.

Since the advent of electronic digital computers in the late 1940's and early 1950's, their organization remained essentially that of Fig. 1.

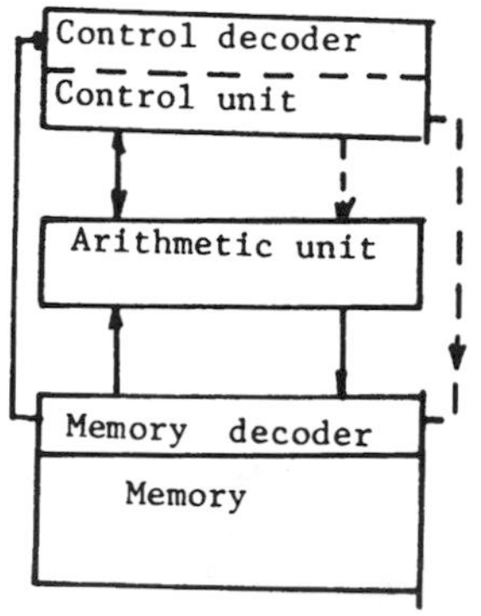

Fig. 1: Computer Organization

It is composed of:

- A memory which holds both program and data
- A control unit which fetches instructions from memory, decodes them and issues commands to the
- Arithmetic/Logic unit which performs the operations on operands fetched from memory and returns the results to that same memory. The addresses of the operands and the results are supplied by the control unit (broken line).

The program, as stored in memory, sequences the instructions so that at any time, a single instruction is processed. The addition of I/O - channels has changed this sequential nature insofar as the system may process input or output concurrently with the processing of the program by the "main" computer. As far as the execution of the program itself is concerned, the notion of the stored program is still responsible for its sequential execution.

This situation forces the algorithm and programs to fit the sequential operation of the machine. The time has arrived to ask the question, "Wouldn't it be better if the machines were adapted to the (possibly) non-sequential nature of some algorithms?" The usual answer seems to be that the known algorithms of numerical analysis are sequential, so why bother? This is putting the cart before the horse. If nature itself is contemplated, it is found that many interrelated processes take place simultaneously and only the fact that the human thought-process seems to be sequential, or that the procedures developed in the last 300 years are such, is responsible for the fact that no trace of the natural parallelism remains in the algorithms. Computers could work in parallel, so why not use this fact in order to adapt them to nature? Lately attempts were actually made to match the natural parallelism by corresponding "hardware". Most of these attempts center around concurrent execution of parts of instructions (with its rather developed graph-model), or subexpressions, microinstructions ("pipeline computers") or at the most, of the same instruction on a set of data ("array computers"). All these require new computer architectures and special languages for expressing the algorithms, and will be discussed later in this book.

The terms above may sound slightly fuzzy and therefore will be clarified by an everyday example.

Suppose that a gasoline station is situated at a road as shown in Fig.2. The most basic "parallelism" is evidenced by the gas-attendant while serving a single

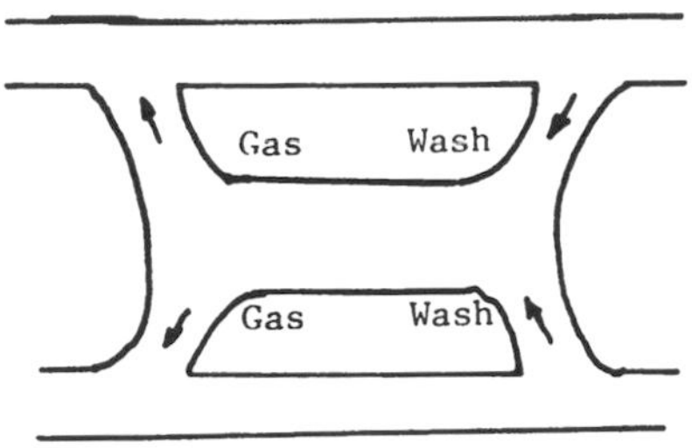

Fig. 2: A gasoline station.

car. His left hand may wipe the windshield; at the same time the right hand is opening the battery for inspection, the leg is kicking the tire and gasoline is flowing into the tank. This is parallelism at the lowest level exemplified by a computer, whose various registers work concurrently in order to supply the result.

Suppose now that there is a constant stream of cars to be serviced during the day (8 am to 4 pm) by two attendants. At each point in time, two independent tasks are performed by two independent attendants - this is a nonfunctional concurrency. For this parallelism the two attendants must be equally intelligent, have the same resources and be independent of each other. Parallelism at the "car service" level, does not prevent lower-level parallelism. So, for instance, each attendant will at some time, kick the tire while gasoline is flowing into the tank.

This case simulates two standalone (multi-) computers which may work concurrently during any given time. The two processors must be intelligent enough to be able to do entire jobs by themselves and the resources (disks, cores, etc.) must be doubled. Such systems are called symmetric, independent, multicomputer systems (or sometimes "duplexes"). Since no overhead is incurred, the price paid for concurrency is the double cost and salary, but cars are also serviced at a double rate (throughput) and the "availability" is higher i.e. even when one of the attendants is sick, the station does not have to close down.

Until now parallelism involved space. Suppose that the (single) attendant tries to time-slice his time, so that for instance he will accept payments from the owner of one car, while the second car is being filled. In the overall picture, there is still parallelism despite the fact that the attendant is doing one job at a time. In computer systems, this "multiprogramming" is exemplified by the processor attending to one job, while the previously interrupted job has its I/O processed by a channel. Multiprogramming is normally enacted by a single processor; if a number of them are used, the system is a "multicomputer".

Next, suppose that the entry lane is so narrow that only a single car can pass it. In this case, if both attendants completed service simultaneously, only one car would advance and the second would have to wait a few seconds. Interference and a consequent time-loss result. In computers, this would be equivalent to storing the entering jobs on a single disk and removing them each time one of the two processors is free. Since only one processor may access the disk at any time, memory interference results. Scarcity of resources (e.g. lane) leads to loss of time, but is obviously cheaper (say, one disk only), so that the total cost/performance is probably higher. If memory replaces the disk above, we have a "multiprocessor".

Suppose that every car requires two different service activities, say, filling and washing. In this case, it may be wise to let two attendants work in a "pipelining" fashion, each specializing on a single task. This might increase the throughput, but unless they are synchronized and the "pipe" is full of cars, there will be times at which one of the attendants is idle.

Let one of the attendants own the place and accept payments. Moreover, let the number of attendants be large and the owner specialize completely - he only organizes the work. The system is then more efficient but asymmetrical and the availability may suffer: who knows if the attendants will work at all if and when the boss is sick? In computer systems this type includes the so called array computers in which a single "master" (control unit) directs all attendants (processing elements or "slaves") to do precisely the same job on different cars (data). Since the slaves are simple arithmetic units and there is only one control unit, the cost is lowered.

The attendants have to be synchronized. Moreover, some of them will be idle for want of work while others are busily obeying the boss's whims. We can then improve the situation if we let one of the attendants be the boss while the real one is sick. In this case the attendants though have to be as intelligent as the boss to be able to take over; we now have a symmetrical system with a "roving" master.

We hope to have made the classification clearer. Multicomputers and duplexes are of no interest since they work in a completely sequential way; they will not be discussed at all. Multiprogramming a single processor or the duplication of hardware in "fault tolerant" computers is of no greater interest. In the next chapter we will discuss multiprocessing, i.e. systems which process k jobs on p cpu's and m memories. They are usually applied in computer centers in order to increase its throughput. We will also discuss parallel processing systems, pps' which process a single job at a time on p processors. Because of their unique position we will also discuss pipeline and an abstract pps (the Apps). Finally, STARAN and PEPE will be mentioned because they use an associative memory and may thus be representative of an entirely different group of pps'. We do not have to dwell too much on it, since [Fo 76] covers more than we need to know about associative memories (and especially STARAN). On the other hand, we will add to the classification of pps' that of being democratic, autocratic and hierarchical (Chapter 3).

The classification usually applied is not into multiprocessors, pipeline, vector, apps and associative pps' but as follows.

A (sequential) computer fetches instructions and operands from memory, executes the instructions and stores results in memory. The instructions form an instruction stream while the operands form a data stream flowing between the cpu and memory. The ordinary computer (Fig.1) is thus a single-instruction, single-data or SISD computer. An array processor uses a single control unit to send a single instruction stream to all its slaves which obey every order synchronously, but each works on its own data. We thus have a Single-Instruction, Multiple-Data, SIMD-system (more on them, in particular, on Illiac, in Chapter 2). Actually, STARAN too may be considered to be SIMD, with the provision that it uses an associative store. Pipeline computers may be considered to be MISD-systems if the view is taken that each data item is processed in different parts of the pipeline. Multiprocessors, Apps' and pps' are representative of Multiple-Instruction, Multiple-Data, MIMD-systems. This is so because in all of them we have the slaves working asynchronously; in pps' the data are different and therefore even if a master is available its "program" is not obeyed in complete synchronism by the slaves. Multiprocessors and apps' do not even have a master and may thus work on completely different jobs altogether. The data is different in all cases, so that they all represent MIMD-systems.

We can picture the systems as in Fig. 3 with PE - the processing, CU - the control units. In the case of MISD, i.e. the pipeline computer, S1 to Sk represent k stages of processing a single instruction. When S_i has computed its result, it passes it to S_{i+1} but since S_{i+1} may still be working on previous data, buffers must

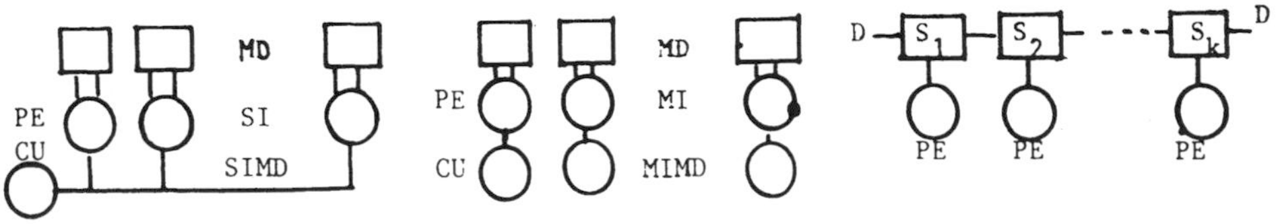

Fig. 3: Parallel Systems

separate the stages. The P's are not really processors but part of a single cpu - each providing a different microinstruction.

1.3 PROBLEM CLASSIFICATION

Aims: To classify the problems into on-line and off-line as well as into inherently parallel Π-problems and non-Π problems. To give examples of every one of the four possible problem areas and introduce in particular the Electric Power Control (EPOC) problem.

Introducing the Cm*-multiprocessor [SFS 76], the authors wrote as follows: "In order to take advantage of the potential high reliability, incremental expandibility and very high throughput of a multiple processor system, a problem must be decomposed into parallel, cooperating processes. To date such decomposition has only been achieved for a few special purpose tasks by individuals familiar with that task. If the multi-processor structure is to become a viable approach to the construction of computer systems, it will need to span a relatively large range of applications. Some areas we hope to investigate include: data base management, signal processing, real time controllers, speech and vision understanding, large numeric computations and text processing." We have mentioned some other fields too.

Frequently mentioned is also the area of weather forecast [Kop 77]. As a matter of fact, 19th century meteorologists used "parallel processing" of a kind:

namely, they used to divide work among themselves. This was possible because each could deal independently of and concurrently with his colleagues on his geographical segment (space decomposition; partitioned data). The interrelationships could be worked out later by a master-meteorologist or a group of them.

The salient feature of this application is that it can easily be partitioned into such independent or quasi-independent parts. We call problems which can be partitioned into independent parts, inherently parallel and denote them by π (without attaching to π any numerical value; thus, we do not know how well partitioned a π-problem is).

Another salient point of weather prediction is that it is an off-line problem. The meteorologists were situated in different locations, sometimes in different countries and the mail service was worse then, a hundred years ago than it is now (despite what everybody believes). Obviously, their calculation was therefore very inaccurate which gave reason for all those jokes about your rheumatism predicting weather better than meteorologists. Today, we compute the weather in a single location but still do not have to do it on-line. If we compute it, say, every 15 minutes that means that satellite pictures are taken every 15 minutes - the computer needs only a few minutes to process it. We see that it still is an off-line problem.

Another problem which usually leads to parallelism is that of Ballistic Missile Defense (Do we check on all "windows" of space from which missiles may be coming at us? Do we follow each possible missile fast enough and accurate so that we know whether it is going to make impact on Novaya Zemlya or on Washington D.C.?).

Let us quote from [Co 72, Co 76] in which the above purpose was summarized as that of verifying, tracking of targets, their discrimination and classification. A computer, PEPE, was introduced there with the following observations:

"It is the job of the computer to initiate a file on each detected object, associate each radar return with its proper file, update the files, perform mathematical functions on them.... The real-time constraint is that for each return (several hundred to several thousand per second), a request for a subsequent radar pulse must be generated and delivered to the radar within a specified time interval (typically 25 to 200 miliseconds). The time interval... can be extremely critical for some functions. A little calculation will show that the foregoing problem is simply not tractable... on conventional sequential computers, even the largest and most powerful ones....

The measurements taken by radar are compared to target data on file. The comparison of m returns with n targets requires normally time of the order of $m*n$, but only of m if the correlation is done by association. Therefore PEPE employs an associative memory.

[For numerical calculations a Kalman filter is used]..." It requires about 3000 machine instructions per execution (about half of these are floating-point arithmetic operations). For 200 targets, each tracked at a radar pulse rate of 20 pulses per second, twelve million instructions per second (Mips) are required.

In additon to the three primary BMD data processing requirements of correlation, scientific computation, and multidimensional file search... the computer must be extremely reliable and this reliability should preferably be an inherent characteristic of the architecture. High reliability is difficult to achieve in a computer suitable for BMD service because of the very large amount of hardware such computers must contain. The latter is true because, in the final analysis, great computational power [as above]... is achieved only via the employment of large amounts of hardware. An architecture acceptable for BMD service must allow high reliability despite the large amount of hardware required. Parallel associative architecture provide opportunities for meeting this requirement, so long as the individual elements in the parallel array can be kept independent of one another. Then, individual elements can fail without affecting others and without affecting the problem solution. Fortunately, many of the data sets dealt with in BMD computations are independent, and lend themselves to assignment to independent processing elements. Since the data sets are independent, there is no need for inter-element communication. This permits the arrangement of processing elements to be almost completely unstructured, so that no particular element or combination of elements is needed for successful problem completion."

We have classified problems according to whether they are or are not inherently parallel and whether they work off- or on-line. In terms of this classification the above is an <u>on-line, π-problem</u>.

In addition to BMD, we might view as on-line π-problems measuring systems for which one author wrote:

"Multi-microcomputer systems will most likely find greatest use in process-control applications. Each slave could be dedicated to a specific task, say testing a particular module, assembly or system. The master could then be used to coordinate the testing, monitor the test results and do data-logging as required. Applications also exist in the data-communication area." Telephone switching centers also present on-line, Π-problems.

<u>Off-Line, non-π-problems</u> are (among others): Signal processing and in particular the Fast Fourier Transform, Sorting, Searching, Optimization and linear algebraic problems.

Having mentioned off-line π and non-π as well as on-line π-problems, we next discuss the most important case, namely an <u>on-line, non-π-problem</u> and in particular control over distribution of electrical energy, the "<u>E</u>lectrical <u>P</u>ower <u>C</u>ontrol" (EPOC) about which the author has more detailed data.

Imagine the control center of a utility company. The operator ("dispatcher") sits there among the minions of push buttons, meters, switches (but not the micro-skirted girls; these are seen in such surroundings only in James Bond movies). The dispatcher has to be aware of the "state of the network", has to make plans for any possible "contingency", has to decide on the "optimum" policy of generation and some supporting activities. To do all these, he has a computer at his disposal, so that the load is shared: the computer makes the calculations, the dispatcher makes the decisions. The backbone of the software system is shown in Fig. 4. We will next review briefly the packages contained therein.

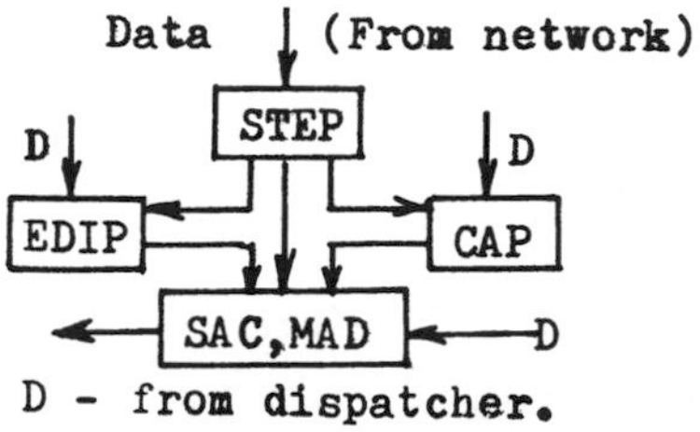

Fig. 4: EPOC - programs

State Estimation Program, STEP

In order to effect all actions and programs, a consistent, accurate and reliable data base is absolutely necessary.

To gather the system data every few seconds and bring it to a central location requires a high-speed digital data-acquisition system. Unfortunately, measured and telemetered data are not accurate enough for the required actions. Errors will certainly result from measurements and in channels and be then amplified in the programs. Some quantities cannot even be measured directly (e.g., phase angles of bus voltages). This has justified providing and then exploiting redundance in measurement so as to obtain "best" estimates of the system variables using least-square estimation, filtering and other stochastic approximation methods. This estimation or filtering can be done by a "state estimation program" STEP.

Altogether, STEP is responsible for filtering all data, detecting outright bad data and setting up the structure of the network. At its completion, there exists a "good" estimate of the state of the network. Since this estimate forms the basis of a number of other control programs, STEP is central (see Fig. 4) to quasi-stationary power dispatch.

Economic Dispatch Program, EDIP

It is hardly necessary nowadays to justify a program which helps saving energy (and hence, money). Since this aim was important even before the energy crisis, EDIP seems to be the oldest of the EPOC (veritably, not OPEC) programs.

The aim of EDIP is to adjust the generation so that all loads are supplied and that the cost of generation is minimal. To this it is necessary nowadays to add remote input, inclusion of interchange of power between neighboring power-pools, scheduling of both own generation and interchange, generation control, reserve analysis and unit commitment. The optimization problem is rather complicated through the addition of a large number of constraints and it will require correspondingly complicated algorithms.

STEP used the information supplied by measuring instruments; EDIP must assume certain data (e.g., generation) and compute the resulting steady-state of the network. This steady-state, or as it is called, the load-flow problem is defined as follows: given all node powers, calculate the node voltages. Since power depends quadratically on voltage, load-flow leads to a set of 2n algebraic, non-linear equations; n is the number of nodes, which for the "average" network is about 1000. Since load-flow is to be solved as part of an iterative loop seeking the optimum, the size of the optimization problem is readily appreciated.

Contingency Analysis Program, CAP

It should be quite obvious that optimum load dispatch is only effected subject to the satisfaction of security constraints, which may considerably modify the minimum operating cost. In particular it may be required to compute the power-flows resulting from the loss of one or more branches of the network and to compare these flows with limits. Moreover, it may be required to find that branch (or branches) which, if removed, cause other parts of the network to be overloaded. In one such case CAP is connected to the state-estimation program, and accepts two lists of outages - a stored one, and a list entered by the dispatcher and then recommends remedial actions for these contingencies. These "corrective actions" may include generation or interchange rescheduling, line-switching, load-shedding, capacitor/reactor switching and voltage schedule modifications. In each case, load-flow will have to be solved (probably, repeatedly).

Actually, we have discussed the static or quasi-stationary contingency analysis. Dispatchers have to deal with dynamic contingency, e.g., stability and blackout problems. In this book, the only material relevant to dynamic contingencies is that on eigenvalues; anyway most of the time spent solving dynamic problems goes to repeated solutions of the load-flow problems.

Supporting Activities "SAC"

This is probably the most time consuming package of programs. It includes after-the-fact interchange billing, scheduling of work orders and maintenance, normal accounting, salaries and the like.

Operating-system support as well as support for the display and data base management are also needed. A separate problems will be that of dealing with the continuously arriving analog information, its conversion and storage.

The first user of STEP will be a "monitoring", alarm, display-system (MAD). In one version the monitoring would involve the system configuration, lists of de-energized systems, open breakers, (which should have but did not operate), of breakers, backup relays and primary relays (which should not have but did operate) and of breaker reclosures. Should any voltage or current etc. be above a prescribed value, an alarm may have to be sounded. The diagrams, alarms, etc. have to be displayed and keeping up the display requires a large amount of computer effort, especially if the procedure suggested in case of any alarm condition should also be displayed. Recently, wall displays have given way to terminals which require less but still sizable amounts of computer time.

A few more functions [DL 74] to be performed by EPOC could probably be added, but even this list is sufficient. It is hoped that the reader is by this time persuaded that there definitely exists a problem.

Mathematically, the problems mentioned above were as follows:

(a) Solution of algebraic, non-linear equations (mostly load-flow) for the STEP, EDIP, and CAP programs.

(b) Solution of linear sets of equations as part of solving the above programs.

(c) Solution of a constrained, non-linear optimization problem for EDIP and unconstrained (least-square) problem for STEP.

The first computers to be used for EPOC were analog, but were replaced by digital computers when these became available. Lately, duplexes, i.e., two computers connected to a common memory, one working and the other on standby, are used. Whether this increases reliability and availability is doubtful.

The duplexes evolved from military installations like the Semi Automatic Ground Environment Air Defense System in which two (tube) processors worked concurrently and compared results from time to time. Such design, commonly called "fault tolerant," may be fine for military use but its low cost/effectiveness, low efficiency and, surprisingly, its insufficient speed precludes use for EPOC. That this is so can be seen by mentioning that the size of the system to be dealt with is usually defined as comprising 500-1200 busses, 1000-1600 lines and 250-900 substations. For a 1000 node network, the number of non-linear complex equations to be solved for load-flow is 1000 or separating real and imaginary parts, it is 2000. Since the solution uses iteratively the Newton-Raphson method, and load-flow as a whole may be repeatedly employed by, say, EDIP or CAP, the amount of arithmetic is so large as to make its response-time critical. The recourse to using a "reduced" instead of the real network obviously reduces the usefulness of all programs. Additional disadvantages are that there are two separate copies of the system's software and that the system cannot be easily expanded. Therefore, we obviously need some other hardware solutions (quite clearly - a pps).

We may conclude as follows:

- EPOC-problems (except those of SAC) are certainly non-π (written $\bar{\pi}$)
- They must be solved on-line, in real-time
- Since the data base is extremely large, none of the existing solutions seem to be able to do this
- We really need another hardware - preferably a parallel one
- If we develop programs of linear algebra, most mathematical problems of EPOC will have been solved

In addition to EPOC, the following are on-line $\bar{\pi}$-problems:

- Particular problems of nuclear reactor control
- Real-time controllers, in general (process control)
- Image processing and pattern recognition

- On-line simulation of control, medical, biological system etc.
- Traffic-control (especially for aircraft)
- Differential analyzers (for simulation which sometimes, say in military applications, may have to run at speeds faster than real time).

A few sentences from [Ko 74] will make this last application easier to understand.

"The very real difficulty in true parallel-arithmetic processing in general-purpose computations is the need for passing information such as intermediate results between the different arithmetic processors. If this is not done cleverly, processors must wait for one another, and the resulting overhead time obliterates the advantage of parallel processing.

Interestingly, the field of continuous system simulation, vital to engineering design, seems especially well suited for parallel digital-computer processing with small processors because the systems of differential equations describing most engineering systems are readily partitioned into blocks requiring relatively little intercommunication. As an example, a plant and its control systems might each be decribed by about 20 differential equations but only 4 or 5 state variables may have to pass between these subsystems. Our idea of multiprocessor simulation is not restricted to systems with such "sparse interconnections," but simulation of these systems will be speeded up very significantly.

The development of useful and efficient multiprocessor systems, especially with inexpensive minicomputers, is one of the significant challenges of the coming decade."

This is what we are going to do in this book and hope to have given the reader enough incentive to follow:

Chapter 2 and 3 on hardware; Chapter 4 on the interface; and starting with Chapter 5, algorithms and speedups to be expected.

2. FUNCTIONAL DESCRIPTION OF SOME PARALLEL SYSTEMS

INTRODUCTION

Various existing parallel processing systems, namely pipelined, SIMD, associative, dedicated on-line systems as well as some general multiprocessors will be discussed. The discussion is not detailed since the aim is only to provide a basis for developing the ASP systems in the next chapter. Each section therefore mentions the disadvantages of the particular system for on-line, non-Π problems. An "Abstract pps", the Apps is introduced with a view of calculating bounds for speedup in various systems and problems. Interconnection networks, especially those needed later are also discussed. If the description of various systems were enlarged, this chapter could serve as a part of a course on "Parallel Processing Hardware".

The systems which will be discussed are as follows: Section 1 deals with pipeline computers and shows that they are no solution for on-line, $\bar{\pi}$-problems. Section 2 introduces the "Abstract pps", the Apps not only as a model, but also to show that memory contention, locking, semaphores, etc. create most of the problems in all MIMD-systems. The speedups of Apps may be used as an upper bound for the hypothetical, though unrealistic, speed to be achieved.

Multiprocessors will be divided into those used in computer-center environments (Sections 2 or 4) and controllers for dedicated systems (Section 7). The first may assume well-partitioned, π-problems, but will suffer from memory interference and are not suitable for our purposes (which include non-π problems). The dedicated systems are not suitable because they cannot provide the availability and are not as cost-effective as we expect from a system to be utilized universally.

The best-known pps, the Illiac-IV is discussed in Section 5. We will find even this computer unsuitable for on-line, non-π problems, although much less so than the previous models.

In Section 6 we discuss associative systems and find even these not to our liking. So, having criticized all existing pps', the question of the appropriateness of the present chapter may be asked. The answers are:

(a) The conclusion is that we, in fact, need a more generalized architecture.

(b) From the review we will collect a large number of facts which will help us design such a solution.

Such design will be the substance of Chapter 3 and to get to it we must muddle through the review of the present chapter.

2.1 PIPELINING

Aims: To define the terms hardware and software pipelining. To give the reasons why pipeline systems are seldom used in on-line process control applications.

A number of different parallel processing systems were either suggested or actually built. Their characteristics may be looked up in the literature, especially in [Thu 76], [TW 75], [YF 77] and [En 77]. Mentioned below will be only those which in some way lead to the basic ASP-design or were actually built.

This book is written in Detroit, so inevitably an assembly line comes to mind and in fact pipelining is the application of an assembly line principle to computers. The basic idea may be grasped from Fig. 1. If a dozen workers along a line assemble a car, the first fastening the chassis to the conveyor, the second putting the first 4 bolts in,..,mounting the engine,.., putting on tires,.., driving out the car and each works on his job exactly 5 minutes, each car is on the assembly 1 hour, but a car is leaving the line every 5 minutes. Thus, the speedup would be 1h/5min or 12 - exactly equal to the "length" of the pipe.

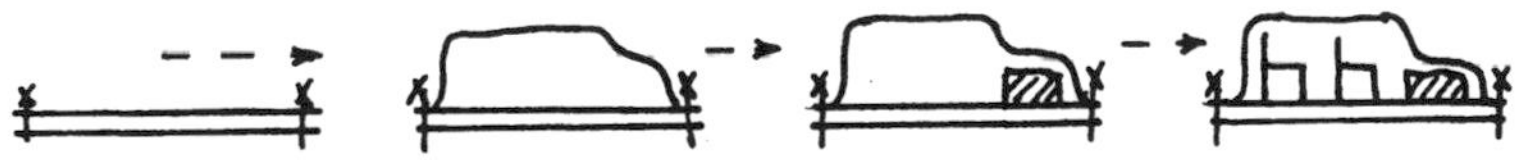

Fig. 1: An assembly line

This being so, we might be tempted to make the pipe as long as possible and subdivide the job in as many subtasks as possible. Even in a car, this has a limit since some jobs cannot be subdivided e.g. putting in a bolt. Moreover there are some precedence relations e.g. the chassis must be on the conveyor before an attempt is made to install the seats and if a subtask is longer than others, all will have to wait for the slowest worker.

In a computer a pipeline consists of processing "segments". Each segment executes a part of the processing and the result appears at the end of the last segment. Full speedup is achieved by having p data items at the same time in the pipe. Buffers must separate the segments but since transfer can be effected only after all buffers have stabilized, the speedup is reduced. Obviously, also, the speed of the pipeline is determined by its slowest element so we should try to make the segment delays as equal as possible.

The simplest pipelining would overlap the Instruction (I) and Execution (E) cycles of computers. Thus, while executing one, the cpu would fetch the next instruction.

The times of I, E i.e. t(I), t(E) depend on the particular instruction, e.g., an unconditional branch is done faster than say a floating-point addition. We must therefore impose the conditions: $I_m <\cdot E_m$; $I_m <\cdot I_{m+1}$ and $E_m <\cdot E_{m+1}$ where $<\cdot$ means "should be done before". The total time will be:

$$T = \Sigma[t(I_m) + t(E_m)];\ m\Sigma=1,\ldots,n \qquad (1)$$

$m\Sigma$ is read "m of the sum." If we allow $E_m <\cdot I_{m+2}$ as long as E_m does not change I_{m+1} (for instance by branching) we will have with $t(I_o) = t(E_{n+1}) = 0$:

$$T = \Sigma\max[t(E_m),\ t(I_m)];\ m\Sigma=0,\ldots,n \qquad (2)$$

and since $\max(t_1,t_2)<(t_1+t_2)$, the speedup will be higher. If for all m, $t(E_m)=t(I_m)$

we would have a speedup $\sigma=2$. If $t(E_m) \gg t(I_m)$, only $\sigma=1$ would be achieved.

We have seen already that σ could be increased by subdividing even more the tasks. Thus if we subdivide the instructions further, e.g. form address of instruction, fetch it, decode it, form operand addres(ses), fetch operand(s), execute and store results then if the pipe is full, and there is no branching, a sevenfold speedup would be achieved.

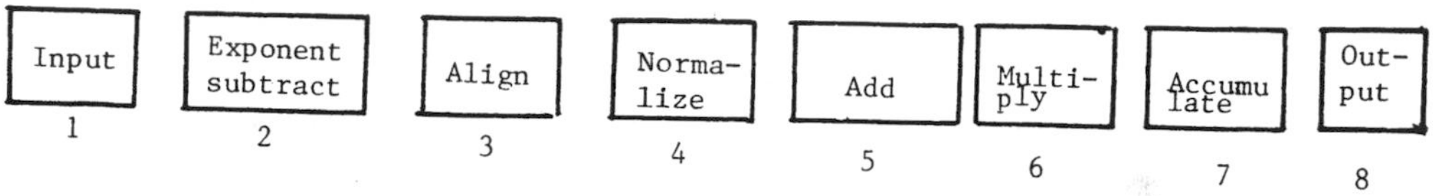

Fig. 2: Segments for floating point operations

The pipeline approach can also speed-up arithmetic. Since floating point operations are longer, that is where the advantages of pipelining will show. Thus, the TI ASC computer has an eight-segment pipeline (Fig. 2) for executing floating-point (and fixed-point) instructions. The eight segments are for:

1. Receiving input operands
2. Comparing mantissas for floating point additions and subtractions
3. Aligning operands
4. Adding and subtracting operands (both fixed and floating point)
5. Normalizing the result
6. Multiplication (with carry-save method). Since operands of 32 bits each are multiplied, a 64 bit result is produced.
7. This segment does effectively an addition but could also accumulate sums.
8. Output segment.

Note that the pipeline is full only if all segments have work to do. Even for floating-point addition where segments 6,7 are not used, this is not the case. For other cases, the speedup will be reduced even more.

We discussed the so-called "hardware pipelining". There also exists "software pipelining". For instance, it was suggested to use an "array processor" the AP-120B attached to a host computer for solving EPOC-problems [Ep 80]. The AP-120B is a pipeline machine (fig. 3) which can add and multiply floating point numbers simultaneously. Suppose that we want to compute a vector $\underline{c} = \underline{a}^2+\underline{b}^2$ i.e. $c_i = a_i^2+b_i^2$ for $i=1,\ldots, n$. In a sequential computer with the programming rules of AP-120B (fig. 4), this would require 21 cycles per iteration (fig. 5), with hardware parallelism 12 cycles (fig.6), and with software pipelining, 12 cycles for each stage (fig. 7); on the average, <u>if</u> the pipe works full time, only 4 cycles per iteration are required.

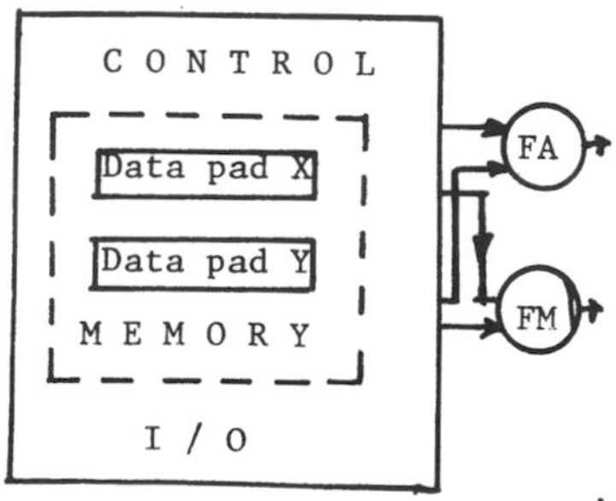

Fig. 3: Data pads (buffers) of AP-120B

Cycle			
1	FMUL A,B	Multiply A and B	Floating
2	FMUL		point
3	FMUL		multiply
4	---	A^*B available here	(FMUL)
1	FADD A,B	Add A and B	FP
2	FADD		Add
3	---	A+B available here	(FADD)
1	FETCH A	Fetch A from memory	Fetching
2	---		Data
3	---		from
4	---	A available here	memory
1	DEC N	Decrement N	Test
2	BGT LOOP	Branch to LOOP if N>0	and
3	---	Here if $N \leq 0$	branch

Fig. 4: Programming rules of AP-120B

```
LOOP:   FETCH A_i  ⎫                    FMUL B_i,B_i  ⎫
        NOP        ⎪                    FMUL          ⎪
        NOP        ⎬ FETCH A_i          FMUL          ⎬ FORM B_i^2
        SAVE A_i   ⎭                    SAVE B_i^2    ⎭
        FETCH B_i  ⎫                    FADD A_i^2,B_i^2  ⎫
        NOP        ⎪                    FADD              ⎬ FORM C_i=A_i^2+B_i^2
        NOP        ⎬ FETCH B_i          STORE C_i         ⎭
        SAVE B_i   ⎭                    DEC N      ⎫ Decrement  loop  count
        FMUL A_i,A_i ⎫                  BGT LOOP   ⎬ and branch if count>0
        FMUL         ⎪           DONE:  RETURN     ⎭
        FMUL         ⎬ FORM A_i^2
        SAVE A_i^2   ⎭
```

Fig. 5: $c_i = a_i^2 + b_i^2$ on a sequential computer

```
LOOP:   FETCH A_i
        FETCH B_i
        NOP
        SAVEX A_i
                  FMUL A_i,A_i;  SAVEY B_i
                  FMUL B_i,B_i
                  FMUL
                  FMUL;   SAVEX A_i^2
                                      FADD B_i^2, A_i^2
                                      FADD
                                      DEC N
                                      STORE C_i; BGT LOOP
DONE:   RETURN
```

Fig. 6: $c_i = a_i^2 + b_i^2$ with hardware pipelining (using data pads)

	Stage 1	Stage 2	Stage 3
	FETCH A_1		
	FETCH B_1		
	NOP		
	SAVEX A_1		
	FETCH A_2;	FMUL A_1,A_1; SAVEY B_1	
	FETCH B_2;	FMUL B_1,B_1	
	NOP;	FMUL	
	SAVEX A_2;	FMUL; SAVEY A_1^2	
LOOP:	FETCH A_i;	FMUL A_{i-1},A_{i-1}; SAVEY B_{i-1};	FADD B_{i-2}^2, A_{i-2}^2
	FETCH B_i;	FMUL B_{i-1},B_{i-1};	FADD
	NOP;	FMUL;	DEC N
	SAVEX A_i;	FMUL; SAVEY A_{i-1}^2;	STORE C_{i-2}; BGT LOOP
DONE:	RETURN		

Fig. 7: $c_i = a_i^2 + b_i^2$ with software pipelining

Suppose we have independent segments like those of Fig. 2 for performing concurrently additions and multiplications of floating-point numbers. If the product of two vectors $\underline{a}^T\underline{b}=\Sigma a_ib_i$; $i\Sigma=1,2,\ldots,$ n is to be calculated in a software pipeline, this can be done as follows. Product $a_1 \cdot b_1$ starts on the multiplication pipeline (4 segments namely 1,6,7 and 8) and one time-step later $a_2 \cdot b_2$ starts. Four clocks, later, the pipe is full and the products arrive at the clock rate; the overall time is 3+n. Addition of the first two products starts and since it requires 6 segments, 6 time-steps later the sums could start coming out of the pipe. Obviously, feedback is needed here to accumulate the partial sums, but if this time-loss is disregarded, each new sum arrives after $5+\log_2 n$. A high speed results.

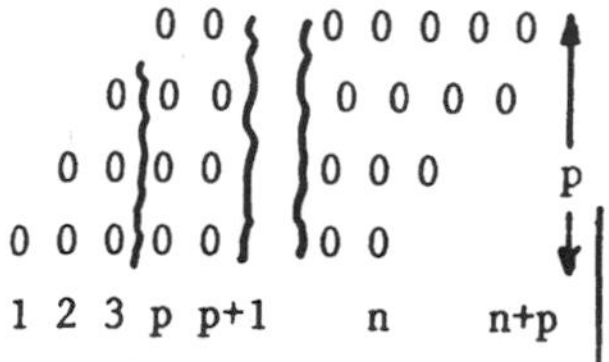

Fig. 8: Work

A generalization of this process is shown in Fig. 8. From it we see that during the initial (p-1) steps, only part of the stages work (water has to flow into the pipe); the same happens at the end (water has to flow out of the pipe). If the number of instructions is n, then the total amount of "work" (circles) is n·p, but it takes the time of (n+p-1) to do it. For part of this time the pipeline is underutilized. If it could be fully utilized all the time, n·p instructions would be done in time n (shift the circles of Fig. 8 left, to form a rectangle). Thus, the "utilization factor" ν and speedup σ are:

$$\nu \cong n/(n+p); \quad \sigma \cong np/(n+p); \qquad (3) \quad (4)$$

In this simple case: $\sigma = p \cdot \nu$ (5)

The speedup and utilization will be further reduced because of the following:

- A segment should access a buffer only after making sure that the buffer contains the data required. To this effect, data is tagged; checking and changing tags takes time.

- In I/E overlap the memory was common and only one data item can be accessed a a time.
- Normally, when an interrupt occurs, the status is saved and work resumed later. With a full pipeline, we must first "let the water run out" and to do this, a point in the program must be selected such that program execution will not pass it. "Filling" and "draining" the pipe occurs not only when work begins and ends but at each interrupt, with even more complicated control.
- The same applies for a case of either branching or feedback.

Pipeline computers are well suited for "repeating" programs, e.g. payroll or sorting. All the instructions of a loop may be stored in an instruction buffer (fast memory) so that no fetching of instructions is required for as long as the program is "in the loop". If each of these loop instructions is used a number of times, this kind of operation, called "loop mode" may decrease the required number of memory accesses and so will the time required for completion of the program assuming the processor is faster than main memory access time.

The following additional reasons may be mentioned for not utilizing the pipeline computers for process-control:

(a) Complicated control, speed reduction by interrupts etc. explained above.

(b) Present day technology supplies complete modules (LSI chips or micro-computers) cheaper and better than specially built pipeline hardware.

(c) The hardware required by pipelined computers seems to be expensive, so the pipes should be kept full most of the time in order to achieve a good cost/effectiveness. No such "filling" of the pipes by the operands or data can be assured in general. Stated differently, once results start coming out of the "pipe", they will do so at the rate of the slowest rather than the fastest unit.

(d) The performance of the pipeline computers depends crucially on performing long strings of identical operations on the data streams; this is not possible in the usual situation, e.g. in electric power control.

2.2 APPS, COMPLEXITY AND SPEEDUP

Aims: To describe Apps, define speedup, time ratio etc., to introduce the "Haydn effect" and fan-in.

In general, a computer may be represented as a processor with memory (Fig. 9). The processor is capable of doing certain operations ("programs") whose operands come from the memory and whose results are stored there. Each operation has a fixed execution time. The memory is random-access.

In analogy, the "abstract parallel-processing system" Apps (Fig. 10) has p identical processors (of the same type as that of Fig. 9). Additionally, we shall

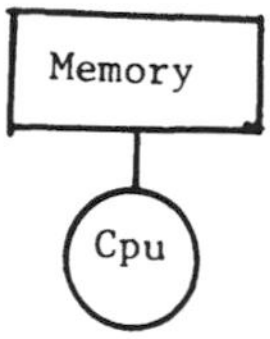

Fig. 9: A computer

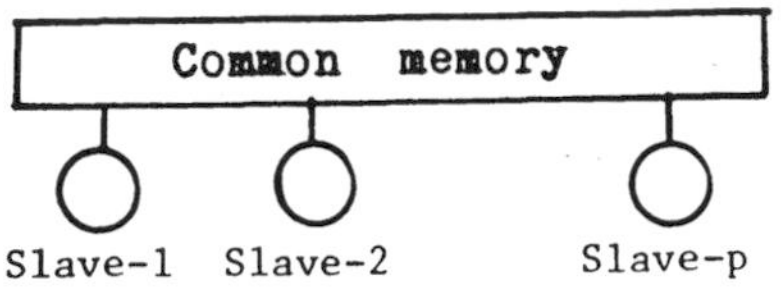

Fig.10: Apps.

assume that processors may access memory simultaneously, even at the same memory location. (It is this feature which makes Apps to be rather unpractical). We shall refer to computations on a pps as p-parallelism; when no limit on p is set as in Apps, we call it unbounded parallelism. We expect a speedup of p for Apps, i.e. it should complete its work in $t_p=1/p$ of the time t_s it takes a single processor to complete the same job. We explore next under what circumstances this will be possible.

In defining the speedup, we follow |St73|: "In any study of computer systems, we need some measure of efficiency.....An appropriate one is the speedup σ, defined as

$$\sigma = \frac{\text{computation time on a serial computer}}{\text{computation time on a parallel computer}} = t_1/t_p \tag{6}$$

where solving a problem on a system with i computers requires time t_i.

To achieve a fair comparison, we always compare the best serial algorithm even when those two algorithms are quite different." This definition will be used whenever such "best" algorithms exist; otherwise, the same algorithm will be used on a serial computer and on ASP.

We will mostly use the inverse of speedup, the

$$\text{Time Reduction Ratio } \rho = 1/\sigma = t_p/t_1 \tag{7}$$

because of the following: The time to do a job with p cpu's includes normally the time t_1, as needed on a single cpu and additionally time pt' for transferring information among the p cpu's and their synchronization. Since $(t_1+pt')=t_p$ is split among p cpu's, the ratio is

$$\rho = [(t_1+pt')/p]/t_1 = 1/p + t'/t \tag{8}$$

Ideally $\rho_0=1/p$; in fact $\rho>1/p$ with a "deterioration" of $\delta=t'/t$. This definition though is wrong as evidenced by the following. For $p=10$, $\rho=1/9$ we would get $\delta=1/9-1/10=1/90\cong 1.1\%$ whereas for $p=100$, $\rho=1/90$: $\delta=1/90-1/100=1/900\cong 0.011\%$. We better use $\delta=pt'/t$ so that in the two cases above are $\delta=11\%$.

Speedup measures the effectiveness of the parallel solution. Ideally σ would be ρ; but in actual practice $\sigma < p$. Heller [He 76] Sameh and Kuck [KS 72] suggest

$$\eta = 100\sigma/p = 100/(\rho\cdot p) \tag{9}$$

which for both cases mentioned above shows an efficiency of 90%.

Let us assume that the processors execute binary operations, that is, each operation is performed on two operands and yields a single result; examples are addition, multiplication, comparision, etc. We also assume that each of these operations requires one unit of time. Let us take a problem which yields a single result for which it needs m operations and try to do it on Apps. We also assume that Apps works in an optimal fashion, i.e. it does no unnecessary operations and at each step it employs the maximum possible number of processors.

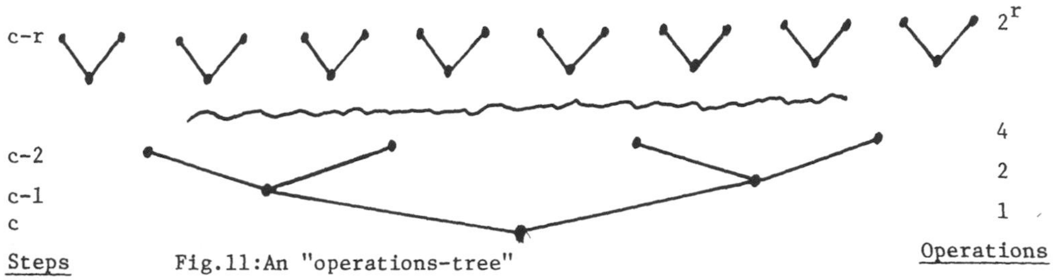

Fig.11:An "operations-tree"

Suppose the program terminates after c time steps (see fig. 11). The final scalar "result" is the outcome of a binary operation on two operands performed by a single slave at a time c; the remaining (p-1) slaves do nothing at time c. Backtracking, at time (c-1) at most two slaves are usefully employed, namely those which produce the two operands for the operations at time c. (We say "at most" since one of the two operands may be ready from a previous step). Since at c only one slave, at (c-1) at most two, and at (c-2) at most 4 slaves are working, it follows that at time (c-r), at most 2^r slaves work. The amount of useful work or the number of operations which can be done in (r+1) stages is thus

$$m \leqq 1 + 2^1 + 2^2 + \ldots + 2^r = 2^{r+1} - 1 \qquad (10)$$

If we assume that each operation requires one unit of time

$$t_p = r + 1 \geqq \lceil \log(m+1) \rceil \qquad (11)$$

where t_p is the running time of Apps, the ceiling operation reflects the "at most" feature and log will always be "base-2".

The previous case is true for as long as 2^r does not exceed the number of available slaves p. Let us next assume that

$$p < 2^{(r+1)} \qquad (12)$$

Here, from the c-(r+1) step for say k steps, we must be satisfied with p slaves (We have no more). The total amount of useful operations done throughout the process by all slaves is $(2^{r+1} - 1 + k*p)$. Since the final result requires at least m operations, but, because of parallelism may require more, we have:

$$m \leqq 2^{(r+1)} - 1 + p*k; \qquad k \geqq \lceil (m+1-2^{(r+1)})/p \rceil \qquad (13)$$

The number of parallel steps is now

$$t_p = r+1+k \geqq r+1+\lceil (m+1-2^{(r+1)})/p \rceil \qquad (14)$$

Assumption (12) leads to

$$r+1 > \lceil \log p \rceil \qquad \text{and} \qquad t_p \geqq \lceil \log p \rceil + \lceil (m+1-2^{(r+1)})/p \rceil$$

We have thus proved the "fan-in" theorem [BM 75] by Munro and Paterson:

<u>Theorem</u>: If a computation of a scalar requiring at least m binary operations is done on an Apps with p slaves, then

$$t_p \geqq \begin{cases} \lceil \log p \rceil + \lceil (m+1-2^{\lceil \log p \rceil})/p \rceil ; & \text{for } m \geqq 2^{\lceil \log p \rceil} \\ \lceil \log(m+1) \rceil & ; \text{otherwise} \end{cases} \qquad (15)$$

Let us examine it for the case that $p=2^v$ when $\lceil \log_2 p \rceil = \log_2 p$, $2^{\log_2 p} = 2^v = p$

$$t_p \geq \begin{cases} \log p + (m+1-p)/p & ; \quad \text{for } m \geqq p \\ \lceil \log(m+1) \rceil & ; \quad \text{for } m < p \end{cases} \tag{16}$$

We have defined the time reduction ratio ρ as the inverse of the speedup. Then, since sequentially we need m steps:

$$\rho = \frac{t_p}{t_s} \geq \left.\begin{matrix} \frac{1}{p} + \frac{\log(p)-1+1/p}{m} & ; \quad \text{for } p \leqq m \\ \lceil \log(m+1) \rceil / m & ; \quad \text{for } p > m \end{matrix}\right\} \tag{17}$$

We see that ρ is always above the ideal 1/p and for an Apps with unbounded p

$$\rho_{opt} = \lceil \log_2(m+1) \rceil / m \tag{18}$$

Review again Fig. 11. If $p = 2^r$ is the number of "tree leaves" then one level further there are p/2 nodes, then p/4 etc. At level w, there are $p/2^w$ nodes and at the root we must have $p/2^r = 1$. Thus the height of the tree is r = logp. Inserting (10) into (18) and $2^r = p$ yields

$$\rho_{opt} = (r+1)/(2^{r+1}-1) \cong r/2^{r+1} = \log p/(2p) = (1/p)(\log p/2) \tag{19}$$

At the start (Fig. 11), all p slaves work; in the next step only half of them work, in step w only $p/2^{w-1}$ and so on, until at the last step (r), only a single slave works. This reminds the author of Joseph Haydn's "Farewell Symphony". To impress upon Graf Esterhazy that it was time to let them depart for Vienna, each musician (slave) in turn bowed and left the stage. Finally only the conductor (master) remained and Count Esterhazy was convinced. We see this "Haydn Effect" in Fig. 11 and it obviously reduces the speedup. Since for $p = 2^r$:

$$\sigma = (2p/\log p) \tag{20}$$

the Haydn effect reduces the speedup by the utilization factor

$$\upsilon = 2/\log p \tag{21}$$

This also shows that in Apps, the equipment is not used efficiently; there is quite a lot of redundancy; the equipment is underutilized.

We have thus far defined the speedup σ, ratio ρ, efficiency η, and the hardware utilization υ. They will be useful later.

We next prove a theorem relating unbounded to p parallelism.

Theorem [Br 74]: If a computation which consists of n unit-time operations can be done in time t using an unbounded number of slaves, then - with p bounded - it can be done in

$$t_p = t + (n-t)/p \tag{22}$$

Proof. We arrange the n operations in levels 1,2,...t, where the levels are defined inductively: level 1 consists of operations performed purely on the input values, i.e. not depending on the results of any previous computations; level i is defined as the set of operations which uses results of level 1 to i-1 and which do not belong to level i-1. Let us assume that the ith level consists of u_i operations.

Now, given p, we shall schedule the operations so that Apps will process with all its processors level after level. If we assume $u_i = m_i p + r_i$, then processing that level will take $m_i + 1$ time units. (We have p processors, so we need m_i time units and then one more for r_i).

The worst case from the point of view of efficiency is when $u_i = 1$, because in that case all processors but one are idle. Therefore, for this worst case:

$$t_p = \Sigma\ (m_i + 1) = \Sigma\ m_i + t\ ;\ i\Sigma = 1,\ldots,t \qquad (23)$$

Since

$$\Sigma u_i = \Sigma(m_i p+1) = t + p\Sigma m_i = n\ ;\ i\Sigma = 1,\ldots,t \qquad (24)$$

we have

$$\Sigma m_i = (n - t)/p \qquad \text{and} \qquad t_p = (n - t)/p + t \qquad \text{Q.E.D.} \qquad (25)$$

(iΣ means in this book the summation over index i, that is "i summed over...")

To compare various systems, we will use as a "benchmark" program, the multiplication of two matrices

$$\underline{C} = \underline{A}\cdot\underline{B} \qquad (26)$$

It is based on computing n^2 scalar products

$$c_{ij} = \underline{a}_{i\cdot}\underline{b}_{\cdot j} = \Sigma a_{ik} b_{kj}\ ;\ k\Sigma=1,\ldots,n \qquad (27)$$

This obviously requires n multiplications and (n-1) additions. If we assume that each multiplication or division takes a single unit of time, then:

$$\ell_{opt} = 2n-1 \qquad (28)$$

Thus $$\log(\ell+1) = \log(2n) = 1+\log n \qquad (29)$$

and application of the fan-in theorem yields:

$$t_p \geq \begin{cases} \lceil \log p \rceil + \lceil (2n-2^{\lceil \log p \rceil})/p \rceil & ;\quad \text{for } 2n-1>2^{\lceil \log p \rceil} \qquad (30) \\ \lceil \log n \rceil + 1 & ;\ \text{otherwise} \qquad (31) \end{cases}$$

Given enough slaves (unbounded parallelism), the optimum of $\lceil \log_2 n \rceil + 1$ can be achieved. The computation would start with one parallel multiplication(for all $a_{ik}b_{kj}$, k=1,...n) followed by log(n) fan-in additions. The number of slaves required here would be n for a single c_{ij} and for the entire matrix-product n^3. Thus, a "lean" matrix of n = 100, would need one million (1,000,000) slaves. Even with the development of cheap VLSI-chips the above is a number much too high and proves the Apps to be a rather abstract model.

2.3 INTERCONNECTION NETWORKS

Aims: To describe various interconnection networks and settle on a single bus.

Apps is a model of a general purpose multiprocessor (an MIMD-system). The basic but abstract assumption is that there is no interference i.e., if two slaves require the same data item from the memory, they get it at the same time. In real life, this is not how memory works. Moreover, for the sake of stability (getting the same results for the same data every time the calculation is done) we must require that no data is read out of part of memory accessed by some other program since that program may very well have modified it. We must "protect" or "lock" such parts of memory.

All decentralized systems such as Apps are based on the principle of each processor finding a new job for itself once its present task is completed. This requires the creation of a special "labor exchange," "superprogram" or "operating system" in the common memory. Since each processor should be able to access it, this would lead to memory contention if done simultaneously by more than a single program. Thus, with the operating system in the common memory, we will have to prevent simultaneous access to it by "locking" the memory. A "test and set" instruction TS is added to the repertoire of many present-day processors so that no two processors might use a resource protected, for example, by "lock A". This locking could be achieved by the "program":

```
TS A  /*test A, set condition code to it, set A=1*/
BNZ -4/*branch 4 bytes back if condition code not 0*/
```

which would first mask out all interrupts for its duration and work as follows.

Suppose A=0 before execution of these two instructions (i.e., the resource (memory) may be used). Then TS will leave 0 in the condition code register and simultaneously set A=1. The BNZ=branch on not zero will not lead to a jump. Overall then, A was set to 1 and the program may access the memory.

If A=1 ahead of the above program, then TS will set both A and the condition code to 1. Hence, the second instruction will be a return to the first instruction. The program is now in a "waiting loop" from which only another program, by making A=0, may release it. This "busy waiting" (like a cat chasing its tail) may take a long time. Altogether, in a pps with decentralized control, a "point of diminishing returns" may be reached rather quickly because of an extended operating system. This is evidenced by Fig. 12 taken from an existing system. (The more units were added, the less work was done because most of the time was wasted on querrying the operating system).

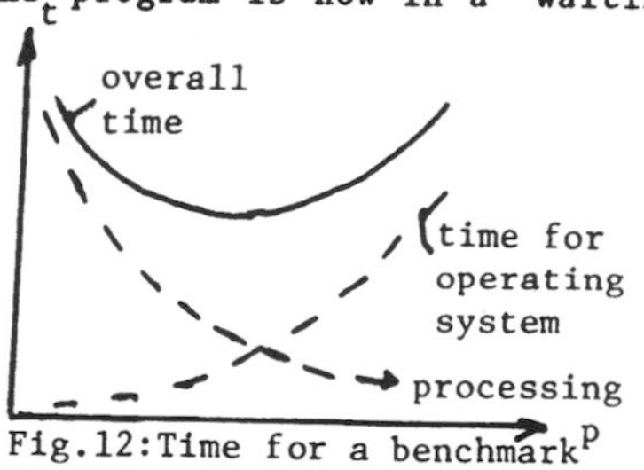

Fig.12:Time for a benchmark

It is seen that a pps with a common memory may require not only a complicated operating system acting as a "labor exchange", but may result in serious interference and time loss, if locks, semaphores etc., are to be used. It was therefore only natural that the idea occurred to many that instead of using a single memory, one should buy them in "blocks", the more so since this is the way they are nowadays produced. Therefore our system will consist of p processing elements (PE's or slaves) and m memory units (ME's) and we have a new problem on our hands, namely how to connect them. Interconnection networks are the subject of the present section.

The simplest way to connect the controller, slaves and memories is by a bus (Fig. 13). There are no continuous connections between functional units and control of transfers between units is accomplished using time-slicing techniques.

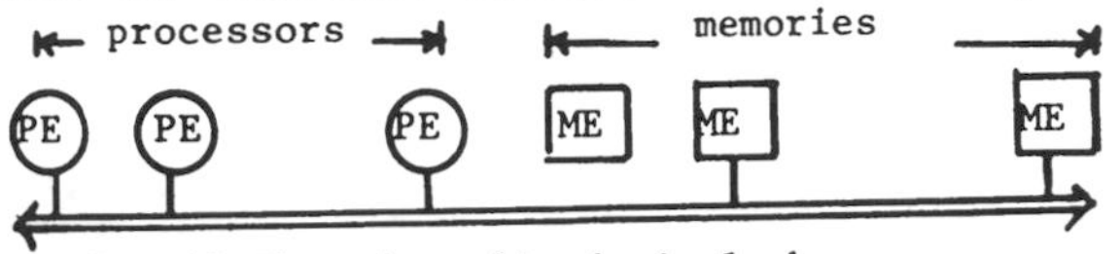

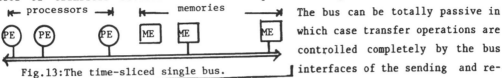

Fig.13:The time-sliced single bus.

The bus can be totally passive in which case transfer operations are controlled completely by the bus interfaces of the sending and receiving units. It is possible to simplify the transfer process by the use of a centralized bus arbiter. The cost required to add or remove functional units to the bus is quite low; usually all that is required is to physically attach or detach the unit. The location to add a unit is also flexible.

The bus may be a full word or one byte wide or it may be able to handle only a single bit at a time. If the bus has fewer bits, the control functions become more complex. Usually all bits of the bus are transferred in parallel to facilitate speed, sometimes using buffer registers. The control lines select a specific device and its mode of operation (talker or listener) and also synchronize data transmission with the computer's operating cycle.

A bus is the basic part of any switching system. Let us deal with it therefore in more detail. A possible switching unit using a single bus is shown in Figs.14,15. This bus will include all data and address lines as well as lines which manage the connections between the processors and memories.

The connection is asynchronous in the sense that it may last any integer number of memory cycles. When the talk is finished, an End-of-Transmission EOT signal from the talking processor interrupts the connection and allows other processors to talk over the bus. The bus is time sliced.

Memory unit j has a device number, say j, which is transmitted on $\log_2(m)$ lines of addressing. The remaining address lines, contain the address inside the j'th memory.

The switch includes a shift register which works as a ring-counter, i.e. it shifts its p bits around (bit p is shifted into position 1, bit 1 into position 2 etc.). At the beginning, this register is loaded by a sequence of 1's and a single 0. When the switch operates, its oscillator shifts this 0 around the register at a clock rate much higher than the memory cycle (at least p).

Each bit of the counter enters an inverter which transmits it to the corresponding processor i by "Enable (i)". Obviously, only the request for which both bit(i)=0 in the ring counter and a memory request MRQ(i)=1 will transfer its MRQ (to all units).

Assuming that the i-th bit of the ring-counter is 0 and processor i requests memory access, the following occurs:

(a) An MRQ is sent to all memories over the MRQ line.

(b) As long as the "busy" flip-flop is "1", the memory bus is transmitting

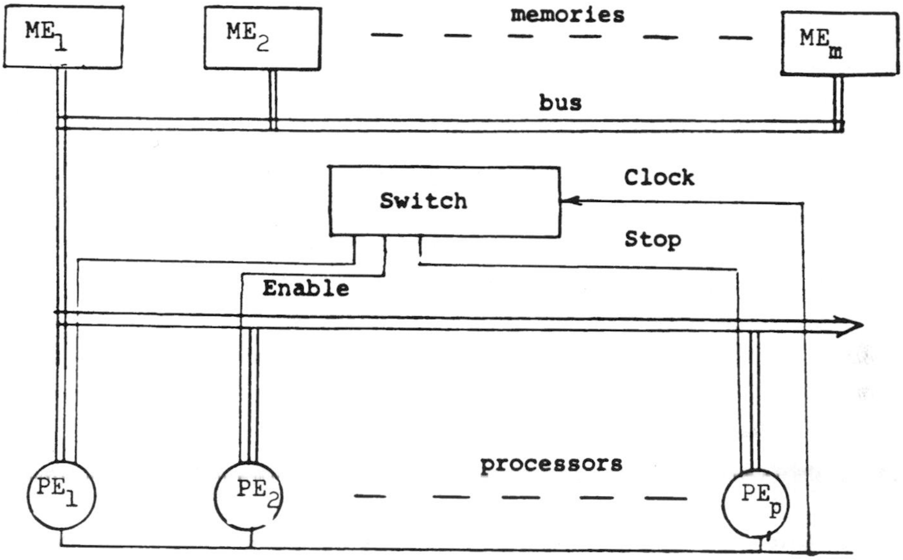

Fig. 14: General diagram of a particular single-bus system.

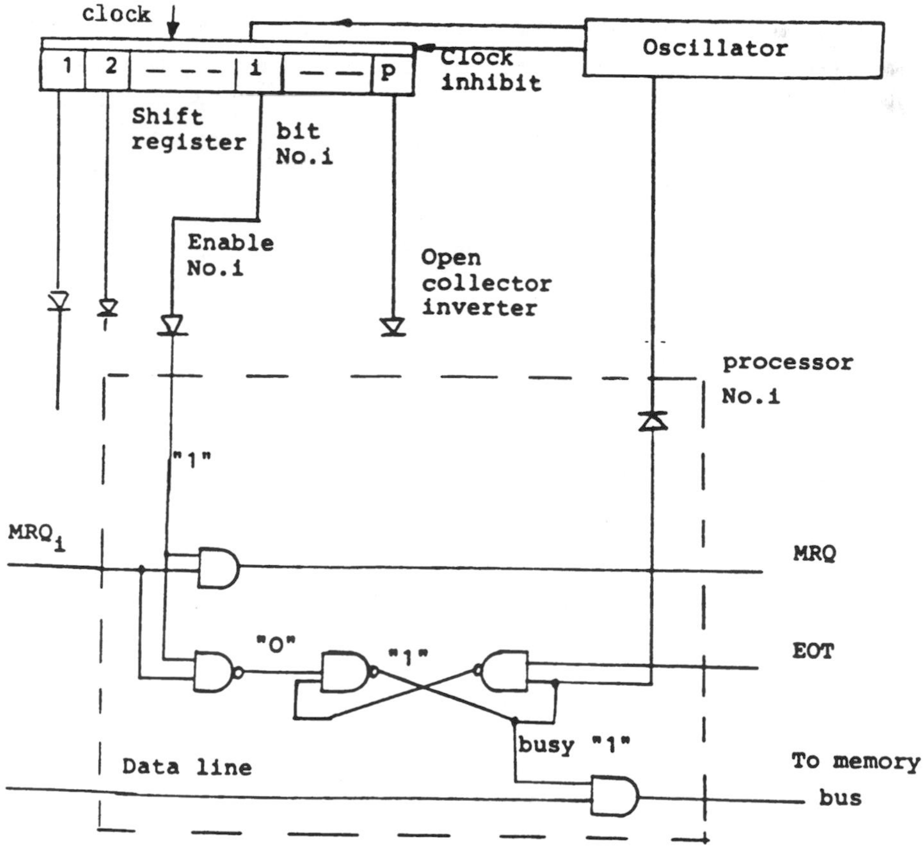

Fig. 15: Some details of the single-bus circuit.

whatever appears on the data lines. The memory bus lines therefore transmit the memory address requested.

(c) An inhibit pulse is sent to the ring counter, stopping (locking) it in its present state until the end of the talk. This inhibits other processors from getting the bus as long as the present talk continues.

The talk itself is started by an AKN acknowledge signal from memory. If none arrives, then a "time out" cancels the memory request.

We have discussed until now the first part of the talk. It is started by the processor issuing the memory request MRQ. Actually two more signals are sent simultaneously:

MOD - when "up", the processor wants to read from memory, when "down" the processor wants to write into memory.

ADT - when "up", the data lines carry an address (of a word in memory), when "down", the data lines carry data.

Those memory units which are not otherwise busy check the addresses of the data lines. If an address applies, it is stored in the memory address register of this particular memory and an acknowledge signal is send to the processor.

(a) Reading: The particular processor receives an AKN signal and consequently interrupts the MRQ-signal and the address from the data lines; it subsequently opens its register lines so as to receive data from a memory. The memory reads from a location specified by the memory address register and puts this data on the lines. At the same time, the memory sends a second AKN-signal to the processor, which stores the information in a register and sends an End-of-Transmission (EOT) signal (Fig. 15); it sets the busy flip-flop to 0 and this in turn interrupts the transmitter/receiver circuits of processor i which connect it with the memory unit. In the case of reading, the memory interrupts its transmitters, thereby stopping the reading phase. The memory (ME_j) is again ready to service any processor.

(b) Writing: PE_i receives the AKN-signal and severs the MRQ and the address as well as opens its transmitter circuits, so that data is transferred to the data lines. Then an additional MRQ-signal is transmitted with the ADT-signal of 0. The memory receives the MRQ signal and checks the ADT-line. If ADT=0, the memory stores the data on the data lines in the memory information register, performs the writing in the location indicated by the memory address register and transmits a second AKN signal to PE_i. Next, PE_i interrupts its transmitters, its MRQ signal and sends an EOT signal to ME_j. It is this pulse which severs the connection.

As seen, in addition to the data lines which must be bi-directional (and accommodate both addresses and data), the following unidirectional lines connect a processor to all memories: MRQ - memory request, ADT - address/data control, MOD - read/write and EOT - end of transmission.

A uni-directional line AKN-acknowledge, connects memories with processors.

Note that during the entire time that PE_i is connected to the memories, all transmitters and receivers of all the other processors from/to the memory bus are interrupted since their enable lines were set 0 - a result of the structure of the ring counter. Note also that a number of messages and acknowledge signals have to be exchanged through the bus; this asynchronous "handshaking" requires considerable time.

Each message that is placed on the bus must contain the data that are to be transferred and the address of the unit to which they are directed. There are no conflicts between multiple messages arriving at a unit simultaneously since only one message is on the bus at a time and a transmitter has to wait until the bus is free to place its message on the line. Each unit in the bus must contain the circuitry necessary to recognize its address in a message and respond correspondingly.

Bus control schemes are usually classified [Thu 72] according to whether they use centralized control or not. In the present case we will make the choice to use a master for other considerations. Hence, only centralized control will be discussed.

A question to be answered is how two units use the bus. Quoting [Thu 72] the following possibilities exist:

Centralized daisy chaining is illustrated in Fig. 16 and works as follows:

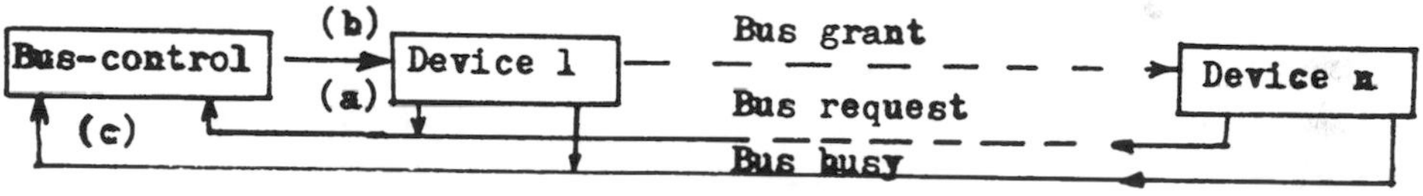

Fig. 16: Daisy chaining bus control.

Devices put requests on the "Bus request" line (a).

The controller returns a signal on the "bus grant" line b. It will ripple through the devices.

When the two signals check, the "Bus busy" line (c) is raised, (a) is dropped and starts data transmission and (b) is held up by (c).

The obvious advantage of such scheme is its simplicity; very few control lines are required and the number of them is independent of the number of devices; hence, additional devices can be added by simply connecting them to the bus.

A disadvantage of the daisy chaining scheme is its susceptability to failure. If a failure occurs in the bus-available circuitry of a device, it could prevent succeeding devices from ever getting control of the bus or it could allow more than one device to transmit over the bus at the same time. A power failure in a single device or the necessity to take a device off-line can also lead to problems with the daisy chain method. However, the logic involved is quite simple.

Another disadvantage is the fixed priority structure which results. The devices which are "closer" to the bus controller always receive control of the bus in preference to those which are "further away." If the closer devices have a high demand for the bus, the distant devices could be locked out.

Since the bus-available signal must sequentially ripple through the devices, this bus assignment mechanism can also be quite slow.

Figure 17 illustrates a central "polling" system. As in the centralized daisy chaining method, each device can place a signal on the bus-request line. When the bus controller receives a request, it begins polling the devices to determine which is making the request. The polling is done by counting on the polling lines. When the count corresponds to a requesting device, that device raises the bus busy line. The controller then stops the polling until the device has completed its transmission and removed the busy signal. If there is another bus request, the count may restart from zero or may be continued from where it stopped.

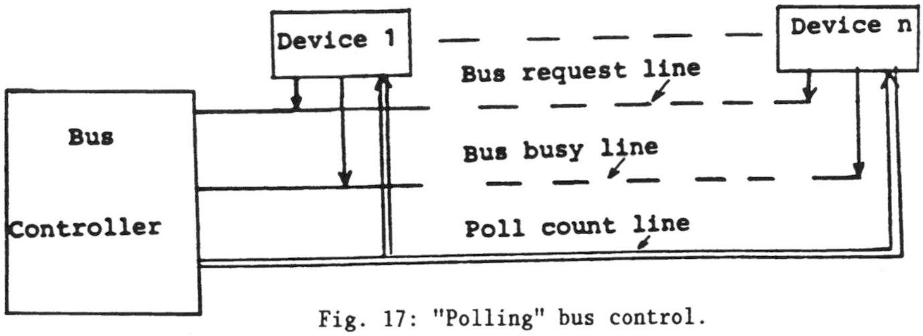

Fig. 17: "Polling" bus control.

Restarting from zero each time establishes the same sort of device priority as proximity does in daisy chaining, while continuing from the stopping point is a round-robin approach which gives equal opportunity to all devices. The priorities need not be fixed because the polling sequence is easily altered.

The bus request line can be eliminated by allowing the polling counter to continuously cycle except while it is stopped by a device using the bus.

Polling does not suffer from the reliability or placement problems of daisy chaining but the number of devices (Fig. 17) is limited by the number of polling lines.

The third method of centralized bus control, "independent request", is shown in Fig. 18. In this case each device has a separate pair of bus request and bus granted lines, which it uses for communicating with the bus controller. When a device requires use of the bus, it sends its bus-request to the controller. The controller selects the next device to receive service and sends a bus-granted to it. The selected device lowers its request and raises bus-assigned, indicating to all other devices that the bus is busy. After the transmission is complete, the device lowers the bus assigned line and the bus controller removes bus-granted and selects the next requesting device.

The overhead time required here for allocating the bus can be shorter than in daisy chaining or polling since all bus requests are presented simultaneously to the bus controller. In addition, there is complete flexibility available for selecting the next device for service. The controller can use prespecified or adaptive priorities, a round-robin scheme or both. It is also possible to disable requests from a

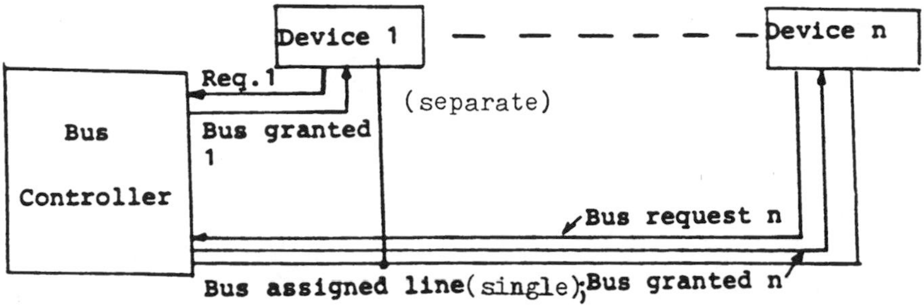

Fig. 18: "Independent request" bus control.

particular device which, for instance, is known or suspected to have failed.

The major disadvantage of independent requests is the number of lines and connectors required for control. Of course, the complexity of the allocation algorithm will be reflected in the amount of bus controller hardware.

Based on the considerations above, the first conclusion may be reached even before the complete hardware is described. It is that the pps should use either polling or independent request, but no daisy chaining.

We discussed asynchronous transmission. There are two basic approaches to synchronous buses: the time slots may be assigned to devices on either a dedicated or nondedicated basis. If time-slots are dedicated, they are permanently allocated to a device regardless of how frequently that device uses them. Each device on the bus is allowed to communicate on a rotational (time division multiplex) basis. The only way that any priority can be established is by assigning more than one slot to a device. More than one device may be assigned to a single time slot by submultiplexing slower or mutually exclusive devices.

Since not all devices will want to transmit at the same time and some may not even be implemented (reserved slots), time is wasted. Also, faster devices will have to wait for slower and, if the time slot rate is made as fast as the fastest device on the bus, then buffers must be incorporated into the slower devices. Depending on the device rate mismatches and the length of data blocks, these buffers could grow quite large. In addition, they must be capable of simultaneous input and output (or one read and one write in a time slot period), or else the whole transfer is delayed until the buffer is filled. Another approach is to run the bus slower than the fastest device and assign multiple time slots to that device, which complicates the control and wastes bus bandwidth if that device is not always transferring data. Special logic must also be included if block transfers are to be permitted since a device normally does not get adjacent time slots.

For reliability, it is desirable even in synchronous control that the receiving device verify and acknowledge correct arrival of the data. This is most effectively done on a word basis. If a synchronous time slot is wide enough to allow a reply for every word, then data transmission will be rather slow because the time slots rely on the slowest device on the bus. One solution is to establish a system convention where verification is by default and if an error does occur, a signal will be returned to the source device, a number of time-slots later. The destination has enough time to test the validity without slowing the transfer rate; however, the source must retain all words which have been transmitted but not verified. With so many faults, it is no wonder that an asynchronous bus is usually chosen for the pps. (As will be seen later, this is not necessarily true for multiprocessors.)

The bus may transfer blocks of data or single words. In the case of parallel-systems, block transfer will be absolutely essential since large amounts of data will have to be transferred through the bus, at least at the start of every job. Moreover, since the block length of data may vary, the block size must be variable. Sometimes single words will have to be transferred. Thus the bus cannot use one of the cheaper and simpler transfer possibilities, like [Thu 72] "single words only, blocks of fixed length only etc.," but must use the most expensive, single word or variable-length blocks. It is the most expensive but also the most flexible and efficient method. No initialization is needed for single words; block length adjusts itself to devices (by direct memory access).

Normally, the single bus introduces a critical system component which can cause a system failure as a result of a malfunction in any circuit component of the bus subsystem. It also is sometimes a serious bottleneck in overall system performance because only one path can be established at any time for data transfers. This may lead to considerable delays.

To obtain more reliability and parallelism, one can use multiple buses, either uni- or bi-directional. The intercommunication functions may be partitioned and a separate bus used for each functional partition. On the other hand, multiple and redundant buses may be used for system reliability. The use of multiple buses also allows multiple simultaneous transfers. However, any benefit derived from the multiple-bus schemes is at the expense of complex bus controls. Some degree of control logic such as arbiter or multiplexer would have to be added.

There are two ways to increase bus reliability. In one of them (Fig. 19a), reconfiguration units would switch so as to bypass a faulty connector ⊠. Any number of malfunctioning interfaces can be so bypassed, but a failure of a reconfiguration unit would break the bus.

In the second, "self-heal" connection, both a faulty unit and connector can be bypassed.

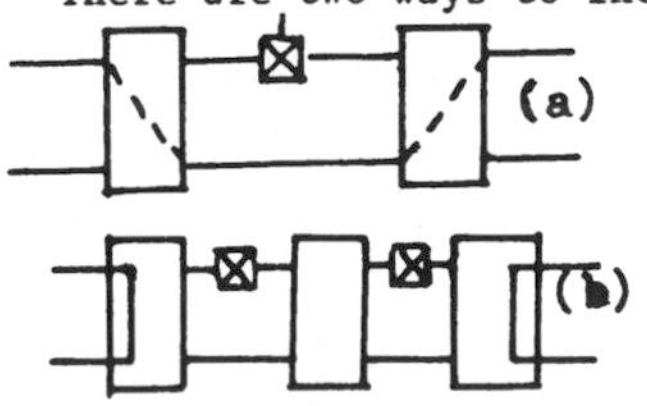

Fig. 19:Reliability enhancement

When the two ends of a bus are connected, a loop results. Normally, a "token" circulates around the loop. The cpu at whose connection it stops is entitled to start a "conversation". When this is finished, the token circulates further. A message may be removed from the loop by the originator of the talk, with a possible check on whether the message was not changed and is error-free. Another advantage of loops over buses is that block and broadcast transmission are easily achieved. The transmitter has simply to keep on entering messages (less than p) onto the loop and each receiver removes a message without destroying it. The transmitter removes it at the end of the loop. The length of the block is variable.

As the next possibility we mention the "common bus switch" (Fig. 20) as suggested recently [BW 75] and quote from it:

"The total transmission time between a processor and a memory bank is composed of three contributions respectively at the time of transmission:

(1) From the processor to the switch;

(2) Across the switch and

(3) From the switch to the memory bank.

The part of transmission time mentioned in (2) is the part that causes interference with other users of the switch and is thus relevant to the throughput restrictions. Reducing this part by keeping the bus switch compact at the expense of longer distances and transmission times as mentioned in (1) or (3) causes the throughput restrictions to be reduced. This is the basic principle of the common bus switch.

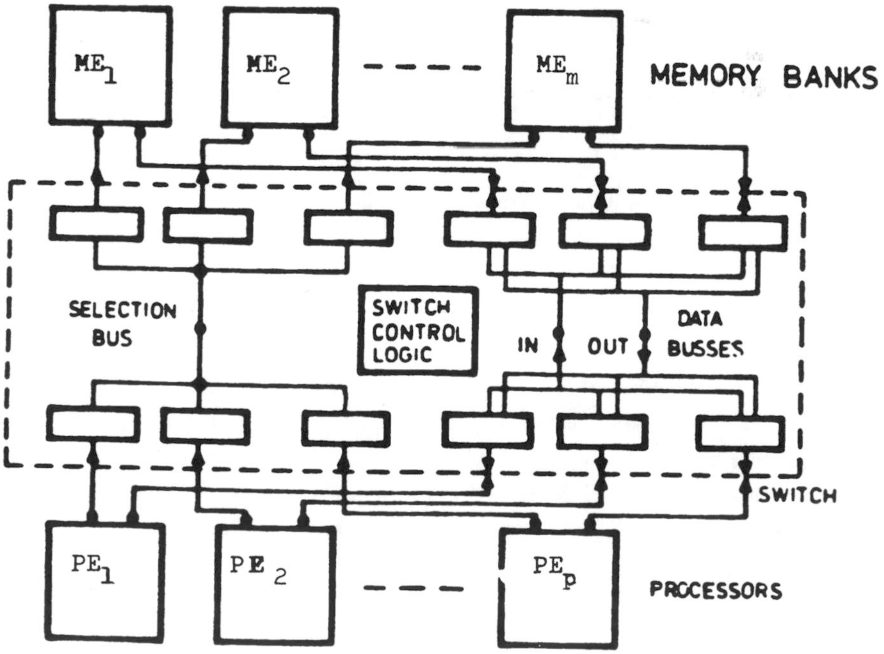

Fig. 20: The structure of the common-bus switch.

The structure of the common bus switch is sketched in Fig. 20. Each processor and memory bank has its own selection register and data register acting as buffers in the switch. If possible these registers are taken out of the processor and the memory banks themselves otherwise they are duplicates. There are three buses shared by the processor and the memory banks. One bus is used to transfer selection-information, one to transport read-data from the memory and one to transport write-data into the memory. Via their bus, the selection registers of each processor can be connected to those of each memory bank. The same is valid for the data registers. The buses may be multiple for reason of reliability and/or efficiency. Because the physical distance between the processor registers and the memory bank registers in the switch can now be very short, the time of transmission along the bus can be reduced to one "register time", i.e. the set time of one flip-flop. This means that although there may be long times of transmission between the processors and the switch and between the switch and the memory banks, a bus is only occupied during one register time per memory cycle (once for the selection bus and once for the input or output bus).

The black box in Fig. 20 called "switch control logic" contains all circuits necessary for controlling the correct operation of the common bus switch. A considerable part of this circuitry would also have to be present in a normal bus switch. The following control logic is required:

- priority circuits to determine which particular request will be granted for a specific memory bank.
- one control counter per memory bank properly adapted to the bank access time and cycle time (the bank timing counter).
- one status flip-flop per memory bank (free or occupied).
- one processor number register per memory bank that indicates which processor is connected to this memory bank.
- priority circuits to determine which request will be granted for a specific bus.
- circuitry which ultimately makes the connection of processor and memory bank registers to the relevant busses".

The authors concluded that:

"The cost of the common bus switch is proportional to the sum of the number of processors (p) and the number of memory banks (m). However, if the memory registers in the switch are duplicates of the registers in the memory banks, there are 2m extra registers (selection and data) as compared to the normal bus switch. If the processor registers in the switch are also duplicates, another 2p registers are required.

In order to investigate the performance of the common bus switch, a simulation program has been written. From a number of runs done with many varying parameters, e.g. number of processors, number of memory banks, cycle times of different memory banks, bus cycle time, access rate, it appeared that extra delays seldom occurred. Thus, the performance of the common bus switch is almost the same as that of the crossbar switch, while the common bus switch is far less expensive."

We next discuss the <u>multiport-multibus</u> scheme of Fig. 21. In this organization, the control, switching and priority arbitration logic are concentrated at the interface to the memory units. Each processor has access through its dedicated bus to all memory units. Access conflicts are resolved by memory ports.

Since each processor has access to all memory modules, it is possible to configure a fully connected topology with a multiport memory system and to have a very high transfer rate in the system. However, the multiport memory system has a large number of interconnections between processors and memories. Also, the multiport memory system has limits on its flexibility since conflicts are resolved through priorities implemented via hardware.

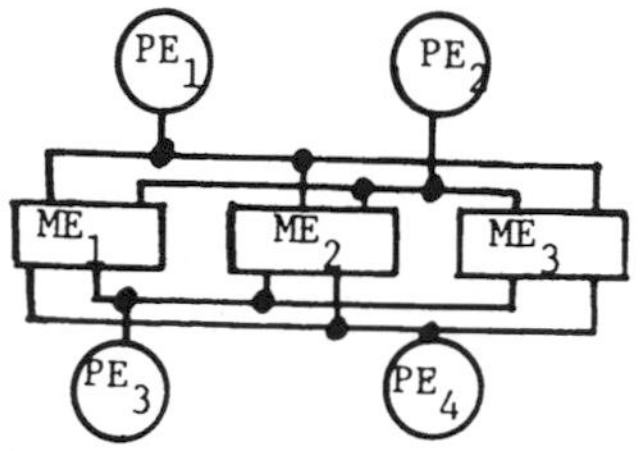

Fig. 21: Another system

Unfortunately, the maximum configuration of this system is limited by the number of ports available on memory units and by the necessity to resolve the conflicts that occur in accessing these units by hardware, making the switch more expensive. Here, again, it is not necessary for every memory to be connected to every processor, but generality is lost if every processor cannot access any memory.

The most complete way to connect all p processors to all m memories is shown in Fig. 22a. This approach is not satisfactory because:

- It is costly in terms of line selection logic and line driving circuits.
- Since only one unit of information can be transferred over a line and since the processors cannot deal concurrently with a number of messages, most of the lines are idle and the circuitry associated with these lines is not being effectively used. This means that we have paid a heavy price, but have used neither the lines nor the circuits efficiently. The connection of Fig. 22a will therefore not be mentioned anymore.

The "crossbar switch" (Fig. 22b) is a bus structure which also connects p processors (PE_i) to m memories (ME_i). It provides simultaneous memory access and communication among the functional units. With this interconnection organization, the maximum number of transfers that can take place simultaneously is limited by the number of memory units (or other functional units) and the band-width- of the buses rather than by the number of paths available. To provide maximum simultaneous transfers, each crosspoint must be capable of switching parallel transmission and resolving possible conflicts among rerequesting units.

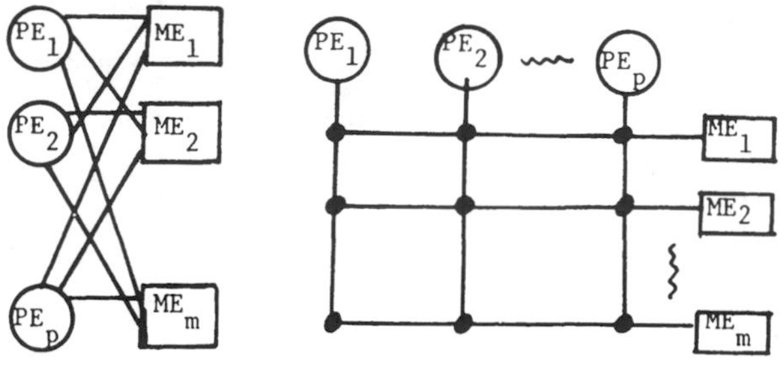

Fig. 22: A complete connection and crossbar switch

Since the number of cross-points grows exponentially, the cost of the circuitry required for the switching facilities becomes significantly high when the number of switch ports is large.

There is only one path between a source-destination pair. If a crosspoint should fail, a destination becomes unreachable from the corresponding source. The expansion of a system can be done by adding additional modules of crosspoints. It may be very complex to control and the reliability of the system will depend crucially on the reliability of the crossbar switch. Note also that each crosspoint must include hardware for resolving access conflicts to a single memory. The switch may therefore be quite expensive, especially since in modern technology, memories are produced in rather small blocks so that m (and even more p·m) may be large.

There are a number of variations of interconnection networks depending on the functional requirements, the control scheme and many other factors. Usually, and especially for very large p and m, the connective logic is organized into several stages of switching elements and connection links to achieve full connections. Such multistage interconnection networks allow processor-to-memory and processor-to-processor communications in a more general way than the organizations described above.

When the number of functional modules in a system increases to a certain level, say the order of 100, the choice of interconnection organizations becomes a critical problem. Multiple-processor systems interconnecting as many as 10^5 functional modules are presently considered. System performance and practical feasibility of such multiple-processor systems would be terribly limited if the conventional interconnection organization such as time shared or common bus, crossbar, or multiport memory were used. Thus one of the challenges in the field of computer architecture is to design an efficient and practical intercommunication subsystem for such massively multiple-processor systems. Mostly these are multistage networks.

Such multistage interconnection networks are used in many areas, e.g. telephone switching, data alignment between memory modules and processors, permutation generators, data sorting, etc. Next is a very brief review on these multistage interconnection networks (with N inputs and N outputs) which are classified into the following four categories: strictly nonblocking, wide-sense nonblocking, rearrangeable nonblocking and blocking networks. (A network which can connect any idle input to any idle output regardless of what other connections are currently in progress is called a strictly nonblocking network.)

An example of a three-stage nonblocking network constructed from a number of smaller crosspoint switches (matrix boxes) is shown in Fig. 23 with $m \geqq 2n - 1$. It is known that the network has less than N^2 crosspoints for $N \geqq 24$ and in general requires asymptotically $cN \exp[2\sqrt{\log_2 N}]$ crosspoints.

Strictly nonblocking networks have found very limited applications since some alternative networks which are simpler to manufacture and to control can be built with very low blocking probability.

A network is called a rearrangeable nonblocking network if it can perform all possible connections between inputs and outputs by rearranging its existing connections so that a connection path for a new inout-outout pair can always be estab-

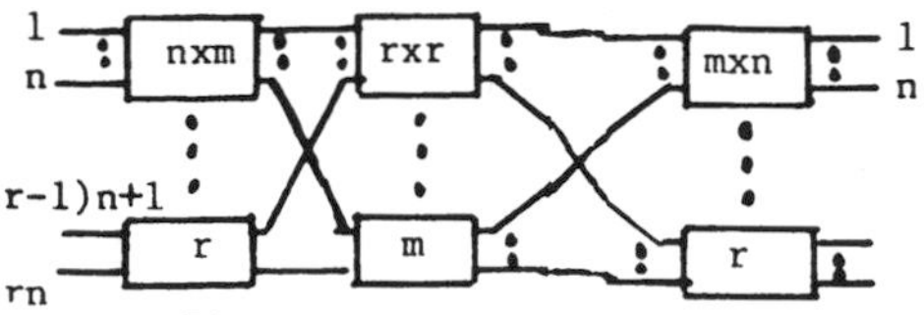

Fig.23:A three stage network.

lished. Benes [Be 65] has given a full description of such networks.

The special case of $N = 2^n$ has been considered for permutation purposes. An example of $N=2^3$ is shown in Fig. 24 where (a) shows the first iteration of a Benes construction scheme and (b) shows the resulting network. In general, 2n-1 stages are needed and the required number of 2x2 switching elements is equal to N(2n-1)/2.

A network which can perform many, but not all possible connections between terminals is called a blocking network. They are popular, but we will mention here only the telephone networks; the others, e.g., a flip or omega network, will be mentioned while discussing parallel systems which use them.

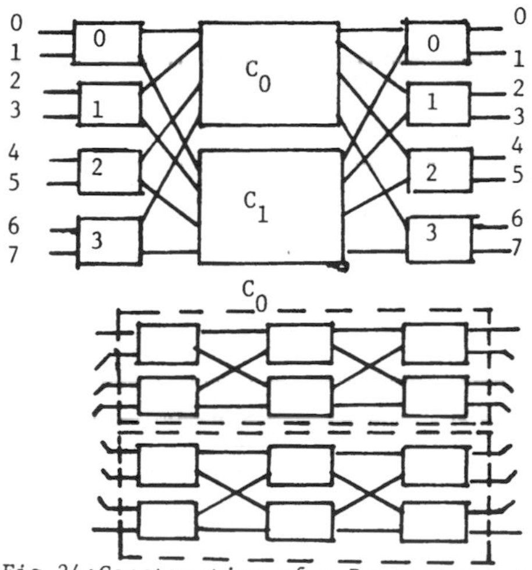

Fig.24:Construction of a Benes network.

The four-stage network shown in Fig. 25 is commonly found in telephone offices. Benes shows [on p. 123] that only a vanishingly small fraction of all possible permutations can actually be achieved by a four-stage network with m = 10 and N = 1000. However, a rearrangeable network of N = 1024 which can achieve all permutations using 2 x 2 switching elements turns out to need 17 stages instead of 4.

The simplicity and the uniform structure of the four-stage networks are attractive for the interconnection network design.

Multistage networks will not be used for a pps - the others may.

Thus, having described the crossbar, common-bus, multiport/multibus and time sliced bus in some detail, we will now compare them.

The time sliced bus is:

- Cheapest and least complex.

- Best suited for modifying system configurations (adding units).

- Since only one message is transferred at any time, the fear was frequently voiced that this might lead to unacceptably long waiting times as the system grew and the traffic became heavier. We will prove later that in the pps, which will serve as our model, this will not happen. As a matter of fact, it was found by simulation [TW 78] that in one application (sorting) the bus was used less than 2% of the total time.

- It is considered to be the least reliable because failure of the bus may be catastrophic for the entire system. This may be remedied by having a second bus in

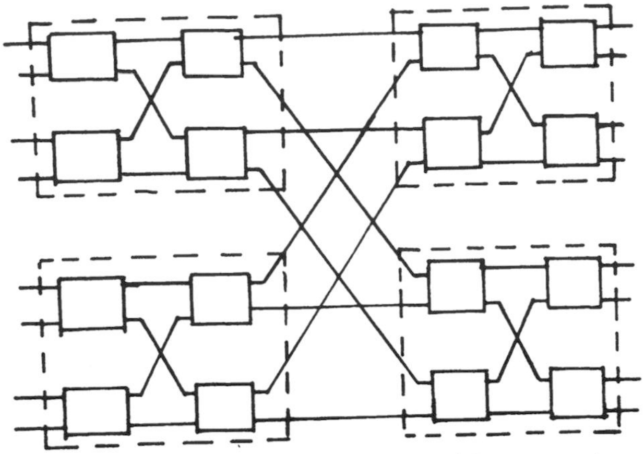

Fig.25: A four-stage telephone switching network.

stand-by. The additional cost is marginal for the system and the reliability higher than that of the crossbar. Addition of reconfiguration units improves reliability.

- Simultaneous use of all available units is lowest.

The crossbar system is:

- The most complex and the most expensive interconnection system.
- It uses simple functional units since none of them needs special circuitry.
- Is suitable only for multiprocessing.
- Has potentially the highest transfer rates, but a number of problems developed in those pps' which used them.
- May usually be expanded without reprogramming.
- Expansion is limited only by the size of the crossbar switch which itself may be expanded within engineering limits.
- Its reliability depends critically on the reliability of the switch.

The Multibus/Multiport system:

- Requires no special switching circuitry.
- Uses the most expensive memory units.
- Has the potential for high transfer rates.
- Is limited in size and configuration by the number and type of memory ports.
- Requires a large number of cables and connectors.

We have not mentioned here the common-bus switch despite the fact that it is probably the best engineering solution to the problem. The reason for the omission was that the common bus switch was not yet produced. We have also not mentioned the multistage networks since we are not going to use them anyway except in Illiac and Staran. A simple time-sliced bus will be all that will be really necessary.

2.4 GENERAL PURPOSE MULTIPROCESSORS

Aims: To describe the C.mmp, Cm* and PRIME as representative of existing multiprocessors.

Apps is a model of what is commonly called a multiprocessor. Its disadvantages for practical applications were already mentioned. Chief among them is the interference which results from the fact that Apps uses a common memory. It is therefore natural to suggest using "private memories" as was done in C.mmp.

C.mmp was developed at Carnegie-Mellon University in Pittsburgh and its origi-

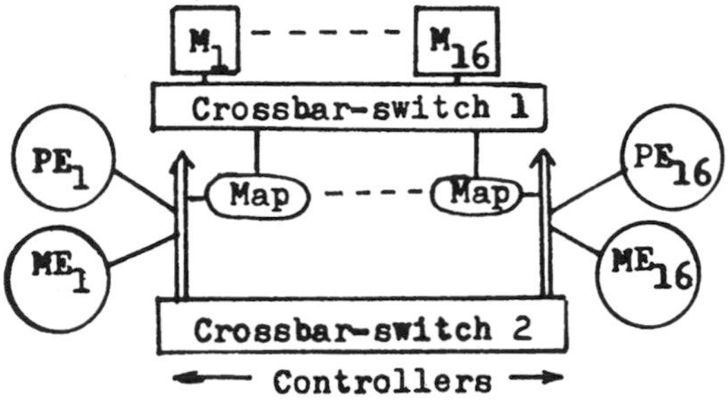

Fig. 26: The C.mmp

nal design is shown schematically in Fig. 26. It had two crossbar-switches: Switch 1 connects any PE_i with any primary memory module M_k, Switch 2, with any controller. These controllers manage secondary memories and I/O devices. When the crossbar switches are set, they define separate processor systems, each with its local private memory ME and controllers for secondary memories and devices. The control of Switch 1 can be by any of the processors, but one processor is always assigned to be the monitoring processor. Switch 2 connects the k unibuses to the processors on a relatively long term basis (miliseconds to hours). The shared primary memory consists of up to 16 blocks M_i containing up to 64K-bits each. There is a local memory attached to the processors; it increases bandwidth, allows completely independent operation and off-line maintenance. The Map attached to each processor translates its address into physical memory addresses to use on the memory and unibuses connected to this Map.

Studies of memory interference for a random distribution of memory references have lead to the view that the C.mmp will have a high cost/effectiveness with 15-30 processors. To reduce conflicts, a cache memory between Map and Switch 1 was also suggested. This would have allowed programs to migrate into the cache, thereby diminishing the number of requests for a single memory and would provide faster access.

The operating system consists of a kernel and extensions. The kernel creates virtual resources (files, read and write operations etc.) and operations for the extensions; these make up the particular operating system. A shared data base is used by the kernel for scheduling and coordinating the many individual processors, thus leading to the contention problem. Since the scheduling of processors is done from a common data base, access to it also requires mutual exclusion provided by "locks." It was found that the number of critical sections to be thus protected should be in the range 2-7 to enable more than one processor to perform monitoring.

The assembled C.mmp is different [FH 78] from that of Fig. 26. It has no caches, only one crossbar (#1) and I/O connected to specific cpu's on a permanent basis. The original design was completely symmetric, the final is not. Since the local memories are used only for interrupt and error-recovery, but not for programs or data, only the common memory is available for programs and memory interference may be quite severe. In fact, as already indicated, the addition of processing units may lead to a decrease instead of increase in processing speed. The decrease in speedup is due further to memory interleaving on the high bits of the addresses.

The reason for it is as follows. An address in C.mmp consists of a block number (one of 16 M_i's) and address local to it. Normally, the local address would occupy high-order, the block-number, the low-order bits. The consecutive instructions of a program numbered, ...0001,...0010,...0011,.. would thus refer to different blocks (enabling simultaneous access). Unfortunately, suppose M_2 has failed: all programs refer to it and would have to be removed - an impossible situation. For the sake of reliability, interleaving in C.mmp is done on the high-order bits, so that all instructions of any program are in the same block. This means that two or more cpu's may try to access the same block with an additional degradation.

The routing of memory requests from the PE's to the M's is done by hardware within the crossbar switch. This increases the price of the switch even more, lowers the overall reliability on account of complicated hardware and may further reduce the speed because of possible queuing delays in the switch.

The MAP-unit permits sharing of data in main memory by translating two addresses into the same physical location. This may lead to interference and downright wrong results as evidenced by the following program to sum the elements of a vector. Each of the processors (say, two) has to do: SUM=SUM+A(I); on its half of indices i (say, 32). PE_1 starts by adding A_1 to the (zero) sum. PE_2 is supposed to do the same with A_{16} but there are two possibilities: if it retrieved the SUM before PE_1 added A_1 to it, it makes it A_{16}, otherwise the SUM will be A_1+A_{16}. We thus have two possibilities only one of which is correct. For the program to be correct (stable), a PE must be able to fetch and update SUM without other PE's having access to it. We must lock them, say through the program:

```
TS     L
BNZ *-4
SUM=SUM+A(I)
Open lock L
```

Actually, "semaphores" are used for locking, but then this is a problem dealt with in courses on operating systems. Here, it will suffice to note that a process can be held waiting for another process to unlock the common memory area.

Another and even more important point is that the shared, main memory may lead to deadlocks. A simple example would be if PE_1 works on $M_1,...,M_8$ at the same time that PE_2 works on $M_9,...,M_{16}$. If both ask for one more block, without releasing the memory blocks they each hold, we have a deadlock. Again - the problem can be solved, but it needs the operating system for it and that in turn means a reduction of efficiency.

The PDP11 computer used as PE has only 16 bits for addresses, resulting in a small address space. Thus only small-sized applications can be processed or the application has to manage its data, thus requiring even more time. In any case, the programming will be difficult.

In conclusion: The C.mmp is a working multiprocessor with a number of good features, e.g., local memories, symmetry through the crossbar switch etc. For general purpose computing, its only disadvantages are in the small address space and contention for memory. For on-line, non-π problems it has all the disadvantages of Apps, a finite p and additional problems because of its crossbar switch and limited use of the local memories.

Another system which emulates Apps is the Cm* also assembled [SFS 76] at Carnegie-Mellon University. It uses "Computer modules", each connected according to Fig. 27; up to 14 such modules connected (Fig. 28) into a "cluster" and a number of clusters into Cm*. Note that each cluster has a (master) controller, the K.map.

Each processor PE is connected to a local memory ME. A teletype (Tty) and disk constitute a controller and are connected to the bus and through it to S.local. This acts as a switch in the following way: it is presented by PE with an address; if this address is in the local memory, the value of it is available right away. Otherwise, the address is transferred with a search code through the "Map bus" to the remaining 13 modules and if not found there, to other clusters (through the K.map controller). We might thus infer that Cm* will have a lot of messages going on simultaneously between the processors wasting time. This may be of no great consequence to an off-line, computer-center environment, but could be worrisome for process control. Even for general purpose computing, it poses some problems.

Local memories form a common store shared by all PE's so that each "sees" the same address space.The only distinction is that there is no delay when accessing own

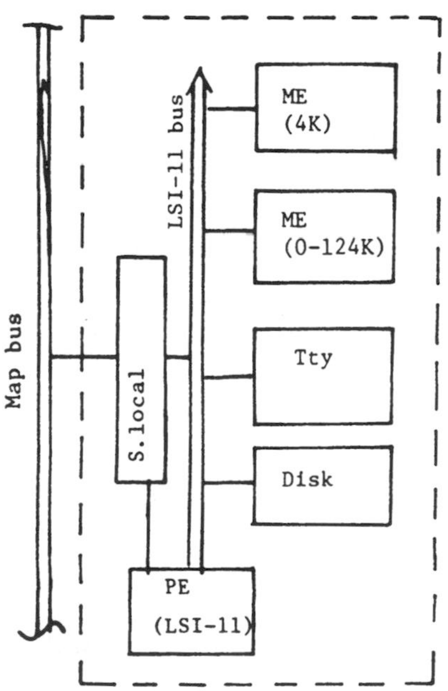

Fig. 27: A Cm* module.

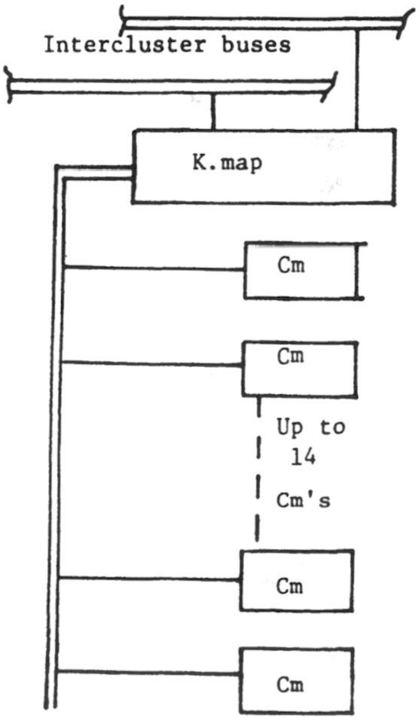

Fig. 28: A cluster of Cm*

memory. The underlying assumption here was that there is program locality, i.e. a processor will seldom require information outside its own local memory. If that assumption should prove wrong, the efficiency of the system will drop considerably.

Processors communicate by asynchronous "message switching" so that every module can access every other module with a minimum number of physical connections. Because software switching is the mode, more time is needed for transfer and only applications which can be decomposed more or less like a π-problem with all the code fitting a single module can be efficiently run on Cm*. A distinct danger brought about by using message switching (and memory "windows") in Cm*, is the possibility of deadlock. The advantage of using a mapping processor (controller) was that it would ensure mutual exclusion on accessing shared data with little overhead. But then this map and its associated map-bus are, for each cluster, also central, critical shared resources and may lead to deadlocks. Quoting: "There are numerous situations where deadlock over bus allocation can occur. Resolving this deadlock requires, at the very least, a timeout and retry mechanism."

An important configuration parameter is the number of processors per cluster. The hardware will accept a maximum of 14; the issue to be evaluated is how many processors the controller-bus combination will support before approaching saturation. A processor which makes all its references to its own local memory places no load on the controller bus. This load is a strong function of the percentage of non-local, i.e. references to neighboring modules in the cluster or to other cluster references. The fraction of accesses a processor makes to its own local memory is analogous to the hit ratio of (uni) processor systems with cache memories.

As in C.mmp, each I/O device is bound to a single module and any module can initiate I/O on a device attached to any other module. However, interrupts can only be serviced locally, so that if a module is lost, all I/O devices attached to it are lost. This is not very desirable from the point of view of reliability, especially since the address space is common.

The discussion of Cm* can be summarized by saying that its common address space may be good for off-line, but not for real-time systems. In particular, we take exception to the fact that in Cm* data of private (local) memories can be shared by other PE's thus creating the locking problem and causing delays because of transfer by packet switching. These delays might be acceptable in a computer-center environment, but not in process-control, dedicated systems.

From all this, it seems advisable not to share memory at all. Such possibility was provided in PRIME (Fig. 29) as developed at the University of California at Berkeley. Here, a processor (one out of five), one or more blocks of memory and some secondary devices are tied through an "External Access Network" and a crossbar switch into a completely independent computer working on a single job. PRIME has centralized control in that at any time one of the subunits (a processor and memory) acts as a control processor directing the activities of the remaining problem-processors. The assignment of the control-monitoring functions, namely job scheduling, buffer management, secondary and primary storage allocation, low-level accounting, system diagnosis and monitoring of all problem processors is dynamic. They are in fact reassigned each time the system is repartitioned into p independently working computers. Once the system is partitioned, there is no further interaction between the monitor and the various processes started on the problem-processors. This is the reason that the monitor-process is relatively small, but also accounts for the

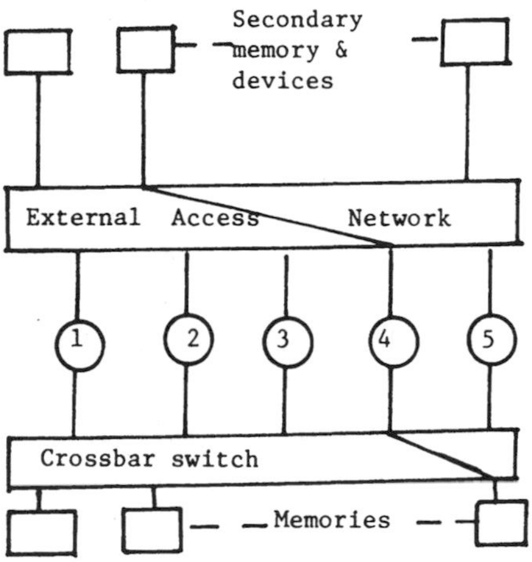

Fig. 29: (a subdivision of) PRIME

fact that each unit must use a local monitor which transfers files and manages both trap programs and the normal I/O routines required by the local functions which, in addition, may include setting and reading memory access maps, saving and restoring the state of the user processes, allocation of virtual addresses etc. The control processor effects global allocation of primary and secondary storage to processes and processors, global error checking and diagnosis, whereas each local monitor effects allocation of virtual addresses, local process-control as well as local error and consistency checks.

It should be emphasized that PRIME is a "terminal oriented" system, i.e. it works on a time-sharing basis with no control of job entry and of sequencing. It was not thought to work on-line at all, and apparently was not assembled.

2.5 ILLIAC-IV

Aims: To describe Illiac and show by way of a matrix-multiplication example its disadvantages. To discuss the omega-network.

MIMD-systems and their disadvantages were already discussed; the best known SIMD-system will be discussed now.

Despite the fact that Illiac and its predecessor SOLOMON are quite well known [SBM 62], it is not yet widely used. Usually the software difficulties are blamed [En 77], but it may be that the total parallelization which it has attempted and the unexpected development of cheap microprocessor-chips are not less of a factor. In any case, it was supposed to consist of four "quadrants", but only one was built. In this section a single quadrant will represent Illiac.

The SOLOMON computer had the following principal features [BBK 68]:

1) A large array of arithmetic units (PE's or "slaves") was controlled by a single control unit (CU or "master") - it was a SIMD computer

2) Information could be broadcast from the master to all slaves

3) Information could be exchanged between neighboring slaves

4) There was very little local control at the slave-level.

Illiac-IV is a SIMD computer which consists of 64 identical slaves driven simultaneously by a single master. The master forces each slave to execute the same instruction at any given time, so that up to 64 operations can go on at once. The instruction sequence represents a single program.

Since at the time Illiac was designed control logic was much more expensive than arithmetic units, it was thought that having a single CU for all 64 slaves and producing them devoid of most control circuitry would save a large percentage of the price. At present, the micro-chips include a CU and the savings seem to be nonexistent. Moreover, Illiac has elaborate and specially built hardware (in the slaves) for arithmetical operations. In the present technological environment this would increase the price very much.

Figure 30 shows one "quadrant" of Illiac-IV [Mc 70]. The single control unit fetches, decodes and broadcasts an instruction to all 64 processing elements. The elements operate synchronously, but have their own local memory so that no memory interference exists. Each has a register R wired directly to four adjacent elements, namely the ith processing element to those numbered i-1, i+1, i-8, i+8. (View the 64 PE's as an 8x8 grid pasted over a torus). Additionally, it has two operand registers A, B and an S-register for temporary storage.

The control unit has limited arithmetic capability and has been provided with a stack-memory. The operating system resides in a host computer not shown in Fig. 30 (initially it was B6700; now it is a PDP-10) which controls program loading and I/O operations and supports system programs (compilers, assemblers etc.).

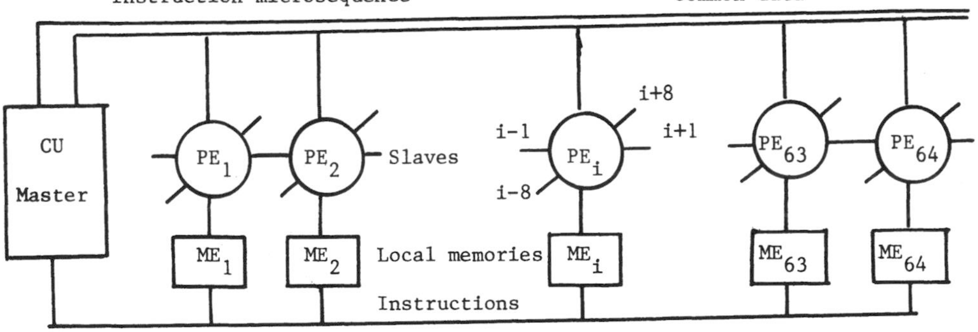

Fig. 30: Schematic diagram of Illiac-IV.

Since each slave has its own memory, it can get data locally much faster than the multiprocessors, which have to access a common memory. It also follows that no deadlock is to be feared, so no locks, semaphores, etc. are needed and the entire problem of memory interference is non-existant. On the other hand, if PE_i requires data stored in ME_j, it gets it by way of "routing" i.e. this data is transferred first to register R of PE_j, from there to R of PE_i and, if so required, stored in ME_i. If the "distance" i to j is ±1 or ±8 (modulo 64), only 100 msecs are spent on routing, but for the outlay of Illiac this distance may be such that up to 7 x 100 = 700 msecs are required. This is quite some time if one considers that 63 elements may have to wait until PE_i gets the data it requires. The problem of software mentioned earlier is mainly that the programmer must not only think in terms of the algorithm but must also allocate memory so as to minimize routing. This in turn may lead to rather complicated data structures.

The CU produces a microsequence for each instruction in the same way that a control unit of a conventional, microprogrammed computer does. Thus all PE's receive the same sequence of enable and disable signals and work in lock-step synchronism. If PE_i multiplies, all multiply.

Well, not necessarily; any slave can be "turned-off" either by the master or by its own data. The master may first broadcast a word of, say, 32 zeros followed by 32 ones, one bit being stored in each slave as a "mode" bit. Only slaves 32-63 which have a mode bit of 1 will process the next instructions; the other slaves must first be turned on (by the master). As seen, conditional branches of conventional computers are accomplished by tests which enable or disable local execution of subsequent commands in the instruction sequence.

Another case is exemplified by the master issuing a command to be obeyed only if the data in an accumulator is, for example, positive. All PE's for which this is not true, will turn their mode bit off and do nothing for as long as the mode bit is not turned on again. This must be done by the master.

The slaves have another degree of freedom. There is an index register X in the master and in every slave. An address a_i (in PE_i) is the sum of that broadcast by the master and the content of X. (The addition effected in an "address adder" provided with each PE.) Thus, if $(X_i)=c$, $(X_j)=b$ and the address sent by the master is a, then PE_i will process a+c but PE_j will "see" a+b. It will be shown later that use of X is quite effective in some problems.

A single word can be broadcast through the upper bus in Fig. 30 to all 64 slaves (e.g. the 64 bits of 1 and of 0, above). On the other hand, the slaves can form a 64-bit word and send it through the lower bus to the master. This allows the master to sense all mode bits and monitor the state of the entire system. Note that the master takes its instructions from the memories of the slaves through this bus.

Having described the overall organization, let us discuss a few details of the local memories (PEM's), processing elements (PE's or slaves), the control unit (CU or master) and additional equipment based on [BBK 68], [Mc 70] and [Da 69].

Every slave has a PEM-memory with 2048 words of 64 bits. Its cycle and access times are 240 and 120 nsecs resp. The memory is independently accessible by its PE, the master and by I/O devices. From Fig. 30 it is seen that a slave can fetch or store operands only in its own memory. The master however, can fetch instructions from any of the 64 memories.

Every slave has the following registers: An accumulator (A) and an operand (B); a carry (C) and routing (R), as well as an S-register for "programmatic storage" of an operand in a slave. In addition to two enable bits, there are six other bits in the mode register (E) which handle fault and test results. There is an index register (X), an address register (MAR) and special hardware for arithmetic operations. This hardware is rather involved [Da 69], since Illiac was designed, in the first place to work on scientific problems which require not only high speed but also high accuracy. There are four kinds of floating and two of fixed point arithmetic on words of 64 bit length. No wonder that floating add, multiply and divide need 350, 450, and 2750 nsecs whereas a fetch and store only 350 and 300 nsec and a register-to-register transfer only 50 nsecs. The slave and memory are connected through a memory logic unit.

The control unit has the following functions: 1) decode the instructions and broadcast them; 2) generate and broadcast common addresses and data to all PE's; 3) receive and process interrupts from the PE's, I/O-units and the host.

The control unit (CU) has the following main components: 1) program look-ahead buffer (PLA) which can hold 64 words each of 64 bits. They constitute a queue of 128 instructions (of 32 bits each), so that the CU can go on decoding for a long time before it needs to fill the buffer. It will fill it when it tests whether the "next" group of 8 words (there are 8 such groups) is not yet in the PLA. Bringing-in a group will destroy the "oldest" group. Queueing will reduce considerably the waiting time for instructions. 2) There is a local data buffer of 64 words which is connected to all PE's and their local memories. 3) The arithmetic unit of the CU is rather simple and restricted to logic operations and fixed-point additions/subtractions on data from the data buffer. 4) There are four 64-bit registers used for indexing, logical operations and broadcasting. 5) The instructions are held in a "final queue" and broadcast as data or as the instruction micro-sequence. Local instructions (indexing, jumps etc) are executed by the arithmetic unit of the PE.

Information transfer between CU and the 64 PE's is effected in several ways: 1) The CU broadcasts a word to all PE's. It goes to the same register of every PE. 2) The CU broadcasts a word such that one bit is transferred to every PE. In this way some PE's are enabled, some disabled through their mode registers. 3) The 64 mode registers can be sampled; the assembled word thus transmitted to the CU indicates the status of the machine. 4) The CU can fetch a single or a block of 8 consecutive words from the local memories. The latter requires only slightly more time than fetching a single word and is used to feed the instruction buffer.

The host affects I/O and works with a disk on the data base. The reliability, i.e. fault detection, test and maintenance procedures will be compared later with that of another system. We conclude this section by discussing programming.

Algorithms must be designed so that all PE's obey the same commands. To illustrate the problem of memory allocation and to show how parallelism is achieved in Illiac, an algorithm for multiplying two matrices X, Y and storing the result in Z will be shown next ($\underline{Z} = \underline{X} * \underline{Y}$).

Matrices X, Y and Z may be stored as in the table below where for instance X(3,2) is stored in location 13 of the memory of PE_2.

PEM_i =	loc 11	12	13	14	loc 21	22	23	24	loc 31	32	33	34
PE 1	X_{11}	X_{21}	X_{31}	X_{41}	Y_{11}	Y_{21}	Y_{31}	Y_{41}	Z_{11}	Z_{21}	Z_{31}	Z_{41}
PE 2	X_{12}	X_{22}	X_{32}	X_{42}	Y_{12}	Y_{22}	Y_{32}	Y_{42}	Z_{12}	Z_{22}	Z_{32}	Z_{42}
PE 3	X_{13}	X_{23}	X_{33}	X_{43}	Y_{13}	Y_{23}	Y_{33}	Y_{43}	Z_{13}	Z_{23}	Z_{33}	Z_{43}
PE 4	X_{14}	X_{24}	X_{34}	X_{44}	Y_{14}	Y_{24}	Y_{34}	Y_{44}	Z_{14}	Z_{24}	Z_{34}	Z_{44}

The program may be summarized in a mixed PL/I and English language, as follows:

DO I=1 TO 4;

Copy row I of X from the PEM's into the control unit; (an instruction "transfer content of location 11 to the CU would transfer row I=1 above)

DO J=1 TO 4;

Broadcast X(I,J) from the control unit to all A-registers;

Fetch row J of Y into the B-register. This must be done as "Fetch element k from local memory to the B-register." (It will be denoted below by k → B-register, e.g. 22 → B transfers Y_{21}, Y_{22}, Y_{23} and Y_{24} into the B registers of the four elements);

Multiply A and B registers (in all elements). Add the result to the S register (of the processing elements); S:=S+A*B

END;

Store S as the new Z. A row will be stored by the command Z → k in the same location k of all elements;

END.

To understand how the algorithm works in parallel, the first few steps for 4x4 matrices X,Y,Z on four PE's are explained as follows:

I=1	Element-1	Element-2	Element-3	Element-4	
J=1	X_{11}	X_{11}	X_{11}	X_{11}	stored in register A
	Y_{11}	Y_{12}	Y_{13}	Y_{14}	k→B is here 21→B
	$X_{11}Y_{11}$	$X_{11}Y_{12}$	$X_{11}Y_{13}$	$X_{11}Y_{14}$	stored in register S
J=2	X_{12}	X_{12}	X_{12}	X_{12}	in A-registers
	Y_{21}	Y_{22}	Y_{23}	Y_{24}	22→B
	$X_{12}Y_{21}$	$X_{12}Y_{22}$	$X_{12}Y_{23}$	$X_{12}Y_{24}$	increments to S; Z+S→S
J=3	X_{13}	X_{13}	X_{13}	X_{13}	in A-registers
	Y_{31}	Y_{32}	Y_{33}	Y_{34}	in B-registers
	$X_{13}Y_{31}$	$X_{13}Y_{32}$	$X_{13}Y_{33}$	$X_{13}Y_{34}$	increments to S
J=4	X_{14}	X_{14}	X_{14}	X_{14}	in A-registers
	Y_{41}	Y_{42}	Y_{43}	Y_{44}	in B-registers
	$X_{14}Y_{41}$	$X_{14}Y_{42}$	$X_{14}Y_{43}$	$X_{14}Y_{44}$	increments to S

At this point the first (I=1) row of Z is stored as the accumulated sum of the increments of S. It is easily verified that in the case above

$$Z_{1J} = \Sigma X_{1k} * Y_{kJ} \quad ; \quad k\Sigma=1,\ldots,4 \quad ; \quad J=1,2,3,4 \qquad (32)$$

is stored. This is indeed the first row of $\underline{Z} = \underline{X} * \underline{Y}$. The storage command is S→31.

Next, I is increased to I=2 and row 2 of X i.e. $X_{21},X_{22},X_{23},X_{24}$ is brought into the controller. Thus, for J=1, all four A-registers will hold X_{21} and after execution of 21→B, the B-registers will hold $Y_{11},Y_{12},Y_{13},Y_{14}$. The S-registers will therefore start their sums from $X_{21} * Y_{11}$, $X_{21} * Y_{12}$, $X_{21} * Y_{13}$ and $X_{21} * Y_{14}$, respectively. If J is increased to 2,3 and 4, the second row of $\underline{Z}$ is calculated etc.

Note that row I of X is copied into the control unit from local memories, column J of Y is fetched into the B-registers from the local memories of the respective PE's. Thus, no "interference" results. The problems, though, stem from the data outlay. In this example it was such that a single command transferred an entire row of $\underline{Y}$ to the B-registers, e.g. 23→B would transfer row 3 of $\underline{Y}$. With proper indexing, we could access the diagonal as well, but what if we want a column of $\underline{Y}$? Since each column is in a separate memory, only a single element would work. The bandwidth would be substantially decreased. We can use "skewed" storage of a matrix (Fig. 31) in which fetching of a column is easy, since columns may be identified if an index register is loaded with 0,1,2,3.Then "load from I incremented by index" would load the (circled) first column. If this index register is shifted to 3,0,1,2, then the same instruction would load the (squared) second column. Unfortunately, storage as in Fig. 31 will not allow simultaneous access to a diagonal. It can even be shown that no arrangement of a pxp matrix in a p-unit memory, with p=even will allow access to arbitrary rows, columns and diagonals without conflicts.

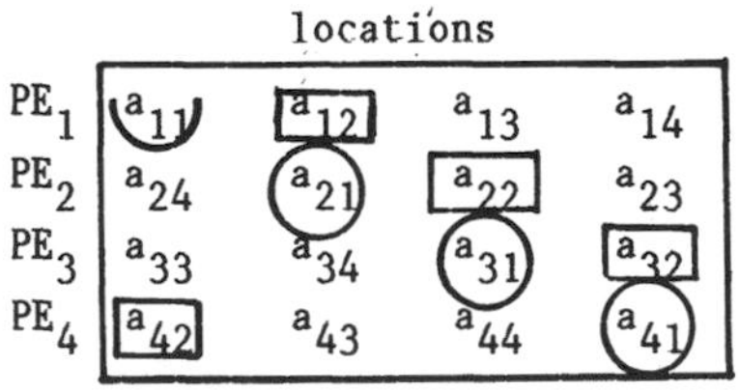

Fig. 31: Skewed storage.

To obtain conflict-free access, we may use a memory with $m=2^{2k}+1$ (any k) such that m>n, where n is the order of the matrix. For the previous example of a 4x4 matrix, using 8 memories and skewed storage as in Fig. 32 would do the trick. Thus, loading the index registers with 0,3,6 and 1 would provide access to column 1, but using 0, 5, 2 and 7 would provide access to the diagonal (in the first, an offset of 3, in the second of 5, both modulo 8 are used). Rows would still have to be routed to other PE's.

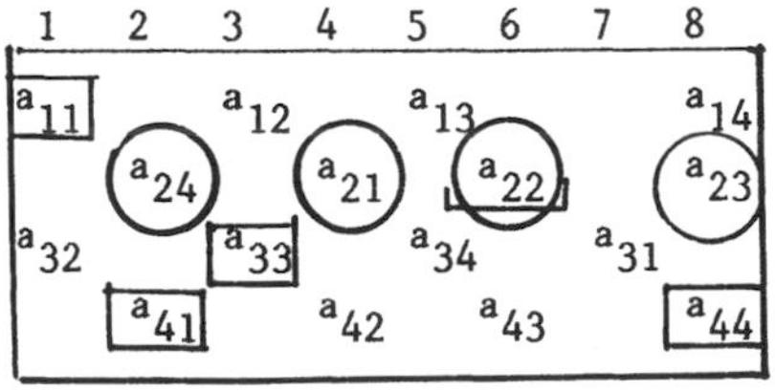

Fig. 32: Skewed storage.

Even if we can store skewed data, we will have wasted a lot of memory (by a factor of two in Fig. 32). With this in mind, STAR and ASC computers have transpose operations, but no independent registers. This leads from a Scylla into a

Charybda in that the time for transposition is essentially wasted and slows down these machines considerably.

The matrix multiplication algorithm has shown that in general data must be arranged in Illiac for efficient computation. This rearrangement is to be done ahead of the actual computation and may take more time than the calculation proper or, for that matter, than some sequential computations. For not completely inefficient use of Illiac, rows and columns must be equally accessible, i.e. skewed storage must be provided. This is part of a higher level (Algol-like) language Glypnir [La 75] developed at the University of Illinois. Still, it is not easy to modify the "natural" arrangement of data. As an example of the difficulties encountered, the data arrangements for eigenvalue calculations as shown in [KS 72] are mentioned. It can be seen there that even without a basic change in the algorithm, a complete outlay of data is required and that it is by no means easy to secure data for each element in its own or in the four neighboring local memories.

We have defined the speedup, ratio and efficiency in (6,7,9). For the matrix-multiplication on Illiac, assuming n=p, we can calculate them by counting the operations in the inner loop on J (the outer, leads to n synchronizations or time of $n\beta$). Two transfers (2τ), one addition α, and one multiplication μ are required for each I-J-pair, i.e. n^2 times. Thus

$$\rho = (n^2(\alpha + \mu) + 2n^2\tau + n\beta)/(n^3\omega) = 1/n + 2\tau'/n + \beta'/n^2$$

$$\eta = 100/(1 + 2\tau' + \beta'/n) \cong 100/(1 + 2\tau')$$

For $\tau' = 0.5$ we would only achieve 50% efficiency. Actually $\tau' \ll 0.5$, but if $n \neq p$, the efficiency decreases.

We shall now examine the construction and properties of the "omega" network as used in Illiac. An example of an 8x8 omega network is shown in Fig. 33. For the present, we shall only consider N x N networks where N is a power of two.

An N x N omega network consists of ℓ=logN identical stages. Each stage consists of a "perfect shuffle" interconnection followed by N/2 switching elements as shown in Fig. 33. The perfect shuffle connection is such that the first four inputs ("a") are connected to the four upper terminals ("u"), the remaining four ("b") to the lower terminals ("l"). Each switching element can have one of the four states shown in Fig. 34. That is, it may either send its inputs straight through, interchange the inputs, or broadcast one of the inputs to both outputs. We do not allow both inputs to be switched to the same output.

In order to switch data through the network, each element in the network is set in one of the above four states (not necessarily all the same) and then the data are allowed to pass from the network inputs to the network outputs.

There is an efficient algorithm for setting the states of the omega network. First, consider switching input number S to output number D. Let $D=d_1d_2...d_\ell$ be the binary representation of the output number to which input number S is to be connected, and let $S=s_1s_2...s_\ell$ be the binary representation of the input number.

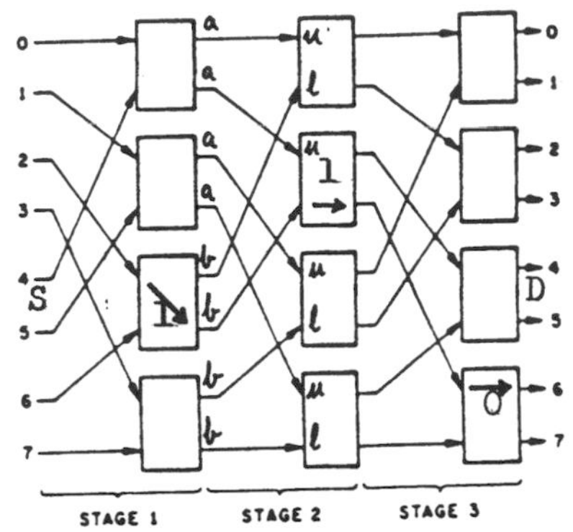

Fig. 33: An 8 x 8 omega network

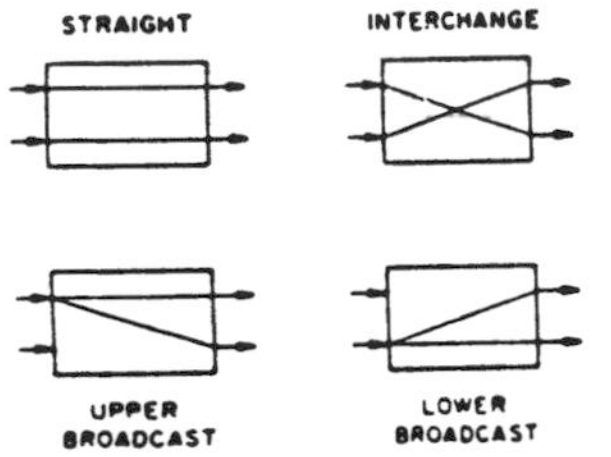

Fig. 34: Four allowed states of the switching elements

Starting at input S, the first switch to which S is connected is set to switch input S to the upper output if $d_1=0$ or the lower output if $d_1=1$. This is shown in Fig. 33 for S=010, D=110. Following this through to a switch in the next stage, we again switch the input to the upper output if $d_2=0$ or to the lower output if $d_2=1$. We continue in this manner, switching on d_i at each stage i, until we get the proper output. It is easy to see that during any given stage i, an input which has been switched to position $s_i s_{i+1} \ldots s_\ell d_1 d_2 \ldots d_{i-1}$ goes through the perfect shuffle and ends up in position $s_{i+1} s_{i+2} \ldots s_\ell d_1 d_2 \ldots d_{i-1} d_i$. Thus, after ℓ=logN operations, the original input must be connected to output $d_1 d_2 \ldots d_\ell$. A similar algorithm works by starting at output $d_1 d_2 \ldots d_\ell$ and working backwards through the network, switching the element at stage i according to s_i.

In order to set up a particular mapping of inputs to outputs, we simply follow the above procedure simultaneously for all inputs or all outputs.

In summary, the major objections to the use of Illiac for solution of non-π, on-line problems or similar computations are as follows:

(a) There are two reasons for using parallel processing. One is speed, the other is availability and/or reliability. Here, the meaning of availability is that even if any of the elements is faulty, the system should be available and function properly (maybe somewhat slower). In Illiac, this is not the case; not only will the entire system be down if the controller (or host processor), but even if one of the elements is removed. By reliability we understand that the system should periodically check itself, amputate any part found faulty and proceed working. It is virtually impossible to check the controller of an array processor.

(b) Thurber [Thu 76] characterizes problems suitable for SIMD-systems as having, "1) a multiplicity of data sets, 2) a requirement for the same computation to be performed on all data sets, 3) no unknown global time relationship between data sets, and 4) all data sets assignable indiscriminately to a processing unit." It must also be such that "the percentage of time spent moving data from one memory to another is small." These characteristics define π-problems - with which we do not deal here.

(c) We have seen that memory assignment for matrices is rather difficult.

This was true for dense matrices. The matrices of power or other networks are very large and extremely sparse (size 2000 * 2000 is considered normal, with only 10-20 nonzero terms in a row). In Illiac, a computing element is either doing what the controller prescribes at any time or is doing nothing. Hence, for the usual sparse type of problems, most of the elements will do nothing most of the time and the computing capability of Illiac will be used very inefficiently.

(d) The original idea of reducing the cost by using a single CU is doubtful at present. 64 microprocessors each with both an ALU and a CU are not necessarily more expensive than 64 specially built PE's.

(e) There is a lot of waste in memory usage. Since memories cost more than cpu's, this tilts the price comparison even more.

(f) The efficiency was not as high as expected.

2.6 ASSOCIATIVE, SIMD- MACHINES

Aims: To describe shortly the Staran and Pepe machines.

In 1945, Dr. Vannevar Bush published a paper in which he discussed the problem of accessing the ever increasing amount of information. Data retrieved was in its infancy then, but it was pointed out by Dr. Bush that selecting it by subclass (as by telephone) or sequentially (as in computer addressing) seemed to be inefficient. Moreover, Bush asserted that the mind does not work in either way but associatively and that "selection by association, rather than by indexing, may yet be mechanized."

It was. A large number of machines were proposed, but apparently not built. The two machines that are available are STARAN and PEPE and we will concentrate on these two. They both work as pps.

The definition of an associative machine seems to include two features: (1) An associative memory from which data can be retrieved or manipulated associatively, i.e., by content instead of address, (2) Operations can be performed on many sets of data with a single instruction, i.e., in parallel.

The difference between associative and (normally addressed) vector memories can be exemplified by a professor asking students if they have a certain book. Vector addressing means to ask every student in turn, according to his seating location, wasting a lot of time. Associative addressing means to ask the students who have the book to raise a hand and then look at the response. In the second case, the process will be definitely shorter (and parallel).

It is seen that in order to retrieve data by content, it must be possible to match items with a search-key word (the title of the book). If we also want to match parts of a word, a "field", we can mask out part of the key. Thus a simplified memory could be as shown in Fig. 35 where a 10-word, 12 bit/word memory is searched for having "1101" in its internal four bits.

The result would be stored in 10 "tag flip-flops" (the hands of the students). The outer eight bits of the words are "masked out" by the 0's of the mask so that the outer eight bits of the key are not compared. The comparison is done sequentially by bits, i.e., bit 5, then bit 6, 7 and finally bit 8 - it is a "word-parallel, bit-sequential" search. Note that the equation: If (key and Mask) = Mask applies.

The memory of STARAN (Fig. 36) has 256 "words" arranged "horizontally" with 256 bits each. Each word has a tag flip-flop (T) associated with it; the collection of all tag bits is called the reresponse store.

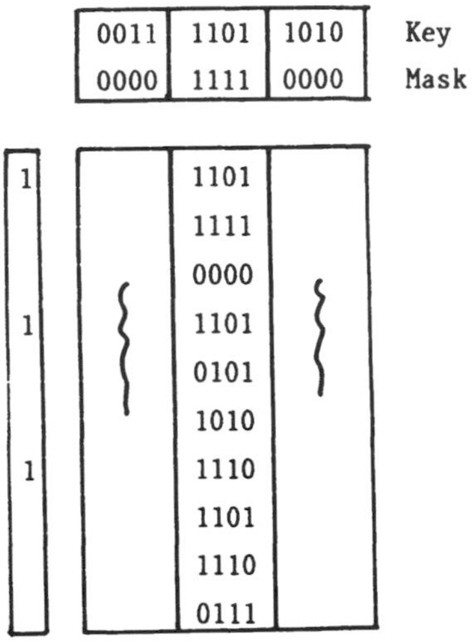

Fig. 35

The Central Control Unit (CCU) should be able to set all T_i=1 by issuing a single command SET. It can broadcast a word which is in its comparand to all 256 words, or it can send a part of the comparand for which the mask bits are 1. If the central control unit issues a COMPARE instruction, all words which do not match the unmasked part of the comparand reset their tag flip-flops to zero. The central control unit can also READ or WRITE into bit positions of words whose tags are on. It can do it sequentially by commands READFIRST or WRITEFIRST which would apply only to the first "top" word whose tag is on.

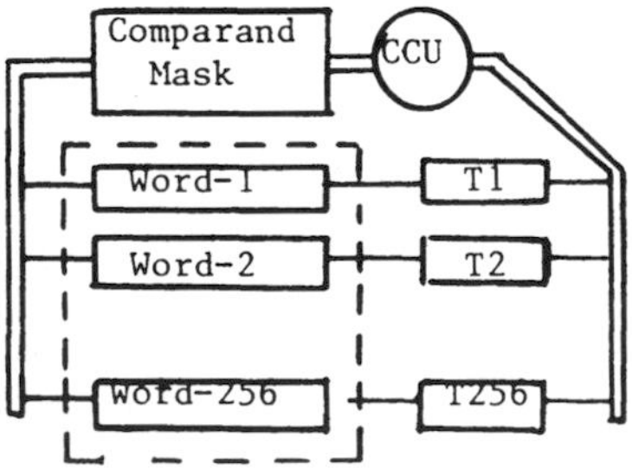

Fig. 36: An associative memory

The correlation of data is seen to require a single time-unit for every bit. The correlation algorithm is thus "bit-serial" and "word-parallel," i.e., all words are processed simultaneously but bit-by-bit, one bit at a time.

Since we have twice mentioned a "bit slice," we should define it. It is a binary vector which includes the i-th bit of every word that was selected and the "don't cares" for all those words that were not selected (tagged).

The circuitry of the memory is such that we can operate on a bit-slice setting it, reading it, or setting the tag bits. We may also select the word which responded first. This is done as indicated in Fig. 37.

All tag flip-flops T_i can be set by the set line. Line R_i of word i is :

$$R_i=\Sigma M_j(C_jS_{ij}'+C_j'S_{ij});ij\Sigma=1,\dots,b \qquad (33)$$

where b is the number of bits in a word and summation or multiplication is to be understood as Boolean "or" and "and" respectively. Thus, if the masking flip-flop is off, M_j=0, the tags will not be reset. If it is on, it will be reset if

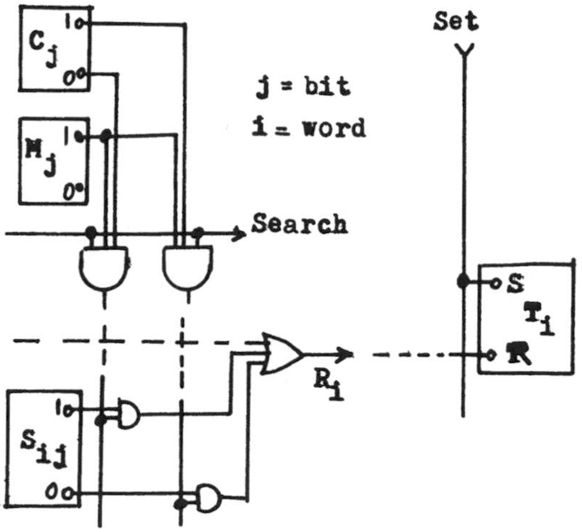

Fig. 37: One bit ($S_{i,j}$) of memory

- we look for C_j=1, but S_{ij}=0 or
- we look for C_j=0, but S_{ij}=1.

In short, when S_{ij} does not correspond to the comparand C_j and C_j is not masked out by M_j.

The first associative memories were special, e.g., cryogenic memories and thus very expensive. Even if we use present or projected memories, Fig. 37 shows that a large amount of hardware is needed. It was shown in [Fo 76] that it is 50% above that needed for vector addressed memories and will thus always be more expensive. Another problem is that we have processed information by bits but input and output requires them to be by word.

In STARAN this problem was solved by using a 256x256 bit array of random access memory with horizontal "word" and vertical "bit slices." A word may be considered to consist of eight "fields" each with 32 bits or in some other combination. I/0 is effected through buses of 256 wires, so that a complete word can be written or read; the circuitry outside the memory is such that it treats bit slices of the memory. It seems to have the best of both worlds (but is expensive).

Associative processors are SIMD-systems, very similar to Illiac, except that they access their memories through association instead of vector addressing and they are arranged differently than those of Illiac. This is why we based the discussion on a distinctive part - the memory. Now we will expand to other parts of STARAN (actually, RADCAP, as discussed in a number of papers in the 1973 Conference on Parallel Processing).

Attached to the memory are three registers: M, X, Y with 256 bits each and a so-called "flip" network for connecting them in various ways. View the M-register as the mask or as a register which tests the response, and X, Y as operand registers. If an operation is written as: $X:=(X*Y)\cdot M$, it is meant as a bit-by-bit operation * (and, or, x etc). This means that any bit i of X will be the result of x_i*y_i for those i for which M_i=1. We may therefore view the three registers as representing 256 one-bit processing elements PE. Each of them receives the same instruction which it either executes or ignores. It cannot do otherwise.

As with any other SIMD machine, STARAN has a single control unit CU (Fig. 38).

It also includes the following functional units: 1) A control memory for storing instructions for the CU. It can also store data; 2) A sequential controller (a PDP11) for peripherals, disk, basic software systems etc.; 3) An external function unit which transfers control and synchronizes information among all units of the

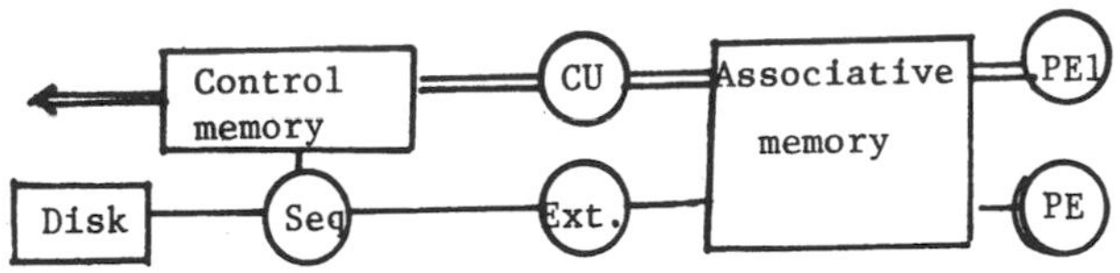

Fig. 38: Functional description of Staran

system; 4) The buses, which serve to transfer information.

The CU is special because of its connection to an associative memory and the instructions it has to broadcast. It includes an instruction register for holding the 32 bits of an instruction, another register to hold the key or operand of 32 bits, an array select register, four field pointers to the associative memory and a few more standard or special registers.

Another non-standard (and thus not cheap) unit is the flip-network [Ba 73]. It gets its 2^n inputs I (Fig. 39) from a "selector", scrambles them according to the

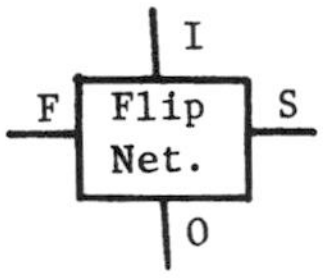

Fig. 39: The flip

flip-control F, shifts them according to the shift-control S and outputs them to the multidimensional access memory through 0. It is composed of a number of 2x2 crossbars (Fig. 40) such that for a 0-input the connection is direct, for 1 is crossed.

Suppose that F = 101. This will establish the connection (6,5,8,7,2,1,4,3). For F being binary numbers: 0,1,2,3,4,5,6 and 7 the connections are: (1,2,3,4,5,6, 7,8), (2,1,4,3,6,5,8,7), (3,4,1,2,7,8,5,6), (4,3,2,1,8,7,6,5), (4,5,6,7,1,2,3,4), (6,5,8,7,2,1,4,3) (7,8,5,6,3,4,1,2) and (8,7,6,5,4,3,2,1) respectively. In the same way we could shift the 8 inputs into (1,2,3,4,5,6,7,8), (8,1,2,3,4,5,6,7), (7,8,1,2, 3,4,5,6), (3,4,1,2,7,8,5,6), (5,6,7,8,1,2,3,4), (4,1,2,3,8,5,6,7) and (2,1,4,3,6,5, 8,7) respectively. With both F and S inputs, a large number of possible permutations can be achieved - unfortunately for a rather high price. The network is blocking.

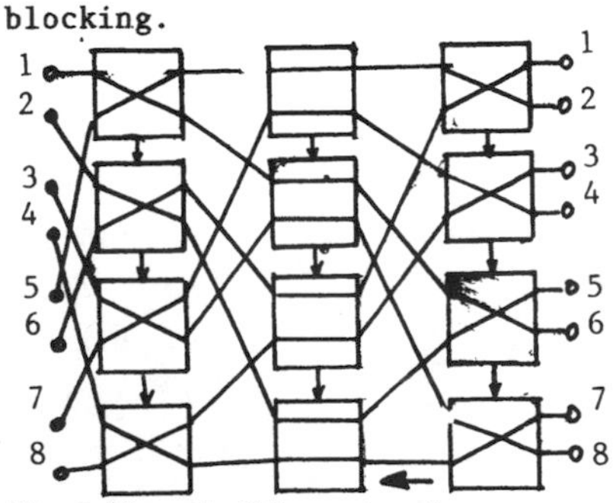

Fig. 40: A flip-network

Let us assume that we want to find the largest of the n words stored in the memory. If the mask stores "100...0" and the key stores "11...1" then we compare the most significant left-most bit of every word with 1. The words r for which T_i remained 1 have in fact a 1 there, the (n-r) which did not, have a zero. Those which have a zero cannot compete for being largest. If all had zeros, we would change the first bit in the key to zero. Next we do the same on bits 2,3,...w of the memory, each time either updating the corresponding bit in the key register or leaving a "1" there. When all w bits are processed, the key register stores the largest word (or words, if a number of them is the same maximum).

We have indicated how a maximum is found but then it seems that comparison is an area for which an associative pps should be efficient by its very fundamental features. Arithmetic vector expressions can also be done.

If we view every word as composed of fields $F1_i, F2_i, \ldots, Fk_i$ where i is the word-number and each field has a number of consecutive bits, then the following operations may be performed:

(a) Fj * Fj → Fk; in all words (with T=1)

(b) C * Fj → Fk; between the comparand and all words

(c) Fj * Fk → Fl; between different words.

* is an addition, subtraction, multiplication, division or comparison (>,≥,=,≤,<) operation. The central control unit may load into or read from the comparand and mask register any word that is there.

Using such operations, we can calculate $\underline{s} = \underline{a} + \underline{b}$ where $\underline{a}$, $\underline{b}$ and $\underline{s}$ are vectors occupying m-bits of a field in a word. If their length is n, we need n words for each of them.

As known, addition can be performed by using Boolean equations: $s_i = a_i \oplus b_i \oplus c_i$; $c_{i+1} = a_i * b_i + a_i * c_i + b_i * c_i$ with *, + and ⊕ denoting "and", "or" and "exclusive-or".

A better way is shown in [Ba 73]. It requires approximately 700 nsecs (for 32 bits, about 22.4 μsecs and amounts to 256 additions). The same time is needed if four arrays are used as in RADCAP - which therefore has 1024 additions in 22.4 μsecs or 40 Mips (million instructions per second).

For other applications, the following times were determined: search=150 nsec/bit, read=150 nsec/bit, write=300 nsec/bit, fetch=150 nsec/instruction. Based on these and other data obtained at RADC it was concluded [Thu 76] that "...an associative processor is useful,...but may not be cost-effective unless it is very carefully tuned to the application." "The study also indicates the potential for disaster that can occur when a special-purpose machine is applied to unsuitable problems." "The spread of throughput increases from 3 to 186 using modifications of the same basic configurations and serves to amplify the need of the user to recognize the special purpose of such processors." (For associative operations high, for arithmetic, low throughputs).

We have encountered a problem, BMD, which was inherently parallel and at the same time required matching real-time data with independent targets - for which it uses associative storage. Because PEPE=Parallel Ensemble of Processing Elements does a lot of scientific calculations, a large number (288) of sequential computers equipped with floating point hardware is used; but because they are standard units, the reliability is not impaired. Since tracking is an on-line, π-problem no lock-step synchronization is needed - each PE can work on its target independently of and concurrently with the other PE's. PEPE is thus completely unstructured.

PEPE can be viewed as 3 SIMD-units (Fig. 41): a correlation, arithmetic and associative-output unit. Each SIMD has a control unit: CCU for the correlation, ACU for the arithmetic and AOCU for the associative output system. The control units are of rather common design with each having its own program and data memory.

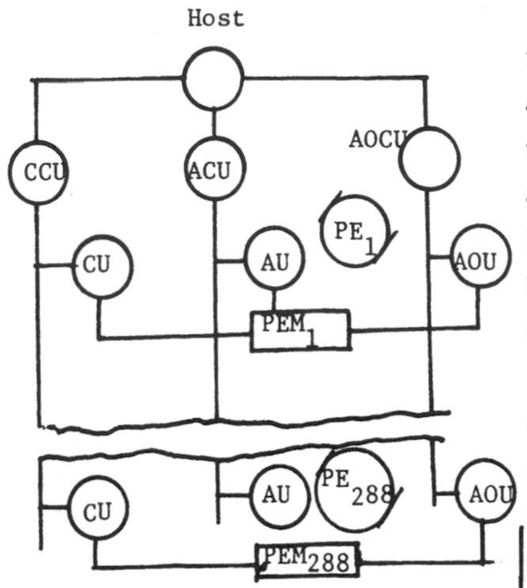

Fig. 41: PEPE

PEPE [ET 73] was designed to suit the particular application of BMD. The "control" units are used mainly for comparison, branching, control of program flow, and supervisory operations, and need only integer, branching, load, store and logical operations. Therefore, no floating-point hardware was provided in the control unit sequential processors.

There are no direct connections among the PE's except through the control units and all timing and control signals come from the control units. Still PEPE is different from Illiac and is called an "ensemble." It was designed specifically for real-time radar tracking and might be called a single-purpose, instead of a special-purpose computer.

Each PE may simultaneously respond to micro steps from each of the three control units, thus effectively executing up to 3x288=864 instructions simultaneously.

The PE's are not of standard design and contain an arithmetic (AU), associative-output (AOU) and correlation (CU) units.

The instruction set of CU is rich in associative "match and compare" operations, so that incoming data can be rapidly and efficiently correlated with data already in element memory, and this be placed in the proper elements.

"The Arithmetic Units had scientific calculations as their primary responsibility; therefore, they were provided with floating-point arithmetic instruction repertoire in addition to all of the other conventional and associative grouping instructions. The CUs and AOUs are mainly required to input/output data and perform associative comparisons, matches, searches, and ordering functions, all of which can be handled with logical and integer arithmetic operations. However, they are occasionally called upon to execute short floating-point subroutines. Rather than provide expensive floating-point hardware in all of the CUs and AOUs to accommodate the rather infrequent requirements, it was decided to include instead provisions for the CCU and AOCU to interrupt the ACU. Then, the ACU could perform the floating-point routines on demand for the CCU and the AOCU. A considerable amount of hardware was thereby saved, and simulations showed that the performance degradation caused by lack of floating-point capability in the CUs and AOUs was insignificant".

As in Illiac, each PE unit (except element memory) contains an Activity register (one bit). When a control unit performs a parallel instruction, all corresponding active (Activity register = "1") PE units respond so that a maximum of 288 PE units may simultaneously execute that instruction.

Each memory element PEM is connected to the AU, ACU, and CU by means of a common data bus. The following priority was established: (1) CU, (2) AOU, (3) AU, the reason being that the CU instructions tend to be short (200-300 nsec) and the AU instructions tend to be considerably longer (floating-point multiply requires 1.9 µsec).

Since PEPE "may be completely unstructured, no element has any positional significance. Thus, the elements can be accessed, ordered and grouped for data manipulation purposes, associatively that is purely on the basis of their contents. An element can fail with no impact on the calculations occurring in the other elements. Moreover, for many problems where data is periodically updated on the basis of continually arriving new data, only the historical state of an independent file is lost when an element fails. New data destined for that element is unable to correlate, so the data is automatically entered into an empty element to begin a new file. Thus, graceful degradation and automatic recovery are achieved naturally. Further, elements can be added as required with no effect on software or program execution. In fact, PEPE programs are oblivious of the number of elements and programmers do not know or care either, as long as there are enough."

The differences between PEPE and the system we are trying to develop stem from the fact that PEPE is suited for a particular (BMD) application whereas we are trying to develop a process-control system. Therefore, we might have to use processors with floating-point hardware to execute the (mostly) arithmetic calculations. As mentioned above, we also want a symmetric system.

PEPE is really a gigantic computer - such as needed for its application. We do not need such speeds (millions of instructions per second) and the computer could consist of mini or even microprocessor units. Price is still a factor.

The main difference is obviously that in general there is no need for extensive associative processing. Finally, because of real-time constraints on the operating systems, we should always try not to share any memory.

Altogether, despite different application areas, the master/slave architecture, broadcast of data in blocks from master to slaves as well as local memories for the slaves will be advocated. Where not needed, the costly associative processing should not be advocated; memory should, if possible, not be shared; because of availability considerations, the master and slaves should be identical (if that is possible and not too costly). The master may then be changed continuously - we will call it a "roving" master. The computers should be mini or microprocessors all with floating point hardware.

2.7 DEDICATED, ON-LINE SYSTEMS

The remark is repeated that the first duty of a designer, the most important categorization depends on the ultimate use of the system. None of the computers above was a dedicated, on-line system for non-π problems, so we will add three systems designed for such use. We hope also to resolve the problems of whether the master/slave or decentralized system and whether a single or p local memories are more suitable for these applications.

One of the earliest multi-microprocessor systems [Re 74] originally without a master was supposed to use MOS/LSI chips connected to a common multiplexed bus (Fig. 42). Since the chips at that time were rather slow but memory and bus were relatively fast, the author claimed that "throughput will be limited by the processors rather than by the memory. This means that several microcomputers can share the same memory since one memory serve all of them . On the other hand shared resources e.g. memory offer an economic advantage by eliminating devices which would have to be duplicated in separate stand-alone systems. Shared resources also provide direct access to data which might otherwise require transmission from one system to another". It was claimed that "throughput increases often almost directly with the number of microcomputers while system cost increases only slightly".

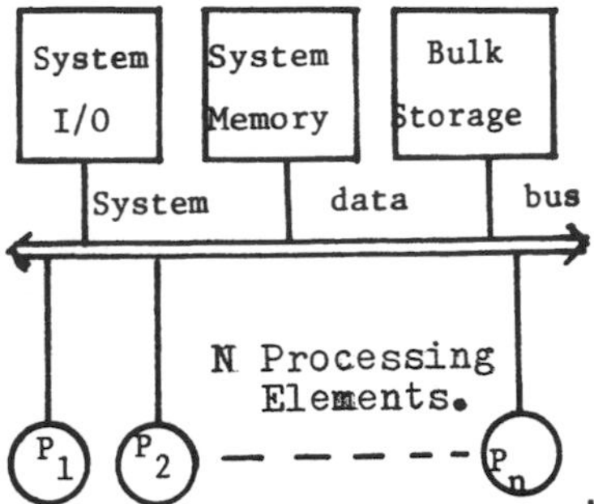

Fig. 42: One of the earliest multiprocessors

These observations are correct as long as they do not include the operating system. If the system routines such as the initial load or interrupt routines are in the common system memory, they have to be protected from simultaneous access by locking. To circumvene these problems, the design of the above pps was modified so that a dedicated controller was added. It was called the resource-allocation processor and represents a "master." When a request is received, this master consults a request table in its memory, while the requesting microcomputer executes a HALT-instruction, busy waiting for an indication on its "grant line" that it may receive the resource required. Obviously, this means a loss of time. There are no local memories; the system was apparently not assembled.

A multiprocessor without a controller but with local memories, the "Pluribus" [He 73], is used as a "dedicated" system in the ARPA network of interconnected computers. This network consists of over 40 sites with the "host" computer at each site connected to the network through a small communication processor, the IMP (Interface Message Processor). When a message from some line arrives, the IMP should receive (and buffer) it; perform error checks; when short enough, process it directly; otherwise route it to another line or to the host and do other housekeeping jobs. In order to be able to perform all these jobs, the IMP must possess enough memory for both programs and buffers and must be very fast. It was this last demand which led the designers of the IMP to the realization that a multiprocessor system would achieve the required bandwidth (speed), reliability and would have the added flexibility no single, fast and powerful machine would provide. The design (Fig. 43) followed an "implicative" reasoning which leads from a particular application to a system design and some of whose conclusions will apply to our system.

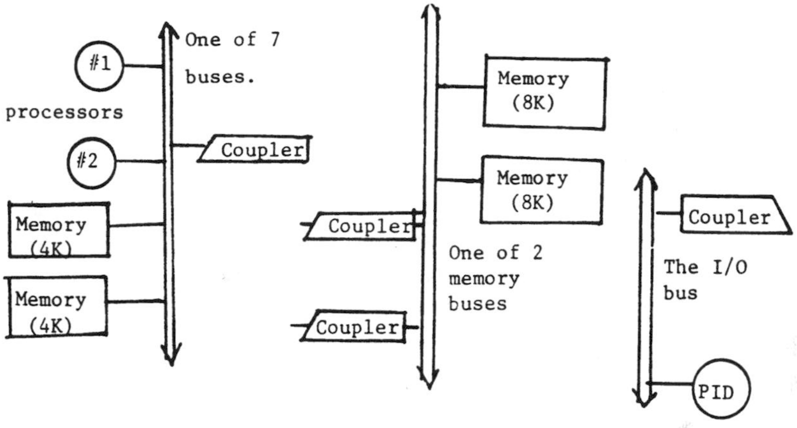

Fig. 43: The Pluribus System

(a) Since requests arrive at unpredictable times it was thought that a bus with asynchronous access is the best solution. Note that each configuration of two processors and two local memories, has one such bus. It may be called a dual-processor unit; there are seven of these. A memory unit includes two 8K memories and bus; there are two of these. There is one I/O unit.

(b) Out of fear that the buses cannot handle all the traffic, 10 were provided with bus couplers providing the "switching arrangement to permit interconnection of all the buses. To adhere to the requirement that all processors must be identical and able to perform any system task, these buses must be connected so that all processors can access all shared memory, I/O can be fed to and from shared memory and each of the processors may control the operation and sense the status of any I/O unit.

(c) Access of shared memory through the switching system will incur time delay. In the given application, some parts of the program are run very frequently, others far less so. This leads naturally to the use of private memories to allow faster local access to the frequently used code, with these local memories all typically containing the same code. With this configuration it was found that the ratio of local vs. shared memory was better than three to one."

(d) Slow (but cheap) cpu's were chosen. "One bus could then service up to four such processors, but it was decided that two was the optimum number, since in simulation studies, serious degradation due to bus contention occurred at 3 processors/bus. Because of the speed advantage of the bus compared to the memories, two logical memory blocks were connected to a single bus with almost no interference. Since this is even more so for I/O devices, a single bus is used for all such devices.

Slowdown of the system due to various interference delays was studied and the results are shown in the table below. Note that software contention leads to the highest percentage of slowdown."

An additional 2 percent slowdown was reported, but even at that point we have 23.5 percent which is not acceptable for process-control applications. We will, therefore, include a master (Pluribus does not have one) and let common memory be

Slowdown	Cause
5.5%	Contention for a processor bus
3%	Contention for the shared memory buses
5%	Contention for the shared memories
10%	Contention for a single system-wide software resource, assuming each processor wants the resource for 6 out of 120 instructions.

accessed only through it, to reduce contention. The master may be required also because of the following.

In the Pluribus system processors on different buses access each other through the I/O bus. The couplers are bidirectional so that the possibility exists that the buses of two processors are trying to get hold of each other through the I/O bus. They may never get it; this is then a case of hardware deadlock. In Pluribus, it is easily detected and removed by preemptive switching every 500 microseconds.

The IMP employs a rather ambitious reliability scheme in which the system is aware at all times of the state of affairs and if something seems to be wrong a "diagnostic" is run, the "bad" unit amputated etc.

One of our systems had a master/slave organization, but a common memory, the other had local memories, but no master. Let us now discuss a system with both a master and local memories.

A good representative of such a system is the COSMAC [Ru 77] of RCA (Fig. 44). It has a master-slave organization with all of the inter-slave communication going through the master. Each of the slaves (up to 256) has a private memory to reduce interference. The connection is really through a single bus which includes both address (I/O) and data. Where it departs from our aims is in its mode of operation, namely that "each of its microcomputers is to perform a dedicated task. Very little data is interchanged between processors relative to the total system data flow. Each microcomputer can operate relatively independently of the others." For telephone exchanges this idea is correct since a number of slaves could for instance process only incoming calls. It would be also true that: "The software in each subsystem is optimally tailored to the processing task for which it has responsibility. Should any processor become overloaded, it cannot be unburdened by any other processor; however, this should not occur with proper system design." In case of process-control, the above clearly does not apply.

"The master-slave organization (Fig. 44) offers many advantages to multimicrocomputer systems" with all interprocessor communication always going through the master.

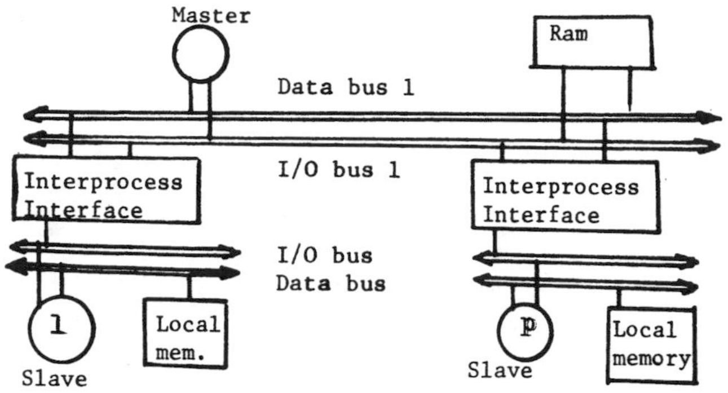

Fig. 44: Functional description of COSMAC

"The master-slave organization appears to be the most suitable for the bulk of multimicrocomputer applications envisioned, i.e. ones where a main processor controls and supervises a multitude of intelligent (microprocessor based) subsystems, each dedicated to a specific task.

It is imperative, if a common memory is used, that reference to it by the individual processors be minimized - hence, some local, random-access memory (RAM) is highly desirable."

We include two more observations from [Ru 77].

"Note that the master-slave multi-microcomputer structure requires each processor to have a local, random-access memory associated with it. It is strongly felt that the shared memory concept is not viable for most multi-microcomputer systems. This is primarily because, even for just a few processors, memory contention problems become severe (especially with low-cost, slow memories). Furthermore, the hardware required to support a multiport memory and to resolve contention is more complex and more expensive than the additional memory required to give each processor at least a minimal memory. Chip costs for static 256 x 4 bit-random-access memories are already below $3.00 and projected to cost about 0.06 cents/bit in 1980" (price projections are always pessimistic).

"Multi-microcomputer systems will most likely find greatest use in process-control applications. Each slave could be dedicated to a specific task, say testing a particular module, assembly or system. The master could then be used to coordinate the testing, monitor the test results and do data-logging as required. Applications also exist in the data-communication area."

We agree with the need for local memories and the use in process control but "task processors" limit the use of COSMAC and decrease its reliability.

There are other multiprocessors [Vi 72, Gr 76] serving as telephone switching centers with processors dedicated to certain tasks. This could be fatal to the availability of the systems since the failure of one unit, say for I/O, incapacitates the entire aggregate unless such functional units are multiplicated. For this reason, the APZ-150 [Gr 76] or some computers for avionics duplicate all processors but this is not desirable in our case either.

2.8 SUMMARY

We have reviewed a number of systems and rejected all of them. Some of the reasons were:

Pipeline computers were too expensive and would not work efficiently on sparse matrix problems we intend to solve. Our problems are not such that an Apps with an unlimited number of processors is required, moreover, both in Apps and the various multiprocessors, the use of a common memory leads to a speed-reduction which we do not intend to tolerate. SIMD systems suffer first of all in respect to availability/reliability: not only will they stop if the control unit, but even if one of the PE's is down. They are also expensive, waste memory and would work inefficiently in sparse matrix problems. We do not need associative memories and since these systems are really SIMD, they have for us all the disadvantages mentioned above.

The systems which will be advocated are to some degree similar to PEPE. It seems thus worthwhile to mention some statements made about the future of (PEPE-like) parallel systems.

"Super-computers will not enjoy a wide and varied market and relatively few will ever be built. The marketing and applications engineering efforts required to sell even one supercomputer is considerable, engineering and other non-recurring costs are high, and software costs are likewise high. Manufacturers are therefore understandably reluctant to invest much effort in supercomputer applications and development; as a result the research investment and hands-on experience necessary to learn how to apply supercomputers effectively is lacking." Because they use massive amounts of hardware to achieve great computational power, they are relatively unreliable and expensive if all that hardware is concentrated in one place. "If the reliability and cost problems can be solved, if the support software can be provided at reasonable cost, and if the problem programming can be made reasonably straightforward and simple, then" there should be "considerable interest and demand for supercomputers and the future of such machines will be assured."

PEPE exhibits some features that provide partial solutions to the above problems. "First, even though it contains a large amount of hardware (about five million gates in the 288-element version), about 95 percent of that hardware is contained in the elements. Therefore, most faults will occur in elements and element failures can usually be tolerated and frequently even ignored in the kinds of problems for which PEPE is suited. Most other architectures, such as sequential and vector machines, do not exhibit this property; a hard failure anywhere in the processing unit cannot usually be ignored.

Cost comparisons likewise favor a PEPE-like machine over other supercomputer architectures having equivalent power and hardware content. Nearly all of the PEPE hardware is contained in the 288 identical elements so that high-volume production methods can be used even though only a few, or even one, PEPE is built. For the same reason, engineering and non-recurrent costs can be kept low, relative to the amount of hardware involved. Since most other supercomputer architectural styles (again, of equivalent hardware content) do not exhibit the high hardware replication inherent in PEPE their costs will be higher.

Current experience with PEPE indicates that support software costs (compilers, assemblers, monitors, link editors, utilities) are roughly equivalent to those encountered in the development of any medium scale general purpose computer. Problem programming is straightforward and simple and presents no difficulties to any FORTRAN programmer."

The above refers to PEPE, a supercomputer (288 rather large elements). Let me now ask the reader to make a mental switch and think about a symmetric system of some 20-30 microprocessors. Next reread the quoted passages and note the following:

(1) The market for supercomputers may be very small; for "our" system it was shown to be considerable.

(2) The cost is low (because of microprocessor prices) and since the production volume is enormous, engineering and non-recurrent costs may really be kept low.

(3) It will be shown in this book that programming the system is very easy. Thus software and reprogramming costs will be low.

(4) The same reasons which make PEPE more reliable will carry over to our model.

(5) The real questions though are to develop such a model, its interface (operating system, language, etc.) and then algorithms and programs for it.

This will be done in the chapters which follow.

3. ALTERNATING SEQUENTIAL/PARALLEL ASP-SYSTEMS

3.1 ASP AND LIMITS OF ITS SPEEDUP

Aims: To provide a better classification system for parallel processing. To define the requirements for the system - they lead to ASP. To calculate the bound of speedup, efficiency, etc for ASP. Based on these, to enumerate the principles for the design of an ASP-systems. To describe existing and projected ASP-systems. To compare them.

In Chapter 2 we reviewed various pps' and can now return to the question of classification. Flynn's scheme is used most often, but even for existing systems it is not unambiguous, especially in respect to pipeline computers. Equally, the classification does not contain any information about the type of connection used. A further difficulty occurs if a computer contains both parallelism and pipelining.

To resolve this difficulty, Enslow suggested that as multiprocessors qualify only systems which include: two or more processors having access to a common memory (whereby private memory is not excluded), shared I/O., a single integrated operating system, hardware and software interactions at all levels, possible execution of a job on different processors and hardware interrupts.

A common memory is mandatory in this definition of a multiprocessor but as the number of processors increases the congestion in the access to the common memory will also increase. Enslow's definition therefore seems to exclude systems containing very large numbers of processors, but since microprocessors for a few dollars are now available systems containing thousands of processors are planned. Some of the more progressive projects of computer architecture such as PRIME are also excluded.

Feng [Fe 72] classifies systems according to the word-length, i.e. the number of bits which are processed in parallel in a word, and the number of words which are processed in parallel. A computer structure is represented by a point in a plane (Fig. 1) where the abscissa is the wordlength and the ordinate is the number of words processed in parallel, as determined by the number of processors. For example, C.mmp which has 16 PE's and words with 16 bits is represented by (16,16). The ordinate can also be determined by the number of arithmetic and logic units instead of PE's, so that ILLIAC IV is represented by (64,64).

Feng's classification does not distinguish between multiprocessors like C.mmp and array processors, i.e. between autonomous processors which execute programs and ALU's which execute operations. It does not distinguish among processing levels.

The TIASC (Texas Instruments Advanced Scientific Computer) is represented as (64,2048). The number 2048 is obtained from the 4 pipelines, each consisting of 8 stages with 64 bits. However, the number 2048 can be obtained in many ways, e.g. 8 pipelines, 8 stages, 32 bits. Thus the classification cannot represent a multiple pipeline structure such as the TIASC unambiguously.

It is also not possible to represent the pipeline structure at the program level of PEPE. PEPE is characterized as (288,16) and the fact that each set of data (up to 288, each representing a target) is processed successively in three different PE's is not represented.

Let us try another, the Erlangen Classification System, ECS [Ha 77]. It is based on the distinctions among three processing levels:

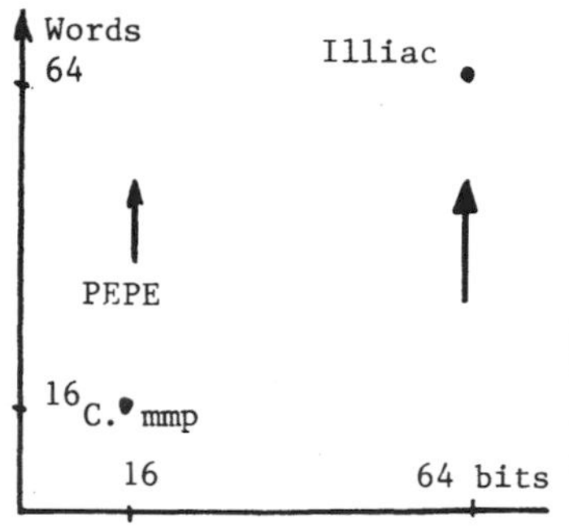

Fig. 1:Feng's classification

1. Program control unit - Using a program counter, some other registers, and, in most cases, a microprogram device, the CU interprets a program instruction by instruction.

2. Arithmetic and logical unit - The ALU uses the output signals of a microprogram device to execute sequences of microinstructions according to the interpretation process performed by the CU.

3. Elementary logic circuit - Each of the microoperations which make up the operation set initiates an elementary switching process. The logic circuits belonging to one bit position of all the microoperations are called an ELC.

A computer configuration can include a number of CU's. Each CU can control a number of ALU's all of which perform the same operation at any given time. Finally, each ALU contains a number of ELC's, each dedicated to one bit position. The number of ELC's is commonly known as the wordlength.

If we disregard pipelining for the moment, the number of CU's, ALU's per CU, and ELC's per ALU form a triple, written t(computer type) = (c, a, w).

We give some examples of the triple: the simplest computer with a single CU & ALU and words 1-bit-long is defined by t(MINIMA) = (1,1,1), t(IBM) = (1,1,32) is an example of the sequential computer, t(SOLOMON) = (1,1024,1) is the historical concept of an array processor, t(ILLIAC IV) = (1,64,64) is the array processor, t(C.mmp) = (16,1,16) is the Carnegie-Mellon University multi-mini project using 16 PDP-11's and t(PRIME) = (5,1,16) is the University of California, Berkeley, project in which time-sharing is replaced by multiprocessing.

The triples above are able to classify all viable parallel structures, but not pipelining. Next the classification is extended to include pipelining implemented at all three levels described earlier.

The multiplication sign will be used at all levels to separate the number representing the degree of parallelism from the number representing the number of stages in the pipeline.

For example, pipelining of the arithmetic unit can be regarded as a "vertical" replication of ECL's compared with "horizontal" replication used in a parallel ECL. We may thus multiply the number of ECL's, by the number of stages in the pipeline, to characterize the ALU. For the TIASC we have then t(TIASC)=(1,4,64x8).

The next higher level of pipelining is instruction pipelining. This involves the existence of a number of functional units which can operate simultaneously to process a single instruction stream. It is based on the inspection of instructions which can be executed simultaneously without conflict. These instructions are executed as soon as a suitable functional unit is free. This technique is referred to as "instruction lookahead" or "instruction pipelining".

Finally we have to consider the pipelining on the PE-level we encountered in PEPE and which may be called "macro-pipelining". Assuming that a data set has to be processed by three different tasks sequentially, then it can be performed in three different processors, each one processing one task. The data stream then passes the first processor, is stored in a buffer, (to which the second processor has also access) and finally passes the second and third processor. Since processors can work at the same time (on different data), the effective processing speed can be ideally tripled in comparison with the use of only one processor. In such a way, stepping from processor to processor data are 'refined' or are 'integrated'. The PEPE array (without the host installation) then is characterized as t(PEPE) =(1x3,288,32).

The triple now reads as follows: t=(c x c', a x a', w x w') and has been extended to a sixtuple to incorporate pipelining. Nevertheless, we keep calling it a triple because the three levels of consideration suggest that we think in three terms, which have to be extended in some cases by an additional term, attached to the other value (of the same level) by using the symbol x.

The values in parantheses are the numbers of:

PCU's in parallel (multiprocessor, MIMD)
PCU's in pipelining (macro-pipelining)
ALU's in parallel (array computer, SIMD)
ALU's in pipelining (instruction pipelining-lookahead)
ELC in parallel (wordlength)
ELC in pipelining (arithmetic pipelining)

All entities are independent of one another. All combinations therefore can appear.

The ECS classification scheme includes all systems mentioned thus far, but gives no indication whether local memories are used or not and about the mode of operation. Also, what about future systems? Are there any other systems?

Since a pps may be viewed as a society of processors, we hope to learn how to organize it by reviewing how human societies are organized to perform some tasks which a single person cannot do by himself.

In any organization we need some coordination for ensuring that its participants work toward the same goal. The more intelligent and independent are the individuals, the easier will the group achieve its goals. Unfortunately, the problems of coordination may be increased so much as to make a society of very independent parts ungovernable.

Precisely as in human societies, we may classify multiprocessor organizations into the following types.

(a) Democratic, decentralized systems

The members know how to do their jobs and are motivated by say, income. Each picks up its jobs and the governement enforces only loose control ("don't kill" laws). In terms of computers the units ("slaves") are very intelligent, complete mini or microcomputers. The switch is as general as possible. There is no central control. Each module seeks its own tasks, secures the resources required (memory, etc.) and the connections. This organization ("multiprocessors") is flexible, but as was shown, too liberal for computers. With more than 4-5 minicomputers it may be bogged down by constant information transfer, locking etc.

(b) Autocratic, centralized systems

The modules are slaves and, as such, follow their leader blindly - be he in Berlin or Moscow. Since each operation is completely described by the master, the only freedom left the slaves is to idle. These systems may achieve very high efficiencies but only for very special applications. Any digression from the beaten path leads to sequentialization and extremely low efficiencies. These systems were exemplified by array processors, e.g. ILLIAC-IV.

(c) Hierarchical systems

If one looks at the Constitution of the U.S., it appears to be neither of the above. It is democratic; but there is, or at least should be, some coordination imposed by the federal government. Washington only sets the goals, - but the states have the right to reject anything patently wrong. A system like this will be called a hierarchical but democratic system.

We next introduce another example of a society - an orchestra. If four members play a quartet, there is no need for a conductor ("master"). Information is transferred either by looking at the same score (C.mmp) or by a few winks (Cm*). If the amount of information is large, both can be unwieldy.

Suppose that an all-string orchestra plays Dvorak's serenade for strings. If no musical scores are in front of them, but they have a sign language, they can look all to the conductor for guidance. This is SIMD: only the conductor has the score ("program") and all slaves who play, do it in unison.

The hierarchical system would ask the conductor to bring first from backstage all scores and put them on the stands. When the concert starts, he only signals when to start or stop playing but the musicians have different scores and thus do not follow him blindly; they only get a few signals from him.

If we "translate" it to a pps, it will have a master but the slaves will be intelligent enough to do rather complicated tasks independently. For this they will need their own programs and data i.e. have each both a control unit and local memory. The system organization then evolves along the lines of Fig. 2.

Let us discuss possible advantages and disadvantages of a hierarchical system:

(a) There is no common address space (as in Cm*). The slaves access main

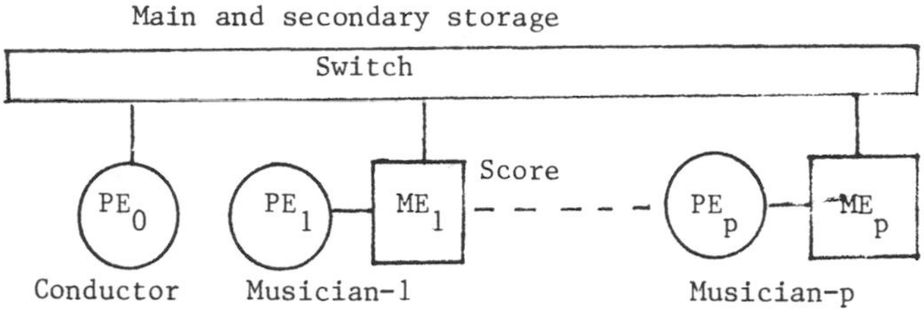

Fig. 2: Organization of a Hierarchical System

memory only through the master (in our orchestra, the conductor distributes the scores prior to the start of the concert). There can be no deadlock and there is no need for locks, semaphores etc. We do not want the conductor running around in order to start musicians, so no multiprogramming. The slaves have just a score: the "Slave Operating System" (SOS) is very simple, it only supports say assembly language. The conductors score is not much more complicated; it only mentions when various instruments start playing and what, generally they are supposed to do. It is a "Control Program" (COP). Summing up: the operating system is simple and will not lead to reduction of speedup. Deadlocks will not occur.

(b) One of the claims for a parallel processing system vs. uniprocessors was that its availability might be higher simply because a loss of one processor would not incapacitate the entire system. This is only true as long as the lost processor is not the master - the availability problem therefore does exist if the control (or for that matter any other function) is centralized. (Can the orchestra play if the maestro is sick?)

It is therefore suggested to use a master, but let it be completely identical to all slaves, so that every processor may act as the master. In fact, in such symmetrical systems every processor may become the master, even on a periodical basis. We might call it then a "roving" master. The symmetry will increase slightly the cost, but also the availability of the pps. Actually, the master could also read new data while the slaves are all working concurrently on their respective memories by "cycle stealing" of a reverse type. Summing it up: A symmetrical pps with a dedicated controller (the master) is the choice. (We are not talking about having the assistant conductor, Mr. Bernstein substitute Mr. Toscanini - we are talking about an orchestra which uses its musicians in turn for conducting.)

The system is thus symmetric, i.e. the master and slaves are identical processors. For solving on-line, process-control problems in general, these processors should have words at least 32 bits long, floating point hardware, etc. Other process-control problems could use shorter words. Both microprocessors and minicomputers may be used. Since microprocessors are dirt cheap we don't mind accepting the fact that the master will probably be very much underutilized.

(c) Each slave should have its own "private" or "local" memory (called simply "memory" in the sequel). This is required in order to enable parallel, autonomous work of the slaves. The master should be able to access all memories as well as the main and secondary memories (to be called "stores"). Most systems reviewed did, in fact, posses such local memories. We should though beware of the following:

If memories are accessed directly by cycle-stealing, this may lead to data deadlocks. The same applies if more than one slave uses them (PEPE). Thus, each local memory should "belong" to a single slave and be accessible only to it or to the master (not at the same time though). The common address space (as in Cm*) is rejected.

In terms of the orchestra: the conductor has access to the scores prior to the musicians playing it - he, in fact, distributed the scores. During the performance, he only watches them play. Obviously, the string player should not even look at the score of the percussionist. In terms of the hierarchical system, the master and slaves access the memories at different times (exclusion).

(d) Cost-effectiveness is assured for mini and microprocessors. It so happens that (p+1) processors each complete with CU and ALU cost less than (p+1) specially built ALU's.

(e) No correlation of data files is needed in general process-control systems; thus, no associative memories need be used. On the other hand, for non-π general programs, with no independent files as was the case in BMD, without its inherent parallelism we cannot use the master as the only source of instructions, as done in ILLIAC, STARAN or PEPE. Not only data, but also programs must be stored in local memories and enable the slaves to work independently.

(f) We will find that a single bus is sufficient as a switch. Thus, a schematic block diagram of the system will be as shown in Fig. 3. The "common switch" was added in order to indicate that the system works as follows: with the common switch in the vertical position, memories 1 to p are part of the master's address space. With the common switch in the horizontal position, memory i is connected only to slave i, for all p slaves but memory zero, the main and secondary stores are connected to the master. Thus, either the master has access to all memories or each memory is used by the slave to which it "belongs". The bus is controlled exclusively by the master.

The block-diagram indicates the mode of operation. Any program must start with an initialization step "I" (see fig. 4) during which the programs and data needed by the slaves are transferred by the master to the memories. During the following parallel step "P", each slave works autonomously using only its memory; all slaves work in parallel. At the end of the P-step, there is some information which must be transferred from the memories to the main store or to the other memories. This, as well as any computations to be done on this information, is the task of the master in the sequential step S. I is also sequential.

The parallel and sequential steps alternate; hence the name "Alternating Sequential/Parallel-Processing." Since this mode of operation is probably more im-

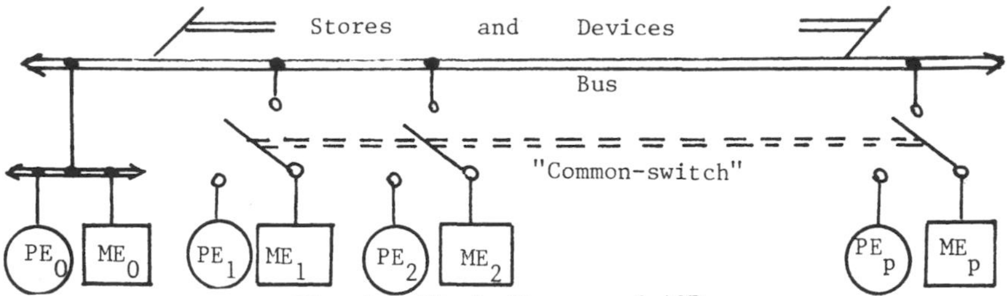

Fig. 3: Block diagram of ASP

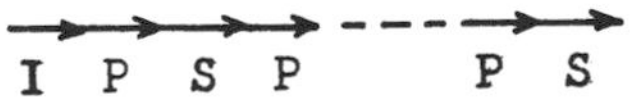

Fig. 4: Step sequence of a program

portant than the hardware and is certainly quite general, we will use it to also indicate all pp's which work according to it. They will be called ASP's.

The memories are accessed first only by the master (common switch "up") and then only by the slaves (switch "down"). In the orchestra with the switch "up" the conductor distributes the scores (programs and data) to the slaves and leaves it there (in private memories). With the switch "down", the common address space disappears: each player has his score (program) to play. In the first step, the single master could only work sequentially; in the second step, the whole orchestra plays simultaneously.

If we had only to solve inherently π-problems, we could work so. For others we can use sequences i.e. having finished the overture, the conductor distributes new scores and invites the pianist. Then, he starts the concerto.

We have mentioned that only the master controls the switch. Since the slaves have to report that they completed their tasks, they cannot do it through the bus, over which they have no control. As we see, the interrupt lines must be separated from the rest of the bus.

It is easy to write programs for ASP. We do not make them completely sequential as they are in books on programming. Neither do we have the compulsion to reduce the sequential times $t(S_i)$ to zero; instead we will try to minimize them. This will always be possible and those more ingenious than I am will get lower minima and therefore higher speedups, but we will all have achieved some speedup.

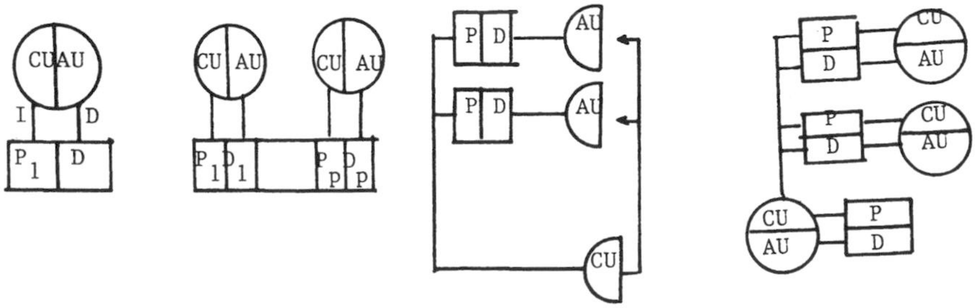

Fig. 5: Classification

We have defined a model and now ask: is it SIMD or MIMD? Well, it is neither.

Since the slaves have their own control units and are not working in lock-synchronism, ASP is not a SIMD-system. On the other hand, there is coordination imposed by the master; the work is synchronous in that each sequential step starts only after all parallel tasks are completed; slaves cannot access common memory (as in C.mmp), there is no single address space and no message switching (as in Cm*). Thus ASP is also not an MIMD-system. It organizes its society of slaves in a democratic way but superimposes some coordination; it is hierarchical.

The classification can be made in yet another way. Since "single data" is used only in monocomputers, we may drop D from our classification. On the other hand, we may add a distinction by "programs". Let us use (Fig. 5) a classification similar to that used in the Illiac manual. A monocomputer (a) has a control (CU) and arithmetic unit (AU) executing a single program on one set of data (SISD or SISP). A multiprocessor (b) has a number of independent processors (CU+AU) each possibly working on a different program. We call it MPMD or MIMD because both the instructions and programs may be independent. SIMD systems (c) have only one CU and work on a single program - SIMD or SPMD.

The ASP system (d) divides a single program into p tasks to be run on p computers (CU+AU) but should it be called MISP or MPSD? It is felt that the name ASP conveys the more fundamental notion of sequential and parallel tasks alternating, the master/slave relationship and coordinaton of the tasks. Both the hardware and the way it works (mode of operation) will be therefore called ASP from now on.

Fig 6. shows in more detail what happens during a P-step. There are n tasks, the longest of which lasts t_m=m. The sum, of t_i, i=...,n is the useful work of step P_k. The important point is that since the data in the memories are different and mostly independent of the program, the time of each "task" may be different. The next sequential step S_{i+1}, should start only when the longest task of P_i is completed (this is not a necessary condition; we could let a slave ask for a new task as soon as it finishes one, but it is easier to visualize the synchronous ASP-mode as in Fig. 6. The difference in task-times influences the speedup, but since most algorithms will be designed so that these differences of tasks are small, the speedup reduction is acceptable). As seen both the instruction and data streams are processed asynchronously in ASP.

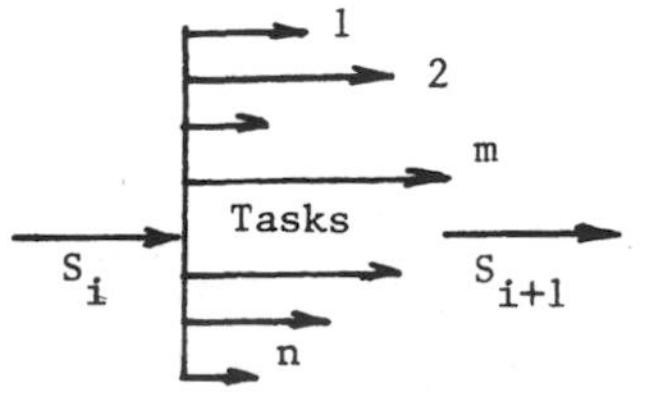

Fig. 6: More detailed step-sequence

We next calculate the bounds on the speedup σ for ASP [SW 78] and make the following simplifying assumptions:

(a) The overhead (synchronization, file transfer, etc.) is at first neglected.

(b) A slave and its memory can complete its task without outside help.

(c) The basic algorithm in abstract form for the serial and parallel computer is the same.

(d) All p+1 processors are identical, so that the time of running a program is unaffected by the choice of cpu(s).

A couple of P and S steps of Fig. 6 would be executed on a uniprocessor in time:

$$u = s + \Sigma t_i \quad ; \quad i\Sigma=1,\ldots,n \tag{1}$$

where n is the number of tasks in the parallel step P, $i\Sigma$ is read "i summed over" and t_i is the time required for executing the i-th (parallel) task. Eq. (1) is not strictly correct since in a uniprocessor the sequential time s (used for transfer of information between memory locations) would be smaller. For now we will disregard this difference.

Let us first discuss the case:

$$n \leqq p \tag{2}$$

i.e., the number of tasks is less or equal (mostly equal) to the number of slaves. If m is the longest of the n parallel tasks, i.e.

$$m = \max_i(t_i) \quad ; \quad i=1,2,\ldots,n \tag{3}$$

then the time it takes ASP to complete a single S and P step is

$$t = s + m \tag{4}$$

The speedup and ratio are therefore:

$$\sigma = u/(s+m) = 1/(f+m/u) \quad ; \quad \rho = f+m/u \tag{5}$$

where $f = s/u$

is the "factor of seriality". From Fig. 6 it is easily seen that the entire time of the parallel step (u-s) is less than if all tasks were of length m, i.e.

$$n*m>(u-s) \tag{7}$$

because it would include the time nothing is done in Fig. 6. This yields:

$$m>(u-s)/n \tag{8}$$

$$(s+m)>(ns+u-s)/n \tag{9}$$

$$\rho = (s+m)/u > ((n-1)s+u)/(u\cdot n) \tag{10}$$

and the speedup is therefore

$$\sigma \leqq n/(f*(n-1)+1) \tag{11}$$

Complexity theory demands that f be strictly 0. ASP will not put itself into a straightjacket. A serial part even if minimal is always required so that the factor of seriality f is never zero. Even if f is small, the speedup will be less than n, or p. On the other hand, for a completely serial program, f=1 and σ=1. Thus,

$$1 \leqq \sigma < p \tag{12}$$

If the number of words sent to and retrieved from a slave by the master is w, the time for transferring a single word through the bus is τ then the overhead time (as part of u) is

$$v = w*\tau/u \tag{13}$$

Adding this part of the overhead to the sequential step S in (11) results in

$$\sigma \leqq n/(f*(n-1)+1+n*v) \tag{14}$$

We have here assumed that the changeover from a P to an S-step is instantaneous; it is not. We need first to wait for all slaves to complete their tasks and then "wake-up" the master. We will find ways to do it rather fast, but not instantaneously. The waiting time plus wake-up time will be called the bus "synchronization", time β. For the time being we will neglect it.

In the second possible case, namely:

$$n > p \tag{15}$$

the time (u-s) is divided into more tasks than there are slaves. For simplicity, assume tasks of equal length and that each slave executes k such tasks. The total time, k(u-s) is clearly not higher than if each slave were to execute the task of maximum length m. Thus

$$k(u-s) \leqq n \cdot m \tag{16}$$

The ratio according to (5) is

$$\rho = 1/\sigma = (s+m)/u = (fu+nm/n)/u = (nfu+nm)/(nu) \tag{17}$$

If we now substitute k(u-s) for nm, we have reduced the numerator so that

$$\sigma \leqq \frac{nu}{nfu+k(u-s)} = \frac{n}{nf+k(u-s)/u} \tag{18}$$

and since nf + k(1-s/u) = nf + k - kf = k + (n-k)f, we have

$$\sigma \leqq n/[f(n-k)+k] \tag{19}$$

We thus see that (11) is a particular case of (19), namely that for which the number of tasks per slave k=1. In the same way, if v=transfer of information over the bus is added, (14) expands into

$$\sigma \leqq \frac{n}{f(n-k)+k+nv} = \frac{n}{(1-f)k+fn+nv} \qquad (20)(21)$$

The number of tasks per slave, k, is in the denominator so that in order to increase the speedup, it should be minimized. This leads to:

$$\sigma \rightarrow \text{optimum for } k=1 \tag{22}$$

$$\text{or } n = p \tag{23}$$

Let us add other conditions for designing an efficient ASP-system:

(a) Both for initialization and for the following parts of an ASP-algorithm, the sequential steps S_i consist of synchronizing the system and the subsequent transfer of information between the master and the slaves. Information (data) may be transferred through the bus either by a single word or by blocks of words.

(b) In the first case, using PDP11-assembly language, the program might be:

```
     MOV SAD, R0; move starting address to R0
     MOV TAD, R1; move target address to R1
     MOV LENGTH, R2; move the number of words to R2
XER: MOV (R0)+,(R1)+; move the word addressed by R0 into core addressed
     ;by R1 and increment the values stored in R0 and R1 by 1 (two bytes).
     ;Auto-increment in the assembly language of PDP11 is marked +.
     DEC R2; decrement the number of words by 1
     BNZ XER; as long as R2≠0, return to XER.
```

Assuming that the block of data to be transferred is long, the three instructions ahead of label XER may be disregarded when compared to those in the loop. Inside the loop, three instructions have to be removed from core, one data word removed and one inserted into core - altogether 5 memory cycles are required for transferring a single word. This transfer requires two memory cycles if done by hardware e.g. by DMA (because DEC R2 is done concurrently and independently). Therefore a loop with block transfer (by DMA) is faster 5/2=2.5 times then without it.

The transfer of data is effected by the master and was seen to be strictly sequential. It influences directly the overall execution time. Thus, block-transfer capability best done by DMA seems to be essential.

(c) As will be shown later, most algorithms will compute data (a single word) in a slave and then have to transfer it to the remaining (p-1) memories. With or without broadcast, the word must be first transferred to the master. With broadcast, transfer to all slaves would require time τ; without it, the time will have to be $(p-1)*\tau$. Without broadcast the total time is $\tau + (p-1)\tau = p\tau$; with broadcast it is 2τ. The advantage of having broadcast is therefore quite obvious in that the time decreases p/2 fold.

(d) Transfer of words over the bus requires time even in block mode. Thus, v of (13) is never zero. Obviously, the higher the overhead time v, the lower the speedup.

(e) The algorithms should be tailored to p, making the number of tasks equal to the number of slaves p.

(f) The factor m/u in (17) measures task-inequality. We see that the higher it is, the lower is the speedup. The attempt must be made to divide the calculations to be done in parallel into equal parts m (thus decreasing it).

(g) Simulation of some algorithms showed that the bus is used for less than 2% of total time, so that bus interference is a minor problem in ASP. Moreover, during step P, the master is idle. It is therefore possible to divide the tasks so that the shortest of them will be done by the master himself. Effectively, this would increase the number of "slaves" from p to (p+1). On the other hand, we will find enough work for the master to do during the time when the slaves work on their P-tasks. The master will therefore not take upon itself any of the P-tasks.

We have come a long way and can now enumerate the principles for the design of an ASP-system (partly from Chapter 2).

(1) For reliability, it should be <u>symmetrical</u> with a roving master
(2) For speed, each slave should have its <u>local memory</u>
(3) The switch should be <u>a single or dual bus</u>
(4) The bus is <u>controlled</u> entirely <u>by the master</u>, thus eliminating the access problem and the risk of deadlocks
(5) In order not to be too expensive, standard <u>off-the-shelf equipment</u> should be used

(6) ASP may be used as a stand-along and as an "auxiliary" system. In the last case, the "main" computer is a "host". ASP will sometimes use separate I/O to each of its slaves and sometimes not; it all depends on the application

(7) We have found that in order to supply a high speedup, it should have broadcast, block-transfer, divide the tasks so that n=p and (for a small f) obey a trivial parallelization principle: do as much work as possible in the P-steps and as little as possible in the S-steps (minimize them). This will make s<<u and f very small.

(8) ASP should be able to work efficiently on non-π problems.

Let us now give an outline of the present chapter.

An organization like that of Fig. 3 was suggested a few years ago by Prof. G. Korn of Arizona. His model, the Kopps (for Korn's pps), will be discussed in Section 3.2 and in particular the features which will have to be improved because they could reduce speedup. We will then discuss existing (working) systems (the SMS'es built by the Siemens Company in Munich, West Germany) and find that even they have a few features which do not fit our requirements. Finally, in 3.4 we design a "Most Efficient pps," the Mopps and a "Tristate operated pps," the Topps. The next chapter will be more specific in the interface for our models, Mopps and Topps, so that we can proceed "using" it.

Three notes complete the introduction:

(a) No matter what we use, Kopps, Mopps, Topps, or SMS, what is completely different is the mode of operation, i.e. the fact that they work neither purely sequential nor purely parallel. From now on, when speaking of systems which work in such "Alternating Sequential/Parallel" mode, we will call them ASP-systems.

(b) The SMS-201 exists and "lives well." (The author had his fun programming it). This is important, since it means that we are not using a hypothetical design model, but an assembled, existing system. All "programs" of the second part of the book can be reprogrammed and run on the SMS-201.

(c) It does not matter whether mini or microprocessors are used. The choice will depend entirely upon the application.

(d) It is the combination of hardware features and modes of operation which makes ASP cheap, fast and reliable!

3.2 KORN'S PPS; THE KOPPS

An ASP-system was originally suggested by Prof. G.A. Korn of Arizona [Ko 72] and will be called Kopps for Korn's pps. Its block-diagram is shown in Fig. 7. In this section we will first copy a part of its description and then add some observations on hardware implementation aspects despite the fact that it was apparently not assembled. Kopps was to be used in place of a differential analyzer.

Kopps consists of (p+1) PDP11/45 minicomputers. One of them (top of Fig. 7) is the master and is connected directly to the system bus. Secondary memory is also connected to the system bus. The slaves are not connected directly to the system bus; instead, two-port, semiconductor memories act as "intermediaries" or buffers. The functions of the various parts, e.g. "solving blocks of differential equations" are shown in Fig. 7. According to [Ko 72]: "The proposed low-cost multiprocessor system employs only standard, quantity produced components; the development effort involves novel interconnection and software.

Referring to Fig. 7, the control processor is an ordinary minicomputer with an interleaved core memory and disk storing all system programs. The control processor handles all input/output, interprocessor communications, and implements the analyzer's system monitor. The latter is an executive program calling for program translation, loading and execution in response to keyboard commands.

The 2 to 16 arithmetic processors are interrupt-driven slaves of the control processor. Each arithmetic-processor has a fast, two-port semi-conductor memory which receives its program and data from common memory through a bus interface. The control processor bus can also transfer data words between arithmetic-processor memories and between these two-port memories and the disk. Finally each arithmetic-processor can interrupt the control processor when a suitable program step is completed.

As the various parallel processors (slaves) finish their computations, they interrupt the control processor (controller or master) which now transfers the data needed by other processors for the next step. At specified times the control processor also moves the data to the graphic display for a run-time display, and to the core memory and/or the disk for post-run displays and data processing operations.

The new PDP-11/45 processors just announced in October 1971, appear to be nearly ideal for the proposed system since they were designed specifically for multiprocessor systems interconnected through common buses (Unibus in Fig. 7) and two-port memories. In addition, the PDP-11/45 comes with both two-word (32 bit) and 4-word (64 bit) formats which will, respectively, permit very fast derivative computation and the needed double-precision integral accumulation. The cost of such a powerful miniprocessor is remarkably low because it is quantity-produced for many diverse applications."..."Thus, a reasonably well partitioned 7-processor system would conservatively match CDC-6400 performance in simulation. Such a system would cost, with applicable discounts, at most $250,000 in 1972, far less than a comparable CDC-6400 installation. We must, of course, not judge the 6400 by our simulation application which favors multiprocessing. In any case, the multiprocessor's advantage will improve with increasing system size, and with decreasing minicomputer prices.

The development of useful and efficient multiprocessor systems, especially with inexpensive minicomputers, is one of the significant challenges of the coming

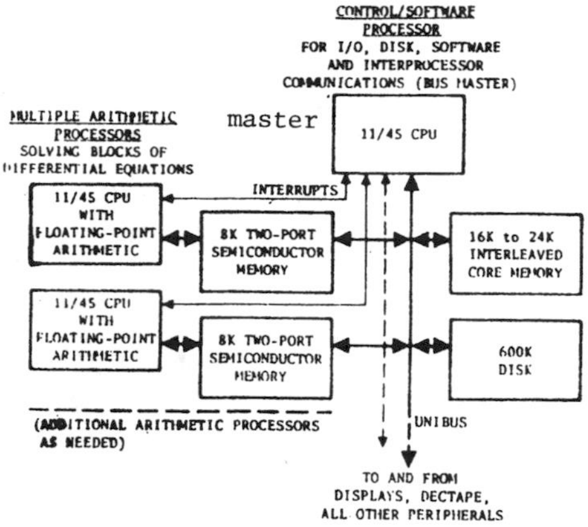

Fig. 7: Korn's original parallel processing system - Kopps

decade."

Kopps is a good starting point to meet this challenge, but is not going far enough. We will discuss its advantages and disadvantages and try to extend it further. Lets start with the disadvantages.

(a) The use of dual-port memories leads to a restriction in the available address space. Since the bus has only 16 bits for addresses, only 64K bytes, or 32K words (of PDP11) may be addressed. Distributed among, say p = 10, slaves, this would amount to less than 3K words per slave (since the master needs a part of the memory space too). We could use the "memory management unit" of the master PDP11/45. This would increase the memory space four-fold but make the overhead so high as to make Kopps impractical. The dual-port memories are also rather expensive.

(b) The system is not symmetrical in that the master does not have a local memory. We could though modify Kopps slightly by adding a (dual-port) control memory to the controller. The advantages of using this additional semiconductor memory would be:

- The sequential parts of the program are executed by the master. It was shown in Section 3.1 that speeding up the sequential parts is of paramount importance to the overall performance of an ASP. It is therefore logical to use a fast semiconductor memory to store the control program, the more so since it is used more often than the other programs.

- The modified Kopps would be completely symmetric and allow an easy reconfiguration even for the case that the master fails. The reliability would therefore be enhanced considerably.

(c) No block-transfer was mentioned.

(d) Apparently, no broadcast-facility was planned.

(e) As already mentioned, every slave may interrupt the master. Note also that interrupts are separated from the bus (Fig. 7). Let us next discuss a possible interrupt interface.

Only standard modules should be used since they are cheaper and are supported by the system software. Since Kopps uses PDP-11 computers, it is suggested to use the standard DEC-interface unit, the DR11-C [Di 73] "connector". It is shown schematically in Fig. 8. For the user, this unit is represented by a 16 bit data output buffer OUTBUF (line DO), a 16 bit data input buffer INBUF (line DI) and a control/status register CSR which includes 2 interrupt enables (IEA, IEB), 2 request lines

(REQA, REQB) and 2 control lines (CSR0, CSR1), as well as other lines.

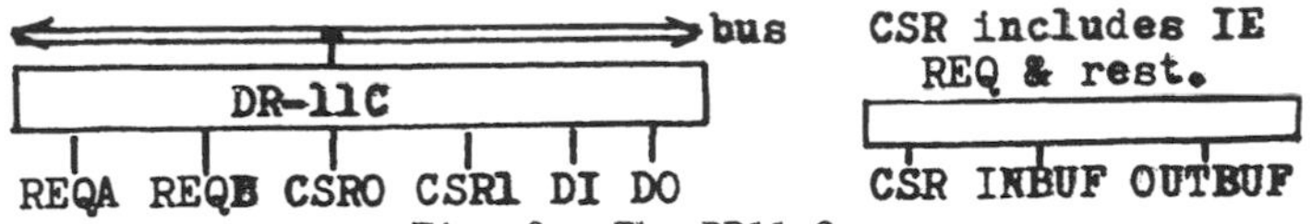

Fig. 8: The DR11-C

Data could be transferred using the buffers in a way exemplified by the following four different instructions:

MOV R0, OUTBUF; Move content of register R0 to the output buffer

ADD R1, OUTBUF; Add to it the content of register R1

CLR OUTBUF; Clear the output buffer

MOV INBUF, R0; Move data from the input buffer to register R0.

If IEA is enabled (logic "1") and a "1" appears on the REQA line, then the connector produces an interrupt signal - provided the priority and other devices connected to the bus allow it. The interrupts on lines REQ-A and REQ-B are completely independent and address different interrupt vectors.

To implement Kopps, two units would have to connect every slave to the control bus (Fig. 9) with the wires crossed so that the REQA-port on one is connected to the CSR0-port of the other unit.

We have assumed throughout (Fig. 6) that the master has started a sequential step only after all slaves have completed their tasks. In Kopps, this was apparently to be done by some counting hardware in the control processor. Since we don't want to interrupt the master all the time for polling, we might add an "and" gate so that all slave interrupts pass through it and its output activates the master.

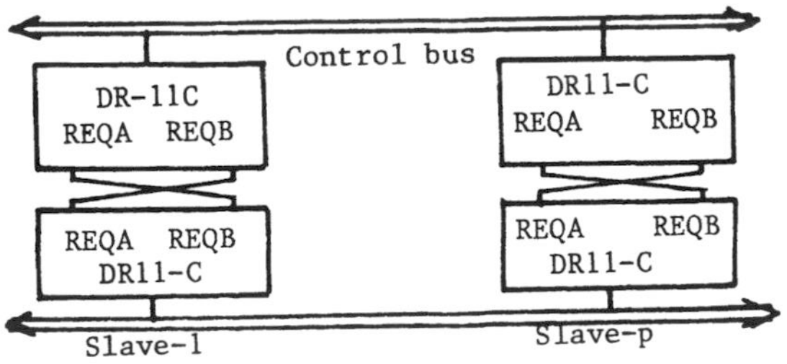

Fig. 9: A possible Kopps-connection

Such an AND-gate may have been added to Kopps and connected as in Fig. 10. It would then provide the following possibilities:

(1) The master may transfer an interrupt simultaneously to all p slaves from its CSR1 line to their REQB lines.

(2) The master will be interrupted on its REQB line if, and only if, all p slaves have sent interrupts on their CSR1 lines ("and' ed" by the additional and-gate).

(3) Crossing the wires of CSR0 and REQA allows the master to send an interrupt

to any one of the slaves and any one of these in turn can interrupt the master.

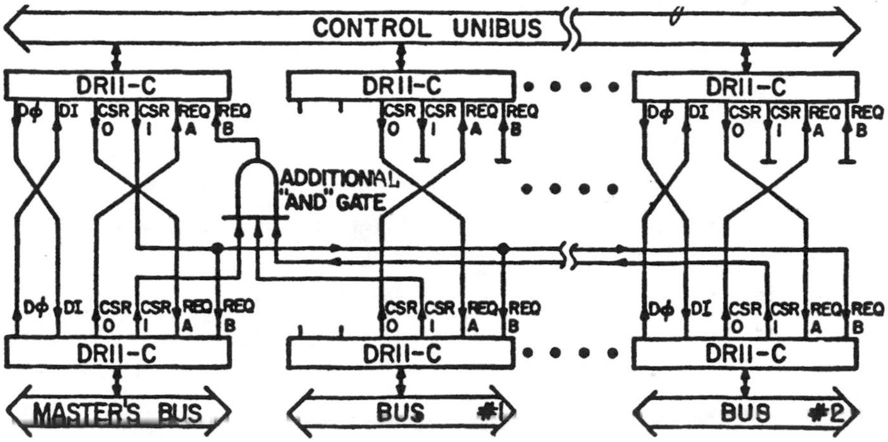

Fig. 10: A possible interrupt interface for Kopps

Even if a dual-port memory would be added to the master, the interrupt handling would probably take a long time. The following idea was therefore explored: It will be seen in later chapters that in ASP-programming the bulk of data stored by the slaves is not to be moved at all during processing of a job. It is a small percentage of data that is used by more than one slave and so it seems a natural improvement to use customary PDP-11 systems and add circuitry which will allow one processor to access data in the memories of other processors (similar to what was done in Cm*).

The Digital Equipment Corporation sells a unit, the DA11-F "Unibus window", which may be used for this purpose. It enables the transfer of data from one bus to another. Each processor may refer to addresses on the bus of the second processor as if they were its own. This is achieved by address mapping as indicated in Fig.11:

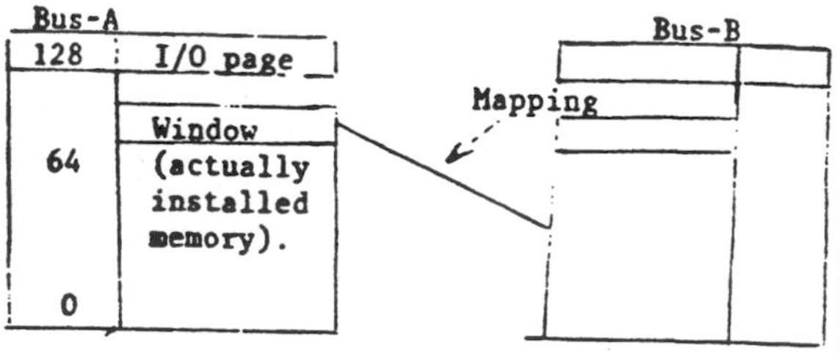

Fig. 11: Address mapping using a "window"

- A continguous block of addresses in the address space of processor A is designated as a window (its size is 512-32K words).

- The window translates these addresses into a corresponding block on the bus of processor B.

- If A refers to an address in its window, the unit translates it automatically into an address on the other bus, synchronizes the two systems and starts the handshaking process. Thus, A will "see" the block of addresses on bus of B as its own.

The window is two-directional, i.e. a block of addresses on the bus of A is seen as part of the address space of A. The two mapping devices and the two blocks are independent of each other.

Due to the way peripherals in the PDP-11 are controlled, the windows enable not only the sharing of memory but also of peripheral units. For instance, A may order a disk controlled by B to transfer a block of data to core of B or even to core of A.

The mapping is effected as follows:

- The size and position of the window in the two address spaces are fixed at the time of installation.

- For every transfer through the bus there exists an addressor and addressee. (They are not synonymous to source and destination; the addressor may be the receiver of data). It follows that

Mapped address=Window displacement + relocation factor. (25)

The window displacement is the (fixed) address of the window on the bus of the addressor and the relocation factor is determined by the addressee. For p processors the windows would have to be cascaded. It will therefore suffice to discuss their use for two processors.

The cooperation of two processors through a window relies on rather complicated software since a "conversation" is required to start some common use of data. This will slow down the process considerably and may even lead to hardware deadlocks, as evidenced by the following case:

The block of A seen by B (Fig. 12) is in the window of A. Recall that for every transfer of data over the bus, there exists a single bus master and a single slave. Suppose that B intends to transfer data to memory; then B is clearly the master and the memory will be the slave. In the case discussed here, this memory address falls into the window of A so that it acts again as a master to the lower register of the window. This register is now trying to be the master of the bus of B in order to transfer the memory address. Recall that B is still the master of bus of B and it will never relinquish its mastership over it; the window will try to get mastership over it, but will never get it. Hence, deadlock occurs.

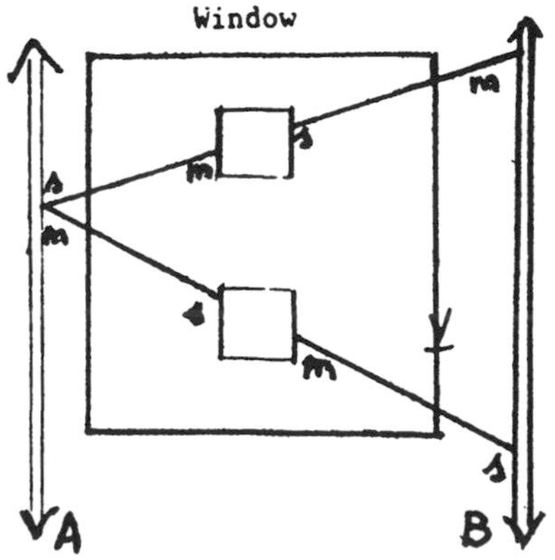

Fig. 12: A deadlock situation

- Still another dangerous (but not deadlock) situation results when A gets access to an I/O page of B. This would allow access to control registers of the unibus by B, i.e. simultaneous access which may lead to disastrous results.

The use of windows has not improved Kopps. On the contrary:

(1) It would restrict even more main memory space

(2) It would increase the number of cycles required for transfer of a data word (from 5 to 6 memory cycles). This increase is due to the fact that two buses and a mapping are involved.

The handshaking is generally a time consuming process (and will not be used).

(3) The window itself is expensive

(4) It complicates the software

(5) Most important: deadlocks are possible; the system is dangerous.

We will not use windows for any of our ASP-systems. Because of the other disadvantages, we will not use Kopps either.

3.3 SMS-SYSTEMS

Kopps was apparently not assembled, but the Siemens Company of West Germany introduced [Ko 76, Kkk 77, Ko 77, Ku77, Kk 79] two ASP-systems, the SMS 101 and SMS 201 (SMS stands for Structured Multimicroprocessor System).

Let us remark at the outset that SMS 101 and SMS 201 were actually built. SMS 201 is in fact running and all the algorithms which we will be developing may be run on it. We do not deal with a model, or a theoretical system - we deal with actually existing pps'.

Let us quote from a description of SMS 101 [Ko 76] with some changes to the text, renumbering of figures etc.

Fig. 13 shows the system components. They are:

- a main processor MPR with private memory M

- an arbitrary number of modules, each consisting of a module processor PR and a private memory M

- the same number of communication memories CM, which are associated to the modules.

These three kinds of functional units are switched together in two manners as shown in Figs 14, 15 and work according to the "phases" of Fig. 16.

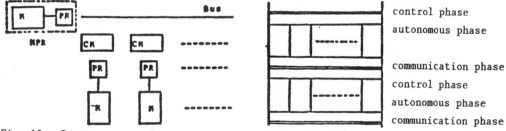

Fig. 13: System components

Fig. 16: Phase sequence of SMS

- In the control phase, the main processor deposits a start address in the communication memories which determines the task to be executed by the modules (hardware connection of 15, common switch in vertical position.) Then it starts the autonomous phase.

- In the autonomous phase the module processor gets the starting address from the communication memory and executes the task. Note that in hardware configuration 14, the module processors have access to their CM's and may operate autonomously.

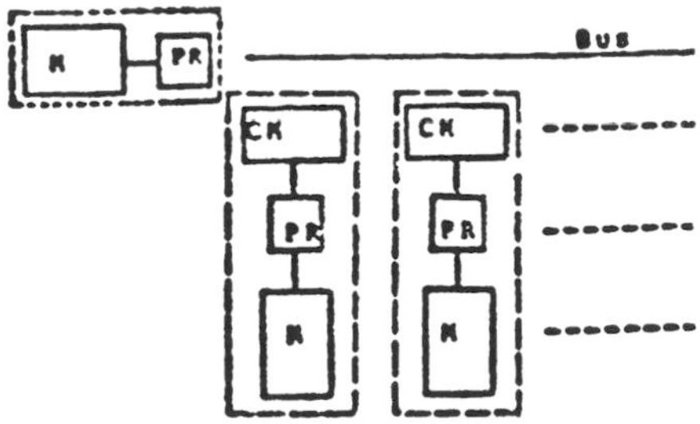

Fig. 14: Memory access mode during the autonomous phase

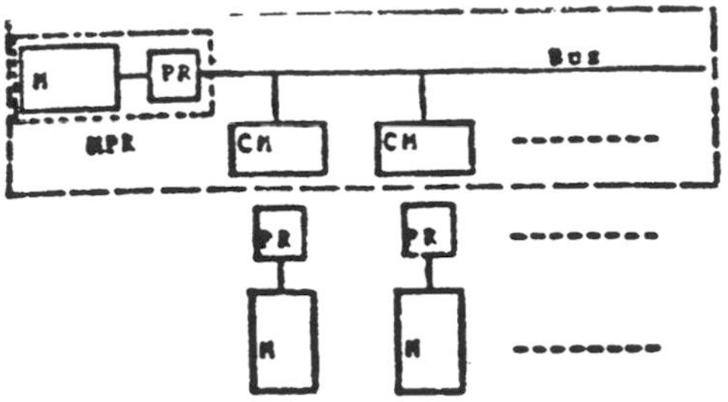

Fig. 15: Memory access mode during control and communication phases

(Common switch of Fig. 3 horizontally.) The data which are needed for computation are taken from the CM and from the private memory M. After completion of the task, the results are stored in the CM and a signal is sent to the main processor. If all modules have finished their tasks, the next phase is started.

- In the communication phase the CM's are disconnected from their module processors, but the main processor again has access to them. It distributes the results of each module simultaneously to the communication memories of all the other modules. In this way every module gets the appropriate data for the next phase cycle."

At this point it is clear that SMS101 was an ASP-system. In particular, no deadlock situations need be feared and no queues are needed; broadcast is provided, but as noted:

"In order to avoid conflicts with common memories, data are distributed and simultaneously stored in the modules if necessary. The advantages are simplicity of organization and the most efficient use of the bus. On the other hand, more memory space is needed."

A first realization of the SMS 101 multiprocessor system consisted of 8 identical modules connected to the main processor by three bus systems. These busses are the control bus, the address and the data-bus (refer to Fig. 17).

Each module consists of the following functional blocks: a Processor Unit (PR), a Module Memory (MM), a Bus Memory Switch (BMS). The following paragraphs briefly describe the function and implementation of these blocks.

"The Processor Unit operates as the Central Processor for the module. It consists of the microprocessor chip 8080 and some support logic for control and for buffering of address and data lines.

The Module Memory stores programs and data, thus combining the task of both private memory and the communication memory. In its standard version, the memory has 2K bytes of Random Access Memory (RAM) and 6K bytes of Programmable Read-Only Memory (PROM). It can be expanded up to 64 bytes in total, limited by the addressing capability of the 8080 chip.

The Bus Module Switch (BMS) is a two-way switch which connects the Module Mem-

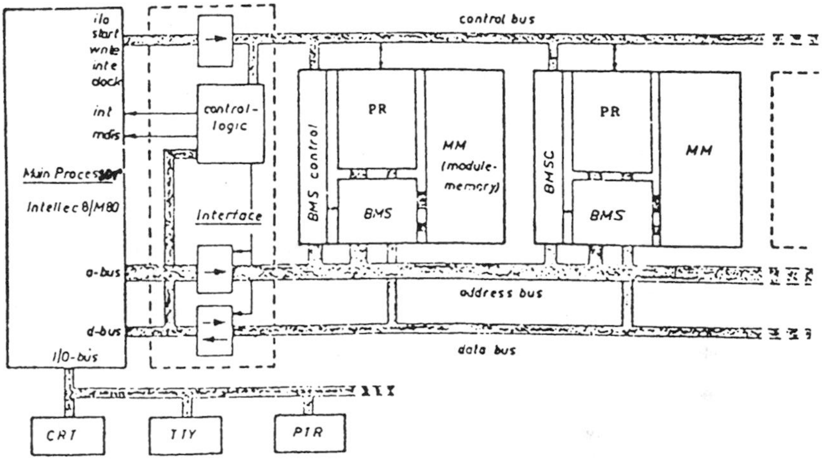

Fig. 17: SMS101 - block diagram

ory (MM) either to the PR or the System Bus.

The SMS is controlled by the BMSC which gets its instructions from the main processor. The status of the switch is saved until a new switch instruction is received. In the autonomous phase, the MM communicates with the PR, whereas in the control and in the communication phases, the information to and from the MM are transmitted over the system bus. These informations consist of data and destination addresses belonging to the data.

The three system busses perform the following tasks: The data and address busses transmit 8 bit data and 16 bit addresses. In addition to that, the address bus carries the control instructions for the BMSC. They consist of a 6 bit switch address which identifies the number of a specific module, and of a 2 bit switch mode information.

The control bus carries signals for the coordination of different parts of the multiprocessor system. First, these are signals which initiate and terminate the program phases (starting the modules, HALT-signals, interrupts to the main processor). Second, together with the address bus, it carries signals for controlling the switches. Finally, it transmits a two-phase clock signal needed for the 8080 chips.

The main processor used in the realized system is the microcomputer Intellec 8/M.80. Containing the same microprocessor chip as the PRs, most of the Intellec's control and signal lines are compatible with the module lines. Hence, interface problems are simplified.

The interface contains several drivers and the following two major functional blocks:

An interrupt logic interrupts the main processor after having received the HALT-signal from all modules.

A transfer logic discerns between memory locations in the main processor memory and the memory locations in the MMs. It is active during the communication and control phases, when the data transfer is controlled by the main processor. Alternately it connects the main CPU either to the main memory to fetch instructions from the control program, or the the MMs for the data exchange between the different modules.

<u>Data Transfers</u>

During the control and communication phases, data transfers over the system bus have to be executed.

The data paths depend on the status of the BM-switches. The following data paths are possible in the realized system:

(a) from the main processor's memory to a specific MM (in order to load specific programs and data in a selected module).

(b) from the main processor's memory to all M-Memories simultaneously (in order to distribute common information needed in all modules). This is broadcast.

(c) from a selected MM to the main processor's memory.

(d) from a selected MM simultaneously to all other M-Memories and the main processor's memory (in order to exchange results of the module computations). This really is broadcast originating in a slave.

Each of these data path's is selectable by a single switch control instruction, sent out by the main processor. Data transfers then are accomplished by the main processor executing one data transfer (MOV) instruction for each data byte.

The SMS 101 has been operational since November 1975. After several malfunctions during the first two weeks due to IC failures, the multiprocessor is now correctly executing test and user programs in continuous operation."

Having satisfied themselves that the SMS 101 has given a good speedup, the SIEMENS Co. then built a larger system, the SMS 201 (and left the SMS 101 as a museum piece). The new SMS 201 was described in [Ko 77] as follows:

Figure 18 "shows the block diagram of the SMS 201.

The main processor is a commercially available minicomputer with peripheral equipment. An interface links it to the multiprocessor system.

The 128 modules are separated into 8 multiprocessor blocks with 16 modules. The drivers are inserted merely because of electrical reasons. They cause no separation of the bus; from the logical point of view, all modules are connected together by a single bus. Thus it is still possible to broadcast the result of one module into the other ones in a single memory cycle.

A module is subdivided into two major units:

The Bus Coupler contains an instruction decoder for transfer and start instructions and a bus--switch. The second unit contains an 8080 microcomputer system with control, 4K bytes PROM and 16K bytes RAM (note: we use 4K bit RAMs; replacing them

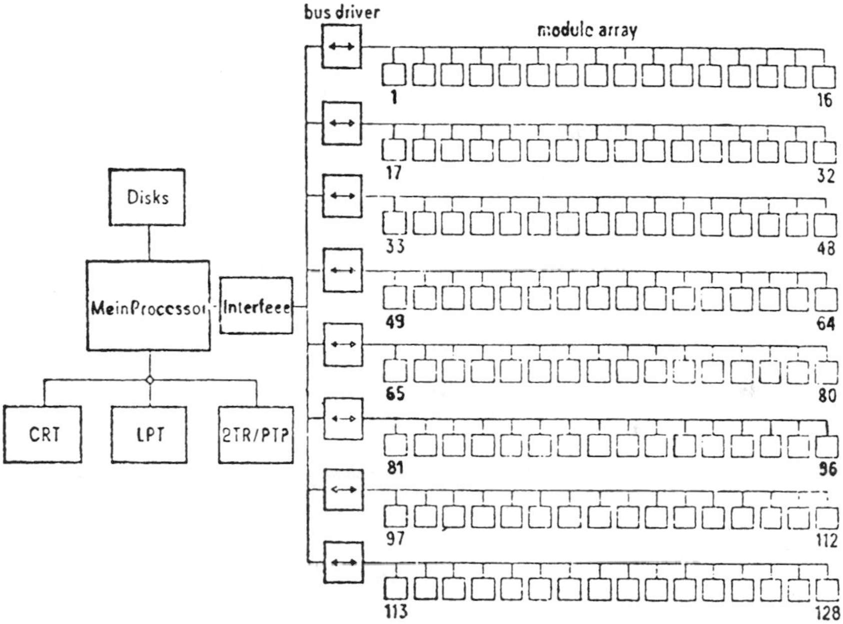

Fig. 18: Block diagram of the SMS 201

with 16K bit-chips, the memory capacity per module should be increased to 64K bytes). An I/O-Interface allows each module to communicate directly with external equipment, e.g. with sensors and regulators in a process control application."

We have shown in Section 3.1 that the duration of the sequential steps determines the speedup. The same conclusion appears in [Ko 76] as follows:

"For a growing number of modules, the duration of the data-exchange phase becomes the limiting factor of the computational speed." In order to improve the situation, a "fast communication processor" CPR was added to the SMS 201 hardware.

In particular, it was observed that although in one memory cycle a result could be read-out of one CM and simultaneously written into all other CM's, and that only 2 clock periods are needed for each switch or transfer cycle, much more time was needed in SMS101. This was because the master was a general purpose computer. Thus, "in a typical program sequence performing one data exchange, 27 clock periods were required. During these 27 cycles, the instructions had to be fetched and decoded and the address pointer had to be loaded. This is a large overhead because only 4 clock periods are used to carry the switch and the data transfer instruction over the system-bus.

The low bus-utilization is also evident. It has been calculated at 11.8% - 16.7%. Improving the system bus utilization is a significant step to reduce the time needed for data exchanges.

For all these reasons a separate communication processor was suggested [Ko 76]:

"Looking at the possibilities of increasing the bus utilization, it is obvious that general purpose computers are not well suited to deal with data transfer problems. Therefore a special communication processor is necessary. Because the main processor must have general capabilities, this has consequences on the multiprocessor architecture: There are two central processors required, a main processor and a communication processor CPR (Fig. 19). The main processor performs the control tasks in the control phase, whereas the communication processor controls the data exchanges in the communication phase.

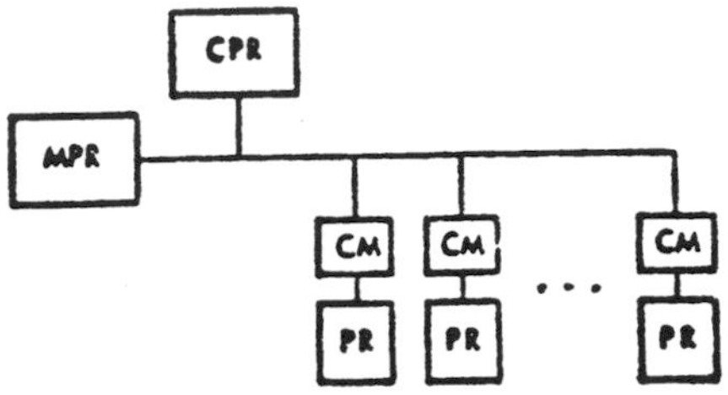

Fig. 19: SMS with separate main and communication processor

Description of the Communication Processor

Simple data transfer controllers are used in computer systems to control the data channels. A commmunication processor, however, must be more flexible and more "intelligent." Its desired features are:

- high transfer rate by efficient bus utilization
- free programmability
- possibility to freely select a distinct program out of several exchange programs
- software-controlled execution of switch and transfer instructions
- processing of single as well as block transfer instructions.

Figure 20 shows the schematic diagram of the developed communication processor providing these features.

Data exchange programs can be stored in the program memory (RAM) via a DMA-channel. The 16 bit instructions consist of a 2 bit operation-code and a 14 bit address. The opcode determines the function of the address:

ØØ switch address

Ø1 starting address for block transfers

1Ø single transfer address or end address for block transfers

11 halt instruction.

In the following, the function of the communication processor will be briefly described:

First the starting address of the selected exchange program is loaded into the program counter; then the processor is started. The instructions addressed by the program counter are read-out of the program memory and are decoded in the instruction decoder. The control logic generates the appropriate control signals for the functional units of the communication processor and for the modules. Switch addresses are gated through the buffer directly onto the systems bus. Starting addresses of block transfers are loaded into the address counter; end addresses of block transfers are directed to the comparator. The address counter generates incrementing transfer addresses on the address bus until the comparator indicates the end of

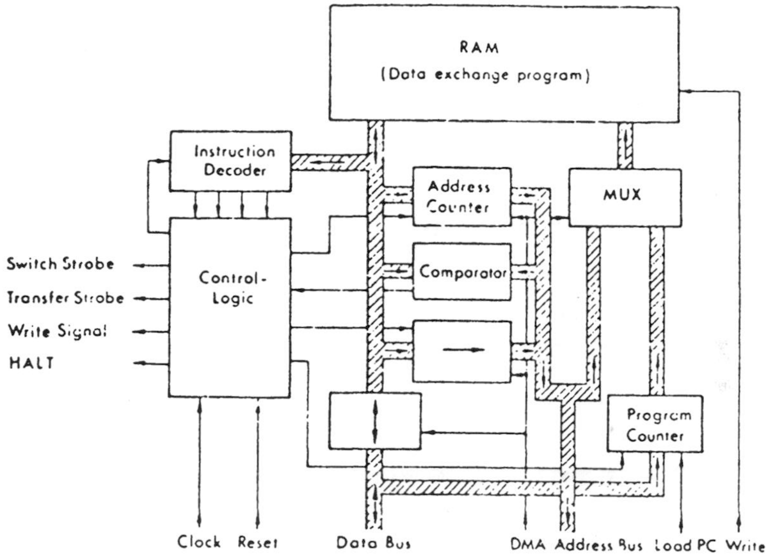

Fig. 20: Schematic diagram of the communication processor

the data block. Single transfer addresses are gated directly to the address bus. A halt-instruction determines the end of the data exchange program which indicates the end of the communication phase. The communication processor passes an interrupt request to the main processor in order to initiate the control phase.

The communication processor achieves high bus utilization using overlapped fetch and execute cycles. After the first fetch cycle (1 clock period), the bus utilization is 100%; it is independent of the sequence of the transfer instructions.

Thus the new concept, with a special communication processor, reduces the communication phase by about the factor 6 to 8.5. It should be pointed out that this improvement is achieved without faster memory chips in the communication memories."

Preliminary design of yet another and more powerful system, the SMS 3, was started by the Siemens Co. [KK 79]. The main difference to SMS 201 was that a dedicated single-chip, Arithmetic-Processing-Unit (APU), was added to each module (slave) to improve floating-point operations.

Part of its description in [KK 79] reads:

"The SMS 3 will provide a performance enhancement of about 20-30 times compared to the SMS 201 achieved by:

- Extending the number of modules

- Using more powerful modules with faster components (bit slice microprocessors) and greater word length

- Speeding up data exchanges by a double-word bus, a communication memory with double-word interface, a faster bus cycle and a special communication processor. The performance characteristics of the SMS 201 with and without APU's and of the

SMS 3 are summarized in the table below. An average module processor utilization of 80% is assumed.

Instruction	SMS 201	SMS 201/APU	SMS 3
Stream	32 $MIPS_8$ 0.03 $MFLOPS_{32}$	32 $MIPS_8$ 0.55 $MFLOPS_{32}$	250 $MIPS_{16}$ 18 $MFLOPS_{32}$
Data Exchange Stream	0,1 MBPS	0,1 MBPS	3,5 MBPS

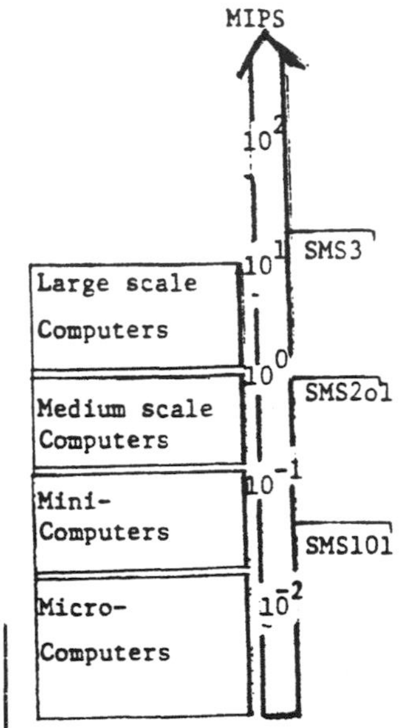

Fig. 21: Comparison of instruction streams.

Figure 21 shows a comparison of the instruction speed of sequential, general purpose computers with SMS-type parallel computers. In order to obtain equivalent values for different word lengths, the following conversion has been applied (with the index being the number of bits):

$1 \text{ MIPS} = 1 \text{ MIPS}_{64} = 6.8 \text{ MIPS}_{16} = 24 \text{ MIPS}_8$

The SMS 101, an 8 module system, reached the minicomputer class; the SMS 201 has an instruction stream comparable to present mainframe computers. The SMS 3 will surpass them for many application problems. Further improvements on the parallel processor side will be possible soon by progress in LSI-technology, whereas further speed-up in sequential processors will be slow due to physical limits."

3.4 MOPPS AND TOPPS

We have described two types of ASP systems, Kopps and the various SMS-systems; do we have to design our own? In view of the fact that the SMS 201 is in fact working and may be commercially available, the question may be rephrased as: "Aren't we reinventing the wheel?"

First of all, it should mentioned that this "wheel" was suggested rather early [Wa 74]. Secondly, it will be shown to be different from Kopps or the SMS-systems. Thus, we start by describing Mopps. The name stands for Multibus-Oriented, Modified, Modern, Modular, Most effective or if you so prefer my own pps, Mopps.

The most important departure from Kopps is that in Mopps data will be transferred between the computers using "Direct Memory Access" DMA units (Fig. 22).

Two advantages are apparent at the outset. First of all DMA-units have hardware to effect block-transfer. Secondly, each is represented by a couple of addresses. Thus, each slave of Mopps is viewed by the master as an address (related to those of local memory). Use of DMA's has extended the memory space.

DMA-controllers are produced by most hardware manufacturers, but in order to

My own pps = Mopps.

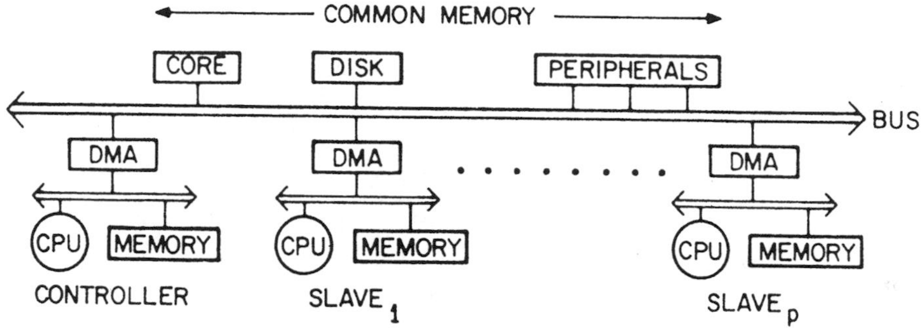

Fig. 22: Basic block-diagram of Mopps

keep to the DEC-hardware of Kopps, we might use its standard DMA unit, namely the DR11-B redrawn in Fig. 23. It is used normally as a general interface unit [Di 73] and is represented by a number or registers. Two 16-bit registers, DRBA for bus address and DRWC for word count receive data from the bus but cannot send it any information. In addition to these two registers this unit includes - as far as the program is concerned - a data buffer DRDB and a fourth 16-bit register DRST (for status, function and control).

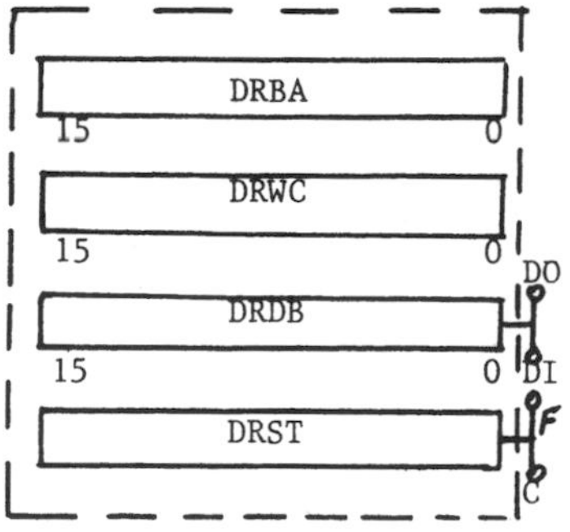

Fig. 23: The DR11-B

The unit works in a half duplex mode; that is, it may be used for input or output, but during a transaction (i.e., transfer of a block of words) only in one direction. Bit 0 of DRST, called the GO-bit, indicates by a "1" the start of an operation. The control bits enable the unit to work in one of the modes:

-"Continuous" mode, where the unit takes possession of the bus for the duration of the entire block-transfer so that the actual (usually high) speed is set by the speed of the external device. It will be as high as the external device will permit and could be as high as one word per memory cycle.

-"Competing" mode, in which the words are transferred by stealing single cycles on the bus. From the end of transferring a word to the start of transferring another word, the unit does not use the bus at all (asynchronous transmission).

On a single computer, the DR11-B is programmed as follows:

-The number of words and their initial address (for output this is the first word to be read-out, for input the address where the first word will be stored) are stored in DRWC and DRBA respectively.

-Control information, including a GO signal is loaded into DRST.

-The operation starts and proceeds in a way transparent to the program which - during this time - may be working on other tasks.

-The end of transfer or a fault are indicated by an interrupt.

A program for the DR11-B might include:

```
INIT:MOV 1000, DRWC; move 1000 into the DRWC register (block length will be 1000)
     MOV STAD, DRBA; move starting address into DRBA
     MOV COM,DRST; move the pattern word COM into DRST (for control)
     ; I/O proceeds here concurrently, until interrupted.
COM:; 16 bits are set up according to a pattern for the control command.
```

Note that this is a hardware implementation of the program in Section 1.

Two units connected crosswise are required to connect each slave to the control bus. A control interface is also added. The DEC-company sells such combined units under the name DA11-B. From now on DA11-B, and where no misunderstanding results, the DR11-B will be called a "connector". In Fig. 22 they were called DMA.

Normally, the DRDB serves as an intermediate, transparent buffer for transferring blocks of data. We next discuss how it can be used for transfer of single words or blocks in a single computer. This will involve handshaking (asynchronous) and will not be used in Mopps. It is given in order to compare the transfer modes.

(a) Transfer of single words.

Since the input and output lines of the connector are crossed, the DRBA registers may be used for transfer of single words in a controlled (not cycle stealing) mode as follows:

-The sender performs an output operation into DRBA (obviously only if the connector is not busy transferring a block of data). At the same time, the direction (i.e., output) and mode (single word) are indicated to the other side using the specified bits of DRST. In order to inform the other side that the word is ready, the sender transmits an interrupt.

-Upon receipt of this interrupt, the receiver may perform an input operation from its DRBA-register. An acknowledgement that the word was received (and that new words may be sent) is then transmitted to the sender in the form of an interrupt.

(b) Transfer of blocks

Blocks may be transferred by the computer (cpu) to some device. Hence, the cpu, as initiator of the operation may:

(1) Load the initial address from common memory into DRBA (bus address).

(2) Load a number also into DRDB (data buffer DRWC).

(3) Load into DRST a word coded to mean: direction is "output" (from cpu), mode is "single word", "ready" to receive interrupts from device and finally "request" an interrupt. Then it WAITS.

During this entire time, the device is waiting, but upon receiving the interrupt, it may

(4) Read the word from DRDB (It was the word count), load it into its DRWC and

(5) Request an interrupt and WAIT. (Up to here, word count was transferred to DRWC.)

The cpu, upon receipt of this interrupt may

(6) Load its DRDB with the memory address required ($DRDB_M$ = address)

(7) Issue an interrupt to the device, waking it up.

The device will then

(8) Load $DRDB_M$ into DRBA (address into DRBA)

(9) Issue an interrupt and WAIT.

Now it is the cpu's turn to service an interrupt. It will

(10) Load: (Mode is block, GO=1) into its DRST

(11) Issue an interrupt to the waiting device and WAIT or start working on some other task.

The wakened device will

(12) Load its DRST with: (mode=block, GO=1) and WAIT for an interrupt which will indicate that the transfer of a block is complete.

This last time unit will see the cpu either WAITing or doing something else, the device also waiting and the block of data being transferred through cycle stealing by the connector. When this transfer is completed, the connector will issue an interrupt both to the cpu and the device whereupon the cpu proceeds with whatever it was doing (for instance, transferring data to another memory) and the device may start its parallel substep.

Note that some features of the protocol may be changed in Mopps. Thus:

(a) The above transfers do not include broadcast.

(b) For the block mode using a connector: It was stated that only two memory cycles are needed per word, but up to 30 cycles may be needed for its start according to the protocol described above. Hence, this mode seems to be useful for transfer of large blocks only. To be more specific: In Kopps, the starting time was negligible, the transfer of a word required 5 cycles. The above transfer (Mopps) is faster for $5 \cdot x > (30 + 2 \cdot x)$ where 30 cycles were needed for the protocol and 2x or 5x for x words; faster if $x > 10$ that is, for blocks of 10 or more words.

(c) There is no need to send interrupts to slaves in order to start them; they will be issued by the connector at the end of the block transfer.

(d) The protocol for transfer from a memory into a common store is similar to the block transfer as described. In this case too, the cpu will initiate the transfer upon receipt of an interrupt which indicates that the device completed processing its parallel substep.

Next we discuss modifications of the software of Mopps to enable much faster block transfer. As described above, the protocol is too general in the sense that every block is a closed entity. The master will start transferring a block only after having informed the slave of the direction, mode, size and starting address of the block. It was the transfer of all this information which required about 30 overhead memory cycles.

Note that the above protocol assumes a completely symmetrical system. This is not the case in Mopps, insofar as only the master may initiate a transfer and determine the mode. The slaves have to ask the master to initiate a transfer to or from their memories. This asymmetry and the fact that Mopps is supposed to execute (at any time) a well defined, specific program lead to a reduction of overhead with a less general protocol. It is based on the ASP-model (Fig. 8) and on using a "WAIT" instruction which is included in PDP11 or for that matter in most minis and micros. In ASP mode:

- All p slaves should start executing a P-step upon receipt of the same interrupt from the master. A single interrupt or rather signal to all slaves is needed.

- The master starts its (sequential) S-step only after it receives interrupts from all p slaves. This could be achieved by letting the master count the incoming interrupts or by adding hardware so that the master receives the interrupt only when the last of the slaves has completed its task. We will add hardware.

Because of this and using the WAIT instruction, we may convince ourselves that there are only three possibilities to use memory (of slave) i:

(a) The master transfers data into or out of memory (i); the corresponing slave (i) WAITs. ("Common switch" in vertical position V.)

(b) Slave (i) uses data (or program) in memory (i) and at the same time the master WAITs (horizontal position H).

(c) Neither processor attempts to get access to memory (i) since (position H):

(i) Slave (i) is WAITing (for the next task).

(ii) The master is WAITing (for all slaves to complete).

Usually "waiting" means a waiting loop, i.e. the processor reads and executes continuously the instruction to "go back" reading, etc. This leads to competition for access to memory (i) in all three cases. As mentioned, the PDP-11 has an instruction WAIT which suspends the processor and even disconnects it from the bus and memories. Therefore none of the three cases leads to competition or time loss.

The ASP-mode is also responsible for the fact that the control bus is not the bottleneck it is thought to be in pps'. As indicated in Fig. 3, the bus is used in the following situations:

(a) The master acts upon the serial S-step. Since at this point all the slaves are WAITing, only the master uses the bus (position V).

(b) The master operates on memory (i), but slave (i) is WAITing. Logically, this means that memory (i) is part of the common memory connected to the bus and used by the (monoprocessor) master. The situation is equivalent to (a).

(c) The master waits for all slaves to finish. This situation, i.e. step P, is equivalent to all memories being disconnected from the bus which therefore is completely inoperative (position H).

(d) The master waits for interrupts from all slaves. During that time it should not respond to any interrupts (except those indicating faults). The "interrupt enable" bits of the connector may be used to achieve this. It is also obvious that no new step or data transfer should begin before interrupts have arrived from all slaves. Summing all this up means that the master should deal with interrupts coming from the slaves only after it has transferred data to them and while it WAITs for the next serial substep to begin.

Points (a) to (d) may be summarized by saying that the bus is not the bottleneck it appears to be. The transfer of data through it is serial and will slow down the process, but this is the result of the fact that a single master controls the bus and not because there is a single bus.

Initiation of a block transfer (input or output) is confined to loading the three registers DRST, DRBA and DRWC. It could be done by the "program":

```
MOV  C,(R3)+; where R3 points to DRWC
MOV  BUFADR, (R3)+; now to DRBA and finally
MOV  <pattern>, (R3)+; move the command pattern to DRST.
```

Each of these instructions needs 3 memory cycles so that 9 are required for initialization. Since two cycles are required for every word transferred in Mopps but five (and no initialization) are needed in Kopps, Mopps will be faster whenever: $9+2x<5$ or $x>3$, i.e. already for blocks of 3 or more words.

Let us review again the need for interrupts in an ASP-system. The master will automatically store in its program counter the location of the "next" control instruction, at the time it suspends itself (to WAIT). Therefore when the slaves signal completion of a P-step, the interrupt handling required is to reactivate the counter. At the end of an S-step, the master may load all program counters of the slaves with the start location of the next program segment, so that again, there is very little interrupt handling required. The bus-synchronization time β, which for asynchronous message switching or common memory systems is quite large, will be reduced in ASP to almost zero, provided the tasks are nearly of equal duration.

As was pointed out in the description of Kopps, broadcast mode is very important for an efficient performance of a pps for simultaneous transfer of an identical program or data to all slaves. In all forms of Kopps and in the Mopps as described up to now, a wasteful loop would have to be programmed to achieve either one of these aims. Since these transfers are part of the serial substep (S_i of Fig. 4), the additional time needed for this substep will obviously reduce the effectiveness of the pps. We therefore need badly a way to broadcast words or blocks of words to all slaves simultaneously. We found no way of doing it in Kopps, but suggest now the following extension to the hardware of Mopps for realizing it.

Connect an additional DR11-B ("Broadcast unit" BUN) to the control bus and add between it and the p connectors 16 data lines (Fig. 24). The idea is to use these lines for broadcast. To do this, certain modifications and additions to the basic hardware are required. They all serve the following purposes:

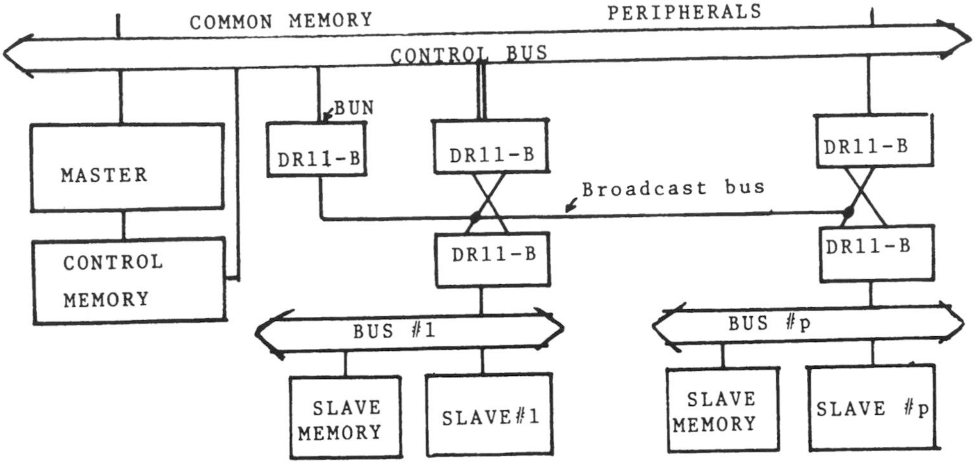

Fig. 24: The Mopps

- To synchronize the transfer of information from BUN to the p connectors.
- To send a single interrupt through BUN to the master in order to indicate that the last slave completed its parallel step.

All this can be achieved by adding the circuit of Fig. 25 to each connector in such a way that BUN operates it as follows:

- Line s selects "simple" or "broadcast" mode
- Its output is:

Out = (s and b) or (not s and p)

i.e., when s=1 (select broadcast), the output is b (from the broadcast bus); otherwise it comes from the opposite part of the connector.

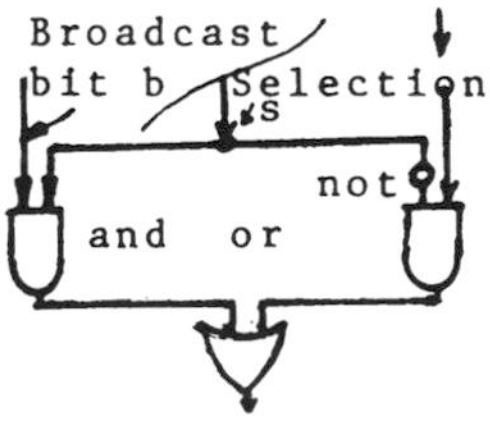

Fig. 25: A switching circuit

Mopps was designed a few years ago. Certain misgivings (e.g., the fact that there is only a single master-bus) led to a new design of Topps (for Tristate operated pps) [TW 81]. It consists of (p+1) identical units (schematically in Fig. 26). At any given time, one of them is the master; the remaining p units are the slaves. The more important connections are:

(a) With only T.2, T.4 closed, the unit acts as an independent computer. p such computers can act together on p tasks of a parallel step. The unit which acts as master is connected to the store through T.2 and T.7 and to its own memory through T.6.

(b) In the sequential step S, the slave units have only T.6 "on," making their memories part of an overall address space.

(c) Mopps had only P and S modes. In Topps there is a third basic mode (and hence the "tristate" in the name). In this "ring" mode, T.2, T.3 and T.5 are "on". Thus each cpu, say i, has access to the private memory of cpu numbered (i-1). The master may be part of the ring in which case it is considered to be also a slave,

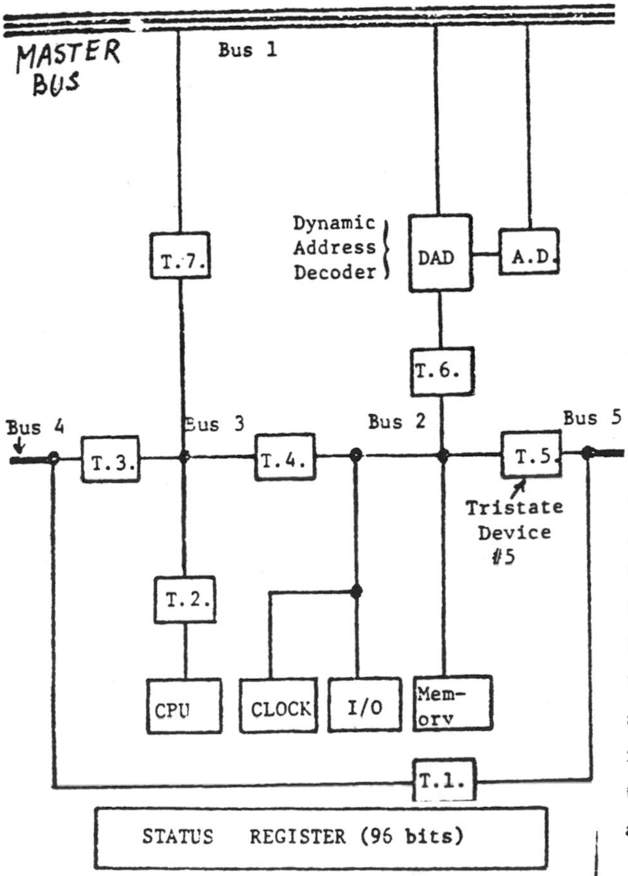

Fig. 26: An element of Topps

numbered 0 (zero).

(d) There are a number of other "combined" modes. For instance, unit "i" may be the master (T.2, T.6 and T.7 connected, but T.4, T.3 and T.5 disconnected) and slaves (i-1), (i+1) connected through T.1.

Compared to Mopps, the following differences and advantages are to be noted:

(a) The system is even more symmetric so that even the master may be replaced. Mopps has a single master-bus which may be thought of as decreasing substantially the reliability. In Topps, if a part of the bus is defective, this part can be removed and the system will be able to go on working. This and the symmetry mentioned above increase reliability and availability.

(b) Each unit has its own I/O. Thus, instead of collecting data in the main memory and block-transferring it through the master bus as in Mopps data is transferred to the slaves individually. In Mopps, I/O operations are part of an S, in Topps of a P-step, a fact which increases the speedup considerably. In some power-system problems, the incoming variables should be checked against limits (overcurrents, low voltages, etc.). In Topps this could be done in parallel, i.e. fast.

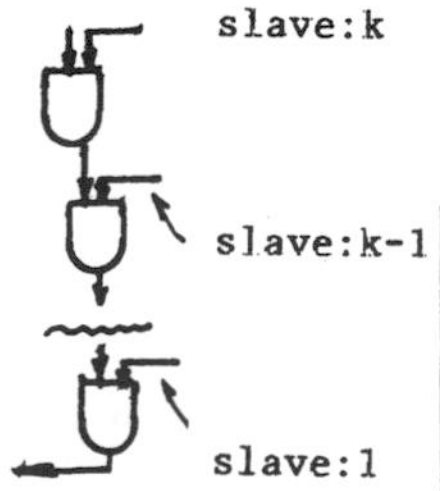

Fig. 27: Interrupts

(c) Expandability of Mopps was hampered by fanin of an and-gate through which all interrupts are strobed into the master. In Topps, the interrupts are transferred to the master as in Fig. 32, ensuring that any number of units can be connected to it.

(d) The particular microprocessors which were chosen have 24 address lines so that 16 Mbytes can be part of a single address space.

(e) The memory addressing of Topps is unique in the fact that <u>each</u> address of the master can be mapped to <u>each</u> address of <u>each</u> slave. This allows for transparent segmentation of the entire memory space. Total memory addressing, as seen by the master, is then $(16 \times 10^6)^2$ bytes. Although this capability exists, it would not be practical since 16 million slaves would be needed to implement the configuration. On the other hand, nobody has ever asked for, nor would they hardly need this much addressing capability. For a practical case, e.g. 128 slaves as in SMS 201, the address space would be 128 x 16 megabytes, which certainly is large enough. This just proves the point that each slave has the ability to act as an intellegent peripheral controller.

(f) The multiple bus switching characteristics of Topps also allow for configurations which included multiple masters and submasters. This is made possible because this switching network is completely micro-programmable. If a new configuration is discovered to be useful, it can be easily implemented by rewriting the microcode of the PROM.

3.5 COMPARISON

We have now described Kopps, Mopps, Topps and SMS 201 (the other SMS-systems do not work at present, so let us not discuss them). All these systems are suitable for ASP-processing and have the following advantages:

(1) The bus is not the bottleneck it appears to be. There is no need to buy much more expensive and less reliable crossbar switches.

(2) No cases of deadlock exist. The way the systems work (centralized control by the master) makes the use of software parallelization features (e.g., semaphores, locks, etc.) unnecessary.

(3) It seems that they promise to yield the two major advantages which were given for ASP earlier: greater speed (of solution) and greater reliability.

There are certain disadvantages to the ASP systems:

(1) There is a limit on their speedup (as computed in 3.1).

(2) There is an overhead for starting a transfer and even with block transfer, some time is wasted.

(3) Processor cooperation requires that some programs be stored in all memories (e.g., interrupt handlers). This leads to a waste of memory space (in the local memories).

Next, we list the specific disadvantages of Kopps (for the application areas we have in mind). Kopps:

(1) Is not symmetric - thereby limiting reliability and availability.

(2) It restricts the size of the memory such that only small programs may be run on it.

(3) It does not have broadcast facilities.

(4) It does not provide block-transfer. The last two were shown earlier to be essential for high speedups.

(5) The cost is high because of the high price of the PDP-series and because dual-port memories are used.

(6) The interrupt system was apparently not adapted to ASP-processing. This may have reduced the efficiency considerably (but made it more general). Keep in mind that no real interrupt handling is required in the ASP mode and times β, τ are very short.

We next compare Mopps and Topps with the SMS-systems.

(1) The two aims of pps' as stated in Chapter 1 were higher availability and speed. It should again be stressed that availability/reliability is more important than speedup and that it depends crucially on the symmetry of the system. The SMS 201 is asymmetric, i.e. the master is completely different from and cannot be replaced by a slave. It is a rather large minicomputer, whereas the slaves are small microcomputers. Hence, for on-line process-control, Mopps and Topps will be more suitable.

(2) Another fundamental difference is in the operating system to be yet described. SMS was built for off-line, Mopps for on-line jobs. Thus the operating system of SMS is just an extension of the standard operating system of the master. In Chapter 4 we will discuss an on-line operating system to be used for Mopps and Topps.

(3) In SMS each slave has I/O and there is no block-transfer of data over the bus. In Mopps, I/O passes through main memory and is then block-transferred to the (slave) memories. Topps has both separate I/O and block-transfer. Since we will show in the next chapter that the master has ample time to deal with I/O while the slaves work on a job cycle, the choice made for Mopps seems reasonable for some jobs, while that of SMS and Topps suits other jobs. The different hardware solutions may be the result of the jobs the designers of SMS had in mind. They assumed "inherent parallelism" (π-jobs), we will not. It is also important whether I/O is through A/D converters or serial input/output.

(4) Mopps transfers data by direct memory access devices, SMS by a communication processor, From the point of view of reliability, centralization is always bad. Both solutions allow block-transfers.

(5) Four connections were possible in SMS, but only three in Mopps. In SMS and Topps we have a path from one (slave) memory to all memories; this path does not exist in Mopps. Whether we need it depends on the algorithms. Let us remark here that Topps has the ring-mode which is certainly useful for band matrices.

4. INTERFACE

Introduction

We have developed a hardware model for ASP-processes but in order to apply it to solving problems, an interface must yet be described.

The first Section will discuss the language problem. It will be shown that it is not necessary to develop a special high-level language for ASP. A few extensions to PL/I (or any other high level language) are sufficient for describing ASP-programs. Discussion of the language used for SMS-201 shows that our approach may be more efficient than using the interrupt facilities of the operating system of the master for information transfer.

Simulation of ASP programs is trivial since all that is required is to "sequentialize" i.e., execute serially all tasks of the P-steps. Two examples show the type of results we may expect. In particular, the matrix multiplication which was already programmed for Apps and Illiac, is programmed in Section 2 for MIMD and ASP systems as well as for the STARAN.

Section 3 deals with the reliability aspect. It is defined numerically and the widely held view that the reliability of a pps is lower than that of a single computer is refuted. Both the theoretical considerations and the experience gathered on SMS201 prove that ASP-systems have very high reliability/availability indeed. This is contrasted with the reliability of Illiac IV, Finally, a test procedure is suggested.

It is shown in Section 4 that the master has the time to handle - if need be - the I/O of the entire system. Guidelines for interrupt handling and memory organization are developed.

The user can view an ASP system through the extended PL/I language. A simpler notation, which we call the SP-notation, is also sufficient. Starting with Chapter 5, both will be used to "program" an ASP-system.

4.1 LANGUAGE PROBLEMS

Aims: To introduce the language for writing programs for ASP and for simulating them on a typical sequential processor. To discuss the way in which the ratio is evaluated and programs are written in the SP-notation. To compare the languages introduced here with that used on SMS-201.

Languages are used in various areas of computer science. In our case they can express programs such as those for:

(a) an existing, working pps

(b) simulation of the ASP program on a sequential computer

(c) the mathematical discussion of the algorithm.

Every computer is ultimately programmed in its machine (assembly) language, but because compilers are available, programs are usually written in high-level languages. The advantages of high-level languages are:

(a) Their syntax is easy to follow and makes the program more transparent and its structure more evident.

(b) High-level languages are concise.

(c) Since the languages are general, a program written in one of these languages may be regarded as the mathematical solution of the problem.

(d) Not only standard instructions but also those particularly applicable to parallel processing were quite extensively discussed in literature, e.g., extensions to Fortran [An 66, Go 66], to Algol-60 [Di 68, De 73], and to Pascal [Br 73].

PL/I was suggested [Wa 74] as a better candidate for the programming language (at least that of the slaves) because of the following considerations:

(a) It can be and is implemented on existing computers. As a matter of fact, it may become the most widely used higher-level computer language. Compilers, even of the optimizing type, exist.

(b) It is a very concise language, especially when dealing with vector and matrix problems. For instance, if A, B, C are nxn matrices then

$$A = B + C \tag{1}$$

means a (simultaneous ?) "element by element" addition of matrices B and C with the result replacing A in core. The same would require in Algol-60 the following program segment:

```
for i:=1 step 1 until n do
    for j:=1 step 1 until m do
        A[i,j]:=B[i,j]+C[i,j];
```

(c) Other features of PL/I, such as multitasking, could be extremely useful.

For the hierarchical ASP's (e.g., SMS, Kopps and Mopps), two types of languages may be needed: For each slave a language which will enable it to perform the (numerical) operations on data in its memory, and one for the the master.

The program tasks of the slaves, being mostly arithmetical, can obviously use PL/I as their language. Let us next check whether it is also a suitable language for the master. In this language, the following features will have to be reflected:

(a) The entire program must be decomposed into sequential and parallel tasks and both the information concerning them and some kind of "precedence graph" showing their sequence, position, etc. must be stored so that the master can follow it.

(b) The part of storage where such programs are stored must be accessible to the master but not to the slaves (as shown earlier, the master does not have to lock these storage areas).

(c) The master is responsible for data movement through the bus and must have instructions effecting such transfers. It should not be able to interleave such transfers in time.

(d) It must accept interrupts from all slaves.

The master's program:

-Is activated by the slaves

-When activated, it finds a new task

-After locating it, the program may

--Move a file from store to a slave memory

--Move variables between the files

--Activate a slave or all of them.

It is seen that the language of the master may be viewed as an extension of the system language (of its OS) - moving files, receiving interrupts, and activating the slaves. This is precisely what was done for the SMS-201 and we will deal with it later. Unfortunately, in our case, debugging such programs would require running them on the actual hardware. This hardware would also be useful for testing various management policies and gathering of statistics - but we do not have it yet. We are therefore led to the conclusions that

(1) We will "program" both the master and the slaves in an "extended PL/I" [CW 80] (actually only the master; for the slaves PL/I is sufficient).

(2) This "parallel PL/I" or PPL/I should be defined so that it may easily be converted into a simulation program.

As mentioned, the usual approach in "programming" parallel systems is through extension of an existing higher level language, e.g., Fortran, Algol or Pascal. The same was done for PEPE with PFOR based on Fortran and for ILLIAC-IV with Glypnir based on Algol-60 [Thu 76, Ma 73, La 75]. For reasons given previously, we use as a basis the PL/I language, to which we add the following extensions:

(1) Indices should identify both arrays and particular memories. In PPL/I, the last is done using paranthesized left-hand indices. For example, the assignment:

(I) A = (J) B; (2)

signifies: "Transfer B from memory J and store it as A in memory I." If I≠J, a bus transfer is involved. If the paranthesized index is zero, or if none is used, the common store is implied.

(2) Two ways of storing variables (especially arrays) are possible: under different or the same name in all memories. In the declaration:

DCL((#)A,(2,5)B(N,N),C(M)) FLOAT (3)

an address for the "distributed" variable A is set aside in all p slave memories, N^2 locations for B in memories 2 and 5 (under the same name B) and an M-vector C in the common store. Each slave can refer only to its copy of A; the master may refer to every one of the A's. If all declared variables have a (#), it may precede the parantheses. Each slave is aware of its number and may use it as (#P). The master stores the number of slaves P.

(3) Since data transfer by broadcast is invariably from the common memory to all slaves, no special identification is needed. Thus

PUT BROADCAST(V) (A); (4)

signifies "broadcast value V to all p memories and store it there as A." If the second name is the same as the first, it may be omitted.

(4) Block transfer is indicated by the operator "≡." Thus

(I)D(1:100,1:6)≡(J)F(101:200,1:6); (5)

effects the block transfer of 600 values F from memory J to I, to be stored there as D. Block transfer may also be combined with broadcast, as in

PUT BROADCAST(V(-8:15)); (6)

which transfers a block of 24 values V by broadcast.

(5) Declaring a "parallel procedure" indicates to the compiler to first compile it and then store it in all memories, e.g.,

PR:PARPROC(X,Y,Z);...;PAREND PR; (7)

where X, Y and Z must have been declared to be distributed variables. The call

PARCALL (I,J,K)PR(A,B,C); (8)

signifies for the master to activate PR with (distributed) parameters A, B, C in memories I, J and K. If PR is to be activated in all slaves, (#) is used.

The above extension is such that a "parallel procedure" would be compiled and transferred to the slaves at the time it is declared. This means that <u>all</u> parallel procedures would be loaded into the local memories <u>ahead</u> of running the program. This would waste a lot of memory.

Suppose that the procedure is transferred to local memories when called in the program. It would not waste memory only if it were overwritten right after being executed once. In that case though, there exists another problem, namely, what to do if the PARCALL is inside of a loop. Transferring the parallel procedure for each iteration of the loop would be a great waste of computer time.

It seems better to let the programmer direct the transfer of a parallel procedure, say by writing PARCALL' if the procedure should be transferred, and kept, PARCALL" when it may be overwritten (after being executed), and PARCALL that it is already stored and may be used ("called"). Memory tables of the operating system will then have to keep a record of which areas of the memories are "used" and which are "free." We will disregard it here and use only PARCALL's.

(6) Topps has more diverse modes of operation. For the "ring" mode the language extension may be:

TRANSFER (I)A ← (J)B; (9)

if only slaves I and J are involved, but if all slaves and the master shift data around

TRANSFER (#)A ← (#)A; (10)

should be used. This keeps in spirit with the five extensions above. If one of the symbols (#) is missing, the p slaves are (but the master is not) part of the ring and may work on another job (say transfer of data into slave memories).

A number of parallel systems were recently developed. Unfortunately, it seems that each new system requires a language to reflect its architecture and facilitate development of efficient algorithms. Thus, Glypnir [La 75] reflects the fact that each processing element of ILLIAC-IV executes the same command (or idles). Although the PPL/1 notation introduced in this section shows some similarity to PFOR [Thu 76, Ma 73] of PEPE e.g., parallel assignment and DO-statements, data-declarations, data-movement through the master (host), broadcast, etc., it also shows differences as a result of different hardware and envisaged application.

Ballistic missile defense for which PEPE is to be applied, exhibits "inherent" parallelism i.e., the job can be partitioned so that each processing element gets a separate, independent task. PEPE will constantly correlate data with existing files - hence its associative store. The ASP-systems assume neither inherent parallelism nor associative storage. The resulting notation, PPL/1 may be used for any system which comprises a common store as well as a separate memory for each slave and employs broadcast, block-transfer and alternating sequential/parallel processing.

We may now restate the reasons behind the extensions to PL/I as defined above:

1) PL/I is very concise and may become the most widely used high-level language.

2) The extensions reflect accurately the hardware properties of ASP, but do not restrict programming to it.

3) It is easy to simulate parallelism.

A simulation program must be composed of a "main" program for the master, which in turn activates the programs of the slaves according to information (probably in form of lists). Since these programs work concurrently, they should be defined as "process" and activated simultaneously by the main program. These processes must communicate with the main program. Thus, some processes may have to wait until some event has occurred or a given time elapsed. This (real) time must be kept by a (simulated) clock.

A simple one-to-one translation converts programs written in the extended language into SIMPL/I [IBM 72] since all features corresponding to underlined words above are part of its simulation language. They are:

(1) The main program of SIMPL/1 activates either serially or concurrently a number of BEHAVIOR's, processes.

(2) It has built-in list-processing facilities of great variety.

(3) It may use a wait instruction.

(4) A process may be reactivated by some condition (event) becoming true. Actually, quite complicated communication patterns between simultaneously running processes may be simulated.

(5) A real-time clock is simulated and synchronizes all programs (main and processes).

Unfortunately, SIMPL/I is also not as widely known as to warrant its inclusion in a book for general readership, but there is another way out of this dillema, namely use of the multitasking facility of PL/I. It will not be as perfect for simulating ASP as SIMPL/I would have been, but has the advantage of being part of standard PL/I and is thus more accessible.

The first four extensions would be programmed in PL/I and each parallel procedure would be a subtask of the main procedure (main task). Multitasking also includes event variables so that a parallel step could be programmed as follows:

```
DO SL=1 TO P;
   CALL PARTASK(SL)EVENT(EV(SL)); END; or
DO SL=1 TO P; WAIT(EV(SL)); END;
```

where PARTASK (declared as a task procedure) would include the event variable EV signalling completion of the task. For this it would have to include timing expressions.

This being so easy, the idea is obvious to use standard PL/I and "sequentialize" the parallel steps. Thus, a procedure, say PARPR, would include an expression for the time it takes (T) and its concurrent execution on all p slaves could be simulated through:

```
MAX=0;
     DO SL=1 TO P;
               CALL PARPR(SL); IF T>MAX THEN MAX=T; END;
```

This will enable us to graph the actual time-execution of ASP-programs. It also shows that if the reader has access to, say, Fortran instead of PL/I, he can rewrite the programs accordingly. We prefer PL/I because of the reasons given above and because the simulation can be improved by multitasking or SIMPL/I.

In terms of the original language definitions, we will use PPL/I for programming the "real" ASP and PL/I without multitasking for simulating it on a sequential computer. We still though need a language for the mathematical discussion of those algorithms which will be described in the second part of this book.

ASP-algorithms are so simple that we will propose for it a notation based entirely on the mode of ASP-processing as given in figures 3-4 and 3-6. Thus any sequential step i will be labelled <u>S(i)</u>: and a parallel step j by <u>P(j)</u>:. The algorithmic parts will use English and the usual mathematical notation.

We will next exemplify this notation, PPL/I and a simulation program by the very simple program for computing

$$y = \Sigma \sin(x_i) \; ; \quad i\Sigma = 1,\ldots,1000 \qquad (11)$$

in an ASP with p=10 slaves. The only assumption we make is that a program to compute sin(x) is prestored in all slaves.

The algorithm in the PS-notation is as follows:

<u>S(1)</u>: Transfer a "slice" of x-values to each of the slaves i.e., x_i, i = 1,...,100 to slave #1, x_i, i = 101,..., 200 to slave #2 and so on until x_i, i = 901,...,1000 to slave #10 (see diagram). Each 100 values are transferred as one block. In each slave, the sum $z = \Sigma \sin(x_j)$; $j\Sigma = 1,\ldots,100$ (12)
will be accumulated.

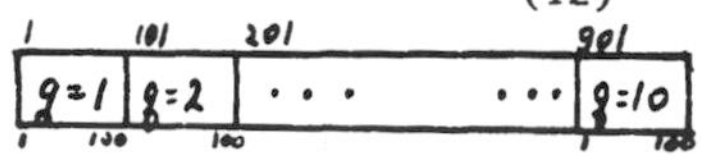

<u>P(1)</u>: Each slave computes "its" z according to (12).

S(2): The 10 values, all named z are transferred to the master and

$$y = \Sigma z^{(q)}; q\Sigma = 1,\dots,10 \tag{13}$$

computed. The superscipt denotes the particular slave.

The same algorithm in the PPL/I notation requires that we keep the x_i's, say as $\underline{w}$, in the main store. The "program" is thus:

```
SN: PROC OPTIONS(MAIN);          /* THIS IS THE NOTATION FOR MAIN PROGRAMS.          */
DCL (I,J,K)FIXED, (Y,W(1000))FLOAT, /* DECLARATION OF COMMON                         */
(#)(Z,X(100))FLOAT,(#)M FIXED;/* AND DISTRIBUTED VARIABLES.                          */
DO I=1 TO P;                     /* IN THIS SEQUENTIAL PART S(1), THE MASTER CHOOSES */
   J=(I-1)*100+1;                /* ALL SLAVES I=1 TO P AND TRANSFERS THE X'S        */
   K=100*I;                      /* ACCORDING TO BOUNDARIES J AND K FROM THE         */
   (I)X(1:100)≡W(J:K);           /* COMMON TO THE SLAVE MEMORIES. EACH STORES A      */
END;                             /* SLICE X(1:100) IN ITS MEMORY.                    */
Y,Z=0;                           /* Z WILL ACCUMULATE 100 SINES                      */
PUT BROADCAST (Z);               /* IT IS FIRST BROADCAST TO ALL SLAVES.             */
PARCALL PR;                      /* PARALLEL PROCEDURE P(1) IS ACTIVATED IN ALL      */
                                 /* P SLAVES. EACH SLAVE ACCUMULATES 100 SINES       */
                                 /* AS ITS Z I.E., AS (#P)Z. THIS SIMPLE CALL IS     */
                                 /* THE ENTIRE PARALLEL PART OF THE PROGRAM.         */
DO I=1 TO P;                     /* IN THIS SEQUENTIAL PART S(2), FOR EVERY SLAVE I  */
   Z=(I)Z;                       /* TRANSFER ITS (I)Z AS Z INTO THE COMMON STORE     */
   Y=Y+Z;                        /* AND ACCUMULATE ALL P Z'S AS THE RESULT Y.        */
END; RETURN(Y);
PR: PARPROC;                     /* THE 100 X'S STORED IN SLAVE (#P)                 */
DO M=1 TO 100;                   /* ARE FIRST CHOSEN AND THEN ADDED TO (#P)Z         */
   Z=Z+SIN(X(M));                /* HERE Z IS REALLY (#P)Z.                          */
END; PAREND PR; END SN;          /* COMPLETES THE PROGRAM                            */
```

Let us calculate the time reduction ratio for the above program. For the computation of y we need two synchronizations (starts of S), bus transfer of 1000 data points (x_i) and 10 partial sums

$$y^{(i)} = \Sigma \sin(x_m); m\Sigma = 1,\dots,100 \tag{14}$$

one in each slave i. Suppose that we need $10(\mu+\alpha)$ to compute a single sine value. Then computing $y^{(i)}$ - that is in the parallel step - we have to do $1000(\mu+\alpha)+100\alpha$ (the last for summation in (14)). We next transferred the 10 partial results $y^{(i)}$ to the master (10τ) and summed them there (9α). Altogether, the two sequential parts require $2\beta + 1010\tau + 1000\mu + 1109\alpha$.

Under the same assumption of computing sin(x) with $10(\mu+\alpha)$, we would need in purely sequential execution $10{,}000(\mu+\alpha) + 100\alpha$. Thus, the time reduction ratio is

$$\rho=(2\beta+1010\tau+1000(\mu+\alpha)+109\alpha)/(10{,}000(\mu+\alpha)+100\alpha) \tag{15}$$

We can clearly approximate this with

$$\rho=(2\beta+1000\tau+1000(\mu+\alpha)+100\alpha)/(10{,}000(\mu+\alpha)) \tag{16}$$

This is then the ratio as computed

$$\rho=1/10 + 0.01\alpha/(\mu+\alpha) + 0.2x10^{-3}\beta' + 0.1\tau' \quad (17)$$

or - since the second part is small - also as

$$\rho=0.1 + 0.1\tau' + 0.2x10^{-3}\beta' \quad (18)$$

Despite the triviality of the problem, a number of features may be noted:

(a) Suppose that y is to be computed repeatedly, say for some k=1,...,m. This would not change ρ at all. We may, however, improve it by using the following "trick." Write S(2) in front of S(1) and make a "jump" to S(1) the first time around - and only then. The sequence is then S(1),P(1),S(2),S(1),P(1),...,P(k-1), S2(k-1) and since for two consecutive S's no bus synchronization is needed, no time β is wasted. Factor 0.2 in (18) is reduced to 0.1 and if β' is large, this rescheduling decreases ρ and increases the speedup σ.

(b) We had stored the "slices" of $\underline{x}$ all as x_i, i=1,...,100. This necessitates some index calculation (I,J,K in S(1)) - a time recovered in PR where no index calculation is needed. Had we transferred the slices with their original indices, we would have had to declare X(1000) in every slave. This would have wasted 10x900 = 9000 addresses.

(c) To change the program into SIMPL/I would require conversion of PR into a BEHAVIOR, its call into START and the transfer of parameters to be effected by PL/I "structures." Similar conclusions apply to other programs we will discuss later - they can easily be simulated by SIMPL/I or by PL/I with multitasking.

The program which follows is self-explanatory - and where it is not, comments are added. The results can be combined into graphs of S, P, S which show how neatly the simulation reflects ASP-processing. In the present case S(1) was 8+101=109, P(1) was AT1+MT1=19768 and the total time on ASP was TOT=19898. In a single computer the required time would have been Σ(AT1+MT1)=50472+104944=155416. Thus the ratio, speedup and efficiency would have been resp:

ρ=19898/155416=0.128; σ=1/ρ=7.811; η=781.1/10=78.11%

The fact that the sine-function cannot be computed each time in 10 operations have reduced σ and η considerably. Another case of 1000 x's but around 60° instead of 45° was run and the results are shown as well; they show a higher speedup.

We will program a slightly more serious and useful problem in the next section and close the present by "repaying a debt." It was mentioned that extensions of the operating system could also have been and were in fact used in SMS-201. Let us discuss this approach next.

In general, SMS-201 interprets PUT, GET, XCH as control instructions for transfer of data from master to slaves, from slaves to the master, exchange between slaves and control (synchronization, etc.) respectively. If data are subdivided physically instead of logically, PT, GT and XC are used instead and letter P is appended to the command. If the letter B is appended to an instruction, it means that bytes, instead of words are meant. We will not deal with these. On the other

```
TEST1: PROCEDURE OPTIONS(MAIN);
      DECLARE (I,J,K,L,M,S,SL,P) FIXED,
              (Y,W(1000),Z(10),X(10,100)) FLOAT;
       DCL PI FLOAT DEC(16) INIT(3.1415920257568);
       DCL (BETA,TAU,MT,AT,TT,ST,TM,TOT) FIXED DEC(10,1);
       DCL (MT1,AT1,AD,MP)FIXED DEC(10,1) EXTERNAL;
       P=10;
       TAU=0.1; BETA=8; AD=2; MP=4; /* ASSUMED VALUES OF "TIMES" */
       TT=0; ST=0; AT=0; MT=0; /* INITIAL VALUES OF TRANSFER,
             SYNCHRONIZATION, ADDITION AND MULTIPLICATION TIMES */
       ST=ST+BETA; /* THERE IS A SINGLE SYNCHRONIZATION, SO ST CAN BE CALCULATED HERE */
       PUT SKIP LIST('ST. 18','ST='||ST);
       /* THE NEXT 8 STATEMENTS CALCULATE 1000 W_VALUES */
       PIO4=PI/2;
       PI12=PI/12;
       INA=PIO4-PI12;
       FIA=PIO4+PI12;
       DELTA=(FIA-INA)/1000;
       DO I=1 TO 1000;
         W(I)=INA+I*DELTA;
       END;
       DO I=1 TO P; /* NEXT WE TRANSFER 100 W_VALUES, L=1,...,100, TO THE SLAVES AS X(SLAVE,L) */
         J=(I-1)*100;
         DO L=1 TO 100;
           X(I,L)=W(J+L);
         END;
       END;
       TT=TT+P*100*TAU;
       PUT SKIP LIST('ST. 33','TT='||TT);
       Y=0.0; /* EACH SLAVE HAS ITS Z(I) INITIALIZED TO 0.0 */
       DO I=1 TO P;
         Z(I)=Y;
       END;
       TT=TT+P*TAU;
       PUT SKIP LIST('ST. 38','TT='||TT);
       /* PAR IS CALLED FOR EACH SLAVE IN TURN. SINCE EACH CALL "USES" UP TIME TOT,
          WE COMPUTE TM AS ITS MAXIMUM AND THUS SIMULATE THE FACT THAT ALL OTHER SLAVES WAIT */
       TM=0;
       DO SL=1 TO P;
         CALL PAR(SL);
         PUT SKIP LIST('AT1='||AT1,'MT1='||MT1);
         TOT=MT1+AT1;
         IF TOT>TM THEN TM=TOT;
       END;
  PAR: PROCEDURE(S);
       DCL S FIXED;
       MT1=0;AT1=0;
       DO M=1 TO 100;
         Z(S)=Z(S)+SIN(X(S,M));
       END;
  END PAR;
  SIN: PROCEDURE(V) RETURNS(FLOAT);
       V2=V*V;
       MT1=MT1+MP;
       D=V;
       SINN=V;
       J=1;
       DO WHILE(ABS(D)¬<1E-20);
         J=J+1;
         D=-D*V2/J;
         J=J+1;
         D=D/J;
         SINN=SINN+D;
       AT1=AT1+3*AD;
       MT1=MT1+3*MP;
       END;
       RETURN(SINN);
  END SIN;

       DO I=1 TO P;
         Y=Y+Z(I);
       END;

                           AT=AT+P*AD;
                           TT=TT+P*TAU;
                           TOT=AT+TT+ST+MT+TM;
                           PUT SKIP(2)LIST('TOT='||TOT);
                           PUT SKIP LIST('AT ='||AT);
                           PUT SKIP LIST('TT ='||TT);
                           PUT SKIP LIST('ST ='||ST);
                           PUT SKIP LIST('MT ='||MT);
                           PUT SKIP LIST('TM ='||TM);
                           PUT SKIP LIST('AT ='||AT);
                           PUT SKIP LIST('TT ='||TT);
                           PUT SKIP LIST(' Y ='||Y);
                       END TEST1;
```

```
ST. 18                   ST=          8.0
ST. 33                   TT=        100.0
ST. 38                   TT=        101.0
AT1=      3012.0         MT1=      6424.0
AT1=      3864.0         MT1=      8128.0
AT1=      4296.0         MT1=      8992.0
AT1=      4800.0         MT1=     10000.0
AT1=      5064.0         MT1=     10528.0
AT1=      5400.0         MT1=     11200.0
AT1=      5580.0         MT1=     11560.0
AT1=      6000.0         MT1=     12400.0
AT1=      6000.0         MT1=     12400.0
AT1=      6456.0         MT1=     13312.0

TOT=     19898.0
AT =        20.0
TT =       102.0
ST =         8.0
MT =         0.0
TM =     19768.0
AT =        20.0
TT =       102.0
 Y = 4.77892E+02
```

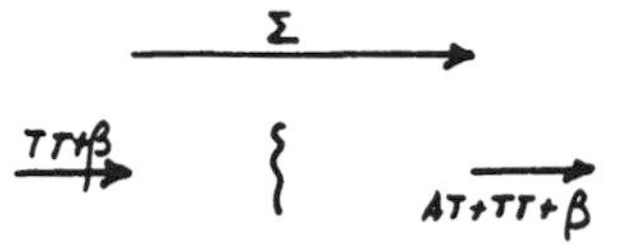


```
ST. 18                   ST=          8.0
ST. 33                   TT=        100.0
ST. 38                   TT=        101.0
AT1=      6600.0         MT1=     13600.0
AT1=      6600.0         MT1=     13600.0
AT1=      6600.0         MT1=     13600.0
AT1=      7032.0         MT1=     14464.0
AT1=      7200.0         MT1=     14800.0
AT1=      7200.0         MT1=     14800.0
AT1=      7200.0         MT1=     14800.0
AT1=      7584.0         MT1=     15568.0
AT1=      7800.0         MT1=     16000.0
AT1=      7800.0         MT1=     16000.0

TOT=     23930.0
AT =        20.0
TT =       102.0
ST =         8.0
MT =         0.0
TM =     23800.0
AT =        20.0
TT =       102.0
 Y = 9.59850E+02
```

hand, a multiple call ("block transfer") is indicated by starting the instruction with the letter M and we will discuss these.

The main PUT - instruction is as follows:

CALL PUTW(IER,MN,MAD,LNG,IAD)

IER is an error code to be used in <u>all</u> procedures. MN is the number of the slave ("module"), with MN=-1 signifying "all modules," that is broadcast. MAD and IAD are the starting addresses in the slave(s) and master respectively, LNG is the length of the block to be transferred. If a single word is to be transferred, LNG must be made 1. PUTS (IER,MN,SAD) transfers a starting address SAD to one or all slaves, MPUTW(IER,MNF,MNL,MAD,LNG,IAD) is a PUTW except that slaves MNF,MNF+1,..., MNL are involved. The number of words transferred is (MNL - MNF+1)*LNG. Finally, MPUTS(IER,MNF,MNL,SAD) transfers (MNL-MNF+1) starting addresses to the named slaves.

The GET-instructions are similar; namely: GETW(IER,MN,MAD,LNG,IAD) and MGETW(IER,MNF,MNL,MAD,LNG,IAD) with the understanding that consecutive locations are always indicated.

The exchange-commands are similar to the TRANSFER instructions of PPL/I as needed in Topps. Thus, calling XCHW(IER,MN,MAD,LNG) would copy a block of data of slave MN to all other slaves starting with the same address MAD and of the same length LNG. An additional instruction is MXCHW(IER,MNF,MNL,MAD,LNG) which deals with multiple slaves. As an example consider:

```
      M=MAD
      DO 1 MN=MNF,MNL
      CALL XCHW(IER,MN,M,LNG)
    1 M=M+2*LNG
```

The same is effected by CALL MXCHW(IER,MNF,MNL,MAD,LNG).

The control functions initialize and stop the interrupt system, start the slaves, test the interrupt status and set-up waiting queues for certain interrupts. INTSY(IER) opens the channels and presents the interrupt routines to the operating system (of the master). It must be called ahead of any other system call. This is precisely the reason why extension of operating system calls is not recommended:

calling INTSY wastes a lot of time. Since all other calls also are activated via the operating system, this type of language is easy to write, but is not very efficient. Stated simply: β and τ would be too high.

CONTROL(IER,SAD) would start all slave-programs from starting address SAD and would let the master wait until all slaves arrive at their respective HLT commands. START(IER) would do the same except that the starting address was first transferred by a PUTS-command and it would let the master go on with its program while the slaves work. WAITF(IER) and WAITL(IER) let the master wait for the first or last HLT respectively.

The language is rather simple and easy to use. Instead of programming in it, let us show how it corresponds to PPL/I. For instance, PUT BROADCAST(V)(A) of PPL/I would be CALL PUTW(IER,-1,V,1,A) and block-transfer could use N instead of 1 for length (LNG). Declaring a parallel procedure would be done by the same PUTW-only now the data being sent is a program. PARCALL would be effected by CALL CONTROL (IER,SAD) and TRANSFER by the XCHW instructions. In all cases INTSY(IER) has to precede the call (wasting time).

Let us repeat that only two "programs" are required: in the PS-notation for a general, mathematical evaluation and in the PPL/I language as a programming solution of the problem at hand. The actual simulation, be it in PL/I with or without multitasking, in SIMPL/I or on the SMS-201 are then easily written.

4.2 MATRIX MULTIPLICATION

Aims: A number of conclusions were reached in the example of the previous section, but to keep more in line with the second part of the book, an example in linear algebra will be given next. It will be that of matrix multiplication - both for dense and sparse matrices. The main goal will be to show that Apps demands an unreasonably high number of slaves, Illiac has a low speedup, but ASP does in fact achieve high speedups with a sensible number of slaves. The data structure to be used in subsequent chapters will also be introduced.

The simplest case of

$$\underline{C} = \underline{A}\cdot\underline{B} \tag{19}$$

is that in which $\underline{A}$ and $\underline{B}$ are (nxl) or (lxn) matrices i.e., are vectors so that

$$c = \underline{a}^T\underline{b} = \Sigma\ a_i b_i;\ i\Sigma = 1,\dots,n \tag{20}$$

is to be computed. We have already seen in 2.2 that this can be done as follows on an Apps: First all n products are formed and if Apps has at least n slaves this would require only a time of 1μ. Then, a fan-in sum requires $\lceil\log_2 n\rceil\alpha$, so that altogether

$$\Omega_p = \lceil\log_2 n\rceil\alpha + 1\cdot\mu \tag{21}$$

operations are required. On a sequential computer, the product requires

$$\Omega_s = (n-1)\alpha + n\mu \tag{22}$$

For larger n, the speedup, (time) ratio and efficiency are respectively:

$$\sigma \cong \frac{n(\alpha+\mu)}{\alpha\log_2 n+\mu}; \qquad \rho \cong \frac{1}{n}[\alpha'\log_2 n+\mu']; \qquad \eta \cong \frac{100}{(\log_2 n)\alpha'+\mu'} \tag{23}$$

At this stage we can already conclude that:

- The number of additions is larger than the number of multiplications. Thus, even if we assume that $\mu>\alpha$, we must count not only multiplications but also additions; the more so, since in present-day computers $\mu\cong\alpha$.
- The utilization factor is very small because of the Haydn effect during the fan-in summation, as evidenced by $\lceil\log_2 n\rceil$. During the last summation only one out of n slaves works.
- The number of slaves must be n; otherwise the speedup would decrease. This may be a very high number.
- This and the fact that memory interference was not included makes the solution rather impractical.
- The form of ρ makes the ratio easier to interpret than the speedup σ.

Next, we make $\underline{A}$ an (nxn) matrix and compute

$$\underline{c} = \underline{A}\ \underline{b}; \quad c_i = \Sigma\ a_{ij}b_j;\ j\Sigma = 1,\ldots,n \tag{24}$$

on Apps. Since every c_i can be viewed as the scalar product

$$c_i = \underline{a}_i{*}\underline{b};\ i=1,\ldots,n \tag{25}$$

the speedup, ratio and efficiency are similar to the previous case except that n^2 slaves are needed - n for every c_i, i=1,...,n. The utilization is slightly better in that at the end n (but out of n^2) slaves add.

Finally, for the general matrix case and n^3 slaves, all n^2 scalar products can be computed with Ω_p. Simple sequential multiplication requires

$$\Omega_s = n^3(\alpha+\mu) = n^3\omega \text{ since } \omega = \alpha + \mu \tag{26}$$

so that $\rho = (\alpha\log_2 n+\mu)/(n^3\omega) = (\alpha'\log_2 n+\mu')/n^3$ (27)

Again, the factor in parantheses appears, but now divided by n^3. For a small (100x100) matrix one million (1,000,000) slaves would be required.

Another way to compute $\underline{C}$ on Apps is by block-decomposition, i.e.,

$$\underline{A} = \begin{bmatrix} \underline{A}_{11} & \underline{A}_{12} \\ \underline{A}_{21} & \underline{A}_{22} \end{bmatrix}; \ \underline{B} = \begin{bmatrix} \underline{B}_{11} & \underline{B}_{12} \\ \underline{B}_{21} & \underline{B}_{22} \end{bmatrix}; \ \underline{C} = \left[\begin{array}{c|c} \underline{A}_{11}\underline{B}_{11}+\underline{A}_{12}\underline{B}_{21} & \underline{A}_{11}\underline{B}_{12}+\underline{A}_{12}\underline{B}_{22} \\ \underline{A}_{21}\underline{B}_{11}+\underline{A}_{22}\underline{B}_{21} & \underline{A}_{21}\underline{B}_{12}+\underline{A}_{22}\underline{B}_{22} \end{array}\right] \tag{28}$$

where all $\underline{A}_{ij}$, $\underline{B}_{ij}$ as well as $\underline{C}_{11}$, $\underline{C}_{12}$, $\underline{C}_{21}$ and $\underline{C}_{22}$ are (n/2)x(n/2) block matrices. From (28) it follows that if an algorithm for efficient multiplication of (n/2)x (n/2) matrices exists, it may be used to calculate the product of nxn matrices. If originally $n=2^k$, matrix multiplication may be reduced to multiplying (2x2) matrices. (Since they include four elements, they will be named quadruplets or "quads" for short.)

V. Strassen proposed the following method for multiplying 2x2 matrices:

$d_1 = (a_{12} - a_{22})(b_{21} + b_{22})$;

$d_2 = (a_{11} + a_{22})(b_{11} + b_{22})$; $\qquad d_5 = a_{11}(b_{12} - b_{22})$

$$d_3 = (a_{11} - a_{21})(b_{11} + b_{12}); \qquad d_6 = a_{22}(b_{21} - b_{11})$$
$$d_4 = (a_{11} + a_{12})b_{22} \qquad ; \qquad d_7 = (a_{21} + a_{22})b_{11} \tag{29}$$

The resulting c's are then:

$$c_{11} = d_1 + d_2 - d_4 + d_6; \quad c_{12} = d_4 + d_5$$
$$c_{22} = d_2 - d_3 + d_5 - d_7; \quad c_{21} = d_6 + d_7 \tag{30}$$

The count of operations shows that

$$\Omega = 7\mu + 18\alpha \tag{31}$$

Strassen was able to prove that for large $n=2^k$, if one does not count additions:

$$\Omega = k\cdot n^{\log_2 7} = k\cdot n^{2.81} \tag{32}$$

instead of n^3. This would indicate that it is a more efficient method of matrix multiplication, except that

- It does not take account of the time for accessing matrix elements
- It does not count additions and is very inefficient for sparse matrices.
- The computation of the d's and c's is not independent and can thus hardly be parallelized.
- No way of numerical error control was found.

On the other hand, if p=8, then each slave could compute one product $\underline{A}_{ik}\underline{B}_{kj}$ of (28) in time of $\omega(n/2)^3$ even if simple-minded matrix multiplication is employed. Four slaves then add the blocks to form $\underline{C}_{ij}$ in time $\alpha(n/2)^2$. Summing up

$$\Omega_p = n^3\omega/8 + n^2\alpha/4 \tag{33}$$

$$\rho = \frac{n^3\omega+2n^2\alpha}{8\cdot n^3\omega} = \frac{1}{8} + \frac{\alpha'}{4n} \cong \frac{1}{8} \tag{34}$$

This is the optimum possible ratio, but - as usual - transfer of data was not included. Additional complications appear when $p\neq 8$.

The conclusion of all this is that no efficient algorithm exists for multiplying the matrices on an Apps. We have also seen that multiplication on Illiac is problematic, mainly because of initial data transfer and subsequent routing. This leaves us with the task of devising methods for STARAN, MIMD and ASP-systems.

Suppose we again deal with 4x4 matrices and store $\underline{Y}$ in the first four words in STARAN as in Fig. 1. We may then denote by A(I,J) an element in the J-th field of location I and by C(J) the word in the J-th field of key-register C. The "program" might be as follows:

```
DO I=1 TO 4;
     C=X(I,*);/*Transfer row I of X into the comparator register C       */
     DO K=1 TO 4;    /*The 4 fields in a word                              */
          DO J=1//4;/*Simultaneously on four locations J                   */
          A(J+4,K)=C(K)*A(J,K);END;/*of J-loop                             */
     END;/*of producing 4 words e.g. words 5 to 8 in Fig. 1                */
     DO J=1//4;/*The sum of the 4 fields of the word is Z(1,m)             */
     A(J+8,I)=A(J,1)+A(J,2)+A(J,3)+A(J,4);END;
END;/*See again for I=1 in Fig. 1.                                         */
```

Word ⟵ Field ⟶

	1	2	3	4
1	y_{11}	y_{21}	y_{31}	y_{41}
2	y_{12}	y_{22}	y_{32}	y_{42}
3	y_{13}	y_{23}	y_{33}	y_{43}
4	y_{14}	y_{24}	y_{34}	y_{44}
5	$x_{11}y_{11}$	$x_{12}y_{21}$	$x_{13}y_{31}$	$x_{14}y_{41}$
6	$x_{11}y_{12}$	$x_{12}y_{22}$	$x_{13}y_{32}$	$x_{14}y_{42}$
7	$x_{11}y_{13}$	$x_{12}y_{23}$	$x_{13}y_{33}$	$x_{14}y_{43}$
8	$x_{11}y_{14}$	$x_{12}y_{24}$	$x_{13}y_{34}$	$x_{14}y_{44}$
9	z_{11}			
10	z_{12}			
11	z_{13}			
12	z_{14}			

Fig. 1: First step of the algorithm

The speedup will not be high because the multiplication (bit-by-bit) is rather slow. Additionally, when the matrices are not 4x4 no such efficient storage of them is possible. Finally, transfer times are difficult to account for.

The problem with the algorithm for MIMD-systems is how to divide the calculations between the rather independent processors and how to reduce contention for the common data. We may use the FORK and JOIN-constructs proposed by Conway [Con 63]. When FORK(L) is encountered, an independent computation is started at label L by a free processor, with the cpu which executed the FORK proceeding linearly in the program. Thus each FORK spawns a new path. JOIN(N) will reduce N by 1 and free a cpu if N remains above zero but proceed if it is in fact zero. In the first case, the freed cpu will seek a new task for itself.

The program for multiplying again 4x4 matrices is as follows:

```
DO K=1 TO N-1;/*Cpu 1 goes on to calculate it for SL=N              */
     FORK(LN);K=N
LN:DO I=1 TO N; S=0;/*Initialization of the sum to zero             */
          DO J=1 TO N;/*The normal loop for computing C(I,J)        */
          S=S+X(I,J)*Y(J,K);END;Z(I,K)=S;
     END;
     JOIN(N);
```

Slave-1 must spawn three paths for K=1,2 and 3 and goes on to compute the fourth column of Z. Since the same X's are to be used by all slaves and reside in the same memory, the interference is considerable. Also, with N>p there is a real problem of scheduling - and as yet it was not solved. Since the speedup depends heavily on the effectiveness of the scheduling algorithm, it will not be discussed further. There were enough reasons given above to expect a low speedup and efficiency.

The matrix multiplication programs for Apps, Illiac, STARAN and MIMD-systems illuminated the problems associated with using these systems. It should also be noted that only dense matrices were treated, but that the efficiencies would drop considerably for the more important case of sparse matrices. In contradistinction, it is shown below that matrix multiplication on an ASP-system is simple and efficient, that the data outlay is trivial and that it may also be applied to the more important case of sparse matrices. In order to develop the program gradually, we first compute the vectors product $c = \underline{a}^T\underline{b}$. For it we would transfer to each slave a "slice" of vector $\underline{a}$ and $\underline{b}$ of width

$h = n/p$ (35)

We will always assume that h is an integer; if it is not, then k "dummy" elements are added to n so that $(n+k)/p = h$ is an integer. All dummy elements will then be stored in slave number p with an instruction not to process them.

Each slave q can now, in parallel, multiply its elements of $\underline{a}$ and $\underline{b}$ producing a scalar $c^{(q)}$. The master would then collect and add $c^{(q)}$, $q=1,\dots,p$. In the P-S-notation the algorithm would therefore be as follows:

S(1): Transfer a slice of $\underline{a}$ and $\underline{b}$ to every slave. Since altogether 2n values are transferred, $2n\tau$ operations are required.

P(1): Each slave q calculates $c^{(q)} = \Sigma\, a_i b_i$; $i\Sigma = (q-1)h+1,\dots,qh$ (36)

and uses for it $h\mu + (h-1)\alpha$ operations.

S(2): p values $c^{(q)}$, $q=1,\dots,p$ have to be transferred to the master and added to form the result: c. For this, $p\tau + (p-1)\alpha$ are needed.

Two bus synchronizations are required - one at the start of every S(i) step.

Altogether: $\Omega_p = 2\beta + 2n\tau + h\mu + (h-1)\alpha + p\tau + (p-1)\alpha$ (37)

Since $h<n$, $p<<n$, both are larger than 1 so that $h-1 \cong h$ and $p-1 \cong p$. Therefore

$$\Omega_p \cong h(\mu+\alpha) + p\alpha + (2n+p)\tau + 2\beta \quad (38)$$

In sequential execution

$$\Omega_s = n\mu + (n-1)\alpha \cong n(\mu+\alpha) = n\omega \quad (39)$$

The speedup and ratio are respectively:

$$\sigma = n\omega/[h\omega + p\alpha + (2n+p)\tau + 2\beta] \quad (40)$$

$$\rho = [h\omega + p\alpha + (2n+p)\tau + 2\beta]/(n\omega) \cong h/n + 2\tau' + 2\beta'/n \quad (41)$$

where $(p\alpha+p\tau)$ was neglected. Since $h/n = 1/p$ we have

$$\rho \cong 1/p + 2\tau' + 2\beta'/n \quad (42)$$

and $\eta = 100/(\rho p) = 100/(1+2\tau' p + 2\beta'/h)$ (43)

A number of conclusions can be drawn from this trivial example:

(a) It is easier to calculate ρ than σ. Therefore in the rest of the book we will compute and approximate ρ and if needed set then $\sigma = 1/\rho$.

(b) Bus synchronization requires much more time than (block) transfer - so much so that serious efforts must be made to reduce the number of synchronizations required (e.g., the trick employed in the $(\Sigma \sin x)$-program we discussed in the previous section).

(c) It is not difficult to include all timing factors: α, μ, τ and β and account for them.

(d) The data structure - slices - is very simple.

A slightly different, but still very simple data structure (Fig. 2) is proposed for $\underline{c} = \underline{A}\,\underline{b}$. Matrix $\underline{A}$ is stored in p horizontal slices but vector $\underline{b}$ is stored in its entirety in every local memory. This will increase the storage demand slightly from $n(n+1)/p$ to $n^2/p+n$ (but $p<<n$). The algorithm then is:

S(1): Transfer the slices of $\underline{A}$ and all of $\underline{b}$ into local memories ($\Omega=n^2\tau + n\tau$)

P(1): Each slave computes c_i of a slice ($\Omega=n\omega h$): $c_i = \Sigma\, A_{ij} b_j$; $i=1,\dots h$; $j\Sigma=1,\dots,n$

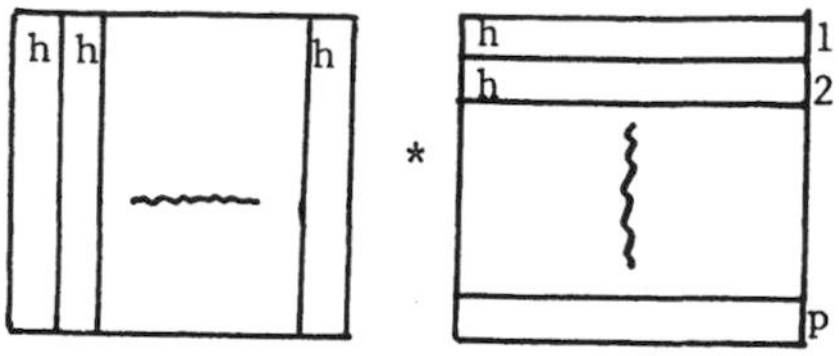

Fig. 3 ~~2~~: Data Structure

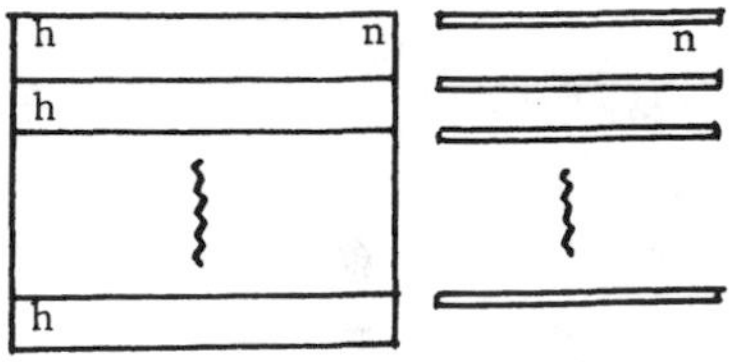

Fig. 2 ~~3~~: Data Structure

S(2): Recall the results from the slaves ($\Omega=p\tau$), including the two synchronizations:

$\Omega_p=2\beta+(n^2+n)\tau+n^2\omega/p+p\tau \cong n^2\omega/p+2\beta+n^2\tau$ (45)

Since sequentially $\Omega_s = n^2\omega$, operations are required, the ratio and efficiency are:

$\rho\cong 1/p+\tau'+2\beta'/n^2$; $\eta\cong 100/(1+p\tau'+2\beta'p/n^2)$ (46)

The deterioration of the ratio ρ due to data transfer has decreased and we may expect a further decrease for real matrix multiplication $\underline{C} = \underline{A}\ \underline{B}$.

In the first algorithm to be proposed for the data structure (Fig. 3) is such that each local memory stores a vertical and the corresponding horizontal slice of matrices $\underline{A}$ and $\underline{B}$ respectively. Each slave q can then compute

$$c_{ik}^{(q)} = \Sigma\, A_{ij}B_{jk};\ q=1,\ldots,p;\quad i,k=1,\ldots,n;\ j\Sigma=\ell,\ldots,u \qquad (47)$$

where ℓ is the lower, u is the upper index of a slice (for slave #1, we have $\ell=1$, $u=h$, for slave p we have $\ell=(p-1)h+1$, $u=n$).

Note that after having evaluated (47), each slave q holds the numerical values of all $n^2=n\times n$ partial elements of $\underline{C}^{(q)}$. To get $\underline{C}$, a summation must be performed

$$c_{i,k} = \Sigma\, c_{ik}^{(q)};\quad q\Sigma=1,\ldots,p \qquad (48)$$

and since this should be done in the master, all n^2 elements of each slave must be transferred first.

The reduction ratio is next calculated (without writing a program). In the initial step, 2hn values have to be sent to each slave over the bus; in the P-step, $h\omega$ are needed for calculating in each slave q the n^2 elements of $C_{i,k}^{(q)}$. Then the system is synchronized, pn^2 words are transferred to the master and added there. In a monocomputer, $n^3\omega$ are needed for matrix multiplication. The reduction ratio and efficiency are therefore

$$\rho = (n^2h\omega+\beta+pn^2\tau(1+2/p))/(n^3\omega) = 1/p+\beta'/n^3+(1+2/p)p\tau'/n + \alpha'/n \qquad (49)$$

$$\eta = 100/[1+p\beta'/n^3+(p+2)p\tau'/n + p\alpha'/n] \qquad (50)$$

Because $n\gg p$, very high speedup and efficiency will be achieved. Note, though, that we need n^2 locations for every $C^{(q)}$ and $2nh=2n^2/p$ for the slices of $\underline{A}$ and $\underline{B}$. Altogether we need $n^2(1+2/p)$ locations in each slave.

If we have that much space, we can store the matrix $\underline{A}$ in all slaves and calculate a slice of $\underline{C}$ using a slice of $\underline{B}$ as in Fig. 4. The address space needed is the same as in the previous algorithm. The new algorithm proceeds as follows:

S(1): Transfer the data of Fig. 4. Here we may send $\underline{A}$ by broadcast i.e., to all slaves at once with $n^2\tau$ units of time. Next, each slave gets its slice of $\underline{B}$ so that another $n^2\tau$ are needed.

P(1): Each slave calculates nh inner products, so that $nh(n\omega)=n^2h\omega$ are needed.

S(2): Transfer of the C-slices back to the master requires $nhp\tau=n^2\tau$ units and no

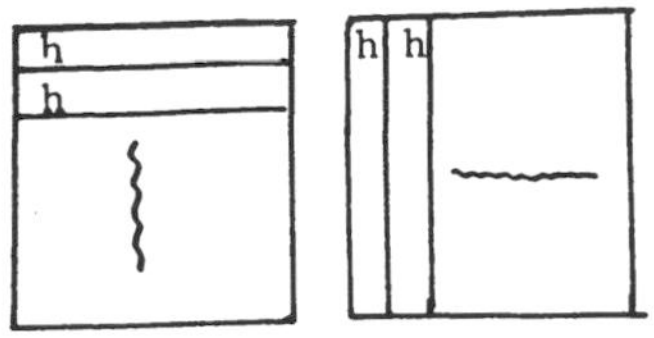

Fig. 4: Data Structure

addition. Thus:

$$\rho=(3n^2\tau+n^2hw+\beta)/(n^3w)=1/p+(3\tau'+\beta'/n^2)/n \quad (51)$$

Comparing (51) with (50) shows that ρ decreased. The results are not always as good as indicated above. It may also be argued that the ideal ratio is $1/(p+1)$ and not $1/p$ as we have used all along, since we use p+1 and not p processors. The efficiency should therefore be lowered to $\eta=100/[(p+1)\rho]$. In any case, no matter what values β', τ', w we use, the second method will be much better than the first.

Concerning the data structures, note that two possibilities of numbering the slices exist. If each slice is numbered as in the original matrices, then n^2 locations would be needed for every slice, so that actually, in the first algorithm, $3n^2$ locations are needed. This may be too much, so that we number every slice from 1 to h. Thus only $n^2+2hn = n^2+2n^2p$ are required, but some renumbering will be needed. Since any $x^{(q)}_{i,j}$ will represent $x_{(q-1)h+i,j}$ or $x_{i,(q-1)h+j}$, a constant $(q-1)h$ has to be added to an index. This is very little additional work so that this solution is preferred.

We have seen that storing rows and columns leads to problems in SIMD systems. Not so in ASP. Any (nxn) matrix is stored as a vector anyway. If the storage is by rows, the access to successive elements of rows requires the index register to store 1, of columns to store n and of the diagonal to store (n+1) and add it, modulo n.

We next discuss the case of sparse matrices. From the practical point of view, these matrices are more important than the dense matrices because they are more prevalent. As already mentioned, a typical power system network would be 2000x2000 with only 10-20 non-zero entries in a row (or column). Numerous other cases exist, but using this as basis, the following are characteristic features of sparse matrices:

(a) Their density i.e., percentage of non-zero elements, is

$$d_a = (100xn_a)/(nxn) \cong (3 \text{ to } 5)\% \quad (52)$$

n is the size, n_a the number of nonzero terms in matrix $\underline{A}$.

(b) The n_a nonzero terms distributed in a non-uniform fashion (very sparse but regular matrices such as those representing partial differential equations are not discussed here).

(c) The diagonal elements are non-zeros.

McNamee [MN 71] has published a sparse matrix multiplication algorithm for sequential execution. Gustavson [Gu 78] has published another with the number of operations Ω less than n^3. We will use the latter. In particular, binary instead of numerical decimal values could be used leading to a known sparsity structure of $\underline{C}$. In the Newton-Raphson or "Hobo" method for solving an algebraic, nonlinear set $\underline{f}(\underline{x})=\underline{0}$, such matrix could be of great value; in these methods, a multiplication $\underline{C}$ =

$\underline{A}*\underline{B}$ is performed repeatedly with the same sparsity structures of $\underline{A}$ and $\underline{B}$. In these cases, n_a^2 instead of n^3 operations would be closer to Ω.

The data-structure and algorithm will be exemplified by the case:

$$\begin{bmatrix} a_{11} & 0 & a_{13} & 0 & 0 & a_{16} \\ 0 & a_{22} & 0 & 0 & a_{25} & 0 \\ a_{31} & 0 & a_{33} & a_{34} & 0 & 0 \\ 0 & a_{42} & 0 & a_{44} & 0 & 0 \\ 0 & 0 & 0 & 0 & a_{55} & a_{56} \\ 0 & 0 & 0 & a_{64} & 0 & a_{66} \end{bmatrix} * \begin{bmatrix} b_{11} & b_{12} & & & & \\ & b_{22} & & b_{24} & & b_{26} \\ & & b_{33} & & b_{35} & \\ b_{41} & & & b_{44} & & b_{46} \\ & & b_{53} & & b_{55} & \\ b_{61} & & & & & b_{66} \end{bmatrix} = \begin{bmatrix} c_{11} & c_{12} & c_{13} & 0 & 0 & c_{16} \\ & c_{22} & c_{23} & c_{24} & c_{25} & c_{26} \\ c_{31} & c_{32} & c_{33} & c_{34} & c_{35} & c_{36} \\ c_{41} & c_{42} & & c_{44} & & c_{46} \\ & & & & c_{55} & c_{56} \\ c_{61} & & & c_{64} & & c_{66} \end{bmatrix} \quad (53)$$

The zero-entries should not be stored, but any compact storage scheme must also be easily accessed. Such a scheme [Gu 78] will actually use only $2n_a+n+1$ or $2n_b+n+1$ storage locations. For the $\underline{A}$, $\underline{B}$ matrices of (53) stored horizontally or vertically, the storage scheme is printed following the program below. Its use is exemplified as follows: a_{31} is accessed by ia(3)=6, ja(6)=1 and $a(6)\equiv a_{31}$; whereas, b_{33} by ib(3)=>ib(1) jb(1)=3 in the second slice and $b(1)\equiv b_{33}$. The first index is used to find a "starting point," the second to find the real index.

The multiplication of two matrices is based on the observation that it can be written as follows:

$$c_{i\cdot} = \Sigma\, a_{ij} b_{j\cdot}\,; \quad a_{ij} \neq 0; \qquad (54)$$

If this is written as:

$$c_{i\cdot} = a_{ij_1} b_{j_1\cdot} + a_{ij_2} b_{j_2\cdot} + \ldots + a_{ij_i} b_{j_i\cdot} \qquad (55)$$

it becomes clear that $c_{i\cdot}$ is a linear combination of those rows of $\underline{B}$ for which $a_{ij}\neq 0$. A similar algorithm storing both $\underline{A}$ and $\underline{B}$ rowwise is given in [Wa 75]. In ASP we may store $\underline{A}$ and $\underline{B}$ in slices with the same ease and write for instance

$$c_{1\cdot} = a_{11} b_{1\cdot} + a_{13} b_{3\cdot} + a_{16} b_{6\cdot} \qquad (56)$$

so that in $$c_{11} = a_{11} b_{11} + a_{13} b_{31} + a_{16} b_{61} \qquad (57)$$

b_{31} would not be found and thus be deleted from the sum.

It is assumed that the matrices are extremely sparse and therefore it may be possible to store larger parts of those matrices. Suppose the entire $\underline{A}$ is stored in <u>every</u> local memory; transfer the vertical slices of B to slaves 1, 2 and 3. Then slave-1 would calculate $c_{11} = a_{11}b_{11}+a_{13}b_{31}+a_{16}b_{61}$; $c_{12} = a_{11}b_{12}+a_{13}b_{32}+a_{16}b_{62}$; $c_{21} = a_{22}b_{21}+a_{25}b_{51}(=0)$; $c_{22} = a_{22}b_{22}+a_{25}b_{52}$; slave-2 would calculate c_{31}, c_{32}, c_{41}, c_{42} and slave-3 would calculate $c_{61}(\neq 0)$. The calculated vertical slice of $\underline{C}$ would be transferred to the master and the second vertical slice of $\underline{B}$ transferred to the master and broadcast.

To compute Ω_p we make the assumption that the non-zero elements are distributed evenly among the slaves. Thus, in each step $(n_b+n_c)/p$, elements have to be trans-

```
SPA_MUL: PROC OPTIONS(MAIN);
  DCL (P,H,H1) FIXED DEC(1);
  DCL E FIXED DEC(3);
  DCL (AT,MT,TT,TA,TM,BETA,TAU,PERC,MAX,E1) FIXED DEC(9,1);
    DCL (AT1,MT1,TOT1) FIXED DEC(9,1);
    DCL (SEQ1,TMAX,SEQ2,PT,NORN) FIXED DEC(9,3);
  GET LIST(P,N,TA,TM,BETA,TAU,MAX,E1);
  N1=N+1;
  H=N/P;
  H1=H+1;

  BEGIN;
    DCL (IB(MAX,P),JB(MAX,P)) FIXED DEC(3);
    DCL B(MAX,P) FIXED DEC(9,3);
    DCL (IA(N1),JA(E1),K) FIXED DEC(5);
    DCL A(E1) FIXED DEC(9,3);
    DCL C(N,H,P) FIXED DEC(15,5);
    FORM: FORMAT(A,COL(7),(20)F(4));
    AT,MT,TT=0.0;
    MAX=0;
    DO JS=1 TO P;
      DO J=1 TO H1;
        GET LIST(IB(J,JS));
      END;
      E=IB(H1,JS)-1;
      TT=TT+H1*TAU; AT=AT+TA;
      DO J=1 TO E;
        GET LIST(JB(J,JS));
      END;
      TT=TT+2*E*TAU;
      DO J=1 TO E;
        GET LIST(B(J,JS));
      END;
    END;   /* END OF TRANSFERRING SLICES OF B */
    DO I=1 TO N1;
      GET LIST(IA(I));
    END;
    E=IA(N1)-1;
    AT=AT+TA;
    DO I=1 TO E;
      GET LIST(JA(I));
    END;
    DO I=1 TO E;
      GET LIST(A(I));
    END;  /* END OF BROADCASTING MATRIX A  */
    TT=TT+N1*TAU+2*E*TAU;
    PUT SKIP LIST('RELEVANT INFORMATION OF A');
    PUT SKIP EDIT('INDEX')(A);
    DO I=1 TO N1;
      PUT EDIT(I)(COL((IA(I)-1)*4+7),F(4));
    END;
    PUT SKIP EDIT('IA=')(A);
    DO I=1 TO N1;
      PUT EDIT(IA(I))(COL((IA(I)-1)*4+7),F(4));
    END;
    PUT SKIP EDIT('JA=',JA)(R(FORM));
    PUT SKIP EDIT('A=',A)(R(FORM));
    PUT PAGE;
    DO I=1 TO P;
      PUT SKIP(3) EDIT('RELEVANT INFORMATION OF B, SLICE:',I)(A,F(2));
      PUT SKIP EDIT('INDEX')(A);
      DO J=1 TO H1;
        PUT EDIT(J)(COL((IB(J,I)-1)*4+7),F(4));
      END;
      PUT SKIP EDIT('IB=')(A);
      DO J=1 TO H1;
        PUT EDIT(IB(J,I))(COL((IB(J,I)-1)*4+7),F(4));
      END;
      PUT SKIP EDIT('JB=',(JB(J,I) DO J=1 TO IB(H1,I)-1))(R(FORM));
      PUT SKIP EDIT('B=',(B(J,I) DO J=1 TO IB(H1,I)-1))(R(FORM));
    END;
    SEQ1=ST+AT+MT+TT;
    TMAX=0;
    PUT SKIP(5);
    DO JS=1 TO P;
      CALL MM(JS);
      IF TOT1>TMAX THEN TMAX=TOT1;
    END;
    SEQ2=NC*TAU+BETA;
    NORN=N*N*N*(TA+TM);
    PT=SEQ1+TMAX+SEQ2;
    PERC=100*PT/NORN;
    PUT SKIP DATA(SEQ1,TMAX,SEQ2,PT,PERC,NORN);
    PUT PAGE LIST('THE PRODUCT MATRIX C IN ROW-WISE');
    DO INA=1 TO N;
      PUT SKIP EDIT(((C(INA,I,J) DO I=1 TO H) DO J=1 TO P))((N)F(5));
    END;

  MM: PROC(JS);
    DCL S FIXED DEC(15,5);
    AT1=0; MT1=0; NC=0;
    DO JNB=1 TO H;
      J1=IB(JNB,JS);
      J2=IB(JNB+1,JS)-1;
      AT1=AT1+TA;
      DO INA=1 TO N;
        I1=IA(INA);
        I2=IA(INA+1)-1;
        AT1=AT1+2*TA;
        S=0.0;
        DO I=I1 TO I2;
          K=JA(I);
          DO J=J1 TO J2;
            IF JB(J,JS)=K
              THEN DO;
                       S=S+A(I)*B(J,JS);
                       AT1=AT1+TA;
                       MT1=MT1+TM;
                       GO TO L;
                     END;
                END;
```

```
L:      END;
        C(INA,JNB,JS)=S;
        IF S¬=0.0 THEN DO; C(INA,JNB,JS)=S; NC=NC+1; END;
      END;
    END;
    TOT1=AT1+MT1;
    PUT SKIP DATA(AT1,MT1,TOT1);
  END MM;
  END;

END SPA_MUL;
```

```
RELEVANT INFORMATION OF A
INDEX   1           2         3           4       5       6       7
IA=     1           4         6           9       11      13      15
JA=     1   3   6   2   5     1   3   4   2   4   5   6   4   6
A=      1   1   1   2   2     3   3   3   4   4   5   5   6   6

RELEVANT INFORMATION OF B, SLICE: 1
INDEX   1           2     3
IB=     1           4     6
JB=     1   4   6   1   2
B=     10  10  10  20  20

RELEVANT INFORMATION OF B, SLICE: 2
INDEX   1       2       3
IB=     1       3       5
JB=     3   5   2   4
B=     30  30  40  40

RELEVANT INFORMATION OF B, SLICE: 3
INDEX   1       2         3
IB=     1       3         6
JB=     3   5   2   4   6
B=     50  50  60  60  60
```

```
THE PRODUCT MATRIX C IN ROW-WISE
 20   20   30    0   50   60
  0   40   60   80  100  120
 60   60   90  120  150  180
 40   80    0  320    0  480
 50    0  150    0  250  300
120    0    0  240    0  720
```

```
AT1=        76.0      MT1=       48.0     TOT1=      124.0;
AT1=        70.0      MT1=       36.0     TOT1=      106.0;
AT1=        76.0      MT1=       48.0     TOT1=      124.0;
SEQ1=       14.799    TMAX=     124.000   SEQ2=        8.625
NORN=     1296.000;
```

ferred to the master and n_b/p rebroadcast. The number of operations in a parallel step is n_c/p^2; initially n_a elements must be broadcast and in the last step no vertical slice of $\underline{B}$ has to be transferred. Thus

$$\Omega_p = p\beta+n_a\tau+n_b\tau/p+pn_c\omega/p^2+(p-2)(2n_b+n_c)\tau/p+n_c\tau/p$$

$$\Omega_p = n_c\omega/p+p\beta+[n_ap+(2p-3)n_b+(p-1)n_c]\tau/p \qquad (59)$$

The number of operations could be reduced if the entire matrix $\underline{B}$ could also be stored in all local memories; the transfer of its vertical slices would be saved.

Obviously in this case, the only way to get meaningful results is by running simulations. The simulation program and one set of results are shown above.

The program itself is self-explanatory, but in order to once again get the reader's attention to sparsity programming, the following were added: (a) The data outlay, (b) Sparse data outlay (Note that for k non-zero elements, 2(k+n+1) elements have to be stored. Thus, for k=3000, n=1000, instead of 1,000,000 only 8002 locations are required). (c) The parallel tasks are of approximately equal duration, so that β is small (d) The ratio and efficiency are resp:

$$\rho=(14.8+124+8.6)/\Omega_s=147.4/\Omega_s;\ \eta=100\Omega_s/(3\cdot147.4)=0.226\Omega_s \qquad (60)$$

but the c in $\Omega_s\cong cn^2\omega$ is still very much debated. In any case, even for sparse matrices, there is considerable speedup.

4.3 THE RELIABILITY ASPECT

Aims: To define reliability numerically and to refute the commonly held view that the reliability of a parallel system is lower than that of a single, large computer. To review triple-modular redundancy, the redundancy schemes of the STAR and Illiac computers and, in more detail, that of SMS-201. To suggest a test procedure.

The first remark is that no discussion of software reliability ("correctness") is attempted, as it is outside the scope here. We should note, however, that simplicity and block-structure of the language is supposed to contribute toward more correct programs. In this respect, the suggested extensions to a high level language should be more advantageous than the design of a completely new language for a pps. Other advantages which could be claimed for PPL/I are the familiarity with PL/I and the opportunity to use "debugged" programs.

The testing procedure which will be suggested will deal neither with software nor even with "acceptability" of data. Take as an example EPOC. Obviously, coding techniques will be employed to check the incoming data. It is also possible to use other testing criteria, for instance the fact that the sum of currents of any node in a network is zero. Thus, if all currents are measured, a check of their sum can be made and the result used as an indication of correctness. We assume such tests are made and will not discuss them further.

Reliability of a system is usually taken to be the measure by which it conforms to the specifications of its behavior. A "failure" is when the system deviates from the specified behavior - a failure is thus an event. The reliability is inversely proportional to the occurrence of failure events. For a single element (say slave), the reliability is usually expressed as $r_1(t) = \exp(-\lambda t)$ where λ is the failure rate of the unit or λ=1/MTBF, the inverse of mean time between failures. Our problem will be to calculate the reliability of a system composed of p units.

For this it will be important to have a clear picture of the structure of the pps. Such structure indicates the components of the pps and how they are interrelated, statically and dynamically. The static structure is important for understanding the kind of faults that might exist; the dynamic structure for understanding the effect of these faults. If, or more realistically, when it is decided that some action must be taken to repair a fault, this mechanical or algorithmic fault must first be located. Obviously our picture of the structure of the pps will guide us in the search for faults. In this respect, the simpler the structure, the better; the less variable it is, the better still. Using a single bus instead of the crossbar switch may pay off in a better search strategy.

The best known reliability-enhancement scheme is TMR (for triple modular redundance). In TMR, each unit is tripled and majority voting equipment is added which checks and compares the output of the three identical units for exact equality. As long as all three, or two out of three, units provide identical results, these are assumed to be correct - the one unit which deviates is "masked out." Thus, the effects of failures are disregarded and viewed from the outside, the system works correctly despite internal faults. TMR is based on the assumption that failures of the units are independent of each other. It is here that software correctness may mess up the picture: if it is incorrect, it is so in all three units, which would then produce identical but incorrect results. The same would apply to the case that the three units of a TMR-scheme have identical design faults.

TMR was suggested for some pps' working as telephone switching centers. For our purposes, in which all (p+1) processors are identical, the TMR solution seems to be unnecessarily expensive; if we agree that not all p slaves are needed and to a decrease in speedup, then we may remove a faulty slave. The testing can be done in a "one-out-of-p" instead of "two-out-of-three" mode and thus be more reliable. The question is how much of performance degradation we find acceptable.

Let P_1 represent the "performance" of a slave [TL 80], so that an ASP would exhibit a combined performance of pP_1. If r slaves were removed because they were found to be faulty, the remaining performance is still pP-rP. The normalized performance π is therefore

$$\pi = (p-r)/p = 1-r/p \qquad (61)$$

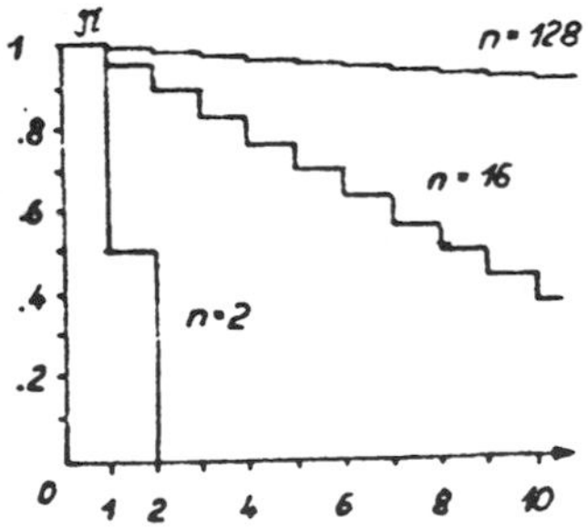

Fig. 5: Performance

It is plotted in Fig. 5 as a function of the removed slaves for systems with p=2, 16 and 128 (the last for SMS-201). Obviously, with p=2 if a unit fails, π is reduced to 50% and the more slaves there are to begin with, the smaller is the loss of performance. The conclusion [TL 80] that "the decrease in performance is insignificant if in the initial stage about a hundred modules or more are present" may be contested on the grounds mentioned in 1.3 for PEPE, namely that the more hardware there is, the more difficult it is to achieve high reliability. On the other hand, this hardware is modular; in PEPE 95% of it is in the elements and since the problem to be solved by it is inherently parallel, there is no interaction between the slaves and they may be replaced easily. This is not the case for problems envisioned for ASP-systems. For ASP-systems a number lower than 128 may in fact be better, the more so, since even for p=16 the removal of a couple of slaves still maintains π>90%.

In Illiac we have a lot of hardware and thus a high probability of system failure. Stated differently, the failure of a single PE causes a system failure and because there are 64 of them, the probability of failure is high. TMR would be much too costly, but a dynamic scheme of enhancing the reliability of Illiac was proposed [BL 80]. In this proposal, a single spare PE is added and replaces any faulty PE (out of the 64). This small hardware redundancy enhances both the availability and the reliability of Illiac and makes its fault-tolerance higher.

The technique proposed would first detect a fault and then restart the program. If such "rollback" fails to correct the error, a permanent fault is assumed and the PE in which the failure was detected is removed (for repair). Unfortunately, Illiac has a very rigid interconnection scheme and the removal of a unit dislocates the entire scheme. If we label by x the PE which failed, removing it removes "neighbors" of the PE's labelled x-1, x+1, x-8, x+8 (all modulo-64) and disturbs the routing interconnection in which x was involved. To restore the routing ability of Illiac, the spare PE is added and all 64 PE's are relabeled. Two relabeling schemes were proposed: either the spare assumed the logical label of the failed PE-x, or all PE's whose number is less than x retain their labels, the others have their numbers reduced by one and the spare is numbered 63 (see Fig. 6 where a "decoupling network" was added to the system).

It can be shown that for $\lambda t=10^{-4}$ the improvement in reliability is better than two orders of magnitude. Still, this is unsatisfactory because only failures of PE's were considered - the decrease of reliability due to the interconnection network, the central control unit, host, etc., may be much higher. In fact if any of these fail, the system is not functionally useful and the availability is zero. Second, reliability assumes that the system can check itself out periodically, but it is virtually impossible to check the controller or host of Illiac (it is an unsymmetric system). Finally, the price of additional hardware may be high and an additional time-delay may have been introduced.

Another system which includes features for reliability enhancement is the STAR (for "Self Testing and Repair") and since it was not mentioned in Chapter 2, a summary on it follows.

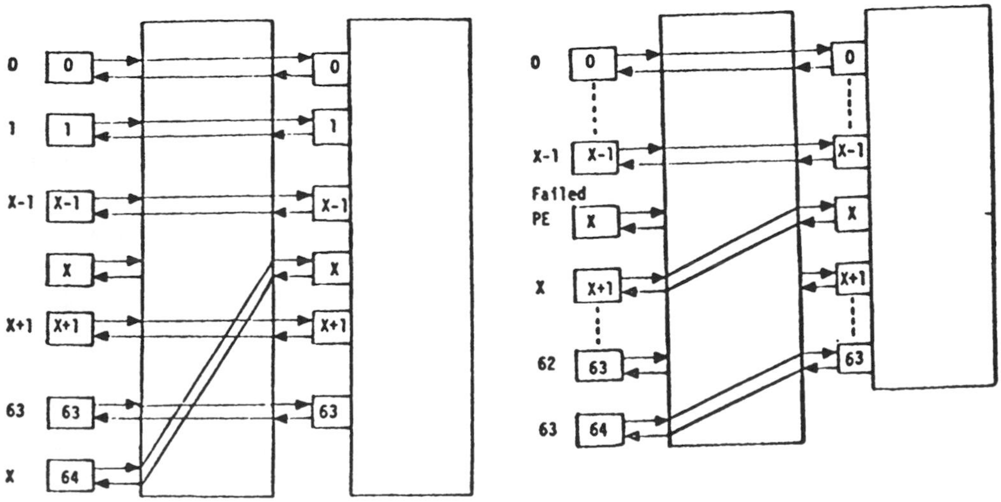

Fig. 6: Addition of a decoupled network

The STAR [AV 72] is functionally divided and consists of: (1) Control processor - contains the index registers and maintains the program location counter; (2) logic processor - performs logical operations; (3) main arithmetic processor - performs arithmetic operations; (4) read only memory; (5) read/write memory; (6) input/output processor; (7) interrupt processor - handles interrupt requests; (8) test and repair processor TARP which monitors the operation of the computer and implements the recovery.

The STAR computer operates in two modes: standard mode and recovery mode. In standard mode the stored programs are executed, and the "normal" algorithms of the TARP issue the principal clocking signals and continually monitor the operation of the system. Each functional unit in the STAR computer generates status messages which are checked in the TARP against the responses that are predicted (independently) by logic internal to the TARP. Thus the TARP can identify, for example, both improperly activated units (unexpected message) and failed units (absence of an expected message).

Finally errors in the TARP itself are detected (and masked) by triple modular redundancy. The intention is that three copies of the TARP will be operational at all times with their outputs decoded by a two-out-of-(n+3) voter. An assumption made, therefore, by the rest of the system is that faults in the TARPs are always masked. The prediction logic of the TARP coupled with the status messages should, in general, enable the TARP to locate the faulty unit causing the error (assuming of course that this prediction logic itself is correct). However, for fault conditions which cannot be resolved by the TARP logic there is a wired-in "cold start" procedure (which is also invoked in the case of temporary power losses).

The reliability of STAR depends crucially on that of TARP. The correct operation of the rest of the system is based on the assumption that TARP is always functioning correctly.

As the STAR was intended for unmanned space missions, permanent faults are treated by the automatic replacement of the faulty unit. There is no provision for their repair. The standard configuration of functional units is supplemented by one or more unpowered spares of each unit, and the TARP implements a spontaneous replacement strategy. A repeated fault indication in a unit leads to its replacement. Spare TARP units are also provided; thus if one of the three operational units disagrees with the other two, then the faulty unit can be replaced by a spare.

When an error is detected and any replacements have taken place, the TARP issues a reset message which causes all operational units to assume an initial state (presumably the contents of the memories are not reset to an initial state). The program that was running is then forced to rollback, that is, to back up to a previous state.

Early analytical studies of redundant systems have indicated that mean-life gains of at least an order of magnitude over that yielded by a non-redundant system could be expected from dynamically redundant systems, with standby spares replacing failed units.

The reliability requirements of most ASP systems are less severe than those mentioned above; at least replacement is possible. It also seems that TARP fits into the STAR-model which is a collection of functionally different units, but could possibly be dropped from ASP which includes (p+1) identical units.

An ASP system exists - it is the SMS-201. If we review its reliability, we can carry it over to a system with fewer than 128 slaves and certainly to the case where the master is just another PE.

Since a reliability study for SMS-201 was conducted [TL 80] we quote from it next:

"Characteristics of reliability

The reliability R(t) of a system is given by the probability of survival for the time from 0 to t. To calculate the reliability for the given system we assume:

- in the initial stage p slaves are present,
- at least p-r slaves are required for minimal performance; failure of more than r slaves is considered a system failure.
- slave failures are statistically independent events."

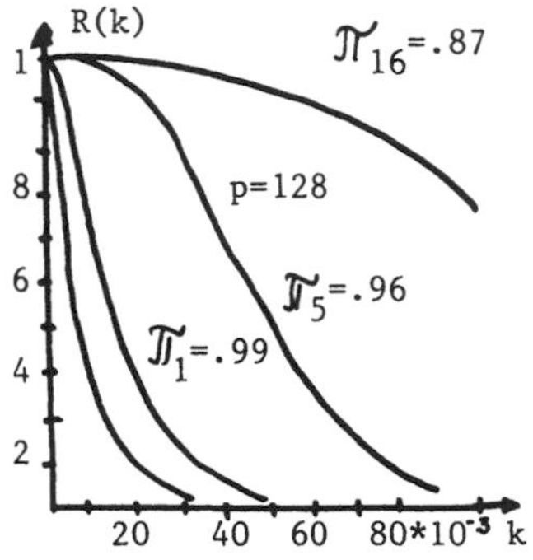

Fig. 7: Reliability of SMS

The reliability R(t) of the given system can be expressed by

$$R(t) = \Sigma\ p'a^i(1-a)^{p-i};\quad i\Sigma = p-r,\dots,p;\ p'=\tfrac{p}{i} \tag{62}$$

as shown in [Ma 74], with a=exp(-xt) being R(t) of a single slave. Thus

$$R(t) = \Sigma\ p'\exp(-\lambda ti)(1-\exp(-\lambda t))^{p-i};\quad i\Sigma = p-r,\dots,p \tag{63}$$

Instead of time, a relative unit k will be used:

$$k=\lambda t \text{ and } R(k) = \Sigma\ p')\exp(-ki)(1-\exp(-k)^{p-i});\quad i\Sigma = p-r,\dots,p \tag{64}$$

R(k) is shown in Fig. 7 as function of k for p=128 and a parameter π_i where i=number of slaves which can fail without causing a total system failure. As can be seen, the performance π increases considerably if a few failing slaves can be accepted.

Next the "mean time between failures" M or the expected time when the (p-r+1) slave fails and the expected time of the first failure M_1:

$$M = \Sigma\ (1/\lambda i),\ i\Sigma = p-r,\dots,p;\quad M = 1/\lambda \tag{65}$$

or are used to define the normalized M namely:

$$m = M/M_1 = \Sigma(p/i);\ i\Sigma = p-r,\dots,p \tag{66}$$

Fig. 8 shows that the more failed slaves (r) accepted, the higher will be m. Thus, if some degradation is accepted (and p must be larger for this) the reliability can be increased significantly without additional redundancy or loss of performance.

The MTBF of SMS may be expressed by

$$M = 1/\Sigma C_i\lambda_i;\ i\Sigma = 1,\dots,n \tag{67}$$

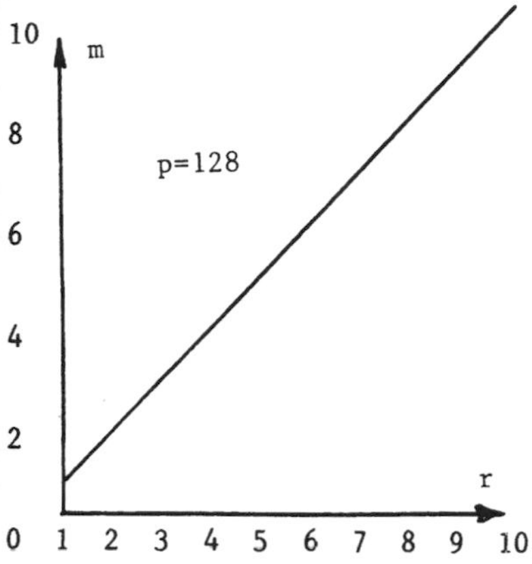

p=normalized performance in case 1. of degradation .96 .92π

Fig. 8: Mean Time Between Failures

where λ_i is the failure rate of component i, C_i is the quantity of each component, n is the total number of the components.

The Table below lists components utilized in the SMS-201 boards including the required quantity of each component. Also listed are the failure rates based on published data. Using these figures, M of a single slave and driver is respectively: M_S=65,000h and M_D=270,000h. As for the entire system, it should be viewed as a serial connection of the master, drivers and the slave. Thus,

$$1/M=1/M_m+1/M_d+1/M_s \quad (68)$$

Since there are 8 drivers and 128 slaves:

$$1/M=1/M_m+8/M_d+1/(M_s\Sigma(1/i)); \; i\Sigma=128-r,\ldots,128 \quad (69)$$

In SMS-201 the master is a single, comparatively large computer. Whether $1/M_m$ should be assumed to be zero is therefore questionable. In ASP, as defined in this book, the master is identical to a slave and only p should be increased. The bus drivers are also simpler, so that no bus blocking failures should be accounted for.

Components	Failure Rate (10^{-6} hrs^{-1})	Device Quantity: Computer Module	Device Quantity: Driver Module
8080 CPU and Support IC's	0.2	13	4
4K dyn. RAM's	0.2	32	-
Other IC's (TTL)	0.1	64	29
Total Failure Rate (10^{-6} hrs^{-1})		15.4	3.7
M (hours)		65.000	270.000

It is therefore of interest to quote verbatim the practical results obtained for SMS-201: "The SMS-201 has been working now for more than two years. After setting up the system the failure rate decreased continuously until it became constant at the end of 1978.

For 1979 all observed failures are listed in Fig. 9. Without repair the number of modules would have decreased from 128 to 116. This corresponds to a MTBF of about 730 hrs. The loss of performance would have amounted to about 9% by the end of 1979.

In reality, we replaced the failing modules. Total system failures caused by failed driver modules or bus blocking did not occur during 1979.

The failure rates discussed above are based on hard errors. The failure rate based on soft errors is about ten times higher and ranges from two to three errors per week. Most of the soft errors occur in the module memories. By using error correction codes, hard and soft errors in the memories can be corrected.

By tolerating a few failing modules, the time intervals between necessary services can be extended without an essential loss of computational power. If the module failure occurs, we reload the program and start computation again. The re-arrangement is done automatically."

The authors concluded that "The aim was to show that large arrays of microcomputers offer high reliability if degradation is acceptable. In the considered system of 128 microcomputers the MTBF of a module array increases from 500 hrs. to about 4000 hrs. if a loss of performance up to 8% is tolerable. The time intervals between two necessary services can be extended. Service costs can be cut."

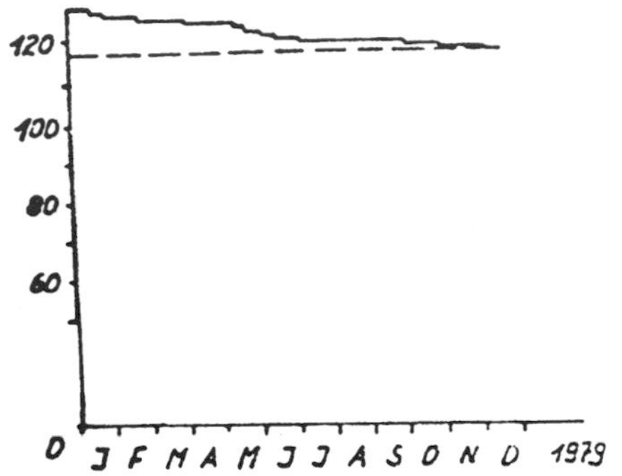

Fig. 9: Number of Operational Units

The most important issue remaining to solve is that of the self-testing program. It was not yet written so only the general principles of how to apply it will be discussed.

On the face of it, the failure of the master incapacitates the entire system and thus defeats the main purpose of using a pps, namely, its higher availability. We intend to deal with it by making the system work in two "states": the production and the self-testing state.

During the production period, with its sequential and parallel steps, the cyclic work is done under the complete and exclusive control of the master. A test-program resides permanently [Rw 81] in all memories as well as in the main and secondary memories. At specified intervals τ a timer initiates a self-testing period i.e., execution of the test program. During the test, the master becomes dependent, with each of the slaves numbered 1 to p being the master for a short testing time. If we consider the p slaves threaded in a circular chain, then <u>first</u> slave 1 checks the master, slave p and 2, <u>then</u> slave 2 checks the master, slaves 1 and 3 and so on. After p test-steps, the system has been redundantly checked and the master regains control. There are two possible failure cases:

(a) The failure of a slave is recognized by three indications: Its "left" and "right" neighbors point to it and the testing slave, when it was itself a master, had to be terminated by the clock. The faulty slave must be removed and since the number of slaves decreases by 1, data must be re-formed.

(b) The failure of the master will be recognized p times (as each of the slaves consecutively checks the master). For a completely symmetrical system, the master will be replaced by one of the slaves and both the system programs reloaded and data transformed.

Note also that:

(a) The test program is run by a slave because the master is more vulnerable and because there are p slaves but only one master. This test-strategy may be called "p out of p+1."

(b) Availability should not be confused with reliability. For reliability of some telephone systems, hardware is duplicated, so that a cpu may be replaced without degrading service. In our scheme, service will decline at faults but the cost is not doubled. It is an open question whether to triplicate the master.

The conclusions are:

- The reliability/availability of ASP-systems will be much higher than those of single computers and even those of other parallel systems.
- For the testing and recovery modes to function properly, the test program must yet be written. Following this, results could supply the numerical data needed for final evaluation of how much more reliable ASP really is.
- The testing procedure will be more effective on a symmetric ASP than on an unsymmetric SMS-201.

4.4 NOTES ON OPERATING SYSTEM SUPPORT

Aims: To prove that the master can handle, if need be, the entire I/O of the system. To provide guidelines for the writing of an interrupt system and for memory organization. For all this, the assumption is made that ASP works within a utility company on electric power control.

The programs EDIP, STEP and CAP are similar in that they rely on the Newton-Raphson method of solution which will "factorize" the system matrix once and reuse it for a number of "back-substitutions." We may assess the required time roughly as follows:

The most efficient algorithm for the first part of all above programs is Poof (see Chapter 6). It will eliminate about half the matrix in say c "steps" each one using

$$t_1' = 2m^2\omega/(pk)\ \mu sec \qquad (70)$$

where m is the size of the matrix, k accounts for sparsity. Thus

$$t_1' = 2c\cdot\omega m^2/(pk)\ \mu sec \qquad (71)$$

are needed to eliminate half of the matrix. The remaining, dense matrix is best solved by "block-elimination" which requires about

$$t_1'' = m^2\omega/(10p)\ \mu sec \qquad (72)$$

For each factorization approximately c "back-substitutions" are needed to complete a solution. Each of them requires:

$$t_1''' = m\omega/(kp)\ \mu sec \qquad (73)$$

and for large m with $m^2 >> m$, this time may be neglected if compared to t_1' and t_1''.

A network has n nodes (buses) and each bus is connected on the average to about two lines, so that the number of lines is 2n. We measure active and reactive power on both ends of each line for STEP (m=8n) and both value and angle of voltage for EDIP and CAP (m=2n) programs.

For simplicity let us assume that we need c solutions for EDIP and STEP to converge and a single solution for each of the c cases of contingency to be checked.

$$t_1 \cong c\omega(n^2/p)[(64+4+4)(1/16 + 10/k)] = 72c(1/16 + 10/k)(n^2/p)\omega \qquad (74)$$

It was found that for networks with n=1000, factor $k \cong 100$ and $c = 5$. Thus the total time would be:

$$t_1 \cong 54n^2\omega/p \qquad (75)$$

For 1000 buses, this would be about $40\omega/p$ minutes. Factor k for small and/or dense systems is much lower than 100 so that the time is higher than that of (75).

Let us now compute the time required by the remaining programs if done by the (single) master.

The number of measurements is 8n (for all lines) and 2n (for all nodes). Assuming χ µsec for a single comparison and that each value is checked against a minimum and maximum point, the required time is

$$t_2' = 10n\cdot\chi \text{ µsec} \qquad (76)$$

The output will use "smart" terminals which normally include 64 Kbytes memory, work at about 9600 baud, have raster scan and good color quality. They will not use more time than t_2'. Additionally, MAD would have to sort the data to be displayed, but this time is inversely proportional to p. Thus, if p displays are assumed, t_2' will also be needed for output. Total time:

$$t_2 \cong 20\chi n \qquad (77)$$

The ratio of times required for other programs to that of limit testing is

$$t_1/t_2 = 2.7(n/p)(\omega/\chi) \qquad (78)$$

Since $\omega > \chi$ and $n >> p$, we arrive at the conclusion that the master will need much less time for completing time-checking and displays than the slaves need for STEP, EDIP and CAP. The master may thus be used for processing interrupts.

We may generalize by saying that t_1 will always be directly proportional to the system size (here n) and inversely proportional to the number of slaves and that the master can be employed during a part of the work cycle.

Let us assume c=5, k=100, ω=1500 and n=1000. Then t_1 = 10/p minutes. If a cycle is to be completed once every minute (this was once required in the United Kingdom), then $p \cong 10$ slaves would be sufficient.

Let us next discuss the interrupts. We may differentiate between internal and external, predictable and unpredictable interrupts. They are summarized in Table 2 which also lists a Greek name, the time of interrupt handling and a priority (with 1 being the highest priority).

The P-steps are so short that we must classify their interrupts π as predictable. With a small variance, they "clock" the cyclic work-load according to the times computed earlier and according to the relevant data. The time of the test interrupt (τ) must be fixed beforehand; the timing of π depends on data which is not constant. Therefore synchronization between π and τ is impossible. Still τ is completely predictable.

We may combine τ with a timer for yet another purpose. The hardware is such that the master is activated only after all slaves finished their P-tasks. Should a hardware failure prevent one of the slaves from issuing its interrupt, no π will appear. τ may then act as a "timer-interrupt" telling the master to take over. We next discuss some of the unpredictable interrupts.

If the dispatcher is dissatisfied with any of the results on the display, he will interrupt the system (δ) and activate one of the query programs. At quiet moments he could also initiate some common functions such as collection of data related to energy exchange with neighboring companies, billings, logs, etc. We should not forget that if an unexpected event occurred in the network, say a thunderstorm, short-circuit etc. then we should not rely completely on the dispatcher. In this case, as well as in the case of a hardware failure, an interrupt (α) should activate both a message on the display and some preventive action by the system.

We may set up a timing diagram for the predictable interrupts ρ and τ but only a probability distribution as far as the unpredictable interrupts δ are concerned. As shown earlier, the first part may be computed for given network size n and given p. The second part can only be assumed on the basis of experience. From talking to industry representatives we gathered that no statistical data actually exists, but that interrupts due to network changes occur "about every half-hour" and "serious trouble, once every few weeks." If this information is taken as an "order of magnitude," the conclusion is drawn that the master can be made responsible for serious network faults and requests by the dispatcher.

The next question is what to do with network-data in the case of an interrupt. Quite clearly, on occurrence of π-interrupts (or signals), data should be retained; it is the normal workload. If any of the other interrupts e.g., α, δ or τ occur, network data can be overwritten. The reason is that until the end of handling the interrupt, the network probably changed, so the results we might get would be based on false data. Moreover, if an external interrupt (α,τ,δ) arrives while the master does I/O, it should stop due to the same consideration.

Table 2: Interrupts

Name	The type of interrupt	Class	Priority	Time
Φ_m	Hardware failure in the master	Internal	1	Varying
Φ_s	Hardware failure in a slave	Internal	2	Varying
δ	Request by the dispatcher	External	3	Long
α	Changes in the electrical network	External	4	Long
τ	Start of the test-procedure	External	5	Very Short
ϕ_m	Program fault, in the master	Internal	6	Long
σ_s	Program fault, in the slave	Internal	7	Short
π	End of parallel, P-step	Internal	8	Very Short

Memory Organization

The system has three levels of memory: the local memories of the slaves, the main memory of the master and a common back-up store. This back-up store contains the entire system i.e., all loadable programs for both the master and the slaves, the self-testing software and the necessary data-files. The local stores are loaded (under control of the master) with the necessary program-partitions for the corresponding P-steps. The main memory of the master holds the root segment of the system with the control program for the periodically changing S- and P-steps.

We intend to support a dedicated system for which the size and behavior of all programs are a priori known and the dimensions of the required data files are predictable. It is therefore natural to suggest a static memory organization. As already mentioned, occasionally the data in both local and main memory have to be repartitioned, but as this depends uniquely on the current state of the program, its behavior is not at all erratic. Thus, storage allocation strategies may be completely fixed and don't need to react to sudden memory constraints.

In order to keep the system completely symmetric and to avoid overloading the master, a "memory processor" (identical to all slaves) may be provided at the interface of the bus and the back-up store (see Fig. 10). Its tasks would be those of managing the back-up store and dealing with I/O and display. A request for any data from the back-up store will be directed by the master to the memory processor which then relieves the master of further direct involvement. At the same time, centralized control as exercised by the master avoids possible conflicts. The master remains responsible for ASP-processing alone.

System operation as discussed in the last section is enhanced by a "status indicator" stored in each of the local, as well as in the main memory. Its bits could indicate:

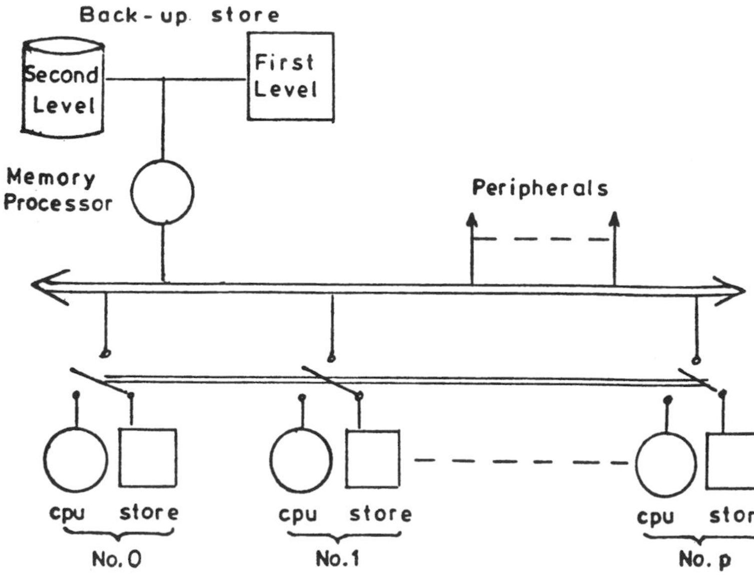

Fig. 10: Another scheme of an ASP-system

Bit 0: 1 if the cpu is a master; 0 if the cpu is a slave

Bit 1: 1 if the system processes the normal workload;
0 if the system processes the self-testing procedure

Bit 2: 1 during the time of an S-step; 0 during the time of a P-step

Bit 3: 1 if active (busy); 0 if idle (waiting or inactive)

Numbering the possible sixteen states as binary numbers of 4 bits, we get the following table in which each cpu is identified as to its role (master or slave), the period (workload or self-test) and whether it is active or not.

The status indicator is part of "resident data" of each of the fast memories. Additionally, each resident part holds:

- The startup address, which holds the location counter after the initial startup
- A small configuration table which defines the number of the current master, the number of the cpu and its left and right neighbors
- An interrupt-indicator field
- A table of free and occupied memory blocks.

Since memories are occupied and recovered, this must be recorded in memory tables as "used" and "free" areas. The same applies to data of the electric network, the com-

Table 3: State Identification

State	Role	Period	Active or Not
0,2	Slave	Test-time	Inactive
1,3	Slave	Test-time	Active
4	Slave	Workload	Inactive (P-step)
5	Slave	Workload	Active (P-step)
6	Slave	Workload	Inactive (S-step)
8-11	Master	Test-time	
12	Master	Workload	Idle (P-step)
14	Master	Workload	Idle (S-step)
15	Master	Workload	Busy (S-step)

and both 7 and 13 are invalid states

piler and some system programs which occupy their areas permanently and some buffers, etc. which are intermittently used and set free. We thus need memory tables which will indicate the status of each block of our statically managed memories.

Conclusions: Some basic principles of an operating system for an "alternating sequential/parallel" ASP-system were defined and it was shown that the load on the master is not too high. The cyclic workload requires a time proportional to the problem size n and inversely proportional to the number of slaves. System control is relatively easy because of the central position of the master. Interrupts can be processed fast; memory management does not require much storage or time. The overall conclusion is that changing from an off-line operating system (as used in SMS) to an on-line operating system should lead to simplification rather than the other way around.

5. ON DIRECT SOLUTION OF A x = b

Introduction

Chapters 5 to 8 deal with the solution of sets of linear equations

$$\underline{A}\ \underline{x} = \underline{b} \tag{1}$$

where $\underline{A}$ is an nxn non-singular matrix, $\underline{b}$ is the nx1 "free" vector and $\underline{x}$, the nx1 vector of unknowns. In the present chapter, known, sequential methods of solving (1) are reviewed. Since these methods are very well described in the literature, the reader is advised to read, say [SB] or [YG] especially for the topics of stability, pivoting or scaling. It is assumed below that this was done and these topics will not be elaborated upon.

Section 1 deals with elimination and in particular shows how the use of Frobenius matrices leads to the LR-decomposition. The number of operations Ω for the Gauss, Jordan and the factorization methods are calculated and the mechanics of the algorithms are described. They will be needed in later chapters.

Elimination and LR-factorization are not the only methods to solve (1). Orthogonalization methods play an increasing role and are therefore covered slightly more in detail in Section 2, the more so since we will need some of the results later on. Additionally, both the Sherman-Morrison and the Kron algorithms are derived by inverting the "elementary" matrix $\underline{U}-\underline{w}\underline{v}^T$.

It is shown in Section 3 that operations on complex sets may be done more efficiently by defining 2x2 matrices of certain types ("quads").

This chapter is a preparation for Chapter 6 in which the methods above will be parallelized. Since this will amount to only rescheduling the algorithms, but does not change them otherwise, the reader is again referred to [SB] for additional reading.

5.1 ELIMINATION

Aims: To review elimination, in particular the methods of Gauss, Jordan, Cholesky and various factorization techniques. To introduce scheduling in which every row in turn is completely transformed. To present elimination as operating on both columns and rows. To introduce Frobenius matrices and show that they form $\underline{L}$ in $\underline{A} = \underline{L}\ \underline{R}$. To calculate the operations count Ω for all methods.

In the linear set $\underline{A}\ \underline{x} = \underline{b}$ only vector $\underline{x}$ is not known. The known $\underline{A}$ and $\underline{b}$ may be combined into an "extended matrix" (2) of dimension nx(n+1) which includes all the known information of (1).

$$[\underline{A},\underline{b}] = \begin{bmatrix} a_{11} & a_{12} & a_{1n} & b_1 \\ a_{21} & a_{22} & a_{2n} & b_2 \\ a_{n1} & a_{n2} & a_{nn} & b_n \end{bmatrix} = \underline{A}^{(0)} \tag{2}$$

It can therefore be operated upon similarly to the equations i.e. two rows (equations) may be interchanged and a multiple of any row i may be added to any row j.

This is precisely what is done in the elimination algorithm named after Gauss.

Its first step would be as follows:

(a) Determine $a_{r1}^{(0)} \neq 0$ in the first column. If no such element exists, then $\underline{A}$ is singular and the procedure is terminated with $\underline{A}^{(0)}$ being the "result",

(b) Interchange rows 1 and r of $\underline{A}^{(0)}$ (we assume for the moment that r=1 so that no interchange is required)

(c) Subtract $f_{i,1} \, \underline{a}_{1,.}$ from rows i=2,...,n where

$$f_{i,1} = a_{i1}^{(0)}/a_{11}^{(0)} \tag{3}$$

and $\underline{a}_{i\cdot}$ is the i-th row (vector) of a matrix $\underline{A}$. This step may thus be summarized as

$$\underline{a}_{i\cdot}^{(1)} = \underline{a}_{i\cdot}^{(0)} - f_{i,1}\,\underline{a}_{1,\cdot}^{(0)}; \quad i=2,\ldots,n \tag{4}$$

Since for all i, i$\neq$1, the element in the first column is made zero:

$$a_{i,1}^{(1)} = a_{i,1}^{(0)} - a_{i,1}^{(0)} \cdot a_{1,1}^{(0)}/a_{1,1}^{(0)} = 0 \tag{5}$$

matrix $\underline{A}^{(1)}$ has the form (6)

Determination of r in (a) is called pivoting. In theory, one could choose $a_{ri} \neq 0$ for any r and i. If it is chosen as the element of maximum value, the process is called "complete" pivoting. Normally, the search is restricted to the operative

$$\underline{A}^{(1)} = \begin{bmatrix} a_{11}^{(0)} & a_{12}^{(0)} & - - - & a_{1n}^{(0)} & b_1^{(0)} \\ 0 & a_{22}^{(1)} & - - - & a_{2n}^{(1)} & b_2^{(1)} \\ & & \diagdown & & \\ 0 & a_{n2}^{(1)} & - - - & a_{nn}^{(1)} & b_n^{(1)} \end{bmatrix} \tag{6}$$

column and the pivoting is referred to as partial pivoting. In complete pivoting, points (a)(b) above are replaced by (a'), (b') in the following way:

(a'): Determine r,s so that r

$$|a_{rs}| = \max|a_{ij}| \tag{7}$$

and continue if $a_{rs} \neq 0$. Otherwise $\underline{A}$ is singular.

(b') Interchange rows 1 and r of $\underline{A}^{(0)}$ as well as columns 1 and s. It is assumed that following the pivoting, all elements of the row are "scaled" i.e. divided by the largest element.

The same algorithm may next be applied to the (n-1) x n matrix which remains if the first row and column of $\underline{A}^{(1)}$ in (6) are removed. Since multiples of the zero in position r,2 are subtracted from the zeros in $a_{r,1}^{(1)}$; r = 3,4,...,n, these zeros are not modified and more.

Applying the algorithm j times results in the matrix $(\underline{A})^{(j)}$ of (8). Note that zeros were introduced into columns 1 to j below the diagonal. As noted, these zeros will not change during the succeeding steps of

$$\underline{A}^{(j)} = \begin{bmatrix} x & x & & x\ x\ x\ x & & x \\ 0 & \diagdown & & x & \\ 0 & & \diagdown\ x & & \\ 0 & & 0\diagdown & x & \\ 0 & & 0\ x\ x\diagdown & & x \\ 0 & & 0\ x\ x & \diagdown & x \\ 0 & & 0\ x\ x & & \diagdown\ x \end{bmatrix} \tag{8}$$

the algorithm. If (9) is taken as an example, (10, 11, 12) results for j=2,3,4.

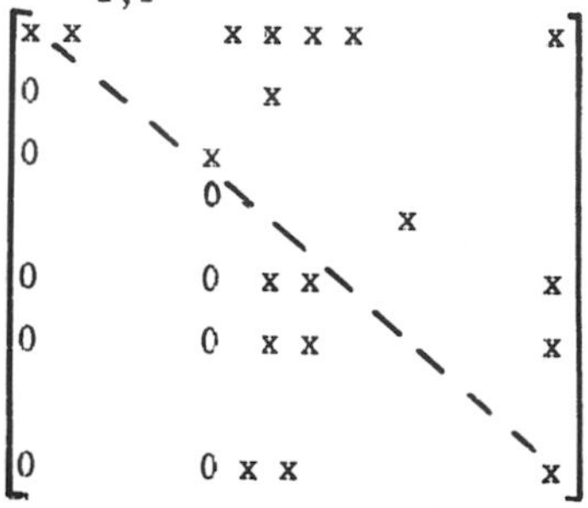

$$\begin{bmatrix} 2 & 1 & 3 & 1 & 13 \\ 1 & 1 & 2 & 1 & 10 \\ 3 & 2 & 4 & -1 & 12 \\ 1 & 4 & -1 & -2 & 1 \end{bmatrix} \begin{bmatrix} 2 & 1 & 3 & 1 & 13 \\ 0 & .5 & .5 & .5 & 3.5 \\ 0 & .5 & -.5 & -2.5 & -2.5 \\ 0 & 3.5 & -2.5 & -2.5 & -5.5 \end{bmatrix} \begin{bmatrix} 2 & 1 & 3 & 1 & 13 \\ 0 & .5 & .5 & .5 & 3.5 \\ 0 & 0 & -1 & -3 & -11 \\ 0 & 0 & -6 & -6 & -30 \end{bmatrix} \begin{bmatrix} 2 & 1 & 3 & 1 & 13 \\ 0 & .5 & .5 & .5 & 3.5 \\ 0 & 0 & -1 & -3 & -11 \\ 0 & 0 & 0 & 12 & 36 \end{bmatrix}$$

Take any element $a_{r,s}$ for which $r>s$, i.e. an element which will ultimately be made zero. It is changed during the first step (4) into

$$a^{(1)}_{rs} := a^{(0)}_{r,s} - f_{r,1} \cdot a^{(0)}_{1,s} \qquad (13)$$

during the second step into

$$a^{(2)}_{r,s} := a^{(1)}_{r,s} - f_{r,2} \cdot a^{(1)}_{2,s} = a^{(0)}_{r,s} - f_{r,1} \cdot a^{(0)}_{1,s} - f_{r,2} \cdot a^{(1)}_{2,s} \qquad (14)$$

and so on. It can be seen that the scheduling of the algorithm could also have been made differently, namely:

(a) Change row two according to

$$a^{(1)}_{2,\cdot} := a^{(0)}_{2,\cdot} - f_{2,1} \cdot a^{(0)}_{1,1} \quad . \qquad (15)$$

(b) Change row three according to

$$\underline{a}^{(1)} := \underline{a}^{(0)} - f_{3,1} \cdot \underline{a}^{(0)} \; ; \quad \underline{a}^{(2)} := \underline{a}^{(1)} - f_{3,2} \cdot \underline{a}^{(1)} \qquad (16)$$

and so on. In row j, there will be (j-1) tranformations as above. This scheduling is basic to some "factorization" algorithms to be discussed in 6.3.

No matter which scheduling is used, $\underline{A}\ \underline{x} = \underline{b}$ is finally transformed into

$$\underline{R}\ \underline{x} = \underline{c} \qquad (17)$$

where $\underline{R}$ is an upper-triangular matrix (see (12)), i.e.,

$$\begin{bmatrix} r_{11} & r_{12} & & r_{1,n} \\ 0 & r_{22} & & r_{2,n} \\ & 0 & \ddots & \\ 0 & & 0 & r_{n,n} \end{bmatrix} \begin{bmatrix} x_1 \\ x_2 \\ \\ x_n \end{bmatrix} = \begin{bmatrix} c_1 \\ c_2 \\ \\ c_n \end{bmatrix} \qquad (18)$$

(Permutations of rows, and therefore of $\underline{x}$, are again disregarded). The unknowns may be calculated from (18) as follows:

$$x_n = c_n / r_{n,n} \; ; \; x_{n-1} = (c_{n-1} - r_{n-1,n}\, x_n)/r_{n-1,n-1} \qquad (19)(20)$$

and so on for $x_{n-2}, x_{n-3}, \ldots , x_3, x_2, x_1$. In our specific case, we consecutively get from (19,20) the values:

$$x_4 = 3,\ x_3 = 2,\ x_2 = 2 \text{ and } x_1 = 1 \qquad (21)$$

Because the sequence is n,n-1,...,1 the process of solving (18) for $\underline{x}$ is called "back-substitution". It can be summarized by:

$$x_i = (c_i - \Sigma\, r_{ij}\, x_j)/r_{i,i}; \; j\Sigma{=}i+1,\ldots,n; \; i = n,n-1,\ldots,1 \qquad (22)$$

with the assumption that no $r_{i,i} = 0$ and with the sum being zero for $j > n$.

The Gauss method, as described above, may be changed so that not only elements below, but also above the diagonal are eliminated. Thus the general equation is not

$$a_{i,k} := a_{i,k} - a_{i,j} \cdot a_{j,k}/a_{j,j}; \; k,i = j + 1,\ldots,n \qquad (23)$$

with j being the pivot, but

$$a_{i,k} := a_{i,k} - a_{i,j} a_{j,k}/a_{j,j}; \; i,k \neq j \qquad (24)$$

Allowing for the necessary pivoting, the result will be:

$\underline{D}\ \underline{x} = \underline{c}$ (25)

instead of $\underline{R}\ \underline{x} = \underline{c}$. $\underline{D}$ is diagonal, so that no back-substitution is necessary; the unknown elements of $\underline{x}$ are determined in any order from:

$x_i = c_i/d_{ii};\ 1 \leqq i \leqq n$ (26)

This method is named after Jordan (in the sequel, the elimination methods of Gauss and of Jordan will be named the G- and the J-method respectively).

Pivoting continues to be disregarded (making $\underline{P} = \underline{U}$) since its application is covered adequately in literature, especially in [SB] and [YG]. The same applies to questions of scaling (equivalencing), accuracy, stability, etc. and to various special methods (Crout, Banachiewicz or Doolittle). They will, however, be mentioned in Chapter 6 whenever needed.

The number of operations Ω_G, Ω_J for the G and J-methods are computed next. For the sake of being able to deal also with the inverse of $\underline{A}$, assume that k free vectors $\underline{b}$, or an n x k matrix $\underline{B}$ is on the right of $A^{(0)}$. For the G-method, we first take the forward elimination $(\underline{A}^{(0)} \rightarrow \underline{R})$, assuming that no pivoting is necessary. The transformation from j to j-1 equations, with k right sides involves:

(a) Calculation of 1/pivot, i.e. $1 \cdot \mu$ (division counts as multiplication)

(b) Formation of the f-multipliers requires $(j-1)\mu$

(c) Each of the $(j-1)^2$ remaining and $k(j-1)$ free elements must be operated upon.

Since j takes all values from 1 to n, steps (a)(b)(c) yield the count:

$\Omega = n\mu + \Sigma\ [(j-1)\mu + (j-1)^2\omega + k(j-1)\omega];\ j\Sigma=1,\dots,n$ (27)

The two sums which appear in (27) may be simplified by:

$\Sigma j = 0.5n(n+1);\ \Sigma j^2 = n(n+1)(2n+1)/6;\ j\Sigma=1,\dots,n$ (28)

With these, (27) reduces to

$6{*}\Omega = n\{2n^2 + 3k(n-1)\}\omega - 3n^2\alpha - n(2\mu-\alpha)$ (29)

For the solution of a single set (k=1), this reduces to:

$6{*}\Omega = n(2n^2 + 3n - 3)\omega - 3n^2\alpha - n(2\mu-\alpha)$ (30)

In back-substitution we need for each k: $1\mu, 2\omega, \dots, n\omega$. Thus

$\Omega_b = k(1+2+\dots+n)\omega - k\alpha = 0.5kn(n+1)\omega - k\alpha$ (31)

Adding (29) and (31) yields the operation count for Gaussian elimination:

$\Omega_G = n(n^2/3 + kn + 2/3)\mu + n(n^2/3 - n/2 + k(n-1) + 1/6)\alpha$ (32)

For k=1, this reduces to

$\Omega_G = n(n^2/3 + n + 2/3)\mu + n(n^2/3 + n/2 - 5/6)\alpha$ (33)

Normally n is large, $n^3 \gg n^2 > n$ (34)

so that $\Omega_G \simeq n^3\ \omega/3;\ \omega = \mu + \alpha$ (35)

In the J-method, each pivot row is applied to (n-1) rows, so that repeating and counting as above yields:

$\Omega_J = \{n(n^2+1)/2 + kn\}\mu + \{n(n-1)/2 + kn\}\alpha$ (36)

For k=1 this reduces to

$\Omega_J = (n^3/2 + n^2 + n/2)\mu + (n^3-n)\alpha/2$ (37)

For large n: $\Omega_J \cong n^3\omega/2$ (38)

Elimination by Gauss is only 2/3 as "expensive" as that of Jordan. When k=n and the initial matrix on the right is $\underline{U}$ (for inversion), we do not have to multiply by 0's or 1's (in known positions). In Jordan's method $\underline{U}$ is transformed directly into $\underline{A}^{-1}$ whereas in the algorithm by Gauss, n back-substitutions are additionally required. We thus get in both cases

$$\Omega_{INV} = (n^3 + n-1)\mu + (n^3 - 2n^2 + n)\alpha \tag{39}$$

For large n, this may be approximated by

$$\Omega_{INV} \cong n^3\omega \tag{40}$$

Matrix $\underline{A}^{(1)}$ of (6) can be calculated by multiplication

$$\underline{A}^{(1)} = \underline{F}_1{}^{(1)} \cdot \underline{A}^{(0)} \tag{41}$$

where $\underline{F}_1$ the Frobenius matrix (of column 1) is

$$\underline{F}_1 = \begin{bmatrix} 1 & & & \\ -f_{2,1} & 1 & & \\ -f_{3,1} & & 1 & \\ \vdots & & & \ddots \\ -f_{n,1} & & & & 1 \end{bmatrix} \quad ; \quad \underline{F}_1 \begin{bmatrix} 1 & 0 & 0 & 0 \\ -.5 & 1 & 0 & 0 \\ -.5 & 0 & 1 & 0 \\ -.5 & 0 & 0 & 1 \end{bmatrix} \tag{42}$$

i.e. is a unit matrix except of its first column, which is

$$\underline{f}_{\cdot 1} = -[-1, f_{2,1}, f_{3,1}, \ldots, f_{n,1}]^T \tag{43}$$

Frobenius matrices are nonsingular. As a matter of fact, $\underline{F}_1$ may be inverted by simply changing all signs for $f_{i,1}$ i.e. using

$$\underline{f}_{\cdot 1} = [1, f_{2,1}, f_{3,1}, \ldots, f_{n,1}]^T \tag{44}$$

For i > 1, $\underline{f}_{\cdot i} = -[0,\ldots,0,-1,\ f_{i+1,i},\ f_{i+2,i},\ldots,f_{n,i}]^T$ (45)

and if the -1 is changed into a zero, we denote it by $\underline{f}'_{.i}$.

In the J-method, the zero's above the diagonal disappear

$$\underline{f}_{\cdot i} = -[f_{1,i},\ldots,\ f_{i-1,i}, -1, f_{i+1,i},\ldots,f_{n,i}]^T \tag{46}$$

Note first that Frobenius matrices can be written as:

$$\underline{F}_i = \underline{U} - \underline{f}'_{.i}\ u^T_{\cdot i} \tag{47}$$

since the unit matrix $\underline{U}$ contributes the 1's and $\underline{f}'_{.i}\ \underline{u}_{i.}$ the i-th column of $\underline{F}_i$. Next calculate column j of matrix $\underline{A}^{(i+1)}$ through:

$$\underline{F}_i\ \underline{a}_{\cdot j} = (\underline{U} - \underline{f}'_{\cdot i}\underline{u}^T_{\cdot i})\underline{a}_{\cdot j} = \underline{a}_{\cdot j} - \underline{f}'_{\cdot i}(\underline{u}_{\cdot i}\underline{a}_{\cdot j}) = \underline{a}_{\cdot j} - a_{ij}\underline{f}'_{\cdot j} \tag{48}$$

This shows that elimination can also be interpreted as follows:

At each stage i, column j of the remaining matrix $\underline{A}^{(i+1)}$ is obtained by subtracting certain multiples of $a_{\cdot j}$ (namely a_{ij}/a_{ii}) from the columns of $\underline{A}^{(i)}$. This leads us to view elimination as operating on columns of $\underline{A}$, instead of on rows.

If instead of the method by Jordan, we revert to that of Gauss:

$$\underline{f}_{\cdot i} = [0,\ldots,0,\ f_{i+1,i}\ldots f_{n,i}]^T \tag{49}$$

Taking $f_{ij} = a_{ik}/a_{jk}$ means that multiplication by $\underline{F}_i$ annihilates elements (j+1,k), (j+2,k),...,(n,k) in row i. Since product (50) is zero, we have for (51):

$$\underline{f}_{\cdot i}\underline{u}_{\cdot i} \cdot \underline{f}_{\cdot j} \cdot \underline{u}_{\cdot j} = 0 \quad (j \neq i) \tag{50}$$

$$\underline{F}_i\ \underline{F}_j = (\underline{U} - \underline{f}_{.i}\ \underline{u}_i)\ (\underline{U} - \underline{f}_{.j}\ \underline{u}^T_{j.}) = \underline{U} - \underline{f}_{.i}\ \underline{u}_{i.} - \underline{f}_{.j}\underline{u}_{j.}\ ;\ (j > 1) \tag{51}$$

On the other hand, the inverse of $\underline{F}_i$ is:

$$\underline{F}_i^{-1} = \underline{U} + f'_{\cdot i}\underline{u}^T_{\cdot i} \qquad (52)$$

Since every step of the G-method is equivalent to a premultiplication by a suitable $\underline{F}_i$, the triangular matrix $\underline{M}$ is

$$\underline{M} = (\underline{F}_{n-1} \cdot \underline{F}_{n-2} \cdot \ldots \cdot \underline{F}_2 \cdot \underline{F}_1) \cdot \underline{A} \qquad (53)$$

The product (51) shows that the $\underline{L}'$ is a lower triangular (left) matrix, e.g.:

$$\underline{L}' = - \begin{bmatrix} -1 & & & & \\ f_{2,1} & & & & \\ f_{3,1} & f_{3,2} & -1 & & \\ & & & & \\ f_{n,1} & f_{n,2} & & f_{n,n-1} & -1 \end{bmatrix} \qquad \underline{L}' = \begin{bmatrix} 1 & 0 & 0 & 0 \\ -0.5 & 1 & 0 & 0 \\ -1 & -1 & 1 & 0 \\ 9 & -1 & -6 & 1 \end{bmatrix} \qquad (54)$$

Since $\underline{L}'$ and $(\underline{L}')^{-1} = \underline{L}$ are lower triangular matrices multiplication by Frobenius matrices yields:

$$\underline{R} = \underline{L}' \cdot \underline{A} \quad ; \quad \underline{A} = \underline{L} \cdot \underline{R} \qquad (55)\ (56)$$

i.e. decomposes $\underline{A}$ into a product of a left ($\underline{L}$) and right ($\underline{R}$) triangular matrices.

For symmetric matrices $\underline{A}$, this decomposition can also be written as:

$$\underline{A} = \underline{L}\ \underline{D}\ \underline{L}^T \qquad (57)$$

where $\underline{D}$ is a diagonal and $\underline{L}$ a unit-triangular matrix (has ones on its diagonal). If we change $\underline{L}$ into $\underline{L}\ \underline{D}^{\frac{1}{2}}$ and $\underline{L}^T$ into $\underline{D}^{\frac{1}{2}}\ \underline{L}^T$ we obtain:

$$\underline{A} = \underline{L}\ \underline{L}^T \qquad (58)$$

which is known as the Cholesky decomposition. (For use of Frobenius matrices, see 6.4.1.)

Suppose that the decomposition (56) is known. The solution of $\underline{A}\ \underline{x} = \underline{b}$ proceeds now in two steps. Since

$$\underline{L} \cdot \underline{R} \cdot \underline{x} = \underline{b} \qquad (59)$$

an auxiliary vector $\underline{z}$ is calculated first from

$$\underline{L} \cdot \underline{z} = \underline{b} \qquad (60)$$

and then $\underline{x}$ is computed by the now familiar back-substitution:

$$\underline{R} \cdot \underline{x} = \underline{z} \qquad (61)$$

Calculation of $\underline{z}$ from $\underline{L} \cdot \underline{z} = \underline{b}$ is known as forward-substitution; a name derived from the way it proceeds. Since

$$\underline{L} \cdot \underline{z} = \begin{bmatrix} 1 & & & & \\ f_{21} & 1 & & & \\ f_{31} & f_{32} & 1 & & \\ & & & & \\ f_{n1} & f_{n2} & & f_{n,n-1} & 1 \end{bmatrix} \begin{bmatrix} z_1 \\ z_2 \\ z_3 \\ \\ z_n \end{bmatrix} = \begin{bmatrix} b_1 \\ b_2 \\ b_3 \\ \\ b_n \end{bmatrix} \qquad (62)$$

$$z_1 = b_1 \ ; \quad z_2 = b_2 - f_{2,1} \cdot z_1 \qquad (63)\ (64)$$

and for a general i:

$$z_i = b_i - \sum f_{i,j} \cdot z_j \ ; \ j\Sigma = 1, \ldots, i-1 \qquad (65)$$

the order is $i = 1,2,\ldots,n$ (a "forward" order). (66)

As in elimination, pivoting and scaling will not be added to the computational complexity. For computing the $(j-1)$ elements of column j of $\underline{L}$ we need $j(n-j)\omega + (j-1)(n-j)\alpha$ and for the corresponding row j of $\underline{R}$: $j(n-j)\omega$. Thus for the $\underline{L}\ \underline{R}$ decomposition we need:

$$\Omega = n\mu+\Sigma\ \{2j(n-j)\mu+2j(n-j)\alpha-(n-j)\alpha\}=n^3\omega/3+2n\mu/3+(n/6-n^2/2)\alpha;\ j\Sigma=1,\ldots,n \quad (67)$$

For the forward substitution of $\underline{L}\ \underline{z} = \underline{b}$ the number of operations is

$$(1 + 2 +\ldots+ n - 1)\omega = 0.5n(n-1)\omega \quad (68)$$

and the same for backward substitution. The total operations count is thus

$$\Omega_{LR} = n(n^2/3 + nk + 2n/3)\mu + n\{n^2/3 + k(n-1) - n/2 + 1/6\}\alpha \quad (69)$$

reducing, for k=1 to

$$\Omega_{LR} = n(n^2/3 + n + 2n/3)\mu + n(n^2/3 + n/2 -5/6)\alpha \quad (70)$$

For large n it is the same as in the G-method, namely, $\Omega_{LR} \cong n^3\omega/3$ (71)

In order to save storage space we may proceed as follows. The elements $a_{jk}^{(i+1)}$ overwrite those of $a_{jk}^{(i)}$ for the R-positions of $\underline{A}^{(i+1)}$; the multipliers f_{jk} are stored in place of the eliminated entries, so that when the decomposition is complete, the extended matrix for k=1 is as in (72). We thus need for it n(n+k) locations and additionally nk for the solution vectors.

If we use pivoting, we need the same storage and number of operations. For inverting the matrix $\underline{A}$, more storage may be needed.

$$\begin{bmatrix} r_{11}^{-1} & r_{12} & r_{13} & \cdots & r_{1n} & c_1 \\ f_{21} & r_{22}^{-1} & r_{23} & \cdots & r_{2n} & c_2 \\ f_{31} & f_{32} & r_{33}^{-1} & \cdots & r_{3n} & c_3 \\ \cdot & \cdot & \cdot & \cdots & \cdot & \cdot \\ f_{n1} & f_{n2} & f_{n3} & \cdots & r_{nn}^{-1} & c_n \end{bmatrix} \quad (72)$$

It was shown that both in storage and operations count the LR-decomposition is completely equivalent to the G-method. It has though a number of advantages:

(a) If $\underline{A}$ is "sparse" i.e. a high percentage of its elements is zero, then $\underline{A}^{-1}$ is "dense", but the $\underline{L}$ and $\underline{R}$ matrices, or equivalently the F-elements and $\underline{R}$ are still sparse (but not as sparse as $\underline{A}$ was).

(b) Sometimes we have to solve $\underline{A}\ \underline{x}=\underline{b}$ for k vectors $\underline{b}$ such that

$$\underline{b}_i=\underline{f}(\underline{x}_{i-1}) \quad (73)$$

The G-method cannot be used, since the values of $\underline{b}_i$ are not known. The LR-method of (60)(61) can be used easily.

(c) Equations (3) to (5) can be generalized

$$r_{k,j} := a_{kj} - \Sigma\ f_{k,s} * r_{s,j};\ s\Sigma=1,\ldots,k-1;\ j = k, k+1,\ldots,n \quad (74)$$

$$f_{i,k} := (a_{i,k} - \Sigma\ f_{k,s} * r_{s,k})/r_{kk};\ s\Sigma=1,\ldots,k-1;\ i = k + 1,\ldots,n \quad (75)$$

i.e. schedule the calculation according to: col.1, row 1, col.2, row.2,...etc., accumulate the sums without intermediate results in a (usually) double-length accumulator. The resulting method will have lower roundoff error.

For symmetric, positive-definite matrices, no pivoting is necessary. With

$$\underline{R} = \underline{L}^T \text{ or } r_{j,k} = f_{k,j};\ r_{kk} = f_{kk} \quad (76)\ (77)$$

the equations are:

$f_{kk}:=(a_{kk}-\Sigma f_{ks}^2)^{\frac{1}{2}}; f_{ik}:=(a_{ik}-\Sigma f_{is}\cdot f_{ks})/f_{kk}; s\Sigma=1,\ldots,k-1$ (78) (79)

This is the original method by Cholesky as used for symmetric, positive-definite matrices. The total number of operations for $\underline{A}=\underline{L}\,\underline{L}^T$ is

$\Omega'_{CH}=n\gamma+(n^3/6+n^2/2+n/3)\mu+(n^3/6-n/6)\alpha$ (80)

with γ being the time of extracting a root. In addition $0.5n(n+1)\mu+0.5n(n-1)\alpha$ are required for forward and backward substitution. Thus altogether, the operations count is

$\Omega_{CH}=n\gamma+(n^3/6+1.5n^2+n/3)\mu+(n^3/6+n^2-7n/6)\alpha$ (81)

or $\Omega_{CH}\cong n\gamma+n^3\omega/6$ (82)

We can solve the system without taking square roots. Write:

$\underline{A}=\underline{L}\,\underline{R}=\underline{L}\,\underline{D}\,\underline{D}^{-1}\,\underline{R}=\underline{L}\,\underline{D}\,\underline{R}'$ (83)

Because of the presence of $\underline{D}$, both $\underline{L}$ and $\underline{R}'$ are unit-triangular. Since in this case

$\underline{A}=\underline{A}^T=(\underline{R}')^T\,\underline{D}\,\underline{L}^T=\underline{L}\,\underline{D}\,\underline{R}'$ (84)

it must also be true that

$\underline{L}^T=\underline{R}'=\underline{D}^{-1}\,\underline{R}=\underline{D}^{-\frac{1}{2}}\cdot(\underline{D}^{-\frac{1}{2}}\,\underline{R})$ (85)

If the matrix in parantheses is named $\underline{R}_{new}$ then:

$\underline{R}_{new}^T\cdot\underline{R}_{new}=\underline{R}^T\,(\underline{D}^{-\frac{1}{2}})^T\,\underline{D}^{-\frac{1}{2}}\,\underline{R}\doteq\underline{L}\,\underline{R}\doteq\underline{A}$ (86)

We can therefore solve $\underline{A}\,\underline{x}=\underline{b}$ by the sequence:

$\underline{R}_{new}^T\,\underline{z}=\underline{b}\;;\;\underline{R}_{new}\cdot\underline{x}=\underline{D}\,\underline{z}$ (87) (88)

Only $\underline{L}$ and $\underline{D}$ as well as $\underline{z}$ and $\underline{x}$ are stored ($\cong 0.5n^2+3n$)

Following the factorization $\underline{A}=\underline{L}\,\underline{R}$, the inverse

$\underline{A}^{-1}=\underline{R}^{-1}\,\underline{L}^{-1}$ (89)

may be found by inverting the two triangular matrices and multiplying them (we will return to this topic later). The inverse of $\underline{L}$: $\underline{M}=\underline{L}^{-1}$ (90)

is determined best by considering that

$\underline{L}\,\underline{m}_{.j}=\underline{u}_{.j}$ (91)

where $u_{.j}$ is the j-th column of unit matrix $\underline{U}$. Vector $\underline{m}_{.j}$ is seen to result from a forward substitution and because $u_{ij}=0$ for $i<j$ so will m_{ij}. Thus $\underline{M}$ is lower triangular with:

$m_{ij}=(u_{ij}-\Sigma f_{ik}\,m_{kj})/f_{ii};\; k\Sigma=j,\ldots,i-1;\; i=j,j+1,\ldots,n$ (92)

In exactly the same way, the elements of $\underline{W}=\underline{R}^{-1}$ are:

$w_{ij}:=(u_{ij}-\Sigma r_{ik}w_{kj})/r_{ii};\; k\Sigma=i+1,\ldots,j;\; i=j,j-1,\ldots,1$ (93)

only that here the elements follow a back-substitution

The inverse $\underline{L}^{-1}=\underline{M}$ requires

$\Omega_M=(n^3/6-n^2/2+n/3)\omega\cong n^3\omega/6$ (94)

and the same for Ω_W. The multiplication of two triangular matrices requires $n^3\omega/3$, so that altogether (with $n^3\omega/3$ for factorization), as before:

$\Omega_{INV}\cong(n^3/3+2n^3/6+n^3/3)\omega=n^3\omega$ (95)

<u>Summary</u>: In this section, direct methods were reviewed. In addition to commonly cited results it was shown that there are two main scheduling policies (4) and (16) and that there is a connection between Frobenius matrices and $\underline{L}$ of $\underline{A}=\underline{L}\,\underline{R}$.

5.2 ADDITIONAL DIRECT METHODS

Aims: Elimination and factorization are not the only direct methods for solving $\underline{A}\,\underline{x} = \underline{b}$; orthogonalization is another method. In some cases e.g. "state estimation" it has distinct advantages. For other problems e.g. "load flow" or general, algebraic non-linear sets, the so-called "modification" methods are very useful. General references [SB], [YG] discuss both approaches, but some additional material will be given in this Section. We will also develop a general inversion formula from which we will derive both the Sherman-Morrison [We68] and the Kron [Br 75] algorithms.

Let us start by generalizing (47) so that matrix $\underline{F}$ is

$$\underline{F}(c,\underline{w},\underline{v}) = \underline{U}-c\underline{w}\,\underline{v}^T \tag{96}$$

where c is a (given) scalar and $\underline{w}$, $\underline{v}$ are (real) column vectors.

A fundamental relationship follows if we form the product of two F-matrices:

$$\underline{F}(c,\underline{w},\underline{v})\cdot\underline{F}(d,\underline{w},\underline{u}) = (\underline{U} - c\underline{w}\,\underline{v}^T)(\underline{U}-d\underline{w}\,\underline{v}^T) =$$

$$\underline{U} - c\underline{w}\,\underline{v}^T - d\underline{w}\,\underline{v}^T + cd\underline{w}\,(\underline{v}^T\underline{w})\underline{v}^T = \underline{F}(e,\underline{w},\underline{v}) \tag{97}$$

Since $\underline{v}^T\underline{w}$ is a scalar, it may be factored out. This yields

$$\underline{F}(e,\underline{w},\underline{v}) = \underline{U}-e\underline{w}\,\underline{v}^T = \underline{U}-(c+d-cd\underline{v}^T\underline{w})\underline{w}\,\underline{v}^T \tag{98}$$

For $\underline{F}(e,\underline{w},\underline{v})$ to be a unit matrix, e must be 0 or d such that

$$d = c/(c\underline{v}^T\underline{w}-1) \tag{99}$$

For this particular d, we have

$$\underline{F}(c,\underline{w},\underline{v})\cdot\underline{F}(d,\underline{w},\underline{v}) = \underline{U} \tag{100}$$

or

$$\underline{F}(d,\underline{w},\underline{v}) = \underline{F}(c,\underline{w},\underline{v})^{-1} \tag{101}$$

$$(\underline{U}-c\underline{w}\,\underline{v}^T)^{-1} = \underline{U}-d\underline{w}\,\underline{v}^T \tag{102}$$

This is a fundamental result. First of all, if the definition (96) is relaxed to that of (47), the formation of $\underline{L}$ in (54) can be seen to consist of accumulation of $\underline{f}\cdot\underline{u}$ terms. Therefore, $\underline{L}^{-1}$ can be calculated by repeated application of (102).

Next, the Sherman-Morrison method will be derived from it. Assume, that a single element A_{ij} is changed in matrix $\underline{A}$ by say $-\Delta$. This is represented by $\underline{w}_1, \underline{v}$ s.t. $w_i = 1$, $v_j=\Delta$ and all other elements $w_k = v_k = 0$. The modified matrix $\underline{B}$ is then

$$\underline{B} = \underline{A}-\underline{w}\,\underline{v}^T = \underline{A}(\underline{U}-\underline{A}^{-1}\underline{w}\,\underline{v}^T) = \underline{A}(\underline{U}-\underline{z}\,\underline{v}^T) \tag{103}$$

where

$$\underline{z} = \underline{A}^{-1}\underline{w} \tag{104}$$

Eq. (102) with c = 1 and $\underline{w}$ replaced by $\underline{z}$ and d from (99) yields

$$(\underline{U}-\underline{z}\,\underline{v}^T)^{-1} = \underline{U} - \underline{z}\,\underline{v}^T/(\underline{v}^T\underline{z}-1) \tag{105}$$

$$\underline{B}^{-1} = (\underline{U}-\underline{z}\,\underline{v}^T)^{-1}\cdot\underline{A}^{-1} \tag{106}$$

$$\underline{B}^{-1} = \underline{A}^{-1}-\underline{A}^{-1}\,\underline{w}\,\underline{v}^T\underline{A}^{-1}/(\underline{v}^T\underline{A}^{-1}\underline{w}-1) \tag{107}$$

This is the celebrated Sherman-Morrison formula which yields the inverse of $\underline{A}$ in which a single element was changed.

It often happens that the number of elements changed in $\underline{A}$ is small but higher than 1. For instance, in electrical networks it often happens that a_{pp}, a_{qq} are changed by a Δ and $a_{pq} = a_{qp}$ by $-\Delta$ (the matrix $\underline{A}$ is symmetric). We could apply the

Sherman-Morrison formula four times, but we can also compute $\underline{B}$ by using $\underline{w},\underline{v}$ as zero vectors except for $w_p=1$, $w_q=-1$, $v_p=\Delta$ and $v_q=-\Delta$.

In this case vector $\underline{z}$ is such that

$$z_i = \underline{A}^{-1}_{ip} - \underline{A}^{-1}_{iq} \tag{108}$$

The inverse is then:

$$\underline{B}^{-1} = \underline{A}^{-1} - \underline{z}\,\underline{v}^T\underline{A}^{-1}/(\underline{v}^T\underline{z}-1) \tag{109}$$

$$\underline{v}^T\underline{A}^{-1} = \Delta\cdot\underline{z}^T \; ; \; \underline{v}^T\underline{z} = -\Delta(2A^{-1}_{pq} - A_{pp} - A_{qq}) \qquad (110\;(111)$$

As a result, all four changes can be included in a single equation

$$\underline{B}^{-1} = \underline{A}^{-1} + \zeta\underline{z}\underline{z}^T \tag{112}$$

where $\zeta = \Delta/[\Delta(2A^{-1}_{pq} - A_{pp} - A_{qq})+1]$ (113)

Note that because of symmetry and (108) a single element equals:

$$B^{-1}_{ij} = (\underline{z}\,\underline{z}^T)_{ij} = (A^{-1}_{ip} - A^{-1}_{iq})(A^{-1}_{jp} - A^{-1}_{jq}) \tag{114}$$

This leads to another way of modifying a matrix $\underline{A}$ of mxm. The addition of the four elements (viewed as the addition of a branch p-q in an electric network) proceeds in two steps.

In the first a column and row n=m+1 is added through

$$A^{-1}_{i,n} = A^{-1}_{ip} - A^{-1}_{iq} \; ; \; A^{-1}_{n,i} = A^{-1}_{i,n} \; ; \; i = 1,2,\dots,m \tag{115}$$

$$A^{-1}_{n,n} = A^{-1}_{pp} + A^{-1}_{qq} - 2A^{-1}_{pp} + 1/\Delta \tag{116}$$

In the second step the matrix is reduced back to size mxm by applying Kron's formula

$$B^{-1}_{pq} = A^{-1}_{pq} - A^{-1}_{pn}\cdot A^{-1}_{n,q}/A_{n,n} \tag{117}$$

to all m^2 elements of $\underline{A}^{-1}$.

This method is often used [Br 75] to "collect" an inverse matrix starting with a 1x1 "matrix" A_{11} for which $\underline{A}^{-1} = 1/A_{11}$ and building the matrix up by consecutive addition of links. On the surface of it, this method does not seem to offer any advantages because of the large number of operations. As shown later this is not so and, additionally, Kron's method has definite advantages for implementation on an ASP-system.

We can generalize this approach by using from [No 69]:

<u>Theorem</u>: If a nonsingular matrix $\underline{H}$ of order n can be written as:

$$\underline{H} = \underline{A} + \underline{B}\,\underline{D}\,\underline{C} \tag{118}$$

where $\underline{B},\underline{D},\underline{C}$ are matrices of order nxp, pxp, pxn respectively and $\underline{A},\underline{D}$ are nonsingular, then

$$\underline{H}^{-1} = \underline{A}^{-1} - \underline{A}^{-1}\underline{B}(\underline{D}^{-1} + \underline{C}\,\underline{A}^{-1}\,\underline{B})^{-1}\,\underline{C}\,\underline{A}^{-1} \tag{119}$$

Kron's method of "diakoptics" (or "tearing") can be viewed as an application of (119) to electrical networks. If a network can be "torn" then its solution can be obtained by solving the torn parts and recombining the results. The network of fig. 4 can obviously be torn, by removing r_6. The original incidence matrix of (135), in which $I_{jk}=-1$ stands for current entering node (column) j through resistor r_k and $I_{jk} = +1$ for leaving it, can be split according to (136) where matrices $\underline{B},\underline{C}$ are those of column 6.

$$\left[\begin{array}{ccccccccccc} -1 & 0 & 0 & 0 & 1 & 0 & 0 & 0 & 0 & 0 & 0 \\ 0 & -1 & 0 & 1 & 0 & 0 & 0 & 0 & 0 & 0 & 0 \\ 0 & 0 & -1 & -1 & -1 & 1 & 0 & 0 & 0 & 0 & 0 \\ \hline 0 & 0 & 0 & 0 & 0 & -1 & -1 & 1 & -1 & 0 & 0 \\ 0 & 0 & 0 & 0 & 0 & 0 & 0 & -1 & 0 & 0 & -1 \\ 0 & 0 & 0 & 0 & 0 & 0 & 1 & 0 & 0 & 1 & 0 \end{array}\right] = \underline{I} \qquad (135) \quad ;$$

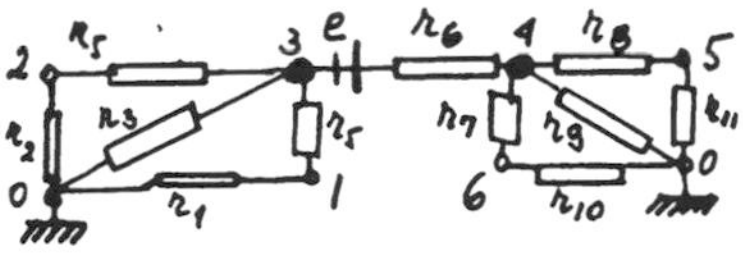

$$\underline{I} = \begin{bmatrix} \underline{A} & \underline{B} & \underline{0} \\ \underline{0} & \underline{C} & \underline{D} \end{bmatrix}$$

As known, Kirchoff's laws for a network can be written as $\underline{v} = \underline{R}\,\underline{c}$; $\underline{I}\,\underline{c} = 0$; $\underline{I}^T\underline{V} = \underline{v} - \underline{e}$ (137)

where $\underline{c}$ is the current vector, $\underline{e}$ a column vector of zeros except for $\underline{e}_6 = e$ and $\underline{V}$ is 6x1 as above. Suppose now that we eliminate $\underline{v}$ and $\underline{c}$ from (137) through:

$$\underline{c} = \underline{R}^{-1}\underline{v} \; ; \; \underline{I}\,\underline{c} = \underline{I}\,\underline{R}^{-1}\underline{v} = \underline{I}\,\underline{R}^{-1}(\underline{I}^T\underline{V}+\underline{e}) = \underline{I}\,\underline{R}^{-1}\underline{I}^T\underline{V}+\underline{I}\,\underline{R}^{-1}\underline{e} = \underline{0} \qquad (138)$$

or $\quad (\underline{I}\,\underline{R}^{-1}\underline{I}^T)\underline{V} = -\underline{I}\,\underline{R}^{-1}\underline{e}$ (139)

$\underline{R}^{-1}$ can be partitioned as per:

$$\underline{R}^{-1} = \begin{bmatrix} \underline{X} & \underline{0} & \underline{0} \\ \underline{0} & \underline{Y} & \underline{0} \\ \underline{0} & \underline{0} & \underline{Z} \end{bmatrix} \qquad (140)$$

where $\underline{X}$, $\underline{Y}$ and $\underline{Z}$ are square matrices of order 5, 1 and 5 respectively. Thus

$$\begin{bmatrix} \underline{A}\,\underline{X}\,\underline{A}^T & \underline{0} \\ \underline{0} & \underline{D}\,\underline{Z}\,\underline{D}^T \end{bmatrix} + \begin{bmatrix} \underline{B} \\ \underline{C} \end{bmatrix} \underline{Y}[\underline{B}^T\underline{C}^T] = \underline{I}\,\underline{R}^{-1}\underline{I}^T \qquad (141)$$

Note that the first part of (141) can be inverted by inverting the (smaller) nonzero blocks, the second part, is even simpler. The overall complexity was thus reduced considerably.

We will return to the basic result later. Next define the scalar product $\underline{v}_1 * \underline{v}_2$ of two vectors $\underline{v}_1, \underline{v}_2$ through

$$\underline{v}_1 * \underline{v}_2 = v_{11}v_{21} + v_{12}v_{22} + v_{13}v_{23} + \ldots + v_{1n}v_{2n} \qquad (142)$$

The length of $\underline{v}_1$ (or of $\underline{v}_2$) and the distance Δ between them are:

$$||\underline{v}_1|| = (v_{11}^2 + v_{12}^2 + \ldots + v_{1n}^2)^{\frac{1}{2}} = (\underline{v}_1 * \underline{v}_1)^{\frac{1}{2}} \qquad (143)$$

$$\Delta^2 = (v_{11} - v_{21})^2 + \ldots + (v_{1n} - v_{2n})^2 = ||\underline{v}_1||^2 + ||\underline{v}_2||^2 - 2\underline{v}_1 * \underline{v}_2 \qquad (144)$$

We can extend the cosine-law

$$\Delta^2 = ||\underline{v}_1||^2 + ||\underline{v}_2||^2 - 2\,||\underline{v}_1||\,||\underline{v}_2||\cos\theta \qquad (145))$$

to n dimensions and get as a result:

$$\cos\theta = (\underline{v}_1 * \underline{v}_2)/(||\underline{v}_1|| \cdot ||\underline{v}_2||) \qquad (146)$$

For complex vectors, we slightly change the definition of $\underline{v}_1 * \underline{v}_2$ and $||v_1||$ namely

$$\underline{v}_1 * \underline{v}_2 = v''_{11}v_{21} + v''_{12}v_{22} + v''_{13}v_{23} + \ldots + v''_{1n}v_{2n} \qquad (147)$$

$$||\underline{v}_1|| = (\underline{v}_1 * \underline{v}_1)^{\frac{1}{2}} = (v''_{11}v_{11} + v''_{12}v_{12} + \ldots + v''_{1n}v_{1n})^{\frac{1}{2}} \qquad (148)$$

where the double-quote denotes a complex-conjugate. In the complex case, the "Hermitian transpose" $\underline{A}^H$ is used instead of $\underline{A}^T$.

Definitions: Two nonzero vectors $\underline{v}_1$, $\underline{v}_2$ are orthogonal if

$$\underline{v}_1 * \underline{v}_2 = 0 \qquad (154)$$

Vectors $\underline{v}_1, \underline{v}_2, \ldots, \underline{v}_n$ are mutually orthogonal or form an orthogonal set, if:

$$\underline{v}_i * \underline{v}_j = 0 \text{ for all } i,j,\ i \neq j \tag{155}$$

If $\underline{v}_1 * \underline{v}_1 = ||\underline{v}_1||^2 = 1$ then $\underline{v}_1$ is a "normalized" vector. An orthogonal set which includes only normalized vectors is called an orthonormal set. A matrix $\underline{Q}$ such that $\underline{Q}^H\, \underline{Q} = \underline{Q}\, \underline{Q}^H = \underline{U}$ is called "unitary". In the real case then $\underline{Q}^T\, \underline{Q} = \underline{Q}\, \underline{Q}^T = \underline{U}$ and such a matrix $\underline{Q}$ is called an "orthogonal" matrix.

Next we develop the Gram-Schmidt orthogonalization procedure. Suppose that an mxn matrix $\underline{A}$ is known and let us denote by $\underline{a}_i$ its i-th column. Then, column $\underline{q}_i$ is calculated so that its length is one:

$$\underline{v}_1 = \underline{a}_1\ ;\ \underline{q}_1 = \underline{v}_1/||v_1|| = \underline{v}_1/r_{11}\ ;\ r_{11} = ||\underline{v}_1|| \tag{156}$$

Next choose $\underline{a}_2$ and subtract from it $r_{12}\, \underline{q}_1$:

$$\underline{v}_2 = \underline{a}_2 - r_{12}\, \underline{q}_1 \tag{157}$$

The scalar r_{12} may be chosen so that $\underline{v}_2$ is orthogonal to $\underline{q}_1$, i.e.

$$\underline{q}_1 * \underline{v}_2 = \underline{q}_1 * \underline{a}_2 - r_{12}(\underline{q}_1 * \underline{q}_1) = 0 \tag{158}$$

The length of $\underline{q}_1$ and thus also $\underline{q}_1 * \underline{q}_1$ was made one so that

$$r_{12} = \underline{q}_1 * \underline{a}_2 \text{ and } \underline{q}_2 = \underline{v}_2/||\underline{v}_2|| = \underline{v}_2/r_{22} \qquad (159)(160)$$

Next set $\underline{v}_3 = \underline{a}_3 - r_{23}\underline{q}_2 - r_{13}\underline{q}_1$ (161)

Vector $\underline{v}_3$ should be orthogonal to both $\underline{q}_1$ and $\underline{q}_2$ so that

$$\begin{aligned} \underline{q}_1 * \underline{v}_3 &= \underline{q}_1 * \underline{a}_3 - r_{23}(\underline{q}_1 * \underline{q}_2) - r_{13}(\underline{q}_1 * \underline{q}_1) = 0 \\ \underline{q}_2 * \underline{v}_3 &= \underline{q}_2 * \underline{a}_3 - r_{23}(\underline{q}_2 * \underline{q}_2) - r_{13}(\underline{q}_1 * \underline{q}_2) = 0 \end{aligned} \tag{162}$$

For i=1,2 we have $\underline{q}_i * \underline{q}_i = 1$ and for $j \neq i$: $\underline{q}_i * \underline{q}_j = 0$. Therefore

$$r_{13} = \underline{q}_1 * \underline{v}_3\ ;\ r_{23} = \underline{q}_2 * \underline{v}_3 \tag{163}$$

The procedure for i=1,...,n is therefore:

$$\underline{v}_i := \underline{a}_i - \Sigma r_{ji}\underline{q}_j\ ;\ j\Sigma = 1, \ldots, i-1 \tag{164}$$

$$r_{ji} := \underline{q}_j * \underline{v}_i\ ;\ \underline{q}_i = \underline{v}_i/||\underline{v}_i|| = \underline{v}_i/r_{ii} \qquad (165)(166)$$

Let us rewrite these equations as

$$\begin{aligned} \underline{a}_1 &= r_{11}\, \underline{q}_1 \\ \underline{a}_2 &= r_{12}\, \underline{q}_1 + r_{22}\, \underline{q}_2 \\ \underline{a}_3 &= r_{13}\, \underline{q}_1 + r_{23}\, \underline{q}_2 + r_{33}\, \underline{q}_3 \end{aligned} \tag{167}$$

$$\underline{a}_k = r_{1k}\, \underline{q}_1 + r_{2k}\, \underline{q}_2 + r_{3k}\, \underline{q}_3 + \ldots + r_{kk}\, \underline{q}_k$$

If $\underline{a}_i$ is the i-th column of an (nxk) matrix $\underline{A}$ and $\underline{q}_i$ of an (nxk) matrix $\underline{Q}$ with orthonormalized columns, then r_{ij} define an upper triangular matrix $\underline{R}$ and (167) is equivalent to

$$\underline{A} = \underline{Q}\, \underline{R} \tag{168}$$

If $\underline{A}$ is a square matrix n=k, then (168) is just another factorization of $\underline{A}$; this time into a product of an orthonormalized and triangular matrix. As a matter of fact, assuming (168), multiplying out and orthonormalizing $\underline{Q}$ is how the Gram-Schmidt procedure is introduced in [SB]. It is shown there that whenever the columns of $\underline{A}$ are nearly linearly dependent, a vector $\underline{v}_k'$ instead of $\underline{v}_k$ of (164) results, due to roundoff error, such that it is not anymore orthogonal to $\underline{q}_1, \underline{q}_2, \ldots, \underline{q}_{k-1}$. We may though "reorthogonalize" it as follows. Compute scalars Δr_{ik} and vector $\underline{z}_k$ from:

$$\underline{z}_k = \underline{v}'_k - \Delta r_{1k}\, \underline{q}_1 - \dots - \Delta r_{k-1,k}\, \underline{q}_{k-1} \tag{169}$$

$$\Delta r_{ik} = \underline{q}_i^H\, \underline{v}'_k \;;\; i=1,\dots,k-1 \tag{170}$$

and "improve" values of q_k, r_{ik} from:

$$\underline{q}_k = \underline{z}_k/||\underline{z}_k||;\; r_{ik}:=r'_{ik} + \Delta r_{ik} \tag{171}$$

where r'_{ik} are the previously computed values. Unfortunately if normally

$$\Omega_{nogs} = mk^2\omega \tag{172}$$

then, orthogonalization which includes the above requires twice as many operations.

The procedure may be rewritten as follows (from 167):

$$\underline{q}_1 = \underline{a}_1 \tag{173}$$

$$\underline{q}_j = \underline{a}_j - \Sigma\, r_{ij}\,\underline{q}_i \;;\; i\Sigma=1,\dots,j-1;\; r_{ij} = (\underline{a}_j^H * \underline{q}_i)/(\underline{q}_i^H * \underline{q}_j) \text{ for } j=2,\dots,k \tag{174}$$

The value of $\underline{a}_j^H * \underline{q}_i$ will not change if $\underline{a}_j$ is replaced by any vector of the form $\underline{a}_j - \Sigma\, c_k\, \underline{q}_k$, $k\Sigma=1,\dots,i-1$ because $\underline{q}_k^H * \underline{q}_i = 0$ for $k \neq i$. Therefore we may compute r_{ij} in (174) using instead of $\underline{a}_j^H$, the vector

$$\underline{a}'_j = \underline{a}_j - \Sigma\, r_{kj}\, \underline{q}_k \;;\; k\Sigma=1,\dots,i-1 \tag{175}$$

but, for efficiency, compute $\underline{a}'_j$ recursively rather than explicitly. Thus, we have the "Modified Gram-Schmidt" method:

$$\underline{a}_j^{(1)} = \underline{a}_j \;;\; j = 1,\dots,n \tag{176}$$

$$\underline{q}_i = \underline{a}_i^{(i)} \;;\; c_i = \underline{q}_i^H * \underline{q}_i \qquad\qquad i=1,\dots,n$$

$$r_{ij} = (\underline{a}_j^{(i)})^H * \underline{q}_i/c_i \;;\; \underline{a}_j^{(i+1)} = \underline{a}_j^{(i)} - r_{ij}\underline{q}_i \;;\; j = i+1,\dots,n \tag{177}$$

If we intend to solve $\underline{Ax} = \underline{b}$ using orthogonalization, then we must also transform $\underline{b}$ into $\underline{b}^{(1)}, \underline{b}^{(2)}, \dots, \underline{b}^{(n+1)}$ as follows ($\underline{A}\ \underline{x} = \underline{Q}\ \underline{R}\ \underline{x} = \underline{b}$; $\underline{R}\ \underline{x} = \underline{Q}^T\underline{b}$):

$$g_k = \underline{q}_k^H * \underline{b}^{(k)}/c_k \;;\; \underline{b}^{(k+1)} = \underline{b}^{(k)} - g_k\underline{q}_k \;;\; k = 1,\dots,n \tag{178}$$

The solution of $\underline{Ax} = \underline{b}$ follows that of

$$\underline{Rx} = \underline{g} \tag{179}$$

where $\underline{g} = (g_1, g_2, \dots, g_n)^T$. This requires only $\Omega = 0.5n^2\omega$ which can be neglected if compared to $\Omega_{nogs} = n^3\omega$. Even this is twice as much as that required for elimination and (176) to (179) will be used only if the fact that Q is orthogonal is of importance.

Three more points on this subject follow:

(a) The difference between the normal and modified Gram-Schmidt methods is that in the first we modify $\underline{a}_1$ to compute $\underline{q}_1$ leaving $\underline{a}_2,\dots,\underline{a}_n$ unchanged, then modify $\underline{a}_2$ to compute $\underline{q}_2$ but leave $\underline{a}_3,\dots,\underline{a}_n$ unchanged etc. In the modified method we compute $\underline{q}_1$ from $\underline{a}_1$ and change $\underline{a}_2,\dots,\underline{a}_n$ (by subtracting $(\underline{q}_1 * \underline{a}_i)\underline{q}_1$) etc.

(b) Since $\underline{Q}\ \underline{Q}^H = \underline{Q}^H\ \underline{Q} = \underline{U}$ we may premultiply $\underline{A} = \underline{Q}\ \underline{R}$ by $\underline{Q}^{-1} = \underline{Q}^H$ and get

$$\underline{Q}^H \cdot \underline{A} = \underline{R} \tag{180}$$

a form used as often as (168).

(c) The normal and modified methods may be summarized in shorter notation:

$$\begin{cases} r_{kk} := \|\underline{a}_{.k}\|;\ \underline{q}_{.k} := \underline{a}_{.k}/r_{kk} & (181) \\ r_{k,j} := \underline{q}_{.k} * \underline{a}_{.j};\ \underline{a}_{.j} := \underline{a}_{.j} - r_{kj} * \underline{q}_{.k};\ j = k+1,\ldots,n & (182) \end{cases}$$

$$\begin{cases} \underline{q}_{.k} := \underline{a}_{.k}^{(k)};\ d_k := \underline{q}_{k.} * \underline{q}_{.k};\ r_{kk} := 1; & (183) \\ \underline{a}_{.j}^{(k+1)} := \underline{a}_{.j}^{(k)} - r_{kj}\underline{q}_{.k};\ r_{kj} := \underline{q}_{k.}\ \underline{a}_{.j}^{(k)}/d_k;\ j=k+1,\ldots n & (184) \end{cases}$$

Let us return to the basic result. $\underline{F}(c,\underline{w},\underline{v})$ of (96) with c=2 is known as the matrix of Householder:

$$\underline{H}(2,\underline{w},\underline{w}) = \underline{U} - 2\underline{w}\ \underline{w}^H\ ;\ \underline{w}^H * \underline{w} = 1 \qquad (185)$$

A matrix $\underline{A} \equiv \underline{A}^{(0)}$ can be reduced step by step using $\underline{H}_j$ through:

$$A^{(j)} = \underline{H}_j\ \underline{A}^{(j-1)}\ ;\ j = 1,2,\ldots,n-1 \qquad (189)$$

where $\underline{w}$ is chosen so that $A^{(n-1)} = \underline{R}$ is an upper triangular matrix. Moreover, [SB] show an Algol-procedure, which determines an nxn unitary matrix:

$$\underline{H} = \underline{H}_n\ \underline{H}_{n-1}\cdots H_1 \qquad (190)$$

and $\underline{R}$ so that $\underline{H}\ \underline{A} = \underline{R}\ ;\ \underline{A} = \underline{H}^{-1}\underline{R} = \underline{Q}\ \underline{R}$ (191)

The reduction of $\underline{A}$ to $\underline{Q}\ \underline{R}$ requires in this method

$$\Omega_H \cong 2n^3/3 \qquad (192)$$

which is more than in Gram-Schmidt orthogonalization, but it has higher accuracy and can be executed on ASP. It is useful also when $\underline{A}$ is sparse.

Suppose now that $\underline{w}$ degenerates into a vector with only two nonzero elements $w_i = s;\ w_j = c$ such that $s^2 + c^2 = 1$. Matrix $\underline{H}$ will therefore be a unit matrix except for the four elements h_{ij}, h_{ii}, h_{ji}, h_{jj} which are:

$$\underline{H}' = \begin{bmatrix} 1-2s^2 & -2sc \\ -2sc & 1-2c^2 \end{bmatrix} \qquad (193)$$

If we write $s = \sin\theta/2;\ c = -\cos\theta/2;\ s^2 + c^2 = 1$ (194)

$$\text{then } \underline{H}' = \begin{bmatrix} \cos\theta & \sin\theta \\ \sin\theta & -\cos\theta \end{bmatrix} * \begin{bmatrix} 1 & 0 \\ 0 & -1 \end{bmatrix} = \begin{bmatrix} \cos\theta & \sin\theta \\ -\sin\theta & \cos\theta \end{bmatrix} \qquad (195)$$

Both forms of $\underline{H}'$ represent "rotations". They were first used by Jacobi in 1846 for reducing a symmetric matrix to a diagonal form, then by Givens 1954 for eigenvalue calculations. We will call them Given's matrices $\underline{G}$. $\underline{G}_{ji}$ is a unitary matrix with

$$G_{ii} = G_{jj} = c;\ G_{ij} = -G_{ji} = s;\quad c^2 + s^2 = 1;\ i < j \qquad (196)$$

To see how it can be used for elimination, note that if a matrix (Fig. 2) is multiplied by $\underline{G}_{2,1}$ of Fig. 3,

$$\underline{A}' = \underline{G}_{2,1} * \underline{A} \qquad (197)$$

of Fig. 4 results. The following should be noted:

- Multiplication by $\underline{G}_{ji}$ changes only rows i and j of $\underline{A}$
- The three elements A'_{ii}, A'_{ij}, A'_{jj} denoted by "*" and A'_{ji} by "0" are

$$A'_{ii}=cA_{ii}+sA_{ji};\ A'_{ij}=cA_{ij}+sA_{jj} \qquad (198)$$

$$A'_{ji}=cA_{ji}-sA_{ii}\ ;\ A'_{jj}=cA_{jj}-sA_{ij} \qquad (199)$$

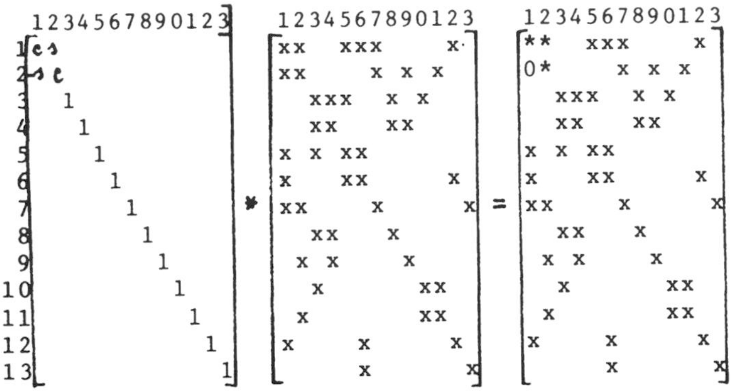

Fig. 3: Rotation Matrix   Fig. 2: Original Matrix   Fig. 4: Result of $\underline{G}_{21}\underline{A}=\underline{A}'$

Therefore A'_{ji} may be eliminated if c,s are chosen according to

$$rt=\sqrt{A_{ii}^2+A_{ji}^2};\ s=A_{ji}/rt;\ c=A_{ii}/rt \tag{200}$$

- Other elements of $\underline{A}'$ are nonzero if A_{ik} or A_{jk} or both were nonzero. Thus, elimination of an element A_{ji} can be pictured easily as follows (Fig. 5):

An asterisk is entered in positions (i,i), (i,j) and (j,j), a zero in position (j,i), symbol "x" whenever both elements A_{ik}, $A_{jk} \neq 0$, for any $1 \leq k \leq n$, $k \neq i,j$ and symbol "." if only one of them was nonzero (symbol "x"). Fig. 5 shows elimination of column 1 of $\underline{A}$. It is known that if elimination proceeds along the columns of $\underline{A}$, then a zero once introduced will not be changed. The result is thus a triangular, "right" matrix $\underline{R}$ and the entire process can be summarized by

$$(\underline{G}_{n-1,n}\cdot\underline{G}_{n-2}\cdot\underline{G}_{n-2,n-1}\cdots\underline{G}_{3,2}\cdot\underline{G}_{n,1}\cdots\underline{G}_{3,1}\cdot\underline{G}_{2,1})\underline{A}=\underline{G}\underline{A}=\underline{R} \tag{201) (202}$$

$$\underline{A} = \underline{Q}\,\underline{R}\ ; \quad (202) \qquad \underline{Q} \equiv \underline{G}^{-1} \tag{203}$$

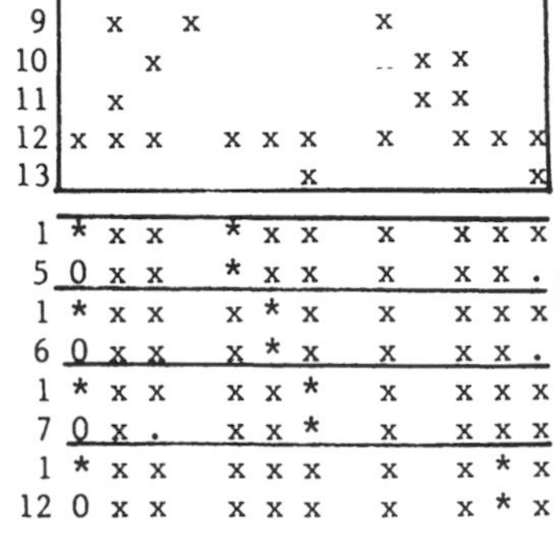

Fig. 5: Elimination of $\underline{A}_{\cdot 1}$

Matrix $\underline{Q}$ is orthonormal i.e.

$$\underline{Q}\,\underline{Q}^T = \underline{U}\ ;\ \underline{Q}^T = \underline{Q}^{-1} = \underline{G} \tag{204}$$

Its inverse is thus identical to its transpose, a fact which will lead to efficient use of orthogonalization

In its present form (198-200) it would require too much effort (especially for the square root), but in 1973, Gentleman showed [Ge 73] that this effort can be reduced. His method will be described below in a slightly different way.

Let us disregard all except the i and j rows and columns so that the G-matrix consists only of c=cosθ and s=sinθ as in (205) below. In order to compute c and s we needed $\alpha+\gamma+4\mu$ and in order to multiply $\underline{G}_{ij}$ by column j of $\underline{A}$, $8\mu+4\alpha$ were required (γ=time for taking a square root). Suppose now that $\underline{A}$ is kept in storage as $\underline{A} = \underline{D}\,\underline{B}$ where $\underline{D}$ is some diagonal matrix and that

$$\underline{G}_{ji} = \begin{bmatrix} c & s \\ -s & c \end{bmatrix} = \begin{bmatrix} d'_{ii} & 0 \\ 0 & d_{jj} \end{bmatrix} \begin{bmatrix} 1 & \varepsilon \\ \delta & 1 \end{bmatrix} = \begin{bmatrix} d'_{ii} & \varepsilon d'_{ii} \\ \delta d'_{jj} & d'_{jj} \end{bmatrix} \tag{205}$$

Multiplying this $\underline{G}_{ji}$ by a diagonal 2x2 matrix with elements $1/d_{ii}$ and $1/d_{jj}$ and comparing with the original $\underline{G}_{ji}$ yields:

$$\psi = d_{jj}/d_{ii} \; ; \; \varepsilon = \psi \cdot tg\theta \; ; \; \delta = -tg\theta/\varepsilon \tag{206}$$

Instead of $\underline{G}_{ji}\ \underline{A}$ we now have (with $\underline{S}$ the ε,δ-matrix):

$$\underline{G}_{ji}\ \underline{A} = (\underline{D}'\underline{S}_{ji}\underline{D}^{-1})(\underline{D}\ \underline{B}) = \underline{D}'\ \underline{S}_{ji}\ \underline{B} = \underline{D}'\ \underline{B}' \tag{207}$$

Multiplication $\underline{G}\cdot\underline{A}$ was replaced by $\underline{S}\ \underline{B}$ with an updating of $\underline{D}$. To eliminate element (j,k) of row j will be therefore done by:

$$d_{jj}\ B_{jk}\cos\theta - d_{ii}\ B_{ik}\sin\theta = 0 \text{ instead of } A_{jk}\cos - A_{ik}\sin\theta = 0 \tag{208}$$

Inserting this into (206) yields

$$\cos^2\theta = d^2_{ii}\ b^2_{ik}/(d^2_{ii}b^2_{ik} + d^2_{jj}b^2_{jk}); \tag{209}$$

Only squares of d_{ii}, d_{jj} appear so that it is better to store $\underline{D}^2$ instead of $\underline{D}$. The comparisons which lead to (206) also yields:

$$\cos\theta = d'_{ii}/d_{ii} = d_{jj}/d_{jj} \; ; \; \sin\theta = d'_{ii}/d_{jj} = -\delta d'_{jj}/d_{ii} \tag{210}$$

so that
$$\varepsilon = d^2_{jj}b_{jk}/(d^2_{ii}b_{ik}) \; ; \; \delta = -b_{jk}/b_{ik} \tag{211}$$

We can summarize the procedure by saying that if $\underline{D}^2$ instead of $\underline{D}$ is kept in storage then ε,δ are calculated as per (211) and $\underline{B}'$ through:

$$b'_{ik} = b_{ik} + \varepsilon b_{jk} \; ; \; b'_{jk} = \delta b_{ik} \tag{212}$$

The dot and · elements result from multiplying the γ,δ-matrix of (205) with $[x,x]^T$ or $[0,x]^T$ and require $\alpha+\mu$ and μ respectively. Thus, in the original method each rotation required $(\gamma+24\omega)$, an x-element 3ω and a dot required 1ω (ω is here either α or μ). In the modified method the corresponding counts are: (17ω), (2ω) and (ω). The reduction in the computational time is thus considerable, especially if a "good" ordering is possible.

On the surface, even the improved method does not seem to be efficient enough to compete with elimination and factorization. It will be shown later that it is a very efficient method for elimination of extremely sparse sets.

Summary: Two Gram-Schmidt orthogonalization prodedures were developed. Equations (99) and (102) show how to invert the matrix $\underline{U} - c\ \underline{w}\ \underline{v}^T$. Using this fundamental result, the formation of $\underline{L}$, its inversion, the Sherman-Morrison, Kron and other methods (e.g. (112) (113)) are easily derived. A generalization leads to the "diakoptic" method. Householder's, and Given's methods were mentioned with the last used both for orthogonalization and elimination.

5.3 COMPLEX NUMBERS AND QUADS

Aims: It is sometimes thought that the most efficient way to solve a set of linear, complex equations is through the use of a high level language which includes operations on complex numbers. Another conclusion will be reached in this section. The aim is to show that by proper definition, sets of equations with 2x2 blocks, "quads", can be solved very efficiently indeed. A theorem about complexity of operations on quads and an efficient way of multiplying $\underline{A}\ \underline{b}$ for a symmetric $\underline{A}$ will also be developed.

Suppose that in $\underline{A}\ \underline{x} = \underline{b}$ matrix $\underline{A}$ and vectors $\underline{x}$, $\underline{b}$ are complex i.e. with $j = \sqrt{-1}$

$$\underline{A} = \underline{B} + j\ \underline{C};\ \underline{x} = \underline{y} + j\ \underline{z};\ \underline{b} = \underline{c} + j\ \underline{d} \tag{213}$$

Insertion into $\underline{A}\ \underline{x} = \underline{b}$ and separation of real and imaginary parts yields:

$$(\underline{B}\ \underline{y} - \underline{C}\ \underline{z}) + j(\underline{C}\ \underline{y} + \underline{B}\ \underline{z}) = \underline{c} + j\ \underline{d} \tag{214}$$

which can also be written in matrix form:

$$\begin{bmatrix} \underline{B} & -\underline{C} \\ \underline{C} & \underline{B} \end{bmatrix} \begin{bmatrix} \underline{y} \\ \underline{z} \end{bmatrix} = \begin{bmatrix} \underline{c} \\ \underline{d} \end{bmatrix} \tag{215}$$

The matrix above may be considered to be a partitioned matrix and

$$\begin{bmatrix} \underline{B} & -\underline{C} \\ \underline{C} & \underline{B} \end{bmatrix}^{-1} = \begin{bmatrix} \underline{W}_1 & \underline{W}_2 \\ \underline{W}_3 & \underline{W}_4 \end{bmatrix} \tag{216}$$

obtained as follows:

$$\underline{Q} = \underline{B} + \underline{C}\ \underline{B}^{-1}\ \underline{C}$$

$$\underline{W}_4 = \underline{Q}^{-1};\ \underline{W}_3 = -\underline{W}_4\ \underline{C}\ \underline{B}^{-1};\ \underline{W}_2 = \underline{B}^{-1}\ \underline{C}\ \underline{Q}^{-1} = -\underline{W}_3;\ \underline{W}_1 = \underline{W}_4 \tag{217}$$

which is in the same form as the B-C matrix above. The solution is thus:

$$\begin{bmatrix} \underline{y} \\ \underline{z} \end{bmatrix} = \begin{bmatrix} \underline{W}_1 & -\underline{W}_3 \\ \underline{W}_3 & \underline{W}_1 \end{bmatrix} \begin{bmatrix} \underline{c} \\ \underline{d} \end{bmatrix} \tag{218}$$

$$\underline{y} = \underline{W}_1\ \underline{c} - \underline{W}_3\ \underline{d}\ ;\ \underline{z} = \underline{W}_3\ \underline{c} + \underline{W}_1\ \underline{d} \tag{219}$$

and only $\underline{B}$ and $\underline{Q}$ have to be inverted. Still, inversion of the matrices in order to solve $\underline{A}\ \underline{x} = \underline{b}$ is time-consuming. Since all matrices and vectors in (215) are real, we may view it as a (2n x 2n) system and solve it by Gaussian elimination. In the following, a similar approach is taken.

Let us for a moment use a 3x3 complex matrix $\underline{A}'$ in solving

$$\underline{A}'\ \underline{x}' = \underline{b}' \tag{220}$$

In full:

$$\begin{aligned} a'_{11}x'_1 + a'_{12}x'_2 + a'_{13}x'_3 &= b_1 \\ a'_{21}x'_1 + a'_{22}x'_2 + a'_{33}x'_3 &= b_2 \\ a'_{31}x'_1 + a'_{32}x'_2 + a'_{33}x'_3 &= b_3 \end{aligned} \tag{221}$$

$$\text{Let } a'_{ik} = c_{ik} + jd_{ik};\ x'_i = y_i + jz_i;\ b'_i = e_i + jf_i \tag{222}$$

Then if each one of the three equations is separated into its real and imaginary parts we get:

$$\begin{aligned} c_{11}y_1 - d_{11}z_1 + c_{12}y_2 - d_{12}z_2 + c_{13}y_3 - d_{13}z_3 &= e_1 \\ d_{11}y_1 + c_{11}z_1 + d_{12}y_2 + c_{12}z_2 + d_{13}y_3 + c_{13}z_3 &= f_1 \\ c_{21}y_1 - d_{21}z_1 + c_{22}y_2 - d_{22}z_2 + c_{23}y_3 - d_{23}z_3 &= e_2 \\ d_{21}y_1 + c_{21}z_1 + d_{22}y_2 + c_{22}z_2 + d_{23}y_3 + c_{23}z_3 &= f_2 \end{aligned} \tag{223}$$

$c_{31}y_1 - d_{31}z_1 + c_{32}y_2 - d_{32}z_2 + c_{33}y_3 - d_{33}z_3 = e_3$
$d_{31}y_1 + c_{31}z_1 + d_{32}y_2 + c_{32}z_2 + d_{33}y_3 + c_{33}z_3 = f_3$

We see that we may have written $\underline{A}'$ as being composed of "quadruplets" (quads for short) i.e. 2x2 submatrices of the form (224)

We call a quad which has an antisymmetric structure, as $\bar{A}$ of (224), an $\bar{O}$-quad. A general quad goes by the name $\bar{D}$.

$$\bar{A} = \begin{bmatrix} c & -d \\ d & c \end{bmatrix} \qquad (224)$$

In some algorithms [WC 79] we use the $\bar{F}$-quads defined by (225): The $\bar{O}$-quads are antisymmetric with identical diagonal elements; they behave like complex numbers (or plane rotations). The $\bar{F}$-quads are symmetric.

$$\bar{F} = \begin{bmatrix} e & f \\ f & -e \end{bmatrix} \qquad (225)$$

All direct methods based on elimination may be carried out with operations on quadruplets replacing similar operations on scalar elements. For instance, Gaussian elimination would start by normalization, that is by multiplying $\bar{Q}_{1,k}$; k=1,...,n by $\bar{Q}_{1,1}^{-1}$ (i.e. inverted quadruplet $\bar{Q}_{1,1}$), thereby making $\bar{Q}_{1,1}$ a unit 2x2 submatrix. In order to make next $\bar{Q}_{2,1} = \bar{O}$ ("elimination") first all $\bar{Q}_{2,m}$; m=1,...,n are multiplied by $\bar{Q}_{2,1}^{-1}$ and then the second row of quadruplets is replaced by

$$\bar{Q}_{2,k} = \bar{Q}_{2,k} - \bar{Q}_{1,k}; \quad k=1,\dots,n \qquad (226)$$

Since inverses of quads are seen to be required, it is noted that $\bar{Q}_{i,k}$ for $i \neq k$ is regular, because $\det(\bar{Q}_{i,k})$ is a sum of squares i.e. positive, $\bar{Q}_{k,k}$ may be singular, in which case renumbering of the nodes ("pivoting") will be required.

The operations to be carried out on row k of quads are thus seen to be:

(a) Instead of division by $A_{k,k}$ make

$$\bar{Q}_{k,m} = \bar{Q}_{k,k}^{-1} * \bar{Q}_{k,m}; \quad m=k,\dots,n \qquad (227)$$

(b) Instead of multiplication by $A_{k,m}$, multiply by the corresponding quads.

(c) Addition of two rows of quads.

Examining the arithmetical operations implied by the algorithms above, we see that the following are required

(a) <u>Multiplication of two $\bar{D}$-type quads</u>: These being of general structure, we may use the straightforward multiplication algorithm, requiring $8\mu + 4\alpha$.

(b) <u>Multiplication of two $\bar{O}$-type quads</u>: It is readily verified, that the map from the field of complex numbers to the set of all $\bar{O}$-type quads, defined by

$$a + jb \rightarrow \begin{bmatrix} a & -b \\ b & a \end{bmatrix} = \bar{O}\,(a,b) \qquad (228)$$

is a field isomorphism. Thus to multiply two $\bar{O}$-quads we may employ the usual algorithm to multiply complex numbers:

<u>Complex</u>: $(a+jb)\,(c+jd) = (ac-bd) + j(bc+ad)$ (229)

<u>$\bar{O}$-type</u>: $\bar{O}(a,b)\cdot\bar{O}(c,d) = \bar{O}(ac-bd,\ bc+ad)$ (230)

which requires $4\mu+2\alpha$.

The Strassen-Winograd algorithm for the multiplication of complex numbers [AHU76], may be used for the multiplication of $\bar{O}$ or $\bar{D}$-quads. For complex numbers, it is defined as follows:

$$p_1 = (a+b)c;\ p_2 = b(d+c);\ p_3 = a(d-c) \qquad (231)$$

$$(a+jb)\ (c+jd) = (p_1 - p_2) + j(p_1 + p_3) \qquad (232)$$

For $\bar{O}$-quads, compute p_1, p_2, p_3 as above. The resulting quad is then:

$$\begin{bmatrix} p_1 - p_2 & -(p_1+p_3) \\ p_1 + p_3 & p_1 - p_2 \end{bmatrix} \qquad (233)$$

This algorithm requires $3\mu+5\alpha$ and is preferable when $\mu>3\alpha$. If $\mu > 11\alpha$, as may happen when multiplication is done in software, then it may also be used for $\bar{D}$ squads, with execution time $7\mu + 15\alpha$.

(c) <u>Multiplication of type $\bar{D}x\bar{O}$, $\bar{O}x\bar{D}$</u>: The multiplication $\bar{D}x\bar{O}$ is equivalent to 2 complex multiplications (zw_1, zw_2).

Indeed

$$\bar{D}x\bar{O} = \begin{bmatrix} a & b \\ c & d \end{bmatrix} x \begin{bmatrix} p & -q \\ q & p \end{bmatrix} = \begin{bmatrix} ap+bq & bp-aq \\ cp+dq & dp-cq \end{bmatrix} = \begin{bmatrix} Re(z\cdot w_1) & Im(z\cdot w_1) \\ Re(z\cdot w_2) & Im(z\cdot w_2) \end{bmatrix} \qquad (234)$$

where $\qquad z = p-jq,\ w_1 = a + jb,\ w_2 = c + jd \qquad (235)$

Similarily,

$$\bar{O}x\bar{D} = \begin{bmatrix} p & -q \\ q & p \end{bmatrix} x \begin{bmatrix} a & b \\ c & d \end{bmatrix} = \begin{bmatrix} pa-qc & pb-qd \\ qa+pc & qb+pd \end{bmatrix} = \begin{bmatrix} Re(st_1) & Re(st_2) \\ Im(st_1) & Im(st_2) \end{bmatrix} \qquad (236)$$

where $\qquad s = p + jq,\ t_1 = a + jc,\ t_2 = b + jd \qquad (237)$

Therefore, each of the algorithms for multiplication of complex numbers may be used. The timings are: $8\mu+4\alpha$ for the straightforward algorithm (which has no advantage over plain multiplication of 2x2 matrices) and $6\mu+10\alpha$ using Winograd's algorithm, which is faster if $\mu>2\alpha$.

(d) <u>Inversion of quads</u>: To invert a $\bar{D}$-quad requires 2 multiplications, 4 divisions and one addition

$$\begin{bmatrix} a & b \\ c & d \end{bmatrix}^{-1} = \frac{1}{a^2+b^2} \begin{bmatrix} d & -b \\ -c & a \end{bmatrix} \qquad (238)$$

and an $\bar{O}$-quad requires 2 multiplications, 2 divisions and one addition:

$$\begin{bmatrix} a & -b \\ b & a \end{bmatrix}^{-1} = \frac{1}{a^2+b^2} \begin{bmatrix} a & b \\ -b & a \end{bmatrix} \qquad (239)$$

Owing to the fact that $\bar{D}$-quads appear in many of the above algorithms, it is worthwhile to carry out the matrix operations in block form, whenever possible. The greatest gain results in computations, where the multiplication consists mostly of $\bar{O}x\bar{O}$ and $\bar{D}x\bar{D}$ quad multiplications. It is of course necessary to keep track of the type of quads being multiplied, which may require additional bits of storage for each quad. This is particularly necessary in Gaussian elimination, where the type of quads may change during the process.

If an $\bar{F}$-quad is multiplied by an $\bar{O}$-quad:

$$\begin{bmatrix} a & b \\ b & -a \end{bmatrix} \begin{bmatrix} c & -d \\ d & c \end{bmatrix} = \begin{bmatrix} (ac+bd) & (bc-ad) \\ (bc+ad) & (bd+ac) \end{bmatrix} \tag{240}$$

an $\bar{F}$-quad results. The above is equivalent to multiplication of $(a+jb)\cdot(c-jd)$ and requires 4 multiplications in the usual, three in Winograd's algorithm. The multiplication of an $\bar{F}$ by $\bar{D}$-quad:

$$\begin{bmatrix} a & b \\ b & -a \end{bmatrix} \begin{bmatrix} c & d \\ e & f \end{bmatrix} = \begin{bmatrix} (ac+be) & (ad+bf) \\ (bc-ae) & (bd-af) \end{bmatrix} \tag{241}$$

is equivalent to two complex multiplications $(a+jb)\cdot(c-je)$ and $(a+jb)\cdot(d-jf)$. Calculation of the products $\bar{O}\times\bar{F}$ and $\bar{D}\times\bar{F}$ as well as inversion of an $\bar{F}$-quad is left as an exercise.

The time for a calculation was expressed in terms of the number of multiplications μ and additions α. In the field of computational complexity, the α's are sometimes neglected, the argument being that $\mu \gg \alpha$. In my view, even counting both μ and α may not be sufficient, since for any arithmetical operation encountered, there are always load, store, bookkeeping and other machine-language operations. However, counting μ and α is meaningful inasmuch as there exists usually a fixed ratio of arithmetical to other operations. For instance, in both

$$Q = P - R;\ Q = P \times R \tag{242}$$

a load and a store operations is required.

If one does assume that α is to be neglected when compared to μ, then the advantages of using quad-algebra are summarized for quad multiplication in the table below.

$\bar{O}\times\bar{O}$	$\bar{D}\times\bar{D}$	$\bar{O}\times\bar{D}$	$\bar{D}\times\bar{O}$	$\bar{F}\times\bar{O}$	$\bar{F}\times\bar{D}$
3	7	6	6	3	6

These numbers should be compared to 8 multiplications normally required for multiplying two quads. Additional savings result in that inversion of a D-quad may be computed by 6, of an O-quad by 4 multiplications and multiplying an $\bar{O}$-quad by a two-vector requires only 3 multiplications.

Remark: The algorithm of Strassen and Winograd used in (a), (b) are known to be optimal in that they require the least possible number of multiplications. A natural question therefore is, whether the multiplication algorithm of (c) is also optimal in this sense; in other words, whether two complex multiplications of the type zw_1, zw_2 can be performed with less than 6 real multiplications. Next is a proof that this is indeed the case, with the additional assumption that commutativity is not to be used. I believe the above to hold even without this assumption.

but this is still an open question.

Consider $\begin{bmatrix} a & b \\ c & d \end{bmatrix} \begin{bmatrix} p & q \\ q & -p \end{bmatrix}$ (243)

to establish the following result:

Theorem: Six multiplications are necessary and sufficient to compute (243) without using commutativity.

The proof of this theorem depends on a number of intermediate results.

Necessity: Product (243) can be written in the form

$$\begin{bmatrix} a & b \\ -b & a \\ c & d \\ -d & c \end{bmatrix} \begin{bmatrix} p \\ q \end{bmatrix} = \begin{bmatrix} ap + bq \\ aq - bp \\ cp + dq \\ cq - dp \end{bmatrix} = \underline{V}. \qquad (244)$$

It will henceforth be assumed that (244) requires at most five multiplications. Since we are assuming non-commutativity, these multiplications are of the form:

$$f_i = (\ell_{1i}a_1 + \ell_{2i}b + \ell_{3i}c + \ell_{4i}d)\,(m_{1i}p + m_{2i}q),\ i = 1,2,\ldots,5 \qquad (245)$$

where $\ell_{i,j}$, m_{ij} are rational constants. All elements of $\underline{V}$ may be expressed as linear combinations in the f_i's.

Lemma: The rank of the matrix $\underline{M}$ is 2.

$$\underline{M}^T = \begin{bmatrix} \ell_{21} & \ell_{22} & \cdots & \ell_{25} \\ \ell_{31} & \ell_{32} & \cdots & \ell_{35} \end{bmatrix}^T \qquad (246)$$

Proof: Assume the opposite, i.e. rank 1 or 0. Hence all rows are rational multiples of one row (which we may assume is the first). Thus there exist rational constants r_2, r_3, r_4, r_5 so that

$$\ell_{2i} = r_i\ell_{21};\ \ell_{3i} = r_i\ell_{31},\ i = 2,3,4,5 \qquad (247)$$

from which follows that

$$\ell_{2i}b + \ell_{3i}c = r_i \cdot (\ell_{21}b + \ell_{31}c) \equiv r_i s(b,c). \qquad (248)$$

Hence, the f_i's of (245) may be written as functions of s rather than of b and c separately, and similarly $\underline{V}$. Setting $a = d = 0$, $b = \ell_{31}$, $c = -\ell_{21}$ results in $s = 0$ and $f_i = 0$, $i = 1,2,3,4,5$, thus $\underline{V} \equiv \underline{0}$. Putting $p = 1$, $q = 0$

$$V = [0, -\ell_{31}, -\ell_{21}, 0]^T \neq 0 \qquad (249)$$

which is a contradiction.

Hence it may be assumed that rows 1 and 2 of $\underline{M}$ are independent and the matrix

$$\underline{N} = \begin{bmatrix} \ell_{21} & \ell_{31} \\ \ell_{22} & \ell_{32} \end{bmatrix} \qquad (250)$$

is nonsingular. We shall denote $D = \det(\underline{N})$.

Next, we reduce the dimensionality of the problem, following the method of [Ho 76]. Suppose $f_i = f_2 = 0$ or

$$\ell_{11}a + \ell_{21}b + \ell_{31}c + \ell_{41}d = 0, \qquad (251)$$

$\ell_{12}a + \ell_{22}b + \ell_{32}c + \ell_{42}d = 0.$

In matrix notation $\underline{K} \begin{bmatrix} a \\ d \end{bmatrix} + \underline{N} \begin{bmatrix} b \\ c \end{bmatrix} = 0$ where $\underline{K} = \begin{bmatrix} \ell_{11} & \ell_{41} \\ \ell_{12} & \ell_{42} \end{bmatrix}$ (252)

Denoting $-\underline{N}^{-1} * \underline{K} = \begin{bmatrix} c_{11} & c_{12} \\ c_{21} & c_{22} \end{bmatrix}$ (253)

we obtain $\begin{bmatrix} b \\ c \end{bmatrix} = \begin{bmatrix} c_{11} & c_{12} \\ c_{21} & c_{22} \end{bmatrix} * \begin{bmatrix} a \\ d \end{bmatrix}$ (254)

When this is substituted in (244), the result is

$$\underline{U} \begin{bmatrix} p \\ \\ q \end{bmatrix} = \begin{bmatrix} a & c_{11}a + c_{12}d \\ -(c_{11}a + c_{12}d) & a \\ c_{12}a + c_{22}d & d \\ -d & c_{21}a + c_{22}d \end{bmatrix} \begin{bmatrix} p \\ q \end{bmatrix} = \underline{V}' \qquad (255)$$

The above is really the original, but reduced problem.

Our assumption being that the original problem can be computed in five multiplications, the reduced problem requires no more than three. Hence, by [Ah 76], p. 433, Theorem 12.1, the rows of $\underline{U}$ are dependent. There exists a vector of rational constants $\underline{w} = (w_1, w_2, w_3, w_4)^T$, not all zero, such that

$$(w_1 w_2 w_3 w_4)\underline{U} = \underline{0}. \qquad (256)$$

Writing this out in detail, and separating the parts depending on a and d yields:

$$\underline{Cw} = \begin{bmatrix} 1 & -c_{11} & c_{21} & 0 \\ 0 & -c_{12} & c_{22} & -1 \\ \\ c_{11} & 1 & 0 & c_{21} \\ c_{12} & 0 & 1 & c_{22} \end{bmatrix} * \begin{bmatrix} w_1 \\ w_2 \\ \\ w_3 \\ w_4 \end{bmatrix} = \underline{0}. \qquad (257)$$

It follows that $\underline{C}$ is singular. Applying the following transformation to $\underline{C}$: (a) multiplying column 2 by (-1), (b) exchanging columns 2 and 4, (c) exchanging columns 3 and 4, we arrive at the matrix

$$\underline{C}' = \begin{bmatrix} 1 & 0 & c_{11} & c_{21} \\ 0 & -1 & c_{12} & c_{22} \\ \\ c_{11} & c_{21} & -1 & 0 \\ c_{12} & c_{22} & 0 & 1 \end{bmatrix} , \qquad (258)$$

which is likewise singular. Denoting

$$\underline{E} = \begin{bmatrix} 1 & 0 \\ 0 & -1 \end{bmatrix}, \quad \underline{F} = \begin{bmatrix} \underline{C}_{11} & \underline{C}_{21} \\ \underline{C}_{12} & \underline{C}_{22} \end{bmatrix}, \tag{259}$$

we may write $\underline{C}'$ in block form as

$$\underline{C}' = \begin{bmatrix} \underline{E} & \underline{F} \\ \underline{F} & -\underline{E} \end{bmatrix}. \tag{260}$$

This matrix is singular if and only if $\underline{X} = \underline{E} + \text{FEF}$ is singular - otherwise

$$(\underline{C}')^{-1} = \begin{bmatrix} \underline{X}^{-1} & \underline{\text{EFX}}^{-1} \\ \underline{\text{EFX}}^{-1} & -\underline{X}^{-1} \end{bmatrix} . \tag{261}$$

$\underline{X}$ is singular iff $\underline{EX} = \underline{E}^2 + \underline{EFEF} = \underline{I} + (\underline{EF})^2$ is; this is equivalent to -1 being an eigenvalue of $(\underline{EF})^2$. Thus $i = \sqrt{-1}$ or $-i$ is an eigenvalue of $\underline{EF}$. It follows that

$$\det \begin{vmatrix} c_{11} \pm i & c_{21} \\ -c_{12} & -c_{22} \pm i \end{vmatrix} = 0, \tag{262}$$

where the $\pm$ sign denotes "either + or -".

Expanding (262) leads to the following conditions which are equivalent to it:

$c_{11} = c_{22}$; $c_{11}c_{22} - c_{12}c_{21} = - \det (\underline{N}^{-1} \ \underline{K}) = -1$ (263)(264)

From (252) and (253) we may derive, by direct computation, the values of c_{11} and c_{22}:

$$c_{11} = -\frac{1}{D} \det \begin{vmatrix} \ell_{11} & \ell_{31} \\ \ell_{12} & \ell_{32} \end{vmatrix}, \quad c_{22} = -\frac{1}{D} \det \begin{vmatrix} \ell_{21} & \ell_{41} \\ \ell_{22} & \ell_{42} \end{vmatrix} \quad (265), (266)$$

and by (263), these two determinants are equal. Consider now a new algorithm, obtained by replacing d with Kd in (243) where K is a rational constant. Carrying the argument throughout for the new algorithm, we should find:

$$c_{11(\text{new})} = -\frac{1}{D} \det \begin{vmatrix} \ell_{11} & \ell_{31} \\ \ell_{12} & \ell_{32} \end{vmatrix}, \tag{267}$$

$$c_{22(\text{new})} = -\frac{1}{D} \det \begin{vmatrix} \ell_{21} & K\ell_{41} \\ \ell_{22} & K\ell_{42} \end{vmatrix} = \frac{-K}{D} \det \begin{vmatrix} \ell_{21} & \ell_{41} \\ \ell_{22} & \ell_{42} \end{vmatrix} \tag{268}$$

Now, since $c_{11(\text{new})} = c_{22(\text{new})}$ for any K, it follows that $c_{11} = c_{22} = 0$.

Again from (252), (253):

$$c_{12} = -\frac{1}{D} \det \begin{vmatrix} \ell_{32} & \ell_{31} \\ \ell_{42} & \ell_{41} \end{vmatrix}, \quad c_{21} = -\frac{1}{D} \det \begin{vmatrix} \ell_{12} & \ell_{11} \\ \ell_{22} & \ell_{21} \end{vmatrix} \quad (269)\ (270)$$

From (264), $c_{12} \cdot c_{21} = 1$ and $c_{12(\text{new})} \cdot c_{21(\text{new})} = 1$, (271) (272)

but $c_{12(\text{new})} \cdot c_{21(\text{new})} = Kc_{12} \cdot c_{21}$, (273) and will be independent of K if and only if $c_{12} \cdot c_{21} = 0$, a contradiction. This proves the necessary part of the theorem.

Sufficiency: We note that (244) is equivalent to two complex multiplications (z_1w, z_2w). In fact, putting $z_1 = a - ib$, $z_2 = c - id$, $w = p + jq$, we find from (244) that

$$\underline{V} = [\text{Re}\,(z_1w),\ \text{Im}\,(z_1w),\ \text{Re}\,(z_2w),\ \text{Im}\,(z_2w)]^T \tag{274}$$

By [AHU76, p. 441], a complex multiplication can be carried out in three real multiplications not requiring commutativity.

Corollary: Two complex multiplications (z_1w, z_2w) require six noncommutative multiplications.

Vector by matrix multiplications

Some cases which may be brought back to complex numbers [WC 79] require multiplication of a vector by a matrix. The special form of $\bar{0}$-quads may also be of advantage here. If the matrix -times- vector multiplication is performed blockwise, then the basic operation is the multiplication of a 2 x 2 quad by a 2-vector. If the quad is of $\bar{D}$-type, then the multiplication is again equivalent to the multiplication of two complex numbers:

$$(a+jb)\ (v+jw) = (av-bw) + j(bv+aw) \tag{275}$$

$$\begin{bmatrix} a & -b \\ b & a \end{bmatrix} \begin{bmatrix} v \\ w \end{bmatrix} = \begin{bmatrix} av-bw \\ bv+aw \end{bmatrix} \tag{276}$$

and may therefore be carried out using $(3\mu+5\alpha)$ rather than $(4\mu+2\alpha)$ operations.

We are dealing here with matrix-times-vector multiplication. If the matrix is symmetric we may further reduce the number of operations.

Let $\underline{A} = (a_{ij})$ be an nxn symmetric matrix, and let $\underline{x}$, $\underline{y}$ be n-vectors. The matrix-times-vector multiplication $\underline{y} = \underline{A}\cdot\underline{x}$ may be arranged so that only $(n^2+n)/2$ multiplications are used (instead of the usual n^2 for a nonsymmetric matrix). This is done as follows:

a) Define the constants b_{ij} through

$$b_{ij} = a_{ij}(x_i+x_j),\ i,j = 1,2,\ldots,n;\ i\neq j. \tag{277}$$

There are n^2-n such constants. Note, however, that $b_{ij}=b_{ji}$ (because $a_{ij}=a_{ji}$); hence, when computing the b's only, $(n^2-n)/2$ multiplications and additions are needed.

b) Define the constants c_i through

$$c_i = (a_{ii} - \Sigma\ a_{ij})x_i,\ \ j\ \Sigma = 1,\ldots,n,\ j \neq i;\ i = 1,2,\ldots,n \tag{278}$$

The computation of the c's requires n multiplications and n(n-1) additions.

c) From the identity

$$y_i = \Sigma\ a_{ij}x_j = \sum_{j\neq i} a_{ij}(x_i+x_j) + (a_{ii}-\sum_{j\neq i} a_{ij})x_i = (\Sigma b_{ij}) + c_i;\ j\Sigma=1,\ldots,n \tag{279}$$

we see that having computed the b's and the c's, no further multiplications are required; this stage calls for $n(n-1)$ additions only.

In sum, the algorithm requires

$t = \mu(n^2+n)/2n+2.5n(n-1)\alpha.$ (280)

Note that this algorithm is efficient also when $\underline{A}$ is sparse; if $a_{ij} = 0$, the corresponding b_{ij} is not computed and the number of multiplications is thus roughly proportional to the number of nonzero elements of $\underline{A}$. Also note that the algorithm remains valid when the a's and b's are 2x2 and $\underline{x}$'s, $\underline{c}$'s and $\underline{y}$'s are 2-vectors.

6. DIRECT, PARALLEL AND ASP METHODS

Introduction

Direct methods of solving $\underline{A}\ \underline{x} = \underline{b}$ i.e. elimination, factorization or modification methods are very popular. There exist a large number of books on the subject and the reader is again referred specifically to [SB]. A few points of interest were also mentioned in Chapter 5. In the present chapter these methods will be adapted to Apps, SIMD and ASP-systems.

A number of methods for Apps were developed lately. Mentioned will be in particular the adaptation of the Gauss-Jordan method. For Apps it will show the by now familiar deficiency of requiring a very large number of slaves and for SIMD of data routing. An algorithm by Csanky is introduced via triangular systems; it is optimal in the number of operations required, but suffers not only from requiring a very large number of processors, but is unstable to bout. This is the result of having to form $\underline{A}^k$ for $k \leq n$. The algorithms are not very practical due to pivoting and data movement which would reduce the speedup considerably.

Data movement is included in computing the speedup of ASP-methods. It is thus found that both the Gauss and Jordan methods have reasonable speedups. The speedup of the Gaussian program is lowered by the Haydn effect. It is shown that various operations on triangular matrices e.g. decomposition, elimination and inversion can be parallelized more or less efficiently. Back-substitution would normally be considered unsuitable for parallelization - a notion disproved in 6.2.

Section 6.3 deals with sparsity. It is shown first that the methods of 6.2 are not suitable for solving $\underline{A}\ \underline{x} = \underline{b}$ if $\underline{A}$ is sparse, because they violate an "ASP-principle". The fill-in is introduced and so are various (sequential) reordering policies which should minimize the fill-in.

These reordering policies have given rise to a number of seemingly different algorithms. As shown in 6.4 they are all based either on the Gauss or the Jordan algorithms. It is therefore sufficient to develop ASP-programs for these two. Unfortunately, the speedups are low and special methods must be developed for sparse matrices. This will be done in Chapter 8.

6.1 KNOWN, PARALLEL METHODS

Aims: To discuss various methods of solving $\underline{A}\ \underline{x} = \underline{b}$ on Apps and SIMD-systems. In particular the speedup and number of slaves will be mentioned, the view being taken that it is not yet practical to build systems with more than 100-200 slaves.

Matrix inversion, solution of $\underline{A}\ \underline{x} = \underline{b}$ and matrix multiplication are related. So, for instance, the inverse of the particular 3n x 3n triangular matrix below is

$$\begin{bmatrix} \underline{U} & \underline{A} & \underline{0} \\ \underline{0} & \underline{U} & \underline{B} \\ \underline{0} & \underline{0} & \underline{U} \end{bmatrix}^{-1} = \begin{bmatrix} \underline{U} & -\underline{A} & \underline{AB} \\ \underline{0} & \underline{U} & -\underline{B} \\ \underline{0} & \underline{0} & \underline{U} \end{bmatrix} \qquad (1)$$

so that an (nxn) multiplication is all that is required. In a more general, but still triangular case:

$$\begin{bmatrix} \underline{A} & \underline{C} \\ \underline{0} & \underline{B} \end{bmatrix}^{-1} = \begin{bmatrix} \underline{A}^{-1} & -(\underline{A}^{-1}\underline{C})\underline{B}^{-1} \\ \underline{0} & \underline{B}^{-1} \end{bmatrix} \tag{2}$$

so that $\underline{A}^{-1}$ and $\underline{B}^{-1}$ could be computed (in parallel) and followed by two matrix multiplications. For some other cases of a dense matrix, inversion can also be reduced to matrix multiplications.

Suppose there exists an efficient algorithm for solving $\underline{Ax}=\underline{b}$ on Apps in time t. Then, $\underline{A}^{-1}$ may also be computed in t as follows (employing however an exorbitant number of slaves). Start from the identity:

$$\underline{A} \cdot \underline{A}^{-1} = \underline{U} \quad ; \quad \underline{A}^{-1} \equiv \underline{B} \tag{3}$$

and rewrite it as n linear systems:

$$\underline{A} \cdot \underline{b}_{.i} = \underline{u}_{.i} \; ; \; i=1,2,\ldots,n \tag{4}$$

Since the number of slaves in Apps is not bounded, all n systems may be solved concurrently, in time t.

The same can be achieved by applying Gauss-Jordan elimination to an "extended" matrix: for $\underline{A}\,\underline{x} = \underline{b}$, the $\underline{A}$-matrix is extended by the $\underline{b}$-column, for $\underline{A}^{-1}$ by an (nxn) unit matrix $\underline{U}$. The following simplified PL/I program describes it (using * to indicate a row of any, declared, length):

```
DO I=1 TO N;                      /* I is the pivoting row             */
   A(I,*)=A(I,*)/A(I,I);          /* Normalization                     */
   DO J=1 TO N; C=A(J,I);         /* J are the rows to be eliminated   */
      IF J=I THEN GO TO L;        /* Row I should not be eliminated    */
EL:   A(J,*)=A(J,*)-C*A(I,*);     /* Elimination, proper               */
 L:END;   END;
```

It does not seem obvious that elimination (statement EL:) can be executed independently for all values of J, but for I=1 we have:

$$\underline{a}_{2.}=\underline{a}_{2.}-a_{21}\underline{a}_{1.};\underline{a}_{3.}=\underline{a}_{3.}-a_{31}\underline{a}_{1.};\ldots;\underline{a}_{n.}=\underline{a}_{n.}-a_{n1}\underline{a}_{1.} \tag{5}$$

and similarly for I=2,...,N-1. The required number of operations is thus: one division, one α and one μ for every I, and for all J's. Altogether $(2\mu+\alpha)$ for every I or totally

$$\Omega_p = n(2\mu+\alpha) \tag{6}$$

The sequential solution of $\underline{A}\,\underline{x} = \underline{b}$ and $\underline{B} = \underline{A}^{-1}$ requires resp. $n^3\omega/3$, and $n^3\omega$ so that

$$\rho_{EL}=3(2\mu'+\alpha')/n^2 \; ; \; \rho_{INV}=(2\mu'+\alpha')/n^2 \tag{7}$$

n(n-1) processors are needed for computing EL in elimination. In inversion, $\underline{A}$ is extended so that its row has width 2n, and $(2n-1)n \cong 2n^2$ slaves are needed in the inner loop. The enormous speedup is achieved by using kn^2 slaves - a number we consider not practical for sizable n.

Inversion of a matrix can also be done on Illiac [Ku 68] as in the following "program":

```
DO I=1 TO N; B=A(I,I);
   DO K=1 TO N: A(I,K)=A(I,K)/B;(SIM)
   DO J=1 TO (N-1)**2:
      A(K,J)=A(K,J)-A(K,I)*A(I,J);(SIM)
END; END;
DO K=1 TO N:
   A(K,I)=-A(K,I)/B;(SIM)END;
A(I,I)=-A(I,I);END ;
```

In the above (SIM) stands for "simultaneous" execution. Following the program will show that routing is required, thus reducing the speedup.

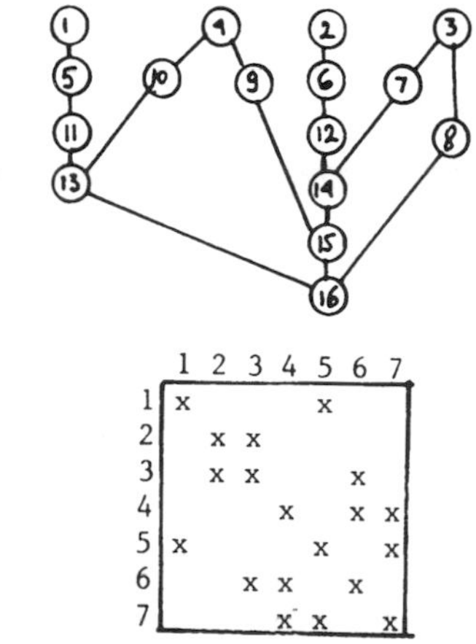

Fig. 1: A task-graph and a matrix

It is tempting to use Strassen's method [St 69] because it uses (at least asymptotically) fewer operations by performing block elimination. Unfortunately, it requires a complicated addressing scheme which may be difficult to achieve and leads to unwanted data movement. Another method, based on "bordering" would require about $n^2\log_2 n$ operations using n slaves [Pe 67,69] and is thus "not as good" as the elimination above. Its main advantage seems to be that it could be executed on special purpose computers which are used anyway for Fast Fourier Transforms.

All of the above algorithms use a large number of slaves. There is a view [KLS 77] that the higher such redundancy, the lower the stability of the algorithms.

A completely different approach is to seek an optimum number of slaves for any particular problem [WH 77]. This number is found by considering the precedence relations i.e. which operations must precede others.

Suppose matrix of fig. 1 is used. Initially, we may normalize:

(1) $a_{15}=a_{15}/a_{11}$; (2) $a_{23}=a_{23}/a_{22}$; (3) $a_{46}=a_{46}/a_{44}$. We could not normalize row (3) since a_{33} will be changed by the new a_{23}. But we could have initially done (4) $a_{47}=a_{47}/a_{44}$ since there are only zeros above a_{44}. Having found a_{15} we may do (5) $a_{55}=a_{55}-a_{51}*a_{15}$, having found a_{23} do (6) $a_{33}=a_{33}-a_{32}*a_{23}$ and then: (7) $a_{66}=a_{66}-a_{64}*a_{46}$; (8) $a_{76}=a_{76}-a_{74}*a_{46}$; (9) $a_{67}=a_{67}-a_{64}*a_{47}$; (10) $a_{77}=a_{77}-a_{74}*a_{47}$; (11) $a_{57}=a_{57}/a_{55}$; (12) $a_{36}=a_{36}/a_{33}$; (13) $a_{77}=a_{77}-a_{75}*a_{57}$; (14) $a_{66}=a_{66}-a_{63}*a_{36}$ (15) $a_{67}a_{67}/a_{66}$; (16) $a_{77}=a_{77}-a_{76}*a_{76}$.

These 16 operations are collected to a task-graph which shows the precedence relations e.g. that operation (13) may be done only after (10) and (11) are completed. It also shows that we need 6 slaves (for doing concurrently operations 5,6,7,8,9,10) and that this system of n=7 can be done in 6 steps (compare to $\frac{343}{6} \cong 57$ slaves and $3^2=9$ steps).

It may be shown that if the rows and columns are arranged according to the sequence 1,5,7,4,6,3,2, a tridiagonal set results but it cannot be solved in less than 12 steps. The authors then proceed to find a (heuristic) method for the search of an optimal ordering - a topic to which we will return later, but apply it to ASP.

We will next discuss an algorithm by Heller for solving $\underline{A}\ \underline{x} = \underline{b}$ with $\underline{A}$ being a lower triangular matrix [He 76]. It is based on three lemmata.

<u>Lemma 1</u>: Let $\underline{A}$ be an (nxn) lower triangular matrix, with $a_{ii}=0$, $i=1,..,n$. Then $\underline{A}^n=0$.

<u>Proof</u>: The characteristic polynomial of $\underline{A}$ equals

$$\det(\underline{A}-\lambda\underline{U})=(-1)^n\lambda^n \tag{8}$$

By the Cayley-Hamilton theorem this polynomial and thus $\underline{A}^n$ equal zero.

<u>Lemma 2</u>: Let $\underline{B} = \underline{U} - \underline{A}$ where $\underline{A}$ is as in Lemma 1. Then

$$\underline{B}^{-1} = \underline{U} + \underline{A} + \underline{A}^2 + \ldots + \underline{A}^{n-1} \tag{9}$$

<u>Proof</u>: Let $\underline{C} = \underline{U} + \underline{A} + \underline{A}^2 + \ldots + \underline{A}^{n-1}$. Then:

$$(\underline{U}-\underline{A})\underline{C} = (\underline{U}+\underline{A}+\underline{A}^2+\ldots+\underline{A}^{n-1})-(\underline{A}+\underline{A}^2+\ldots+\underline{A}^n) = \underline{U}-\underline{A}^n=\underline{U}-0=\underline{U} \tag{10}$$

Hence: $$\underline{C} = (\underline{U}-\underline{A})^{-1} = \underline{B}^{-1} \tag{11}$$

<u>Lemma 3</u>: $$(\underline{U}+\underline{A}^1)(\underline{U}+\underline{A}^2)(\underline{U}+\underline{A}^{2^2})\ldots(\underline{U}+\underline{A}^{2^{k-1}})=\underline{U}+\underline{A}+\underline{A}^2+\ldots+\underline{A}^{2^k-1} \tag{12}$$

<u>Proof</u>: For k=1 we have $2^k-1=1$, $2^{k-1}=1$ and $\underline{U} + \underline{A} = \underline{U} + \underline{A}$ i.e. identity. Inductively, for a given k>1:

$$(\underline{U} + \underline{A} + \underline{A}^2 + \ldots + \underline{A}^{2^k-1})\ (\underline{U} + \underline{A}^{2^k}) = (\underline{U} + \underline{A} + \underline{A}^2 + \ldots + \underline{A}^{2^k-1}) +$$

$$(\underline{A}^{2^k} + \underline{A}^{2^k+1} + \ldots + \underline{A}^{2^k-1+2^k}) = \underline{U} + \underline{A} + \underline{A}^2 + \ldots\ \underline{A}^{2^{k+1}-1} \tag{13}$$

which is again of the required form, but now for k+1. Q.E.D.

To solve $\underline{A}\ \underline{x} = \underline{b}$ where $\underline{A} = \underline{U} - \underline{B}$ is a lower unit and $\underline{B}$ a strictly lower triangular matrix, we first insert:

$$\underline{x} = \underline{A}^{-1}\ \underline{b} = (\underline{U}-\underline{B})^{-1} \cdot \underline{b} \tag{14}$$

then use Lemma 2 to get

$$\underline{x} = (\underline{U}+\underline{B}+\underline{B}^2 + \ldots + \underline{B}^{n-1}) \cdot \underline{b} \tag{15}$$

and finally use Lemma 3 to get the result:

$$\underline{x} = (\underline{U}+\underline{B})(\underline{U}+\underline{B}^2)\ldots(\underline{U}+\underline{B}^{2^c})\underline{b} \tag{16}$$

$2^k-1 \geq n$ operations are required in the sum, so that $2^k \geq n+1$, $2^{k-1} \geq (n+1)/2$ and:

$$c = k-1 \geq \log_2(n+1)/2 \tag{17}$$

The number of operations is at most d^2+d where $d= \log_2 n$. The number of slaves can be calculated using the tableaux below, where summation (by columns) yields:

$$\begin{bmatrix} 1 & & & \\ 2 & 1 & & \\ 3 & 2 & 1 & \\ & \ddots & \ddots & \\ n & & 2 & 1 \end{bmatrix}$$

$$(1+2+\ldots+n)+(1+2+\ldots+n-1)+\ldots+(1+2)+1=\Sigma i(i+1)/2 =$$
$$0.5(\Sigma i+\Sigma i^2) = 0.5\ n(n+1)/2 + 0.5\ n(n+1)(2n+1)/6 \cong n^3/6 \tag{18}$$

This is a very high number of slaves, even for purely theoretical considerations and we next discuss another method [CK 75]. It is a variation on the Gauss-Jordan elimination scheme and might be called "elimination by diagonals". Given a unit, lower-triangular matrix $\underline{A}$; $a_{ii}=1$, $i=1,\ldots,n$ with $\ell-1$ diagonals equal to zero

$$a_{ik} = 0, \text{ for } i-k=1,\ldots,\ell \tag{19}$$

it is possible, in parallel, to eliminate ℓ further diagonals. The "program" would be:

```
DO J=1 TO (N-1);
   DO I=J+1 TO N;
   A(I,*)=A(I,*)/A(I,I);
   DO K=J TO (J+J-1);
   A(I,*)=A(I,*)-A(I,I-K)*A(I-K,*)
END;END;END;/* of loops j,i,k to be done in parallel  */
DO I=1 TO N; /* this loop too can be done in parallel */
   X(I)=A(I,N+1);END;
```

The method is seen to proceed as follows: Initially, the first subdiagonal is zeroed and we have a "strip" of diagonals of width w=2. Next, set the next two diagonals to zero etc. The process may be described as one in which w is doubling itself each time. To calculate the number of operations and slaves we use fig. 2. The first step would be to multiply rows in order to zero a strip. This can be done in a single, parallel operation and we can calculate the number of slaves p by adding the number of multiplications for areas A,B and C respectively.

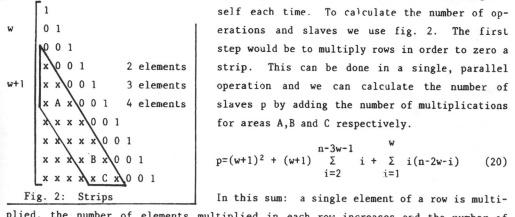

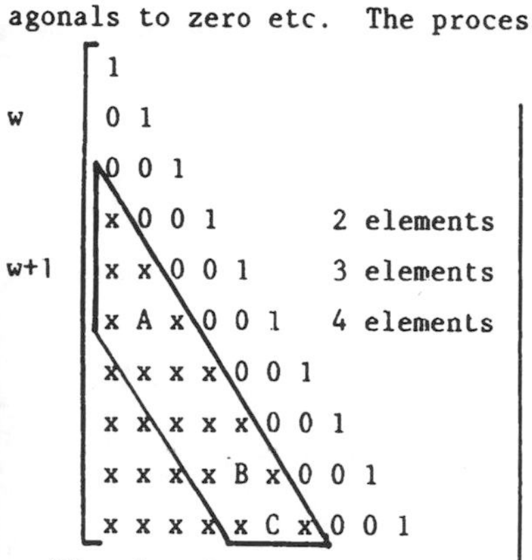

Fig. 2: Strips

$$p=(w+1)^2 + (w+1) \sum_{i=2}^{n-3w-1} i + \sum_{i=1}^{w} i(n-2w-i) \qquad (20)$$

In this sum: a single element of a row is multiplied, the number of elements multiplied in each row increases and the number of elements in a row increases but the number of those zeroed already in a column decreases. In sum total, we have:

$$p = (w+1)^2 + 0.5(w+1)(n-3w+1)(n-3w-2)+(n-2w) \Sigma\, i - \Sigma\, i^2;\; i\Sigma=1,\dots,w \qquad (21)$$

For $w \gg 1$, $n \gg 1$ this is approximately

$$p = 0.5w(n-3w)^2 + (n-2w)w^2/2 - w^3/3 \qquad (22)$$

Differentiating and comparing to 0 yields

$$w_{1,2} = (5n\pm\sqrt{6n})/19 = (0.39 \text{ or } 0.134)n \qquad (23)$$

$$p_{min} = 0.0037n^3 \cong n^3/270;\; p_{max} = 0.0299n^3 \cong n^3/34 \qquad (24)$$

for the first step. For zeroing a "strip", we need at most (w+1) subtractions or (w+1)/2 slaves. The number of elements in an area would be

$$1+2+3+\dots+n - 2(w+1) \cong 0.5(n-2w)^2 \qquad (25)$$

The number of slaves to process all these elements is

$$p \cong 0.5w \cdot 0.5(n-2w)^2 = 0.25(4w^3-4nw^2+wn^2) \qquad (26)$$

$\partial p/\partial w=0$ will yield $w=(8n\pm 4n)/24$ or

$$w_{min}=n/2;\; w_{max}=n/6;\; p_{max}=0.25(4n^3/216-4n^3/36+n^3/6)=n^3/54 \qquad (27)$$

The number of slaves needed when only essential operations are performed is slightly lower, namely $n^3/68$. The number of operations is:

$$\Omega=\log_2 2+\log_2 4+\ldots+\log_2(n/2)=1+2+\ldots+\log_2(n/2)=0.5(\log_2 n/2)^2 \tag{28}$$

As already mentioned, block elimination can be used. Thus since

$$\begin{bmatrix} \underline{A} & \underline{0} \\ \underline{B} & \underline{C} \end{bmatrix}^{-1} = \begin{bmatrix} \underline{A}^{-1} & \underline{0} \\ -(\underline{C}^{-1}\underline{B})\underline{A}^{-1} & \underline{C}^{-1} \end{bmatrix} \; ; \quad \begin{array}{l} \underline{A} \text{ is } (m\times m) \\ \underline{A},\underline{C} \text{ are lower triangular} \end{array} \tag{29}$$

$\underline{A}$ and $\underline{C}$ would be inverted simultaneously, $\underline{C}*\underline{D} = \underline{B}$ would be solved and finally $\underline{D}$ and $\underline{A}^{-1}$ would be multiplied. As proved in [BM 75] the number of slaves and the number of operations are of the order of n^3 and $(\log_2 n)^2$ respectively.

The inverse of $\underline{L}$ can be expressed as a product of Frobenius matrices, $\underline{F}_i$ which are $\underline{U}$ except for the i-th column which is

$$\underline{f}_{.i} = [0,\ldots,0,1/\ell_{ii},-\ell_{i+1,i}/\ell_{ii},\ldots,-\ell_{n,i}/\ell_{ii}]^T \tag{30}$$

The solution of $\underline{A}\,\underline{x} = \underline{b}$ is therefore $\underline{x} = \underline{F}_n \cdot \underline{F}_{n-1} \ldots \underline{F}_1 \cdot \underline{b}$ (31)

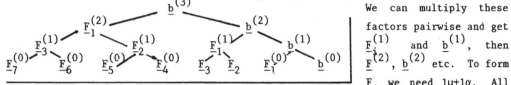

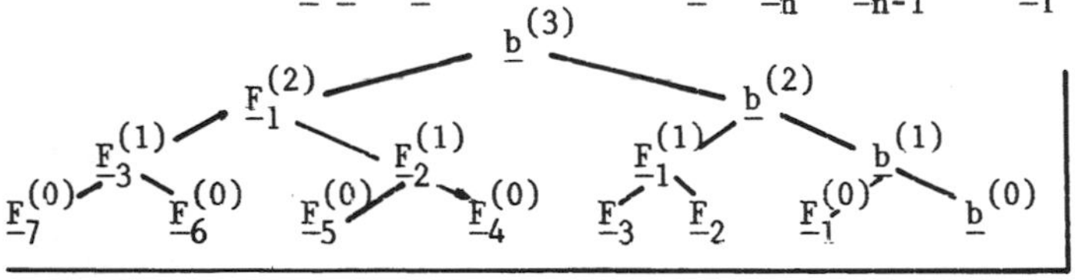

We can multiply these factors pairwise and get $\underline{F}_i^{(1)}$ and $\underline{b}^{(1)}$, then $\underline{F}^{(2)}$, $\underline{b}^{(2)}$ etc. To form $\underline{F}_i$ we need $1\mu+1\alpha$. All products can be done in parallel for $(1+j)(\mu+\alpha)$ where j is the level of the tree [SB 77]. Since one additional multiplication is required

$$\Omega_p = 3\mu + \Sigma\,(2+j)\omega = 3\mu + 3\omega \log_2 n/2+0.5\omega(\log_2 n)^2; \; j\Sigma=0,\ldots,\log_2 n \tag{32}$$

or if we assume $\alpha=\mu=0.5\omega$

$$\Omega_p = 3\mu + 0.5\mu \log_2 n(3+\log_2 n) \tag{33}$$

It is also shown in [SB 77] that the number of slaves needed is

$$p \cong 15\, n^3/1024 \cong n^3/68 \tag{34}$$

i.e. the same as in (27). The number of operations is also the order of $(\log_2 n)^2$ as in (28), so that the importance of this method is not so much by itself as because it points to a general approach, may be applied to band-systems [SB 77] and mainly because (31) is applicable to back-substitution for a dense, quadratic matrix and we have to discuss this, more general, case too.

This leads us to an algorithm by Csanky [Cs 75] for computing $\underline{x} = \underline{A}^{-1}\underline{b}$ for a general matrix $\underline{A}$. We need for it some Lemmata:

<u>Lemma 1</u>: Let λ_j be an eigenvalue of $\underline{A}$, s_i the "trace" of $\underline{A}^i$ and

$$\psi(z) = \Pi\,(z-\lambda_j) = \det(z\underline{U}-\underline{A}) = z^n+c_1 z^{n-1}+\ldots+c_{n-1}z+c_n; \; j\Pi=1,\ldots,n \tag{35}$$

Then: $\quad s_i = \Sigma\,\lambda_j^i \; ; \; j\Sigma=1,\ldots,n$ (36)

<u>Proof</u>: The trace of $\underline{A}$ is Σa_{ii}, or the coefficient of z^{n-1} in the expansion of $\det(z\underline{U}-\underline{A})$. Next expand the matrix with $z-a_{ii}$, $i=1,\ldots,n$ on the diagonal, by its first row: All, but the main diagonal will contain terms of maximum degree n-2. Hence, the only contribution to z^{n-1} comes from:

$$(z-a_{11})(z-a_{22})\ldots(z-a_{nn})=z^n-(\Sigma a_{ii})z^{n-1}+\ldots \tag{37}$$

and $\quad c_1 = -\Sigma a_{ii} = -$ trace of $\underline{A}_i$ (38)

Since c_1 is the negative sum of all roots we have

$$\text{trace}(\underline{A}) = \Sigma\, \lambda_j^1 \;;\; j\Sigma=1,\ldots,n \tag{39}$$

With $(\lambda_1,\lambda_2,\ldots,\lambda_n)$ as eigenvalues of $\underline{A}$, we have that $(\lambda_1^i,\lambda_2^i,\ldots,\lambda_n^i)$ are the eigenvalues of $\underline{A}^i$ and by the same token, that

$$s_i = \Sigma\, \lambda_j^i = \text{trace}\,(\underline{A}^i) \;;\; j\Sigma=1,\ldots,n \tag{40}$$

Lemma 2 (The Newton identities):

$$\begin{bmatrix} 1 & & & & & \\ s_1 & 2 & & & & \\ s_2 & s_1 & 3 & & & \\ s_3 & s_2 & s_1 & 4 & & \\ \sim\sim\sim & & \ddots & \ddots & & \\ s_{n-1} & s_{n-2} & & & s_1 & n \end{bmatrix} * \begin{bmatrix} c_1 \\ c_2 \\ c_3 \\ c_4 \\ \vdots \\ c_n \end{bmatrix} = -\begin{bmatrix} s_1 \\ s_2 \\ s_3 \\ s_4 \\ \vdots \\ s_n \end{bmatrix} \tag{41}$$

$$s_i = -s_{i-1}c_1 - s_{i-2}c_2 - \ldots - s_1 c_{i-1} - ic_i \;;\; i=1,2,\ldots n \tag{42}$$

Proof: The first row of (41) yields $c_1=-s_1$, the second $s_1c_1+2c_2=-s_2$ which points to roots of polynomials. Thus if

$$\psi(x)=x^n+c_1x^{n-1}+c_2x^{n-2}+\ldots+c_{n-1}x+c_n \tag{43}$$

is a polynomial with distinct roots $\gamma,\delta,\ldots,\varepsilon$, then

$$\psi'(x)=nx^{n-1}+(n-1)c_1x^{n-2}+(n-2)c_2x^{n-3}+\ldots+c_{n-1} \tag{44}$$

and $\psi'(x)=\psi(x)/(x-\gamma)+\psi(x)/(x-\delta)+\ldots+\psi(x)/(x-\varepsilon)$ (45)

By a long division, and because γ is a root of $\psi(x)=0$:

$$\psi(x) = (x-\gamma)P(x)+0 \tag{46}$$

$$\begin{aligned}\psi(x)/(x-\gamma)&=x^{n-1}+(\gamma+c_1)x^{n-2}+[(\gamma+c_1)\gamma+c_2]x^{n-3}+\ldots((\gamma+c_1)\gamma+c_2)\gamma+\ldots)\gamma c_{n-1}\\ &= x^{n-1}+(\gamma+c_1)x^{n-2}+(\gamma^2+c_1\gamma+c_2)x^{n-3}+\ldots+(\gamma^{n-1}+c_1\gamma^{n-1}+\ldots)\end{aligned} \tag{47}$$

$$\psi(x)/(x-\delta)=x^{n-1}+(\delta+c_1)x^{n-2}+(\delta^2+c_1\delta+c_2)x^{n-3}+(\delta^3+c_1\delta^2+c_2\delta+c_3)x^{n-3}+\ldots \tag{48}$$

and so forth. Therefore:

$$\begin{aligned}\psi'(x)=nx^{n-1}&+[(\gamma+\delta+\ldots+\varepsilon)+nc_1]x^{n-2}+[(\gamma^2+\delta^2+\ldots+\varepsilon^2)+c_1(\gamma+\delta+\ldots+\varepsilon)+nc_2]x^{n-3}+\ldots\\ &\ldots+(s_i+c_1s_{i-1}+c_2s_{i-2}+\ldots+c_{i-1}s_1+nc_i)x^{n-i-1}\end{aligned} \tag{49}$$

but because of (44), we have by comparing coefficients that

$$s_i+c_1s_{i-1}+c_2s_{i-2}+\ldots+c_{i-1}s_1+nc_i=(n-i)c_i \tag{50}$$

and $s_i=-s_{i-1}c_1-s_{i-2}c_2-\ldots-ic_i$ Q.E.D. (51)

Lemma 3: $\underline{A}^{-1}=-(\underline{A}^{n-1}+c_1\underline{A}^{n-2}+\ldots+c_{n-2}\underline{A}+c_{n-1}\underline{U})/c_n$ (52)

Proof: By the Cayley-Hamilton theorem

$$\underline{A}^n + c_1\,\underline{A}^{n-1} + \ldots + c_{n-1}\,\underline{A} + c_n = 0 \tag{53}$$

$\underline{A}$ was assumed nonsingular, $c_n=\Pi(\lambda_i)\neq 0$ so that

$$\underline{A}(\underline{A}^{n-1}+c_1\underline{A}^{n-2}+\ldots+c_{n-1})+c_n=0 \tag{54}$$

Rearranging (54) yields (52).

We are now ready for the algorithm of Csanky. Let $k=\log_2 n$ and compute z^i,

$1 \leqq i \leqq n$ in n operations using n/2 slaves. Thus $\underline{A}^i$, $1 \leqq i \leqq n$ can be computed, in an obvious way in k(k+1) operations using n^4 slaves. To compute $s_i = \text{trace}(\underline{A}^i)$, i=1,2,...,n will take also nω on $0.5n^2$ slaves. Next solve for the c_i's the system of Lemma 2 by (31) in (k+1)(k+2)/2 with about n^3 slaves. Finally, $\underline{A}^{-1}$ may be computed in (k+2)ω using n^3 slaves. Since $\underline{x} = \underline{A}^{-1}\underline{b}$ requires (k+1)ω on n^2 slaves

$$\Omega_p \leqq 1.5\,(\log_2 n)^2 \tag{55}$$

Unfortunately, the calculation of c_n is extremely sensitive to rounding errors committed in the evaluation of the traces s_i. Csanky's method is therefore an excellent theoretical result of no great help in creating actual programs. It also requires n^4 slaves which we consider prohibitively large; the solution by way of elimination seems more practical.

However, in dealing with elimination, we have neglected the need for pivoting. If $a_{ii}=0$, then (n-i) elements of column i have to be searched for $a_{ji} \neq 0$. With k= log(n-1) this will add

$$\Sigma\,[\log(n-j)] = kn-2^k - k + 1\ ;\ j=1,\ldots,n-1 \tag{56}$$

comparisons. If we assume that comparison also needs time ω, then 3nω were needed for Gauss-Jordan elimination, but $n\log_2 n$ for pivoting. It is seen that <u>the effort on pivoting can completely overwhelm the arithmetic effort</u> and it is not surprising that ways of evading the pivoting were attempted. They rely on Given's rotations and will be discussed later.

Data movement, even more than pivoting, will increase the time of a solution on Apps or SIMD-systems. This is convincingly proved in [Mo 78] for Apps, Illiac and even computers with the shuffle network and will not be repeated here.

<u>Conclusions</u>: We have discussed block and nonblock elimination as well as Csanky's methods for a general and a number of algorithms for triangular matrices. All required a prohibitively large ($>n^2$) number of slaves, show low utilization and (probably) low stability. Their time bounds are good only if pivoting and data transfer are not accounted for. Next we discuss whether the same applies to ASP-systems.

6.2 ASP-ELIMINATION

<u>Aims</u>: In this section we discuss the application of ASP to elimination methods e.g. Gauss, Jordan, Cholesky and similar algorithms. Then we apply ASP to triangular matrices and for back-substitution. The ratios of all methods are computed.

6.2.1 General, dense matrices

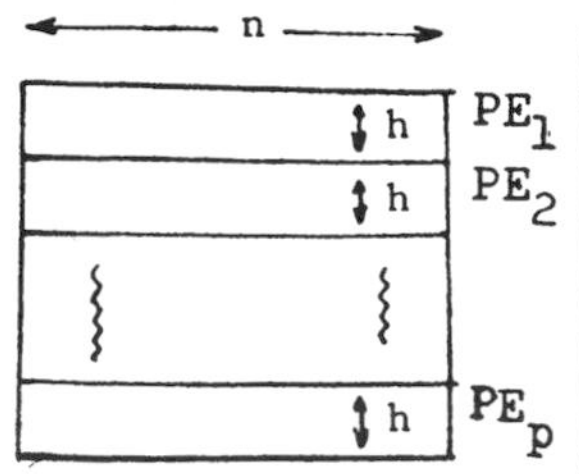

Fig. 3: Data structure

It was noted in 6.1 that the data structure required for solving $\underline{A}\,\underline{x} = \underline{b}$ on SIMD-systems is very complicated and is one of its main weaknesses. The data structure for ASP-execution is based on "slicing" (Fig. 3), that is, a slice of width

$$h = n/p \tag{57}$$

and length n, is assigned to each slave (h is assumed to be an integer; if $n \neq h{*}p$, some zero rows are added to the slice residing in memory of slave p). These slices could have been stored so that rows are numbered as in the original matrix A. This would require a large storage space (n^2 words for A) in every (slave) memory. Instead, we will number all slices of A starting with row 1 (and thus reaching h). This means that we have saved storage, but will have to compute the correspondence between the row indices in slices and those of the entire matrix A as stored in the (common) store.

The first to be discussed is the method of Jordan since it is easily implemented on ASP. The pivoting row is sent from the memory which holds it to the master and is broadcast to all processors. Having received this vector (stored as T), each processor performs the Jordan elimination process on its slice of rows. In the following example, the pivoting rows are taken in natural order.

```
JORDAN: PROC;
DCL (H,I,LO(P),H1(P),P)FIXED, (#)(H,I,IP,J,K,N)FIXED,
(A(N,N),B(N),X(N),T(N+1),D)FLOAT.(#)(A(H,N+1),B(H),X(N),T(N+1),D,B)FLOAT;
GET DATA; H=N/P
DO I=1 TO P;                           /*FOR EVERY SLAVE CALCULATE THE LOW     */
   LO(I)=(I-1)*H+1;H1(I)=I*H;          /*AND HIGH BOUNDS OF A SLICE.           */
   (I)A(1:H,1:N)≡A(LO(I):H1(I),1:N);   /*SLICES OF A AND B ARE TRANSFERRED     */
   (I)B(1:H)≡B(LO(I):H1(I));           /*TO THE SLAVES BY BLOCKS.              */
END;                                   /*END OF INITIALIZATION                 */
DO IP=1 TO P;                          /*PIVOTING ROW IS TAKEN FROM MEMORY IP. */
   DO J=LO(IP) TO H1 (IP);             /*J IS THE INDEX OF THE PIVOT ROW       */
                                       /*LO & HI ARE THE LIMITS OF THE SLICE.  */
      T(J:N+1)≡(IP)A(J,J:N+1);         /*TRANSFER NONZERO PART OF PIVOTING     */
                                       /*ROW TO THE MASTER.                    */
      PUT BROADCAST (J);               /*NUMBER OF PIVOTING ROW AND THE        */
      PUT BROADCAST (T(J:N+1));        /*ROW ITSELF ARE BROADCAST.
      (#) PARCALL ELIM1;               /*ELIMINATE IN PARALLEL.                */
END; END;
/*  The only parallel part above, was the call on the (parallel) procedure ELIM1.
This procedure computes and stores the factor table F (i.e. the left and right tri-
angular matrices L and R) needed for back-substitution and for other purposes - to
be mentioned.                                                                  */
ELIM1:PARPROC;
D=1.0/T(J):                    /* NEXT IS NORMALIZATION OF THE PIVOT ROW       */
DO K=J+1 TO N+1; T(K)=T(K)*D; END;
LOOP: DO I=1 TO H;
   IF LO+I-1=J THEN DO; /* SPECIAL TREATMENT OF PIVOTING ROW                   */
F1:A(I,J)=D;                   /* FOR FACTOR TABLE                             */
   DO K=J+1 TO N+1; A(J,K)=T(K); END;
   GO TO E1; END;
```

```
SAVE:  B=A(I,J);
IF B=0 THEN GOTO E1;
F2:A(I,J)=-B*D;                  /* THIS PART CONSTRUCTS THE FACTOR TABLE     */
DO K=J+1 TO N+1;
   A(I,K)=A(I,K)-T(K)*B; END;
E1:  END;                        /* END OF THE LOOP                           */
END;                             /* END OF ELIM1                              */
END;                             /* END OF THE JORDAN PROCEDURE               */
```

The only row not operated on is naturally the pivoting row itself, which is merely replaced in memory by its normalized replica (see special treatment of pivoting row in the program). Statements F1 and F2 replace the matrix A with elements of the factor table. Statement SAVE will save operations in case of a sparse matrix (the treatment of sparsity will be given later).

The J'th call of ELIM1 results in:

(a) (N-J+2) multiplications for normalization.

(b) H(N-J+2) multiplications and H(N-J+1) subtractions (inner loop following F2).

The total time spent in the parallel step equals therefore

$$t_1 = \Sigma\ (H+1)(N-J+2)\mu + \Sigma\ H(N-J+1)\alpha = .5(H+1)(N+1)(N+2)\mu + .5HN(N+1)\alpha + \{N\beta + 0.5(N+1)(N+2)\tau\}\ ;\ J\Sigma=1,\ldots,n \quad (58)$$

where the part in braces includes the time for synchronization and $2(N-J+1)\tau$ for transfer. The time required for purely sequential execution is

$$t_s = (N^3/2+N^2+N/2)\mu + 0.5(N^3-N)\alpha \quad (59)$$

Combining these results and assuming N>>p we have, after some algebra

$$\rho_J = (t_1+t_2)/t_s \cong 1/p + 2\beta'/n^2 + \tau'/n \quad (60)$$

It is seen that when n is large, the reduction approaches ideal 1/p.

Gaussian elimination differs from the method of Jordan in that the elimination of non-zeros occurs only below the diagonal. This difference can be easily incorporated into the JORDAN program if ELIM1 is changed into ELIM2 as follows.

```
ELIM2:  PARPROC;
IF J>H1 THEN RETURN;                     /* INITIAL CONDITION         */
DO K=J+1 TO N+1; T(K)=T(K)*D;  END;
LOOP:  DO I=MAX(1,J-LO+1) TO H;
```

with the rest of the procedure unchanged.

Let us next calculate the time t required for factorization of the (nxn) matrix A (assumed to be dense) on ASP according to Gaussian elimination (to be called the G-method). It is

$$t_G \cong \Sigma\ (i^*\mu + n^*i(\mu+\alpha)/p + \beta + i^*\tau)\ ;\ i\Sigma=1,\ldots,n \quad (61)$$

where the first summand ($i^*\mu$) is required for normalization of rows, the second for introducing zeros (parallel step), the third for transfer synchronization (securing the bus) and the last for actual data-transfer over the bus. The actual time t_G is smaller than that of (61) because when the last slave works, it does not have either to send information to the other slaves nor eliminate its upper triangular part.

The summation results in

$$t_G = n(n+1)\mu/2 + n^2(n+1)\omega/(2p) + n\beta + n(n+1)\tau/2 \qquad (62)$$

If - as is usually the case

$$h = n/p >> 1 \qquad (63)$$

then the first expression may be neglected when compared to the second. The remaining three expressions represent the total computing time t_C, the total synchronization time t_S and the total bus transfer time t_B, namely

$$t_C = n^2(n+1)\omega/(2p);\ t_S = n*\beta;\ t_B = n(n+1)\tau/2 \qquad (64)$$

It is seen that t_B is negligible compared to the other two parts, so that

$$t_G \cong n^3(\mu+\alpha)/(2p) + t_S \qquad (65)$$

As was shown in Chapter 5, Gaussian elimination on a monocomputer requires

$$T_G = \Sigma\ (i*\mu+(i-1)(i*\mu+i*\alpha) \cong n^3(\mu+\alpha)/3 \quad ;\ i\Sigma=1,\dots,n \qquad (66)$$

Hence, for Gaussian elimination

$$\rho_G = 1/p + 1/(2p) + 3\beta'/n^2 + 3\tau'/(2n) \qquad (67)$$

In this case the synchronization part may also be neglected.

The foregoing shows that the J-method is more suitable for being used on ASP since it almost achieves the ideal speedup i.e. is about p times faster than if executed on a conventional computer. Usually (see Chapter 5), Gaussian elimination is considered to be more efficient by a factor of 3/2 so the reason for this discrepancy should be discussed.

ASP executes the G-method as follows: The first row is normalized in the first memory, is sent over the bus and only then do all p slaves work in parallel. The same sequence is repeated for rows 2,3,...,h but when the second slave starts working on rows h+1,h+2,...,2h, the first slave becomes idle and henceforth drops out completely. Similarly, after the second slave completes its work on row 2h, the third slave starts and the first two slaves are effectively removed from the process. Finally, when row (p-1)h has been broadcast over the bus, only the last slave remains working.

We have again the Haydn effect and it seems to be responsible for Gaussian elimination being less suited for ASP, than Jordan's method. To find more accurately how this effects elimination, we next discuss more thoroughly the use of both ELIM-procedures.

Suppose that in the main program IP=1, that is the pivoting row J is taken from the memory of slave 1. In other words, LO≦J≦H1 for slave 1 and J<LO for all other slaves. Therefore, for slaves 2,...,p the initial condition of ELIM2 does not hold; moreover, since J<LO then J-LO+1≦1 and thus MAX(1,J-LO+1)=1. It follows that for these slaves invoking ELIM2 has the same effect as invoking ELIM1. In general, when the pivoting row is taken from memory of slave K, then all slaves numbered K+1,K+2, ...,p do the same work in Gaussian as in the Jordan elimination. It follows that with the exception of the last slice, both take the same time when executed on ASP.

Yet when executed on a sequential machine, the method of Gauss is faster than that of Jordan by a factor of 3/2. Thus, the ratio of the above implementation of the G-method tends to 2/(3p) as n grows, rather than to the ideal value 1/p.

This ratio-increase is due to poor utilization of the slaves. To observe this, let IP=3. Hence J>H1 for slaves 1 and 2. When parallel procedure ELIM2 is started by these slaves, it is immediately terminated by the initial condition. In general, when IP=K only slaves K,K+1,...,p remain active and slaves 1,2,...,K-1 are idle. As elimination proceeds the slaves drop out one-by-one due to the Haydn effect.

A simple remedy to this situation is to take the first pivoting row from slave 1, the second pivoting row from memory of slave 2 and so on cyclically. This is done in the following PPL/1 program.

```
GAUSS2:  PROC;
DCL((#)(T(N),K1,K2,J),T(N),K1,K2,J)FLOAT;
J=1;                            /* COUNT OF ROWS WHICH HAVE BEEN USED   */
DO K1=1 TO H;                   /* K1=INDEX OF THE PIVOTING ROW,        */
DO K2=1 TO P;                   /* K2 INDICATES THE NUMBER OF MEMORY    */
                                /* FROM WHICH THE PIVOTING ROW COMES.   */
T(J:N+1)≡(K2)A(K1,J:N+1);       /* TRANSFER PIVOTING ROW TO MASTER.     */
PUT BROADCAST (K1,K2,J);
PUT BROADCAST (T(J:N+1));       /* BROADCAST IT TO ALL SLAVES.          */
PARCALL ELIM2;                  /* ELIMINATE IN PARALLEL.               */
J=J+1;  END;  END;
ELIM2:  PARPROC;
D=1/T(J);
DO K=J+1 TO N+1;T(K)=T(K)*D;END;     /* NORMALIZATION OF PIVOT ROW.      */
DO I=K1 TO H;                        /* I POINTS TO A ROW IN THE SLICE.  */
   IF (I=K1)&(K2=NAME) THEN DO;      /* IF I POINTS TO THE PIVOTING ROW  */
   A(I,J)=D;
   DO K=J+1 TO N+1; A(I,K)=T(K); END;
   GOTO E1;  END;
B=A(I,J); IF B=0 THEN GOTO E1;
A(I,J)=-B*D;                         /* ELIMINATION PROPER               */
DO K=J+1 TO N+1;
   A(I,K)=A(I,K)-T(K)*B;
END;
E1:  END; END; END;
```

The calculation of the ratio ρ for this elimination method, being different from the previous, will be presented in some detail.

It takes $n*\mu$ to normalize the first row (from memory 1) and each slave (with the exception of the first) eliminates h elements in the first column; this requires $hn(\mu+\alpha)$ operations. The second column requires $(n-1)\mu$ for row normalization and

$h(n-1)(\mu+\alpha)$ for elimination; thus when $k<p$, the k'th row (taken from the k'th memory) calls for $(n-k+1)\mu+h(n-k+1)\omega$. When we arrive at the p'th slave, the length of the vector to be normalized is $(n-p+1)$. However, there are now only h-1 zeroes in each memory to introduce. The result is thus $(n-p+1)\mu+(h-1)(n-p+1)\omega$.

The continuation of the process is readily perceived. The normalization terms form an arithmetical sequence with distance $d=-\mu$, starting with $n\cdot\mu$ and ending with $1\cdot\mu$, the sum of which yields $t_n=0.5h(n+1)\mu$. The elimination terms may be expressed as follows

$$t_e=[h\sum_{i=1}^{p-1}(n-i+1)+(h-1)\sum_{i=p}^{2p-1}(n-i+1)+,..,+(h-k)\sum_{i=k\cdot p}^{(k+1)p-1}(n-i+1)+,..,+\sum_{i=(h-1)p}^{hp-1}(n-i+1)]\omega \quad (68)$$

Expanding and writing in reverse order yields

$$t_e/\omega=(2+3+,\dots,+(p+1))+2((p+2)+(p+3)+,\dots,+(2p+1))+\dots+h((h-1)p+2)+\dots+hp) \quad (69)$$

Adding $h(hp+1)$ to the last parenthesis (and to the left-hand side), yields with A

$$A=(1+2+\dots+p+1)=p(p+3)/2 \quad (70)$$

$$t_e/\omega+h(hp+1)=A+2(p^2+A)+3(2p^2+A)+..+h((h-1)p^2+A)=0.5h(h+1)A+(2*1+3*2+..+h(h-1))p^2 \quad (71)$$

Because of the identity $2*1+3*2+\dots+h(h-1)=(h-1)h(h+1)/3$ (72)

and with $h=n/p$, (71) yields:

$$t_e = n(n/p+1)[p(p+3)/4+(n/p-1)p^2/3]\omega/p \quad (73)$$

which with the obvious approximation $n/p\cong n/p-1\cong n/p+1$ yields

$$t_e = [n^3/(3p)+n(p+3)/(4p)]\omega \quad (74)$$

The times for synchronization and data transfer equal those of the Jordan method and can be added. Hence

$$\rho_G\cong[(n^3/(3p)+n(p+3)/(4p)]\omega+n\beta+[(n+1)(n+2)\tau/2]/(n^3\omega/3)$$
$$\cong 1/p+3(p+3)/(4*p*n^2)+3\beta'/n^2+3\tau'/(2n) \quad (75)$$

With large n, the reduction approaches the ideal value of 1/p. It is also readily seen, that the order of choosing the pivoting rows is not important as long as the first row is taken from the memory of slave 1, the second from the domain of slave 2 and so on cyclically. This allows a certain freedom in the choice of pivots, which may be necessary for maintaining numerical stability.

Both methods approach optimal speedup, but the G-method is actually faster. It should be again stressed that the above calculations apply to non-sparse matrices $\underline{A}$. Elimination of sparse matrices is treated later.

6.2.2 Triangular matrices

Decomposition

If $\underline{A}$ is symmetric and positive-definite, it can be decomposed as

$$\underline{A} = \underline{R}^T\,\underline{R} \quad (76)$$

where $\underline{R}$ is upper-triangular. There are two algorithms [Ru 76] for computing $\underline{R}$, the first calculating iteratively for $i=1,\dots,n$:

$$r_{ii} := \mathrm{sqrt}(a_{ii}) \quad (77)$$

$$r_{ij} := a_{ij}/r_{ii} \text{ for } j=i+1,\dots,n \quad (78)$$

$a_{jk} := a_{jk} - r_{ij}r_{ik}$ for $j=i+1,\dots,n$ and $k=j,\dots,n$ (79)

This algorithm is not suitable for ASP since each r_{ii} can be calculated only after the corresponding a_{ii} has been changed by (79) in a previous iteration on i. Hence in this (and a second) algorithm of [Ru 76], the taking of the square roots cannot be spread among the slaves and the resulting sequentialization will decrease the speedup.

The LDL^T decomposition can be adapted for ASP with the equations written for $i=1,\dots(n-1)$ as follows:

$c_{ki} := d_{kk}r_{ki}$, $k=1,\dots,(i-1)$; $d_{ii} := a_{ii} - \Sigma\, c_{ki}r_{ki}^2$, $k\Sigma=1,\dots,i-1$ (80)

$r_{ij} := (a_{ij} - \Sigma\, c_{ki}r_{kj})/d_{ii}$; $j=(i+1),\dots,n$; $k\Sigma=1,\dots,i-1$ (81)

The upper triangle of $\underline{A}$ is stored in the memory of the master. Each slave operates on a vertical "slice" of $\underline{R}$ of width $h(=n/p)$. If we let each slave store consecutive h columns, then for $i>h$ the first slave will be idle, after $i>2h$ the second etc. This process shows again the "Haydn effect" mentioned earlier. It will increase ρ and reduce speedup. We may achieve a better balance of work if we note that each slave needs only its own columns of $\underline{R}$. The algorithm is rephrased so that it includes the following sequential S- and parallel P-steps for $i=1,\dots,(n-1)$:

S(i): Retrieve from the slaves r_{ki}, $k=1,\dots,(i-1)$. Compute c_{ki}, d_{ii} as per (80). Broadcast them and a_{ij}, $j>i$ to the slaves.

P(i): Compute r_{ij} as per (81), h columns j in a slave.

The ratio depends on how well the job is divided among the slaves. As an example take n=9, p=3 and let the slices include columns (2,6,7), (3,4,8) and (5,9) respectively. r_{ij} for the following i,j would be computed:

Slave1:	1,2;1,6;1,7	2,6;2,7	3,6;3,7	4,6;4,7	5,6;5,7	6,7		
Slave2:	1,3;1,4;1,8	2,3;2,4;2,8	3,4;3,8	4,8	5,8	6,8	7,8	
Slave3:	1,5;1,9	2,5;2,9	3,5;3,9	4,5;4,9	5,9	6,9	7,9	8,9

Work is divided more evenly and the Haydn effect appears only at the very end. For larger h, the ratio can be even more improved but as mentioned - can only be calculated for specific cases.

The advantages of the method are that it has a good ratio, because no square roots are calculated, the work is divided about evenly among the slaves, there is little transfer of data in step S(i) and the transfer if needed, is done mostly by broadcast.

Forward Substitution

Insertion of (76) leads to solving $\underline{A}\,\underline{x} = \underline{b}$ by a "forward substitution": $\underline{R}^T\underline{y}=\underline{b}$ followed by a "back-substitution" $\underline{R}\,\underline{x} = \underline{y}$ as discussed in Chapter 5 and below. Forward substitution is written in full as follows:

$$\begin{aligned}
&r_{11}y_1 &&=b_1\\
&r_{12}y_1+r_{22}y_2 &&=b_2\\
&r_{13}y_1+r_{23}y_2+r_{33}y_3 \;-\;-\;-\;- &&=b_3 \qquad (82)\\
&r_{1n}y_1+r_{2n}y_2+r_{3n}y_3+ \qquad\qquad +r_{nn}y_n &&=b_n
\end{aligned}$$

It suggests itself as parallelization that the master computes an y_i and all slaves adjust their sums $b-\Sigma r_{ij}y_i$ by subtracting $r_{ij}y_i$ for each i of their (horizontal) slice. The trouble with this approach is that after calculating y_h, the first slave is idled, after y_{2h} - the second etc. and from i=(n-1)h+1 only slave p works. Because of the Haydn effect, the ratio will be high (and speedup low).

We can improve the algorithm by organizing it in the way exemplified in Fig. 4 for n=12, p=3. The y_i's and elements marked "-" are computed by the master, the others by slaves working concurrently. The algorithm would initially set

$$c_{ij}: = 0 \text{ for } i=1,\ldots,n \text{ and } j=1,\ldots,p \qquad (83)$$

(Here p=3). Next follow i=1,...,(h-1) sequential and parallel steps:

<u>S(i)</u>: $m=(i-1)p+1$ (84)

$$\text{For } j=m,\ m+1,\ldots,m+p-1: \quad y_j: = (b_j - \sum_{q=1}^{p} c_{jq} + \sum_{k=m}^{j-1} r_{kj}y_k)/r_{jj} \qquad (85)$$

<u>P(i)</u>: m=ip+1; k=m-p. Each slave q=1,...,p computes for j=m, m+1,...,n:

$$c_{mq}: = c_{mq} + r_{kj}y_k \qquad (86)$$

y_1											
-	y_2										
-	-	y_3									
v	v	v	y_4								
v	v	v	-	y_5							
v	v	v	-	-	y_6						
v	v	v	x	x	x	y_7					
v	v	v	x	x	x	-	y_8				
v	v	v	x	x	x	-	-	y_9			
v	v	v	x	x	x	/	/	/	y_{10}		
v	v	v	x	x	x	/	/	/	-	y_{11}	
v	v	v	x	x	x	/	/	/	-	-	y_{12}

Fig. 4: Forward elimination schedule

In order to compute ρ note that

(a) Compared to others, the times for (84) are negligible

(b) In (85) the elements "-" of Fig. 4 are calculated. In the worst case $p\alpha$ are required for the first and $p\mu+(p-1)\alpha$ for the other sums (here $5\alpha+3\mu$). Thus, in every S(i) the required number of operations is

$$\Omega_{S(i)}=p\alpha+p\mu+(p-1)\alpha=p(\mu+2\alpha)-\alpha \qquad (87)$$

(c) Counting "backwards" the number of operations for (86), yields

$$\Omega_{(86)}=[p+2p+\ldots+(h-1)p](\omega)= 0.5p(h-1)h\omega\cong 0.5n^2/(p\omega) \qquad (88)$$

(d) At the start of every S(i), a synchronization and transfer of about $0.5\,n^2$ elements r_{ij} is needed. Thus

$$\Omega'_{S(i)} = \beta+0.5n^2\tau \quad ; \; e = h-1 \qquad (89)$$

(e) In purely sequential execution of (88) $\Omega_{(88)} \cong 0.5n^2\omega$ so that

$$\rho = \{0.5n^2\omega/p+e[p(\mu+2\alpha)-\alpha]+e\sigma+0.5n^2\tau\}/(0.5n^2\omega) \qquad (90)$$

Neglecting α compared to $2p\alpha$ and making $e\cong h$ yields:

$$\rho\cong 1/p+2(\mu+2\alpha)/(n\omega)+2\beta'/(pn)+\tau' \qquad (91)$$

It is seen that ρ approaches the optimum value of 1/p.

Back Substitution

The inverse of an (nxn) matrix $\underline{A}$, is given in the Gauss form as

$$\underline{A}^{-1} = \underline{F}_n * \underline{F}_{n-1} * \ldots * \underline{F}_1 \tag{92}$$

where $\underline{F}_i$ is a unit matrix except for column i:

$$\underline{F}_{1,.i} = [F_{1i}, F_{2i}, \ldots, F_{ni}]^T \tag{93}$$

This column is that of the "factorization" or Frobenius table $\underline{F}$ as was stored in, say, the GAUSS program. The solution of $\underline{A}*\underline{x}=\underline{b}$ by back-substitution is then

$$\underline{x} = \underline{A}^{-1}*\underline{b} = \underline{F}_n*\underline{F}_{n-1}*\ldots*\underline{F}_1*\underline{b} \tag{94}$$

It is assumed that following the factorization [WC 76], the slices of F and b are stored in the slave memories.

Equation (94) would normally be considered unsuitable for parallelization; $\underline{b}^{(1)}=\underline{F}_1*\underline{b}$ must precede $\underline{b}^{(2)}=\underline{F}_2*\underline{b}^{(1)}$ etc., so that a rigid sequence of operations is called for. Still, it may be programmed for ASP as follows:

Let us rewrite (94) in the form of recurrence relations with $\underline{b}^{(0)}=\underline{b}$

$$\underline{b}^{(i)} = \underline{F}_i * \underline{b}^{(i-1)} \quad , \; i=1,2,\ldots,n \tag{95}$$

resulting in $\underline{x} = \underline{b}^{(n)}$. Using notation $b_k^{(m)}$ for the k-th element of $\underline{b}^{(m)}$, we obtain

$$\underline{b}^{(i)}=\underline{b}^{(i-1)}+b_i^{(i-1)}*(F_{1i},F_{2i},\ldots,F_{ii}-1,\ldots,F_{ni})^T=\underline{b}^{(i-1)}+b_i^{(i-1)}*g_i \tag{96}$$

where g_i was defined as

$$g_i = (F_{1i},F_{2i},\ldots,F_{i-1,i},F_{ii}-1,F_{i+1,i},\ldots,F_{ni})^T \tag{97}$$

Each application of (96) may be done concurrently by all slaves for their range h, provided each holds the constant $b_i^{(i-1)}$. The entire process is a sequence of n parallel steps calculating

$$b_j^{(i)}=b_j^{(i-1)}+b_i^{(i-1)}*g_j^{(i)}; \quad j=1,2,\ldots,h \tag{98}$$

by each slave simultaneously. Assuming that the initialization was in fact done, back-substitution proceeds according to the following program.

```
BSS:  PROC OPTIONS(MAIN);   /*   BSS STANDS FOR BACK SUBSTITUTION SIMPLE   */
DCL (H,I,J,K,M,N) FIXED, (B(N),F(N,N),V) FLOAT,
    (#)L FIXED,(#)(B(1:H),F(1:H,1:N),V) FLOAT;
DO I=1 TO N; F(I,I)=F(I,I)-1; END;  / *FOR VECTOR G                      */
DO I=1 TO P;   /* TRANSFERRING BY BLOCKS SLICES OF B AND F TO SLAVES     */
   J=(I-1)*H+1; K=I*H; (I)J=J; (I)K=K;
(I)B(1:H)≡B(J:K); (I)F(1:H,1:N)≡F(J:K,1:N); END;
DO I=1 TO P; J=(I-1)*H;
   DO K=1 TO H; M=J+K;
      V=(I)B(K); PUT BROADCAST (V);
      PARCALL (#)PA(M); END; END;
PA: PARPROC (M);
DO L=1 TO H;
   B(L)=B(L)+V*F(L,M); END;
PAREND;               /* END OF PARALLEL PROCEDURE PA                    */
END;   /* END OF THE BLOCK SUBSTITUTION SIMPLE PROGRAM BSS               */
```

With c nonzero elements per row and average density of d=100 c/n, the entire program contains n broadcasts of V, n synchronizations and dn^2/p multiplications and additions. Sequential execution requires $dn^2\omega$. Hence, the time reduction achieved with this program is

$$\rho_{BSS}=(dn^2\omega/p+n\tau+n\beta)/(dn^2\omega)=1/p+(\beta'+\tau')/(dn) \quad (99)$$

Ideally, ρ should be 1/p. The additional term, the "interference" is small as long as $\beta'/(dn)$ is small. However, β' increases with the system size p, and if in addition $\underline{F}$ is sparse, $\beta'/(dn)$ may be larger than 1/p i.e. the loss would exceed the gain. In order to reduce interference and in particular the synchronization part, other algorithms will be developed in a later chapter.

<u>Inversion of Triangular Matrices</u>

We will deal with lower triangular, non-singular matrices $\underline{A}$ (the case for upper matrices is similar). They are normally inverted by iterative computation of

$$b_{ik}: = -(\Sigma a_{ij}b_{jk})/a_{ii}, i>k;\ b_{ii}: = 1/a_{ii};\ i=1,\ldots,n \quad j\Sigma=k,\ldots,i-1 \quad (100)$$

and seem to imply a strictly sequential scheduling. This can be changed if all diagonal elements b_{ii} are computed and broadcast first. Equation (100) describes then a column k

$$b_{ik}: = -b_{ii}\ \Sigma\ a_{ij}b_{jk};\ j\Sigma=k,\ldots,i-1;\ i=k+1,\ldots,n \quad (101)$$

such that each b_{ik} depends only on those b_{jk} for which j<i.

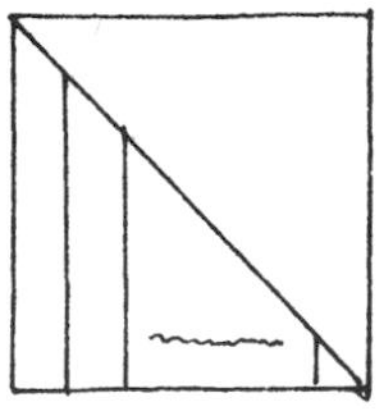

Fig. 5: Data

Let us assume that $\underline{A}$ is stored in all slave memories and that each slave is to compute a vertical slice of $\underline{B}$ (Fig. 5). The algorithm consists of only two steps:

<u>S(1)</u>: The master computes all b_{ii} and broadcasts them

<u>P(1)</u>: Every slave computes b_{ik} for its slice of columns k.

The following may be noted.

(a) a_{ik} are not needed after the corresponding b_{ik} are computed and $\underline{A}$ could be overwritten. Unfortunately, $\underline{A}$ is needed row-wise whereas $\underline{B}$ is computed column-wise, so that overwriting may require complicated programming and is hardly worth the effort.

(b) The simplest way to divide the work among the slaves is to let each compute $0.5n^2/p$ elements of $\underline{B}$. Since all slaves have to wait for the longest task to be completed, we may assume these to be in the first k columns, so that

$$0.5n^2/p = n+(n-1)+\ldots+(n-k) \quad (102)$$

Obviously, for k only the integer root applies in

$$k = (n+0.5) \pm \mathrm{sqrt}(n^2(1-1/p)+n-0.5) \quad (103)$$

Matrix $\underline{A}$ of $\cong .5n^2$ elements and all b_{ii}'a have to be computed and transferred during S(1). This requires $\beta+n\mu+(0.5n^2+n)\tau$. For the longest task (first k columns), the number of operations is about $0.5[n(n+1) + (n-1)n+\ldots+(n-k+1)(n-k)-k(k+1)]\omega$. The ratio can therefore be computed for any specific case, e.g., for n=8, p=2, k=2:

$$t_p \cong 70\mu + 62\alpha + 38\tau + \beta \quad (104)$$

Since in sequential execution t_1=n+0.5[6+(2.3)+...+n(n-1)-2n]ω or, here 73μ+65α, the ratio will be the rather good

$$\rho \cong (35\mu + 31\alpha + 38\tau + \beta)/(73\mu + 65\alpha) \cong 1/2 + \tau'/2 + \beta'/70 \qquad (105)$$

(c) Work could have been equalized as for decomposition, but since here it would mean splitting the columns, it is hardly worth it.

6.3 SPARSITY

Aims: To show that elimination is inefficient for very sparse matrices. To postulate a "principle" of parallelization. To define fill-in and discuss its implications. To show that reordering the equations may result in lower fill-in. To give some numerical evidence for this.

6.3.1 Introduction

The parallel algorithms developed earlier have one common characteristic; they disregard the topology of the network. This is of no disadvantage when the system under consideration is dense, and indeed these algorithms perform best on full matrices. As the network becomes sparse, they become increasingly inefficient. To analyze this deterioration and point out possible solutions, we will first describe a modified version of the Gaussian elimination as developed earlier for ASP.

The set to be solved is still $\underline{A}\ \underline{x} = \underline{b}$. In elimination algorithms, a row i operates on row k by replacing

$$a_{kj} = a_{kj} - a_{ij}a_{ki}/a_{ii},\ j=1,2,\ldots,n \qquad (106)$$

to eliminate a_{ki}. This will be called "basic Gaussian operation" or bag(i,k). Row i is here the "pivot", row k will henceforth be called simply "row".

It is now assumed that each slave memory holds the entire matrix $\underline{A}$ and the vector $\underline{b}$ (earlier on, these memories were supposed to hold only a "slice" of $\underline{A}$ each, but since now $\underline{A}$ is extremely sparse, the present assumption is justified). Each slave though is assigned a subset of rows of $\underline{A}$ as its "rows".

The algorithm is as follows:

(a) The master chooses a pivot i (according to some optimal strategy to be yet suggested) and broadcasts it over the bus to all slaves.

(b) Each slave performs basic elimination on all its rows with pivot i i.e. bag(i,k) for all of its rows k.

(c) Elements which will constitute row i and column i of the factor table $\underline{F}$ required for factorization are now available, as are those of row i of the upper triangular matrix required for back substitution. If the slaves have insufficient storage, these elements will have to be transferred over the bus to the common store.

All three steps above have to be repeated (n-1) times. Steps (a) and (c) are sequential, step (b) is parallel.

Analysis of elimination shows that the reduction achieved for dense matrices is nearly 1/p. However, most practical cases e.g. electric power systems and other networks yield extremely sparse matrices; the percentage of zeros may even exceed 99%. For such matrices the above algorithm shows the following disadvantages:

(1) Step (a) is executed (n-1) times and each time:

- The master starts its sequential step only after all p slaves have completed their jobs. Since the number of non-zero terms is unequal, this forces some slaves to wait. The synchronization time increases.
- The master needs a time-interval to set-up the system for transferring the pivot over the bus. This time-interval is independent of the amount of information transferred, so that the bus is not used efficiently.
- Transfer of data over the bus is required.

(2) In step (b) each slave works only on those of its rows k for which $A_{ki} \neq 0$. This means that for a sparse matrix, there is little work for each slave to be done in each substep. An extreme case is a tridiagonal matrix $\underline{T}$ where $T_{ij}=0$ for all $|i-j|>2$. Let the rows of slave 1 be numbered 1,2,...,h, those of slave 2 as h+1, h+2,...,2h etc. Then it is easily seen that step (b) becomes sequential, because bag(i,i+1) is the only operation performed with pivot i. In other words, only one processor works at a time and there is no parallelism! We thus arrive at an obvious <u>Principle of efficiency</u>: <u>When scheduling an algorithm for ASP-execution, it is desirable that the bulk of arithmetical operations fall into the parallel steps</u>. There are two reasons for this. First, it enables a larger number of slaves to work concurrently, and secondly since the total amount of work is constant, it reduces the number of parallel steps. This is important, because each parallel step is preceded by some overhead work (synchronization, data-transfer etc.) done sequentially by the master. Hence, minimizing the number of steps reduces overhead and increases speedup. Solving an extremely sparse system by the above algorithm is against this principle and consequently results in poor time reduction.

Another disadvantage of the ASP-versions for sparse matrices is the "<u>fill-in</u>", that is the fact that whereas $\underline{A}$ is sparse, $\underline{F}$ is less so.

The algorithms were checked for their effectiveness when applied to sparse matrices. The smaller the fill-in and the lower the number of required arithmetic operations - the higher the "effectiveness".

All factorization methods substitute zeros for some elements of $\underline{A}$ and insert non-zero elements into the "factorization" or F-table. To trace this process, the $\underline{A}$ and $\underline{F}$-matrices may be represented by Boolean matrices [Re 71].

In order to calculate the number of non-zero elements of row i of $\underline{B}$ (the Boolean matrix which stands for $\underline{A}$), inserted there, we compute

$$b_{i,m} = b_{i,m} \vee b_{k,m} \;;\; \forall m \neq k, \qquad (107)$$

and count the number of non-zero bits in the disjunction $\vee$. Similarly, the conjunction:

$$b_{i,m} = b_{i,m} \wedge b_{k,m} \;;\; \forall m \neq k, \qquad (108)$$

yields by count the number of arithmetic operations.

A percentage of p_{in} null elements in $\underline{B}$ is chosen, and a random-number generator inserts Boolean values into $\underline{B}$ according to the chosen p_{in} and so that the resulting matrix is non-singular. For straight-forward application with no ordering or scaling whatsoever, tests on a matrix of n x n = 80 x 80 were performed with results shown in Table 1. For instance for p_{in} = 94%, the method based on Gaussian elimination created p_{out} = 43%, and for the Jordan algorithm p_{out} = 45%. The corresponding numbers of operations were Ω = 2.82 and 10.1%. These percentage values were computed relative to the normally required $n^3/3$.

	Gauss		Jordan	
p_{in} %	p_{out} %	Ω_{out} %	p_{out} %	Ω_{out} %
94	43.19	2.82	45.13	10.10
89	31.08	10.18	25.20	23.62
84	20.02	16.09	13.34	33.14
79	12.55	22.03	8.34	39.78
74	10.52	23.61	6.61	41.82
69	7.41	23.88	4.51	41.86
64	6.48	24.98	4.73	43.31

Table 1: Percentage of zeros and multiplications introduced into an 80*80 matrix

It is seen that as far as the sparsity of the $\underline{F}$-table is concerned neither elimination nor the J-method seems to be preferable. Yet, the sparsity of $\underline{F}$ is not the only consideration involved. As will be shown, the number of the F-matrices to be used in the Jordan methods is smaller and their structure lends itself better to programming. Since the ordering policy has a much greater influence on the sparseness than the differences shown in the table, no method is advocated at this stage.

6.3.2 Fill-in

Let us first rephrase the Cholesky decomposition for a symmetric matrix $\underline{A}$. Suppose that

$$\underline{A}^{(0)} = \begin{bmatrix} a & \underline{r}^T \\ \underline{r} & \underline{A}' \end{bmatrix} \tag{109}$$

where a is a scalar, $\underline{r}$ is a (n-1)x1 vector and $\underline{A}'$ an (n-1)x(n-1) matrix. The first step of factorization may be effected through

$$\underline{A}^{(1)} = \begin{bmatrix} 1 & 0 \\ -\underline{r}/a & \underline{U} \end{bmatrix} * \begin{bmatrix} a & \underline{r}^T \\ \underline{r} & \underline{A}' \end{bmatrix} * \begin{bmatrix} 1 & -\underline{r}^T/a \\ 0 & \underline{U} \end{bmatrix} = \begin{bmatrix} a & 0 \\ 0 & \underline{A}'-\underline{r}\,\underline{r}^T/a \end{bmatrix} \tag{110}$$

In the next step, $\underline{A}'-(\underline{r}*\underline{r}^T)/a$ is factored in the same way etc.

Gaussian elimination on symmetrical matrices may be interpreted in terms of graph theory. Given a symmetric nxn matrix $\underline{A}=(a)_{ij}$ we form its corresponding undirected graph $G_A=(V,E)$, where $V=(v_1,v_2,\ldots v_n)$ are the vertices of $\underline{A}$. An elimination step (110) can then be viewed as an operation transforming $G_A^{(0)}$ into $G_A^{(1)}$. As is seen from (110) $G_A^{(1)}$ has an isolated vertex v_1 which we will disregard, and an (n-1) node graph corresponding to $\underline{A}^{(1)} = \underline{A}-\underline{r}*\underline{r}^T/a$. If $a_{ij}^{(0)}\neq 0$ for some (i,j) then, barring a chance cancellation, $a_{ij}^{(1)}\neq 0$; hence the edges of $G_{\underline{A}}(0)$ not adjacent to v_1 (which we removed) are preserved in $G_{\underline{A}}^{(1)}$. However, $G_{\underline{A}}^{(1)}$ may contain additional edges, which were not present in $G_{\underline{A}}^{(0)}$. Denoting $G_{\underline{A}}^{(0)}=(V_0,E_0)$, $G_A^{(1)}=(V_1,E_1)$, we have the following characterization of these edges.

Lemma: $(V_s,V_t) \in E_1 \wedge (V_s,V_t) \notin E_0$ is equivalent to

$(V_1,V_s) \in E_0 \wedge (V_1,V_t) \in E_0$; $(V_s,V_t) \notin E_0$

Proof: From $(V_s,V_t) \in E_0$ we have $a_{1s}=r_s \neq 0$

From $(V_1,V_t) \in E_0$ we have $a_{1t}=r_t \neq 0$

Hence, $a^{(1)}_{st}=a^{(0)}_{st}-r_s r_t/a$, and $(V_s,V_t) \in E_1$ (Note that $a^{(0)}_{st}=0$)

Next note that from $(V_s V_t) \in E_1$ it follows that $a^{(1)}_{st}=a^{(0)}_{st}-r_s r_t/a \neq 0$. Since $(V_s,V_t) \notin E_0$, $a^{(0)}_{st}=0$. Therefore $r_s \neq 0$, $r_t \neq 0$. Q.E.D.

A "clique" is a subset $C \subset V$, such that for every $v,w \in C$, $(v,w) \in E$. We arrive at the following rule of elimination on graphs:

(a) Add new edges such that all vertices adjacent to v_1 form a clique.

(b) Delete v_1 and its incident edges.

Following [RTL76] we define the <u>deficiency</u> of vertex v as the set of edges which is added to the graph upon elimination of V. Formally

$$D(v) = \{(x,y) \mid v-x,\ v-y,\ x \neq y\} \tag{111}$$

where u-v means $(uv) \in E$. We also define the v-elimination graph as the graph remaining after (a) and (b). Formally

$$G \equiv (V-\{v\}, E(V-\{v\}) \vee D(v)) \tag{112}$$

were E(S) denotes the induced graph.

Suppose that rows of $\underline{A}$ are eliminated one-by-one. This results in a sequence of elimination graphs $G_o=G$, $G_1=(G_o)_v$, $G_2=(G_1)_{v2}\ldots$ At each step, define the fill-in F_i as the set of edges added to graph G_{i-1} upon elimination of v_i. The total accumulated fill-in F(G) is defined as $F(G)=\bigcup F_i$ with i=1 to n-1, so that the elimination graph of G is the original graph plus the total accumulated fill-in:

$$G' = (V, E \cup F(G)) \tag{113}$$

The phenomenon of fill-in has important computational implications. The following lemma clearly belongs to the folklore of the subject, but curiously enough, has never been formulated.

Lemma: Let $\underline{F}_i$ be as in (5-41). Denote by $\hat{\underline{F}}_i$ the matrix formed by setting all but the i'th diagonal element of $(\underline{F}_i)^{-1}$ to zero. Then

$$\underline{L}=\underline{F}_1^{-1} * \underline{F}_2^{-1} * \ldots * \underline{F}_n^{-1} = \hat{\underline{F}}_1 + \hat{\underline{F}}_2 + \ldots + \hat{\underline{F}}_{n-1} \tag{114}$$

Proof: The proof can be done by direct multiplication. Note that the sum is nonoverlapping i.e. two non-zero elements are never summed.

Corollary: $|E \cup F(G)|$ = number of non-zero terms of $\underline{L}$.

Proof: Each non-zero off-diagonal term of $\underline{F}^{(i)}$ corresponds to an edge removed at some stage. Since all edges of $E \cup F(G)$ are finally removed and each one only once, it follows from (114) that

$$E \cup F(G) = \Sigma \text{ (number of non-zero elements in } \underline{L}\text{); } i\Sigma=1,\ldots,n-1 \tag{115}$$

which establishes the result.

This result is significant when it is desired to solve $\underline{A}*\underline{x}=\underline{b}$ where $\underline{A}$ is sparse and symmetric. Using the Cholesky decomposition, we end up with a lower triangular matrix $\underline{L}$, which - due to fillin - may contain more non-zeros that the original matrix $\underline{A}$. This may lead to difficult problems of storage. In fact, the following example shows an almost empty matrix A (with only n elements to store) such that elimination leads to a full lower ~~diagonal~~ triangular matrix ($\cong n^2/2$ elements).

$$\underline{A}^{(o)} = \begin{bmatrix} 1 & a_1 & a_2 & a_3 & \cdots & a_n \\ a_1 & 1 & & & & \\ a_2 & & 1 & & & \\ & & & \ddots & & \\ a_n & & & & & 1 \end{bmatrix}$$

$G_A^{(0)}$ is

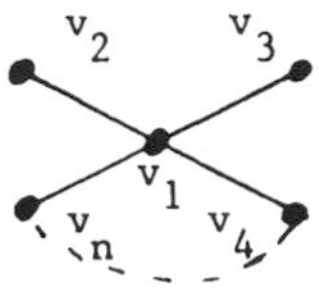

Fig. 6: A matrix and its graph

This is most easily seen from the graph interpretation (Fig. 6): Gv_1 is the full graph on n-1 vertices.

Apart from increase in storage demand, fillin also influences the number of operations required. As seen from (110) the first step of elimination requires $0.5\ (\psi(r_1)+\psi^2(r_1))$ where $\psi(r_1)$ is the number of non-zero elements of $\underline{r}_1=\underline{r}$. $\psi(r_1)$ divisions are also required. Repeating:

$$\Omega = 0.5\ \Sigma\ [(\psi(\hat{r}_i) + \psi^2\ (\hat{r}_i)] + \psi\ (\hat{r}_i) * 2 \qquad (116)$$

This shows that the number of operations increases with fill-in.

6.3.3 Reordering

The obvious remedy to fill-in is reordering, i.e. prior to factorization, rearrange the rows in an order which minimizes fill-in. To preserve the symmetry of the matrix, apply the same rearrangement to the columns. This is equivalent to factorization of the matrix $\underline{P}^T\ \underline{A}\ \underline{P}$, where $\underline{P}$ is a permutation matrix. Having found a solution $\underline{y}$ to the system $\underline{P}^T\ \underline{A}\ \underline{Py} = \underline{P}^T\ \underline{b}$ which is equivalent to $\underline{A}\ \underline{P}\ \underline{y} = \underline{b}$ and thus to $\underline{y} = \underline{P}^{-1}\ \underline{A}^{-1}\ \underline{b}$ one multiplies $\underline{y}$ by $\underline{P}$ to obtain $\underline{x} = \underline{A}^{-1}\underline{b}$. This multiplication is but a reordering of the elements of $\underline{y}$.

If in the example of Fig. 6 we had reversed the ordering of the vertices ($i\to n-i+1$) we would have obtained the matrix $\tilde{\underline{A}}$ and its corresponding graph of Fig. 7. Applying the elimination process to $\tilde{\underline{A}}$, or its graph version to $G_{\tilde{\underline{A}}}$, we see that no fill-in occurs. In view of the fact that fill-in depends on the ordering and we shall be interested in finding "good" orderings we slightly modify the previous definitions to reflect the dependence on ordering. Let γ be a bijection γ: $\{1,2,\ldots n\}\leftrightarrow V$; γ will be called an ordering of V. $G_\gamma = (V,E,\gamma)$ is an ordered graph. The elimination process $P(G_\gamma) = (G = G_o,\ G_1,\ G_2,\ldots,G_{n-1})$ is the sequence of elimination graphs defined recursively by $G_o=G, G_i=(G_{i-1})v_i$. The fill-in $F(G_\gamma)$ is defined by

$$\tilde{\underline{A}} = \begin{bmatrix} 1 & 0 & 0 & \cdots & 0 & a_n \\ & 1 & & & 0 & \\ & & \ddots & & & \\ & 0 & & & 1 & \\ & & & & & 1 \end{bmatrix}$$

$G_{\tilde{\underline{A}}}$ is

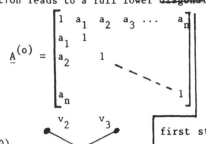

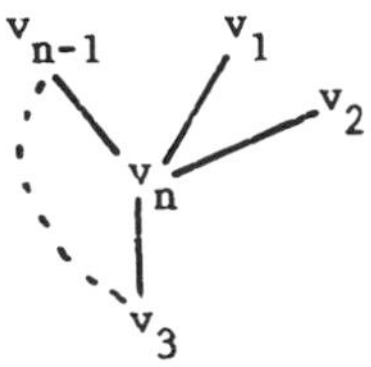

Fig. 7: Network

$F(G_\gamma) = \bigcup F_i$; $i=1,\ldots,n-1$ where $F_i D(V_i)$ in G_{i-1}, and the elimination graph $G_\gamma{*}=(V,E \bigcup F(G_\gamma))$ is to be called G_γ^*.

The above remarks imply, that an ordering is sought which minimizes fill-in. However, reordering of equations is sometimes necessary for purpose other than fill-in minimization, notably for numerical stability. Such ordering was mentioned as a pivoting procedure, and is not necessarily identical to those which minimize fill-in. In fact, there is no connection between the two; the order of pivoting is primarily determined by the absolute value of matrix coefficients - (usually, the largest element is chosen as pivot) and many pivoting policies purposefully destroy symmetry. However, it is known ([Wi 65], p. 231) that for positive definite symmetrical matrices, a symmetrical reordering does not cause instability. Still another ordering will be derived later and its purpose will be to make parallelization more effective.

Large electrical networks in particular power networks were among the prime reasons behind the quest for good ordering. A power system may consist of hundreds or thousands of buses, with each bus connected to an average of c buses, where c has been estimated as being less than 3 [Al 76]. For such sparse networks, a good ordering policy may lead to great savings in storage and computation time.

The goal of finding good orderings has been pursued in two directions: the graph-theoretical and heuristic direction.

The foundations for the first of these were laid by Rose [Ros 70] who investigated what is known as perfect elimination graphs. These are graphs for which an ordering exists, such that $F(G_\gamma) = \emptyset$, i.e. no fill-in is introduced. He gave a characterization of these graphs, and in a recent paper [Ro 77] an efficient algorithm to determine whether a graph is perfect, and if so, what is the ordering that produces no fill-in. However, many graphs encountered in practice are not perfect, and some fill-in must be introduced.

The problem of finding an ordering called the minimum ordering which gives the least fill-in of all possible orderings is very difficult. In fact, for a non-symmetrical matrix it has been shown to be so-called NP-complete [Ro 77], (solvable only by brute force) and the authors conjecture, that the same problem for symmetrical matrices is also NP-complete. Having despaired of attaining that objective, the theorists defined a goal which could be attained - the so called minimal ordering. A minimal ordering is one which produces a fill-in such that no proper subset thereof can be produced by any other ordering. In other words, γ is minimal, if and only if any ordering δ satisfying $F(G_\delta) \subseteq F(G_\gamma)$ also satisfies $\gamma=\delta$. Ingenious algorithms for finding a minimal ordering have been devised. Clearly, a minimum ordering ($|F(G_\gamma)| = \min$) is also minimal but the converse is far from true. Indeed, it is shown in [Ro 76] that in certain cases a minimal ordering is much inferior (in terms of fill-in) to a non-minimal one, let alone a minimum solution. It is rather sad that such deep graph-theoretical investigations as lie behind the minimal ordering theory have led to results whose impact on practical problems is small. No theoretical treatment of minimizing other objective functions, such as the total count of operations, has been attempted.

Confronted with the acute problem of memory and computing time limitation when dealing with large matrices, scientists devised a number of heuristic policies to determine good orderings. These policies have no deep theoretical basis, and are motivated by common sense and experience. They work very well on real-life problems, although can be shown to fail when applied to certain artificial counter examples. Three policies which have received attention in power system applications [TW 67] and others are

(1) The permutation is chosen so that the number of nonzero terms is non-decreasing.

(2) The permutation is constructed during the process of elimination itself according to the rule: Having eliminated k rows, the k+1'th row to be eliminated is chosen as the one which has the least number of non-zero terms.

(3) Having eliminated k vertices, the k+1'th vertex is chosen as the one whose elimination causes the least fill-in in G_k.

The policies work remarkably well when applied to sparse power systems. Usually policy 2 is the favorite one, because it gives much better results than policy 1, although requiring more work. Policy 3 is better than 2, but the computational work involved in 3 is so much greater, that 2 is chosen as the best compromise. It should be noted that all three methods greatly reduce the number of arithmetical operations. In short, though not optimal, they have proved very useful. Next, some comparison between the methods will be given.

The following tables describe the process of elimination from the point of view of fill-in, number of operations etc. The matrix on which elimination is performed is a sparse 150x150 symmetrical matrix, with an average of 5.6 nonzero elements per row. Table 2 describes the process when no ordering is used; Tables 3 and 4 depict the results of ordering policies 1 and 2 respectively.

The leftmost column lists the number k of the bus to be eliminated at that point. The corresponding figure in column 2 is the number of multiplications/divisions to be performed in order to carry elimination of the k'th bus to the end.

k	Number of μ's	nonzeroes in factor table	nonzeroes in remaining matrix	% of nonzeroes
1	301,921	10,840	854	3.7
20	300,426	10,541	1,335	7.7
40	291,788	9,851	2,867	23.2
60	222,790	7,851	6,365	76.8
80	117,548	5,013	4,653	92.3
100	44,250	2,601	2,601	100.0
120	9,950	961	961	100.0
140	450	121	121	100.0

Table 2: Elimination without ordering

Thus the first entry of this column shows how many μ's are required for the entire process. Comparing these values in the three tables, it can be seen that an ordering policy substantially reduces the total number of operations. Policy 2 results in 4 times less operations than policy 1 and 7 times less than no-ordering policy. The third column gives the number of nonzero elements in the factor table for the remaining matrix (before the elimination of the k'th bus). Thus the first entry of column 3 gives the total number of nonzeros in the factor table. Again, the advantages of ordering policies are manifest. The fourth column lists the number of nonzero elements in the remaining (non-eliminated) part of the matrix, and the fifth shows the percentage of nonzeroes. The phenomenon of fill-in is evident. By comparing the three tables, it can be seen that policy 2 has by far the least fill-in. However, even the best ordering method cannot in the general case avoid fill-in and, consequently, at a certain stage the remaining matrix becomes so full that no ordering policy is of any noticeable advantage. If we set this limit of efficiency (rather arbitrarily) at 80%, it can be seen from Table 4 that this point is reached at k=100. We are then left with a 50x50 matrix, almost full, with over 80% of multiplications still to be done, as can be seen from the entries in column 2. From this point on, no conventional approach can further reduce the amount of work, and we are thus led naturally to parallel processing. This is the object of the next section.

k	Number of μ's	nonzeroes in factor table	nonzeroes in remaining matrix	% of nonzeroes
1	170,557	7,574	854	3.7
20	170,340	7,451	819	4.7
40	169,776	7,255	929	7.5
60	165,960	6,809	1,835	22.1
80	115,714	4,985	4,331	85.9
100	44,250	2,601	2,601	100.0
120	9,950	961	961	100.0
140	450	121	121	100.0

Table 3: Elimination with ordering policy 1

k	Number of μ's	nonzeroes in factor table	nonzeroes in remaining matrix	% of nonzeroes
1	43,737	3,784	854	3.7
20	43,520	3,661	819	4.7
40	43,172	3,449	833	6.7
60	42,652	3,229	925	11.7
80	41,580	3,011	1,219	24.1
100	36,436	2,407	2,135	82.0
120	9,950	961	961	100.0
140	450	121	121	100.0

Table 4: Elimination with ordering policy 2

6.4 ASP-FACTORIZATION

Aims: To redefine factorization in terms of Frobenius matrices. To show that all the different factorization methods developed are based on the Gauss or Jordan algorithms. To program two representative cases for ASP.

6.4.1 A reminder

The reader is reminded that Gaussian elimination may be viewed as a transformation of matrix $\underline{A}$ by consecutive, elementary row operations:

$$\underline{A} \equiv \underline{A}^{(o)} \rightarrow \underline{A}^{(1)} \rightarrow \underline{A}^{(2)} \rightarrow \ldots \rightarrow \underline{A}^{(n-1)} \equiv \underline{R} \qquad (117)$$

into an upper, "right", triangular matrix $\underline{R}$. For example, (5-9) led to:

$$\underline{A}^{(o)} = \begin{bmatrix} x & x & x & x \\ x & x & x & x \\ x & x & x & x \\ x & x & x & x \end{bmatrix} \rightarrow \begin{bmatrix} x & x & x & x \\ o & x & x & x \\ o & x & x & x \\ o & x & x & x \end{bmatrix} \rightarrow \begin{bmatrix} x & x & x & x \\ o & x & x & x \\ o & o & x & x \\ o & o & x & x \end{bmatrix} \rightarrow \begin{bmatrix} x & x & x & x \\ o & x & x & x \\ o & o & x & x \\ o & o & o & x \end{bmatrix} = \underline{R}$$

Thus, the elementary row operations eliminate nonzeroes in consecutive columns below the diagonal elements. The i'th transformation is effected by multiplying $\underline{A}^{(i-1)}$ on the left by a factor or "Frobenius" matrix $\underline{F}_i$ which is equal to the unit matrix except for its i'th column, which is:

$$[0,0,\ldots,1, -f_{i+1,i}, -f_{i+2,i},\ldots,-f_{n,i}]^T \;;\; f_{k,i} = F_{k,i}^{(i-1)}/F_{i,i}^{(i-1)} \qquad (118)$$

Transformation (117) can therefore be written as the sequence:

$$\underline{A}^{(i+1)} = \underline{F}_{i+1} \cdot \underline{A}^{(i)} \text{ for } i=0,1,\ldots,n-2 \qquad (119)$$

The upper triangular matrix $\underline{R}$ equals the product:

$$\underline{R} = \underline{F}_{n-1} \cdot \underline{F}_{n-2} \cdots \underline{F}_2 \cdot \underline{F}_1 \cdot \underline{A} \qquad (120)$$

from which it is seen, that $\underline{A}$ can be expressed as:

$$\underline{A} = (\underline{F}_1^{-1} \cdot \underline{F}_2^{-1} \ldots \underline{F}_{n-1}^{-1}) \cdot \underline{R} = \underline{L} \cdot \underline{R} \qquad (121)$$

Since $\underline{F}_i$ is lower triangular, so is its inverse. As a matter of fact, $\underline{F}_i^{-1}$ has the same structure as $\underline{F}_i$, with all minus signs changed to plus. Hence $\underline{L}$ is lower-triangular and equation (121) is known as the $\underline{L}\cdot\underline{R}$ decomposition of $\underline{A}$. Having decomposed $\underline{A}$ into this form, it is easy to solve $\underline{A}\ \underline{x} = \underline{b}$ in two stages; first, solving the triangular system $\underline{L}\ \underline{z} = \underline{b}$ and then the triangular system $\underline{R}\ \underline{x} = \underline{z}$.

Another method of elimination, which we named after Jordan eliminates zeroes not only below the diagonal, but also above it. The process is exemplified by:

$$\underline{A}^{(o)} = \begin{bmatrix} x & x & x & x \\ x & x & x & x \\ x & x & x & x \\ x & x & x & x \end{bmatrix} \rightarrow \begin{bmatrix} x & x & x & x \\ o & x & x & x \\ o & x & x & x \\ o & x & x & x \end{bmatrix} \rightarrow \begin{bmatrix} x & o & x & x \\ o & x & x & x \\ o & o & x & x \\ o & o & x & x \end{bmatrix} \rightarrow \begin{bmatrix} x & o & o & x \\ o & x & o & x \\ o & o & x & x \\ o & o & o & x \end{bmatrix} \rightarrow \begin{bmatrix} x & o & o & o \\ o & x & o & o \\ o & o & x & o \\ o & o & o & x \end{bmatrix} = \underline{D}$$

and the end result is a diagonal matrix $\underline{D}$. Again, the process may be viewed as a sequence of transformations on the matrix $\underline{A}$. The i'th transformation is effected by premultiplying $\underline{A}^{(i-1)}$ on the left by a factor matrix $\underline{F}_i$, where $\underline{F}_i$ equals the unit matrix except for the i'th column shown below:

$$[-f_{1i}, -f_{2i},\ldots,-f_{i-1,i}, 1, -f_{i+1,i},\ldots,-f_{n,i}]^T \qquad (122)$$

As in (120) we have:

$$\underline{F}_n * \underline{F}_{n-1} * \underline{F}_{n-2} \dots \underline{F}_1 * \underline{A} = \underline{D}; \text{ or } \underline{A} = \underline{D} * (\underline{F}_1^{-1} \dots \underline{F}_{n-1}^{-1}\, \underline{F}_n^{-1}) \tag{123}$$

As in the case of Gaussian elimination, $\underline{F}_i^{-1}$ has the same structure as $\underline{F}_i$, with minus signs changed to plus.

$$\underline{A}^{-1} = \underline{F}_n * \underline{F}_{n-1} * \dots * \underline{F}_1 * \underline{D}^{-1} \tag{124}$$

Thus, having computed the factors $\underline{F}_i$ as well as $\underline{D}$ and having stored them, the solution of the system reduces to multiplying the vector $\underline{b}$ by the product above. No back substitution is necessary.

In the case that $\underline{A}$ is symmetrical, we may obviously write

$$\underline{A} = \underline{L} \cdot \underline{R} = \underline{L} \cdot \underline{L}^T \tag{125}$$

As in elimination, Frobenius matrices may be used to effect (125). Premultiplying $\underline{A}^{(i-1)}$ by $\underline{F}_i$ (as before) and post-multiplying by $\underline{F}_i^T$ eliminates all nonzeroes in row and column i, except the diagonal element. Thus

$$\underline{F}_n * \underline{F}_{n-1} * \underline{F}_{n-2} * \dots * \underline{F}_1 * \underline{A} * \underline{F}_1^T * \dots * \underline{F}_n^T = \underline{D} \tag{126}$$

where $\underline{D}$ is diagonal matrix. As before $\underline{A} = \underline{L}*\underline{D}*\underline{L}^T$ i.e.

$$\underline{A} = (\underline{F}_n * \underline{F}_{n-1} * \dots * \underline{F}_1)^{-1}\, \underline{D} * ((\underline{F}_n * \underline{F}_{n-1} * \dots * \underline{F}_1)^{-1})^T = \underline{L}\, \underline{D}\, \underline{L}^T \tag{127}$$

This representation is unique, provided diag $(\underline{L}) = \underline{U}$. Moreover it is known ([No 69]), that $\underline{A}$ is positive definite iff $\underline{D} > 0$. In this case, with $\underline{L} * \underline{D}^{\frac{1}{2}} = \underline{G}$ one has $\underline{A} = \underline{G} * \underline{G}^T$ where $\underline{G}$ is lower triangular. This is the Cholesky factorization.

6.4.2 Equivalence of methods

The three forms (121), (124) and (127) are obviously equivalent to elimination, Jordan and Cholesky decomposition. The reason that they are advocated is that for sparse matrices, with a change of scheduling and reordering, the fill-in will be lower. Thus if all Frobenius matrices are stored in a single F-table, memory space and also time, will be saved [SB].

Four different factorization methods [TW 67, Zo 71, We 68, Ha 63] were suggested in practice so that we may question which of them should be used and whether they are really different methods at all (they are not).

In order to describe the algorithms we will use for a while the notation of Fig. 8 to indicate that the statement S_i or vertically lower boxes are to be performed with i taking all values between j and k (with a "step" of 1). Having completed the iteration on i, the box is left horizontally. Also needed will be the definition of the three functions rt(i), ta(m,i) and tb(m,i) of Fig. 8.

As already mentioned $\underline{A}$ is transformed and at the same time the F-table is recorded. All Frobenius matrices are copied from $\underline{F}$, so that comparison of various

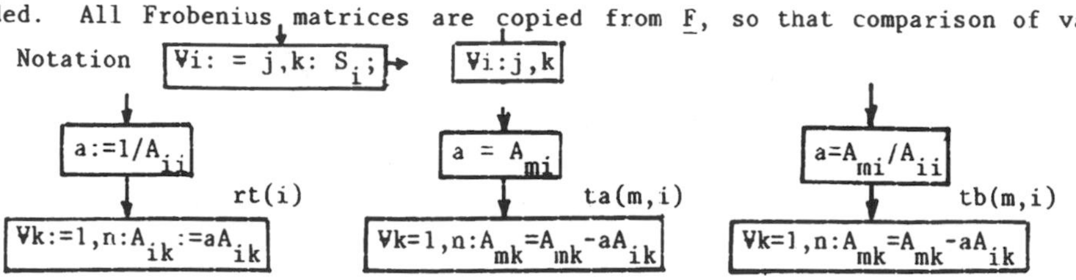

Fig. 8: Three basic functions and notation

methods should start from the F-tables that they yield. Moreover, since A is not anymore required, transformations on A may be made, provided that F does not change. On the other hand, all operations which store values f_{ij} should and will be recorded. Throughout, the algorithm will be exemplified by matrix A of [TW 67]:

$$A = \begin{bmatrix} 2 & 1 & 3 \\ 2 & 3 & 4 \\ 3 & 4 & 7 \end{bmatrix}$$

Fig. 9: A-Matrix

The best known factorization method [TW 67] is called OOTF for "Optimally Ordered Triangular Factorization". If no use of optimal ordering is made, the triangular factorization program of Fig. 10 results. Applying it to matrix A, the F-table of Fig. 11 results.

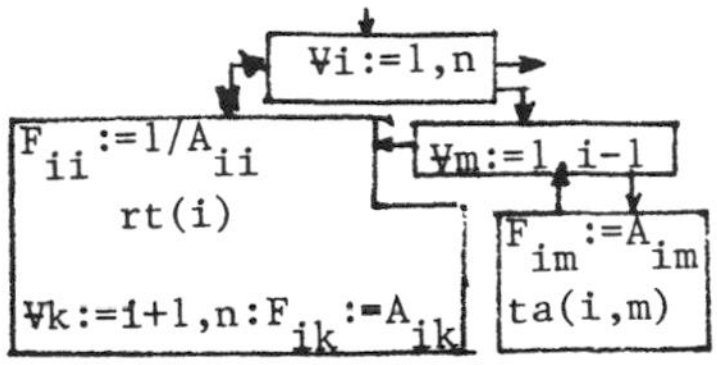

Fig. 10: OOTF

$$\begin{bmatrix} 2 & 1/2 & 3/2 \\ 2 & 3 & 4 \\ 3 & 4 & 7 \end{bmatrix} \rightarrow \begin{bmatrix} 2 & 1/2 & 3/2 \\ 2 & 2 & 1/2 \\ 3 & 5/2 & 7 \end{bmatrix} \rightarrow \begin{bmatrix} 2 & 1/2 & 3/2 \\ 2 & 2 & 1/2 \\ 3 & 5/2 & 5/4 \end{bmatrix} \rightarrow \begin{bmatrix} 1/2 & 1/2 & 3/2 \\ 2 & 1/2 & 1/2 \\ 3 & 5/2 & 4/5 \end{bmatrix}$$

Fig. 11: Transformation by OOTF

Another well-known method [Zo 71], the "Bi-Factorization" method, Fig. 12, yields for the same A, a different F-table (Fig. 13) so it behooves to ask for the reason underlying this difference.

Both algorithms use functions rt and ta and since these are basic to Gaussian elimination, this method is next shown (Fig. 14). Comparing Fig. 14 with Fig. 12 shows them to be identical except for storage of F.

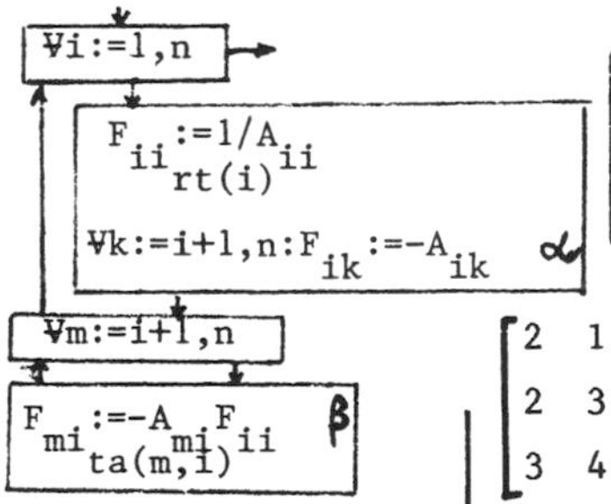

Fig. 12: Bifactorization

$$\begin{bmatrix} 1/2 & -1/2 & -3/2 \\ -1 & 2 & 1 \\ -3/2 & 5/2 & 5/2 \end{bmatrix} \rightarrow \overset{L_1D_1 \;\; L_2D_2}{\begin{bmatrix} 1/2 & -1/2 & -3/2 \\ -1 & 1/2 & -1/2 \\ -3/2 & -5/4 & 4/5 \end{bmatrix}} \begin{matrix} \leftarrow R_1 \text{ of OOTF} \\ \leftarrow R_2 \text{ of OOTF} \\ \leftarrow D_3 \end{matrix}$$

Fig. 13: Transformation by bifactorization

$$\begin{bmatrix} 2 & 1 & 2 \\ 2 & 3 & 4 \\ 3 & 4 & 7 \end{bmatrix}$$

This could be added to Fig. 12 and thus proves Gaussian elimination and Bifactorization are equivalent. If for the storage operations marked by α and β in Fig. 12, the operations $F_{ik}:=A_{ik}$ and $F_{mi}:=A_{mi}$ resp. are used, the F-table of OOTF (Fig. 11) results. Thus OOTF is yet another storage method of elimination. The contribution of OOTF and Bifactorization seems to be in scheduling elimination strictly by rows and most of all in enforcing a reordering policy.

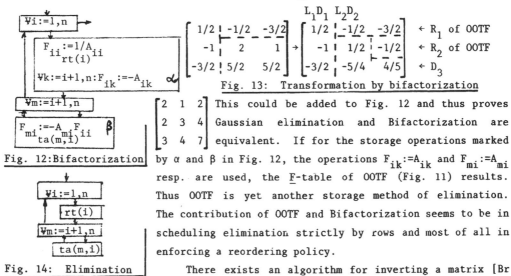

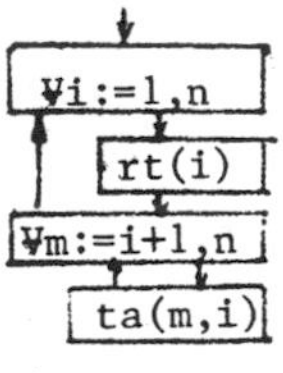

Fig. 14: Elimination

There exists an algorithm for inverting a matrix [Br 75] commonly called "Kron's method" and described as follows:

(a) Denote by a the i-th row, by b the i-th column of A

(b) Calculate $c := -1/A_{ii}$ and modify all elements of A except in its i-th row or column according to

$$a_{km} := a_{km} + c * b_k * a_m \tag{128}$$

(c) Replace the i-th row by the values c*a, the i-th column by c*b and a_{ii} by (-c)

Repeating these steps for all values of i (in any order!) yields $\underline{A}^{-1}$.

Adding storage operations explicitly would transform this algorithm into the Bi-Factorization method except for

$$F_{ik} := - a_{ik}/a_{ii} \tag{129}$$

at α. Since a_{ii} was made 1 by the preceding rt(i), this division is superflous.

Summing up, we may say that as far as the transformations of $\underline{A}$ are concerned, OOTF, Bi-Factorization and the here modified Kron's method, are all equivalent to Gaussian elimination. Only the scheduling, reordering policy, the order of storing and hence the resulting $\underline{F}$ are different.

This being so, let us extend the elimination method (Fig. 15) so that $\underline{A}$ is used only for the calculation of $\underline{F}$. Then, $\underline{F}$ will be the same as in the OOTF method, but the number of operations on $\underline{A}$ will have been reduced.

There are two more, known factorization algorithms [We 68, Ha 63]. If - as previously - only the resulting $\underline{F}$ is of interest they are both represented by the program in Fig. 16. The fact that $\underline{A}$ is transformed by this program into a unit matrix, leads to the suspicion that both methods are based on the Jordan algorithm. The proof is shown in Fig. 17 which, represents the straightforward Gauss-Jordan [Be 66] method with storage of $\underline{F}$ explictly mentioned. As with Gaussian elimination, since the order of storing $\underline{F}$ is different, two tables (Figs. 18, 19) result.

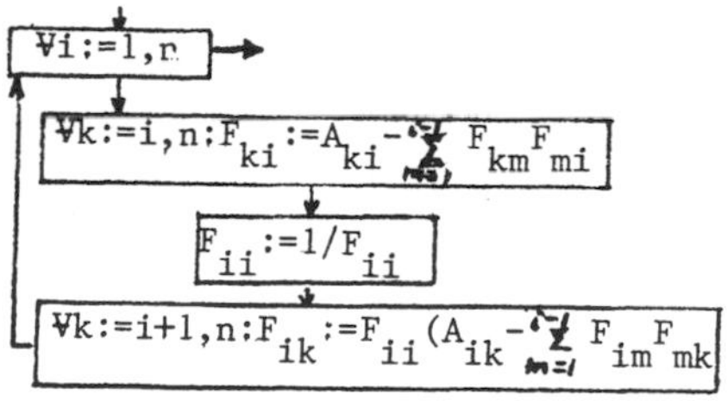

Fig. 15: Modified

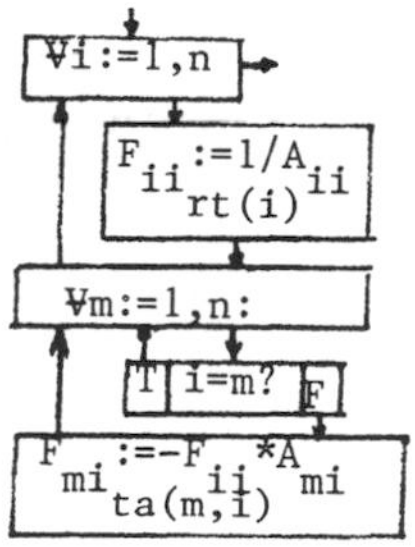

Fig. 16: Flowchart

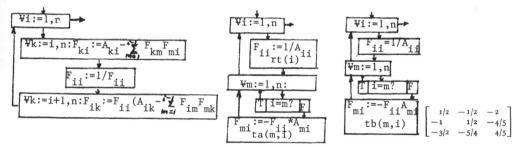

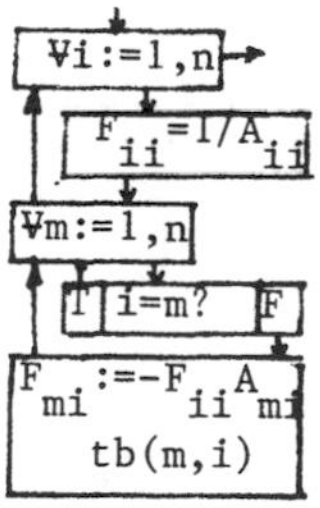

Fig. 17: Jordans method

$$\begin{bmatrix} 1/2 & -1/2 & -2 \\ -1 & 1/2 & -4/5 \\ -3/2 & -5/4 & 4/5 \end{bmatrix}$$

Fig. 18: End-table

$$\underline{A}_1 = \begin{bmatrix} 1/2 & 0 & 0 \\ -1 & 1 & 1 \\ -3/2 & 0 & 1 \end{bmatrix}; \quad \underline{A}_2 = \begin{bmatrix} 1 & -1/4 & 0 \\ 0 & 1/2 & 0 \\ 0 & -5/4 & 1 \end{bmatrix}; \quad \underline{A}_3 = \begin{bmatrix} 1 & 0 & -1 \\ 0 & 1 & -2/5 \\ 0 & 0 & 4/5 \end{bmatrix}; \quad \underline{A}^{-1} = \begin{bmatrix} 1 & 1 & -1 \\ -2/5 & 1 & -2/5 \\ -1/5 & -1 & 4/5 \end{bmatrix}$$

Fig. 19: Tables of basic factorization $\qquad \underline{A}^{-1} = \underline{A}_3\underline{A}_2\underline{A}_1$

To find whether and which methods are equivalent, the $\underline{F}$-tables will be next used as a substitute for $\underline{A}$. To this end, non-singular matrices are next defined (following [TW 67]). They differ from the unit matrix only in the row or column indicated:

$$\underline{F}_{i,+}\text{:row } (i) = (0,\ldots,0,1,F_{i,i+1},\ldots,F_{i,n}) \tag{130}$$

$$\underline{F}_{i,-}\text{:row } (i) = (0,\ldots,0,1,-F_{i,i+1},\ldots,-F_{i,n}) \tag{131}$$

$$\underline{F}_{-,i}\text{:col } (i) = (0,\ldots,0,1,-F_{i+1,i},\ldots,-F_{n,i})^T \tag{132}$$

$$\underline{F}'_{+,i}\text{:col } (i) = (F_{1i},\ldots,F_{i-1,i},1,F_{i+1,i},\ldots,F_{n,i})^T \tag{133}$$

$$\underline{F}'_{*,i}\text{:col } (i) = (0,\ldots,0,F_{ii},F_{i+1,i},\ldots,F_{n,i})^T \tag{134}$$

and similarly for $\underline{F}'_{i,+}$ or $\underline{F}'_{i,-}$. Also, $\underline{F}_d$ is the diagonal part of $\underline{F}$ and

$\underline{F}_i$: row (i) = $(0,\ldots,0,F_{ii},0,\ldots,0)$. (135)

With the above notation, and using Figs. 10 and 12 the following (product) matrices may be computed:

$$\underline{C} = \left(\prod_{i=1}^{n-1} \underline{F}_{i,-}\right) * F_n * \left(\prod_{i=n-1}^{1} \underline{F}_{-,i} * \underline{F}_i\right),\quad \underline{B} = \left(\prod_{i=1}^{n-1} \underline{F}_{i,+}\right) * \left(\prod_{i=n}^{1} \underline{F}'_{+,i}\right) \qquad (136)$$

It is obvious that the different signs result from the fact that $f_{i,m}$ were stored with + or - respectively and that $\underline{F}_n$ is inserted in (136) because the product Π following it starts with index (n-1). A check of Fig. 11 and 13 will show that any $\underline{F}_{-,i}*\underline{F}_i$ of the first equals $\underline{F}'_{+,i}$ of the second. Summing up: Both $\underline{C}$ and $\underline{B}$ are the same matrix, (namely, $\underline{A}^{-1}$).

We now claim that OOTF, Bi-Factorization and Kron's method are all equivalent to Gaussian elimination. This claim is supported by:

(a) The transformations rt(i), ta(m,i) and their place in flowcharts Figs. 10, 12 and 14 are identical,

(b) Every transformation rt(i) is preceded and followed by identical storage operations - except for the sign,

(c) Recalling that postmultiplication of any matrix $\underline{A}$ by matrix $\underline{F}_k$ results in $\underline{A}$ whose k-th column is multiplied by f_{kk} explains the difference between the two resulting tables (Figs. 11 and 13). This postmultiplication though should not be performed since it is implied (together with the sign difference), in (136). In the remaining three algorithms, we compute

$$\underline{C} = \underline{F}_d * \prod_{i=n}^{1} \underline{F}'_{*,i}, \quad ; \quad \underline{B} = \prod_{i=n}^{i} \underline{F}_{*,i} \qquad (137)$$

and find them both to be $\underline{A}^{-1}$ (see Figs. 18,19). The equivalence rests here on the fact that a transformation tb(i,m) is - as far as $\underline{F}$ is concerned - completely identical to ta(i,m) preceded by rt(i) and on the above post-or here premultiplication by a matrix $\underline{F}_d$. Additionally, note that the two flowcharts are otherwise identical.

6.4.3 ASP-algorithms

We will deal now with the two basic methods but have first to decide which algorithm in each of the two groups will be suitable for execution on ASP. This will amount to not only an addition of such "new" factorization methods as those of Jordan, Gauss or Kron, but to the development of parallel algorithms of factorization covering all seven sequential methods.

In both algorithms to be discussed, all "steps" will be done for index i changing sequentially from 1 to n.

For the first group, Kron's algorithm [Br 75] will be scheduled for execution on an ASP. This choice was made because of the fact that the rows and columns, treated during an iteration may be chosen at will, hence optimally ordered.

The algorithm proceeds by the following steps (for each i):

(a) Recall the i-th column and row of $\underline{A}$ from store or (private) memories and broadcast it on the bus to all slaves. Each memory stores now as $\underline{d}$ the i-th row, as $\underline{b}$ the i-th column of $\underline{A}$, and as $c = -1/d_i$.

(b) Each slave, concurrently with the others, corrects its slice of $\underline{A}$ (it resides in its memory) by $\forall\ m = 1,n : a_{km} := a_{km} + c*b_k*d_m$; where $k := (p-1) * h + 1,\ p * h$ is the index running through the slice.

(c) Still very much in parallel, each slave corrects: $d_k = c*d_k$; $b_k = c*b_k$; for k inside its slice, as in (b).

(d) The corrected slices of $\underline{d}$ and $\underline{b}$ are transferred to the store and stored there as parts of $\underline{F}$.

(e) It is not necessary to "collect" the new $\underline{A}$ in core, since it is both left in the memories at the end of step (b) and needed there for the subsequent indices i. The value (-c) is to be transferred to the memory where it replaces a_{ii}.

Table $\underline{F}$ resides in core at the end of execution. In steps (b) and (c), which include the overwhelming part of operations, all p slaves work concurrently. Steps (a), (d) and (e) are sequential, and are executed by the master.

The algorithm is seen to be rather efficient, hence the reason for its limited use outside the electric power system group must be questioned. It is said that in purely sequential programs step (b) requires two multiplications for each of the $(n^2 - 2n + 1)$ elements $a_{k\ell}$; $k,\ell \neq i$. The remaining $(2n - 2)$ elements are multiplied once (in (c)) by c, so altogether

$$n[2(n^2 - 2n + 1) + 2n - 2] = 2n^2(n - 1) \cong 2n^3 \qquad (138)$$

multiplications are required instead of n^3 in Crouts algorithm (in [Be 66] it is called "the compact scheme"). Actually, the factor $c*b_k$ in (b) is the same for all columns m of a given row k, so that we may store it in the accumulator for reuse. This reduces the work back to about n^3. Moreover, as noted in [Pe 69] "with parallel processing, the total number of operations is not significant. What matters is the number of sets of operations, where each set involves those being done in parallel". In the algorithm above most of the work is done concurrently on all p slaves with insignificant bus-transfer times. Hence, the number of sets of operations is $S \cong n^3/p$. It is seen to depend on the number of slaves, and this proves that the program is well suited for parallel execution.

In algorithms based on the Jordan method, at each stage a column of $\underline{A}$ (except its diagonal entry) instead of only its "lower-triangular" part is transformed to zero. Hence work is more evenly distributed among the p processors, and these methods should lend themselves even better to parallelization.

It is suggested that in this group, the "base-substitution" algorithm [Ha 63] should be re-scheduled for ASP. Hence, each memory holds initially its slice of a unit matrix $\underline{U}$. The steps (for each i) are:

(a) Transfer (blockwise if possible) column i of $\underline{A}$ from core to all slaves and

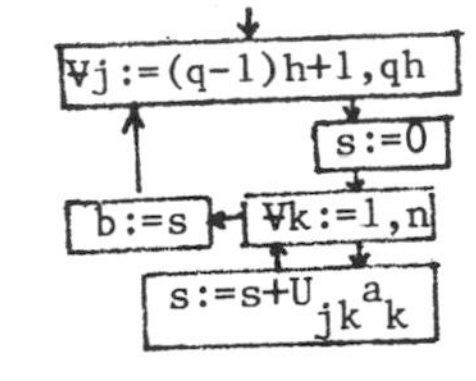

Fig. 20:Another method

store it there as, say, $\underline{d}$

(b) Multiply concurrently each slice of $\underline{J}^{-1}=\underline{U}$ (as stored in the memories) by $\underline{d}$ according to Fig. 20 and store (retain) the resulting slices $\underline{b}$ in the slaves. Next, each processor computes its part of table $\underline{F}$ through

$$c=b_i;\ \forall k=(p-1)*h+1,\ p*h\ :\ f_{ki} := -b_k/c;\ f_{ii}=1/c. \qquad (139)$$

(c) "Correct" $\underline{A}^{-1}=\underline{U}$ by calculating concurrently in all slaves their new slices by $\underline{U}:=\underline{F}'_i*\underline{U}$ where $\underline{F}'_i$ is a unit matrix whose i-th column is computed in (139).

(d) Transfer slices of $\underline{F}$ into core. Hence at the end of the program, the entire $\underline{F}$ is stored in the core.

This program is even more parallel than the previous, because only steps (a) and (d) require the services of the bus and master. Moreover the interference is small in both algorithms because the parallel parts are not interrupted by an action of the master. Unfortunately both are inefficient for sparse matrices, and will have very low speedups if pivoting is required. In such cases, we better use orthogonalization which is our next topic.

6.5 ORTHOGONALISATION ON ASP

We have introduced orthogonalization in 5.2 and shown how to use it for elimination or for factorization.

$$\underline{A} = \underline{Q} * \underline{R} \qquad (140)$$

For dense matrices, orthogonalization is less efficient than factorization. There is though an argument concerning the number of operations Ω in both and we start by discussing Ω of factorization.

Since most computers are equipped nowadays with floating-point hardware, the times of a single multiplication or addition are approximately equal, call it here the "operation" time ω. Moreover, checking of conditions requires not much less than ω. Thus A=B+C may require the "program": MOV B,R; ADD C,R and MOV R,A whereas <u>if</u> B=C <u>then</u> <u>goto</u> L would need: MOV C,R; SUB B,R and BZ L. In the "programs" R is a register, MOV B,R fetches B from memory to R, BZ means "branch on zero" and ADD, SUB have the obvious interpretation. It is seen that both programs require approximately the same time.

The time of factorization is usually calculated by counting the number of operations, but not condition-checking. In that case, factorization of dense matrices requires

$$\Omega_{LR} \cong 2n^3\omega/3 \qquad (141)$$

For sparse matrices and optimally ordered factorization, the claim was made in [TH67] that:

$$\Omega_{LR} \cong n\omega + \Sigma\psi_i + \Sigma\psi_i^2\ ;\ i\ \Sigma = 1,\ldots,(n-1) \qquad (142)$$

where ψ_i is the number of nonzero terms of row i. Thus, assuming that every row of $\underline{A}$ has ψ non-zero elements

$$\Omega_{LR} \cong n\omega + (n-1)\psi\omega + (n-1)\psi^2\omega = (\psi^2+\psi+1)n\omega = cn\omega \qquad (143)$$

This is clearly an undercount since even for a diagonal matrix, solving $\underline{D}\ \underline{x} = \underline{b}$ requires $n\omega$. We will assume therefore that

$$\Omega_{LR} = cn^2\omega \tag{144}$$

and base it on the following observations:

- There is always a considerable "fill-in" especially when using the static policy, so that ψ increases during factorization. For $\psi^2+\psi+1 = n$, we would have (144) with c=1.
- The authors of [TH67] were aware of it and mentioned that "large networks are composed of subnetworks with relatively few interconnections and the optimal ordering scheme takes advantage of this property." In the last 14 years, the interconnections grew considerably more dense.
- It is instructive to follow factorization of the 10 x 10 matrix shown in [TH67]. Without ordering, it requires 356ω, with a static ordering 206ω so that c = 3.56 and c = 2.06 respectively.
- The main point is that Ω_{LR} did not count checking of conditions. The number of these depends on the storage scheme: If $\underline{A}$ is stored in an nxm array, it is proportional to n, but the whole point of OOF is to store only the nonzero elements. If the storage of [TH67] is used, the number will be very high, as evidenced by the following quotes: "If the sign... is positive, the first three entries are... followed by m; if m is positive it is followed by...; if m is negative,... ." "Similarly, if the sign... is negative... ." A more efficient storage scheme was used in matrix multiplication, but even then c > 2 should be used in (144).

As already mentioned, $\underline{A} = \underline{L}\ \underline{R}$ is only part of the computational effort - the rest is reusing it, say k, times. Each of these requires $0.5n^2\omega$ for a dense matrix and $\underline{L}$, $\underline{R}$ are much more dense than $\underline{A}$. Assuming that their density is d, the entire computational effort of solving $\underline{A}\ \underline{x} = \underline{b}$ by factorization is

$$\Omega_{LR} = cn^2\omega + 0.5kdn^2\omega = (c+d\cdot k/2)n^2\omega \tag{145}$$

It is seen that Ω depends substantially on k i.e. on how many times F can be reused.

The next characteristic of the method, is the memory size required. For the storage scheme proposed it will be

$$S_{LR} = 2\psi_i+s\cdot n \tag{146}$$

With prices of memory decreasing, this storage is not a determining factor anymore.

It is mentioned in [TH67] that "there are some cases which cannot be solved." One is if a flat start is not followed by a Gauss-Seidel iteration (which requires $cn\omega$). Another, can best be shown for two equations, say

$$3x + 4y = 7; \quad 6x + 8.02y = 14.02 \tag{147}$$

for which obviously x=y=1. Since the two lines are almost parallel, elimination will not be stable. A small error of say 0.01 may lead to 0.01y = 0.02 and y=2 instead of 0.02y = 0.02 and y=1.

Equations (5-196) to (5-212) and Fig. 5-5 show how to use Givens' method for solving $\underline{A}\ \underline{x} = \underline{b}$. Fig. 5-5 indicates that the original matrix can be used to insert symbols 0,* and . and that the fill-in (number of dots) is considerable. The same in a condensed form as shown in Fig. 21.

$$\begin{matrix} i \\ j \end{matrix}\begin{bmatrix} c & s \\ -s & c \end{bmatrix} * \overset{\begin{matrix} i & j & k & l & m \end{matrix}}{\begin{bmatrix} x & x & & x & x \\ x & x & x & & x \end{bmatrix}} = \overset{\begin{matrix} i & j & k & l & m \end{matrix}}{\begin{bmatrix} * & * & \cdot & x & x \\ 0 & * & x & \cdot & x \end{bmatrix}}$$

Fig. 21: Proof

In this form, orthogonalization is rather time consuming. The elements of row i in Fig. 21 are computed according to $A_{ik} := s*A_{jk}$; $A_{il} := c*A_{il}$; $A_{im} := c*A_{im}+s*A_{jm}$ (145)

and similarly for row j. A fill-in requires 1ω, other non-zero 3ω operations and both rows i, and j have to be calculated (in elimination-only one). Additionally, $\underline{A} = \underline{Q}\ \underline{R}$ requires a square-root calculation. The total amount of computation can though be reduced [Ge 68]. Below is a slightly different proof of this method.

Let us factor $\underline{A}$ into the product of a diagonal matrix $\underline{D}$ and matrix $\underline{B}$ i.e.

$$\underline{A} = \underline{D}\ \underline{B} \tag{146}$$

Any element A_{km} may then be written as

$$A_{km} = D_m B_{km} \tag{147}$$

Instead of the rotation matrix $\underline{G}_{ji}$ we may use

$$\underline{M}_{ij} \triangleq \underline{D}'\ \underline{E}_{ji}\ \underline{D}^{-1} \tag{148}$$

where

$$\underline{D}' = \begin{bmatrix} d_i' & 0 \\ 0 & d_j' \end{bmatrix}; \quad \underline{E}_{ji} = \begin{bmatrix} 1 & e_{ij} \\ e_{ji} & 1 \end{bmatrix} \tag{149)(150}$$

The transformation is therefore equivalent to

$$\underline{D}'\ \underline{B}' = \underline{D}'\ \underline{E}_{ji}\ \underline{D}^{-1}\ \underline{D}\ \underline{B} = \underline{D}'\ \underline{E}_{ji}\ \underline{B} \tag{151}$$

Inserting (150) into (151) yields

$$\begin{bmatrix} d_i' & 0 \\ 0 & d_j \end{bmatrix}\begin{bmatrix} 1 & e_{ij} \\ e_{ji} & 1 \end{bmatrix}\begin{bmatrix} 1/d_i & 0 \\ 0 & 1/d_j \end{bmatrix} = \begin{bmatrix} d_i'/d_i & e_{ij}d_i'/d_j \\ e_{ji}d_j'/d_i & d_j'/d_j \end{bmatrix} = \begin{bmatrix} c & s \\ -s & c \end{bmatrix} \tag{152}$$

By comparing elements:

$$e_{ij} = s\cdot d_j/d_i' = sd_j/(c\cdot d_i) = t\cdot d_j/d_i \tag{153}$$

$$e_{ji} = -s\cdot d_i/d_j' = -sd_i/(c\cdot d_j) = -t\cdot d_i/d_j \tag{154}$$

We therefore have for tanθ:

$$t=s/c = A_{ji}/A_{ii} = D_jB_{ji}/(D_iB_{ii}) \tag{156}$$

so that

$$e_{ij} = \left(\frac{D_j}{D_i}\right)^2 \frac{B_{ji}}{B_{ii}}\ ;\ e_{ji} = -\frac{B_{ji}}{B_{ii}} \tag{156}$$

From (152) it follows that

$$D_i' = c\cdot D_i\ ;\ D_j' = c\cdot D_j \tag{157}$$

so that c must yet be calculated. From (148):

$$c^2(A_{ii}^2 + A_{ji}^2) = c^2(D_i^2B_{ii}^2 + D_j^2B_{ji}^2) = D_i^2B_{ii}^2 \tag{158}$$

This c^2 inserted into (157) yields:

$$(D_i')^2 = \frac{D_i^2B_{ii}^2}{D_i^2B_{ii}^2+D_j^2B_{ji}^2} D_i^2\ ;\ (D_j')^2 = \frac{D_i^2B_{ii}^2}{D_i^2B_{ii}^2+D_j^2B_{ji}^2} D_j^2 \tag{159}$$

Note that for transformation (144), no square root taking is required provided $\underline{D}{*}\underline{D}$ instead of $\underline{D}$ is stored. The calculation would actually be according to (156) and $c^2 = 1/(1-e_{ij}e_{ji})$; $(D'_k)^2 = c^2 D_k^2$ for k=i,j (160)

If instead of the c,s - matrix, we insert the $\underline{E}$-matrix in Fig. 21, we get for columns k, ℓ and m respectively:

$B'_{ik} := e_{ij}{*}B_{jk}$; $B'_{jk} := B_{jk}$; $B'_{i\ell} := B_{i\ell}$; $B'_{j\ell} := e_{ji}{*}B_{i\ell}$ (161)(162)

$B'_{im} := B_{im} + e_{ij}{*}B_{jm}$; $B'_{jm} := B_{jm} + e_{ji}{*}B_{im}$ (163)

Compared to the original method, no square-root is taken, the fill-in requires a single (161,162) and other elements 4 operations ω. Thus we have to compare ω,ω and 4ω with 0,3ω and 3ω resp. and whether orthogonalization or elimination requires more operations (and time) depends really on the amount of fill-in.

To reduce fill-in, policy (2) is used in factorization. In order to arrive at a comparable policy for orthogonalization, we will first orthogonalize "by hand" the original net and matrix (Figs. 22,23). From it we deduce that:

- The further "lower-right" is an element the less work it generates. Thus $A_{13,2}$ generated (3*) and (6x) and 2·) elements, but $A_{13,9}$ only (3*), (5x) and a single · despite the fact that the two rows right of the diagonal were full for $M_{13,9}$.
- The closer we get to the lower-right corner, the more operations are needed. Thus, $M_{13,7}$, filled all elements $A_{13,j}$, 7<j<13.
- $\underline{M}_{5,1}$ enters fill-in $A_{1,3}$ which itself generates $A_{6,3}$, $A_{7,3}$ and $A_{12,3}$. Thus fill-in, even in the right matrix $\underline{R}$ contributes (indirectly) to the operations count.
- It is obvious that the less "linkage", the better. Thus, consecutive numbering of nodes should be discouraged.

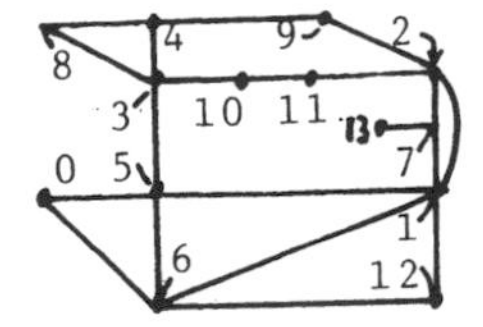

Fig. 22: Network

	1	2	3	4	5	6	7	8	9	0	1	2	3
1	*	x	.		x	x	x		.		.	x	.
2	⊗	*	.	.	.	.	x		x		x	.	.
3			*	x	x	.	.	x	.	x	.	.	.
4			⊗	*	.	.	.	x	x	.	.	.	.
5	⊗	⊙	⊗	⊙	*	x	.	.	.	.	.	.	.
6	⊗	⊙	⊙	⊙	⊗	*	.	.	.	.	.	x	.
7	⊗	⊗	⊙	⊙	⊙	⊙	*	.	.	.	.	.	x
8			⊗	⊗	⊙	⊙	⊙	*	.	.	.	.	.
9		⊗	⊙	⊗	⊙	⊙	⊙	⊙	*	.	.	.	.
10			⊗	⊙	⊙	⊙	⊙	⊙	⊙	*	x	.	.
11		⊗	⊙	⊙	⊙	⊙	⊙	⊙	⊙	⊗	*	.	.
12	⊗	⊙	⊙	⊙	⊙	⊗	⊙	⊙	⊙	⊙	⊙	*	.
13							⊗	⊙	⊙	⊙	⊙	⊙	*

Fig. 23: A=QR, Original Network

These points lead to the following ordering policy: Number the nodes in order of increasing number of branches. A number of nodes which have the same number of branches should be numbered in a non-consecutive order if possible.

The same network with the nodes renumbered according to the policy as stated results in orthogonalization as in Fig. 25. Other examples also justify the policy.

OOF is used normally so that $\underline{A}$ is factored into $\underline{L}\cdot\underline{U}$ and the $\underline{L}$, $\underline{U}$ matrices reused a number of times, say k. Tests were conducted to ascertain whether the same could be used when $\underline{A} = \underline{Q}\,\underline{R}$, i.e. is orthogonalized. It was found that k could be increased compared to OOF because $\underline{Q}\,\underline{R}$ is less sensitive to perturbations. Most importantly: no pivoting is necessary This makes orthogonalization even more efficient.

Next we calculate how the two methods compare when applied to the full solution of $\underline{A}\ \underline{x} = \underline{b}$. Instead of factorization, forward and back-substitution, solution of $\underline{A}\ \underline{x} = \underline{b}$ would proceed according to

$$\underline{A} = \underline{Q}\ \underline{R};\ \underline{z} = \underline{Q}^{-1}\ \underline{b};\ \underline{R}\ \underline{x} = \underline{z} \qquad (164)$$

but since $\underline{Q}^{-1} = \underline{Q}^T$, the second of these leads to

$$\underline{z} = \underline{Q}^T \underline{b} = (\underline{G}_{n-1,n}\underline{G}_{n-2,n} \cdots \underline{G}_{3,1} \cdot \underline{G}_{2,1})\underline{b} = (\underline{G}_{n-1,n} \cdots (\underline{G}_{3,1}, (\underline{G}_{2,1}\underline{b}))\cdots) \qquad (165)$$

Each $\underline{G}_{j,i}$ was stored as a pair of values and each of the indicated multiplications requires only 4ω. The number of multiplications equals the number of rotations. If every column of $\underline{A}$ had initially ψ nonzero elements, it had $\psi/2$ of it below the diagonal and this number was increased by fill-in but certainly not more than twice. Thus, we would need for (165) $\Omega = 4\psi n\omega$ for solving $\underline{R}\ \underline{x} = \underline{z}$

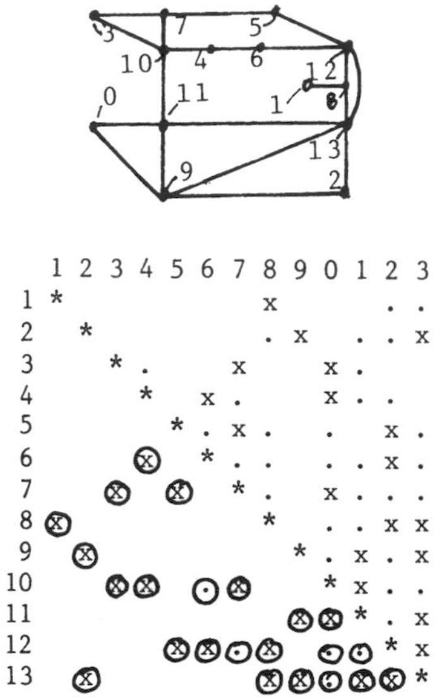

Fig. 24: A Renumbered Net

$$\Omega_{SOL} = n^2\omega + 4\psi n\omega \cong n^2\omega \qquad (166)$$

which is only 50% of that required by factorization.

We next discuss the possibility of modifying the method for execution on ASP. For it note that if $\underline{A}$ is multiplied by $\underline{G}_{jk}$, only its k and j row change. A number of transformations can therefore be done simultaneously if and only if no index repeats itself. Thus, for our matrix $\underline{G}_{8,1}\underline{A}$ and $\underline{G}_{9,2}{*}\underline{A}$ and $\underline{G}_{7,3}{*}\underline{A}$ can be done concurrently, but $\underline{G}_{13,2}{*}\underline{A}$ cannot since index 2 appeared twice.

This leads to a very simple ordering policy for ASP-execution: Divide the network into p "clusters" connected each to a node with as many branches as possible and so that there is no direct connection between cluster centers. The resulting speedup, ratio and efficiency are being investigated at present. They clearly depend on the network. Since the matrices are sparse, the same row may be stored in more than one memory. In a number of equations, the orthonormal matrix $\underline{Q}$ had to be multiplied by a vector, say $\underline{b}$. For parallel execution, we better rewrite these equations and instead of, say (166), write:

$$\underline{Q}^T\underline{b} = (\underline{G}_{n-1,n}\underline{G}_{n-2,n}\cdots)\cdots(\underline{G}_{h,1}\cdots\underline{G}_{3,1}\underline{G}_{2,1})\cdot\underline{b} = \underline{Q}_p\underline{Q}_{p-1}\cdots\underline{Q}_1\underline{b} \qquad (167)$$

where $h = n/p$ is assumed to be an integer. In fact, the above produces each product $(\underline{G}_{ij}\cdots\underline{G}_{k,1})$ in a different slave and if we form the products so that no index is repeated inside a pair of parantheses, there is no multiplication involved; this is done at the end of multiplying the p product matrices as in Chapter 4. As seen, there is very little actual computing to be done and whatever there is can be easily parallelized so that the speedup approaches p and efficiency approaches 100%. Because of the way the $\underline{Q}_i$ are produced the roundoff error is smaller - an important consideration for cases where accuracy is not less important than speed.

Next, algorithms for executing the Gram-Schmidt methods on ASP are discussed.

Each iteration of the normal algorithm could be done in ASP as follows (with $\delta=(q-1)h+1$, $\Delta=qh$).

$$P(k_1):\quad \text{Each slave } q \text{ computes } r_{kk}^{(q)} := \sum_{i=\delta}^{\Delta} a_{ik}^2 \tag{168}$$

$$S(k_1):\quad r_{kk} := \sqrt{\Sigma\, r_{kk}^{(s)}};\ q\Sigma = 1,\ldots,p. \quad \text{Broadcast } r_{kk} \tag{169}$$

$$P(k_2):\quad s_{ik} := a_{ik}/r_{kk};\ i = \delta,\ldots,\Delta \tag{170}$$

$$r_{kj}^{(q)} := \Sigma\, s_{ik} a_{ij};\ j = k+1,\ldots,n;\ i\ \Sigma = \delta,\ldots,\Delta \tag{171}$$

$$S(k_2):\quad r_{kj} := \Sigma\, r_{kj}^{(q)};\ j = k+1,\ldots,n;\ q = 1,\ldots,p \tag{172}$$

$$P(k_3):\quad a_{ij} := a_{ij} - r_{kj} s_{ik};\ i = \delta,\ldots,\Delta;\ j = k+1,\ldots,n \tag{173}$$

Obviously, we would combine $P(k_3)$ with $P(k_1)$, start at $P(1)$ and stop at $P(n)$, but we do need 2β for each k. For the five steps above the processing times are $[h\omega + p\tau]$, $[p\alpha + \tau]$, $[h\mu + (n-k)h\omega + p(n-k)\tau]$, $[n-k)(p\omega + \tau)]$ and $[(n-k)h\omega]$ resp. For n iterations, with $n(n-1)/2 \cong 0.5n^2$ we have

$$\Omega_p \cong 0.5n^2(2h+p)\omega + 0.5n^2(p+1)\tau + 2n\beta \tag{174}$$

and since $\Omega_1 \cong n^3\omega$ we have (without counting sqrt in Ω_p or Ω_1)

$$\rho = 1/p + (1+\tau')/(2h) + 2\beta'/n^2 \tag{175}$$

In the modified Gram-Schmidt algorithm, the calculation of the r_{kj}'s can be combined with that of d_k. For instance,

$$r_{12} = \frac{\sum_{k=1}^{n} a_{k2} s_{kl}}{\sum_{k=1} s_{kl} s_{kl}} = \frac{\sum_{k=1}^{h}(\cdot) + \sum_{k=h+1}^{2h}(\cdot) + \ldots + \sum_{k=n-h}^{n}(\cdot)}{\Sigma(\cdot) + \Sigma(\cdot) + \ldots + \Sigma(\cdot)} \tag{176}$$

and the respective sums may be done in the slaves. The ASP program is:

$P(k_1)$: Rename a_{jk} as s_{jk} for $j = \delta,\ldots,\Delta$ in each slave

Compute $v^{(s)} := \Sigma s_{jk}^2$ and $r_{jk}^{(s)} := \Sigma\, a_{jk} s_{ik}$; $i = k+1,\ldots, n$ and j as above. Transfer p a's and n(n-k) r's to the master

$S(k_1)$: $d_k = \sum_{k=1}^{p} v^{(s)}$ and $r_{kj} = \sum_{q=1}^{p} r_{kj}^{(q)}/d_k$ for $j = k+1,\ldots,n$. Transfer all r_{kj}'s

$P(k_2)$: $a_{kj} := a_{kj} - r_{kj} s_{jk}$; $j = k+1,\ldots,n$

We would again combine $P(k_2)$ with $P(k_1)$. In the substeps above the number of operations are $[h\mu + (h-1)]$, $(n-k)[h\mu + (h-1)\alpha]$, $[p + n(n-k)]\tau + \beta$, $p\alpha$, $(n-k)[\alpha p + \mu]$, $(n-k)\tau$ and $(n-k)(\alpha + \mu)$ resp. Thus for the usual simplifications e.g., $h - 1 \cong h$, $m \cong n$ and summation over k, the result will be:

$$\Omega_p \cong hn^2\omega + 0.5n^3\tau + n\beta; \qquad \rho = 1/p + \tau'/2 + \beta'/n^2 \tag{177)(178}$$

Compared to (175) we have reduced the synchronization and increased the transfer part; altogether since $\beta >> \tau$ the ratio is closer to being optimal.

7. ITERATIVE METHODS

Introduction

Linear sets can be solved not only by direct, but also by iterative methods. These methods which include the algorithms of Jacobi, Gauss-Seidel and various relaxation schemes are thought to be strictly sequential. It will be shown that using a new general approach, called "vertical programming" they can be easily programmed for ASP. Moreover using vertical programming, entirely new methods can be developed. One such method discussed in Section 3 uses only 50% of the number of operations used by other methods. It is shown that in this respect, it is in fact optimal: no other "alternating" method can reduce the operations count further.

Since this book deals with ASP, new methods must be checked not only for their convergence, but also for the time ratios. This is done for both old and new methods. Certain less-well known methods e.g. Aitken's acceleration scheme or the conjugate-gradient scheme are also discussed in terms of execution on ASP.

Iterative methods of solving $\underline{A}\ \underline{x} = \underline{b}$ are normally advocated only for sparse and in particular band matrices. For such systems the methods above are inefficient, but numerical evidence obtained from actual runs on the SMS201 shows that the situation is not as bad as it seems. On Staran too, quite reasonable results were obtained, especially for the Jacobi method. Moreover, numbering the nodes in the black-red scheme improves the speedup both on Staran and on SIMD systems. We expect it to be also more efficient on ASP-systems.

To summ-up: in this chapter we will parallelize algorithms which seem completely sequential.

7.1 SEQUENTIAL METHODS

Aims: To introduce various iterative methods for solving sets of linear equations. Since most of these are well-known, particular attention will be paid to less known techniques e.g. Aitken's acceleration, iterative improvement and gradient methods.

7.1.1 Splitting

In this chapter, we will discuss the iterative solution of a set of linear equations:

$$\underline{A}\ \underline{x} = \underline{b} \qquad (1)$$

Solving (1) is important on its own but since in most applications of iterative methods, matrix $\underline{A}$ is extremely large and sparse, some considerations must be given to problems raised by its size and sparsity.

In this section, only the mechanics of some fundamental algorithms will be described. $\underline{A}$ is a general n x n matrix and $\underline{x}$ and $\underline{b}$ are (column) n-vectors, but for didactic purposes we will first follow the solution of the particular system:

$$\begin{aligned}
-20x_1 + x_2 + x_3 + 6x_4 + 2x_5 + x_6 &= -17 \\
x_1 - 20x_2 + 2x_3 + x_4 + 4x_5 + 3x_6 &= -25 \\
x_1 + 2x_2 - 20x_3 + 2x_4 + x_5 + 2x_6 &= -8 \\
6x_1 + x_2 + 2x_3 - 20x_4 + 3x_5 + x_6 &= -60 \\
2x_1 + 4x_2 + x_3 + 3x_4 - 20x_5 + 5x_6 &= -13 \\
x_1 + 3x_2 + 2x_3 + x_4 + 5x_5 - 20x_6 &= -1
\end{aligned} \qquad (2)$$

Set (2) may be rewritten so that x_1 is calculated from the first, x_2 from the second equation and so on. The resulting set is:

$$\begin{aligned}
x_1 &= 0.85 + 0.05x_2 + 0.05x_3 + 0.30x_4 + 0.10x_5 + 0.05x_6 \\
x_2 &= 1.25 + 0.05x_1 + 0.10x_3 + 0.05x_4 + 0.20x_5 + 0.15x_6 \\
x_3 &= 0.40 + 0.05x_1 + 0.10x_2 + 0.10x_4 + 0.05x_5 + 0.10x_6 \\
x_4 &= 3.00 + 0.30x_1 + 0.05x_2 + 0.10x_3 + 0.15x_5 + 0.05x_6 \\
x_5 &= 0.65 + 0.10x_1 + 0.20x_2 + 0.05x_3 + 0.15x_4 + 0.25x_6 \\
x_6 &= 0.05 + 0.05x_1 + 0.15x_2 + 0.10x_3 + 0.05x_4 + 0.25x_5
\end{aligned} \qquad (3)$$

In the simplest method (of Jacobi), a vector $\underline{x}^{(0)}$ is assumed and inserted into (3). This yields $\underline{x}^{(1)}$ which is again inserted into the right side of (3) etc. For instance if all $x_i^{(0)} = 1$, then (3) yields:

$$\underline{x}^{(1)} = (1.40,\ 1.80,\ 0.80,\ 3.65,\ 1.40,\ 0.65)^T \qquad (4)$$

where superscript (1) means "result of first iteration" and T means "transpose".

The algorithm is seen to consist of a repeated application of

$$\underline{x}^{(i+1)} = \underline{k} + \underline{I} * \underline{x}^{(i)} \qquad (5)$$

where the elements of constant vector $\underline{k}$ and iteration matrix $\underline{I}$ are calculated from

$$k_j = b_j/A_{jj} \qquad (6)$$

$$I_{kl} = -A_{kl}/A_{kk}\ ;\ k \neq \ell \qquad (7)$$

$$I_{kk} = 0 \qquad (8)$$

We might have written the algorithm without introducing $\underline{k}$ and $\underline{I}$, namely as

$$x_k^{(i+1)} = (b_i - \Sigma\ a_{kj} * x_j^{(i)})\ /\ a_{kk};\ k = 1,2,\dots,n;\ j\Sigma\neq k \qquad (9)$$

A "sweep" includes the updating of all $x_k^{(i+1)}$; $k = 1,2,\dots,n$ and is seen to use only values of the previous sweep $x_k^{(i)}$; $k = 1,2,\dots,n$. This is the reason why the name "method of simultaneous displacements" is used in the literature for the Jacobi or <u>JA-method</u>.

For every iteration (i+1), residuals r_k may be computed per:

$$r_k = x_k^{(i+1)} - x_k^{(i)} \qquad (10)$$

and the algorithm terminated whenever

$$e = \Sigma\ r_k * r_k < \varepsilon \quad \text{or } e = \max(r_k) < \varepsilon;\ k = 1,\dots,n \qquad (11)$$

ε being a predetermined accuracy factor.

The JA-method seems to be natural for ASP-programming since the entire vector $\underline{x}^{(i+1)}$ may be computed using only $\underline{x}^{(i)}$. We will next introduce other iterative methods in which this is not the case and start with the Gauss-Seidel method.

In the Gauss-Seidel algorithm, if $\underline{x}^{(0)} = \underline{1}$ then from (2):

$$x_1^{(1)} = 1.40 \qquad (12)$$

as it was in the J-method. But, when computing $x_2^{(1)}$, the corrected new value of $x_1^{(1)}$ namely 1.4 will be used. This yields

$$x_2^{(1)} = 1.25 + 0.05*1.4 + 0.5 = 1.82 \qquad (13)$$

In the same way, both $x_1^{(1)}$ and $x_2^{(1)}$ are used for correcting $x_3^{(1)}$ etc.

$$x_3^{(1)} = 0.4 + 0.05*x_1^{(1)} + 0.1*x_2 + 0.25 = 0.9$$
$$x_4^{(1)} = 3.0 + 0.3*1.4 + 0.05*1.82 + 0.1*0.902 + 0.2 = 3.8 \qquad (14)$$
$$x_5^{(1)} = 0.65 + 0.14 + 0.364 + 0.045 + 0.57 + 0.25 = 2.019$$
$$x_6^{(1)} = 0.05*2.4 + 0.15*1.82 + 0.09 + 0.05*3.8 + 0.25*2.019 = 1.18.$$

The next step (or rather "sweep") would start by computing

$$x_1^{(2)}=0.85+0.05*1.82+0.05*0.902+0.3*3.8+0.1*2.02+0.05*1.18=2.39 \qquad (15)$$

which is much closer to the final value of x_1.

As presented, this method is a good example of algorithms which are considered to be <u>inherently sequential</u>. Already, when $x_1^{(i+1)}$ is corrected it uses $x_2^{(i)}$, $x_3^{(i)}$, $x_4^{(i)}$, $x_5^{(i)}$, $x_6^{(i)}$; then $x_2^{(i+1)}$ uses not only the above x_3, x_4 x_5 x_6 but also the recently corrected $x_1^{(i+1)}$; then $x_3^{(i+1)}$ uses $x_1^{(i+1)}$ and $x_2^{(i+1)}$ etc. Note that each of these x's had to "<u>wait</u>" until the previous x's were computed; it appears that <u>correction of every</u> $x_k^{(i+1)}$ <u>can be done only after all</u> $x_{k-1}^{(i+1)}$, $x_{k-2}^{(i+1)}, \ldots, x_1^{(i+1)}$ <u>have been computed i.e. in a rigid sequence</u>. We might therefore be justified in our question as to whether this algorithm can at all be scheduled efficiently for ASP.

It can and will later. Right now we add two more methods.

To increase the speed of the JA- and S-methods, a modification, known as over or under-relaxation was devised. The computation of each component $x_i^{(m+1)}$ proceeds in two steps. First, an intermediate result $\tilde{x}_i^{(m+1)}$ is defined through:

$$\tilde{x}_i^{(m+1)} = \Big(b_i - \sum_{j=1}^{i-1} a_{ij}x_j^{(m+1)} - \sum_{j=i+1}^{n} a_{ij}x_j^{(m)}\Big) / a_{ii} \qquad (16)$$

and then the final result is obtained through

$$x_i^{(m+1)} = x_i^{(m)} + w(\tilde{x}_1^{(m+1)} - x_i^{(m)}) = (1-w)x_i^{(m)} + \tilde{x}_i^{(m+1)} \qquad (17)$$

where w is a constant known as the "relaxation" factor.

When $w>1$, the method described by (16), (17) is known as successive over-relaxation (SOR); $w<1$ corresponds to under-relaxation and is seldom used. For $w=1$ the method reduces to the Gauss-Seidel method.

Another method is known as the Symmetric Succesive Over-Relaxation method - SSOR. It was proposed by Sheldon [YG] to overcome certain difficulties in SOR. Each iteration consists of two half-steps: the first is a normal SOR-step, the second is a SOR-step with the order of equations reversed. The method has advantages, but is usually considered to be more laborious as SOR. This is not correct; as a matter of fact, it requires exactly the same number of operations as SOR, as will be discussed later when "vertical programming" is introduced on ASP.

The methods of Jacobi and Seidel (and by a simple extension, SSOR and SOR) are members of a subfamily of linear iterations derived by splitting the matrix $\underline{A}$. Expressing $\underline{A}$ as a difference of two matrices

$$\underline{A} = \underline{B} - \underline{C} \qquad (18)$$

where $\underline{B}$ is nonsingular, one defines an iterative method for the solution of (1) by the recursion:

$$\underline{B} * \underline{x}^{(i+1)} = \underline{C} * \underline{x}^{(i)} + \underline{b} \qquad (19)$$

where the iteration index provides the clue to the reason for splitting $\underline{A}$.

In the same way as in (5), we can write for the S,SOR and SSOR methods the general formula of "linear iterations" namely:

$$\underline{x}^{(i+1)} = \underline{I} * \underline{x}^{(i)} + \underline{k} \qquad (20)$$

The previously mentioned algorithms can be derived from this formula as follows.

Let $\underline{L}$, $\underline{R}$ and $\underline{D}$ denote the strictly lower-triangular "left", upper-triangular "right" and diagonal submatrices of $\underline{A}$. We may then write for the method of Jacobi that $\underline{A}$ was split according to

$$\underline{B} = \underline{D} \ ; \quad \underline{C} = -(\underline{L} + \underline{R}) \qquad (21)$$

(19) is then: $\underline{D}\,\underline{x}^{(i+1)} = -(\underline{L} + \underline{R})\underline{x}^{(i)} + \underline{b}$ (22)

The diagonal matrix $\underline{D}$ is certainly nonsingular and we may write

$$\underline{x}^{(i+1)} = -\underline{D}^{-1}(\underline{L} + \underline{R})\underline{x}^{(i)} + \underline{D}^{-1}\underline{b} \qquad (23)$$

Thus: $\underline{I} = -\underline{D}^{-1}(\underline{L} + \underline{R})$; $\underline{k} = \underline{D}^{-1}\underline{b}$ (24)

The S-method results from splitting $\underline{A}$ according to

$$\underline{B} = \underline{D} + \underline{L} \ ; \quad \underline{C} = -\underline{R} \qquad (25)$$

so that (19) is: $(\underline{D} + \underline{L})\underline{x}^{(i+1)} = -\,\underline{R}\,\underline{x}^{(i)} + \underline{b}$ (26)

$$\underline{I} = -(\underline{D} + \underline{L})^{-1}\underline{R} \ ; \quad \underline{k} = (\underline{D} + \underline{L})^{-1}\underline{b} \qquad (27)$$

From (26) we have:

$$\underline{x}^{(i+1)} = -(\underline{D} + \underline{L})^{-1}\,(\underline{R}\,\underline{x}^{(i)} - \underline{b}) \qquad (28)$$

which can also be written as:

$$\underline{x}^{(i+1)} = \underline{D}^{-1}(\underline{b} - \underline{L}\,\underline{x}^{(i+1)} - \underline{R}\,\underline{x}^{(i)}) \qquad (29)$$

The methods of Jacobi and Gauss-Seidel are seen to be derived from explicit splittings. Eq. (19) may be regarded as a system of linear equations in n unknowns (the vector $\underline{x}^{(i+1)}$). It may be asked, why expand effort on the solution of this system rather than solve (1) directly as originally written. Indeed, if $\underline{C}$ is the zero matrix, then (19) reduces to (1). The answer though is that the splitting (18) is usually chosen so as to make the solution of (19) easy. One way is to impose the condition that $\underline{B}$ be lower (or upper) triangular, thereby reducing the solution of (19) to simple back-substitution. It is readily seen, that the two methods (Jacobi and Gauss-Seidel) conform to this requirement and are therefore known as explicit methods.

Suppose we subtract $\underline{D}\,\underline{x}^{(i)}$ from both sides of (22). This yields

$$\underline{D}(\underline{x}^{(i+1)} - \underline{x}^{(i)}) = \underline{b} - (\underline{L} + \underline{R} + \underline{D})\underline{x}^{(i)} = \underline{b} - \underline{A}\,\underline{x}^{(i)} \qquad (30)$$

which may be interpreted as follows: The change in $\underline{x}$ is proportional to the residual vector

$$\underline{r} = \underline{b} - \underline{A}\, \underline{x}^{(i)} \tag{31}$$

with $\underline{D}^{-1}$ being the factor of proportionality. We might therefore "overrelax" (or overshoot), and multiply $\underline{r}$ by the overrelaxation factor w:

$$\underline{x}^{(i+1)} = \underline{x}^{(i)} + \underline{D}^{-1}\, w\, \underline{U}\, (\underline{b} - \underline{A}\, \underline{x}^{(i)}) \tag{32}$$

$$\underline{x}^{(i+1)} = (\underline{U} - w\, \underline{D}^{-1}\, \underline{A})\underline{x}^{(i)} + w\, \underline{D}^{-1}\, \underline{b} \tag{33}$$

Comparing this with (20) yields:

$$\underline{I} = \underline{U} - w\, \underline{D}^{-1}\, \underline{A}; \quad \underline{k} = w\, \underline{D}^{-1}\, \underline{b} \tag{34}$$

This method might be called Jacobi-overrelaxation or JOR. It is seldom used, but shows, that in order to change (29) we write

$$\underline{D}(\underline{x}^{(i+1)} - \underline{x}^{(i)}) = \underline{b} - \underline{L}\, \underline{x}^{(i+1)} - \underline{R}\, \underline{x}^{(i)} - \underline{D}\, \underline{x}^{(i)}$$

$$= \underline{b} - \underline{A}\, \underline{x}^{(i)} - \underline{L}(\underline{x}^{(i+1)} - \underline{x}^{(i)}) \tag{35}$$

Applying $w^{-1}\, \underline{U}$ to both sides yields:

$$(w^{-1}\, \underline{D} + \underline{L})\underline{x}^{(i+1)} = \underline{b} - \underline{R}\, \underline{x}^{(i)} - (1 - w^{-1})\underline{D}\, \underline{x}^{(i)} \tag{36}$$

Comparing with the general iteration formula (20) yields:

$$\underline{I} = -(w^{-1}\, \underline{D} + \underline{L})^{-1} * ((1 - w^{-1})\underline{D} + \underline{R}); \; k = (w^{-1}\, \underline{D} + \underline{L})^{-1}\underline{b} \tag{37}$$

or still better if we take w instead of w^{-1}:

$$\underline{I} = (\underline{D} + w\, \underline{L})^{-1}\, ((1 - w)\underline{D} + w\, \underline{R}); \; \underline{k} = w(\underline{D} + w\, \underline{L})^{-1}\, \underline{b} \tag{38}$$

Before we handle SSOR, let us deal with the case w = 1 i.e., the symmetric S-method for a symmetric matrix i.e. for

$$\underline{R} = \underline{L}^T \tag{39}$$

Eq. (26) yields for the two "half"-sweeps respectively:

$$(\underline{D} + \underline{L})\underline{x}^{(i+\frac{1}{2})} = \underline{b} - \underline{L}^T\, \underline{x}^{(i)} \tag{40}$$

$$(\underline{D} + \underline{L}^T)\underline{x}^{(i+1)} = \underline{b} - \underline{L}\, \underline{x}^{(i+\frac{1}{2})} \tag{41}$$

Inserting $\underline{x}^{(i+\frac{1}{2})}$ from (40) into (41) and comparing with (20) shows that

$$\underline{I} = (\underline{D} + \underline{L}^T)^{-1}\, \underline{L}\, (\underline{D} + \underline{L})^{-1}\underline{L}^T = (\underline{D} + \underline{L}^T)^{-1}\, \underline{L}\, \underline{D}^{-1}(\underline{U} + \underline{L}\, \underline{D}^{-1})^{-1}\, \underline{L}^T \tag{42}$$

The equations of this method are normally written as follows:

$$\underline{x}^{(i+\frac{1}{2})} = \underline{x}^{(i)} + w\cdot(\underline{b} - \underline{x}^{(i)} - \underline{L}{*}\underline{x}^{(i+\frac{1}{2})} - \underline{R}\, \underline{x}^{(i)}) \tag{43}$$

$$\underline{x}^{(i+1)} = \underline{x}^{(i+\frac{1}{2})} + w\cdot(\underline{b} - \underline{x}^{(i+\frac{1}{2})} - \underline{L}{*}\underline{x}^{(i+\frac{1}{2})} - \underline{R}{*}\underline{x}^{(i+1)}) \tag{44}$$

where the superscript $i+\frac{1}{2}$ denotes a half-step. The "forward" and backward steps (43) (44) are derived in an obvious way from the way $\underline{A}$ was split.

For the SSOR method

$$\underline{I} = (\underline{D} + w\, \underline{L})^{-1} \cdot ((1 - w) \cdot \underline{D} - w\cdot\underline{R}); \quad k = w\cdot(\underline{D} + w\cdot\underline{L})^{-1} \cdot \underline{b} \tag{45}$$

and $\underline{x}^{(i+1)}=(1-w)\cdot\underline{x}^{(i)}+w\cdot\tilde{\underline{x}}^{(i+1)}=\underline{x}^{(i)}+w\cdot\underline{D}^{-1}\cdot(\underline{b}-\underline{D}\cdot\underline{x}^{(i)}-\underline{L}\underline{x}^{(i+1)}-\underline{R}\underline{x}^{(i)})$ (46)

There is a large body of knowledge concerning the convergence, speed, stability etc. of iterative methods. Summaries of them may be looked up in [SB] or [YG] and for the special case of $\underline{A}$ being a tridiagonal matrix, in [Yo 70]. In this section we add a few pages on less well-known methods.

7.1.2 Aitken's Acceleration Method

When $\underline{A}$ is real and symmetric with positive diagonal elements, its iteration matrix $\underline{I}$ has real and positive eigenvalues and the convergence may be accelerated using Aitken's method. The resultant convergence will then be better than that of SOR even with the best w. For a positive definite $\underline{A}$, a unique optimum w exists so that using it together with Aitken's scheme will yield a method with convergence higher than that of SOR by an order of magnitude. Since we prove below that the method can be applied to a vector componentwise, it can be obviously of use in an ASP system, with every slave processing independently its slice.

Given a sequence of numbers $x_n \to s$, the so-called Δ^2-acceleration proposed by Aitken, forms the following transformed sequence x'_n:

$$x'_n = x_n - (x_{n+1} - x_n)^2/(x_{n+2} - 2x_{n+1} + x_n); \; n = 0,1,\ldots \tag{47}$$

It may be shown [He64] that under certain conditions the transformed sequence converges faster to s than the original. Precisely speaking, define

$$d_n = x_n - s; \quad d'_n = x'_n - s; \quad n = 0,1,\ldots \tag{48}$$

and assume that the sequence $\{d_n\}$ is "asymptotically geometrical" i.e. as n tends to infinity the quotient of consecutive d's approaches a limit of

$$d_{n+1}/d_n = a + e_n \; ; \quad n = 0,1,\ldots \tag{49}$$

where $|a| < 1$ is a constant and e_n tends to 0 as n tends to infinity.

Under these conditions, the following identity holds [He64, p. 73]:

$$d'_n/d_n = (a + e_n)\,(e_{n+1} - e_n)/((a - 1)^2 + e'_n) \tag{50}$$

where $e'_n = a(e_n + e_{n+1}) - 2e_n + e_n e_{n+1}$ (51)

As n approaches infinity, d'_n/d_n tends to zero, which shows that for large n, x'_n is a better approximation to s than x_n.

How much better is this approximation? The answer depends on e_n. We shall examine the behaviour of d'_{n+1}/d'_n. By (50)

$$d'_{n+1}/d'_n = (\, a + e_{n+1})\,(e_{n+2} - e_{n+1})/((a - 1)^2 + e'_{n+1}) \tag{52}$$

Dividing by (50) and using (49) we find that

$$d'_{n+1}/d'_n=((a+e_{n+1})((a-1)^2+e'_n)/((a-1)^2+e'_{n+1}))*(e_{n+2}-e_{n+1})/(e_{n+1}-e_n)$$
$$=((a + e_{n+1})((a-1)^2+e'_n)(e_{n+2}/e_n-e_{n+1}/e_n))/(((a-1)^2+e'_{n+1})(e_{n+1}/e_n-1)) \tag{53}$$

Assume that the sequence $\{e_n\}$ is asymptotically geometrical i.e.

$$\lim(e_{n+1}/e_n) = b, \quad |b| < 1 \qquad \text{for } n\to\infty \tag{54}$$

Hence $\lim(e_{n+2}/e_n) = b^2$ for $n\to\infty$ (55)

Passing to the limit in (53) and using (54) (55) we obtain

$$\lim(d'_{n+1}/d'_n) = a * (b^2 - b)/(b - 1) = a\cdot b; \text{ for } n\to\infty \tag{56}$$

From it we see that the sequence $\{d'_n\}$ is asymptotically geometrical, with quotient $a\cdot b$. Since $|b| < 1$, this sequence converges faster than $\{d_n\}$, the increase in speed depending on $|b|$. In any case, the convergence of x'_n is linear. Since the sequence $\{d'_n\}$ is asymptotically geometrical, the Aitken transform may be applied again to the sequence x'_n resulting in an even faster converging sequence x''_n. It may be shown to be asymptotically geometrical with quotient $a\cdot b^2$, but this asymptotical behavior may be delayed and obscured by round-off error.

It is remarkable that Aitken's acceleration method may be adapted so as to yield quadratic convergence. This is known as the diagonal Aitken procedure [He64] or Steffenson's method. It may be arrived at heuristically as follows.

Let $x_n \to s$, and let the sequence $d_n = x_n - s$ be asymptotically geometrical; therefore Aitken's method is applicable. Assume further that the sequence x_n is generated by a recursion formula $x_{n+1} = f(x_n)$. Given an initial value x_0, we calculate $x_1 = f(x_o)$, $x_2 = f(x_1)$, $x_3 = f(x_2)$ and then perform an Aitken acceleration step (47) which yields x_3'. Since x_3' is a better approximation to the limit than x_3, it makes sense to continue the recursion starting with x_3' rather than x_3. So we compute $x_4 = f(x_3')$, $x_5 = f(x_4)$, $x_6 = f(x_5)$, followed by computation of x_6' with (47). Again, x_6' is incorporated into the main sequence.

The series of iterates resulting from Aitken accelerations converges quadratically to s [He64]. It is also possible to attain quadratic convergence even if the Aitken step is incorporated less often (say after every L "normal iterations" where L > 3), which requires less arithmetics and is particularly important when accelerating SSOR. (See numerical example below).

Aitken's process is suitable for speeding up the convergence of certain linear iterations. Let

$$\underline{x}^{(n+1)} = \underline{I} * \underline{x}^{(n)} + \underline{k} \tag{57}$$

define a linear iteration sequence, $\underline{x}^{(n)} \to \underline{s}$. Passing to the limit in (57) yields

$$\underline{s} = \underline{I} * \underline{s} + \underline{k} \tag{58}$$

and subtracting (58) from (57) yields

$$\underline{d}^{(n+1)} = \underline{I} * \underline{d}^{(n)} \text{ where } \underline{d}^{(n)} = \underline{x}^{(n)} - s \tag{59}$$

Suppose next that $\underline{I}$ is symmetrical and positive definite with eigenvalues $1>\lambda_1>\lambda_2\ldots>\lambda_k>0$ and the corresponding vectors $\underline{v}_1,\ldots\underline{v}_k$ form an orthonormal set. Expanding $\underline{d}^{(0)}$ in terms of the eigenvectors results in

$$\underline{d}^{(0)} = \Sigma\ \underline{u}_i * \underline{v}_i;\ i\Sigma=1,\ldots,k \tag{60}$$

Therefore

$$\underline{d}^{(n+1)} = \underline{I}^n * \underline{d}^{(o)} = \Sigma\ u_i * \underline{I}^n * v_1 = \Sigma\ u_i{*}\lambda_1^n * v_i;\ i\Sigma=1,\ldots,k \tag{61}$$

Let w_i denote the first component of the eigenvector $\underline{v}_1$, i =1,..,k and let $d^{(n)}$ denote the first component of $\underline{d}^{(n)}$. From (61)

$$d^{(n+1)} = \Sigma\ u_i * \lambda_i^n * w_i;\ i\Sigma=1,\ldots,k \tag{62}$$

Assuming that $w_1 u_1 \neq 0$, we have

$$\frac{d^{(n+1)}}{d^{(n)}} = \frac{u_1 w_1 \lambda_1^{n+1} + u_2 w_2 \lambda_2^{n+1} + \ldots + u_k w_k \lambda_k^{n+1}}{u_1 w_1 \lambda_1^{n+2} + u_2 w_2 \lambda_2^{n+2} + \ldots + u_k w_k \lambda_k^{n+2}} \tag{63}$$

$$d^{(n+1)}/d^{(n)} = [\lambda_1 + \sum_{i=2}^{k} \frac{\lambda_i w_i u_i}{w_1 u_1} (\frac{\lambda_i}{\lambda_1})^n]/[1 + \sum_{i=2}^{k} \frac{w_i u_i}{w_1 u_1} (\frac{\lambda_i}{\lambda_2})^n] \tag{64}$$

Since $\lambda_i < \lambda_1$ for i=2,...,k we have that (λ_i/λ_1) tends to 0 which results in $(d^{(n+1)}/d^{(n)})$ tending to λ_i. Hence $\{d^{n+1}\}$ is asymptotically geometrical and Aitken's acceleration process may be used. It is interesting to calculate the actual acceleration to be thus obtained. Using (64) we have

$$d^{(n+1)}/d^{(n)} = \lambda_1 + [\sum_{i=2}^{k} [(\frac{\lambda_i w_i u_i}{w_1 u_1})(\frac{\lambda_i}{\lambda_1})^n - (\frac{\lambda_i w_i u_i}{v_1 u_1})(\frac{\lambda_i}{\lambda_1})^n]/[1 + \sum_{i=2}^{k} (\frac{w_i u_i}{w_1 u_1})(\frac{\lambda_i}{\lambda_1})^n] \quad (65)$$

$$d^{(n+1)}d^{(n)} = \lambda_1 + [\sum_{i=2}^{k} f_i (\frac{\lambda_i}{\lambda_1})^n]/[1+\sum_{i=2}^{k} h_i (\frac{\lambda_i}{\lambda_i})^n] \equiv \lambda_1 + g_n; g_n \to 0 \quad (66)$$

It may be seen (the cumbersome algebra is omitted) that g_n is also asymptotically geometrical with quotient λ_2/λ_1. Hence the accelerated sequence d'_n has by (56) the quotient $a*b=\lambda_2$, and the smaller λ_2 in comparison with λ_1, the better will be this acceleration method.

It is seen that the argument $u_i w_i \neq 0$ is not crucial to the result. Assuming $u_1 w_1 = u_2 w_2 = \ldots = u_r w_r = 0$, $u_{r+1} w_{r+1} \neq 0$ and reasoning similarly reveals that $\{d'_n\}$ has quotient λ_r etc.

The same reasoning can of course be applied to any component of the vectors in question. Hence the acceleration can be applied componentwise to the entire vector.

If we assume that in the original system of equations $\underline{A}*\underline{x} = \underline{b}$, matrix $\underline{A}$ is symmetric with positive diagonal elements, then by [Yo 70] the eigenvalues of the iteration matrix $\underline{I}$ of the SSOR process are real and non-negative. (Nothing can be asserted as to their being distinct). If the overrelaxation factor is between 0 and 2 and $\underline{A}$ is positive definite, the process converges.

Many important practical computations have a symmetrical and positive definite (hence having positive diagonal elements) matrix $\underline{A}$. This occurs for instance in the solution of the least squares approximations as used in the state estimation and measurement evaluation problems. These problems lead to the solution of a linear system of the type $\underline{J}^T * \underline{J} * \underline{x} = \underline{b}$ (67)

where $\underline{J}$ is an m x n matrix. $\underline{J}^T\underline{J}$ is obviously symmetrical and non-negative, definite; mostly it is also positive definite. For this class of problems, SSOR accelerated by Aitken's method appears to be very effective. As mentioned, it is also applicable to certain SSOR sequences.

A numerical example.

Let $\underline{A}\ \underline{x} = \underline{b}$ be a system of linear equations. $\underline{A}$ is an n x n matrix, whose elements are given by $a_{ij}=2$ for i=j; $a_{ij}=-1$ for $|i-j|=1$ and $a_{ij}=1$ otherwise (68)

This matrix, recommended as a test case in [We 68] has a number of interesting properties:

(a) It is the admittance matrix of the "ring" network of Fig. 1, where R=1 and bus 0 is taken as reference. (b) The eigenvalues of $\underline{A}$ are known [OR 70] to be:

$\lambda_k(\underline{A}) = 4\sin^2(k\pi/(2(n+1))$ (69)

The Jacobi iteration matrix equals

$\underline{I}_j = -\underline{D}^{-1}*(\underline{L}+\underline{R}) = \underline{C}-\underline{U}$ (70)

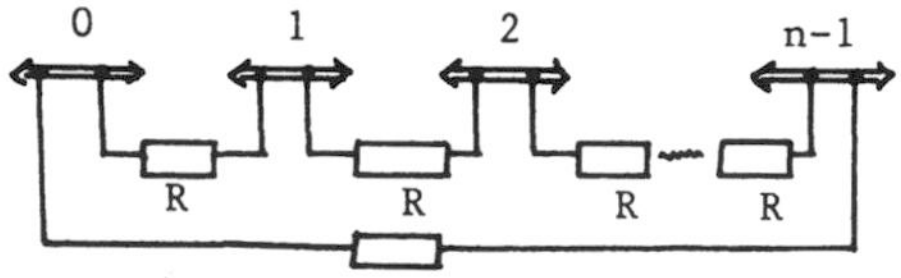

Fig. 1: A ring network.

where $c_{ij}=1$ for $i=j$; $c_{ij}=-0.5$ for $|i-j|=1$ and 0 otherwise (71)

It is seen that $\underline{C}=0.5*\underline{A}$; hence $\lambda_k(\underline{C})=0.5*\lambda_k(\underline{A})$ and

$$\lambda_k*(\underline{C}-\underline{U})=\lambda_k(\underline{C})-1=0.5\lambda_k(\underline{A})-1=2\sin^2(k\pi/(2(n+1))-1=-\cos(k\pi/(n+1)) \quad (72)$$

Therefore the spectral radius $r(\underline{C})=\cos(\pi/(n+1))$. Moreover, the matrix $\underline{A}$ is "2-cyclic" [Va 62] and thus the optimal relaxation factor w_L for SSOR is

$$w_L = \frac{2}{1+(1-r(\underline{C})^2)^{1/2}} = \frac{2}{1+\sin(\pi/(n+1))} \quad (73)$$

and the radius of convergence of the SOR-method is

$$r_L = w_L-1 = (1-\sin(\pi/(n+1)))\ /\ (1+\sin(\pi/(n+1))) \quad (74)$$

In the following example n=40, hence

$$w_L=1.85778;\ r_L=0.857787 \quad (75)$$

Therefore we are able to compare the convergence of the method of Aitken with optimal successive over-relaxation. The table below lists the results of the comparison. The leftmost column indicates iteration count and the other two show a measure of convergence

$$||\underline{x}^{(k+1)}-\underline{x}^{(k)}|| = \max |x^{(n+1)}-x^{(n)}| \ , \text{ for } 1\leq k\leq 40 \quad (76)$$

The second column lists these values for optimal SOR and the third column for Aitken's accelerated SSOR. No attempt was made to find the optimal over-relaxation factor for SSOR (the value w_L was used) so it is likely that the optimal SSOR with Aitken's acceleration is even better than the results indicate. It is evident from the comparison that the accelerated SSOR is superior to optimal SOR, although its superiority is revealed when the iterates are relatively close to the limit.

The most interesting results are shown in the last column. Here the results of Aitken's acceleration were used every 6'th main iteration. Since convergence may be expected only when $\underline{x}^{(k)}$ is close to the limit, this process was started after 40 iterations. The resulting numbers indicate clearly that this is a further improvement over the usual Aitken acceleration process during advanced stages of the calculation.

Method: Iteration Count	SOR $w_L=1.85778$	Accelerated SSOR $w_L=1.85778$	Steffensen L=6
10	$4.917\ 10^{-1}$	$2.772\ 10^{-1}$	
20	$3.331\ 10^{-1}$	$5.035\ 10^{-2}$	
30	$1.630\ 10^{-1}$	$4.770\ 10^{-3}$	
40	$3.680\ 10^{-2}$	$5.358\ 10^{-4}$	
50	$9.080\ 10^{-3}$	$9.385\ 10^{-5}$	$4.171\ 10^{-5}$
60	$2.190\ 10^{-3}$	$1.890\ 10^{-5}$	$1.452\ 10^{-6}$
70	$6.995\ 10^{-4}$	$4.642\ 10^{-6}$	$4.872\ 10^{-9}$
80	$1.364\ 10^{-4}$	$1.106\ 10^{-6}$	$9.690\ 10^{-11}$

Table 1: Comparison of three iterative methods.

7.1.3 Iterative Improvement Techniques

Assume that $\underline{A}\ \underline{x} = \underline{b}$ has been solved by a direct method. The solution $\underline{x}^{(1)}$ will be inaccurate due to the inevitable roundoff error. The residual:

$$\underline{r}^{(1)} = \underline{b} - \underline{A}\ \underline{x}^{(1)} \tag{77}$$

will not be a zero vector. Suppose we also define the "error" vector

$$\underline{e}^{(1)} = \underline{x} - \underline{x}^{(1)} \tag{78}$$

where $\underline{x}$ is the correct solution. Insertion of (78) into $\underline{A}\ \underline{e}^{(1)}$ yields:

$$\underline{A}\ \underline{e}^{(1)} = \underline{A}\ \underline{x} - \underline{A}\ \underline{x}^{(1)} = \underline{b} - \underline{A}\ \underline{x}^{(1)} = \underline{r}^{(1)} \tag{79}$$

It is tempting to say that all that is required is to solve

$$\underline{A}\ \underline{e}^{(1)} = \underline{r}^{(1)} \tag{80}$$

and then insert $\underline{e}^{(1)}$ into

$$\underline{x} = \underline{e}^{(1)} + \underline{x}^{(1)} \tag{81}$$

to get the absolutely correct result. Unfortunately, it is precisely (80) that we cannot solve - otherwise we could have solved $\underline{A}\ \underline{x} = \underline{b}$ in the first place more accurately. What we may assume, is that $\underline{x}$ (let's call it now $\underline{x}^{(2)}$) of (81) is a better approximation to $\underline{x}$ than $\underline{x}^{(1)}$ was. We may thus proceed iteratively improving $\underline{x}^{(i)}$ by this process, but note the following:

(a) The original system $\underline{A}\ \underline{x} = \underline{b}$ was probably solved using $\underline{L}\cdot\underline{R}$ decomposition. (80) may thus be written as

$$\underline{L}\cdot\underline{R}\ \underline{e}^{(i)} = \underline{r}^{(i)} \tag{81}$$

and solved, as usually in two steps

$$\underline{L}\ \underline{z} = \underline{r}^{(i)}\ ;\ \underline{R}\ \underline{e}^{(i)} = \underline{z} \tag{82}$$

The computation of $\underline{r}$ requires $n^2\omega + n\alpha$, that of $\underline{e}$ only $n\alpha$ and the solution of (82) only $2n^2(\omega)/2$. Altogether

$$\Omega \cong 2n^2\omega \tag{83}$$

instead of the $\omega n^3/3$ are required - an order of magnitude reduction.

(b) The computation of $\underline{r}^{(i)} = \underline{b} - \underline{A}\ \underline{x}^{(i)}$ involves subtraction of nearly equal quantities and so cancellation may take place. It is therefore advisable to compute $\underline{r}^{(i)}$ using double-precision and round-off results only when finished. There is no reason for higher precision work while correcting $\underline{x}^{(i)}$.

(c) The convergence of the process can be proved as follows. For $\underline{E}$ being an error matrix

$$(\underline{A} + \underline{E})\ \underline{e}^{(i)} = \underline{r}^{(i)} \tag{84}$$

can be viewed as the source of the error and we might use a perturbation on $\underline{e}^{(i)}$ to find out its influence i.e. assume that $\underline{e}^{(i)}$ is its exact solution. Then

$$\underline{r}^{(i)} = \underline{A}(\underline{U} + \underline{A}^{-1}\ \underline{E})\ \underline{e}^{(i)} = \underline{A}(\underline{U} + \underline{F})\ \underline{e}^{(i)} \tag{85}$$

There is a theorem [YG] which shows that if for some matrix norm:

$$||\underline{F}^{(i)}|| \leqq \delta < 1/2 \tag{86}$$

for all i, then for any vector norm we can write

$$||\underline{x}^{(i)} - \underline{x}|| \leqq (\delta/(1-\delta))^i\ ||\underline{x}|| \tag{87}$$

and since $\delta < 0.5$ we have $\Delta = \delta/(1-\delta) < 1$ so that Δ^i is an ever decreasing quantity.

We might prove convergence also by using $\underline{\tilde{A}}^{-1}$ as an approximation to $\underline{A}^{-1}$. Then:

$\underline{r}^{(1)} = \underline{b} - \underline{A}(\tilde{\underline{A}}^{-1}\,\underline{b}) = (\underline{U} - \underline{A}\,\tilde{\underline{A}}^{-1})\,\underline{b}$ (88)

$\underline{r}^{(2)}=\underline{b}-\underline{A}(\underline{x}^{(1)}+\underline{e}^{(1)})=(\underline{U}-\underline{A}\,\tilde{\underline{A}}^{-1})\underline{b}-\underline{A}\,\underline{e}^{(1)}=(\underline{U}-\underline{A}\,\tilde{\underline{A}}^{-1})\underline{b}-\underline{A}\,\tilde{\underline{A}}^{-1}\underline{r}^{(1)}$ (89)

$\underline{r}^{(2)} = (\underline{U} - \underline{A}\,\tilde{\underline{A}}^{-1})\,\underline{b} - \underline{A}\,\tilde{\underline{A}}^{-1}(\underline{U} - \underline{A}\,\tilde{\underline{A}}^{-1})\,\underline{b} = (\underline{U} - \underline{A}\,\tilde{\underline{A}}^{-1})^2\underline{b}$ (90)

or in general $\underline{r}^{(i)} = (\underline{U} - \underline{A}\,\tilde{\underline{A}}^{-1})^i \cdot \underline{b}$ (91)

The process will converge if all eigenvalues of $\underline{U} - \underline{A}\,\tilde{\underline{A}}^{-1}$ are $|\lambda|<1$. The convergence of the process is linear and

$\underline{x}^{(i)} = \underline{x}^{(1)} + \underline{e}^{(1)} + \underline{e}^{(2)} +\ldots+ \underline{e}^{(i)} \cong \underline{x}$ for $i \to \infty$ (92)

7.1.4 Gradient Methods

The solution of $\underline{A}\,\underline{x} = \underline{b}$ minimizes $\underline{r}^T\underline{r}$ where the residual $\underline{r}$ is

$\underline{r} = \underline{A}\,\underline{x} - \underline{b}$ (93)

We can therefore start with some vector $\underline{x}^{(o)}$ and iteratively "improve" it until $\underline{r}^T\underline{r}$ is a minimum. Thus we have the iterative scheme:

$\underline{x}^{(i+1)} = \underline{x}^{(i)} + C_i\,\underline{w}^{(i)}$ (94)

where C_i and $\underline{w}^{(i)}$ have yet to be determined. If $(\underline{r}^T\,\underline{r})^{(i)} = s^{(i)}$ then

$s^{(i+1)} - s^{(i)} = C_i^{\,2}(\underline{u}^{(i)})^T\,\underline{u}^{(i)} - 2C_i(\underline{u}^{(i)})^T\,\underline{r}^{(i)};\ \underline{u}^{(i)} = \underline{A}\,\underline{w}^{(i)}$ (95)

and $s^{(i+1)} < s^{(i)}$ only if

$C_i < s(\underline{u}^{(i)})^T\,\underline{r}^{(i)}/[(\underline{u}^{(i)})^T\,\underline{u}^{(i)}]$ (96)

This may supply a value of C_i which corresponds to a minimum of s. If $\underline{w}$ is chosen along the line of "steepest descent", its components will be the derivatives of $s^{(i)}$ with respect to $\underline{x}^{(i)}$ so that $s^{(i)}$ will change rapidly. This gives $\underline{w}^{(i)} = \underline{A}^T\,\underline{r}^{(i)}$ so that the algorithm is

$\underline{r}^{(i)} = \underline{b} - \underline{A}\,\underline{x}^{(i)};\ \underline{w}^{(i)} = \underline{A}^T\,\underline{r}^{(i)};\ \underline{u}^{(i)} = \underline{A}\,\underline{w}^{(i)}$ (97)

$C_i = [(\underline{u}^{(i)})^T\,\underline{r}^{(i)}]/[\underline{u}^{(i)})^T\,\underline{u}^{(i)}];\ \underline{x}^{(i+1)} = \underline{x}^{(i)} + C_i\,\underline{w}^{(i)}$ (98)

There are three matrix-times-vector multiplications here, but only two are needed since $\underline{r}^{(i+1)} = \underline{b} - \underline{A}\,\underline{x}^{(i+1)} = \underline{r}^{(i)} - \underline{A}[\underline{x}^{(i+1)} - \underline{x}^{(i)}]$

$\underline{r}^{(i+1)} = \underline{r}^{(i)} - C_i\underline{A}\,\underline{w}^{(i)} = \underline{r}^{(i)} - C_i\underline{u}^{(i)}$ (99)

The computation is still rather lengthy, but according to the results of Section 6.1 can be easily and efficiently parallelized.

For symmetric matrices, $\underline{A} = \underline{A}^T$ and (98) yields

$C_i = (\underline{w}^T\,\underline{r})/(\underline{w}^T\,\underline{A}\,\underline{w})$ (100)

where the iteration superindex (i) was dropped. We can then use the "conjugate gradients" method as follows. For $\underline{w}^{(i)}$ take

$\underline{w}^{(i)} = \underline{r}^{(i)} + k_{i-1}\,\underline{w}^{(i-1)}$ (101)

so that the process will terminate exactly after n steps. This can be achieved if $\underline{w}^{(i)}$ is made orthogonal to $\underline{A}\,\underline{w}^{(i-1)}$. Thus

$[\underline{w}^{(i)}]^T[\underline{A}\,\underline{w}^{(i-1)}]=0$ and $k_{i-1}=-[(\underline{r}^{(i)})^T(\underline{A}\,\underline{w}^{(i-1)})]/[(\underline{w}^{(i-1)})^T(\underline{A}\,\underline{w}^{(i-1)})]$ (102)

The algorithmic steps start with k_{i-1} and $\underline{w}^{(i)}$ of (102) (101) and proceed with

$C_i = [(\underline{r}^{(i)})^T\,\underline{w}^{(i)}]/[(\underline{w}^{(i)})^T(\underline{A}\underline{w}^{(i)})];\ \underline{x}^{(i+1)} = \underline{x}^{(i)} + C_i\underline{w}^{(i)}$ (103)

$\underline{r}^{(i+1)} = \underline{b} - \underline{A}\,\underline{x}^{(i+1)} = \underline{r}^{(i)} - C_i(\underline{A}\,\underline{w}^{(i)})$ (104)

The n vectors $\underline{w}^{(0)}, \underline{w}^{(1)}, \ldots, \underline{w}^{(n-1)}$ are independent i.e. no relation

$m_0\underline{w}^{(0)} + m_1\underline{w}^{(1)} +\ldots+ m_{n-1}\underline{w}^{(n-1)} = 0$ (105)

exists, except if every m_i or some $\underline{w}^{(i)}$ is null. In fact because of conjugacy, premultiplying (105) by $(w^{(i)})^T \underline{A}$ would yield $m_i = 0$ directly. Since all $\underline{w}$'s are independent and $\underline{r}^{(n)}$ is orthogonal to all of them, it follows that $\underline{r}^{(n)} = \underline{0}$ and the process should terminate exactly after n steps.

This is precisely what prevented wide acceptance of this method initially [HS52]. Because of round-off error, the process did not terminate after n iterations and could thus not compete with elimination. It was made again popular by Reid [Re71] who regarded it "not as a direct method for the solution of full systems of equations, but as an iterative method for the solution of large and sparse sets". For tridiagonal or block-tridiagonal sets there are other methods, but for very sparse, large but irregular sets, the method is one of the best. Since power system matrices are of this type, since it is also efficient for state estimation and is easily programmed for ASP, it has its place in our scheme of things.

Actually, a number of variants of the original method were developed, eight of them being mentioned in [Re71]. The one usually preferred requires proofs that

$$\underline{r}_i^T \underline{r}_i = \underline{r}_i^T \underline{w}_i \text{ and } k_i = (\underline{r}_{i+1}^T \underline{r}_{i+1})/(\underline{r}_i^T \underline{r}_i) \qquad (106)$$

(with iteration index as subscript). The first is obviously correct for i = 0 since then $k_i = 0$ and $\underline{w}_i = \underline{r}_i$ in (101). For $i > 0$, we may use (101) as in:

$$\underline{r}_{i+1}^T \underline{r}_{i+1} = (\underline{w}_{i+1} - k_i \underline{w}_i)^T \underline{r}_{i+1} = \underline{w}_{i+1}^T \underline{r}_{i+1} - k_i \underline{w}_i^T \underline{r}_{i+1} \qquad (107)$$

If C_i of (103) is used, then obviously $\underline{w}_i^T r_{i+1} = 0$ so that $r_{i+1}^T \underline{r}_{i+1} = \underline{w}_{i+1}^T \underline{r}_{i+1}$ Inductively, if for any i, $\underline{r}_i^T \underline{r}_i = \underline{r}_i^T \underline{w}_{i+1}$ then $\underline{w}_i^T \underline{r}_{i+1} = 0$. Q.E.D.

Insert $\underline{A}\ \underline{w}$ into definition (102) of k_i, then exchange $\underline{w}_i$ in the denominator through (101) and use orthogonality relations:

$$\underline{r}^T \underline{w} = 0 \text{ for } i > j;\ \underline{w}^T (\underline{A}\ \underline{w}) = 0 \text{ for } i \neq j \text{ and } \underline{r}^T \underline{r} = 0 \text{ for } i \neq j \qquad (108)$$

As a result of all this, k_i will be as in (106) namely:

$$k_i = - \frac{\underline{r}_{i+1}(\underline{A}\ \underline{w}_i)}{\underline{w}_i^T (\underline{A}\ \underline{w}_i)} = - \frac{\underline{r}_{i+1}^T (\underline{r}_{i+1} - \underline{r}_i)}{\underline{w}_i^T (\underline{r}_{i+1} - \underline{r}_i)} = \frac{\underline{r}_{i+1}^T \underline{r}_{i+1}}{\underline{r}_i^T \underline{r}_i} \qquad (109)$$

The algorithm is thus the sequence:

$$C_i = (\underline{r}_i^T \underline{r}_i)/(\underline{w}_i^T (\underline{A}\ \underline{w}_i)) \qquad (110)$$

$\underline{x}_{i+1}$ from (94), $\underline{r}_{i+1}$ from (99), k_i from (109) and $\underline{w}_i$ from (101). We need for it the product $(\underline{A}\ \underline{w})$, two scalar products and three scalar-by-vector products.
In all these, the methods of chapter 6 may be used - especially those for sparse systems. Since the vectors can be overwrittern, storage can also be conserved. The same algorithm is advocated in [DB74] and [SB].

Order and signs are changed in [SRS73], but Rutishauser eliminates $\underline{w}_i$ as follows. If we multiply (101) by $\underline{A}$, replace i by i-1 and then use (104) twice,

$$(\underline{r}_i - \underline{r}_{i+1})/C_i = \underline{A}\ \underline{r}_i + (k_{i+1}/C_{i-1})\ (\underline{r}_{i-1} - \underline{r}_i) \qquad (111)$$

results. Still another version, particularly suited for sparse systems was also proposed. We may summarize all of them as follows:

$C_i = (\underline{r}_i^T \underline{r}_i)/([\underline{w}_i^T (\underline{A}\ \underline{w}_i)]$	$\underline{s} = \underline{A}\ \underline{w}_i;\ C_i = \underline{u}_i^T \underline{u}_i)/(\underline{s}_i^T \underline{s}_i)$
$\underline{x}_{i+1} = \underline{x}_i + C_i\ \underline{w}_i$	$\underline{x}_{i+1} = \underline{x}_i + C_i\ \underline{w}_i$
HS: $\underline{r}_{i+1} = \underline{r}_i - C_i\ (\underline{A}\ \underline{w}_i)$	$\underline{r}_{i+1} = \underline{r}_i - C_i \underline{s}_i;\ \underline{u}_{i+1} = \underline{A}^T \underline{r}_{i+1}$
$k_i = (\underline{r}_{i+1}^T\ \underline{r}_{i+1})/(\underline{r}_i^T\ \underline{r}_i)$	$k_i = (\underline{u}_{i+1}^T\ \underline{u}_{i+1})/(\underline{u}_i^T\ \underline{u}_i)$
$\underline{w}_{i+1} = \underline{r}_{i+1} + k_i\ \underline{w}_i$	$\underline{w}_{i+1} = \underline{u}_{i+1} + k_i\ \underline{w}_i$

$$\underline{s}_i = \underline{A}\ \underline{r}_i;\ C_i = (\underline{r}_i^T\ \underline{s}_i)/k_{i-1} - e_{i-1}$$
$$\underline{sr}_{i+1} = (e_{i-1}\ \underline{\Delta r}_i - \underline{s}_i)/C_i$$
$$\underline{r}_{i+1} = \underline{r}_i + \underline{sr}_{i+1};\ \underline{s}_{i+1} = \underline{A}\ \underline{r}_{i+1}$$
$$k_i = \underline{r}_{i+1}^T\ \underline{r}_{i+1};\ e_i = C_i(k_i/k_{i-1})$$
$$\underline{\Delta x}_{i+1} = (\underline{r}_i + e_{i-1}\ \underline{\Delta x}_i)/(C_i;\ \underline{x}_{i+1} = \underline{x}_i + \underline{\Delta x}_{i+1}$$

7.2 BASIC ASP-METHODS

Aims: To program the Jacobi method for ASP. To demonstrate that even the Gauss-Seidel algorithm normally considered to be strictly sequential can be programmed for ASP by "vertical" techniques. To start development of new methods which will be more efficient even on monocomputers than those known today .

7.2.1 The JA-Method

The data for most algorithms of this section is essentially the same, so we start with it.

Each slave memory holds a "slice" of matrix $\underline{A}$ and vector $\underline{b}$ as well as the "current" vector $\underline{x}^{(i)}$. For (2) and sweep 1, the storage in an ASP with p=2 slaves is shown in Figure 2.

The width of a slice h = n/p will again be assumed to be an integer.

↑	-20	1	1	6	2	1	-17	1 1 1 1 1 1	memory
h	1	- 20	2	1	4	3	-25		of slave
↓	1	2	- 20	2	1	2	-8		1
↑	6	1	2	- 20	3	1	-60	1 1 1 1 1 1	memory
h	2	4	1	3	- 20	5	-13		of slave
↓	1	3	2	1	5	- 20	-1		2

Figure 2: A Storage Scheme

Eq. (9) shows that each $x_k^{(i+1)}$ may be computed using values $x_k^{(i)}$ of the previous sweep. Hence, each slave may compute its slice of $\underline{x}^{(i+1)}$ independently of and concurrently with all other slaves. In the sequential step which then follows, every slave transfers its slice of $\underline{x}^{(i+1)}$ to the other slaves.

A PPL/1 program may thus be written directly:

```
JACOBI:  PROC OPTIONS(MAIN);
DCL (H,I,N,L(P),P,U(P)) FIXED, (A(N,N),B(N),X(N),D,EPS,R)FLOAT,
```

```
(#) (A(H,N),B(H),X(N),R,S)FLOAT, (#) (H,J,K,N)FIXED;
GET DATA (N,P); H=N/P;
CALL INIT; /*INITIALIZATION                                                 */
PUT BROADCAST (X(1:N)); /* BROADCAST INITIAL VALUES OF                      */
                        /* VECTOR X TO ALL P SLAVES.                        */
L: PARCALL PR;   /*  PR IS ACTIVATED IN ALL P SLAVES SIMULTANEOUSLY.        */
                 /* IT COMPUTES A SLICE OF X(J) AT FIRST AS S               */
                 /* AND ACCUMULATES R=SUM(S-X)^2 IN EACH SLAVE.             */
D = 0;           /* D WILL ACCUMULATE THE SUM OF ERRORS.                    */
DO I=1 TO P:     /* FOR EVERY SLAVE I                                       */
  R=(I)R;        /* TRANSFER ITS ERROR R TO THE COMMON MEMORY               */
  D=D+R:         /* AND ADD IT THERE TO D.                                  */
  X(L(I):U(I)) ≡ (I)X(1:H); /* THE SLICE OF X'S IS BLOCK                    */
                 /* TRANSFERRED FROM SLAVE I TO COMMON MEMORY               */
                 /* AND THEN REBROADCAST TO ALL SLAVES.                     */
  PUT BROADCAST(X(L(I):U(I));  END;
IF D>EPS THEN GO TO L;    /* DECISION AS TO WHETHER TO PROCEED              */
RETURN;                   /* OR TO RETURN THE RESULTING X.                  */
INIT: PROC;
DO I=1 TO P;              /* FOR EVERY SLAVE CALCULATE BOUNDS               */
  L(I)=(I-1)*H+1;U(I)=I*H           /* OF ITS SLICE.                        */
  (I)A(1:H,1:N)≡A(L(I):U(I),1:N);  /* BLOCK TRANSFER SLICES OF A            */
  (I)B(1:H)≡B(L(I):U(I));/*AND B FROM COMMON TO THE I'TH MEMORY             */
END;
PR:  PARPROC;
R=0;  /* R ACCUMULATES THE SUM OF SQUARES OF ERRORS OF EACH SLAVE           */
DO J=1 TO H;
  S=B(J);            /* S WILL BE THE NEW VALUE OF X(J)                     */
  DO K=1 TO N;
    IF K≠J THEN      /* WITH THE SUM OVER ALL K EXCEPT K=J                  */
    S=S-A(J,K)*X(K); END;
  S=S/A(J,J);        /* THIS IS NEEDED IF A(J,J) ≠ 1                        */
  R=R+(S-X(J))**2;   /* SUM OF SQUARES OF THE RESIDUALS                     */
  X(J)=S;            /* UPDATING THE X-VALUE                                */
PAREND; END          /* END OF PARALLEL PROCEDURE PR AND OF JACOBI          */
```

7.2.2 The S-Method; Vertical Programming

Programming the JA-method for ASP was trivial. As for the S-method, some doubts were expressed as to even the possiblity of parallelization. To show that it can in fact be parallelized, rewrite the general equation

$$\Sigma \ A_{jk}\, x_k = b_j;\ j = 1,2,\ldots,n;\ k\Sigma=1,\ldots,n \qquad (112)$$

not in the usual way: $A_{jj}\ x_j = b_j - \Sigma\ a_{jk}\ x_k;\ k\Sigma\neq j$ (113)

but as

$$a_{jj}{*}x_j^{(i+1)} = b_j - \sum_{k=1}^{j-1} a_{jk}{*}x_k^{(i+1)} - \sum_{k=j+1}^{n} a_{jk}{*}x_k^{(i)} \quad (114)$$

In this equation, the sum was split so as to show in an explicit way which x's are from the present and which are from the previous sweep.

Using (114) we may program the algorithm of Gauss-Seidel (S-method) in an unconventional way. Suppose we define two vectors $\underline{t}$ and $\underline{z}$ as:

$$t_j = -b_j + \Sigma\ a_{jk}{*}x_k;\quad j = 1,2,\dots,n;\ k\Sigma=j+1,\dots,n \quad (115)$$

$$z_j = \Sigma\ a_{jk}{*}x_k;\quad j = 1,2,\dots,n;\ k\Sigma=1,\dots,j-1 \quad (116)$$

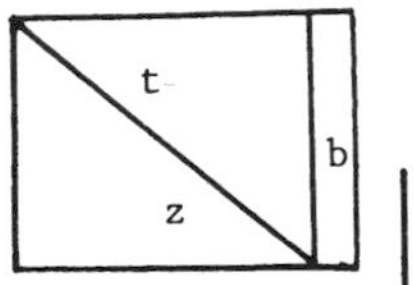

Fig. 3: t,z and b.

and store them sliced in the memories of the slaves (see Fig. 3) together with $\underline{x}$. These vectors store the upper-triangle-minus-b and the lower-triangle respectively. If superscripts (i) attached to $\underline{t}$ and $\underline{z}$ indicate the sweep-number, then (114) becomes simply

$$x_j^{(i+1)} = -(t_j^{(i)} + z_j^{(i+1)})/a_{jj};\ j = 1,2,\dots,n \quad (117)$$

This shows that in order to compute an x_j only the values of z_j should be updated whereas the values of t_j may be taken from the previous sweep.

The parallel version of the S-method relies on the way the vectors $\underline{t}$ and $\underline{z}$ are updated. Assume for instance as before that $\underline{x}^{(o)}=1$ and $\underline{z}^{(o)}=\underline{0}$ so that for set (2):

$$\underline{t}^{(o)} = (28,35,13,64,18,1)^T \quad (118)$$

It is important to note that t_n, z_1 are constant, i.e. for any i:

$$t_n^{(i)} = -b_n;\ z_1^{(i)} = 0 \quad (119)$$

The new value of x_1 is calculated from (117) as:

$$x_1^{(1)} = -(28+0)/20 = 1.4 \quad (120)$$

Next, instead of computing $x_2^{(1)}$ we correct vectors $\underline{t}$ and $\underline{z}$. We do it for i=2,...,n; hence the name "vertical programming". x_1 does not appear in any t_i; therefore $\underline{t}$ does not change yet. Neither does z_1 (since it is not a function of $\underline{x}$), but we may start already the accumulation of $\underline{z}_j^{(1)}$ by collecting

$$z_j^{(1)} = z_j^{(0)} + a_{j1}{*}x_1^{(1)};\quad j = 2,3,\dots,6 \quad (121)$$

i.e. columnwise. In our case then

$$\underline{z}^{(1)} = (0,1.4,1.4,8.4,2.8,1.4)^T \quad (122)$$

It is important to note that $z_2^{(1)}$ does not depend on $x_2,\dots,x_6$. It will be 1.4 as long as $x_1^{(1)}$ is not changed. Since we also know the value of $t_2^{(0)}$:

$$x_2^{(1)} = (1.4 + 35)/20 = 1.82 \quad (123)$$

This x is a parameter of both $\underline{t}$ and $\underline{z}$. It may be used to update $\underline{t}$ of (115) to be

$$t_1^{(1)} = t_1^{(0)} + a_{12}{*}x_2^{(1)} - a_{12}{*}x_2^{(0)} \quad (124)$$

Hence, if we define the residuals through

$$r_k = x_k^{(i+1)} - x_k^{(i)} \quad (125)$$

we may rewrite (115) in the simpler form

$$t_1 = t_1 + a_{12}*r_2 \qquad (126)$$

In the same way, i.e. using column 2, the $\underline{z}$-vector may be updated:

$$z_j = z_j + a_{j2}*x_2 \ ; \ j=3,\dots,6 \qquad (127)$$

Since $\underline{t}$ was completely initiated, but $\underline{z}$ set to $\underline{0}$, we use the next x-value for updating $\underline{z}$ but the residual $\underline{r}$ for updating $\underline{t}$.

We may now develop an ASP-program for this algorithm. It stores the matrix $\underline{A}$ and vectors $\underline{b}$, $\underline{x}$ as in the previous method. Additionally, slices of $\underline{t}$ and $\underline{z}$ are stored in the corresponding memories.

The steps of the algorithm are as follows:

(a) Slices of $\underline{A}$ and $\underline{b}$ as well as the initial value $\underline{x}^{(0)}$ of vector $\underline{x}$ will be stored in all slave memories. Hence the part of the JA-method ahead of and including CALL INIT; may be copied. Additionally vectors $\underline{t}$ and $\underline{z}$ should be initialized. This is done by calling an initialization procedure

PARCALL IN2;

Steps (b) and (c) constitute the main body of the algorithm. Index k identifies the slaves and thus runs sequentially from 1 to p; index i runs then - also sequentially - along the slice stored in slave k. Altogether, index i runs from 1 to h*p = n.

(b) An i is chosen. A new x_i is computed but stored temporarily as y (in the k'th memory). Next, a residual r is calculated and its square added to e (error accumulator). Finally, the values of r and y are transferred through the bus and via the common store to all slave memories, where y is stored as the new value of x. In the k's memory, y is simply renamed as x.

```
LB:DO K=1 TO P; /* K IS THE INDEX OF THE SLAVE                         */
  DO I=L(K) TO U(K); /* I RUNS SEQUENTIALLY OVER ALL VALUES            */
  PARCALL (K)PA(I); /* STORED IN SLAVE K.  PA WILL COMPUTE             */
                    /* THE NEW X(I), THE DIFFERENCE BETWEEN            */
                    /* IT AND OLD X(I) AND ACCUMULATE R*R              */
                    /* IN E - ALL IN MEMORY OF SLAVE K                 */
  (0)Y = (K)Y;      /* TRANSFER THE NEW X(I) AND                       */
  (0)R = (K)R;      /* R FROM SLAVE K INTO COMMON MEMORY.              */
  BROADCAST (Y) (X(I));  /* BROADCAST BOTH TO ALL SLAVE MEMORIES       */
  BROADCAST (R);         /* INCLUDING THE K'S FROM WHICH IT CAME       */
```

(c) Each (slave) memory has now stored the new value of x_i and r. The correction of all values of $\underline{t}$ and $\underline{z}$ which use these r and x_i respectively, <u>may proceed concurrently in the (slave) memories</u>.

```
  PARCALL PB;       /* THIS PROCEDURE UPDATES ALL VALUES OF VECTORS    */
                    /* T AND Z, EACH AS A SLICE OF A DIFFERENT SLAVE.  */
  END;              /* THIS COMPLETES THE SEQUENTIAL ITERATION ON I    */
END;                /* IN WHICH A SET OF NEW VALUES FOR X, NEW VECTORS */
                    /* T AND Z AND E + R* R WERE COMPUTED IN EACH SLAVE. */
```

When the sequential iteration on i ("sweep") is completed, vector $\underline{t}^{(i)}$ as computed above becomes $\underline{t}^{(i+1)}$ as needed for the next sweep. Note that most of the arithmetic operations are done during the parallel step (c) which adjusts t and z (columnwise).

(d) In step (b), each slave memory stored the sum of the squares of its residuals as e. In the next step these will be summed and the program terminated if their sum is less than ε. Else, the program reverts to step (c).

```
G=0;                  /* G IS THE OVERALL ERROR.                              */
DO I=1 TO P;          /* FOR EACH OF THE P SLAVES, TRANSFER ERROR E TO
  G = G + (I)F;                COMMON MEMORY    AND ADD IT THERE TO G.        */
END;
```

(e) If the process has not yet converged, initial values for the next sweep must be prepared. They include setting all error accumulators e and all z's to zero. Then the process reverts to step (b).

```
IF G<EPS              /* IF G IS SMALLER THAN EPSILON THEN THE PROCESS         */
THEN GO TO LE;        /* IS TERMINATED-OTHERWISE ALL ERROR-ACCUMULATORS        */
LD:PARCALL PC;        /* E AND ALL Z'S ARE SET TO ZERO BY PC AND               */
GOTO LB;              /* A NEW SWEEP STARTS AT LABEL LB.                       */
PA:PARPROC(I);        /* THERE IS NO NEED TO INDEX ALL VARIABLES WITH          */
                      /* THE NUMBER K OF THE SLAVE .                           */
Y = -(Z(I)+T(I))/A(I,I);/* Y IS THE NEW X(I)                                   */
R = Y-X(I);           /* R IS THE RESIDUAL                                     */
E = E+R*R; PAREND;    /* E ACCUMULATES R*R OF SLICE K IN MEMORY K.             */
IN2:  PARPROC;        /* NEW PARALLEL PROCEDURE.                               */
DO I=1 TO H;          /* GO ALONG THE SLICE                                    */
  Z(I)=0; T(I)=-B(I); /* INITIATING Z TO 0 AND T AS                            */
  DO K=I+1 TO N;      /* INDICATED.  THIS REQUIRES A                           */
   T(I)=T(I)+A(I,K)*X(K); /* SUMMATION ON T.                                   */
END; END; PAREND;     /* END OF PARALLEL PROCEDURE IN2.                        */
PB:PARPROC;           /* EACH VARIABLE WITH INDEX I MAY                        */
                      /* BE USED TO CHECK WHETHER IT IS                        */
                      /* BELOW OR ABOVE SOME SLICE.                            */
IF I<(K)L(K)          /* FOR THIS CONDITION, THE SLICE                         */
THEN DO;              /* OF K LIES BELOW ROW I, SO THAT                        */
DO J=L(K) TO U(K);    /* HERE ONLY THE Z'S ARE CORRECTED                       */
  Z(J)=Z(J)+A(J,I)*X(I);
END;  END;
ELSE; IF I> (K)U(K) /* HERE ONLY THE T'S ARE CORRECTED.                        */
THEN DO J=L(K) TO U(K); /* NOTE THAT HERE THE R AND NOT Y
  T(J)=T(J)+A(J,I)*R;  /* ARE USED.                                            */
```

```
END;  ELSE; DO;       /* THIS IS THE CASE OF I BEING                          */
DO J=L(K) TO I-1;     /* "INSIDE" THE SLICE.  FIRST THE                       */
  T(J)=T(J)+A(J,I)*R /* T'S ARE CORRECTED.                                    */
END;
DO J=I+1 TO U(K);     /* NOW THE Z'S ARE CORRECTED                            */
  Z(J)=Z(J)+A(J,I)*X(J);  /* BOTH COLUMNWISE!                                 */
END; PAREND;          /* END OF PARALLEL PROCEDURE PB.                        */
PC:PARPROC;
E=0;                  /* IN ALL SLAVES SET E AND ALL                          */
DO I=L(K) TO U(K); Z(I)=0; END; /* Z'S IN THE SLICE TO ZERO.                  */
PAREND;               /* END OF PARPROC PC &                                  */
LE:END;               /* OF THE ENTIRE PROGRAM                                */
```

The final result, vector $\underline{x}$ is identical to that obtained by application of the sequential algorithm of Seidel, though in order to apply ASP, vectors $\underline{t}$ and $\underline{z}$ were introduced and use was made of the following facts:

<u>The values</u> t_i <u>in sweep k+1 are those calculated in sweep k</u>.

<u>The values</u> z_i <u>are used as soon as they are computed</u>.

<u>The values</u> t_i, z_i <u>for i=1,2,...,n are computed so that whenever an</u> x_i <u>is corrected, all terms</u> $A_{ji}*r$ <u>and</u> $A_{ji}*x_i$ <u>are added to</u> t_i <u>and</u> z_i <u>respectively</u>.

Next we will follow the developed program as it solves our problem for n=6, p=3 and therefore h=2. The essential part in (b) is the (parallel) call on PA. It computes y and r=y-x(i) (it also accumulates e=sum(r^2), but this part is not essential in our discussion). The BROADCAST statements set all x(i) as y and transfered r to the slaves. In step (b) procedure PB is called; it updates the $\underline{t}$ and $\underline{z}$ vectors.

Let us start again with $\underline{x} = \underline{1}$ and $\underline{z} = \underline{0}$. Then $\underline{t} = (28,35,13,64,18,1)^T$ as before. We will next painstakingly follow the calculations:

<u>SLAVE K=1</u>

I=1: (1)PA(1): $y=(z_1+t_1)/20=(0+28)/20=1.4$; $r=y-x_1=0.4$; $x_1=1.4$

<u>Note</u>. PB(J) will mean "Routine PB as executed by slave J computes."

PB(1): $z_2=z_2+x_1=0+1.4=1.4$. Note: z_1 will not change in this sweep.

PB(2): $z_3=z_3+x_1=0+1.4=1.4$; $z_4=0+6*1.4=8.4$

PB(3): $z_5=z_5+2x_1=2.8$; $z_6=z_6+x_1=1.4$

I=2: (1)PA(2): $y=(z_2+t_2)/20=(1.4+35)/20=1.82$; $r=y-x_2=0.82$; $x_2=1.82$

PB(1): $t_1=t_1+r=t_1+x_2^{(1)}-x_2^{(0)}=(\Sigma A_{1j}*x_j+A_{12}*x_2^{(0)})+A_{12}x_2^{(1)}-A_{12}x_2^{(0)}$; $j\Sigma\neq 2$

<u>Note</u>. The expression in parantheses is the previous t_1; in the result, only $A_{12}x_2^{(0)}$ was changed into $A_{12}x_2^{(1)}$. Thus $t_1=28+0.82=28.82$.

PB(2): $z_3=z_3+2x_2=1.4+3.64=5.04$; $z_4=z_4+x_2=8.4+1.82=10.22$

PB(3): $z_5=z_5+4x_2=2.8+7.28=10.08$; $z_6=z_6+3x_2=1.4+5.46=6.86$

<u>Note</u>. z_3 will not change anymore in this sweep.

SLAVE K = 2

I=3: (2)PA(3); $y = (z_3+t_3)/20=(5.04+13)/20=0.908$; $r=-0.098$; $x_3=0.902$.

PB(1): $t_1=t_1+r=28.82-0.098=27.732$; $t_2=t_2+2r=35-0.196=34.804$

Note again how t_2 was changed: $t_2= \Sigma A_{2i}x_i+2x_3^{(o)}+2(x_3^{(1)}-x_3^{(0)})$; $i\Sigma\neq 3$

$t_2 = \Sigma A_{2i}x_i + 2x_3^{(1)}$; $i\Sigma\neq 3$

PB(2): $z_4=z_4+2x_3=10.22+1.804=12.024$. Note: it will not change.

PB(3): $z_5=z_5+x_3=10.08+0.902=10.982$; $z_6=z_6+2x_3=6.86+1.804=8.664$

I=4: (2)PA(4): $y=(z_4+t_4)/20=3.8$; $r=y-x_4=2.8$; $x_4=3.8$

PB(1): $t_1=t_1+6r=44.5$; $t_2=t_2+r=34.8+2.8=37.6$

PB(2): $t_3=t_3+2r=13+5.6=18.6$

PB(3): $z_5=z_5+3x_4=10.98+11.4=22.38$; $z_6=z_6+x_4=8.66+3.8=12.46$

Note: z_5 will not change anymore in this sweep.

SLAVE K=3

I=5: (3)PA(5): $y=(z_5+t_5)/20=2.02$; $r=y-x_5=1.02$; $x_5=2.02$

PB(1): $t_1=t_1+2r=46.5$; $t_2=t_2+4r=41.6$

PB(2): $t_3=t_3+r=19.6$; $t_4=t_4+3r=65$

PB(3): $z_6=z_6+5x_5=17.56$

Note that at every i, the value z_{i+1} is the final value to be computed. For I=6, $t_1,\ldots,t_5$ will get their final values; $t_6=1$ is anyway constant.

I=6: (3)PA(6): $y=(z_6+t_6)/20=1.18$; $r=y-x_6=0.18=0.2$; $x_6=1.18$

PB(1): $t_1=t_1+r=46.4$; $t_2=t_2+3r=41.6+0.6=42.2$

PB(2): $t_3=t_3+2r=19.6+0.4=20$; $t_4=t_4+r=65.2$

PB(3): $t_5=t_5+5r=18.2$

The author is sorry for having lead the reader through all this sordid and may be wrong detailed calculation, but he found no other way to convince the reader that the algorithm works and that at this stage both vectors $\underline{t}$ and $\underline{z}$ correspond precisely to (115,116). If required, a new iteration could be started provided $\underline{z}$ is made zero again (seems a pity). <u>To conclude: We have Asp'ed the Gauss-Seidel, a seemingly inherently sequential algorithm</u>.

7.2.3 Improvement

The S-algorithm may be improved as follows. Instead of four vectors $\underline{x},\underline{b},\underline{t}$, and $\underline{z}$, two, namely $\underline{x}$ and $\underline{t}$ will suffice. Values of $\underline{b}$ are read-in initially as $\underline{t}$ which later stores

$$t_i = b_i - \Sigma\ a_{ij}*x_{ij};\quad j \neq i;\ j\Sigma=1,\ldots,n \tag{128}$$

This t_i is the corrected x_i provided a_{ii} was set to 1 and the x_j-values were corrected earlier. Each time an x_j is corrected all t_i may be corrected through

$$t_i^{(m+1)} = t_i^{(m)} + a_{ij}(x_j^{(m)} - x_j^{(m+1)}) = t_i^{(m)} - a_{ij}*r \tag{129}$$

Thus, we do not need vector $\underline{z}$ at all.

It was pointed out in Chapter 4 that the speedup depends crucially on the number of synchronizatons; the fewer of these, the better. We even had a parallelization principle underlining this and will use it next in a fundamental change to the program. If you followed the steps of the S-method above, the master is called for transfer of every new x_i and r which it broadcasts to all slaves, then for gathering all errors e. By computing each $x_j^{(m+1)}$ and $r=x_j^{(m+1)}-x_j^{(m)}$ one step ahead of it being used, the number of set-up times ("synchronizations") may be reduced. Incidentally, the program will then use also fewer subroutines (and linkages), but since the t_i's are corrected using small values $(x_j^{(m)}-x_j^{(m+1)})$ of (125) the roundoff error may be larger. A program of this type appears next.

The GS program below uses in fact fewer synchronizations than the previous programs. This is achieved simply by calculating $x_1^{(1)}$ and $d=x_1^{(1)} - x_1^{(0)}$ and broadcasting it before starting the iterations at label LLB. Note that the synchronization is then required in only one place - when calling the PR-subroutine. Note also, that for K=N, the value of x_1 is computed so that the iteration may go on undisturbed. Finally note, that only two n-vectors are needed.

```
GS:PROC OPTIONS(MAIN);      /* THE MAIN CONTROL PROGRAM                          */
DCL (I,J,K,L,LB(P),N)FIXED, (D,DX,RM,RMAX,W,X(N),T(N),A(N,N))FLOAT,
     (#)(I,J,K,L,LB)FIXED, (#) (DX,XX,X(N),A(H,N),T(H)) FLOAT;
GET DATA(N,RMAX);           /* N=DIMENSION, RMAX=MAXIMAL RÉSIDUAL               */
GET LIST(X(I),I=1 TO N);    /* INITIAL VALUE OF VECTOR X                         */
GET LIST(T(I),I=1 TO N);    /* ACTUALLY THIS IS VECTOR B.                        */
GET LIST ((A(I,J) DO I=1 TO N) DO J=1 TO N)); /* THE MATRIX A.                   */
H=N/P;                      /* THE WIDTH OF A SLICE .                            */
DO I=1 TO N;  W=T(I)+X(I);
  DO J=1 TO N; W=W-A(I,J)*X(J); END;
  T(I)=W; END;              /* T(I)=B(I)-A(I,J)*X(J),J=1,...,N BUT J≠I           */
DO I=1 TO P;
  J=(I-1)*H+1; K=I*H;       /* J AND K ARE THE BOUNDS OF THE SLICE I.            */
  (I)A(1:H,1:N)≡A(J:K,1:N); (I)T(1:H)≡T(J:H); (I)LB=J-1;
END; /*  LB AND SLICES OF A AND T NUMBERED 1:H WERE TRANSFERRED .                */
PUT BROADCAST (X(1:N));  /* INITIAL VALUE OF VECTOR X IS TRANSFERRED.            */
W=(1)T(1); D=W-X(1); I=1; /* W=NEW X(1), D=(NEW-OLD)X(1), I=SLAVE .              */
PUT BROADCAST (W) (X(1)); PUT BROADCAST (D) (DX);
LLB:RM=ABS(D);  /* RM WILL HOLD THE LARGEST VALUE |XNEW-XOLD|                    */
DO K=1 TO N; L=K+1;  /* CHOOSE SEQUENTIALLY ROW K                                */
  IF REM(K/H) = 0 THEN I=I+1;  /*  I=NUMBER OF SLAVE OF SLICE OF K               */
  IF L>N THEN DO; L=1; I=1; END;
  PARCALL (#)PR(K,L);  /* ADJUST T CONCURRENTLY AND FIND X(L)                    */
  W=(I)XX; PUT BROADCAST(W) (X(L));  /* XX FOUND IN SLAVE L                      */
  D=(I)DX;  PUT BROADCAST(D) (DX);  /* DX = (XNEW-XOLD)                          */
  R=ABS(D); IF R>RM THEN RM=R; /* UPDATING RM                                    */
END;  /*  COMPLETED CORRECTING ITERATIVELY X(2),X(3),...,X(N),X(1)               */
  IF RM>RMAX THEN GOTO LLB;  /* START OF A NEW ITERATION                         */
```

```
PR:  PARPROC(K,L);
DO J=1 TO N;  /* CORRECTING THE SLICE OF T EXCEPT WHERE J+LB=K        */
  IF (J+LB)≠K THEN T(J)=T(J)-A(I,K); END;
IF I=(#P) THEN DO;  /* CALCULATE NEW X(L) AND DX IN SLAVE I          */
J=L-LB;  XX=T(J); DX=XX-XL; END;
END;  /* PR ADJUSTED A SLICE OF VECTOR T AND COMPUTED NEW DX AND X  */
END; /*END OF GS=GAUSS SEIDEL PROCEDURE WITH FEWER SYNCHRONICATIONS */
```

<u>An ASP-version of SOR</u>

The algorithm of this section uses only a single auxiliary vector AUX - instead of <u>t</u> and <u>z</u>. AUX is divided among the (slave) memories in slices. AUX(I) will be updated so that immediately before calculation of a new X(I), it will hold the sum of A(I,J)*X(J) for J=1 to N, using the most recently calculated values of X(J). The algorithm consists of an initialization during which AUX(I) is initialized to hold the sum A(I,J)*X(J) where X(J) are the initial values-and an iterative stage. The stopping criterion is by R and W stands for the overrelaxation factor.

```
PAR_SOR:  PROC(OPTIONS) MAIN;
DCL (#) (LO,HI,J) FIXED;  /*  BOUNDARY OF SLICE INDICATORS              */
DCL (#) (X(N), A(H,N+1), AUX(H)) FLOAT;
DCL (A(H,N+1), X(N)) FLOAT, (LOW(P), HIGH(P)) FIXED;
DO I=1 TO P;
  LOW(I) =(I-1)*H+1; HIGH(I)=I*H;  /* THE SLICE BOUNDARIES             */
  (I)LO=LOW(I);  (I)HI=HIGH(I);  /* ARE TRANSFERRED TO SLAVES .        */
  GET FILE(A) DATA ((A(L,M) DO M=1 TO N+1) DO L=LOW(I) TO HIGH (I));
  (I)A=A;  /*  BLOCK TRANSFER OF SLICES OF A                           */
END;  /* END OF INITIALIZATION EXCEPT FOR VECTOR AUX.                  */
PARCALL INIT;  /* INITIALIZES VECTOR AUX .                             */
LOOP:  RMAX=0.0;
DO K=1 TO P;  /*  K IS HERE THE NUMBER OF THE SLAVE.                   */
  M=0;
  DO J=LOW(K) TO HIGH(K);
  M=M+1;
  (K)PARCALL NEWX(XNEW,M,J); XNEW=(K)XNEW; /* COMPUTE NEW X(J)         */
  PUT BROADCAST (XNEW,J);  /* AND TRANSFER IT TO ALL SLAVES .          */
  PARCALL UPDATE(J);  /*  IN ALL MEMORIES COMPUTE A(S,J)*X(J)          */
     R=ABS(XNEW-X(J)); /* FOR S=1 TO N AND ACCUMULATE THEM .           */
     IF R>RMAX THEN R = RMAX;
END;END;
IF RMAX<EPS THEN RETURN;
GOTO LOOP;
INIT:  PARPROC;
PREP:  DO I=1 TO H;
```

```
  AUX(I)=0;
  DO J=I+LO-1 TO N;
     AUX(I)=AUX(I)+A(I,J)*X(J);
END;END PREP; PAREND INIT;
NEWX:  PARPROC(XNEW,M,J);
XNEW=X(J)-W/A(M,J)*(B(M)-AUX(M));  /* CLASSICAL OVERRELAXATION              */
AUX(M)=0; X(J)=XNEW;
PAREND NEWX;
UPDATE:  PARPROC(J);
DO I=1 TO H;
  AUX(I)=AUX(I)+A(I,J)*XNEW;
END;PAREND UPDATE;
END;  /*   OF THE ENTIRE PAR-SOR                                          */
```

There exists another version of this algorithm which does not require additional storage at all. The idea is the same as in 7.2.3 namely: Vector x contains as before the most recently computed values of the x_i's. There is another n-vector named AUX, whose i'th component equals

AUX(I) = B(I) - Σ A(I,J)*X(J);JΣ=1,...,N (130)

using the most recently computed values of X. Given these two vectors, it is straightforward to calculate a new X(I) using overrelaxation; the formula is simply

XNEW = X(I) + W*AUX(I)/A(I,I) (131)

Having updated X(I), one updates the vector AUX in the following fashion

AUX(I) = AUX(I) + A(I,K)*(XNEW - X(K)), I = 1,2,...,N (132)

and it is easily seen that the new AUX(I) conforms to (17) with the old X(K) on the right side replaced by XNEW. Note in particular, that I above is from 1 to N i.e. now AUX accumulates the entire sum of A(I,J)*X(J) from 1 to N except where I=J.

In ASP, XNEW is broadcast over the bus as soon as it is computed by one of the slaves and all slaves correct their respective components of AUX through (132). The entire procedure is very similar to PAR_SOR, with the following changes.

The loop PREP of procedure INIT becomes

```
PREP:  DO I=1 TO H;
     AUX(I) = B(I);
     DO J=1 TO N;
          AUX(I) = AUX(I) - A(I,J)*X(J);
     END;END; /*  OF PREP  */
```

It still seems that another vector B is needed. Note, however, that it is used only in initialization and is not needed at all during the iterative process itself. Therefore, as before, AUX may be initialized as part of the masters routine using values read once from external storage, thus obviating the need for B.

Procedures NEWX and UPDATE become:

```
NEWX:  PARPROC(XNEW,M,J);                 UPDATE:PARPROC(J);
XNEW=X(J)-W/A(M,J)*AUX(M);                DELX=XNEW-X(J);
X(J)=XNEW;                                DO I=1 TO H;
PAREND NEWX;                          AUX(I) = AUX(I)+A(I,J)*DELX;
                                      END; END OF UPDATE;
```

7.2.4 Other Methods

Aitken's acceleration method, especially the version by Steffenson was shown to speed-up convergence (Table 1). Since the scheme can be applied componentwise to entire vectors, we can easily program it for ASP. All that is needed, is for the slaves to store three vectors (or three slices of vectors), $\underline{x}_i$, $\underline{x}_{i-1}$, $\underline{x}_{i-2}$ and compute the next $\underline{x}_{i+1}$ not by iteration, but by (47). The speed-up is optimal, since there is no need for additional information transfer, but more storage space is needed.

Let us review again the iterative improvement technique. A single iteration would consist of:

$$\underline{r}^{(i)} = \underline{b} - \underline{A}\,\underline{x}^{(i)}; \quad \underline{A} = \underline{L}\,\underline{R} \tag{133}$$

$$\underline{L}\,\underline{z} = \underline{r}^{(i)}; \quad \underline{R}\,\underline{e}^{(i)} = \underline{z}; \quad \underline{x}^{(i+1)} = \underline{x}^{(i)} + \underline{e}^{(i)} \tag{134}$$

The above procedure involves matrix and matrix-by-vector multiplications, forward and backward substitutions and vector additions. These operations were either already "programmed" for ASP or - as is the case with vector addition - are inherently parallel and thus trivially executable on ASP.

Next we program the HS-algorithm of conjugate gradients (7.1.4) for a possible ASP execution. There are two products which can be "prepared". At the start of an iteration, we might compute $\underline{s}_i = \underline{A}\,\underline{w}_i$ and right after computing $\underline{r}_{i+1}$ use it in $y = \underline{r}^T_{i+1}\,\underline{r}_{i+1}$ so that at the beginning of an iteration it can be used as z. The algorithm is therefore as follows:

$$\underline{s}_i = \underline{A}\,\underline{w}_i; \quad c_i = z/(\underline{w}_i^T \underline{s}_i); \quad \underline{x}_{i+1} = \underline{x}_i + c_i \underline{w}_i \tag{135}$$

$$\underline{r}_{i+1} = \underline{r}_i - c_i \underline{s}_i; \quad y = \underline{r}^T_{i+1}\,\underline{r}_{i+1}; \quad k_i = y/z; \quad \underline{w}_{i+1} = \underline{r}_{i+1} + k_i \underline{w}_i; \quad z=y \tag{136}$$

Only a single matrix-vector multiplication is required and it can be performed by each slice of $\underline{A}$ multiplying the entire vector $\underline{w}$. A scalar product, say of $\underline{w}_i^T \underline{s}_i$ can be written as

$$\underline{w}_i^T \underline{s}_i = \sum_{j=1}^{n} w_j^{(i)} s_j^{(i)} = \sum_{q=1}^{p} \Big(\sum_{j=(q-1)h+1}^{qh} w_j^{(i)} s_j^{(i)} \Big) \tag{137}$$

This is an inherently parallel calculation of the inner loop even if only slices of $\underline{w}$ and $\underline{s}$ are stored (even more so for $\underline{r}^T_{i+1}\,\underline{r}_{i+1}$). There are then p values to be added for the "price" of pτ. Other parts of the algorithm hardly need to be considered, but the number of synchronizations may be large. It is left as an exercise to compute it and thus the ratio for this algorithm.

7.3. ALTERNATING METHODS

Aims: To develop a new iterative method which is both more efficient by 50% than the Gauss-Seidel algorithm and lends itself easily to an ASP-program. To prove that in some respect this algorithm is optimal. To introduce other methods and to compute the time ratios for all of them. To discuss convergence.

7.3.1. New Algorithms

The methods of Jacobi, Gauss-Seidel and SOR have been known for a long time now (the method of Jacobi dates back to 1845) and there is a vast literature on the subject [We68,Va62]. In this Section we shall present two methods, one of which (SSOR) has been analyzed in literature and the other (SJ) has only recently been published [CW77a]. These methods seem also to be well suited for various power-system problems ([WC76],[WC77]). They are all the more interesting because new and faster algorithms have been devised for them. (See [CW77b] and [CW80]).

In order to use the Gauss-Seidel method on ASP, we have used the $\underline{t}$ and $\underline{z}$ vectors. The "correction" of an x_j is then (similar to 7.2.7)

$$x_j^{(i+1)} = -(t_j^{(i)} + z_j^{(i+1)}) \tag{138}$$

where we have assumed that the set ($\underline{A}\ \underline{x} = \underline{b}$) is already normalized i.e. that all $a_{ii}=1$. We have not used $\underline{t}$, $\underline{z}$ in the JA-method, since that seemed unnecessary, but if we do this, then the general equation of the JA-method becomes

$$x_j^{(i+1)} = b_j - \sum_{k=1}^{j-1} a_{jk}\, x_k^{(i)} - \sum_{k=j+1}^{n} a_{jk}\, x_k^{(i)} \tag{139}$$

Using the $\underline{t}$ and $\underline{z}$ vectors this is equivalent to

$$x_j^{(i+1)} = -(t_j^{(i)} + z_j^{(i)}) \tag{140}$$

The fact that in the S-method (see 7.2.7) $z_j^{(i+1)}$, but here in the JA-method $z_j^{(i)}$ is required made the ASP-programming of the JA-method trivial.

Recall now the situation at the end of a full sweep, say i, i.e. after solving (127). As was pointed out there, all values $t_j^{(i)}$ and $z_j^{(i)}$ are known at that point and all x_j's could be corrected by a Jacobi sweep using (140). This requires only an insignificant additional effort.

It should be noted that the above renders the t's obsolete for the next S-sweep and it is therefore necessary to revert to step (a) of the program to compute $\underline{t}$ again (for the next sweep).

The new algorithm then consists of an S-sweep followed by a JA-sweep; it will be called the "SJ-algorithm". It may be programmed both for ASP and for a mono-computer (sequential program). In both cases the S- and JA sweeps alternate.

The ASP-program of the SJ-method is identical to that of the S-method except that the parallel procedure PC is now:

```
PC:PARPROC;                          /* PC IS CALLED BY SLAVE K          */
DO I=L(K) TO U(K);                   /* SO THAT ALL ITS VARIABLES        */
  X(I)=-(Z(I)+T(I))/A(I,I);          /* ARE TO BE INDEXED AS P#          */
END;E=0;END;                         /* END OF PC                        */
```

As mentioned, since the call on PC (J-sweep) destroys the t-vector, the program reverts to L instead of to LB.

Let us define the $\underline{R}$ and $\underline{L}$ matrices as earlier. Then, with only a single additional vector, the algorithm proceeds as follows:

(a) Compute $\underline{R}*\underline{x}^{(m)}$

(b) S-sweep: Compute $\underline{x}^{(m+1/2)}$ simultaneously forming $\underline{L}*\underline{x}^{(m+1/2)}$ and saving it in an auxiliary vector.

(c) Compute $\underline{B}*\underline{x}^{(m+1/2)}$

(d) JA sweep: Compute

$$x_i^{(m+1)} = b_i - \underline{L}*\underline{x}^{(m+1/2)} - \underline{R}*\underline{x}^{(m+1/2)};\ i=1,2,\ldots,n \qquad (141)$$

(e) Revert to step (a).

(The use of the half index is justified by a sweep count).

Let us now count the operations and storage required for both the JA and S-methods. Defining the set:

$$S = \{(i,j) \mid a_{ij} \neq 0\} \qquad (142)$$

we see that the total number of operations per iteration equals $|S|$. For a full matrix $|S| = n^2$. Comparing this with approximately $n^3\omega/3$ required for the direct solution of linear equations by Gaussian elimination, it is seen that as long as the number of iterations required for convergence is smaller that n/3, iterative methods are preferable to direct methods. The memory space required equals $|S|$ locations to store the matrix plus 2n locations for vectors $\underline{x}$ and $\underline{b}$. Here iterative methods are at a clear advantage over direct methods when $\underline{A}$ is sparse, because of the phenomenon of fill-in encountered in Gaussian elimination (see Chapter 6).

The first three steps of the SJ-method require about 0.5 $|S|\mu$ each (assuming equal numbers of non-zero elements in lower and upper triangle, as in the case of a symmetric matrix). The last step entails no μ's at all. Hence the total count is about 1.5 $|S|\mu$ (only 50% more for a single J-sweep).

Another algorithm which alternately uses two known methods results if at the end of the scan-down in the S-method, we start a scan-up. In this case, though, during the scan-down the t's will not be recalculated; instead they are changed according to: $t_1=-b_1$ right after x_1 is calculated, $t_2=-b_2$ right after x_2 is calculated and so on. These t's are not changed more during the scan-down. Then at the end of the scan-down (i=2,...,n) we may start a scan-up (i=n-1,..,1) as follows.

FOR I=6: X(6) = -(T(I)+Z(I))/A(I,I);

Note that $x_1^{(1)}, x_2^{(1)}, \ldots, x_5^{(1)}$ which are included in the above are all from the iteration numbered (1). Therefore the computed x_6 should have superscript (2). Then make $z_6 = 0$ and

FOR J=1,...,5: $t_1=-b_1+A_{16}x_6^{(2)}$, $t_2=-b+A_{26}x_6^{(2)}$, ..., $t_5=-b_5+A_{56}x_6^{(2)}$

In the same way, the scan-up proceeds for I=5,4,3,2 and 1.

Note that at this stage, the t's and z's are ready for the next scan-down. The two scans were symmetric and since each required for a full matrix $n^2/2$ operations, altogether n^2 operations were required. If this is compared with $2n^2$ normally required for two sweeps, the conclusion is drawn that in this method 50% of the operations are saved.

This being so, one wonders if the same could not be done for the SSOR method as normally executed on a single computer. If it can, then there is no basis for the frequently voiced opinion that SSOR requires twice as much effort as, say, SOR. As shown earlier, nearly half the number of arithmetic operations can be saved if storage space is available to hold an auxiliary n-vector in the main memory. Indeed, if at the beginning of the m'th step $\underline{x}^{(m)}$ and $\underline{b}-\underline{R}\underline{x}^{(m)}$ are stored (the latter in an auxiliary vector) one can simultaneously compute the i'th component of $\underline{x}^{(m+1/2)}$ and $\underline{L}\underline{x}^{(m+1/2)}$ for i=1,2,...,n and write the latter over $\underline{b}-\underline{R}\underline{x}^{(m)}$ which is no longer needed. In the same fashion, one forms the i'th component of $\underline{b}-\underline{R}\underline{x}^{(m+1)}$ along with that of $\underline{x}^{(m+1)}$ overwriting $\underline{L}\underline{x}^{(m+1)}$ as one proceeds with i=1,2,...,n. This requires only half as many additions and multiplications as the straightforward approach. The algorithm proceeds as follows: Let $\underline{D}=\underline{U}$ for simplicity (i.e. $a_{ii}=1$), $\underline{x}=(x_1,...,x_n)^T$, $\underline{y}=(y_1,...,y_n)^T$ be two storage vectors initially holding $\underline{x}^{(0)}$ and $\underline{b}-\underline{R}*\underline{x}^{(0)}$ respectively. The algorithm then iterates the following two steps:

Forward step:

$$\left.\begin{aligned} z &= \Sigma\ l_{ij}*x_j;\ j\Sigma=1,...,i-1 \\ x_i &= x_i + w*(y_i-x_i-z) \\ y_i &= z \end{aligned}\right\}\ i = 1,...,n \qquad (143)$$

Backward step:

$$\left.\begin{aligned} z &= b_i - \Sigma\ r_{ij}*x_j;\ j\Sigma=i+1,...,n \\ x_i &= x_i + w*(z-y_i-x_i) \\ y_i &= z \end{aligned}\right\}\ i = n,n-1,...,1 \qquad (144)$$

We see that the forward step requires (1+2+...+n-1)=n*(n+1)/2 multiplications because of the sum of $l_{ij}*x_j$ (and n multiplications by w). The backward step requires the same amount of operations. The total count for both steps yields $n*(n+1)\cong n^2$ i.e. about the same as for a single SOR-iteration.

7.3.2. A Generalization [CW79]

The computational savings resulting from the algorithms described above, are special cases of a general scheme whereby any two explicit iterations may be combined in an alternating fashion. Let

$$\underline{A} = \underline{B}_1 - \underline{C}_1 = \underline{B}_2 - \underline{C}_2 \qquad (145)$$

be two explicit splittings of the matrix $\underline{A}$ associated with the iterative methods

$$\underline{B}_1*\underline{x}^{(m+1)} = \underline{C}_1*\underline{x}^{(m)} + \underline{b} \qquad (146)$$

$$\underline{B}_2*\underline{x}^{(m+1)} = \underline{C}_2*\underline{x}^{(m)} + \underline{b} \qquad (147)$$

Suppose, the two methods are to be applied in an alternating way i.e. $\underline{x}^{(1)}$ is obtained from $\underline{x}^{(0)}$ using (146), and $\underline{x}^{(2)}$ from $\underline{x}^{(1)}$ using (147), $\underline{x}^{(3)}$ from $\underline{x}^{(2)}$

using (146) and so on. The equations describing this "alternating" method are

$$\underline{B}_1 * \underline{x}^{(m+1/2)} = \underline{C}_1 * \underline{x}^{(m)} + \underline{b} \tag{148}$$

$$\underline{B}_2 * \underline{x}^{(m+1)} = \underline{C}_2 * \underline{x}^{(m+1/2)} + \underline{b} \ ; \ m \geq 0 \tag{149}$$

We next define the following sets of pairs of indices

$$B_1 = \{(i,j) \mid (\underline{B}_1)_{ij} \neq 0,\ i \neq j\}; \quad B_2 = \{(i,j) \mid (\underline{B}_2)_{ij} \neq 0,\ i \neq j\} \tag{150}$$

$$C_1 = \{(i,j) \mid (\underline{C}_1)_{ij} \neq 0,\ i \neq j\}; \quad C_2 = \{(i,j) \mid (\underline{C}_2)_{ij} \neq 0,\ i \neq j\} \tag{151}$$

As in the case with most iterative methods, we consider the splittings to correspond to a decomposition of the matrix $\underline{A}$ i.e.

$$B_1 \cup C_1 = S; \quad B_1 \cap C_1 = \emptyset; \quad B_2 \cup C_2 = S; \quad B_2 \cap C_2 = \emptyset \tag{152}$$

where $S = \{(i,j) \mid (\underline{A}_{ij} \neq 0,\ i \neq j\}$ (153)

Next denote $B_2 \cap C_1 = N; \quad B_1 \cap C_2 = M$ (154)

Theorem: The alternating method described by (148,149) requires no more than

$$\Omega = (2|S| - |M| - |N|)*\mu \tag{155}$$

per iteration.

Proof: We outline an algorithm which achieves this bound. It is assumed that we have at our disposal an auxiliary n-vector $\underline{y}$. We also assume that initially $\underline{y}$ holds $\underline{C}_1 * \underline{x}^{(m)}$. As earlier $a_{ii} = 1$.

(a) The iteration starts by computing $\underline{x}^{(m+1/2)}$ through (148). Since the splitting is explicit, this amounts to back-substitution. While calculating $x_i^{(m+1/2)}$, we form the sum of all $a_{ij} * x_j^{(m+1/2)}$ for i,j in M and store it in y_i. This step requires $|B_1|$ multiplications μ.

(b) Next $\underline{x}^{(m+1)}$ is evaluated through (149). We note that some of the operations required in computing $\underline{C}_2 * \underline{x}^{(m+1/2)}$ have already been done in step (a) and stored in $\underline{y}$. In fact,

$$(\underline{C}_2 * \underline{x}^{(m+1/2)})_k = \Sigma a_{kj} * x_j^{(m+1/2)} \quad \text{for } k,j \ \varepsilon \ C_2 \tag{156}$$

$$(\underline{C}_2 \ \underline{x}^{(m+1/2)})_k = \sum_{(k,j)\varepsilon M} a_{kj} * x_j^{(m+1/2)} + \sum_{(k,j)\varepsilon C_2 - M} a_{kj} x_j^{(m+1/2)} \tag{157}$$

and the first sum is stored in y_k and need not be computed again. Since by (154) $M \subset C_2$, it follows that $|C_2 - M| = |C_2| - |M|$. Therefore the second summation calls for $|C_2| - |M|$ multiplications. After computing $(C_2 * \underline{x}^{(m+1/2)})_k$, y_k is not needed and may be overwritten. In analogy with step (a), we calculate next $\underline{x}^{(m+1)}$, the back-substitution requiring $|B_2|$ multiplications to form the sum of $a_{ij} * x_j^{(m+1)}$ for $(i,j) \varepsilon B_2$. For each k, the partial sum of $a_{ij} * x_j^{(m+1)}$ for $(k,j) \varepsilon N$ is computed separately and saved in y_k.

(c) Before reverting to (a) to start a new iteration, the auxiliary vector must contain $\underline{C}_1 * \underline{x}^{(m+1)}$ i.e.

$$y_k = \sum_{(k,j)\varepsilon C_1} a_{ij} * x_j^{(m+1)} = \Big(\sum_{(k,j)\varepsilon N} + \sum_{(k,j)\varepsilon C_1 - N} \Big) a_{ij} x_j^{(m+1)} \tag{158}$$

must hold. Only the second sum must be computed (the first is already stored in y_k). This calls for $|C_1| - |N|$ multiplications, so that altogether:

$$\Omega/\mu = |B_1| + |C_2| - |M| + |B_2| + |C_1| - |N| = 2|S| - |M| - |N| \tag{159}$$

Remark 1: Relaxation may be easily incorporated into the above scheme. After computing $x_j^{(m+1/2)}$, one replaces it by $x_j^{(m+1/2)} + w*(x_j^{(m+1/2)} - x_j^{(m)})$ where w is the relaxation factor. A similar formula applies to the second half-step.

We shall now show how various algorithms are derived from the above general scheme. Suppose first that $\underline{B}_1 = \underline{B}_2$, hence $\underline{C}_1 = \underline{C}_2$ by (154) and the number of multiplications is $2|S|$; therefore if two half-steps are identical, there is no gain. (This shows that stationary processes, like the original Gauss-Seidel or Jacobi-algorithms do not benefit from the above result).

Consider now the case

$$\underline{B}_1 = \underline{L} + \underline{D};\ \underline{C}_1 = -\underline{R};\ \underline{B}_2 = \underline{D};\ \ \underline{C}_2 = -(\underline{L} + \underline{R}) \tag{160}$$

which corresponds to the SJ-method. Defining

$$L = \{(i,j) | (\underline{L})_{ij} \neq 0,\ i \neq j\};\quad R = \{(i,j) | (\underline{R})_{ij} \neq 0,\ i \neq j\} \tag{161}$$

we see that in this case

$$N = \emptyset,\quad M = L \tag{162}$$

and the composite iteration requires $2|S| = n^2$, $|L| \cong n^2/2$ so that $1.5n^2$ multiplications are required - a saving of 25%. Finally if

$$\underline{B}_1 = \underline{D} + \underline{L},\ \ \underline{C}_1 = -\underline{R},\ \ \underline{B}_2 = \underline{D} + \underline{R},\ \ \underline{C}_2 = -\underline{L} \tag{163}$$

which corresponds to the "back and forth Seidel" (or SSOR if over-relaxation is used) we see that

$$M = R,\ N = L \tag{164}$$

so that $\Omega/\mu = |B_1| + |C_1| + |B_2| + |C_2| - |M| - |N| = |L| + |R| = |S|$ (165)

which is a gain of 50% over the straightforward algorithm for the case of a full matrix.

Remark 2: The gain achieved in the last case is the highest obtainable through the above scheme. Since $M \subset B_1$ and $N \subset C_1$ by (154) and also $B_1 \cap C_1 = \emptyset$ by (152) it follows that

$$|M| + |N| \leqq |B_1 \cup C_1| = |S| \tag{166}$$

Substituting this in (155) we get

$$\Omega \geqq (2|S| - |S|) * \mu = |S| * \mu \tag{167}$$

We see that SSOR attains this bound.

Being very proud of having made more efficient a method bearing the name of Karl Gauss, it seemed only natural to program it. The ASP version was already given earlier, but more programmers for years to come will use single computers - not parallel or ASP systems. Therefore, a PL/I program is presented below.

We will have to minimize storage and therefore proceed as follows.

The original SJ-method required four n-vectors: $\underline{x}, \underline{b}, \underline{z}$ and $\underline{t}$; the best SSOR-method only three: $\underline{x}, \underline{y}$, and $\underline{b}$. If we assume that all $A_{ii} \neq 0$ then we may normalize i.e. divide each row by A_{ii} ahead of starting the iterations. Hence, all $A_{ii} = 1$ and their locations may be used for storing b_i/A_{ii} in the diagonal of $\underline{A}$. This not only reduces storage requirement to two n-vectors, say $\underline{x}$ and $\underline{y}$ but will also simplify the correction of x_j's since no multiplication or division by A_{ii} is needed.

```
FASSOR:  PROC OPTIONS (MAIN);
DCL (I,J,K,N,N1,NUMIT,MANIT) FIXED,
(A(N,N),D,OM,R,RMAX,T,X(N),Y(N),Z) FLOAT;
/* THE NEXT LINE SHOULD HAVE BEEN READ-IN BEFORE CALLING FASSOR.             */
GET DATA (N,MANIT,OM,RMAX); /* MANIT=MAXIMUM NUMBER OF ITERATIONS            */
               /* OM=OVERRELAXATION FACTOR, RMAX=MAX-RESIDUAL .              */
GET LIST (A);  /* A=THE MATRIX, ASSUMPTION IS A(I,I)≠0 .                     */
GET LIST (Y);  /* THIS READS IN THE RIGHT HAND SIDE B .                      */
N1=N+1; GET LIST (X); /* INITIAL VALUE OF VECTOR X .                         */
DO I=1 TO N;   */ THIS IS THE LOOP WHICH NORMALIZES A                        */
     D=A(I,A); */ SO THAT WE KEEP IT INTACT.                                 */
     DO J=1 TO N; A(I,J)=A(I,J)/D; END;
     Z=Y(I)/D; A(I,I)=Z; /* A(I,I) HOLDS THUS B(I)/A(I,I).                   */
     K=I+1; /* NEXT WE COMPUTE Y(I)=B(I)-SUM(A(I,J)*X(J)).                   */
     DO J=K TO N; Z=Z-A(I,J)*X(J); END; Y(I)=Z;
END; /* THIS IS THE END OF INITIALIZATION.                                   */
NUMIT=1; /* NUMIT=NUMBER OF ITERATION.  THE DOWNWARD SWEEP FOLLOWS.          */
L1:  R=0.0; /* BOTH NUMIT AND R WILL BE USED AS STOPPING CRITERIA .          */
DO I=1 TO N;
     Z=0.0; K=I-1; T=X(I);
     IF K=0 THEN GOTO L2;  /* THIS MIGHT BE MORE EFFICIENT.                  */
     DO J=1 TO K;  Z=Z-A(I,J)*X(J); END;
L2: D=Z+Y(I)-T;  /* THIS IS THE "DISTANCE" (XNEW-XOLD).                      */
     X(I)=T+OM*D; Y(I)=Z;
     /*  THE FIRST IS OVERRELAXATION.  THE SECOND STORES - SUM(A*X).         */
     T=ABS(D); IF T>R THEN R=T;  /* R STORES MAXIMAL T.                      */
END;  /* THIS IS THE END OF THE DOWNWARD SWEEP.  NEXT IS UPWARD.             */
DO I=N BY(-1) TO 1;
     K=I+1; Z=A(I,I); T=X(I); /* Z IS INITIALIZED TO B(I)/A(I,I).            */
     IF K>N THEN GOTO L3;
     DO J=K TO N; Z=Z-A(I,J)*X(J); END;
L3:D=OM*(Z+Y(I)-T); /* THIS IS THE DISPLACEMENT OF X                         */
     X(I)=T+D; Y(I)=Z;
     T=ABS(D); IF T>R THEN R=T;
END;            /* THIS IS THE END OF THE UPWARD SWEEP                       */
NUMIT=NUMIT+1;
IF (NUMIT>MANIT) | (R<RMAX) THEN RETURN;
GOTO L1;  /* GO BACK SINCE NEITHER STOPPING CRITERIAE STOP YOU               */
END;       /* END OF FASSOR = FAST SSOR PROCEDURE                            */
```

Note that the corrections were such that vector $\underline{y}$ replaced $\underline{t}$.

7.3.3. Properties of the methods

Reduction ratios

The matrices of practical problems are rather sparse. As mentioned, the "typical" matrix of, say, power systems would have about n=2000 but only 8-12 non-zero entries in a row (or column). The computations must take account of this fact.

Let us introduce parameter d - the density of the matrix. To make our deliberations simpler, we shall assume that the non-zero terms are distributed uniformly over the matrix (in practice they are not). Thus if their number per row is c, we have

$$d = c/n \tag{168}$$

For a dense matrix, d will tend to one and the equations we shall develop, will apply for this case too.

An important factor was introduced through the examples of the SOR and SSOR-programs. When trying to parallelize SSOR in its faster form (FASSOR, where 50% of operations are saved), but according to ideas used in the ASP-version of SOR, one finds that the forward-step is similar to PAR_SOR with one exception: the updating procedure would have to be invoked only for those slaves which contain rows with indices K greater than the index of the currently corrected x_i. This is so because we update only the $\underline{z}$-vector and set $\underline{t}=-\underline{b}$. Thus after a while, when i>h, the first slave will have nothing to update, when i>2h the first 2 slaves will have nothing to update etc. and when i>n-h only a single slave, the p-th will work - all others will idle. This is again the "Haydn effect" so that the reduction ratios ρ will have to be multiplied by $\log_2 n$.

Let us first note that we will disregard completely the times for checking the convergence and base the calculation of ρ on a single sweep. Also that for purely sequential algorithms and execution, the time required for a single sweep is

$$\Omega_s = d * n^2 * \omega \tag{169}$$

where we have not counted assignments, branches etc. (this means that the actual reduction of time is greater than indicated by that ρ which will be computed; we are going to penalize ASP).

The simplest program was certainly that for the JA-method as described in 7.2.1. A sweep starts at label L where one bus-synchronization is required. Every one of the p slaves has to do n*h times the loop on K. Additionally, there are 4h assignments (counted as α's), one addition and one squaring (μ). Altogether this step requires

$$t_1 = d*n^2*h*(2\alpha+\mu) + 4h*\alpha*d*n+\alpha+\mu+\tau \tag{170}$$

Another synchronization is needed for gathering and distributing data. In this, sequential phase, we have to transfer separately the p errors (I)R, twice the h-slices of $\underline{x}$ and make p additions. Altogether

$$t_2 = \beta+p*\tau+2h*\tau*d*n+p*\alpha \tag{171}$$

The total time for a single sweep is then:

$t_p = d*n^2*h*(2\alpha+\mu)+4h*\alpha*d*n+\alpha+\mu+2\beta+(100p+2h*d*n)\tau+p*\alpha$ (172)

If we disregard $\alpha+\mu+p*\alpha$ in t_p and the $4\alpha/(n*p*\omega)$ in ρ then:

$\rho_{JA} = 1/p + [(100p+2d*n^2/p)\tau'+2\beta']/(dn^2)$ (173)

where we have defined as usually $\tau'=\tau/\omega$ and $\beta'=\beta/\omega$.

The reduction of time consists of two parts: the optimal reduction 1/p and deterioration due to bus-transfer (τ') and synchronization (β'). This second part will heavily depend on the density d of A because no matter how few elements in a row, synchronization must be done for it.

We may write $\rho_J = 1/p + k_{JA}*n/d$ (174)

For dense matrices d approaches 1 and

$\rho_{JA} = 1/p + 2\tau'/p + 2\beta'/n^2$ (175)

so that the interference is rather small (or negligible for large n). For extremely sparse matrices (d<<1) we have:

$\rho_{JA} = 1/p + 2(50p*\tau'+\beta')/(d*n^2)$ (176)

Since d*n=c, the number of non-zero elements of a row, $d*n^2=c*n$ may be such as to make the second part of consequence.

One conclusion we may draw here is that we do not have to count every addition or multiplication; only those inside loops really count.

We had two ASP-programs for the SOR-method. Both algorithms require about $n^2*d*\omega/p$ for actual computation, $n*\beta$ synchronizations and $2n*\tau$ transfers and $(\mu+2\alpha)$ operations per sweep. The effective reduction of time is therefore

$\rho_s = 1/p + k_S/d*n$ where $k_S = \beta'+2\tau'+(\mu+2\alpha)/\omega$ (177)

It is obvious that SOR is not as efficiently programmed as was the JA method. It is also more sensitive to changes in density d.

For the SJ-method we have

$\rho_{SJ} = 4((1/p-1/(4p^2))+(0.5\beta'+\tau'+0.5(\mu+2\alpha)/\omega))/3$ (178)

Two remarks to this ρ:

- When computing it, the time of one SJ-sweep was divided by t_S (the time of the sequential sweep). Thus we should yet divide by 2 (but also by d).
- The Haydn effect is pronounced in this method, so its ρ reflects the worst-case time in which all slaves wait for one.

We have given ρ for the JA,S and SJ-methods; the reader is invited to compute it for the SSOR method.

All three reduction ratio's were functions of α,μ,τ,β,p,n and d. If we assume α,μ,τ and β as 1.36, 5.44, 0.04, 13.6 respectively (which are those of one well known minicomputer) and compute the ρ's for a Mopps with p=10 working on a network of n=1000 elements, we find that in addition to the optimal value of ρ=0.1 we have Δ's as in Table 2.

It can clearly be seen that with increasing sparsity the reduction ratios deteriorate and speed advantages gained by ASP may be entirely nullified. For d=0.01

Table 2: Comparison

d	1	0.5	0.2	0.1	0.05	0.02	0.01
Δ_{JA}	0.1186	0.1188	0.1206	0.1275	0.1374	0.1671	0.2162
Δ_S	0.0321	0.0642	0.0161	0.0321	0.0642	0.1606	0.3212
Δ_{SJ}	0.0363	0.0692	0.0498	0.0626	0.0919	0.1798	0.3260

the increase completely overshadows the optimal ratio of 0.1. The conclusion is that: These methods should be used only for relatively dense matrices. Sparse matrices are better solved by the conjugate gradient method.

Turning now to the higher d's we observe that the SOR method seems to be the better one.It is not, since we should yet divide the numbers for the SJ-method by 2. Even better results shows the SSOR method. The next conclusion is then: For relatively dense matrices, the SSOR and SJ-methods are best.

Applicability and Consistency

In the Gauss-Seidel or Jacobi methods, the original matrix $\underline{A}$ may be decomposed according to Figures 4,5 as

$$\underline{A}=\underline{A}_1+\underline{A}_2 \quad (179)$$

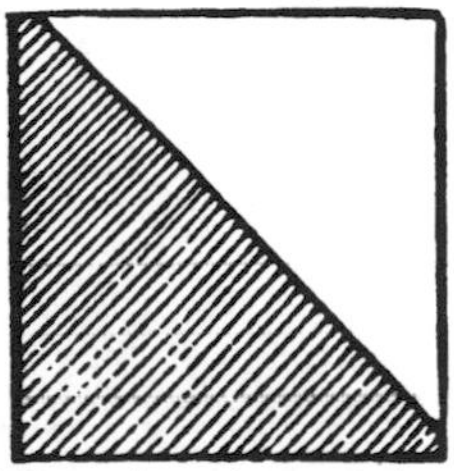

Fig. 4: $\underline{A}_1$ and $\underline{A}_2$ of the J-method.

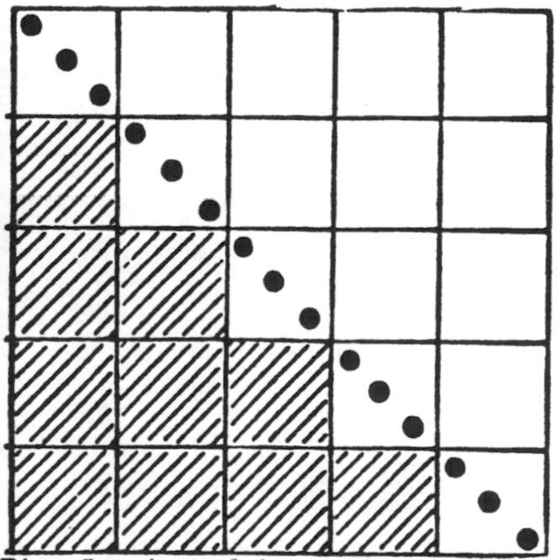

Fig. 5: $\underline{A}_1$ and $\underline{A}_2$ of the GS-Method.

$\underline{A}_1$ corresponds to the shaded area and $\underline{A}_2$ to the unshaded submatrix (Figs. 4, 5) $\underline{A}\ \underline{x} = \underline{b}$ may next be rewritten as $\underline{A}_1\underline{x}^{(k+1)}+\underline{A}_2\underline{x}^{(k)}=\underline{b}$

or $$\underline{x}^{(k+1)} = -(\underline{A}_1^{-1}*\underline{A}_2)\underline{x}^{(k)}+\underline{A}_1^{-1}*\underline{b} \quad (180)$$

where $-(\underline{A}_1^{-1}*\underline{A}_2)$ is the iteration matrix $\underline{I}$ mentioned earlier. (180) requires that $\underline{A}_1$ be nonsingular. In the two methods discussed here

$$\det(\underline{A}_1) = \prod a_{ii};\ i\prod = 1,\ldots,n \quad (181)$$

and therefore the applicability condition of $\underline{A}^{-1}$ is that all diagonal terms of $\underline{A}$ be non-zero.

In the SJ-method, the iteration matrix $\underline{I}_{SJ}$ is a product of $\underline{I}_S$ and $\underline{I}_{JA}$. The same condition is therefore required for the SJ-method as well.

An iterative method is said to be consistent if the limit $\underline{x}$ to which $\underline{x}^{(k)}$ converges, satisfies $\underline{A}\ \underline{x} = \underline{b}$.

For any method for which (179) applies, we replace $\underline{x}^{(k+1)}$ and $\underline{x}^{(k)}$ by their limit-value $\underline{x}$ to obtain

$$\underline{x} = -\underline{A}_1^{-1}*\underline{A}_2*\underline{x} + \underline{A}_1^{-1}*\underline{b} \quad (182)$$

Multiplying by $\underline{A}_1$ and rearranging terms yields

$$(\underline{A}_1+\underline{A}_2)\underline{x} = \underline{b} \quad \text{or} \quad \underline{A}*\underline{x} = \underline{b} \quad (183)$$

which proves consistency of these methods.

It can be verified that the SJ, SSOR or for that matter any method which consists of applying two iterative consistent methods alternately, is also consistent.

Convergence

The SJ-method is composed of an S followed by a JA-sweep. It may easily be shown that if the S and JA-methods converge, then SJ converges too. This follows from

$$||\underline{I}_{SJ}|| = ||\underline{I}_S*\underline{I}_J|| < ||\underline{I}_S|| * ||\underline{I}_J|| \qquad (184)$$

The convergence of the JA and S methods were investigated in the literature [We68,Va62]. For particular types of matrices (e.g. non-negative, Stjeltjes, cyclic etc.) various sufficient conditions were derived and the relation between their speed of convergence established. In the general case, no such relationship exists (see [Va62] p. 73, bottom paragraph). It would be equally futile to try to establish such a general relationship between S, JA and SJ-methods. Except for the obvious result of (184), analysis must be confined to particular cases. Similarly, no general statements comparing convergence of two sweeps of S with a single sweep of JA will be attempted.

In the following, two examples in which the SJ methods outperforms both the JA and S-methods are given. (The SSOR method is treated in depth in the literature).

$$\begin{bmatrix} 1 & d & g \\ a & 1 & f \\ b & 0 & 1 \end{bmatrix}$$

Fig.6.

Consider the matrix of Fig. 6. The characteristic polynomials for JA, S and SJ iteration matrices are respectively

$$P_{JA}(\lambda)=\lambda^3-v*\lambda+w,\ P_S(\lambda)=\lambda(\lambda^2+v*\lambda+w),\ P_{SJ}(\lambda)=\lambda^2(\lambda-(v-w)) \qquad (185)$$

$$\text{where } v=a*d+b*g,\ w=b*d*f,\ \det(\underline{A})=w-v+1 \qquad (186)$$

(a) As a first example, set b=2, d=f=1, a=0 and g=1. Thus w=2 and the following relationships exist for the spectral radii:

$$r(\underline{I}_{JA})>1,\ r(\underline{I}_S)>1,\ r(\underline{I}_{SJ})=0 \qquad (187)$$

Hence, the JA and S-methods diverge, whereas the SJ-methods converges (in three iterations because $\underline{I}_{SJ}$ is nilpotent). Similar examples may be constructed using other values of matrix elements; more specifically, if $\underline{b}$ is made arbitrarily large, then the JA and S methods diverge arbitrarily fast, while the SJ-method still converges.

(b) Set a=b=d=1, g=-1 and f=1/4 The spectral radii are now

$$r(\underline{I}_J) = (1/4)^{1/3} = 0.63;\ r(\underline{I}_S) = 0.5;\ r(\underline{I}_{SJ}) = 0.25 \qquad (188)$$

It is evident that all three methods converge and in this particular example the SJ-method converges twice as fast as the S-method. (Double S-iteration yields iteration matrix $\underline{I}_{SS}=\underline{I}_S\underline{I}_S$ with $r(\underline{I}_{SS})=0.25$ too). It is thus seen that in this case too the SJ-algorithm is superior to two Seidel iterations because fewer operations are required.

The discussion of the ratios ρ should not let us forget that the time in which a problem is solved depends both on its ρ and convergence of the algorithm. Thus, when suggesting an algorithm as a solution for a particular set of linear equations on ASP, not only its ρ but also the convergence properties of this method should be taken into account.

7.4 OTHER IMPLEMENTATIONS AND METHODS

Aims: To introduce tridiagonal sets and show that previously discussed methods are not efficient in solving them. To list results of running the JA, S and SSOR programs on SMS201, of running JA on STARAN and S on Illiac.

Iterative methods of solving $\underline{A}\ \underline{x} = \underline{b}$ are normally advocated only for sparse sets. The reasons are that direct methods would require too much storage, because of the size of $\underline{A}$ and the fill-in and that the convergence of iterative methods is high enough. This last is true only if the overrelaxation factor w can be calculated.

Sets of linear equations often derive from discrete approximations to partial (elliptic) differential equations. These systems are tridiagonal. There is a large body of knowledge concerning tridiagonal sets ([SB],[Yo 70]). We are going only to touch upon the topics which directly serve our aims.

Iterative solution of partial differential equations effects a cyclic "sweep" over mesh-points of a superimposed grid, during which pointwise approximations are refined. Numerically, this means solving $\underline{T}\ \underline{x} = \underline{b}$.

The structure of the matrix is such that each "row" has three nonzero blocks (Fig. 7), with $\underline{B}'$ and $\underline{B}''$ having coefficients different from B because they reflect boundary conditions. If the points are numbered so that two "colors" alternate ("black and red" numbering), then the set of equations may be written so that $\underline{T}$ is diagonally block tridiagonal. Such matrices have "property A": A square matrix possesses it, if through permutations of both rows and columns it may be rewritten as a diagonally block tridiagonal matrix. The important fact is that for such matrices an optimal overrelaxation factor:

$$\underline{T} = -\begin{bmatrix} \underline{B}' & \underline{U} & & & \\ \underline{U} & \underline{B} & \underline{U} & & \\ & \underline{U} & \underline{B} & \underline{U} & \\ & 0 & & & \\ & & \underline{U} & \underline{B} & \underline{U} \\ & & & \underline{U} & \underline{B}'' \end{bmatrix}$$

$$\underline{B} = \begin{bmatrix} -4 & 1 & & & \\ 1 & -4 & 1 & 0 & \\ & & & & \\ & 0 & 1 & -4 & 1 \\ & & & 1 & -4 \end{bmatrix}$$

Fig. 7: Tridiagonal Set

$$w_{opt} = 2/(1+\sqrt{1-\lambda_1^2});\ \lambda_1^2 \cong \underline{r}^{(i+1)}/\underline{r}^{(i)} \tag{189}$$

may be computed using as approximate value of λ_1^2 the ratio of two consecutive residuals (For λ_1^2, the Raleigh quotient should be taken).

Even with w_{opt} known, a SSOR-solution of $\underline{T}\ \underline{x} = \underline{z}$ will be rather inefficient on ASP as can be seen from the following. Suppose that each memory holds a horizontal slice of h=n/p equations:

$$c_j x_{j-1}^{(i)} + a_j x_j^{(i)} + b x_{j+1}^{(i-1)} = z_j;\quad j=2,\dots,n \tag{190}$$

where blocks degenerated to single elements, (i) is the sweep number. Slave k in whose memory row-j is stored, calculates $x_j^{(i)}$, transfers it to the master which broadcasts it to all slaves for updating of all sums (of $a_{r,s}x_s$). In the general, (not tridiagonal) sparse case the other slaves ($\neq$k) would do very little work so that most of the work would be done in S-instead of in P-steps. In the tridiagonal case, no work at all would be done outside slave-k, so that there would be no speed-up at all. We will improve this in Chapter 8.

We now turn to the method of conjugate gradients. Since the elements of $\underline{T}$ do not have to be really stored, the product $\underline{T}\ \underline{w} = \underline{s}$ can be calculated whenever needed and - for ASP-does not have to be collected by the master and redistributed to the slaves. Additionally eigenvalues and w_{opt} are not required making the application of the method relatively simple. The ASP-program is therefore left as an exercise.

Iterative methods for general matrices were programmed for the SMS 201. At first, a modification of the JA-program and then the S-method was run (in summer 1978, by Dr. Nagel, Prof. L. Richter and myself). It is important to note at the outset that the results will not be very encouraging because of the way synchronization and data transfer is effected on SMS201, namely by its master operating system (calls on its interrupt handling routines). Thus, β=770μs, τ = 370μs, for broadcast from master and τ = 280μs from one slave to all others. This should be compared to 10ms for $x_i=x_i+a_{ij}x_j$ and to 3ms for $x_i=-t_i-z_i$, both for i=1,2,...,128 (the number of slaves). For an idea of what is achievable, one should reduce synchronization and transfer times considerably in all results given below for SMS201.

The results were worse for the Jacobi method, because of the data structure. In the program of [Na79], each slave stored only one row of $\underline{A}$ say $\underline{a}_{k.}$ (and obviously $\underline{x}$, b_k). Each slave calculates a single x_k

$$x_k^{(i+1)} = (b_k-\Sigma a_{kj}x_j^{(i)})/a_{kk};\ j\Sigma\neq k \tag{191}$$

and then broadcasts it to all other slaves (in an S-step). Each slave checks if its $|x_k^{(i+1)} - x_k^{(i)}|<\varepsilon$ and sets a flag accordingly. The master checks all flags and stops the computation if all were set.

It is easily seen that the P-step is here very short compared to the S-steps, thus disobeying the "parallelization principle". It is therefore not surprising that it required more time than a parallel elimination procedure programmed and run on the same problems. Still, the remarks were made that even this variant of the Jacobi iterative method had some advantages: simpler programming, faster execution for lower accuracy and for nonlinear equations. The last results from the idea of starting each iteration with the results of a previously computed solution to the linearized problem (which was solved with lower accuracy).

The S-program was run for various matrices (dimension n) and the times t_s, t_e, t_p for sequential (and synchronization), exchange of data and parallel steps were measured. The hardware utilization was calculated according to

$$v = t_p*(t_s+t_e+t_p)^{-1} = t_p/t \tag{192}$$

Time t_s was constant for a given n and is shown in Table 3, other times and v in Table 4. Since theoretically the times (for τ,β etc. as above) are:

$$t_s=(n+3)0.77+3\cdot 0.37=(3.4+0.77n)\text{ms};t_e=(0.067p+0.314n)\text{ms};t_p=20n^2/p+3(2+1/p)n \tag{193}$$

we can also compare the calculated and measured (total) times (Figure 8).

n	15	30	60	128	256	512	1024
t_s	14.95	26.50	49.6	101.96	200.52	397.64	791.88

Table 3: Sequential-synchronization times

$$t' = 0.067p + (20n^2 + 3n)/p \qquad (194)$$

is the part of time dependent on the number of slaves p. The increase in the ex-

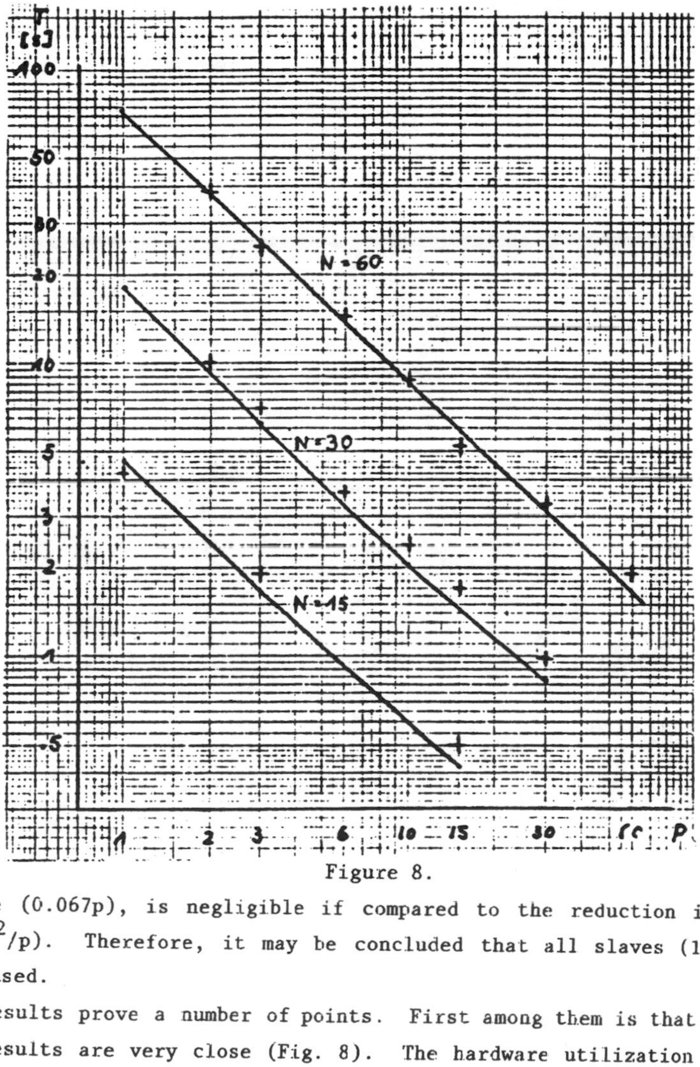

Figure 8.

change-time (0.067p), is negligible if compared to the reduction in the parallel time ($\cong 20n^2/p$). Therefore, it may be concluded that all slaves (128 in SMS 201) should be used.

The results prove a number of points. First among them is that calculated and measured results are very close (Fig. 8). The hardware utilization factor is over 95%, and this disproves the notion that the bus or the exchange of information are in any way the bottlenecks of the program. This is the more encouraging, since in this case of the Gauss-Seidel method, the parallel steps are extremely short and data is exchanged much more often (n times more often) than in the Jacobi method (as it should be programmed).

n	T_{ex}	T_A	T	p	v_2
n=5	4.777	4635.000	4654.727	1	0.996
	4.911	1605.000	1624.861	3	0.988
	5.045	999.000	1018.995	5	0.980
	5.715	393.000	413.665	15	0.950
n=30	9.487	18270.000	18305.990	1	0.998
	9.554	9225.000	9261.055	2	0.996
	9.621	6210.000	6246.121	3	0.994
	9.755	3798.000	3834.255	5	0.991
	9.822	3195.000	3231.322	6	0.989
	10.090	1989.000	2025.590	10	0.982
	10.425	1386.000	1422.925	15	0.974
	11.430	783.000	820.930	30	0.954
n=60	18.907	72540.000	72608.500	1	0.999
	18.974	36450.000	36518.570	2	0.998
	19.041	24420.000	24488.640	3	0.997
	19.108	18405.000	18473.710	4	0.996
	19.175	14796.000	14864.770	5	0.995
	19.242	12390.000	12458.840	6	0.994
	19.510	7578.000	7647.109	10	0.991
	19.644	6375.000	6444.242	12	0.989
	19.845	5172.000	5241.445	15	0.987
	20.180	3969.000	4038.780	20	0.983
	20.850	2766.000	2836.450	30	0.975
	22.860	1563.000	1635.460	60	0.956
n=128	40.259	328832.000	328974.200	1	1.000
	40.326	164800.000	164942.300	2	0.999
	40.460	82784.000	82926.440	4	0.998
	40.728	41776.000	41918.690	8	0.997
	41.264	21272.000	21415.220	16	0.993
	42.336	11020.000	11164.300	32	0.987
	44.480	5894.000	6040.441	64	0.976
	48.768	3331.000	3481.728	128	0.957
n=256	80.451	1313024.000	1313305.000	1	1.000
	80.518	657280.000	657561.100	2	1.000
	80.652	329408.000	329689.200	4	0.999
	80.920	165472.000	165753.400	8	0.998
	81.456	83504.000	83786.000	16	0.997
	82.528	42520.000	42803.050	32	0.993
	84.672	22028.000	22313.190	64	0.987
	88.960	11782.000	12071.480	128	0.976
	97.536	6659.000	6957.055	256	0.957
n=512	160.835	5247488.000	5248046.000	1	1.000
	160.902	2625280.000	2625839.000	2	1.000
	161.036	1314176.000	1314735.000	4	1.000
	161.304	658624.000	659182.900	8	0.999
	161.840	330848.000	331407.500	16	0.998
	162.912	166960.000	167520.600	32	0.997
	165.056	85016.000	85578.690	64	0.993
	169.344	44044.000	44610.980	128	0.987
	177.920	23558.000	24133.560	256	0.976
	195.072	13315.000	13907.710	512	0.957
n=1024	321.603	20980740.000	20981860.000	1	1.000
	321.670	10493440.000	10494550.000	2	1.000
	321.804	5249792.000	5250906.000	4	1.000
	322.072	2627968.000	2629082.000	8	1.000
	322.608	1317056.000	1318170.000	16	0.999
	323.680	661600.000	662715.600	32	0.998
	325.824	333872.000	334989.700	64	0.997
	330.112	170008.000	171130.000	128	0.993
	338.688	88076.000	89206.560	256	0.987
	355.840	47110.000	48257.720	512	0.976
	390.144	26627.000	27809.020	1024	0.957

Table 4: Execution times and utilization

The time to set up vector $\underline{t}$ was also measured and found to be rather unequal for various slaves. Since this time is a considerable part of the GJ-method, a possible improvement might be achieved by making the slice width h unequal; this could equalize the initialization time, but then again, it is better to use SSOR, for which the above problem will not exist.

Gilmore has programmed [Gi74] the Jacobi algorithm for STARAN and extended it to other methods, e.g. overrelaxation. The equation of Jacobi's are (for $\underline{A}=\underline{D}-\underline{E}-\underline{F}$):

$$\underline{x} = \underline{D}^{-1} (\underline{E} + \underline{F})\, \underline{x} + \underline{D}^{-1}\, \underline{b} \qquad \text{or} \qquad \underline{x}^{(i+1)} = \underline{I}\, \underline{x}^{(i)} + \underline{c} \tag{195}$$

Exactly as in SOR, we may view vector $\underline{x}^{(i+1)}$ of (195) as an estimate of $\underline{x}$, call it $\bar{\underline{x}}$ and specify $\underline{x}^{(i+1)}$ as a weighted average of $\bar{\underline{x}}$ and $\underline{x}$ i.e.

$$\underline{x}^{(i+1)} = w\, \bar{\underline{x}}^{(i+1)} + (1-w)\, \underline{x}^{(i)} \quad \text{or} \quad \underline{x}^{(i+1)} = [(1 - w)\, \underline{U} + w\underline{D}^{-1}(\underline{E}+\underline{F})]\underline{x}^{(i)} + w\underline{c} \tag{196}$$

Evidently, for w=1 this "parallel relaxation" program reduces to the J-method. Its two parts can easily be executed in parallel on ASP.

For implementation on STARAN, field operations will be used. They can be written (with ⊛ standing for +,-,* or /) as

$$(Fn_1)_i \circledast (Fn_2)_j \rightarrow (Fn_3)_k \tag{197}$$

with n_1,n_2,n_3 being the number of fields, i,j and k equal or not to each other. With 7 fields per word, n=9, p=3, h=3 we would store initially (C_1,C_2,C_3) in F1, the three rows of $\underline{I}$ in F2 and a complete vector $\underline{x}$ in F3. This initial assignment (and subsequent additions) are shown in Table 5 in its first three columns. In step 1:

F1	F2	F3	F4	F5	F6	F7	Word
C_1	I_{11}	x_1	$I_{11}x_1$	Σ_1	Σ_1+C_1	Δx_1	1
	I_{12}	x_2	$I_{12}x_2$				2
	I_{13}	x_3	$I_{13}x_3$				3
C_2	I_{21}	x_1	$I_{21}x_1$	Σ_2	Σ_2+C_2	Δx_3	4
	I_{22}	x_2	$I_{22}x_2$				5
	I_{23}	x_3	$I_{23}x_3$				6
C_3	I_{31}	x_1	$I_{31}x_1$	Σ_3	Σ_3+C_3	Δx_3	7
	I_{32}	x_2	$I_{32}x_2$				8
	I_{33}	x_3	$I_{33}x_3$				9

Table 5: Jacobi Method on STARAN

$$(F2)_i \cdot (F3)_i \rightarrow (F4)_i \tag{198}$$

an "in-word" multiplication. In step 2 these products are summed, so that for instance:

$$\Sigma_2 = I_{21}x_1 + I_{22}x_2 + I_{23}x_3 = \Sigma I_{jk}x_k \tag{199}$$

We have to assume that, in practice, the slices will be much larger and all products $I_{jk}x_k$ can be added as in Apps. Thus for $h = 2^m$, we do m/2, m/4,...,2 and a single addition - altogether for $h\log_2 h$ additions in time m (since in parallel). In step 3, C_i is added to each Σ_i, for t=α and for the new x_i. In step 4, the new x_i's are compared to the old ones and the absolute value of their difference Δx_i is entered into F7. In step 5, Δx_i's are compared to some ε and the response flip-flop set accordingly. If a new sweep is needed, each new x_i has to be transferred from F6 of a word u to F3 of words u+3,u+6,.. (obviously, modulo 9).

Let us compute ρ. For the initial assignment of data, all n^2 values I_{jk} have to be transferred and n values x_i have to be broadcast; the time is $(n^2+n)\tau$. In step 1 all h·p=n multiplications can be done at once, so t=μ. For the Σ's, time of

$\alpha \cdot \log_2 h$, for steps 3, 4 and 5 only single α are required, but for starting a new sweep, n values are to be transferred - each to (p-1) words into F3. This is best done by broadcast, so that only $n\tau$ transfers are needed. A synchronization is needed to start it. Altogether:

$$t_p = \mu+(3+\log_2 h)\alpha + (n^2+2n)\tau + \beta; \; t_s=n^2\mu+n^2\alpha=n^2\omega \qquad (200)$$

Note that only a single multiplication μ instead of $n^2\mu$ and only $\log_2 h = \log_2 n - \log_2 p \cong \log_2 n$ additions α instead of $n^2 d$ are required. Were it not for $(n^2+2n)\tau+\beta$, we would be inclined to say that STARAN achieves the logarithmic speed bound of Apps. Unfortunately, we must reduce the speedup on account of the fact that in STARAN, α and μ are much higher than in standard computers. Storage space was also wasted: if each field is considered a word, then $7n^2$ words are needed, as compared to n^2 in a sequential computer. Parallel relaxation is different from the Jacobi method in its iteration matrix-but we had not accounted for the work of setting it up anyway. The actual times obtained are shown in Table 6.

TABLE 6. EXECUTION TIME IN MILLISECONDS FOR ONE ITERATION

	Time per iteration, msec		
	System size		
Computer configuration	5 x 5	25 x 25	50 x 50
C1 (μ = 21.5 μsec)	1.0	22.0	85.0
C2 (μ = 4.5 μsec)	0.3	6.0	22.0
Standard AP 20 bit fixed point	0.6	1.1	1.6
Standard AP 32 bit floating pt.	3.0	4.3	5.2
Optional AP 32 bit floating pt.	0.4	0.9	1.4

It is interesting to note that a relation was found in [Gi74] between the eigen values of the Jacobi λ_j and parallel relaxation λ_ρ. It is

$$\lambda_p=1-w(1-\lambda_j) \qquad (201)$$

Based on it:

$$w_{opt}=21(2-\lambda_{j,1}-\lambda_{j,n}) \qquad (202)$$

where $\lambda_{J,i}$ is the i-th (ordered) eigenvalue of the Jacobi iteration matrix.

Iterative methods are used for tridiagonal sets more than for other sparse systems of equations. If N(i),E(i),W(i) and S(i) denote the "north", "east", "west", and "south", neighbours of any point at iteration i respectively, then the Jacobi method would substitute for x(i+1) according to a "5-point" formula:

$$x(i+1) = [N(i) + E(i) + W(i) + S(i)]/4 \qquad (203)$$

A disadvantage of this method is that two copies have to be stored for each point: the present and next value (of potential). We compute <u>all</u> x(i+1) before throwing away all x(i). This, and the better convergence, lead to the use of the Gauss-Seidel method in Illiac [St73] in which the points of a mesh are scanned from left to right and the rows from top to bottom. Thus:

$$x(i+1) = [N(i) + E(i) + W(i+1) + S(i+1)]/4 \qquad (204)$$

and updated data for W and S are used after being computed. Since they may be overwritten, only one copy has to be stored for x-values and the convergence is better than in the Jacobi method. For Illiac other methods are suggested, as per quote:

"In a naive implementation of the algorithm for a parallel computer, say the ILLIAC IV, it is reasonable to update the points of an entire row at a time, and to scan the rows of the mesh say from bottom to top. In this case, the iteration formula is:

$$x(i) = [N(i+1) + E(i-1) + W(i-1) + S(i)]/4 \qquad (205)$$

Note that only the southern neighbor contributes new data in this formula, because only the southern neighbor has been updated before x is updated. Thus (205) has slower convergence than (204). In fact, it requires roughly 50% more iterations. The programmer may be quite surprised that his ILLIAC IV program runs somewhat slower than expected. The iteration scheme appears to be ideally suited to ILLIAC IV because every processor has something to do. Yet, even when N processors are kept busy throughout the calculation, the speed-up is roughly (2/3) N instead of N, as expected. Table 7 shows typical iteration counts for various methods. Fortunately, it is possible to achieve the Gauss-Seidel convergence rate on a parallel processor. Instead of scanning the mesh by rows, we scan the mesh by diagonals. In particular, we do two diagonals at a time, and choose the diagonals to be N diagonals apart on an N x N mesh". "The number of points updated in each iteration will then be constant and equal to N. In this scheme, it is easy to show that the iteration formula is (204) so that the rate of convergence is the same as the serial algorithm."

Table 7. Numerical Solution of Poisson's Equation on a Square

Mesh Size	Algorithm	Iterations
8 x 8	Jacobi	378
8 x 8	Line parallel	288
8 x 8	Gauss-Seidel	194
16 x 16	Jacobi	282
16 x 16	Line parallel	222
16 x 16	Gauss-Seidel	159

Let us now return to STARAN. If the normal ordering (Fig. 9) is called "typewriter" ordering, that of Fig. 10 is called "checkerboard" in [Gi74] and "red-black" in other references [54].Since in the typewriter ordering the N,W-values are updated but S,E are not, the iteration can be viewed as using half-updated values all the time. When the "black points (1,2,3,4,5) are updated, we cannot use the "red" points (6,7,8,9) since they have not been neighbors. So we use no updated points half the time. By contrast, on the second half of the sweep (points 6 through 9), we necessarily use nothing but new estimates in our updating procedure and we use all updated points half the time. This is because we labeled points as red and black in such a fashion that red points had only black neighbors and conversely. This potential of the grid for a checkerboard ordering corresponds to Property (A) in the coefficient matrix of the related system of linear equations. The interesting thing for us here is that use of the typewriter and checkerboard orderings for

GS (and SOR) give equivalent results in terms of convergence rate. In other words using half updated points all the time is equivalent to using all updated points half the time.

Note that for each half-sweep (red or black) the arithmetic is the same as in the Jacobi method i.e. inherently parallel. Thus, instead of using the Jacobi method or complicate the Gauss-Seidel process, it seems better to split the sweep into red and black halves and use simple, inherently parallel programs.

x	x	x	x	x
x	1	2	3	x
x	4	5	6	x
x	7	8	9	x
x	x	x	x	x

Figure 9: Normal Ordering

x	x	x	x	x
x	1	6	2	x
x	7	3	8	x
x	4	9	5	x
x	x	x	x	x

Fig. 10: Red-black Ordering

PE_{k-1}		PE_k		PE_{k+1}	
r	b	r	b	r	b
b	r	b	r	b	r
r	b	r	b	r	b
b	r	b	r	b	r

b=black cell; r=red cell
Figure 11: Ordering of cells

Normally, the Dirichlet problem is written as follows:

$$U_{ij}-L_{ij}U_{i-1,j}-R_{ij}u_{i+1,j}-B_{ij}U_{i,j-1}-T_{ij}U_{ij+1} = G_{i,j} \tag{206}$$

where L,R,B and T are constants (not necessarily 1 and 4), and the unknowns u_{oj} are known from the boundary conditions. In a "red-black" SOR method, each iteration consists of a "red" and a "black" half step. In the red step, all "red" iterates (i+j even) are updated according to

$$u_{ij}^{n+1} = (1-w)\, u_{ij}^{n}+w(L_{ij}U_{i-1,j}^{n}+R_{ij}U_{i+1j}^{n}+B_{ij}U_{ij-1}^{n}+T_{ij}U_{ij+1}+G_{ij}) \tag{207}$$

and in the subsequent black step all "black" iterates (i+j odd) are updated through

$$u_{i,j}^{(n+1)} = (1-w)u_{ij}^{n} + w(L_{ij}u_{i-1j}^{n+1} + R_{ij}u_{i+1j}^{n+1} + B_{ij}u_{ij-1}^{n+1} + T_{ij}u_{ij+1}^{n+1} + G_{ij}) \tag{208}$$

This method must not be confused with the Jacobi overrelaxation method, where (207) is used for the black iterates as well and which is by far too slow to be competitive with the optimally overrelaxed red-black SOR-method [Sch 75].

With regard to the execution of the red-black SOR-method on an array computer, (See Fig. 11) we firstly remark that due to the underlying mesh, all data relevant to the computation can be arranged in a two dimensional array of "cells" c_{ij}, such that cell c_{ij} contains just the data associated with mesh point (ih,jh). Secondly, as a consequence of the five point formula and the red-black ordering, all red iterates are decoupled and so are the black. Hence all red (black) iterated can be updated simultaneously. Thirdly, the form of the formulas (207) and (208) is the same for all i,j. Finally, the data needed for updating any iterate are contained either in its associated cell or its neighbouring cells.

Now assume that the array of data has been stored into the array of PEs as indicated in Fig. 11. Then it is clear from the above remarks that a red half step can run on an array computer by first updating the top row of red iterates, then the second row of red iterates, and so on. The black step runs analogously. Other algorithms were mentioned in [Tr 73].

8. SPECIAL APPROACHES FOR SOLVING Ax=b ON ASP

Introduction

Up to this point only one group of methods specially adapted for ASP was introduced. It was that of "vertical programming" and the alternating methods which were derived from it. All the other ASP-methods were based on rescheduling known algorithms.

In this chapter additional general approaches as to how best to program linear algebraic problems for ASP are developed. One is based on the realization that the bus synchronization time β is responsible for speedup reduction more than anything else. If blocks instead of single elements are processed, the number of β's may be reduced by these "block methods". Another approach is based on "tearing": Suppose we decompose $\underline{A}\ \underline{x} = \underline{b}$ into m^2 subproblems, each of size (n/m) x (n/m) then, instead of $\Omega(n^3)$ we would need only $\Omega(n^3/m^3)$ - an enormous reduction. The problem is only, how to decompose the original problem and how to "paste" the partial results. A good example for this approach is given in a later chapter.

The application of these approaches to the direct and iterative solution of sparse sets leads to "parallel, optimally ordered factorization" (poof) and block-iterative methods of Sections 3 and 4 respectively. For the special case of tridiagonal sets, "chasing, tearing and shooting" is given some preliminary thought in Section 5.

8.1 REORDERING AND TEARING

Aims: To discuss the BD, BT and BBD decompositions as representative of reordering methods. To supply a different justification for tearing than in Chapter 5 and show the connection between the two.

This type of method is widely known and has been discussed extensively. The point we will make is that if they can be applied to any parallel system, they can be implemented even more efficiently on ASP.

While discussing factorization we noted that its usefulness for sparse systems (as compared to elimination) rests on the fact that whereas $\underline{A}^{-1}$ is full even if $\underline{A}$ is very sparse, the factorization

$$\underline{A} = \underline{L}\ \underline{R} \qquad (1)$$

or the F-table retain a certain degree of sparsity. As a matter of fact, it is the "reordering policy" which is the heart of the algorithm and a key to its success (or failure). The reordering was done so as to minimize the fill-in and the number of operations, but reordering could also be done for the sake of parallelization.

The idea behind all reordering schemes is to rearrange the rows and columns of a matrix $\underline{A}$, thus transforming it into a matrix $\hat{\underline{A}}$, whose particular form lends itself to efficient parallelization. Since reordering the rows of $\underline{A}$ has no effect on the solution vector $\underline{x}$ (disregarding round-off errors) and reordering the columns results simply in permuting the components of $\underline{x}$, the solution of the original system $\underline{A}\cdot\underline{x} = \underline{b}$ is readily obtained from the reordered system $\hat{\underline{A}}\ \hat{\underline{x}} = \hat{\underline{b}}$. Precisely speaking, if $\underline{P}$ is the permutation matrix acting on the rows, and $\underline{Q}$ is the permutation matrix of the columns, then the transformed system is

$$\hat{\underline{A}}\ \hat{\underline{x}} = (\underline{PAQ})\ \underline{x} = \underline{Pb} = \hat{\underline{b}} \tag{2}$$

and it is easily seen that $\underline{Qx}$ solves the original system

$$\underline{A}\ \underline{x} = \underline{b} \tag{3}$$

The most desirable form of $\underline{A}$ is the block-diagonal (BD) form. The matrix consists of p square submatrices $\underline{D}_1, \underline{D}_2,\ldots,\underline{D}_p$ of dimensions $\ell_1,\ell_2,\ldots,\ell_p$ respectively, situated along the main diagonal, as shown in Fig. 1.

The parallel solution of BD-systems is obvious. If the first ℓ_1 rows are assigned to slave 1, the next ℓ_2 rows to slave 2 etc., then the decomposed solution vector $\underline{x}_k$ may be obtained in parallel so that slave-k solves the subsystem:

$$\underline{D}_k * \hat{\underline{x}}_k = \hat{\underline{b}}_k \tag{4}$$

independently of all others. Thus no interprocessor communication is necessary and the solution is obtained in one parallel step.

$$\begin{matrix}\ell_1\\ \ell_2\\ \vdots\\ \ell_p\end{matrix}\begin{bmatrix}\underline{D}_1 & & \\ & \underline{D}_2 & \\ & & \ddots \\ & & & \underline{D}_p\end{bmatrix} * \begin{bmatrix}\hat{\underline{x}}_1\\ \hat{\underline{x}}_2\\ \vdots\\ \hat{\underline{x}}_p\end{bmatrix} = \begin{bmatrix}\hat{\underline{b}}_1\\ \hat{\underline{b}}_2\\ \vdots\\ \hat{\underline{b}}_p\end{bmatrix}$$

Fig. 1: Block diagonal decomposition

$$\begin{bmatrix}\underline{D}_1 & & & & \\ \underline{A}_{21} & \underline{D}_2 & & & \\ \underline{A}_{31} & \underline{A}_{32} & \underline{D}_3 & & \\ \sim\sim\sim & & & \ddots & \\ \underline{A}_{p1} & \underline{A}_{p2} & & & \underline{D}_p\end{bmatrix} * \begin{bmatrix}\hat{\underline{x}}_1\\ \hat{\underline{x}}_2\\ \hat{\underline{x}}_3\\ \vdots\\ \hat{\underline{x}}_p\end{bmatrix} = \begin{bmatrix}\hat{\underline{b}}_1\\ \hat{\underline{b}}_2\\ \hat{\underline{b}}_3\\ \vdots\\ \hat{\underline{b}}_p\end{bmatrix}$$

Fig. 2: Block-triangular decomposition

A slightly more general form of $\underline{A}$ is the Block Triangular (BT) form. It differs from the BD form in that the blocks below the diagonal are not zero (Fig. 2).

With the assignment of rows as in BD decomposition, the process proceeds as follows. All slaves, working in parallel, invert (or decompose into the $\underline{LR}$ form) their respective diagonal blocks $\underline{D}_i$. Then, slave 1 solves $\underline{D}_1 \cdot \hat{\underline{x}}_1 = \hat{\underline{b}}_1$ and transmits $\hat{\underline{x}}_1$ to all other slaves; with the transfer completed, the i'th slave forms the partial sum $\underline{A}_{i1} \cdot \hat{\underline{x}}_1$. At this point, slave 2 solves $\underline{D}_2\hat{\underline{x}}_2 = \hat{\underline{b}}_2 - \underline{A}_{21}\hat{\underline{x}}_1$ and $\hat{\underline{x}}_2$ is transmitted to slaves 3,4,...,p etc. The process is one of block elimination.

Two obvious questions suggest themselves at this point. The first is a question of existence: Given a sparse matrix $\underline{A}$, does a "good" BT ordering exist? By a "good" ordering we mean one which has enough diagonal blocks $\underline{D}_i$ to assign to all processors and whose blocks have reasonable sizes. The second question is: if such an ordering exists, how do we find it efficiently? The second question is answered by the depth-first search algorithm of Tarjan [Ta 72]; an adaptation of this algorithm to sparse matrix decomposition is given in [GG 76]. Unfortunately, the answer to the first question is that a BT ordering is unique (up to reordering of the blocks and reordering of rows and columns within a block). Therefore, the solver has no freedom in choosing the blocks and their sizes. It often happens that a matrix A is irreducible, i.e. its BT form consists of one block only. In this case nothing is gained by BT decomposition.

Another form of decomposition, called the Bordered Block Diagonal (BBD) form, affords great freedom of choice to the solver. We shall discuss this form under the assumption that the matrix A is symmetrically structured (i.e. its nonzero elements form a symmetrical pattern). A BBD with p=5 is shown in Fig. 3.

$$\begin{bmatrix} D_1 & 0 & 0 & 0 & A_{15} \\ 0 & D_2 & 0 & 0 & A_{25} \\ 0 & 0 & D_3 & 0 & A_{35} \\ 0 & 0 & 0 & D_4 & A_{45} \\ A_{51} & A_{52} & A_{53} & A_{54} & D_5 \end{bmatrix} * \begin{bmatrix} \hat{x}_1 \\ \hat{x}_2 \\ \hat{x}_3 \\ \hat{x}_4 \\ \hat{x}_5 \end{bmatrix} = \begin{bmatrix} \hat{b}_1 \\ \hat{b}_2 \\ \hat{b}_3 \\ \hat{b}_4 \\ \hat{b}_5 \end{bmatrix}$$

Fig. 3: Bordered, block-diagonal decomposition

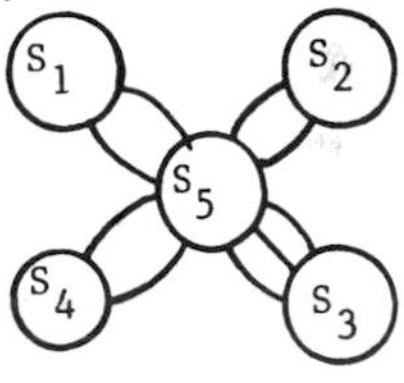

Fig. 4: The graph $G(\hat{A})$

Gaussian elimination may be performed simultaneously on blocks 1,2,3 and 4. The process is most easily described by using inversion of diagonal blocks (though LR factorization can also be used). Slave 1 diagonalizes D_1 and introduces zeroes into block A_{51}; this amounts to modifying D_5 by subtracting the matrix $B_1 = A_{51} D_1^{-1} A_{15}$ from it. The actual modification, however, is deferred to a later stage; at this point B_1 is formed and stored. None of the other blocks is affected, so at the same time slave 2 diagonalizes D_2 and forms $B_2 = A_{52}\, D_2^{-1}\, A_{25}$. When all 4 processors have completed this parallel operation, D_5 is modified by subtracting from it the sum $(B_1+B_2+B_3+B_4)$ (The summation and the subtraction may also be performed in parallel). Then D_5 is diagonalized. The resulting matrix is then upper-triangular and the solution follows by back-substitution.

Further insight into this problem may be gained when we consider $\hat{A}$ of Fig. 3 as the adjacency matrix of an undirected graph $G(\hat{A})$ (i.e. $(\hat{A})_{ij} \neq 0$ iff vertex i is connected to vertex j). Denote the set of vertices whose indices are $1,2,\ldots,\ell_1$ by S_1, those of indices $\ell_1+1,\ldots,\ell_2$ by S_2 etc. It follows from the form of A that vertices of S_1 are connected to vertices of S_1 or to vertices of S_5; similarly, vertices of S_2 are disconnected from any other vertices but those of S_5, and so on. S_5 is called a separating set, for if its vertices and their adjacent edges are removed from $G(\hat{A})$, the resulting graph is a union of 4 mutually disjoint subgraphs. The structure of $G(A)$ is depicted in Fig. 4.

The questions raised in connection with the BT form, namely, the existence of a good decomposition and of an efficient algorithm for finding it, apply to the BBD form as well. The situation in the case of BBD is the opposite of that of BT. Given a sparse graph G, there are many possible ways to choose a separating set S; if $|G|$ is small, they can be even found by inspection. However, no universally applicable and efficient algorithm for automatic generation of good decompositions

has been found. A good decomposition is characterized by a small separating set S and a large number of subsets S_i, with the variance of the set $\{|S_i|\}$ as small as possible. A good algorithm faces a difficult task, because these conditions may be conflicting.
For references, see [Du 77].

One application area in which the BBD form may be easily obtained is that of finite-difference schemes arising from the discretization of differential equations. The "networks" encountered there are two or three-dimensional regularly interconnected grids. It is then possible to find a separating set S in such a way that the separated components S_i resemble in form the parent graph. The resulting "offspring" may be decomposed again, thus giving rise to even smaller subnetworks etc. The process is called nested dissection and it leads to efficient decompositions (from the point of view of parallel processing) even if the separating sets generated during the dissection are quite large. The application of nested dissection to other problems, say electric power networks has been attempted [Er 77] but with limited success, because of the irregularity of the interconnections. The method proposed depends ultimately on the human eye to find good dissections.

Suppose we have a good decomposition of matrix $\hat{\underline{A}}$ in BBD (or BT, or BD) form with the exception of a small number of nonzero elements, which "spoil" the decomposition. The matrix $\hat{\underline{A}}$ may then be written as $\hat{\underline{A}}_1 + \underline{B}$, where $\hat{\underline{A}}_1$ is in true BBD form, and $\underline{B}$ consists of the above mentioned elements. It is therefore natural to ask, whether a solution to $(\hat{\underline{A}}_1+\underline{B}) \cdot \hat{\underline{x}} = \underline{b}$ can be obtained with few operations given $\underline{A}_1^{-1}$ ($\underline{A}_1^{-1}$ itself can be computed in parallel). This process has a simple graph interpretation. Fig. 5 shows the graph of an "almost" BBD matrix. If the edges (V_9,V_{10}) (V_2,V_4) were removed, the resulting matrix would be in a perfect BBD form. These edges are then artificially "torn", the meaning of "tearing" (or removing links) being readily perceived.

If the matrix $\underline{B}$ of the torn elements is of low rank, say r, when r < n, then it can always be expressed in the form

$$\underline{B} = \underline{V} * \underline{W}^T \tag{5}$$

where $\underline{V}$ is nxr and $\underline{W}$ is rxn. Often the matrices $\underline{V}$ and $\underline{W}$ can be derived very simply from $\underline{B}$, for instance when $\underline{B}$ has only one nonzero element b_{ij}; then $\underline{V}$ may be taken as an nx1 matrix with $V_{i,1} = 1$ and $V_{k,1} = 0$ for $k \neq i$ and $\underline{W}$ as an nx1 matrix with $W_{k,1} = \delta_{ki} b_{ij}$. Matrices $\underline{V}$, $\underline{W}$, are now vectors and (5) shows that the Sherman-Morrison equation as formulated in Chapter 5 may be applied

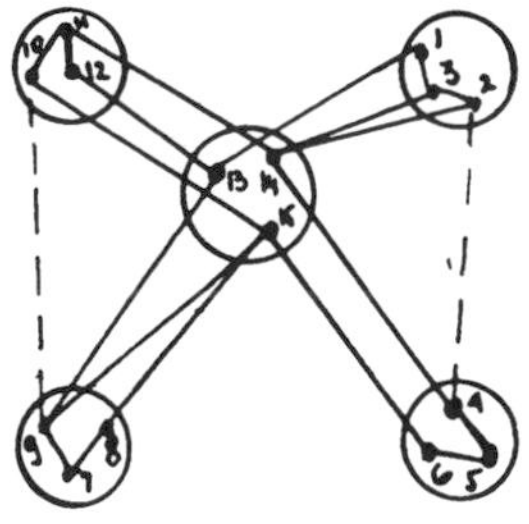

Fig. 5: The graph of an "almost BBD" matrix

$$\hat{\underline{A}}^{-1} = (\hat{\underline{A}}_1 + \underline{v}\,\underline{w}^T)^{-1} = \hat{\underline{A}}^{-1} - \hat{\underline{A}}^{-1} \cdot \underline{v}\,(\underline{U} + \underline{w}^T \hat{\underline{A}}_1^{-1} \underline{v})^{-1}\, \underline{w}^T \hat{\underline{A}}_1 \tag{6}$$

The advantage of (6) over direct inversion of $(\underline{A}_1+B)$ is that the inversion of $\underline{U} + \underline{w}^T \underline{A}_1^{-1} \underline{v}$ is often very easy. For the example cited above, $\underline{w}^T \hat{\underline{A}}_1^{-1} \underline{v}$ consists only of one nonzero element, and the inversion is trivial. It can be seen that (6) may be used for the solution of a system of linear equations since we have:

$$\hat{\underline{A}}^{-1}\ \hat{\underline{b}} = \hat{\underline{A}}_1^{-1}\ \underline{b} - (\hat{\underline{A}}^{-1}\ \underline{v}\ (\underline{U} + \underline{w}^T\ \hat{\underline{A}}_1^{-1}\ \underline{v})^{-1}\ \underline{w}^T\ \hat{\underline{A}}_1^{-1})\ \underline{b} \tag{7}$$

and, given $\hat{\underline{A}}_1^{-1}$ the process of solving $\hat{\underline{A}}\ \hat{\underline{x}} = \hat{\underline{b}}$ breaks into the following stages:

(i) Compute $\underline{y} = \hat{\underline{A}}^{-1}\underline{b}$ (an n-vector)

(ii) Compute $\underline{z} = \underline{w}^T\underline{y}$ (an r-vector)

(iii) Solve the linear system $(\underline{U} + \underline{w}^T * \underline{A}_1^{-1}\ \underline{v}) \cdot \underline{u} = \underline{z}$ for $\underline{u}$ (an r-vector)

(iv) Compute $\underline{s} = \underline{vu}$ (an n-vector)

(v) Compute $\underline{t} = \underline{A}^{-1}\underline{s}$ (an n-vector)

(vi) The final result is given by $\underline{x} = \underline{y} - \underline{t}$

It may be added that a matrix in the BBD form may be reduced to the BD form by means of (6), if all the links connecting S with the sets S_i are "torn". When the separating set S is small, the number of operations necessary to include the effect of those links (i.e. the operations implied by (6) or (7)) is likewise small. This again stresses the importance of a small separating set. Useful applications of (7) are to be found in [No 69] chapter 5. Techniques of tearing derived from it are also known as diakoptics, a subject mentioned in Chapter 5 and intensely studied in some circles of electrical engineering.

Yet another the D-method which in some cases may be viewed as a reordering method was developed and applied to ASP. Since it relies on similarity transformations and these are properly treated in the chapter on eigenvalues, the discussion of the D-method is delayed until then.

8.2 DIRECT BLOCK METHODS

Aims: To develop block-elimination and block factorization methods. To show that the methods reduce transfer and synchronization times if applied on ASP. To show that block-methods can also be applied to back-substitution.

8.2.1 Block-elimination

When programming for Mopps, Topps or related ASP systems one should strive to maximize the part of work done in parallel. In other words, the total duration of the sequential steps in the parallel-sequential model should be minimized. Since much of the time taken by the sequential steps is spent on system synchronization, an activity which includes a constant amount of time, reducing the number of sequential steps will result in more efficient algorithms.

To illustrate this point, consider a single step of the Gauss or Jordan method as described earlier. It is seen to consist of (n-1) repetitions of the following three operations:

(i) One of the slaves computes a value f (the "multiplier")

(ii) f is transmitted to the master and broadcast to all slaves

(iii) Each slave performs approximately h·n·d additions and multiplications, where d is the average part of nonzeroes, i.e. d=c/n for c=the number of nonzero elements per row.

Suppose now that the matrix is sparse (d<<1) and we want to increase p. The time of step (iii) will decrease, whereas (ii) does not change, because f must still be transmitted each time. Actually, the time of (ii) may even grow with p (the more processors, the more synchronizing time is required). We may reach a stage, where an overwhelming part of the system-time is taken up by synchronization, with little or no calculation done by the slaves.

A technique which partly alleviates this difficulty is to divide matrix $\underline{A}$ into blocks of size mxm so that interprocessor communication will be needed only when an entire block has been processed. This technique is quite general and will be used extensively; here we deal with its application to direct (elimination) methods of solving $\underline{A}\ \underline{x} = \underline{b}$.

Suppose that $\underline{A}$, an nxn matrix, is divided into p^2 square blocks of size h=n/p. Set $\underline{A}\ \underline{x} = \underline{b}$ can then be solved using block operations i.e. inversions, multiplications and additions of (hxh) matrices. The blockwise solution follows exactly the steps of ordinary solution with the normal arithmetical operations replaced by their block counterparts. The idea itself is not new, and many authors (e.g. [We 68], [St 73]) have used if for various purposes. We will use it as a starting point for developing some methods especially suitable for application of ASP. In this section, the aim is more modest: to introduce the basic technique as applied to various stages of elimination. One such program (the BE-method) is next described in general terms and exemplified by Fig. 6 for the case of n=16, p=4.

$$
\underset{a}{\begin{bmatrix} \underline{U} & \underline{X} & \underline{X} & \underline{X} \\ \underline{U} & \underline{X} & \underline{X} & \underline{X} \\ \underline{U} & \underline{X} & \underline{X} & \underline{X} \\ \underline{U} & \underline{X} & \underline{X} & \underline{X} \end{bmatrix}}
\rightarrow
\underset{b}{\begin{bmatrix} \underline{U} & \underline{X} & \underline{X} & \underline{X} \\ \underline{0} & \underline{X} & \underline{X} & \underline{X} \\ \underline{0} & \underline{X} & \underline{X} & \underline{X} \\ \underline{0} & \underline{X} & \underline{X} & \underline{X} \end{bmatrix}}
\rightarrow
\underset{c}{\begin{bmatrix} \underline{U} & \underline{X} & \underline{X} & \underline{X} \\ \underline{0} & \underline{U} & \underline{X} & \underline{X} \\ \underline{0} & \underline{U} & \underline{X} & \underline{X} \\ \underline{0} & \underline{U} & \underline{X} & \underline{X} \end{bmatrix}}
\rightarrow
\underset{d}{\begin{bmatrix} \underline{U} & \underline{X} & \underline{X} & \underline{X} \\ \underline{0} & \underline{U} & \underline{X} & \underline{X} \\ \underline{0} & \underline{0} & \underline{X} & \underline{X} \\ \underline{0} & \underline{0} & \underline{X} & \underline{X} \end{bmatrix}}
\rightarrow
\underset{e}{\begin{bmatrix} \underline{U} & \underline{X} & \underline{X} & \underline{X} \\ \underline{0} & \underline{U} & \underline{X} & \underline{X} \\ \underline{0} & \underline{0} & \underline{U} & \underline{X} \\ \underline{0} & \underline{0} & \underline{0} & \underline{U} \end{bmatrix}}
$$

Fig. 6: Reduction of matrix by block-elimination.

In the first stage, all slaves carry out simultaneously and independently a "Gauss-Jordan" operation on their respective slices. The result is shown in Fig. 6a in which $\underline{U}$ is as usual a unit and $\underline{X}$ a dense hxh submatrix. In the second step, the content of the first slice (excluding the $\underline{U}$ portion) is broadcast to slaves k=2, ...,p, which use it to reduce the previously eliminated rows to zeros. Practically, slaves whose number k≠1 will subtract all rows 1,2,...,h from rows kh+1,...,(k+1)h. The result is shown in Fig. 6b in which $\underline{0}$ stands for an h*h, zero-matrix. In the third stage slaves for which k=2,3,...,p diagonalize (in a Jordan step) the adjacent blocks, with the result shown in Fig. 6c. In stage 4, the contents of slice 2 is broadcast to memories k=3,4,...,p for zeroing of their previously diagonalized slices - resulting in Fig. 6d. Proceeding in the same fashion will, after 2p-1 steps yield Fig. 6e, which looks like an upper triangular matrix. In passing, it will be noted that block elimination as described above, accomplishes more than the usual Gaussian elimination because in the first the diagonal submatrices are unit matrices whereas in the second they are not (i.e. block elimination will zero the shaded parts of Fig. 7, elimination will not).

$$\begin{bmatrix} 1 & / & / & / \\ 0 & 1 & / & / \\ 0 & 0 & 1 & / \\ 0 & 0 & 0 & 1 \end{bmatrix}$$

Fig.7: Block

The number of operations required for the odd stages is:

$$t_{odd} = \Sigma\ (i\mu+(h-1)i(\mu+\alpha))=n(n+1)\mu/2+(h-1)n(n+1)\omega/2;\ i\Sigma=1,\dots,n \qquad (8)$$

The even stages comprise t-computing, t-synchronization and t-transfer i.e. t'_C, t'_S and t'_T so that

$$t_{even} = t'_T+t'_S+t'_C = h^2\tau p(p-1)/2+p\beta+h^2\alpha p(p-1)/2 \qquad (9)$$

Lumping together computations from odd and even stages, yields:

$$t_C=n^2(n+1)\omega/(2p)-n/(h+1)\alpha/2\cong n^2(n+1)\omega/(2p)-n^2\alpha/2p \qquad (10)$$

$$t_T=(n^2/p^2)(p^2-p)/2)\tau)=n^2(1-1/p)\tau/2;\ t_S = p\beta \qquad (11)$$

Note, that all three values t_C, t_T, t_S have decreased compared with elimination - because of substituting $p\tau$ for $n\tau$ and $p\beta$ for $n\beta$ ($p<<n$). Altogether

$$\rho_{BE} = 1/p+1.5(\tau'/n+2p\beta'/n^3)+0.5/p \qquad (12)$$

The improvement of ρ has not been achieved for nothing:

1) The slave memories required in block elimination have to be twice as large as those for the elimination by the Gauss-method.

2) The number of row operations increases, which increases the number of nonzero terms introduced in the process. However, the increase is very slight.

Block elimination degenerates into a modification of Gaussian elimination if executed on a monocomputer. In short: it is a method suited exclusively for parallel and especially ASP execution.

This method of elimination may be cast into a factorization form in the following two steps:

(a) The upper (right) triangular supermatrix $\underline{R}$ is the result of applying

$$\Pi\ \underline{T}_i*(\Pi\ \underline{Q}_{ki})*\underline{A} = \underline{R};\ i\Pi=1,\dots,p;\ k\Pi=1,\dots,i \qquad (13)$$

where the h*h submatrices of $\underline{T}$ are defined through:

$$\underline{T}_{ij} = \underline{U} \text{ for } i=j;\ T_{ij} = -\underline{U} \text{ for } j=k,i<j \text{ and } \underline{T}_{ij} = \underline{0} \text{ otherwise} \qquad (14)$$

and $\underline{Q}_{ki}$ is a unit matrix whose k'th column in slice i, (k+h)'s in slice (i+1) and generally the (k+(i-1)h)=s column in slice q consists of $1/a_{sk}$ on the diagonal and of $-a_{jk}/a_{sk}$ on the remaining entries of slice i. Fig. 8 shows one example of each of these two matrices, for n=12, p=3, namely of Q_{21} and T_1, and Fig. 9 shows the entire process for n=6, p=3. Note, that the entries a_{st} are not the original values; for instance the a_{st} of Q_{21} in Fig. 9, are those resulting from multiplying the original $\underline{A}$ by Q_{11} etc. The number of terms to be saved is the same as in the elimination method.

It is to be noted that the method as described is not applicable to very sparse matrices because no procedure to control fill-in is included. This can be amended to a large extent by introducing an ordering strategy into the odd stages of the

$$
\begin{bmatrix}
1 & -a_{12}/a_{22} & 0 & 0 & & & & & & & & \\
0 & 1/a_{22} & 0 & 0 & & & & & & & & \\
0 & -a_{32}/a_{22} & 1 & 0 & & & & & & & & \\
0 & -a_{42}/a_{22} & 0 & 1 & & & & & & & & \\
 & & & & 1 & -a_{52}/a_{62} & 0 & 0 & & & & \\
 & & & & 0 & 1/a_{62} & 0 & 0 & & & & \\
 & & & & 0 & -a_{72}/a_{62} & 1 & 0 & & & & \\
 & & & & 0 & -a_{82}/a_{62} & 0 & 1 & & & & \\
 & & & & & & & & 1 & -a_{92}/a_{10,2} & 0 & 0 \\
 & & & & & & & & 0 & 1/a_{10,2} & 0 & 0 \\
 & & & & & & & & 0 & -a_{11,2}/a_{10,2} & 1 & 0 \\
 & & & & & & & & 0 & -a_{12,2}/a_{10,2} & 0 & 1
\end{bmatrix}
\begin{bmatrix}
1 & & & & & & & & & & & \\
 & 1 & & & & & & & & & & \\
 & & 1 & & & & & & & & & \\
 & & & 1 & & & & & & & & \\
-1 & & & & 1 & & & & & & & \\
 & -1 & & & & 1 & & & & & & \\
 & & -1 & & & & 1 & & & & & \\
 & & & -1 & & & & 1 & & & & \\
-1 & & & & & & & & 1 & & & \\
 & -1 & & & & & & & & 1 & & \\
 & & -1 & & & & & & & & 1 & \\
 & & & -1 & & & & & & & & 1
\end{bmatrix}
$$

Fig. 8: Factor matrices of block-elimination

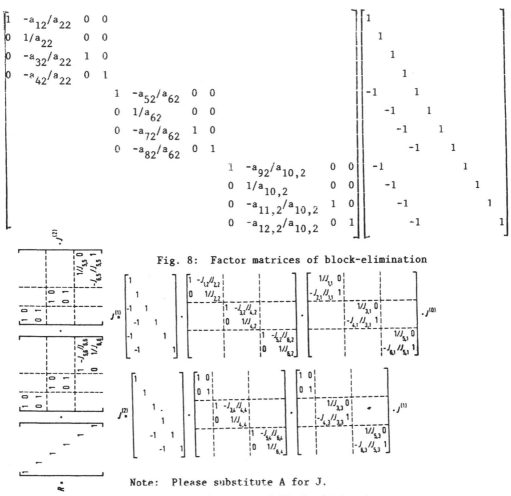

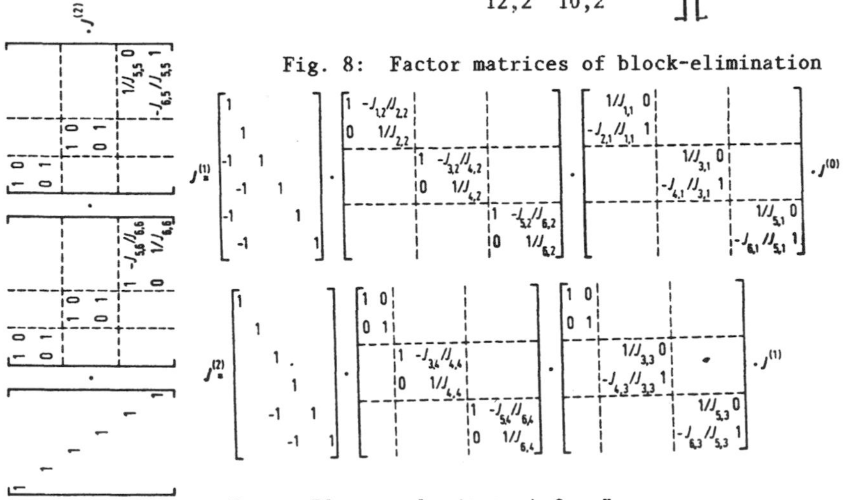

Note: Please substitute A for J.

Fig. 9: A particular case of block-elimination

algorithm. At those stages, each slave reduces one of its blocks to unity by row operations; a row reordering policy within each slice would result in partial suppression of fill-in with no extra inter-processor communication. A further fill-in reduction can be obtained in the even stages, with the master deciding which block is to be the pivoting one (e.g. the block whose rows contain the least number of nonzeroes - in analogy with policy 2 of subsection 6.3.3).

If zero submatrices are introduced not only below, but also above the diagonal, then the method can be called "block Jordan". The student is asked to write a simulation program for it. It should be more efficient than BE on account of removing the Haydn effect and because no back-substitution is required. The fact that the diagonal submatrices are themselves diagonal helps too.

8.2.2 Block-back-substitution

We have already shown in 6.2.2 that back-substitution can be adapted to ASP despite the fact that it seems an inherently sequential algorithm. Unfortunately, as shown by Eq. 6.52 the time reduction ratio includes a term $\beta'/(d*n)$ which may, for very sparse matrices ($d<<1$) be larger than $1/p$ and thus nullify the speed advantage of ASP. We should try to reduce the harm.

Summing 6.51 on $i = 1,2,\dots,n$ yields:

$$\underline{x} = \underline{b}^{(n)} = \underline{b}^{(o)} + b_1^{(o)} \underline{g}^{(1)} + b_2^{(1)} \underline{g}^{(2)} + \dots + b_{n-1}^{(n-2)} \underline{g}^{(n-1)} + b_n^{(n-1)} \underline{g}^{(n)} \qquad (15)$$

Subdividing this sum into blocks of h terms each, we have

$$\underline{x} = \underline{b}^{(o)} + \Sigma_k \left(\Sigma\, b_j^{(j-1)} \underline{g}^{(j)}\right); \; k\Sigma=1,\dots,p; \; j\Sigma=L(k)\dots U(k) \; (\text{"lower,upper"}) \qquad (16)$$

Each inner sum in (16) may be evaluated in parallel [CW 80]. Since $p<<n$ and the number of parallel steps is reduced from n in BSS to p, this will result in considerable savings in synchronization time. There is however an overhead to be paid (in step A of algorithm below).

The k-th parallel step (computing the k-th inner sum of (16)), consists of three stages, which follow sequentially upon each other.

Step A: All $b_j^{(j-1)}$ of the innermost sum of (16) are computed in slave k as its slice of $\underline{b}$. For example, all h elements of slice $\underline{b}_1$ (see Fig. 10) are computed by slave 1 according to:

$$\begin{aligned} b_i &= b_i + b_i * f_{i,1} \; ; \; i = 1,2,\dots,h \\ b_i &= b_i + b_2 * f_{i,2} \; ; \; i = \quad 2,\dots,h \\ b_i &= b_i + b_h * f_{i,h} \; ; \; i = \qquad\quad h \end{aligned} \qquad (17)$$

Step B: The block of coefficients b_i; $i=1,\dots,h$ computed in step A, is broadcast to all slaves (via the master).

Step C: All slaves compute concurrently the k'th inner loop of (16).

Fig. 10 explains the process. For $k = 1$, slice b_1 is computed in step A with the aid of the lower triangular block $\underline{t}_1$. In step C, slice $\underline{b}_1$ is used to compute all blocks $\underline{w}_1$ concurrently. The same applies to slaves $k = 2,\dots,p$.

In the BSF program (for block-substitution, faster), we have omitted the declarations and initialization since they are the same as earlier.

```
BSF:  PROC OPTIONS (MAIN);
DO NP = 1 TO P;
     PARCALL (NP) COEFF;
     V(1:H)≡(NP)V(1:H); PUT BROADCAST (V);
     PARCALL (#)PSUM(NP);   END;
COEFF:PARPROC;
IND=((#P)-1)*H+1; V(1)=B(1);
DO I=1 TO H-1; BF=B(I);
     DO J=I+1 TO H;
          B(J)=B(J)+BF*F(J,IND); END;
     IND=IND+1; V(I+1)=B(I+1); END; PAREND COEFF;
PSUM:PARPROC(M);
IND=(M-1)*H+1; IF(#M) THEN GO TO SPEC;
DO I=1 TO H;
```

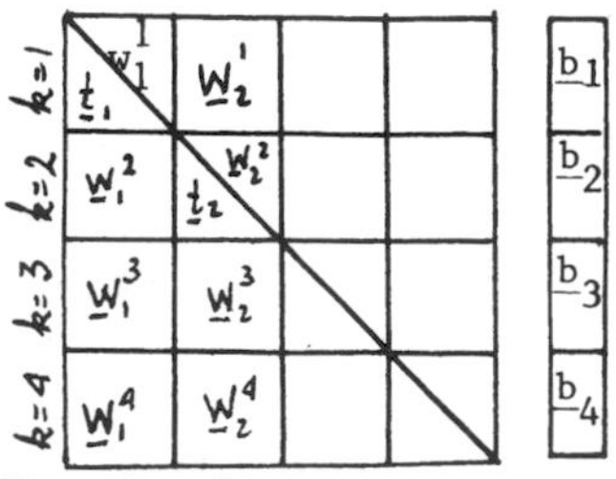

Fig. 10: Division in blocks.

The operations count yields for step (a): $((h-1) + (h-2) + \dots + 1)\ (\mu+\alpha)d \cong 0.5dh^2\omega$, for step (b): $h\tau+\beta$ and for step (c): $dh^2\omega$. The cycle is repeated p times so that

```
    DO J=1 TO H;
          B(J)=B(J)+V(I)*F(J,IND); END;
    IND=IND+1; END; GO TO FINAL;
SPEC:  DO I=1 TO H;
    DO J=1 TO I;
          B(J)=B(J)+V(I)*F(J,IND); END;
    IND=IND+1;
END;
FINAL:  END PSUM; END BSF;
```

for BSF:

$\rho_{BSF}=(1.5\ dhn\omega+n\tau+p\beta)/(dn^2\omega)= 1.5/p+\tau'/(dn)+(p\beta')/(dn^2)$ (18)

Judging by their first term, ρ_{BSS} seems better than ρ_{BSF}. Indeed, the latter spends more time on arithmetics at its step A.

The comparison which follows shows that in certain circumstances, this disadvantage is offset by the reduced time required for synchronization. Indeed, $\rho_{BSF} < \rho_{BSS}$ if $0.5/p<\beta'(1-1/h)/(dn)$ or, for $p<<n$, approximately when $\beta'>dn/(2p)$. For a realistic situation with $n = 500$, $d = 0.02$ and, say, $p = 20$, we have $\beta' > 0.25$ or $\beta > 0.25\ \omega$. This is obviously valid, since no matter how fast the hardware and how clever the synchronization, it takes more than $0.25\ \omega = (\alpha+\mu)/4$ to synchronize a 20-processor system. It may be shown that $\beta' > dn/(2p)$ holds for a wide range of parameters, for which BSF is then faster indeed.

A generalization

Algorithms BSS and BSF may be viewed as special cases of a general block method with block size=1 for BSS and h for BSF. In the general algorithm, we subdivide h into k blocks of size v each, i.e. $n=p\cdot v\cdot k$ and the sum into $k\cdot p$ blocks of size v. Eq. 6.51 may now be rewritten as

$$\underline{x} = \underline{b}^{(o)} + \sum_{j=0}^{p-1} \sum_{s=0}^{k-1} \sum_{q=0}^{v-1} b_{jh+sv+q+1}^{(jh+sv+1)} \cdot \underline{g}^{(jh+sv+q+1)} \tag{19}$$

This may be "programmed" as follows:

LOOP 1 on index $j=0,1,\ldots,p-1$, with index $(j+1)$ denoting the "leading" slave.

LOOP 2 on index $s=0,1,\ldots,k-1$ with $(s+1)$ pointing to a block within the leading slave.

LOOP 3 on index $q=0,1,\ldots,v-1$ consists of three steps:

(1) The v coefficients $b_r^{(r-1)}$, with r in the current block ($r=jh+sv+1$) are evaluated by formulae similar to (17). (These equations have been omitted due to the complicated indexing).

(2) The coefficients $b_r^{(r-1)}$ are broadcast;

(3) A parallel loop in which all slaves compute concurrently the inner sum of their respective slices;

END OF ALL LOOPS;

Steps (1,2,3) require $d((v-1) + (v-2) + \ldots + 1))\ \omega$, and $dhv\omega$ respectively. Summing these values, multiplying the sum by $p\cdot k$ and dividing by $dn^2\omega$ yields

$$\rho_{GBS} = 1/p + [(v-1)/2 + \tau'/d + \beta'/(dv)]/n \tag{20}$$

which reduces to ρ_{BSF} for v=h and to ρ_{BSS} for v=1.

The additional degree of freedom v makes it possible to optimize the algorithm for a given computer and data. Part "g" of (20) which depends on v is minimum for v_o:

$$g = [(v-1)/2 + \beta'/(dv)]/n \quad ; \quad v_o = \sqrt{2\beta'/d} \qquad (21)$$

The best ρ is achieved if v is chosen as the divisor of n nearest to v_o.

8.3 PARALLEL, OPTIMALLY ORDERED FACTORIZATION POOF

8.3.1 Preliminaries

Let "zet" stand for a zero-term (element) and "nozet" for a non-zero term of matrix $\underline{A}$. The following considerations will be based on the well-known fact that some matrices exhibit a symmetrical pattern of zets - they will be called zet symmetric matrices.

The basic idea of the algorithm will be that for zet symmetric matrices, basic Gaussian steps, called bag (i,k) and bag (j,k) are commutative operations, provided

$$a_{ij} = 0 \qquad (22)$$

For sparse matrices this will enhance parallelism by enabling a large number of pivots to be applied simultaneously. We now pursue this more rigorously.

Theorem 1: In a zet symmetric matrix, bag (i,k) and bag (j,k) commute if $a_{ij} = 0$.

Proof: Let i,j be two pivots and k a "row" (to be operated on). If bag (i,k) is applied first and bag (j,k) later, the result for m>i is

$$a'_{km} = a_{km} - a_{im}*a_{ki}/a_{ii} \qquad \text{(following bag (i,k))} \qquad (23)$$

$$a''_{km} = a'_{km} - a_{jm}*a'_{kj}/a_{jj} \qquad \text{(following bag (j,k))} \qquad (24)$$

The assumption was that $a_{ij} = 0$ so that if we substitute j for m in (23), $a'_{kj} = a_{kj}$ results. Substituting this and (23) into (24) yields

$$a''_{km} = a_{km} - a_{im}*a_{ki}/a_{ii} - a_{jm}*a_{kj}/a_{jj} \qquad (25)$$

In (25) indices i,j may be interchanged. Hence, the operations may be also performed in the reverse order. Q.E.D.

Theorem 1 shows the condition for a number of pivots to act interchangeably and simultaneously on the same row. Obviously, elimination of rows j,k by pivot i are also independent operations.

Theorem 2: If after bag (i,m); m>i, both row and column i are discarded, the symmetric pattern of zets is retained.

Proof: Suppose that $a_{ki} = 0$, $a_{\ell i} = 0$ and $a_{ji} \neq 0$. Since $a_{ki} = 0$, the zets in row and column k will not be changed. Element $a_{\ell j}$ will be changed, but so will $a_{j\ell}$. The zet-symmetry is thus retained. Q.E.D.

Corollary: If a matrix $\underline{A}$ is zet symmetric and $a_{ij} = 0$ then all operations using pivots i and j may be performed independently and simultaneously and the matrix which remains after rows and columns i and j are eliminated, is also zet symmetric. In an obvious way, this result applies to a set of indices i,j...

We next formulate the preceding result in terms of elimination on graphs.

Definition: Let G = (N,E) be an undirected graph, with N the set of nodes and $E \subset (N\times N)$ the set of edges. Then $S \subset E$ is called an independent subset if for any pair x ε S, y ε S it is true that (x,y) ∉ E.

<u>Result</u>: Let S be an independent set, then all x ε S may be eliminated independently (hence simultaneously).

8.3.2 The algorithm

It is obvious that parallelism is enhanced by employing the maximal subset of nodes as pivots. In 8.3.1, it was shown that there should be no links connecting the pivot nodes. This leads naturally to the following optimization problem: given a graph G, find a maximal independent subset S.

In [AHU 76] this is shown to be an NP-Complete problem, which has no known, efficient solution. An enumerative approach seems to be the best that can be done.

Another, much more practical approach is to suggest a suboptimal (instead of optimal) policy. The following solution is recommended for the posed problem:

1) The node with the least number of links is given index 1. (If there are several, one is chosen arbitrarily).

2) Assume nodes 1,...,k have been chosen. Next, assign index k+1 to the node which has the least number of links and is not directly connected to any of the first k nodes.

3) When rule (2) cannot be applied any more (with k=m), number the remaining nodes (m+1,...,n) arbitrarily.

The poof algorithm which uses the above renumbering scheme, is best exemplified (figures 11,12,13 and tables 1,2,3) by a concrete example. (In order to exemplify the characteristics of poof, matrices of at least 100x100 should be used - otherwise it is difficult to have meaningful sparsity. The network of Fig. 11 is therefore intended only for description of the algorithm. Experimentation with large, sparse matrices is reported in 8.3.3).

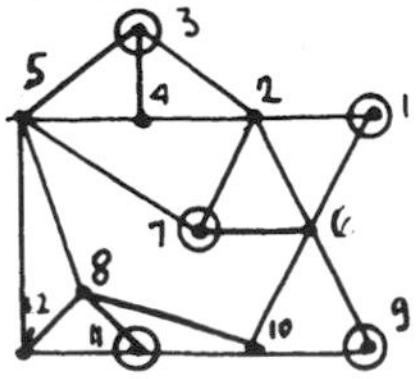

Fig. 11: A network

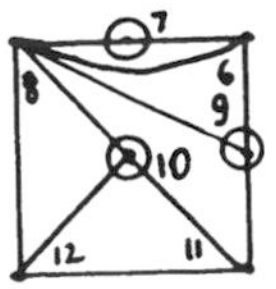

Fig. 12: Reduced network

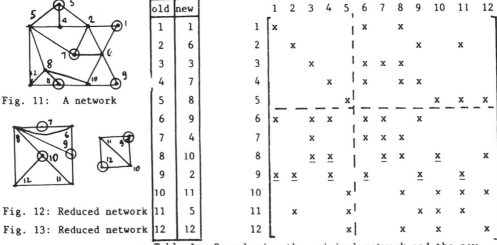

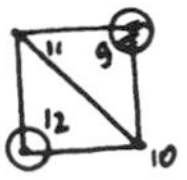

Fig. 13: Reduced network

old	new
1	1
2	6
3	3
4	7
5	8
6	9
7	4
8	10
9	2
10	11
11	5
12	12

	1	2	3	4	5	6	7	8	9	10	11	12
1	x					x		x				
2		x							x		x	
3			x			x	x	x				
4				x		x		x	x			
5					x					x	x	x
6	x		x	x		x	x		x			
7			x			x	x	x				
8			x	x			x	x		x		x
9	x	x		x		x			x		x	
10					x			x		x	x	x
11		x			x				x	x	x	
12					x			x		x		x

Table 1: Renumbering the original network and the new adjacency graph.

Following the initial renumbering step by step (Fig. 11) leads to: 1) Node 1 is chosen as the first node.

2) Nodes 2,6 are "crossed out", 9 chosen as pivot, 10 crossed out, 3 chosen as pivot, 4 and 5 crossed out, 7 and 11 chosen as pivots. Pivots are encircled in Fig. 11.

3) The renumbering of the original network and the resulting adjacency matrix are shown in Table 1. It can be seen that the rows and columns corresponding to the chosen 5 pivots, form a diagonal block.

According to the corollary, all 5 pivots may next be eliminated simultaneously. For example, if two slaves work in parallel, the first could eliminate pivots 1,2 at the same time that the second eliminates pivots 3,4 and 5. The network which corresponds to non-eliminated nodes is shown in Fig. 12, its renumbering and adjacency matrix in Table 2. Fig. 13 and Table 3 show the next stage of elimination. The elimination of the two remaining nodes (11,12) completes the poof algorithm.

old	new
6	9
7	6
8	10
9	7
10	8
11	11
12	12

	6	7	8	9	10	11	12
6	x			x	x		
7		x		x	x	x	
8			x		x	x	x
9	x	x		x	x		
10	x	x	x	x	x		x
11		x	x			x	x
12			x		x	x	x

Table 2: As Table 1 but for the reduced network

old	new
9	9
10	11
11	12
12	10

	0	10	11	12
9	x		x	x
10		x	x	x
11	x	x	x	x
12	x	x	x	x

Table 3: Final renumbering and adjacency table

The set of operations which includes the choice of a set of pivots and their subsequent (parallel) elimination, will be called a "poof step".

The poof-algorithm is an elimination process, but if the factor-table is stored during the elimination then poof is also a factorization algorithm.

8.3.3 Discussion

The poof algorithm may be executed on ASP in the following way:

(a) The master decides on the basis of the remaining adjacency table, which nodes are pivots and assigns rows to be operated on to each slave. This information (in form of indices) is broadcast to the slaves.

(b) Each slave performs bag(i,k) for all its rows k. Every slave uses all pivots i in this (parallel) substep.

(c) Each slave sends (blockwise) its modified rows to the master which then broadcasts them to all slaves.

(d) If elimination is not complete, revert to (a).

Steps (a) and (c) are sequential and reduce the speed-up. Both substeps may be improved as follows:

(a') The work of the master: choosing the pivots and assigning rows so as to achieve equal work for the slaves does not depend on the numerical values, but only on the adjacency table. It is therefore possible for the master to compute the indices for the next step during the time that the slaves work on substep (b).

Actually, choosing the indices for the entire process can be carried out before the elimination starts. Such preconditioning is advantageous if elimination is to be performed a number of times on the same network (as is the case in optimization and contingency programs). In both cases speed-up is increased.

(c') It is possible to assign rows to slaves at the start of the program for its entire duration. In that case, only pivot rows have to be sent in step (c'), so that much less transfer time is needed. However, such rigid assignment may lead to uneven load balance on the slaves. As poof (or any other factorization method) proceeds, the remaining matrix becomes less sparse due to the effect of fill-in. When the percentage of nozets exceeds a certain value, it may be better to switch over to one of the parallel methods suggested earlier for non-sparse matrices.

To determine this value, a large number of numerical experiments were conducted. In each experiment a network with a given number of nodes n and a given average node-degree k (the number of links emanating from a node) was randomly generated. This method was an improved version of the one discussed in [Al 76] and did not generate any nodes connected to the rest of the network by a single link.

PS \ NO	60	80	100	120	140	160	180	200
1	5.60	4.20	3.39	2.85	2.12	2.42	1.85	1.67
2	12.0	8.81	7.17	6.39	5.18	4.64	3.81	3.53
3	25.0	19.7	16.5	14.6	11.8	10.9	8.23	8.14
4	55.8	42.4	37.4	33.7	28.7	25.5	19.8	19.1
5	84.1	77.7	68.7	63.9	60.0	52.9	44.7	42.0
6	100.0	98.3	93.0	91.7	88.8	80.6	78.1	73.7
7		100.0	100.0	99.0	96.7	97.0	97.9	94.6
8				100.0	99.2	100.0	100.0	99.0

Table 4: Fill-in f(%) for k=2.4

Tables 4 to 7 summarize 128 out of a much larger number of cases which were tested. Tables 4 and 6 show the fill-in "f", Tables 5 and 7 the percentage of operations "p" both as functions of the number of nodes (NO) and of the poof steps (PS). Each entry is an average of 8 different test cases generated. For example, the encircled entry in Tables 4 and 5 shows that for N=160, the fill in was 0.8060 and that 81.38% of the total number of operations were done after having completed only 6 poof steps.

Let us assume that at f=60% it is better to switch over from poof to the Block Elimination (BE) algorithm. As seen in the tables (heavy lines), this occurs after 4 or 5 poof steps. At these points, p for k=2.4 is between 73.17% and 91.05%. This proves that this algorithm completes the bulk of its numerical work in a very

PS	NO 60	80	100	120	140	160	180	200
1	41.0	36.9	34.7	31.0	29.2	28.0	26.5	25.9
2	61.7	57.9	54.9	47.4	45.6	43.6	41.1	41.1
3	77.2	71.9	68.0	59.0	58.0	53.7	51.1	51.1
4	87.9	82.5	78.4	69.3	69.2	64.4	60.2	60.4
5	95.1	91.0	87.1	79.2	78.5	73.2	70.6	69.5
6	97.9	95.5	92.9	87.4	86.4	81.4	80.5	78.7
7	99.3	97.8	96.0	92.0	92.0	88.9	86.9	85.8
8	99.9	99.2	98.0	95.0	95.0	92.4	91.0	90.5

Table 5: Percentage of Operating p(%)

small number of poof steps. To emphasize this point, Table 8 shows how many nodes would have remained not eliminated, had we switched to the BE algorithm at the points mentioned above.

PS	NO 60	80	100	120	140	160	180	200
1	6.58	4.91	3.93	3.26	2.78	2.46	2.18	1.96
2	15.7	12.1	9.73	7.97	6.88	6.20	5.49	5.03
3	35.6	29.1	24.3	20.6	17.1	15.4	14.0	12.5
4	68.7	59.3	51.0	43.2	40.2	38.1	32.7	28.9
5	94.9	85.7	80.3	69.6	66.6	66.2	60.8	53.3
6	99.7	98.6	96.2	89.6	89.8	88.4	85.1	79.9
7	100.	100.	99.9	97.3	97.9	96.9	97.0	94.8
8			100.	99.6	99.6	99.3	99.7	99.7
9						99.8	100.	99.9

Table 6: Fill-in f(%) for k=3

PS	NO 60	80	100	120	140	160	180	200
1	21.7	16.9	13.1	11.6	9.89	8.03	6.86	6.25
2	38.2	30.7	23.9	21.6	18.2	14.5	12.5	11.2
3	54.4	44.9	35.5	31.1	27.5	22.2	19.0	16.7
4	68.4	58.7	48.0	41.6	37.4	31.6	27.1	23.3
5	80.4	71.3	59.9	52.9	48.9	42.6	36.2	31.7
6	87.1	79.7	71.4	62.5	58.4	51.3	47.3	41.1
7	91.7	85.0	77.8	71.2	68.7	61.1	56.0	50.0
8	95.0	89.3	82.7	77.0	76.0	67.6	62.6	56.1
9	97.3	92.7	87.0	81.6	80.3	72.9	67.3	61.8

Table 7: Percentage of operations for k=3

The execution of poof on ASP may also be organized so that instead of assigning rows, the master assigns pivots to slaves - i.e. each slave works on the entire matrix with its assigned pivots. If for instance, row k is operated upon by pivot i (in slave "x") and by pivot j (in slave "y"), the two resulting rows k are changed as follows:

$$a_{km}^{(x)} = a_{km} - a_{im}*a_{ki}/a_{ii} \quad , \quad m>k \tag{26}$$

$$a_{km}^{(y)} = a_{km} - a_{jm}*a_{kj}/a_{jj} \quad , \quad m>k \tag{27}$$

To get the final result - $a''_{k,m}$ of (25), replace

$$a''_{km} = a_{km}^{(x)} + a_{km}^{(y)} - a_{km} \tag{28}$$

This represents an additional computational effort which lowers the speed-up, because it is necessary to transfer rows over the bus and perform the merging in (28) sequentially in the master.

Poof is but one policy of choosing pivots to enhance parallelism. Other procedures could be conceived, e.g. choose as pivots at each step those nodes which are connected to the largest number of other nodes (but not to other pivots).

N	k=2.4	k=3
60	5	9
80	6	10
100	9	16
120	11	20
140	12	21
160	15	23
180	13	30
200	15	32

Table 8: Number of remaining (uneliminated) nodes for f=50%

Both methods try to enlarge the amount of work in parallel substep (b) - elimination proper - as compared to the other substeps which represent overhead. In poof, the maximum number of nodes are choses as pivots at each step; the other policy chooses pivots so as to maximize the number of rows to be operated upon.

This section is concerned with speeding up the factorization process. Paralization is of no avail, if it is achieved at the expense of increasing the overall number of operations too much. This is precisely what would happen, were the reverse policy chosen, because fill-in would be maximized.

N	p'	q'	p'	q'
60	0.94	1.03	0.98	1.02
80	0.95	1.03	1.04	1.03
100	0.95	1.03	1.06	1.03
120	0.96	1.02	0.98	1.01
140	0.99	1.03	0.96	1.00
160	0.96	1.02	1.13	1.05
180	0.97	1.02	1.09	1.05
200	1.02	1.03	1.13	1.06

Table 9: Comparison of poof with policy 2 for k=2.4 and k=3

Poof is a policy which could also be applied in programs run on standard (single) computers. It is therefore of interest to compare it under these conditions with policy 2 discussed earlier. The same 128 matrices generated for the previous tests, were also solved using "policy 2". The results are summarized in Table 9 in which the ratios of fill-in for policy 2(p') and poof (q') are given. It may be seen that the number of operations and the fill-in of the two methods are about the same.

In conclusion, it may be stated that poof was shown to be very well suited for parallel factorization. It may be viewed both as a reordering and block method.

8.4 BLOCK, ITERATIVE METHODS

Aims: A number of block-iterative methods will be developed and their ratios calculated. The convergence of these methods is also discussed.

In this section we present first a re-scheduling of the Gauss-Seidel method and evaluate its efficiency. Let the nxn matrix $\underline{A}$ be subdivided into p horizontal slices which reside in their respective memories, as usual. Each slice is vertically subdivided into p square major blocks of size h*h. Each major block is next subdivided into k^2 minor blocks (Fig. 14) of size (q*q) where

$$n = p*k*q = p*h \tag{29}$$

Vector $\underline{t}$ is initialized to:

$$t_\ell = - \Sigma\, a_{\ell j}*x_j \;;\; j\Sigma=\ell+1,\dots,n \tag{30}$$

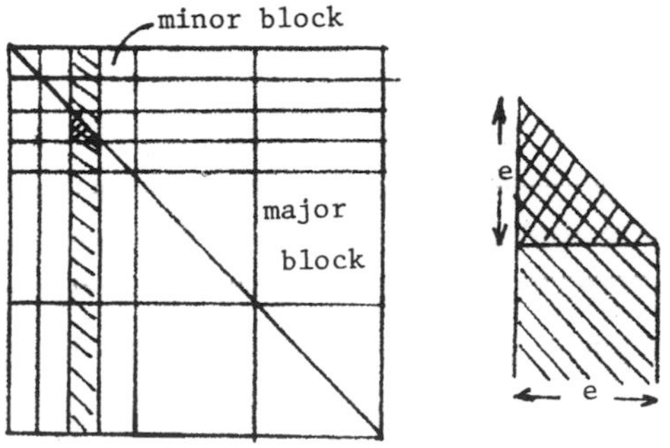

Fig. 14: Subdivision of matrix $\underline{A}$

Next the Gauss-Seidel algorithm will be "programmed" according to the blocks defined above.

Loop 1 on index i = 1,2,...,p where i denotes the (sequentially) chosen slave.

Loop 2 on index j = 1,2,...,k chooses (sequentially) a minor diagonal block within major block (i,i).

Loop 3 is the innermost loop and consists of three steps:

(a) Correct x_1-values in the chosen minor block, within slice i, according to

$$x_\ell = (q_\ell + t_\ell)/a_{\ell\ell} \tag{31}$$

and update the t_ℓ's partially through

$$t_\ell = t_\ell + a_{r\ell}*x_j \tag{32}$$

where $a_{i\ell}$ is in the strictly lower triangle of the chosen minor block (cross-hatched in Fig. 14).

(b) Transfer (sequentially) the corrected x's to all slaves.

(c) All slaves update their t-values according to (32), where the indices i,ℓ range over their slices of the hatched area of Fig. 14.

The three loops are nested. Note that only step (c) of Loop 3 is executed concurrently by all p-slaves.

Next, the reduction ratio is computed. Loop 3 is executed p·k times, and each time: Step (a) takes approximately $0.5q^2$ dω, step b takes $(\beta+q\tau)$ and, disregarding the fact that slave i has less work to do, step (c) takes $kq^2d(\mu+\alpha)$. Altogether, the time of one iteration of the algorithm above is

$$T = p\cdot k(q^2d(k+0.5)\omega+\beta+q\tau) \qquad (33)$$

Since sequential execution of the Gauss-Seidel procedure requires approximately $n^2d\omega$ operations, we have:

$$\rho=1/p+(\tau'+(0.5qd+\beta'/q))/(nd)=1/p+0.5q/n+(\beta'/q+\tau')/(nd) \qquad (34)$$

If the part g of (34) which depends on p, is minimized, the optimum value g of a given matrix (i.e. n and d) is:

$$g = 0.5qd+\beta'/q \quad ; \quad q = \sqrt{2\beta'/d} \qquad (35)$$

Actually q must be chosen an integer and a divisor of h. Therefore, (35) is only an approximation. For instance, for a matrix of n = 200, d = 0.025 (i.e. 5 non-zeros per row) and an ASP with p = 10, the optimal value is $q\simeq 13$, but 10 or 20 will be chosen, since h = 20. For all possible q-values, g is much larger than τ' and equals 2.85, 1.45 and 1.779 for q = 20, 10 and 1 respectively. The last case corresponds to blocksize 1, i.e. to the Gauss-Seidel algorithm. It is seen that the block method reduced the time ratio ρ considerably. Since this result will be amplified for larger, sparser matrices, the conclusion is that this block-version of the Gauss-Seidel method, solves sparse systems efficiently on ASP.

Proper Block-Iterative Methods

Below is a description of two iterative methods which are by their very nature amenable to block execution. Both methods are derived from the general scheme of "splitting". In this scheme, the nonsingular matrix $\underline{A}$ is split into

$$\underline{A} = \underline{A}_1 - \underline{A}_2 \qquad (36)$$

The iterative method for solving $\underline{A}\ \underline{x} = \underline{b}$ with the above splitting of $\underline{A}$ forms the i+1'th iterate $\underline{x}^{(i+1)}$ from $\underline{x}^{(i)}$ through

$$\underline{A}_1 * \underline{x}^{(i+1)} = \underline{A}_2 * \underline{x}^{(i)} + \underline{b} \qquad (37)$$

As pointed out in chapter 7, the classical iterations of Jacobi and Gauss-Seidel can be derived from this scheme; e.g., taking $\underline{A}_1$ to be the diagonal part of $\underline{A}$ leads to the method of Jacobi. For all methods we assume that computing $\underline{A}_2*\underline{x}^{(0)}$ is part of initialization.

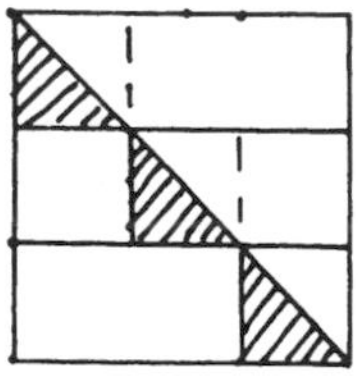

Fig. 15: $\underline{A}_1,\underline{A}_2$ of method B_1

(i) Method B1 [CW 77a]

The appropriate splitting is given in Fig. 15 with the cross-hatched part corresponding to $\underline{A}_1$ (including the diagonal). The figure also shows the rows of $\underline{A}$ divided into 3 slices, to be stored in the memories for a 3-slave system. The B1 algorithm consists of cyclic repetition of steps (a) and (b) below:

(a) Each slave corrects its slice of x's independently of the others and in the fashion of the S-method. That is, if for example n=30, then slave 1 corrects x_1, uses the corrected value to correct x_2 etc., while at the same time slave 2 corrects x_{11} using x's from the previous iteration, then corrects x_{12} using the recent x_{11}, and so on. Simultaneously, slave 3 operates similarly on x_{21} through x_{30}.

(b) The corrected values of all x's are transmitted to the master, which checks convergence and, if necessary, broadcasts the new vector $\underline{x}$ to all slaves, which, working in parallel compute their corresponding parts of $\underline{A}_2 * \underline{x}$. The reduction achieved by this method can be calculated to be

$$\rho_{B1} = 1/p+(p\beta'/n+\tau')/(nd) \tag{38}$$

The ratio is seen to be smaller than that of BGS for any q. This shows that, from the point of view of ASP processing, B1 is superior to Gauss-Seidel, even if the latter is implemented in block form. Note, however that a fair comparison between the two methods must take their convergence properties into account (see below).

(ii) Method B2

The splitting for this method is given in Fig. 16 and is similar to that of the Gauss-Seidel method. The two splittings differ only in the lower triangular parts of their diagonal blocks. In fact, when the block size is 1, the two methods are identical. Therefore, one is naturally led to apply a parallelization similar to the block Gauss-Seidel method described earlier. With h=n/p, each slave in turn corrects its slice of x's in a Jacobi fashion, while the others wait, then transmits x's via the master, to all other slaves. The method is thus seen to be complementary to B_1; it is a Jacobi iteration within each block, followed by a Seidel-like use of previously computed values. The reduction of time obtained by this process is

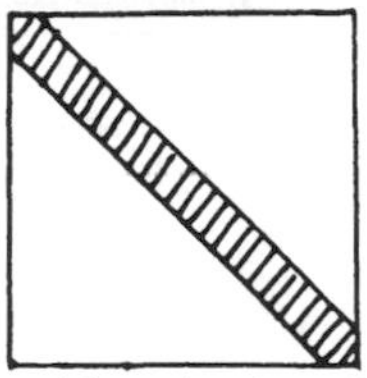

Fig. 16: $\underline{A}_1, \underline{A}_2$ of method B_2

$$\rho_{B2} = 1/p+(p\beta'/n+\tau'+1)/(nd) \tag{39}$$

and exceeds ρ_{B1} of (38) by 1/(nd). This is a consequence of the fact that during the Jacobi phase of B_2 all slaves but one are idle.

Another approach to the parallelization of this iterative method, advocated in [CW 77a] and, implicitly in [Rb 70], is to execute the Jacobi phase in parallel. Let us reverse the roles of p and h; the n rows of $\underline{A}$ are now divided into h slices of p rows each, residing in the corresponding memories. The ordering of rows is different: slave 1 holds now the rows whose numbers in the original ordering were 1, h+1, 2h+1,...,(p-1)*h+1, i.e. the first rows of the original slices; slave 2 holds rows 2, h+2, ..., (p-1)*h+2, and in general slave k holds rows k, h+k,..., (p-1)*h+k.

Once more, we employ an auxiliary vector $\underline{t}$ which is initialized to hold

$$t_\ell = b_\ell - \Sigma\, a_{j\ell} x_j^{(o)} \; ; \; j\Sigma = 1,\dots,n; j\neq\ell \tag{40}$$

In the first parallel step the first slave updates x_1 using

$$x_1^{(1)} = t_1/a_{11} \tag{41}$$

Simultaneously slave 2 updates x_2 using the first row (now numbered p+1 in the general matrix) through $x_2^{(1)} = t_{p+1}/a_{p+1,2}$ and in general, the k'th slave computes

$$x_k^{(1)} = t_{(k-1)p+1}/a_{(k-1)p+1,k} \tag{42}$$

In other words $x_1^{(1)}$ to $x_h^{(1)}$ have been computed independently and simultaneously, corresponding to a Jacobi step. Each processor updated its corresponding x by applying relaxation to the first row in its slice. In addition, each processor forms the difference $x_k^{(1)} - x_k^{(o)}$ for "its" value of k.

In the following sequential step, the differences $x_k^{(1)} - x_k^{(o)}$ are sent to every memory including that of the master (which needs them to check convergence at the end of an iteration).

The last step in a cycle is the updating of all t_ℓ through

$$t_\ell = t_\ell + \Sigma a_{\ell j}(x_j^{(1)} - x_j^{(o)}) \ ; \ j\Sigma=1,\dots,h;(j\neq\ell) \tag{43}$$

which is again performed in parallel by all h processors.

The cycle now repeats itself with the processors updating simultaneously $x_{h+1}, x_{h+2}, \dots, x_{2h}$, applying relaxation to the second equation of their corresponding slices. The differences $x^{(1)} - x^{(o)}$ are formed and sent to all processors, and the parallel updating of $\underline{t}$ terminates the cycle.

Clearly, to complete one iteration of the method, p such cycles are necessary, followed by a convergence check.

The first step of each cycle requires the time $\omega=\mu+\alpha$, the transfer of data $\beta+h\cdot\tau$, and the parallel updating of $\underline{t}$ takes $2\cdot p\cdot h\cdot d\cdot\omega$ (each processor applies the updating formula to its p rows). Since there are p cycles, the total time equals

$$T = p(p\cdot hc(\mu+\alpha) + \beta + h\cdot\tau + 1) = p\cdot n\cdot q\cdot\omega+p\cdot\beta+n\cdot\tau+1 \tag{44}$$

The resulting ρ_{B2a} equals (B2a stands for the above implementation of B2)

$$\rho_{B2a} = p/n + (\beta'/p+\tau'+1/p)/(nd) \tag{45}$$

To make a fair comparison with B2, one should employ the same number of slaves for both implementations. To this end, we consider a system for which p=n/p (which is feasible for $n \leqq 500$). Denote this quantity by u. Then

$$\rho=1/u+(\beta'/u+\tau'+1)/(nd);\ \rho_{B2}=1/u+(\beta'/u+\tau'+1/u)/(nd) \tag{46}$$

which constitutes an improvement over B2, the significance of which increases as d becomes small.

<u>Convergence of Block Iterative Methods</u>

As is well known, there exist no universal iteration methods. To justify an iterative method, one has to show its convergence for a practically important family of matrices, or to exhibit this convergence empirically. The following statements will be shown to hold for B1 and B2.

<u>Theorem</u>: A sufficient condition for the convergence of the B1, B2 methods is the (time honored) condition of diagonal dominance, i.e.

$$|A_{k,k}| > \Sigma\ |A_{k,j}| \ ; \ j \neq k;\ j\Sigma=1,\dots,n \tag{47}$$

<u>Proof</u>: Matrix $\underline{A}$ was decomposed into matrices $\underline{A}_1$ and $\underline{A}_2$ by (36). Let λ be an eigenvalue of $\underline{A}_1^{-1} \cdot \underline{A}_2$. Then

$$\det\ (\underline{U}-\underline{A}_1^{-1}\cdot \underline{A}_2) = 0 \tag{48}$$

where $\underline{U}$ = identity matrix. Taking determinants of both sides of

$$\underline{A}_1 \cdot (\lambda\underline{U}-\underline{A}_1^{-1}\cdot \underline{A}_2) = \lambda\underline{A}_1 - \underline{A}_2 \tag{49}$$

yields $\det(\lambda \underline{A}_1 - \underline{A}_2) = 0$ (50)

Therefore the matrix $\underline{M} = \lambda \cdot \underline{A}_1 - A_2$ is singular.

By Hadamard's theorem applied to $\underline{M}$, there exists one k for which

$$\left.\begin{array}{l} |\lambda||\underline{A}_{kk}| \leq |\lambda| \sum_{P_1} |A_{k,j}| + \sum_{P_2} |A_{k,j}| \\ \text{or } |\lambda| \, (|A_{k,k}| - \sum_{P_1} |A_{k,j}|) \leq \sum_{P_2} A_{k,j} \end{array}\right\} \text{over } P_1, P_2 \qquad \begin{array}{r}(51)\\(52)\end{array}$$

where P_1, P_2 are the sets of indices of elements of $\underline{A}_1$, $\underline{A}_2$ resp. $(k,j)\Sigma\varepsilon P_1$ and $(k,j)\Sigma\varepsilon P_2$ resp. and in the first sum $j \neq k$.

By the assumption of diagonal dominance

$$|A_{k,k}| > \sum_{\substack{j=1 \\ j\neq k}}^{n} |A_{k,j}| = \sum_{\substack{(k,j)\varepsilon P_1 \\ j\neq k}} |A_{k,j}| + \sum_{(k,j)\varepsilon P_2} |A_{k,j}| \qquad (53)$$

$$\text{so that } (|A_{k,k}| - \sum_{(k,j)\varepsilon P_1} |A_{k,j}|) > \sum_{(k,j)\varepsilon P_2} |A_{k,j}| \qquad (54)$$

In order for both (52) and (54) to hold, $|\lambda|$ must be smaller than 1. This is true for any eigenvalue of $\underline{A}_1^{-1} \cdot \underline{A}_2$, so that the spectral radius $r(\underline{A}^{-1}\, \underline{A}_2) < 1$ and the method converges.

The second statement employs the definitions and results of [Rb 70]. Let $\underline{A}$ be an M-matrix. Denote by $\underline{I}_{method}$ the iteration matrix $\underline{I}$ for an iterative method applied to $\underline{A}\ \underline{x} = b$. Assume further that the Jacobi iteration converges, i.e. $r(I_j)<1$. Then both B1 and B2 converge faster than Jacobi, but slower than Gauss-Seidel;

$$r(I_{G-S}) < r(I_{B1}) < r(I_J); \quad r(I_{G-S}) < r(I_{B2}) < r(I_J) \qquad (55)$$

Proof. The proof is identical for B1 and B2. Let $\underline{A} = \underline{M}_1 - \underline{N}_1 = \underline{M}_2 - \underline{N}_2 = \underline{M}_3 - \underline{N}_3$ be the splittings corresponding to the methods of Gauss-Seidel, B1 and Jacobi respectively. By theorem 3.14 of [Va62] we have that all three splittings are regular. We can also see from the Figures 15, 16 that $N_3 \geq N_2 \geq N_1$. The result now follows from Theorem 3.15 of [Va62].

It is seen that from the point of view of asymptotic convergence, methods B1 and B2 are inferior to Gauss-Seidel. In the case of B2, it is interesting to observe the behavior of the method as p increases. It has been shown in [Rb70] that $r(I_{B2})$ monotonically decreases as p increases; in the limit, when p=n, $r(I_{B2}) = r(I_{G-S})$. Therefore, convergence improves. The ratio, however, may behave different. We have

$$d(\rho_{B2})/dp = (\beta'/d-1)/n^2 \qquad (56)$$

which is positive for most applications. Hence the efficiency of parallelization decreases. Between those two conflicting trends there exists a certain value of p which yields a minimal ρ. This value must be determined experimentally, for lack of any precise information concerning the behavior of $r(I_{B2})$ as a function of p.

8.5 CHASING, TEARING AND SHOOTING TRIDIAGONAL SETS

Aims: To suggest a modification of Southwell's relaxation method and "tearing", for ASP. To indicate that both block and "shooting" methods seem to lead to efficient ASP implementation. Finally, to show that if Topps is used, a particularly efficient method of "chasing" may be employed. The present section advances some ideas about possible solutions of tridiagonal sets; no proofs or results are given.

The field of solving $\underline{T}\ \underline{x} = \underline{z}$ is really too big for this chapter, but we only intend to get an idea of how ASP-methods might be developed. To do this, we advance now a few, very tentative, completely unproven ideas.

The original version of relaxation did not use a computer. The area, say a rectangle (fig. 17) with known values on its borders, had a superimposed grid of points. Initially, some values were given to these points. Then, an equation for improving x was applied to the point with the highest residual and so on. Each time, the largest residual vanishes.

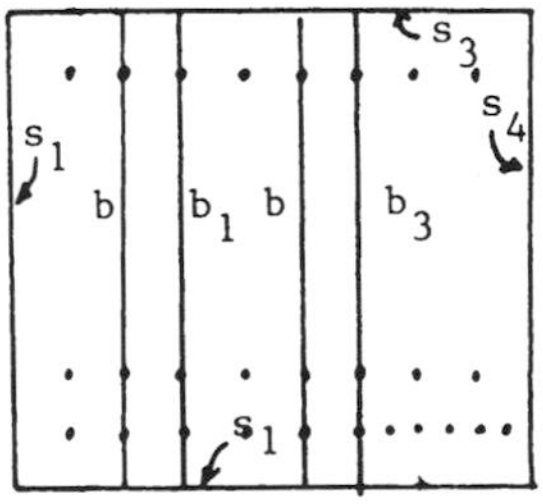

Fig. 17: Relaxation

Suppose we "tear" (quite artifically) the area into p subareas. For instance, suppose that in fig. 17 one area stretches from side s_2 to b_1, the second from b_2 to b_3 and the third (p=3) from b_4 to s_4. Each subarea can be solved once by the SSOR method on a computer. The slaves can next transfer to the master the values computed for the points on or near the (fictitious) boundaries. In a sequential step, the master adjusts these values and broadcasts them so that a new parallel step may start.

We have no results to prove that the method converges and if so how fast. Being similar to Southwell's original relaxation method, it should though converge. Its ratio will obviously be excellent since relatively little information is to be exchanged. In chapter 10, a similar "tearing" algorithm for state estimation will be discussed; its convergence is very fast indeed. Thus, the idea is worth looking into.

Next, the "implicit block-relaxation" [SRS 73] will be adapted for ASP. If the free vector $\underline{b}$ and the unknown $\underline{x}$ are subdivided in the same way as $\underline{T}$ and if we write the equation in a general way, we get for $\underline{T}\ \underline{x} = \underline{b}$:

$$\begin{bmatrix} \underline{D}_1 & \underline{E}_1 & & & & \\ \underline{C}_1 & \underline{D}_2 & \underline{E}_2 & & & \\ & \underline{C}_2 & \underline{D}_3 & \underline{E}_3 & & \\ & & \ddots & \ddots & \ddots & \\ & & & \underline{C}_{p-2} & \underline{D}_{p-1} & \underline{E}_{p-1} \\ & & & & \underline{C}_{p-1} & \underline{D}_p \end{bmatrix} * \begin{bmatrix} \underline{x}_1 \\ \underline{x}_2 \\ \underline{x}_3 \\ \vdots \\ \underline{x}_{p-1} \\ \underline{x}_p \end{bmatrix} = \begin{bmatrix} \underline{b}_1 \\ \underline{b}_2 \\ \underline{b}_3 \\ \vdots \\ \underline{b}_{p-1} \\ \underline{b}_p \end{bmatrix}$$

If we also assume $\underline{C}_o = \underline{E}_p = 0$ then we can write for each block-row:

$$\underline{C}_{j-1}\underline{x}_{j-1}^{(i+1)} + \underline{D}_j\underline{x}_j^{(i+1)} + \underline{E}_j\underline{x}_{j+1}^{(i)} = \underline{b}_j \qquad (57)$$

In this equation only $\underline{x}_j^{(i+1)}$ is not known, so that if ahead of starting the iterations, Choleski decomposition of the $\underline{D}_i$ submatrices is prepared, (57) can be solved by forward and backward substitutions. Also, (57) can be rewritten as:

$$\underline{x}^{(i+1)} = - (\underline{C} + \underline{D})^{-1} \underline{E}\,\underline{x}^{(i)} + (\underline{E} + \underline{D})^{-1}\underline{b} = \underline{I}_B\,\underline{x}^{(i)} + \underline{c} \tag{58}$$

with $\underline{I}_B$ being the iteration matrix of block-relaxation.

There is no reason why overrelaxation or for that matter symmetric overrelaxation should not be also used in block form. (57) will then be split into 1/2 of the iterations "down" and 1/2 going "up" to yield:

$$\underline{C}_{j-1}\,\underline{x}_{j+1}^{(i+\frac{1}{2})} + \underline{D}_j\,\underline{x}_j^{(i+\frac{1}{4})} + \underline{E}_j\,\underline{x}^{(i)} = \underline{b};\ \underline{x}_j^{(i+\frac{1}{2})} = \underline{x}_j^{(i)} + w(\underline{x}_j^{(i+\frac{1}{4})} - \underline{x}_j^{(i)}) \tag{58}$$

$$\underline{C}_{j-1}\,x_{j+1}^{(i+\frac{1}{2})} + \underline{D}_j\,\underline{x}_j^{(i+3/4)} + \underline{E}_j\,\underline{x}^{(i+1)} = \underline{b};\ \underline{x}_j^{(i+1)} = \underline{x}_j^{(i+\frac{1}{2})} + w(\underline{x}_j^{(i+\frac{1}{2})}) \tag{59}$$

In (58), $\underline{x}_j^{(i+\frac{1}{4})}$ and $\underline{x}_j^{(i+\frac{1}{2})}$ are computed for $j=1,2,\ldots,p$; in (59) $\underline{x}_j^{(i+\frac{1}{2})}$ and $\underline{x}_j^{(i+1)}$ are computed for $j=p,p-1,\ldots,2,1$ in the same way in which successive symmetric overrelaxation was done earlier, i.e., by using only 50% of operations. For programming it on ASP note that:

(a) The forward and backward substitutions can be done according to previously discussed ASP-methods.

(b) Since an entire block of values is transferred at a time, only h (instead of n) synchronizations are needed - a p-fold reduction.

(c) Despite all this, the method will hardly be efficient, mainly because some slaves will be idle while others work.

Another method which might be tried on ASP is that of "shooting". Consider again fig. 17 and specify in some way x_i on the first horizontal line above side s_1. This allows the computation of all values, ("shooting") upward $\underline{x}^{(1)}$ including those on side s_3 i.e. $\underline{x}^{(1)}$. Next for $j=1,2,\ldots,p$ assume $x_j = 1$ on that first horizontal line and $x_{k\neq j} = 0$ for all other points on the same line. In each of these p cases, a sweep upwards with $\underline{b} = \underline{0}$ is made yielding all vectors $\underline{x}_j^{(2)}$ and a vector $\underline{x}_j^{(2)}$ on side s_3. Then

$$\underline{x} = \underline{x}^{(1)} + \Sigma\,\chi_j\,\underline{x}_j^{(2)}\ ;\ j\Sigma = 1,\ldots,p \tag{60}$$

is a solution which satisfies the boundary conditions on sides s_1, s_2 and s_4. It also satisfies the conditions on s_3, if χ_j are chosen so that

$$\underline{x}^{(1)} + \Sigma\,\chi_j \cdot \underline{x}_j^{(2)} = \underline{b}'\ ;\ j\Sigma = 1,\ldots,p \tag{61}$$

where $\underline{b}'$ represents the boundary conditions on s_3. Set (61) for χ_j, $j=1,\ldots,p$ (but not $j=1,\ldots,np$) tends to be very ill-conditioned, but can probably be solved (at least in some cases) by iterative improvement techniques. Note that set (61) has dimension p, whereas the number of points is p·n; it is not a very large set. Note also that all computations for calculating $\underline{x}_j^{(2)}$, $\underline{\underline{x}}_j^{(2)}$, $j=1,\ldots,p$ can be done completely in parallel, with no exchange of information required.

Other and direct methods of solving $\underline{T}\ \underline{x} = \underline{b}$ were proposed: marching and nested dissection being mostly mentioned. In particular let us mention the algorithm of Buneman [SB] as representative of "reduction methods". These methods exploit the special structure of $\underline{T}$ to reduce the solution of $\underline{T}\ \underline{x} = \underline{b}$ recursively to the solution of another set which is structured as $\underline{T}$ but has only half as many unknowns. Recursively, the number of unknowns is halved. The method can quite obviously be programmed for ASP; I suspect that a similar method which was developed without any thought of parallelization [WB 69] can also be so programmed - but then these are really direct methods.

Finally, let's advance another method, which for obvious reasons will be called "chasing". View (57) as having elements c_i, a_i, b_i instead of blocks $\underline{C}_i$, $\underline{D}_i$, $\underline{E}_i$ and $\underline{z}$ replacing $\underline{b}$. For any j, j≠1, j≠n we have then:

$$c_j\, x_{j-1}^{(i)} + a_j\, x_j^{(i)} + b_j\, x_{j+1}^{(i-1)} = z_j \qquad (62)$$

where (i) indicates the iteration ("sweep") number. The SSOR program can be improved by changing the algorithm. Suppose n=8, p=2, $x_j^{(0)}=0$ for j=0,...,9. Apply then the following "chasing" program":

P(1): Slave - 1 calculates $x_j^{(1)}$, j=1,...,4 from (62).

S(1): Transfer $x_4^{(1)}$ from slave-1 to slave-2, solve there

$$c_5 x_4^{(1)} + a_5\, x_5^{(1)} + b_5\, x_6^{(0)} = z_5 \qquad (63)$$

for $x_5^{(1)}$ and transfer it back to slave-1.

P(i): Calculate $x_j^{(2)}$, j=1,...,4 in slave-1 and simultaneously $x_j^{(1)}$, j=6,7,8 in slave-2, both by applying (62) iteratively. Note that slave-1 is one sweep ahead of slave-2.

S(i): Transfer $x_4^{(i)}$ to slave-2, compute there $x_5^{(i)}$ and return it to slave-1.

Steps P(i), S(i) go on for i=2,3,... For each P(i), every slave k accumulates:

$$\delta_k = \Sigma\{x_j^{(i)} - x_j^{(i-1)}\}^2 \qquad (64)$$

for all j's of its slice. These p values are transferred to the master and whenever

$$e = \Sigma\, \delta_k \ ;\ k=1,\dots,p \qquad (65)$$

is smaller than some given accuracy, the solution has converged. Unfortunately, for p=2, δ_2 is that of sweep (i-1) while δ_1 is of sweep (i), so that summation (65) can be done only every p iterations.

Let us disregard P(1), S(1) and count the number of operations required for a sweep (i). In each P(i), (62) is applied (h-1) times so that

$$\Omega_p = (h-1)\ (3\mu + 2\alpha) \qquad (66)$$

For each S(i), a synchronization β, the transfer of two x-values and of δ_k to the master and broadcast of it, as well as one (3μ + 2α) are required

$$\Omega_s = \beta + 5(p - 1)\tau + (3\mu + 2\alpha) \qquad (67)$$

The ratio (inverse of speedup) for Mopps is therefore

$$\rho_m = (\Omega_p + \Omega_s)/\{n(3\mu + 2\alpha)\} \cong 1/p + \{\beta + 5(p - 1)\tau\}/\{n(3\mu + 2\alpha)\} \qquad (68)$$

Let us now assume that Topps replaces Mopps. In Topps all (p - 1) values x_j may be sent to their "right" neighbor slaves simultaneously. All δ_k are sent along with slave p adding them to e. Use of Topps leads therefore to the following advantages:

- The transfer time was reduced from 5(p - 1)τ to 2τ at each sweep. For p=128 as in SMS 201, the reduction is considerable. Accordingly, the ratio is

$$\rho_t \cong 1/p + (\beta + 2\tau)/\{n(3\mu + 2\alpha)\} \qquad (69)$$

- The convergence criterion was tested every single instead of every p'th sweep.

Let us now return to more general cases. The finite-difference equations of a two-dimensional Dirichlet problem in a convex region, may be written for a uniform mesh as in (57) except that now a_k, b_k, c_k represent submatrices of order $n_k \times n_k$, $n_k \times n_{k+1}$ and $n_k \times n_{k-1}$ respectively, x_k is a vector of unknowns in the k-th mesh line and z_k a subvector which depends on boundary values. Obviously, the order of the matrix in (57) is

$$N = \Sigma n_i;\ i = 1,\ldots,m \qquad (70)$$

The main difference to the previous case is that (57) was tridiagonal, but is now block-tridiagonal. The a's are tridiagonal, the b's and c's are negative-unitary submatrices, a "row" of $[c_j, a_j, b_j]$ comprises therefore mostly zeros, but c_j, a_j and b_j must be stored in their entirety in order not to complicate programming too much. Moreover in other cases e.g. field problems in electrical machines, in multilevel filters and even for Dirichlet problems using a 9-point instead of a 5-point formula, the "width" of a row is even larger. In all these cases k words (k>2) have to be transferred, so that the additions to ρ_m and ρ_k the "deteriorations" are respectively:

$$\rho - 1/p = \{(2k + 1)(p - 1)\tau\}/\{n(3\mu + 2\alpha)\} \qquad (71)$$

$$\rho - 1/p = \{(k + 1)\tau\}/\{n((3\mu + 2\alpha)\} \qquad (72)$$

The advantage of using Topps instead of Mopps is seen to increase.

9. OTHER PROBLEMS OF LINEAR ALGEBRA

Two disparate areas of linear algebra will be discussed: linear programming and eigenvalue analysis. The reader is asked to excuse it on the ground that linear programming (ℓ_ρ) will be needed in the next chapter, so it has to be discussed, eigenvalue analysis is probably the most important part of linear algebra, so it certainly has to be discussed. (We will discuss mostly the practically more important case of a real, symmetric matrix).

The treatment of ℓ_ρ is not too detailed. Actually, it serves only to demonstrate that block methods are indeed useful. In any case, a family of ASP-ℓ_ρ (or ALP)-programs will be developed. They differ in policies and since these are heuristic, the best proof of their effectiveness is numerical. Some policies lead to a high speedup indeed.

Similarity transformations lead to Jacobi's method. It is shown that an ASP-program for it may be developed such that it has a rather high speedup. ASP methods are developed for Given's, Householder's and other methods. Again the treatment is not detailed; developing the methods is still in progress. They do compare favourably with the few programs developed for SIMD-systems.

9.1 LINEAR PROGRAMMING

Aims: To develop an ASP-program for the simplex algorithm, so that it can serve for comparisons. To improve its speedup by block-methods. To calculate the efficiencies. The chapter is based on [WL 80].

In its simplest canonical form the linear programming problem ℓ_ρ is defined as follows:

Find min $z = \underline{c}^T \underline{x}$ (1)

of the cost function $\underline{z}$ such that the following constraints are satisfied:

$\underline{A}\ \underline{x} = \underline{b}\ ;\ \underline{x} \geqq 0$ (2)

All vectors are column vectors, the number of linear constraints (dimension of $\underline{A}$ and $\underline{b}$) is m, dimension of $\underline{c}$ and $\underline{x}$ is n ($n > m$) and all $b_i \geqq 0$. Initially $a_{ij} = 1$ for $i = j$, $i = 1,\ldots,m$, $a_{ij} = 0$ for $i \neq j$, $i,j = 1,\ldots,m$, and $c_j = 0$, $j = 1,\ldots,m$.

The well-known Simplex method is readily adapted for an ASP system. The data structure is as follows: Matrix $\underline{A}$ and vector $\underline{b}$ are stored in private memories (Fig. 1) by "slices" of (equal) integer width

$h = m/p$ (3)

The entire vector $\underline{x}$ is stored in each of the p private memories.

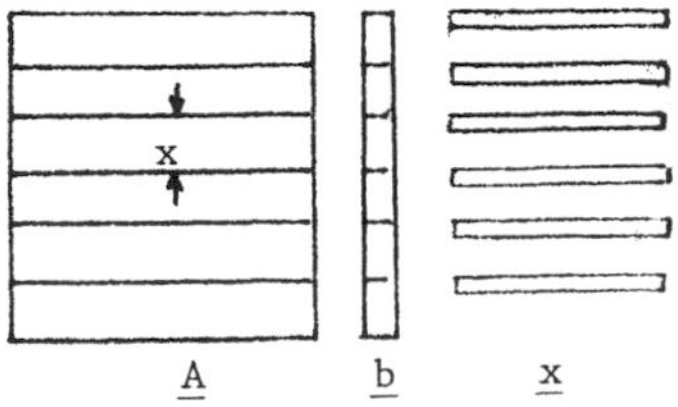

Fig. 1: Data Structure

The first version of the parallel Simplex algorithm, to be called PAS, is introduced only in order to be able to compare it with other algorithms. It consists of:

Step S (sequential step, executed by the master)

(a) Select column s of the tableaux, such that

$$c_s = \min c_i \quad (\text{for } c_i < 0) \tag{4}$$

If no $c_i < 0$ exists, the procedure is completed and the solution optimal.

(b) To find the x_r to be removed (from the basis), calculate

$$b_r/a_{rs} = \min (b_i/a_{i,s}) \text{ for } a_{i,s} > 0 \text{ and } i = 1,\ldots,m \tag{5}$$

If no $a_{is} > 0$, the procedure is terminated with an unbounded solution.

(c) Divide row r by a_{rs}, i.e.

$$a'_{r,j} = a_{r,j}/a_{rs} \;;\; j = 1,\ldots m;\; j \neq i \tag{6}$$

$$b'_r = b_r/a_{rj};\; a'_{rs} = 1 \tag{7}$$

(d) Broadcast the new row r and index s to all p slaves.

Step P (parallel step, executed by the p-slaves concurrently, each on its slice of $\underline{A}$ and $\underline{b}$)

$$b'_i = \begin{cases} b_{rs}/a_{rs} & i = r \\ b_i - b_r * a_{is}/a_{rs}; & i \neq r \end{cases} \quad i = 1,\ldots,m \tag{8}$$

$$a'_{ij} = \begin{cases} a'_{rj}/a'_{rs} & ;\; i = r; \\ a_{ij} - a_{is} * a'_{rj}/a'_{rs} & \end{cases} \quad \begin{matrix} i = 1,\ldots,m \\ j = 1,\ldots,n \end{matrix} \tag{9}$$

While the slaves are executing (8) (9) the master updates $\underline{c}$ according to

$$c'_j = c_j - a_{rj} * c_s/a'_{rs};\quad j = 1,\ldots n \tag{10}$$

In the parallel step, variables x_r and x_s were exchanged and new $\underline{A}'$, $\underline{b}'$, $\underline{c}'$ result. When all p-slaves have completed step P, the master initiates a new S-step with ($\underline{A}'$, $\underline{b}'$, $\underline{c}'$) instead of the original ($\underline{A}$, $\underline{b}$, $\underline{c}$).

Only eqs. (8) and (9) are executed in parallel. The master is scheduled so that it initiates an S-step as early as possible and broadcasts a new row $\underline{r}$ of $\underline{A}$ and index s ("selected" column) when completing the S-step.

We shall next compute the effective time ratio ρ of this algorithm. Since we do not know how many iterations are required, the times to be compared relate to a single iteration. In keeping with the accepted practice of complexity calculations, this "time" Ω will here be proportional to the required number of multiplication/division operations (μ).

Problems normally encountered [BAH76] have very large m and n but are extremely sparse. We may assume that each column of $\underline{A}$ has only d% nonzero entries. The number of μ's in each task of the algorithm is now as follows:

Step a requires none.

Step b has as many divisions as there are positive elements in columns. In the worst case (all positive), $\Omega_b = d*m*\mu$

There are $d*(n-m)$ multiplications in (6) and one in (7), so that for step c, $\Omega_c = d*(n-m)+1$.

Step d requires a bus-synchronization β and $(d*(n-m)+1) * \tau$ transfer (τ) times for broadcasting (simultaneously) the $d^*(n-m)+1$ elements of row r to all slaves.

In step P, all factors a'_{rj}/a'_{rs} are known, so that only one μ is required for each application of (9). Since every row r has $d(n-m)$ and every column s has d^*m-1 non-zero elements, the time to update matrix $\underline{A}$ is $t' = d^*(n-m)^*(d^*m-1)\mu$. In the same way, $(d^*m-1)\mu$ and $(d^*(n-m)+1)\mu$ are required for the updating of $\underline{b}$ and $\underline{c}$ resp.

Altogether, a single iteration requires

$$\Omega/\mu = d^*m+d(n-m)+1+d^2(m-1)(n-m)+d(m-1)-d(n-m)+1. \tag{11}$$

If we assume that work is divided evenly among the p slaves during the P-step, the total time will be:

$$\Omega_p = [2dm+d^2(n-m)m]\mu/p+\beta+[d(n-m+1)]\tau \tag{12}$$

The effective time ratio ρ (with $d(n-m)+1$ omitted in the denominator) is

$$\rho \cong 1/p + \beta/[d^2(n-m)m\mu] + [1/(dm) + 1/(d^2(n-m)m]\tau/\mu \tag{13}$$

Since the ideal $\rho = 1/p$, we can see that the proposed algorithm is efficient for large but not too sparse matrices. For very sparse matrices, d is small and the increment to $1/p$ increases accordingly. For sparse matrices we will next develop four algorithms, to be called ALP/1, 2, 3, and 4 (for ASP LP). They will all be basically the same as PAS, except that instead of replacing single pairs (x_s, x_r), blocks of variables (B) are interchanged simultaneously (during various P-steps).

Low effectiveness of the PAS-algorithm for very sparse matrices, is due to violation of the "parallelization principle". In fact, for such matrices, the bulk of arithmetical operations may fall in the sequential steps, with only a few (non-zero) elements of each slice to be changed simultaneously during the parallel step. In order to improve the situation, the algorithm must be rescheduled so that as much work as possible is shifted to the P-step. This may be achieved by using blocks of variables $\underline{x}_r$ and $\underline{x}_s$ to be removed and selected respectively. This approach proved successful in factorization and back-substitution and was also mentioned in the more distant past [Da63] for a different computational environment, on which occasion it was correctly called "block pivoting". We now proceed to illustrate its possible implementation on ASP.

Certain conditions must be imposed on blocks of columns $\underline{x}_r$ and $\underline{x}_s$ for them to be exchanged simultaneously.

Condition 1: A necessary and sufficient condition for simultaneous exchange of x_{r1} with x_{s1} and x_{r2} with x_{s2} is that matrix $\underline{C}$ below is nonsingular, so that

$$\underline{g} = \underline{C}^{-1} \begin{bmatrix} b_{r_1} \\ b_{r_2} \end{bmatrix} = \begin{bmatrix} a_{r_1 s_1} & a_{r_1 s_2} \\ a_{r_2 s_1} & a_{r_2 s_2} \end{bmatrix}^{-1} \begin{bmatrix} b_{r_1} \\ b_{r_2} \end{bmatrix} \geq 0 \tag{14}$$

$$b_j - [a_{js_1}, a_{js_2}]\, \underline{g} \geq 0 \text{ for } j \neq r_1, r_2 \tag{15}$$

The calculations are simpler if we state just the sufficient condition:

$$a_{r_1 s_2} = a_{r_2 s_1} = 0 \tag{16}$$

The change of $\underline{A}$, $\underline{b}$, and $\underline{c}$ (8, 9, 10) is effected by row r. Thus, simultaneous exchange is possible only if r_1 does not alter row r_2 and vice versa.

Suppose we exchange x_{r1} and x_{s1} in the basis. Row r_2, with elements a_{i,r_2}, will be changed into $a'_{r_2 i} = a_{r_2 i} - a_{r_1 i} * a_{r_2 s_1} / a_{r_1 s_2}$ (17)

Hence, the condition of $a'_{r_2 i} = a_{r_2 i}$ is that $a_{r_2 s_1} = 0$, (18)

and the second part of (16) is necessary for $a'_{r_1 i} = a_{r_1 i}$.

By induction we have the proposition: The condition for simultaneous exchange of blocks of variables

$$B^{(k)} = \{(x_{s_1}, x_{r_1}), \ldots, (x_{s_k}, x_{r_k})\} \tag{19}$$

is that

$$x_{ri,sj} = 0 \text{ for all } i,j = 1,\ldots,k; \quad i \neq j \ . \tag{20}$$

Note: The above conditions are also sufficient for ensuring that the objective function z does not decrease, provided all selected, non-basic variables $\underline{x}_s$ have negative values c_s. Indeed, if we set $a_{rj} = 0$ in (10),

$$c'_{s_2} = c_{s_2} \tag{21}$$

results. Hence, if $c_{s_2} < 0$, it will remain negative following the exchange.

We have already stated certain conditions for choice of block B^k; we still need to know how to select the set $\{x_r\}$ so as to ensure that the solution remains feasible (5). This will form part of the algorithms to be explained below.

The ALP-algorithms depend on the choice of the set $\{x_r\}$. A "block pivoting" method for the choice of $\{x_r\}$ is mentioned in [Da63]. It discusses the question of how many pivots can be chosen en block. We will extend this method so as to ensure that the result is also feasible (but will retain the name "block pivoting").

Choose a nonbasis x_{s_1} s.t. $c_{s_1} = \min c_i$ for $c_i < 0$. If no $c_i < 0$ exists, the minimum has been found. Otherwise, the variable to be removed from the basis is

$$\text{that } x_{r_1} \text{ for which } b_{r_1}/a_{r_1 s_1} = \min (b_i/a_{is_1}) \text{ for } a_{is_1} > 0 \tag{22}$$

Vector $\underline{b}$ is adapted through assignments (8) in which r,s are replaced by r_1, s_1.

Next, a nonbasic x_{s_2} is chosen such that for $c_i < 0$

$$c_{s_2} = \min_i c_i; \text{ s.t. } a_{r_1 s_2} = 0 \text{ and } a_{r_2, s_1} = 0. \tag{23}$$

Column r_2 is chosen in accordance with (23) in which r_2, s_2 replace r_1 and s_1, respectively. If none of the x_{s_2}, x_{r_2} satisfy the conditions of (23), block $B^{(k)}$ cannot be extended.

We now generalize this process. Let us assume that the set

$$B^{(k)} = \{(x_{r_1}, x_{s_1}), \ldots, (x_{r_k}, x_{s_k})\}, \tag{24}$$

satisfying all conditions, is already selected and vector $\underline{b}^{(k)}$ updated accordingly. Next, find the set $X^{(k)} = \{x_t\}$ such that

$$x_t \notin \{x_{s_1}, \ldots, x_{s_k}\}, \tag{25}$$

$$\text{all } c_t < 0, \tag{26}$$

$$a_{r_i t} = 0 \text{ and } a_{w,s_i} = 0 \text{ for } i = 1,\ldots,k, \tag{27}$$

and w was chosen so that

$$b_w^{(k)}/a_{wt} = \min (b_i^k/a_{it}) \text{ for } a_{it} > 0. \tag{28}$$

If the set $X^{(k)}$ is empty, the selection is completed. Otherwise

$$x_{s_{k+1}} = \{x_t \mid x_t \in X^{(k)}, \ c_t = \min, \ c_i, \ x_i \in X^{(k)}\} \tag{29}$$

and the extended set is $B^{(k+1)} = B^{(k)} \cup \{(x_{r_{k+1}}, x_{s_{k+1}})\}$ (30)

where r_{k+1} obeys for $a_{i_1 s_{k+1}} > 0$:

$$(b_{r_{k+1}}/a_{r_{k+1}s_{k+1}}) = \min (b_i/a_{i_1 s_{k+1}}) \tag{31}$$

Suppose that after each extension of B, vector $\underline{b}^{(k)}$ is recalculated according to:

$$b_i^{(k+1)} = \left\{ \begin{array}{ll} b_{r_{k+1}}^{(k)}/a_{r_{k+1}s_{k+1}}, & i = r_{k+1} \\ b_i^{(k)} - b_{r_{k+1}}^{(k)} * a_{i,s_{k+1}}/a_{r_{k+1}s_{k+1}}, & i \neq r_{k+1} \end{array} \right\} \ i = 1,\ldots,m, \tag{32}$$

then we can claim that all conditions are satisfied. Indeed, because of (28), the set $B^{(k+1)}$ satisfies the proposition. (27) ensures that the objective function does not increase at each iteration; (32) yields a vector $\underline{b}^{(k+1)}$ whose elements are all positive, so that all basic solutions are also feasible.

The first of the ALP family of algorithms - to be denoted ALP/1 - proceeds therefore as follows:

<u>Step A</u> (1) Let the master find the set of pairs to be exchanged (according to cost).

(2) Each time a new pair (x_r, x_s) is selected, interrupt the slave which holds row r and let it divide it by a_{rs}.

(3) Transfer rows $(r_1,\ldots,r_k)$ and indices $(s_1,\ldots,s_k)$ to all p-slaves.

<u>Step P</u>: Update the tableau (in parallel by all slaves, simultaneously) and repeat from (1).

Stage (2) of step A proceeds simultaneously with (1) and therefore step A is not called "sequential".

We next describe the <u>ALP/2</u> algorithm. Heuristically speaking, we would like the blocks of pivots to be as large as possible, to enhance parallelism. Since the cost function has no connection with the nonzero pattern of the constraints, choosing the pivots according to the cost criterion does not necessarily lead to large blocks of pivots. Therefore it is suggested that <u>x_s should be that variable which has the maximum number of zero elements in its column</u>. Intuitively, this should lead to a large set of columns which satisfy the conditions of the proposition. The new choice will be shown to be preferable to that of ALP/1; in fact, the sparser the column, the better chance there is of finding a large group $B^{(k)}$.

Thus, ALP/2 is identical to ALP/1 except for the policy of choosing the pivots (step A(1) of ALP/1). Below we exhibit results of simulations, which show that this change constitutes an improvement.

ALP/3 is another member of the ALP family. The reasoning behind it is as follows: step A of ALP/1 and ALP/2 starts with a search for variables to be exchanged simultaneously. The search process has a disadvantage in that many division operations may be "wasted". This can be seen as follows. Suppose $B^{(k)}$ of (24) is given and we want to augment it. We search for a new variable x_t which is to enter the basis. To determine whether x_t is a possible candidate we have to check (a) that $c_t < 0$ (in the case of ALP/1), (b) that $a_{r_i t} = 0$ for $i = 1,2,\ldots,k$. If x_t passes these criteria, we have (c) to make all the divisions implied by (28) to determine w (i.e., the variable which leaves the basis). But having computed w, we may find that the other condition of (27), namely $a_{w_i s} = 0$ is not fulfiled and x_t is not eligible; however, the division operations implied by step (28) were already wasted.

To avoid this, condition (31) must be dropped. If so, the submatrix A' composed of rows $r_1,r_2,\ldots,r_k$ and columns $s_1,s_2,\ldots,s_k$ of A will be lower triangular (instead of diagonal as in the case of ALP/1 and ALP/2). Therefore, prior to sending rows $r_1,\ldots,r_k$ to all processors for parallel Jordan operations, matrix A' must be diagonalized.

An additional step is inserted in which all $a_{r_i s_j}$; $i,j = 1,\ldots,k$; $i < j$ are made zero iteratively. First, all elements $a_{r_i s_1}$ for $i = 2,\ldots,k$ are reduced to zero by eliminating rows $r_2,\ldots,r_k$ with row r_1. Then, row r_2 is applied to rows $r_3,\ldots,r_k$ etc.

Note that since rows $r_1,\ldots,r_k$ are divided among slave memories, this intermediate step may be executed in parallel by sending rows $r_1,\ldots,r_k$ to the slaves which then "reduce" the elements of a column simultaneously.

Algorithm ALP/4 is derived from ALP/3 in the same way as ALP/2 is derived from ALP/1; namely, instead of choosing the new basic variables according to cost, the columns with the least number of nonzeros are chosen.

To sum up: the four algorithms of the ALP family are parallel implementations of the block-pivoting technique. They differ mainly in the way in which the pivots are chosen. In ALP/1 and ALP/3 the choice is based on cost, in ALP/2 and ALP/4 on sparsity. Furthermore, ALP/3 and ALP/4 require an elimination operation on the pivoting rows, prior to the exchange proper.

ALP programs have two advantages over PAS.

(1) Work is divided more evenly among the slaves. At the outset the matrix is very sparse, so that a large block of variables can be exchanged simultaneously, thus satisfying the parallelization principle. The assumption that the matrix is fast changing into a dense one (correct for factorization) is not always valid as shown by the following, simple example.

The tables below show a problem in which the original 8 nonzero elements increase to 12 when x_1 enters and x_5 is removed from the basis, but drop back to 8 when, next, x_2 enters and x_1 is removed. It is obvious that when the constraint

	x_1	x_2	x_3	x_4	x_5	x_6	x_7	x_8	b
	4	2	0	3	1	0	0	0	5
	-8	0	4	0	0	1	0	0	2
	0	0	3	0	0	0	1	0	1
	-2	0	5	0	0	0	0	1	1
c	-4	-3	5	3	0	0	0	0	0

	x_1	x_2	x_3	x_4	x_5	x_6	x_7	x_8	b
	1	.5	0	.75	.25	0	0	0	1.25
	0	4	4	6	2	1	0	0	12
	0	0	3	0	0	0	1	0	1
	0	1	5	1.5	.5	0	0	1	3.5
c	0	-1	5	6	1	0	0	1	5

	x_1	x_2	x_3	x_4	x_5	x_6	x_7	x_8	b
	2	1	0	1.5	0.5	0	0	0	2.5
	-8	0	4	0	0	1	0	0	2
	0	0	3	0	0	0	1	0	1
	-2	0	5	0	0	0	0	1	1
c	1	0	5	1.5	1.5	0	0	0	7.5

matrix is no longer sparse, the work of updating it is so heavy that PAS satisfies the parallelization principle.

(2) Obviously, the number of iterations required by ALP is smaller than that of Simplex or PAS, since cost-at least in the initial stages - is reduced faster. This advantage is especially marked when treating extremely large problems, which require external I/O-means.

Since all algorithms are heuristic, the only way to compare their ratio ρ, is through simulation. In the simulation process, a large number of n x n matrices were chosen at random. The matrices were very sparse, with 2, 3 or 4 non-zero elements per row. For each of these matrices, the program simulated the behavior of ALP/1, ALP/2, ALP/3 and ALP/4 on an ASP with p processors. Each simulation involved counting the number m of μ's, the number of synchronizations s and the number of bus transfers w; following which, the running time

$$T = m\mu + s\cdot\beta + w\cdot\tau \qquad (33)$$

was computed, using values of μ,β,τ from a manufacturer's handbook (equalling 5, 10 and 0.04 microseconds respectively). Then ρ was computed

$$\rho = T/T_{simplex} \qquad (34)$$

where $T_{simplex}$ is the time to solve the particular instance by the Simplex method. An average $\bar{\rho}$ of the effectiveness factor over all instances of random matrices of given size was computed, and so was the standard deviation σ^2 of this "random variable". A sample of results appear in the following table (σ^2 is given in parentheses). The only exception is row #1; the matrices considered in this case were rather dense (40 x 40 matrices with d = 0.5)

Table 1 - Effective Time Ratios

#	n	p	PAS	ALP/1	ALP/2	ALP/3	ALP/4
1	40	6	.21(.001)	-	-	-	-
2	70	6	.49(.120)	.61(.29)	.48(.25)	.46(.28)	.44(.26)
3	100	6	-	.46(.24)	.38(.21)	.42(.40)	.32(.16)
4	150	6	-	-	.36(.37)	-	.31(.21)
5	70	12	.41(.120)	.45(.21)	.37(.20)	.33(.19)	.33(.19)

Table 1 leads to the following conclusions:

(1) PAS deteriorates rapidly as sparseness increases (Compare rows 1 and 2)

(2) In all algorithms, ρ improves with larger matrices. For instance, for 100 x 100 matrices, ρ of ALP/4 with 6 slaves is better than ρ of (70 x 70) matrices with p = 12

(3) Choice of B^k based on sparseness (i.e., ALP/2, ALP/4) is better than the corresponding (ALP/1, ALP/3) programs based on cost criteria. Thus, "block pivoting" should be used in this form only

(4) ALP/2 and ALP/4 are also more effective than PAS. It seems that the larger the matrices, the greater these differences.

9.2 SIMILARITY TRANSFORMATION METHODS

Aims: To introduce similarity transformations and to show how they are used for transforming a (dense) matrix into one whose eigenvalues can easily be found. To describe the Jacobi, Householder and Givens methods. To program them for ASP and calculate the speedups. Only real matrices are treated. To show that both Givens' and Danilevsky's method can be used not only for the eigenvalue, but also for solvings $\underline{A}\,\underline{x} = \underline{b}$.

9.2.1 Similarity transformation

Transformations of a matrix $\underline{A}$ of the form $\underline{S}^{-1}\,\underline{A}\,\underline{S}$ where $\underline{S}$ is nonsingular are known as similarity transformations. Their usefulness is primarily the result of the fact that the eigenvalues of $\underline{A}$ and of $\underline{S}^{-1}\,\underline{A}\,\underline{S}$ are the same. For if we premultiply $\underline{A}\,\underline{x} = \lambda\,\underline{x}$ by $\underline{S}^{-1}$ and insert $\underline{S}\,\underline{S}^{-1} = \underline{U}$, we get

$$\underline{S}^{-1}\underline{A}(\underline{S}\underline{S}^{-1})\underline{x} = (\underline{S}^{-1}\underline{A}\underline{S})(\underline{S}^{-1}\underline{x}) = \lambda(\underline{S}^{-1}\underline{x});\ \underline{z} = \underline{S}^{-1}\underline{x};\ (\underline{S}^{-1}\underline{A}\underline{S})\underline{z} = \lambda\underline{z} \qquad (35)$$

with the same λ. Clearly the eigenvector was changed from $\underline{x}$ to $\underline{z} = \underline{S}^{-1}\underline{x}$.

Similarity is a transitive property for if $\underline{B} = \underline{S}_1^{-1}\underline{AS}_1$ and $\underline{C} = \underline{S}_2^{-1}\underline{BS}_2$, then $\underline{C} = \underline{S}_2^{-1}\ \underline{S}_1^{-1}\ \underline{A}\ \underline{S}_1\ \underline{S}_2 = (\underline{S}_1\underline{S}_2)^{-1}\ \underline{A}\ (\underline{S}_1\underline{S}_2) = \underline{S}_3^{-1}\ \underline{A}\ \underline{S}_3$ where $\underline{S}_3 \equiv \underline{S}_1\underline{S}_2$. Well-conditioning

will be insured if the condition number of $\underline{S}$ is not too large [SB].

Let $\underline{A}$ have eigenvalues and vectors $\lambda_1,\lambda_2,\ldots,\lambda_n$ and $\underline{x}_1,\underline{x}_2,\ldots,\underline{x}_n$ resp. and let Λ be a diagonal matrix with λ_i on the diagonal and $\underline{X}$ an nxn matrix s.t. its i-th column is $\underline{x}_i$. Then

$$\underline{A}\ \underline{x}_i = \lambda_i\ \underline{x}_i \text{ for } i=1,\ldots,n \text{ or } \underline{A}\ \underline{X} = \underline{\Lambda}\ \underline{X} \tag{36}$$

If the eigenvectors are linearly independent, then $\underline{X}^{-1}$ exists and $\underline{X}^{-1}\ \underline{A}\ \underline{X} = \underline{\Lambda}$ so that $\underline{A}$ is similar to a diagonal matrix whose diagonal elements are the eigenvalues of $\underline{A}$. This is the basis of the method of Jacobi. Other methods use the sequence:

$$\underline{A}_i = \underline{S}_1^{-1}\ \underline{A}_{i-1}\ \underline{S}_i;\ i = 1,2,\ldots,n \tag{37}$$

in order to transform $\underline{A} = \underline{A}_o$ into a matrix $\underline{B}$ of simpler form:

$$\underline{B} = \underline{A}_n = \underline{S}^{-1}\ \underline{A}\ \underline{S};\ \underline{S} = \underline{S}_1\ \underline{S}_2,\ldots,\underline{S}_n \tag{38}$$

The eigenvalues of $\underline{B}$ are those of $\underline{A}$ and $\underline{B}$ is such that they can be more easily calculated than those of $\underline{A}$.

Let us introduce a "plane rotation" matrix $\underline{S}_{p/q,r}$ such that it is a unit matrix $\underline{U}$ except for the four elements.

$$s_{pp} = s_{qq} = \cos\theta;\ s_{qp} = -s_{pq} = \sin\theta \tag{39}$$

Note that postmultiplication (premultiplication) of $\underline{A}$ by $\underline{S}$ changes only columns (rows) p,q of $\underline{A}$. It follows that the only elements of $\underline{A}$ which change in $\underline{S}^{-1}\ \underline{A}\ \underline{S}$ lie in the p-th and q-th rows and columns of $\underline{A}_r$ namely:

$$a_{pi} = a_{ip} := c_{pq}\cdot a_{pi} - s_{pq}\cdot a_{qi};\ i\neq p,q \tag{40}$$

$$a_{qi} = a_{iq} := s_{pq}\cdot a_{pi} + c_{pq}\cdot a_{qi};\ i\neq p,q \tag{41}$$

$$a_{pp} := c_{pq}^2\cdot a_{pp} + s_{pq}^2\cdot a_{qq} - 2\cdot a_{pq}\cdot s_{pq}\cdot c_{pq} \tag{42}$$

$$a_{qq} := s_{pq}^2\cdot a_{pp} + c_{pq}^2\cdot a_{qq} + 2\cdot a_{pq}\cdot s_{pq}\cdot c_{pq} \tag{43}$$

$$a_{pq} = a_{qp} := (a_{pp} - a_{qq})\cdot s_{pq}\cdot c_{pq} + a_{pq}(c_{pq}^2 - s_{pq}^2) \tag{44}$$

Suppose we multiply $\underline{S}^T$ by $\underline{S}$. The entries which count are shown below

$$\begin{bmatrix} \cos\theta & \sin\theta \\ -\sin\theta & \cos\theta \end{bmatrix} \begin{bmatrix} \cos\theta & -\sin\theta \\ \sin\theta & \cos\theta \end{bmatrix} = \begin{bmatrix} b & 0 \\ 0 & b \end{bmatrix}$$

with $b = \sin^2\theta + \cos^2\theta$ which can be made 1 by a proper choice of θ.

It is seen that $\underline{S}$ leads to a unitary (and orthogonal) transformation:

$$\underline{S}^T\ \underline{S} = \underline{U};\ \underline{S}^{-1} = \underline{S}^T \tag{45}$$

Another similarity transformation uses Householder's matrix:

$$\underline{H}_i = \underline{U} - 2\ \underline{h}_i\ \underline{h}_i^T;\ \underline{h}_i^T\ \underline{h}_i = 1;\ h_i^T = [0,\ldots,0,h_{i+1},\ldots,h_n]$$

We encountered this matrix in Chapter 5 and will return to it later. Here, it suffices to note that premultiplication of $\underline{A}$ by $\underline{H}_i$ affects only rows (i+1) to n of $\underline{A}$ and that $\underline{H}_i\ \underline{A}\ \underline{H}$ is defined through [YG]:

$$s_{i-1} = (a_{i,i-1}^2 + a_{i+1,i-1}^2 + \ldots + a_{n,i-1}^2)^{\frac{1}{2}};\ a'_{i,i-1} = a_{i,i-1} + s_{i-1}(\operatorname{sgn} a_{i,i-1}) \tag{46}$$

$\underline{v}_i^T=[0,\ldots,0,a'_{i,i-1},a_{i+1,i-1},\ldots,a_{n,i-1}]; \; 1/\gamma_i=s_{i-1}^2+s_{i-1}|a_{i,i-1}|$ (47)

The transformation $\underline{H}_i\ \underline{A}_{i-1}\ \underline{H}_i$ by $\underline{H}_i = \underline{U} - 2\ \underline{v}_i\ \underline{v}_i^T$ yields a new column:

$$a'_{i-1,i-1} = a_{i-1,i-1};\ a'_{i,i-1} = s_{i-1},\ a'_{i+1,i-1}=\ldots=a'_{n,i-1} = 0 \quad (48)$$

We are next going to review how transformations by $\underline{S}$ or $\underline{H}$ can be used for computing eigenvalues and solving sparse linear sets $\underline{A}\ \underline{x} = \underline{b}$.

9.2.2. Jacobi's method

The classical Jacobi method reduces a symmetric matrix $\underline{A}_o \equiv \underline{A}$ to diagonal form by a sequence of orthogonal transformations:

$$\underline{A}_{k+1} = \underline{R}^T_{p/q,r}\cdot\underline{A}_k\cdot\underline{R}_{p/q,r}\ ;\ r=p,\ k=0,1,2,\ldots \quad (49)$$

where element $a_{p,q}$, $p<q$ is chosen as the "pivot" to be eliminated. Matrix $\underline{R}$ is identical to that of S in (39).

The condition $a_{pq}=a_{qp}=0$ determines $c_{pq}\equiv\cos\theta$, $s_{pq}\equiv\sin\theta$ as:

$$u := 0.5(a_{qq}-a_{pp})/a_{pq}\ ;\ v := \mathrm{sign}(u)/(\ u\ +\mathrm{sqrt}(1+u^2)) \quad (50)$$

$$c_{pq} := (\mathrm{sqrt}(1+v^2))^{-1}\ ;\ s_{pq} := c_{pq}\cdot v \quad (51)$$

Note again that (40) to (44) change only rows and columns p and q of matrix $\underline{A}_k$.

Parallel versions of this algorithm attempt to ensure that a number of rotations occurs independently and may thus proceed in parallel. In [KS72] the rotation matrix of each major step (Fig. 2) is composed of n/2 submatrices (2 by 2) on the diagonal. Each transformation (49) is followed by a permutation.

$$\underline{A}_{k+1} := \underline{P}\cdot\underline{A}_{k+1}\cdot\underline{P}^T \quad (52)$$

$$\underline{P} = (\underline{u}_1,\ \underline{u}_n,\ \underline{u}_2,\ \ldots,\ \underline{u}_{n-1}) \quad (53)$$

where $\underline{u}_i$ is the i-th column of the identity matrix $\underline{U}$. (The permutation above is not the only one possible; a similar result would be achieved by

$$\underline{P} = (\underline{u}_n,\ \underline{u}_2,\ \underline{u}_3,\ \ldots,\ \underline{u}_{n-1},\ \underline{u}_1) \quad (54)$$

and others.) Each "major step" (49, 52) annihilates n off-diagonal terms of $\underline{A}_k$ simultaneously and permutes the matrix so that after (n-1) permutations the original order of elements is restored.

This method can easily be implemented in ASP, with the following two steps being iterated

$\underline{P}$: Each slave performs h/2 rotations

$\underline{S}$: Permute according the (52, 53).

For each of the h/2 blocks, the time of $4\alpha+6\mu+2\gamma$ (γ is the time to take a square-root) is required. Altogether, the sum for the "top" slice is $(2\alpha+4\mu)((n-h)^2+0.5h^2)$. For the lower slices work decreases until hardly anything remains to be done by slave p, but unfortunately it will have to wait for slave 1. For the permutation, p rows of $\underline{A}_{k+1}$ must be shifted vertically between the slaves (horizontal shifts cost nothing) and this amounts to $n\beta+pn\tau$. Altogether, the time required for a major step is

$$\Omega_p = 0.5h(4\alpha+6\mu+2\gamma)+(2\alpha+4\mu)(n^2-2nh+1.5h^2)+n\beta+pn\tau \quad (55)$$

Had the same algorithm been programmed for a sequential machine, the time:

$$\Omega_1 = 0.5n\ (6\mu+4\alpha+2\gamma)+(2\alpha+4\mu)n^2/2 \tag{56}$$

would have been required. From (55), (56) it follows that the ratio is:

$$\rho = \frac{0.5n(4\alpha+6\mu+2\gamma)/p+n^2(1-2/p+1.5/p^2)(2\alpha+4\mu)+n\beta+pn\tau}{0.5n(4\alpha+6\mu+2\gamma)+0.5n^2(2\alpha+4\mu)} \tag{57}$$

If n is large and γ small, this may be approximated by

$$\rho \cong \frac{2(p^2-2p+1.5)}{p^2} + \frac{\beta+p\tau}{n(\alpha+2\mu)} \tag{58}$$

If the second term is neglected, the efficiency will be

$$\eta \cong \frac{50p}{p^2-2p+1.5} \tag{59}$$

p	1	2	3	4	5	6	7	8	9	10
η	100	66.5	33.3	21.0	15.1	11.8	9.6	8.2	7.0	6.1

Table 2: Efficiencies of the method

These efficiencies were computed (Table 2) as in [KS72], that is without account for either the time to arrange the data (to be neglected in ASP, but not in Illiac) or to the shifts (to be neglected in Illiac, but not in ASP).

We noted already some general disadvantages, which also apply specifically to this method, namely:

- A very complicated data base (see Figs. 1-5 of [KS72])
- A correspondingly long time to arrange it prior to computation
- Difficult programming.

There are disadvantages also in the ASP version, namely:

- The threshold method [Co63] was not applied
- The work was distributed rather unequally among the slaves so that slave p had to wait for most of its P-step. "Scrambling" will not help, since it may increase the number of row-shifts between slaves.
- The efficiencies (Table 2) are rather low.

We next suggest an ASP-method in which data movement is reversed: instead of moving rows and columns, it will move the diagonal elements and the sines and cosines between the master and the slaves. The method will be exemplified on a 12x12 matrix and an p=3-slave system. Its various parts are marked as in Fig. 3 and h=n/p=4. The first step is exemplified by Fig. 3 and consists of:

S1: Transfer the diagonal elements $a_{i,i}$ and those of the subdiagonal (marked by V) for which in $a_{i,i+1}$, i is odd to the master. The master computes the sines and cosines according to (50), (51) and adjusts the diagonal elements according to (42) (43). The new elements as well as all $s_{i,\ i+1}$, $c_{i,\ i+1}$ values are broadcast to all slaves.

P1: Each slave performs the horizontal and then the vertical changes in a part of its slice. Thus, slave 1 works employing (40) (41) on parts γ, δ, slave 2 on Ψ, ψ

and slave 3 on ζ, ε'.

<u>S2</u>: The master replaces ε in slave 1 with ε' as calculated in slave 3. It then repeats S1 for i even.

<u>P2</u>: Repeats P1, but with even i.

The next step (marked Λ in Fig. 4) would annihilate $a_{i,\ i+2}$ in the same way as the first did for $a_{i,\ i+1}$. Unfortunately, we would then need to "cross over" from one slave into another. In order to make the programming simpler, we will store in each slave, the entire upper triangle of $\underline{A}$ (but work on slices as previously). Thus we need to transfer not only ε', but about $n^2/2$ elements first to the master and then broadcast them to all slaves.

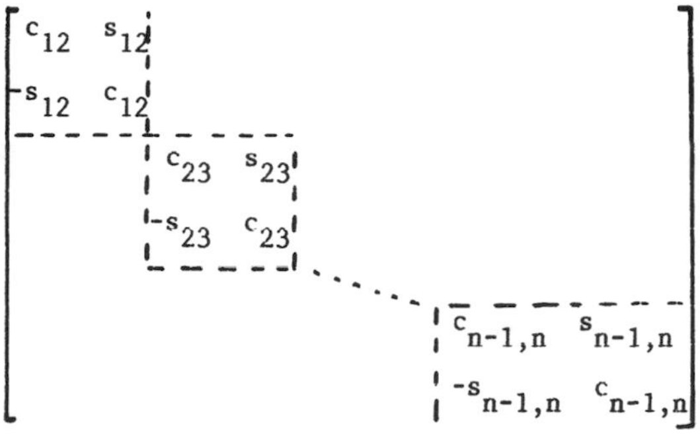

Fig. 2: A rotation matrix

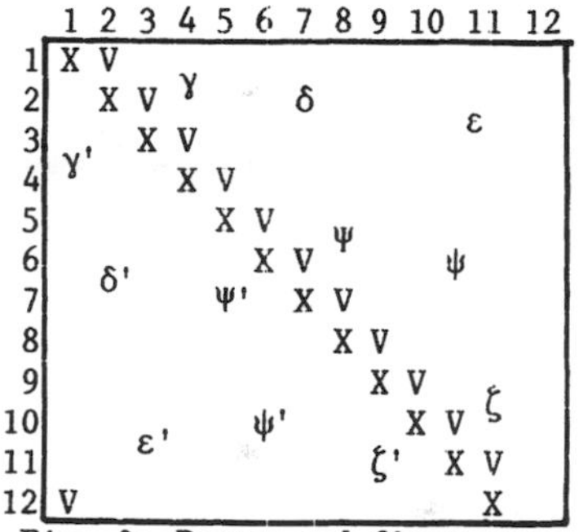

Fig. 3: Parts and first step

Let us now calculate the ratio of this method:

(a) The time of synchronization β is usually 100-200 times as large as τ. An efficient algorithm will therefore minimize the number of synchronizations required. We might start the algorithm above by transferring the upper "new" triangle followed by sequential step S(1). We will then be able to combine steps S(2) and S(1), thus reducing the number of synchronizations by 1.

(b) We can proceed choosing subdiagonals according to Fig. 4. Each time, there are n diagonal, subdiagonal, sine and cosine values (except for subdiagonal a(i,i+6) which has only n/2=6 elements) to be computed and exchanged. For each sequential step we thus need for the various parts of what was S(2) and S(1) above:

$$\Omega' = \beta+n^2\tau+2n\tau+2n(6\mu+4\alpha+2\gamma)+2n(9\mu+4\alpha)+4n\tau \qquad (60)$$

In the sequential case we would have only needed $2n(6\mu+4\alpha+2\gamma)$ for the computation of sines, cosines and $2n(9\mu+4\alpha)$ for correcting the diagonal terms; no data transfer (τ) or bus synchronization (β) would be required.

(c) Whether we do it serially or on ASP, we have to correct all elements of the upper triangle (actually only $1+2+\ldots+(n-2)=(n-2)(n-1)/2 \cong n^2/2$) 4 times: twice horizontally and twice vertically. In the sequential case, n pivots as in Fig. 3 would require

$$\Omega'' = (4\mu+2\alpha)4n^2/2 = 4n^2(2\mu+\alpha) \qquad (61)$$

but only Ω''/p in the parallel case.

(d) In both the sequential and ASP-algorithms we will have to choose n/2 subdiagonals. Thus, the time ratio:

$$\rho = \frac{4n^2(2\mu+\alpha)/p+\beta+n^2\tau+2n\tau+2n(6\mu+4\alpha+2\gamma)+2n(9\mu+4\alpha)+4n\tau}{4n^2(2\mu+\alpha)+2n(6\mu+4\alpha+2\gamma)+2n(9\mu+4\alpha)} \qquad (62)$$

$$\rho = \frac{4n^2(2\mu+\alpha)/p+n(30\mu+16\alpha)+4n\gamma+n(n+6)\tau+\beta}{4n^2(2\mu+\alpha)\ +\ n(30\mu+16\alpha)+4n\gamma} \qquad (63)$$

For large n, this ratio may be approximated by

$$\rho \cong \frac{4n^2(2\mu+\alpha)/p+4n\gamma+\tau n^2+\beta}{4n^2(2\mu+\alpha)\ +\ 4n\gamma} \qquad (64)$$

If it wouldn't be for the taking of the square root (γ), data-transfer (τ) and bus-synchronization (β) we would have achieved the ideal ratio $\rho=1/p$ and 100% efficiency. Even counting γ, τ and β, the efficiencies will be very high - certainly much higher than those of Table 2.

Let us add the following notes concerning this method:

(a) The threshold search method [Co63] can be easily added. All that is needed is to precede each sequential step by a search for elements above the threshold. Since this search can be performed entirely in parallel i.e., each slave searches its own slice independently of and concurrently with other slaves, the efficiency of the threshold method will be even higher. (If needed, any ASP-version of searching could be used.)

(b) For sparse matrices the following method is suggested. Suppose slave 1 chooses pivot $a_{p,q}$, slave 2 chooses $a_{r,s}$. Element $a_{p,r}$ would have been changed into

	1	2	3	4	5	6	7	8	9	0	1	2	3
1		V	Z	O	X	/	Y						
2			V	Z	O	X	/	Y					
3				V	Z	O	X	/	Y				
4					V	Z	O	X	/	Y			
5						V	Z	O	X	/	Y		
6							V	Z	O	X	/	Y	
7								V	Z	O	X	/	
8	/								V	Z	O	X	
9	X	/								V	Z	O	
	0	X	/								V	Z	
	Z	O	X	/								Z	
	y	Z	O	X	/								

Fig. 4: A complete sweep

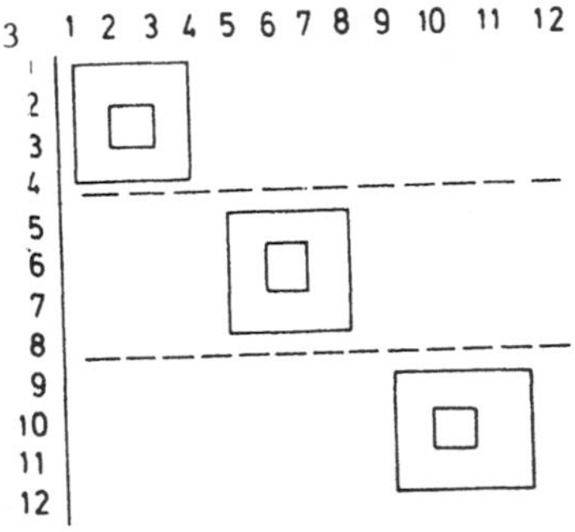

Fig. 5: Another set of rotations

$$a'_{pr} := c_{pq}\cdot a_{pr} + s_{pq}\cdot a_{rq} \qquad (65)$$

because of the first rotation and into

$$a''_{pr} := c_{rs}\cdot a'_{pr} + s_{rs}\cdot a'_{ps} \qquad (66)$$

because of the second. If

$$a_{rp}=a_{sp}=a_{rq}=a_{sq}=0 \qquad (67)$$

then $a''=a$ and the two slaves can work <u>independently</u>, each correcting its rows and columns. In terms of the "program", this means that the slaves should choose <u>all</u> possible pivots, but the master will have to reduce it to s subsets obeying (67).

(c) The method of Jacobi was not changed; only its scheduling was. Therefore, the convergence was not affected.

(d) The set of rotations (Fig. 4) used above is not the only one possible. Indeed, any set of <u>independent</u> rotations, e.g., that of Fig. 5 will do.

(e) Instead of using the sines and cosines s_{pq}, c_{pq} as in (40)-(44), we may follow [RR78], add calculation of

$$d = s_{pq}/(1+c_{pq});\ e = v\cdot a_{pq} \tag{68}$$

and then express the calculation of all elements of $\underline{A}_{k+1}$ as perturbations of elements of $\underline{A}_k$, namely as:

$$a_{pp} := a_{pp}-e;\ a_{qq} := a_{qq}+e \tag{69}$$

$$\left.\begin{array}{l} a_{pi} = a_{ip} := a_{pi}-s_{pq}(a_{qi}+d\cdot a_{pi}) \\ a_{qi} = a_{iq} := a_{qi}+s_{pq}(a_{qi}-d\cdot a_{qi}) \end{array}\right. \quad i \neq p \text{ or } q \tag{70}$$

Not only will this yield more accurate results, but it also requires fewer operations and is particularly well suited for our algorithm; d and e are calculated by the master and broadcast to all slaves (along with other values of S1) and (70) is then used in the parallel step.

(f) If it is desired to compute the eigenvectors along with the eigenvalue, we normally do it as follows. Initialize matrix $\underline{S}$ as an identity matrix $\underline{U}$. For each chosen pivot a_{pq}, modify the p and q columns of $\underline{R}$ as follows:

$$r_{ip} := c_{pq}\cdot r_{ip}-s_{pq}\cdot r_{iq} \tag{71}$$

$$r_{iq} := s_{qp}\cdot r_{ip}+c_{qp}\cdot r_{iq} \tag{72}$$

There is not much work at the beginning, but the matrix $\underline{S}$ will be dense after the first sweep and stay so later. We may therefore assume that each slave works on its slice correcting columns p,q according to (71, 72). This part requires no additional synchronization or data transfers. Its efficiency is thus 100%.

9.2.3. Given's method

This method [Wi65,RR78] uses the same orthogonal rotations

$$\underline{A}_{k+1} = \underline{R}^T_{p/q,r}\cdot\underline{A}_k\cdot\underline{R}_{p/q,r} \tag{73}$$

and (40)-(44) as does the method of Jacobi except that in Given's method, s_{pq} and c_{pq} are chosen so as to annihilate elements a_{qr}, a_{rq}, i.e.,

$$s_{pq} := -a_{rq}/sq;\ c_{pq} := a_{rp}/sq;\ sq = \sqrt{a^2_{rp} + a^2_{rq}} \tag{74}$$

and that the rotations are scheduled strictly according to

$$p/q,r = j/i,j-1;\ j=2,3,\ldots,n-1 \text{ and for each } j:i=j+1,\ldots,n \tag{75}$$

This schedule preserves zeros and transforms the algorithm into a noniterative one but it leaves a tridiagonal matrix to be yet solved.

ASP algorithms will be discussed as in [Wi65] namely by showing how they apply to the first row and column with the understanding that the method carries over to other rows and columns in the same way. This is shown for n=12, p=3 in Fig. 6 where "x" denotes elements (p,p), (q,q), (p,q), and (q,p) and "V" all the others (p = 1, q=2). The simplest method would let the master store row 2 and would proceed as in:

(a) The master recalls row q(q=3,...,n) from the respective slave, computes s_{pq}, c_{pq} ((74) for r=2) and broadcasts them to all slaves.

(b) Each slave changes columns p and q of its slice according to (40)(41) and one of them also a_{pp}, a_{qq} and a_{pq}, a_{qp} ((42),(43)).

For the first transformation with $\underline{R}_{2/3,1}$ this amounts to:

(a) The master calculates $sq=\sqrt{a^2_{21}+a^2_{31}}$, $c_{21}=a_{21}/sq, s_{21}=-a_{31}/sq$ and broadcasts them

(b) Slaves 1, 2 and 3 (Fig. 6) calculate $\{a_{33},a_{43},a_{22},a_{23}=a_{32}\}$, $\{a_{i2}$ and a_{i3} for $i=4,5,6,7\}$ and $\{a_{i2}$ and a_{i3} for $i=8,9,10,11\}$ respectively.

It is obvious that this method is rather inefficient on account of large data movement and unequal distribution of work. To a large degree the algorithm may be improved if careful attention is paid to the sequence of transformations. Written if full, they are:

$$\underline{R}^T_{2/n,1}\cdots\underline{R}^T_{2/5,1}\underline{R}^T_{2/4,1}\underline{R}^T_{2/3,1}\underline{A}_1\underline{R}_{2/3,1}\underline{R}_{2/4,1}\underline{R}_{2/5,1}\cdots\underline{R}_{2/n,1}=\underline{A}_2 \tag{76}$$

$$\underline{R}^T_{3/n,2}\cdots\underline{R}^T_{3/6,2}\underline{R}^T_{3/5,2}\underline{R}^T_{3/4,2}\underline{A}_2\underline{R}_{3/4,2}\underline{R}_{3/5,2}\underline{R}_{3/6,2}\cdots\underline{R}_{3/n,2}=\underline{A}_3 \tag{77}$$

$$\vdots$$

$$\underline{R}^T_{n-1/n,n-2}\underline{A}_{n-2}\underline{R}_{n-1/n,n-2}=\underline{A}_{n-1} \tag{78}$$

$$\underline{R}^T_{p/q,p-1}\,\underline{A}_{p-1}\,\underline{R}_{p/q,p-1}=\underline{A}_n \tag{79}$$

where each transformation annihilates element $a_{q,p-1}=a_{p-1,q}$ by a rotation in plane (p,q), $p<q$.

Note that for every row (76-79), the p and r in $R_{p/q,r}$ are the same. Thus, we may call p, the "basic row" and r the "annihilated column". Note also, that because of symmetry $a_{ij}=a_{ji}$, $j\neq i$. This leads to another algorithm in which

```
 1| X X 0 0 0 0 0 0 0 0 0 0
 2| X X V V V V V V V V V V
 3| 0 V
 4| 0 V
 5| 0 V
 6| 0 V
 7| 0 V
 8| 0 V
 9| 0 V
10| 0 V
11| 0 V
12| 0 V
```

Fig. 6: Annihilating elements of first column

```
|1 w 0 0 0 0 0 0 0 0 0 0
|w X X X X X X X X X X X
|0 X X
|0 X X X
|0 X X X X
|0 X X X X X
|0 X X X X X X
|0 X X X X X X X
|0 X X X X X X X X
|0 X X X X X X X X X
|0 X X X X X X X X X X
|0 X X X X X X X X X X X
```

Fig. 7: Matrix R_2

<u>all</u> sine and cosine values for any annihilated column r are computed in the master. Thus, for (76), the master holds row 1 and the single value $w=a_{21}$. It then computes <u>recursively</u>:

$$\left.\begin{aligned} &sq=\sqrt{w^2+a^2_{1,i}}\ ;\ c_q=a_{1q}/sq\ ;\ s_q=a_{1q}/sq \\ &w:=w\cdot c_q+a_{1q}\cdot s_q \end{aligned}\right\}q=3,4,\ldots n \tag{80}$$

All c_q and s_q values are then broadcast as a single block and the slaves thus given <u>repeated</u>, <u>independent</u> work. Note also that because $i>p>q$ in each basic row, the values $\{a_{pp},a_{qq}, a_{pq}=a_{qp}\}$ may be calculated at the very end <u>in a slave</u> thus saving one synchronization.

Next we compute the efficiency. For each basic row m, the initial transfer requires (β+mτ). (80) is computed (n-m) times, so that (n-m)(6μ+2α+γ) are required for it and (n-m)τ for broadcast. Initially, all slaves except the first need 0.5h(h-1)(4μ+2α) for repeatedly performing (40)(41). Unfortunately, after the first (h-2) steps, the first slave stops working entirely, after (2h-2) two slaves are idle, etc. For the last h steps of the algorithm only the last slave works; we again encounter the Haydn effect and in this case, scrambling the rows will be of no help. Hence, even if only a single slave works, still

$$\Omega' = 0.5h(h-1)(4\mu+2\alpha) = h(h-1)(\alpha+2\mu) \qquad (81)$$

are needed. The time for one basic row on an ASP-system is thus

$$\Omega_p = \beta+m\tau+(n-m)(6\mu+2\alpha+\gamma)+(n-m)\tau+0.5h(h-1)(4\mu+2\alpha) \qquad (82)$$

with m being n-1, n-2,...,3, 2. Since $h^2=n^2/p^2>>n$ we may write

$$\Omega_p \cong \beta+n\tau+(n-m)\gamma+h^2(2\mu+\alpha) \qquad (83)$$

This must be multiplied by (n-2) to yield the entire count. In sequential execution [RR78] the same requires

$$\Omega \cong 4n^3(2\mu+\alpha)/3 + 0.5n^2\gamma \qquad (84)$$

Inserting these values yields the (time reduction) ratio of:

$$\rho = \frac{n(2\mu+\alpha)/p^2+0.5\gamma}{4n(2\mu+\alpha)/3+0.5\gamma} + \frac{\beta+n\tau}{4n^2(2\mu+\alpha)/3+0.5n\gamma} \qquad (85)$$

For n/p=4/3, the first part approaches the ideal, optimal ratio of 1/p. For n/p>4/3, the ratio increases, but will still be rather good.

It is tempting and possible to calculate on ASP all rotations for a basic row p:

$$\underline{R}_p = \underline{R}_{p/q,p-1}\cdot\underline{R}_{p/q+1,p-1}\cdot\ldots\cdot\underline{R}_{p/n,p-1} \qquad (86)$$

at once. (For p=2, this is shown in Fig. 7.) Unfortunately, it is then necessary to compute

$$\underline{A}_p = \underline{R}_p^T\cdot\underline{A}_{p-1}\cdot\underline{R}_p \qquad (87)$$

There are two ways to compute a matrix product (Chapter 4), but they cannot easily be adapted to calculate $\underline{A}_p$ of (87). In any case, the previous method seems to be better. On the other hand, Gentleman's method (Ge73) will reduce the number of operations (recall, Chapters 5, 6 and 8).

9.2.4. Householder's method

This algorithm was also adapted [KS72] for Illiac, but in a form to which we raise the same objections, mostly that the data structure is complicated, would take too much set-up time and that it depends on the number of processing elements. It is better to start from basic premises [Wi65]. In order to compute the new elements a_{ij}, i=r+1,...,n only the corresponding elements a_{ij} of $\underline{A}_r$ are required. Because of symmetry (of S), these elements may be computed row-wise ("in-slice") through:

$$a_{ij} := \Sigma\ s_{ik}\cdot a_{kj} = \Sigma\ s_{ik}\cdot a_{jk};\ k\ \Sigma = r+1,\ldots,n \qquad (90)$$

The algorithm, exemplified again for the first step on the (12x12) matrix of Fig. 6 would be as follows:

P(1): Slaves 1, 2 and 3 compute: $s_1^2 = a_{21}^2+a_{31}^2+s_{41}^2$; $s_2^2 = a_{51}^2+a_{61}^2+a_{71}^2+a_{81}^2$ and $s_3^2 = a_{91}^2+a_{10,1}^2+a_{11,1}^2+a_{12,1}^2$ respectively. These values and row 1 are then blocktransferred to the master.

S(1): The master computes the scalars:

$$s^2 = s_1^2+s_2^2+s_3^2;\ s = +\sqrt{s^2};\ \psi = 1/(b^2+|a_{12}|b) \tag{91}$$

and the vector:

$$\underline{w}^T = (0, a_{12}+b\cdot \mathrm{sgn}(a_{12}), a_{13}, \ldots, a_{1,12})^T \tag{92}$$

It then broadcasts ψ and $\underline{w}$ to all p=3 slaves.

P(2): Each slave calculates its slice of vector $\underline{u}=\psi A \underline{w}$ through

$$u_i = \psi \Sigma\ a_{ik}\cdot w_k;\ k\ \Sigma=1,\ldots,12 \tag{93}$$

with i=(1,2,3,4)(5,6,7,8) and (9,10,11,12) for the three slaves. Additionally they compute each

$$k_j = 0.5\cdot\psi\cdot\sum_i w_i\cdot u_i \tag{94}$$

where i runs the range of indices given for each slave j as above. All k_j's and vector $\underline{u}$ are then transferred to the master.

S2: The master calculates

$$k = \Sigma\ k_j\ ;\ j\ \Sigma = 1,\ldots,p;\ \underline{q} = \underline{u} - k\underline{w} \tag{95}$$

and broadcasts vector $\underline{q}$ to all slaves.

P(3): Each slave replaces

$$a_{ij} := a_{ij}-(w_i q_j+q_i w_j);\ j=2,\ldots, n \tag{96}$$

and i over the entire slice (except for the first row which need not be computed). This completes the first major step; the next step is identical except that it operates on an (n-1)x(n-1) matrix. The "times" for each of the steps in turn is:

$$\Omega_{p1} = h\mu+(h-1)\alpha+\gamma+p\tau_s+n\tau_b+\beta \tag{97}$$

$$\Omega_{s1} = (p-1)\alpha+2\alpha+3\mu+\gamma+\tau_s+(n-1)\tau_b \tag{98}$$

$$\Omega_{p2} = (hn+1)\mu+h(n-1)\alpha+(h+2)\mu+(h-1)\alpha+p\tau_s+n\tau_b+\beta \tag{99}$$

$$\Omega_{s2} = p\alpha+n\alpha+n\mu+n\tau_b \tag{100}$$

$$\Omega_{p3} = h(n-1)(2\alpha+2\mu) \tag{101}$$

(We have not taken into account that slave 1 has one row less to compute, since it will have to wait for other slaves to finish). The overall, ASP-time for an nxn matrix is:

$$\Omega_p = (3hn+n+6)\mu+(3hn+n-h+2p-1)\alpha+2\gamma+(2p+1)\tau_s+(4n-1)\tau_s+2\beta \tag{102}$$

We may approximate this by

$$\Omega_p = 3hn(\alpha+\mu)+4n\tau+2(\gamma+\beta) \tag{103}$$

The size of the matrix decreases by one for each transformation so that Ω_p should use not n but $(n)+(n-1)+(n-2)+\ldots+2+1 = n(n+1)/2 \cong 0.5n^2$. The total time on ASP is therefore of order:

$$\Omega_p = 1.5hn^2(\alpha+\mu)+2n^2\tau+2n(\gamma+\beta) \tag{104}$$

The total time for sequential execution [RR78] is of order $2n^3(\alpha+\mu)/3$ so that if we neglect $2n\gamma$, the ratio will be:

$$\rho \cong (2.25/p) + 3(n\tau'+\beta')/n^2 \qquad (105)$$

This ratio is worse than that of Given's method. Including $2n\gamma$ (taking of the square-root does take considerable time) in both parallel and sequential execution will improve ρ, but it will not be as good as that of Given's method. As is often the case, the best sequential method (Householder's) is not necessarily the best for ASP.

9.2.5 Danilevski's method

All previously discussed methods of solving $\underline{A}\ \underline{x} = \underline{b}$ can be traced back to the Gauss or Gauss-Jordan elimination algorithms.

These methods while reducing the matrix into triangular or diagonal form, are based on operations which preserve only one invariant of the original matrix, namely its rank (which in the case of loadflow is known anyway). If, in addition to solving the set of equations, it is required to compute the coefficients of the characteristic polynomial - as it often happens in control problems - then similarity transformations must be used.

We have already seen that Given's method can be used for elimination in $\underline{A}\ \underline{x} = \underline{b}$. Next, an approach will be described which uses the Danilewski (D-) method for factorization and produces at the same time the characteristic polynomial. It will use matrices in the Frobenius normal form i.e.

$$\underline{F} = \left[\begin{array}{cccccc|c} 0 & \cdot & \cdot & \cdot & 0 & 0 & A_{1,n} \\ \hline 1 & & & & & & A_{2,n} \\ & 1 & & & & & \\ & & \cdot & & & & \\ & & & \cdot & & & \\ & & & & \cdot & & \\ & & & & & 1 & A_{n,n} \end{array}\right] = \begin{bmatrix} \underline{0} & A_{1,n} \\ \underline{U}_{n-1} & \underline{t} \end{bmatrix} . \qquad (106)$$

In the above matrix, $\underline{0}$ and $\underline{t}$ are a (zero) row and a (non-zero) column vector respectively. $\underline{U}_{n-1}$ is an (n-1) x (n-1) identity matrix.

Since the inverse of $\underline{F}$ is

$$\underline{F} = \left[\begin{array}{c|cccccc} -A_{2,n}/A_{1,n} & 1 & & & & & \\ -A_{3,n}/A_{1,n} & & 1 & & & & \\ & & & \cdot & & & \\ & & & & \cdot & & \\ & & & & & \cdot & \\ & & & & & & \cdot \\ -A_{n,n}/A_{1,n} & & & & & & 1 \\ \hline 1/A_{1,n} & & 0 & & \cdot & \cdot\ \cdot & 0 \end{array}\right] = \begin{bmatrix} -\underline{t}/A_{1,n} & \underline{I}_{n-1} \\ 1/A_{1,n} & 0 \end{bmatrix} \qquad (107)$$

it follows that the similarity transformation

$$\underline{A}^{(1)} = \underline{F}_1^{-1} * \underline{A} * \underline{F}_1, \tag{108}$$

may be calculated according to the following equations:

$$A_{i,k}^{(1)} = A_{i+1,k+1} - A_{i+1,n} * (A_{1,k+1}/A_{i,n}); \tag{109}$$
$$i,k = 1,2,\dots,n-1,$$

$$A_{n,k}^{(1)} = A_{1,k+1}/A_{1,n}; \quad k = 1,2,\dots,n-1 \tag{110}$$

$$A_{i,n}^{(1)} = \Sigma \ (A_{i+1,k} - A_{i+1,n} * A_{1,k}/A_{1,n}) * A_{k,n}; \ k\Sigma=1,\dots,n; \tag{111}$$
$$i = 1,2,\dots,n-1,$$

$$A_{n,n}^{(1)} = (\Sigma \ A_{i,k} * A_{k,n})/A_{1,n}; \ k\Sigma=1,\dots,n \tag{112}$$

Transformation (108) is performed again, except that the elements of the Frobenius matrix $\underline{F}_2$, take their last column from $\underline{A}^{(1)}$ instead of from the original $\underline{A}$. Proceeding in this way, matrix

$$\underline{F} = \underline{A}^{(n-1)} \tag{113}$$

of Frobenius form is produced. Hence

$$\underline{F}_{n-1}^{-1} * \dots * \underline{F}_2^{-1} * \underline{F}_1^{-1} * \underline{A} * \underline{F}_1 * \underline{F}_2 * \dots * \underline{F}_{n-1} = \underline{F}, \tag{114}$$

$$(\underline{F}_1 * \dots * \underline{F}_{n-1}) * \underline{F} * (\underline{F}_{n-1}^{-1} * \dots * \underline{F}_1^{-1})$$
$$= \left(\prod_{i=1}^{n-1} \underline{F}_i \right) * \underline{F} * \left(\prod_{i=n-1}^{1} \underline{F}_i^{-1} \right) = \underline{A} \tag{115}$$

and this is a valid factored form of A with the factorization-matrices being supplanted by the Frobenius matrices $\underline{F}_i$ and $\underline{F}$.

The above is valid as long as $A_{1,n} \neq 0$. If it happens that $A_{1,n} = 0$, then:

(a) If at least one element $A_{m,n} \neq \emptyset$, the rows and columns 1 and m are interchanged and the process may proceed.

(b) All elements $A_{3,n}^{(j)}, \dots, A_{n-j,n}^{(j)}$ are zero. Then, matrix A has the form

$$\underline{A}^{(k)} = \begin{bmatrix} \underline{B} & \underline{0} \\ \underline{B}_1 & \underline{F}' \end{bmatrix} \tag{116}$$

where $\underline{F}'$ is a Frobenius-matrix of order k+1, which is itself a factorization matrix. The process may therefore proceed by factorization of the (n-j-1) order matrix $\underline{B}$.

For the matrix of [TH 67], similarity transformations (108) yield:

$$\underline{F} = \begin{bmatrix} -4/3 & 1 & 0 \\ -7/3 & 0 & 1 \\ 1/3 & 0 & 0 \end{bmatrix} * \begin{bmatrix} 2 & 1 & 3 \\ 2 & 3 & 4 \\ 3 & 4 & 7 \end{bmatrix} * \begin{bmatrix} 0 & 0 & 3 \\ 1 & 0 & 4 \\ 0 & 1 & 7 \end{bmatrix} = \begin{bmatrix} 5/3 & 0 & 14/3 \\ 5/3 & 0 & 5/3 \\ 1/3 & 1 & 31/3 \end{bmatrix} = \underline{A}, \tag{117}$$

$$\underline{F}_1^{-1} * \underline{A} * \underline{F}_1 = \underline{F}; \quad \underline{F}_2^{-1} * \underline{A}^{(1)} * \underline{F}_2 = \underline{F}, \tag{118}$$

$$\underline{F} = \begin{bmatrix} -5/14 & 1 & 0 \\ -31/14 & 0 & 1 \\ 3/14 & 0 & 0 \end{bmatrix} * \begin{bmatrix} 5/3 & 0 & 14/3 \\ 5/3 & 0 & 5/3 \\ 1/3 & 1 & 31/3 \end{bmatrix} * \begin{bmatrix} 0 & 0 & 14/3 \\ 1 & 0 & 5/3 \\ 0 & 1 & 31/3 \end{bmatrix} = \begin{bmatrix} 0 & 0 & 5 \\ 1 & 0 & -14 \\ 0 & 1 & 12 \end{bmatrix} \quad (119)$$

$$\begin{bmatrix} 3 & 14/3 & 5 \\ 4 & 5/3 & -14 \\ 7 & 31/3 & 12 \end{bmatrix}$$

Fig. 9: Resulting $\underline{F}$

In the above, as well as in the general case, all elements of column (n-1) are zero except $A_{n,n-1} = 1$ and therefore contain no information necessary for the subsequent operations. This column may therefore be overwritten by column n of $\underline{F}_1$. At the next transformation, column (n-2) may be overwritten by $\underline{F}_{1,n}$ etc. The final storage keeps only the above columns of $\underline{F}$ as in Fig. 9.

The parallelization of the D-method proceeds as follows: For each of the (n-1) similarity transformations

(a) Transfer row number 1 to all p local memories

(b) Each slave independently and concurrently with others calculates the new values (109) using only data in its memory.

(c) Transfer column n to all local memories.

(d) Correct, in parallel, row and column n (110,111,112)

In sequential execution the D-method requires $\cong n^3(\alpha+\mu)$. Since, in steps (b) and (d) above, the size of the table is reduced (by 1) in each consecutive step, the ratio is

$$\rho_D = (n-1)(2(\beta+n\tau) + 0.5(n-2)(\mu+h\mu+h\alpha) + h(2\alpha+\mu))/(n^3\omega)^3$$
$$\cong 1/p + 2\beta'/n^2 + 2\tau'/n \quad (120)$$

Conclusions

Three similarity and the Danilevski transformation were introduced. Using rotations, the Jacobi method arrives at the eigenvalues (and vectors) of a symmetric matrix. The methods of Givens and Householder produce a tridiagonal matrix for symmetric and a Hessenberg matrix for a not symmetric $\underline{A}$. All three methods can be programmed for ASP with high speedups. The solution of tridiagonal or Heisenberg matrices will follow the description and parallelization of power methods.

9.3 POWER METHODS

9.3.1 Direct power methods

For the direct power method the same simple data structure of slices is used. Each slave holds a "slice" of matrix $\underline{A}$ such that its width h=n/p is assumed to be an integer (if not, then add zero rows). The slave memories hold also entire vectors or matrices - as specified.

The methods are described in words with the S(i), P(i)-notation. It is assumed throughout that there are no multiple eigenvalues; the extension of the algorithms to complex, multiple eigenvalues can follow standard methods.

In the direct power method [Wi65, GW73] an initial vector $\underline{z}$ is chosen, preferably as $\underline{z}^{(o)} = (1,1,\ldots,1)^T$ (121)

and then iterated through

$$\underline{z}^{(k)} = \underline{A} \cdot \underline{z}^{(k-1)}; \quad k=1,2,\ldots \tag{122}$$

The dominant eigenvalue of $\underline{A}$ is calculated as follows. Compute for all elements i of vectors $\underline{z}^{(k)}$, $\underline{z}^{(k-1)}$:

$$\lambda_i' = z_i^{(k)}/z_i^{(k-1)} \tag{123}$$

If $|\lambda_1|>|\lambda_j|$ j=2,...,n then $\lambda_1 = \lambda_i'$ (124)

In ASP, this algorithm consists of iterating $\underline{P}(1)$ and $\underline{S}(1)$:

P(1): Each slave multiplies its slice of $\underline{A}$ with the latest value of $\underline{z}$

$$\underline{z}_m' = \Sigma A_{jm} z_j^{(j-1)}; \quad m = (p-1)h+1,\ldots,ph \quad j\ \Sigma = 1,\ldots,n \tag{125}$$

S(1): The master gathers all slices $\underline{z}_i'$; i=1,...,p forms from them a new $\underline{z}^{(k)}$ and broadcasts it to all slaves.

Following the k'th step, $\underline{z}^{(k)}$ is retained in the memories (as slices), $\underline{S}(1)$, $\underline{P}(1)$ and $\underline{S}(1)$ done once more and (123) applied. If most λ_i' values differ by less than a prescribed accuracy, then λ_1 was found; otherwise, the iterative process is restarted.

Steps P(1), S(1) require:

$$\Omega_p = h(n\mu+(n-1)\alpha) + ph\tau + \beta \cong hn\omega+ph\tau+\beta \tag{126}$$

Sequentially the method needs $\Omega_s=n^2\omega$ so that

$$\rho = (hn\omega + ph\tau + \beta)/(n^2\omega) = 1/p + (\beta' + 2n\tau')/n^2 \tag{127}$$

For power matrices and for the usual values of τ,β etc. we have $(\beta+n\tau) \ll n^2\omega$ so that nearly optimal reduction is achieved. The algorithm requires little data transfer.

It is customary [GW73] to normalize vector $\underline{z}$ at each iteration, so that in fact computed is

$$\underline{z}' = \underline{A} \cdot \underline{z}^{(k-1)}; \quad \underline{z}^{(k)} = \underline{z}'/\max(\underline{z}'); \quad k=1,2,\ldots \tag{128}$$

where $\max(\underline{z}')$ is the largest element of $\underline{z}'$. If such normalization is done, $\max(\underline{z}')$ approaches the eigenvalue λ_1.

There are two ways to normalize $\underline{z}$ in ASP. In the first, the master broadcasts $\max(\underline{z}')$ to all slaves which perform (128), each on its slice of $\underline{z}'$. The additional work is

$$\Omega' = hn\tau + \beta + h \cdot \mu = \beta + h(n\tau + \mu) \tag{129}$$

In the second method, the master normalizes $\underline{z}'$, so that the additional work is only $\Omega' = n\mu$ (130)

(In both cases, the time to search for $\max(\underline{z}')$ is not included in τ'). Since in most cases $\beta^2 + n^2\tau/p > n(p-1)\mu/p$ (131)

the second method is more effective, and the reduction increases only by the small time of μ'/n^2. The search could have been done in parallel making the first method competitive but only barely because of an additional synchronization.

The convergence of the method is satisfactory only if (124) applies; otherwise various acceleration devices are employed. Since methods based on an origin shift [Wi 65, GW 73] are essentially serial and ad-hoc, they are unsuitable for ASP. The methods suitable are:

(a) Aitken's acceleration method.

Let the slaves keep slices of $\underline{z}^{(k)}$, $\underline{z}^{(k-1)}$ and $\underline{z}^{(k-2)}$ and every m steps, m>3 compute: $z_i^{(k+1)} = (z_i^{(k-2)} z_i^{(k)} - z_i^{(k-1)})/(z_i^{(k-2)} - 2z_i^{(k-1)} + z_i^{(k)})$ (132)
for all i. This yields better approximations to the eigenvalues than λ_i'. Since in ASP this may be done as part of $\underline{P}(1)$,ρ will hardly increase, and the method can be employed for symmetrical and unsymmetrical matrices. If, on the other hand we let the master do the normalization, it can also decide when to quit.

(b) Rayleigh's quotient method (GW73.)

In a symmetric matrix, the eigenvectors may be chosen so that they are orthonormal. Thus

$$\lambda_1 = (\underline{z}^T * \underline{A}\ \underline{z}^{(k)})/(\underline{z}^T * \underline{z}^{(k)}) \tag{133}$$

$\underline{z}^T$ being the transpose of $\underline{z}^{(k)}$. In ASP, calculation of the scalar products should be part of step S1 since $\underline{Az}^{(k)}$ is stored anyway in the master. The additional t'=2nμ is not significant.

ASP shows a subtle advantage when used for sparse matrices. In a 100x100 matrix with ten non-zeroes in a row, $\underline{A} \cdot \underline{z}^{(k-1)}$ would require 100x100 checks for 100,000/p multiplications. In ASP the number of checks is smaller and only 1000/p checks instead of 1000 are wasted per row. No matter which acceleration device we employ the ratio ρ will include the 2τ'/n term of (127). We next try another method which may lower ρ substantially.

9.3.2 Inverse power method

This method is based on the fact that if λ is an eigenvalue [Wi65,GW73] of a non-singular matrix $\underline{A}$, then 1/λ is an eigenvalue of $\underline{A}^{-1}$. Reversing (122) we may compute iteratively

$$\underline{A}^{-1}\ \underline{z}^{(k)} = \underline{z}^{(k-1)}; \quad k=1,2,... \tag{134}$$

Since for the eigenvalue next to say λ' we have

$$(\underline{A} - \lambda'\ \underline{I})^{-1}\ \underline{z}^{(k)} = \Sigma\ \alpha(\lambda_i-\lambda')^{-k}\ z_i^{(o)}; \ i\Sigma=1,...,n \tag{135}$$

the process will converge to that λ_i which is closest to λ'. Actually, λ_i is found from $1/(\lambda_i-\lambda') = z_j^{(k+1)}/z_j^{(k)}; \quad j=1,...,n$ (136)
This is a stable and fast method, to wit p. 622 of [Wi65]: "I have found inverse iteration to be by far the most powerful and accurate of those methods I have used for computing eigenvectors"

Fortunately also, it is easily adapted to ASP. The "program" is:

S(1): Send the approximate values λ_q one to each slave. The time required for it is only pτ and is not part of the iterations. Neglect it.

P(1): Let slave q decompose its matrix into a right $\underline{R}$ and left $\underline{L}$ triangular matrix:

$$(\underline{A} - \underline{\lambda}_q \cdot \underline{I})^{-1} = \underline{L}_q \cdot \underline{R}_q \tag{137}$$

for which it needs about n^3/p operations. Next

$$\underline{L}_q \cdot \underline{z}'' = \underline{z}^{(k-1)} \tag{138}$$

$$\underline{R}_q \cdot \underline{z}' = \underline{z}'' \tag{139}$$

$$\underline{z}_i^{(k)} = \underline{z}_i'/\max(\underline{z}'); \quad i=1,2,\ldots,n \tag{140}$$

may be iterated independently and concurrently in each slave. Each iteration (without normalization) requires n^2 operations. Synchronization was not required; neither was data-transfer. p eigenvalues were found and since this would require normally $pn^2\omega$, the reduction ratio is

$$\rho = n^2\omega/(pn^2\omega) = 1/p \tag{141}$$

We have thus achieved optimal speedup. The reason for this low ratio was that we used an "inherently parallel" and therefore, optimal method. The catch is that we have first to find p different λ_q eigenvalues. How to do this is discussed below.

In order to remove a few difficulties, let us confine ourselves to a matrix $\underline{A}$ of order n that is symmetric and positive definite. The problem of finding the p largest eigenvalues ($p<n$) with their eigenvectors will now be attacked with the simultaneous iteration of p linearly independent initial vectors. The eigenvectors of differing eigenvalues form an orthogonal system, but nonetheless the sequences of iterated vectors in the power method exhibit the tendency to approach a multiple of the first eigenvector asymptotically. In order to prevent the p simultaneously iterated vectors from becoming proportional to the same vector, and to do justice to the orthogonality, at every step a system of orthogonal vectors is formed from the iterated vectors.

Assume that the p initial vectors $\underline{x}_1^{(0)}, \underline{x}_2^{(0)}, \ldots, \underline{x}_p^{(0)}$ have been orthonormalized and have been assembled into a tall nxp matrix $\underline{X}^{(0)}$ whose columns are vectors $\underline{x}_j^{(0)}$. The method described here can fail if, by accident or unwise selection, the p-dimensional subspace of initial vectors is orthogonal to any one of the eigenvectors of the p largest eigenvalues. The iterated vectors $\underline{z}_1^{(1)}, \underline{z}_2^{(1)}, \ldots, \underline{z}_p^{(1)}$ of $\underline{z}_j^{(1)} = \underline{A}\underline{x}_j^{(0)}$ analogously produce the matrix

$$\underline{Z}^{(1)} = \underline{A}\underline{X}^{(0)} \tag{142}$$

which has maximum rank p. The columns of $\underline{Z}^{(1)}$ are orthonormalized by the Schmidt orthogonalization technique prior to the next iteration. Matrix $\underline{Z}^{(1)}$ is decomposed into

$$\underline{Z}^{(1)} = \underline{X}^{(1)}\underline{R}^{(1)}, \tag{143}$$

where $\underline{X}^{(1)}$ indicates an n x p matrix with p orthonormalized columns, and $\underline{R}^{(1)}$ a regular upper triangular matrix. The general kth iteration step is then

$$\underline{Z}^{(k+1)} = \underline{A}\underline{X}^{(k)}; \quad \underline{Z}^{(k+1)} = \underline{X}^{(k+1)}\underline{R}^{(k+1)}; \quad k = 0,1,2,\ldots \tag{144}$$

[SRS] Theorem: If the (p+1) largest eigenvalues λ_j of a symmetric definite matrix $\underline{A}$ are different, with a suitable choice of $\underline{X}^{(0)}$ the columns of $\underline{X}^{(k)}$ converge to the normalized eigenvectors $\underline{y}_1, \underline{y}_2, \ldots, \underline{y}_p$ of the p largest eigenvalues $\lambda_1 > \lambda_2 > \ldots > \lambda_p$. The sequence of upper triangular matrices $\underline{R}^{(k)}$ converges with increasing k to a diagonal matrix whose diagonal elements are the eigenvalues.

Note: The method converges even if several of the p largest eigenvalues are multiple eigenvalues.

Algorithm (144) has the drawback that the iterated vectors $\underline{z}_j^{(k)}$ are orthonormalized by the Schmidt technique from left to right, while the first vector is merely normalized. With an unfavorable choice of initial vectors, especially in $x_1^{(0)}$, the first eigenvector may be developed very slowly, thereby slowing the convergence of the p iterated vectors to the system of p eigenvectors which are sought.

A first improvement of this situation is possible in that after the orthonormalization process

$$\underline{Z}^{(k+1)} = \underline{X}^{(k+1)}\underline{R}^{(k+1)} \qquad (145)$$

the vectors $\underline{x}_1^{(k+1)}, \underline{x}_2^{(k+1)}, \dots, \underline{x}_p^{(k+1)}$ are arranged according to the magnitude of the normalization constants. Thus an iterated vector with a strong component of the first eigenvector leaps into first place.

Another improvement for ASP is to try the bi-iteration method.

As mentioned earlier, more than a single dominant eigenvalue may be required. We will assume that c·p are required with c an integer, but that they may be crude approximations.

There are a number of methods [Wi65,GW73] which calculate rough approximations, but since they are based on "deflation", they are all inherently sequential. Instead, it is suggested to use the bi-iteration [Ba 58] method, modified for symmetric matrices [CJ 70]. Its ASP - version starts by storing in all slaves a matrix, say $\underline{U}$ whose p columns approximate p eigenvectors of $\underline{A}$, namely $\underline{u}^{(1)}, \underline{u}^{(2)}, \dots, \underline{u}^{(p)}$ with

$$\underline{U}^T \cdot \underline{U} = \underline{I} \qquad (146)$$

Each slave stores (Fig. 10) a slice of $\underline{A}$ and the matrix $\underline{U}$. The steps of the method are:

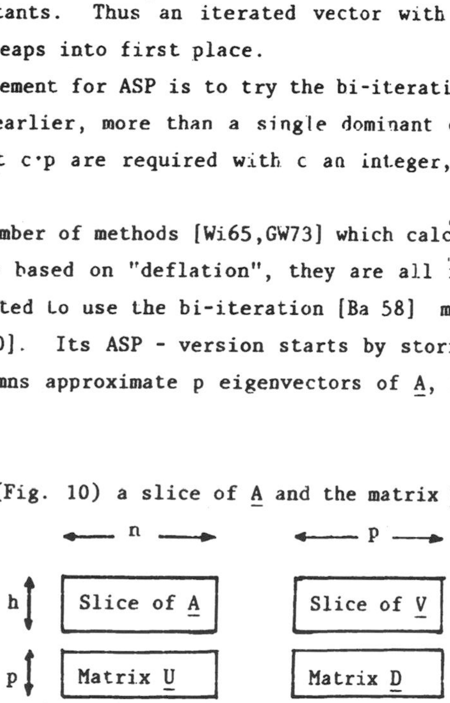

Fig. 10: Data structure

P(1): Compute (in slices) the nxp matrix $\underline{V}$ and the pxp matrix $\underline{D}$ through

$$\underline{V} = \underline{A}\ \underline{U}; \quad \underline{D} = \underline{U}^T\ \underline{V} \qquad (147)(148)$$

Computation of (147) is straightforward. For (148)

$$\sum_{k=1}^{h} u_{ki}\, v_{kj} + \sum_{k=h+1}^{2h} u_{ki}\, v_{kj} + \sum_{k=(p-1)h}^{ph} u_{ki}\, v_{kj}$$

$$= \sum_{q=1}^{p} \sum_{k=(q-1)h+1}^{qh} u_{ki}\, v_{kj} = \sum D_{ij}^{(q)} \qquad (149)$$

Each slave may thus compute independently its share of $\underline{D}$. The operation count yields $t_1 = hpn\omega + hp^2\omega$ (150)

S1: The master gathers p^2 elements $D_{ij}^{(q)}$ from each of its slaves and forms $\underline{D}$. Note that $\underline{D}$ has order p and is thus much smaller than $\underline{A}$.

The next substep is to compute eigenvalues of $\underline{D}$ and a matrix $\underline{C}$ of its eigenvectors. Since $\underline{D}$ is a rather small matrix and resides already in the master, it is advisable to do this part serially (it requires $p^3f\omega$ with f given) or by the method of Jacobi - in parallel. Then $\underline{C}$ is broadcast to all slaves, which now store the full data of Fig. 10. Altogether, this time:

$$t_2 = p^3\tau + \beta + p^3\alpha + fp^3\omega \qquad (151)$$

$\underline{P2}$: Another matrix $\underline{W}$ is formed through

$$\underline{W} = \underline{V} \cdot \underline{C} \qquad (152)$$

with slave q=1,...,p computing

$$W_{ij} = \Sigma\, V_{ik}\, C_{kj};\ k\Sigma 1,\dots,p;\ i=(q-1)h+1,\dots,qh;\ j=1,\dots,p \qquad (153)$$

i.e. each slave calculates a slice of $\underline{W}$ which corresponds to its slice of $\underline{V}$.

In general, $\underline{W}$ will not be an orthogonal matrix and so either the process of [CJ 70], or a simple ASP-version of an orthogonalization process as in Chapters 5 and 6 is employed. Altogether, in P2:

$$t_3 = p^3\omega + n(n-1)(\beta+2p\tau+n\omega/p)/2 \qquad (154)$$

$\underline{S2}$: The orthogonalized $\underline{W}$ is transferred as the new $\underline{U}$ to the master where a convergence test determines whether to return to $\underline{P1}$ for another iteration or stop. This step (excluding the test) requires

$$t_4 \cong p^3\tau + \beta \qquad (155)$$

The above method, if done sequentially requires

$$t_s = (pn^2 + p^2n + fp^3 + p^3 + n^3/3)\omega \qquad (156)$$

Even if we assume that factors without n can be neglected, the time reduction ratio will be

$$\rho = 1.5/p + 1.5(\beta' + 2p\tau')/n \qquad (157)$$

Both parts of ρ are too high, and the method is recommended only for computing p crude approximations λ_q for starting the inverse iteration method.

Concluding we may advise to use a two-step approach in the case that p>1 eigenvalues are sought: compute a crude approximation by biorthogonalization and then use the inverse power method to calculate $\lambda_1,\lambda_2,\dots,\lambda_p$. (If only a single, dominant λ_1 is sought, use the direct power method).

The speedup was nearly optimal except for bi-orthogonalization. We could invert the simultaneous power method by writing

$$\underline{A}\ \underline{Z}^{(1)} = \underline{X}^{(0)} \qquad (158)$$

This is equivalent to p sets:

$$\underline{A}\ \underline{z}_{\cdot q}^{(1)} = \underline{L}\ \underline{R}\ \underline{z}_{\cdot q}^{(1)} = \underline{x}_{\cdot q}^{(0)},\quad q = 1,2,\dots,p \qquad (159)$$

If $\underline{L}$ and $\underline{R}$ were transferred to the p slaves, each does:

$$\underline{L}\ \underline{s}_q = \underline{x}_{\cdot q}^{(0)}\ ;\ \underline{R}\ \underline{z}_{\cdot q}^{(1)} = \underline{s}_q \qquad (160)$$

the first by a forward, the second by backward substitution. The new $\underline{z}_{\cdot q}$ can be used to calculate $\underline{x}_{\cdot q}^{(1)}$ etc., the question though is whether orthogonalization is required. Another question - left as an exercise - is the following: Each slave stores $\underline{L}\ \underline{R}$ of $\underline{A} = \underline{L}\ \underline{R}$. In the second step (inverse iteration) it needs $\underline{L}_q,\underline{R}_q$ of (160). How can $\underline{L}_q,\underline{R}_q$ be computed efficiently and in ASP if $\underline{L},\underline{R}$ are given?

9.4 COMPLETING THE SOLUTION

Aims: To "program" the algorithms of completing the solution, e.g. Sturm sequences for ASP and to calculate their ratios.

Sturm sequence solution

The result of applying Householder's or Given's method to a symmetric matrix is a symmetric, tridiagonal matrix $\underline{T}$. There are a number of ways to calculate its eigenvalues, but the method of bisection, coupled with the property of Sturm sequences (pp. 300-307 of [Wi65]) is so admiringly suited for ASP programming and is so stable that no other method need be mentioned. Moreover, this algorithm will be defined in a straightforward way without changing in any way its classical form. The program then is:

S(1): Calculate $g=(|c_i|+|d_i|+|c_{i+1}|)$, where d is a diagonal and c a non-diagonal element. The range in which the eigenvalues lie is -g,g. This range is divided into p subranges and the p+1 demarcation values

$$k = -g,\ -g+\Delta, \ldots, g-\Delta,\ g \tag{161}$$

send to the p slaves. By broadcast, the values c_i, d_i are also sent to all slaves.

P(1): Each slave calculates its recurrent sequence

$$u_0 = 1;\ u_1 = d_1 - \lambda \text{ ("its" } \lambda_q); \tag{162}$$

$$u_i = (d_i - \lambda)u_{i-1} - c_i^2 u_{i-2};\ i = 2,\ldots,n \tag{163}$$

and the number of sign agreements x. Then x and λ are sent to the master.

S(2):For $x(k_1)=m$; $x(k_2)=m+1$ with $k_2<k_1$ there is an eigenvalue in the range k_2 to k_1.

This is usually enough to find ranges of eigenvalues. If the eigenvalues themselves are to be calculated, this is best done by bisection. If we assume that we use all p slaves to calculate p eigenvalues, then this process will be inherently parallel.

Let us exemplify the above by an example. Matrix $\underline{T}$ is shown in Fig. 11. Suppose that one of the slaves has to find, during step P1, whether there is an eigenvalue in range 0-4. Applying (162-163) to $\underline{T}$ with 0 and 4 for λ will yield u_i = 1,-3,2,-5,-3 and u_j = 1,-7,40,-313,1831 respectively. There is one sign agreement in the first case and none in the second. Since 0<4 there is an eigenvalue in the range 0 to 4.

$$\begin{bmatrix} -3 & 2 & 0 & 0 \\ 2 & -2 & 1 & 0 \\ 0 & 1 & -4 & 3 \\ 0 & 0 & 3 & -3 \end{bmatrix}$$

Fig. 11: T-matrix

Next, the master may instruct the same slave to decide whether λ is in range 0-2 or 2-4. The slave applies (162, 163) without having to ask again for the c and d values (as they still reside in its memory). The result is the sequence u_i=1,-5,16,-91,311 and therefore the eigenvalue lies in the range 0 to 2.

As usually, after m such tests, the range of eigenvalues will shrink with factor 2^{-m}. The above calculation is especially efficient since no function values are to be computed; the number of sign agreements is sufficient.

Since the algorithm is almost inherently parallel we may assume that $\rho \cong 1/p$.

Note here that ρ will be even closer to $1/p$ if in step S(2), the range $[-g,+g]$ is subdivided not into equidistant parts, but so that each has the same number of eigenvalues λ_i, $i=1,\ldots,n/p=h$. In an additional parallel step P(2), each slave uses bisection to calculate all h of "its" eigenvalues. This part of the algorithm is inherently parallel.

Next consider the calculation of eigenvectors of $\underline{T}$. It is usually done by the inverse power method - and we have already seen that this method leads to a high speedup for ASP. One might be even tempted to decompose $\underline{T} = \underline{L} \cdot \underline{R}$ according to ($e_o = 0$): $b_{i-1} = e_{i-1};\ a_i = d_i - e_{i-1}^2/a_{i-1};\ c_i = e_i/a_i;\ i=1,\ldots,n$ (164)
exemplified for n=5 in

$$\begin{bmatrix} a_1 & & & & \\ b_1 & a_2 & & & \\ & b_2 & a_3 & & \\ & & b_3 & a_4 & \\ & & & b_4 & a_5 \end{bmatrix} \begin{bmatrix} 1 & c_1 & & & \\ & 1 & c_2 & & \\ & & 1 & c_3 & \\ & & & 1 & c_4 \\ & & & & 1 \end{bmatrix} = \begin{bmatrix} d_1 & e_1 & & & \\ e_1 & d_2 & e_2 & & \\ & e_2 & d_3 & e_3 & \\ & & e_3 & d_4 & e_4 \\ & & & e_4 & d_5 \end{bmatrix} \qquad (165)$$

For every approximate λ_i' we would decompose $\underline{T}'=\underline{T}-\lambda_i'\underline{U}$ in another slave and compute

$$\underline{L}_i\ \underline{R}_i\ \underline{z}^{(i+1)} = \underline{Z}^{(i)};\ i = 0,1,\ldots \qquad (166)$$

by simple substitutions.

Unfortunately, this method proves to be frequently unstable so that a method proposed in [SRS] is suggested for ASP. It really reduces $\underline{T}-\underline{\lambda}\ \underline{U}$ to triangular form (Fig. 12) by (n-1) steps s.t. at step k we only deal with two rows of form:

$$\begin{matrix} \alpha & \beta & \\ e_k & d_{k+1} - \lambda' & e_{k+1} \end{matrix}$$

$$\begin{bmatrix} a_1 & b_1 & c_1 & & \\ & a_2 & b_2 & c_2 & \\ & & \ddots & \ddots & \ddots \\ & & & & c_{n-2} \\ & & & & b_{n-1} \\ & & & & a_n \end{bmatrix}$$

Fig. 12: $\underline{R}$ of $\underline{T}-\lambda'\underline{U}$

If $|\alpha|\geq|e_k|$, the multiplier $f_k=e_k/\alpha$ is formed. If $|\alpha|<|e_k|$, $f_k= \alpha/e_k$ and the two rows are interchanged. Next, f_k-times the first row is subtracted from the second row to produce a zero instead of e_k.

Before using $\underline{R}$ for back-substitution, let us remark that a good choice of $\underline{z}^{(0)}$ is such [Wi63] that in $\underline{R}\ \underline{z}^{(1)} = \underline{q}$, vector $\underline{q}$ has all its components as 1. This was found to simplify the computation of

$$\underline{R}\ \underline{z}^{(1)} = \underline{q};\ (\underline{T} - \lambda'\underline{U})\underline{z}^{(2)} = \underline{z}^{(1)} \qquad (167)$$

Since $(\underline{T}-\lambda'\underline{U})$ was already transformed to triangular form, the use of the f_k's and interchange record will generate a vector $\underline{z}'$ and $\underline{R}\ \underline{z}^{(2)} = \underline{z}'$, the desired $\underline{z}^{(2)}$.

The first part can be done efficiently only on Topps; for Mopps, it seems to be inefficient, except if you note that each slave will do the entire procedure by itself. No information transfer is necessary, except at the end, when the p resulting eigenvectors are tranferred to the master.

There still remains the problem of computing the p eigenvectors $\underline{z}_i$ of $\underline{A}$. Since $\underline{T} = \underline{H}\ \underline{A}\ \underline{H}^T$ (or $\underline{G}\ \underline{A}\ \underline{G}^T$), and $\underline{A} = \underline{H}^T\ \underline{T}\ \underline{H}$ we find that if $\underline{z}_i'$ is an eigenvector of $\underline{T}$ i.e. $\underline{T}\ \underline{z}_i' = \lambda_i\ \underline{z}_i'$ then:

$$\lambda_i\ \underline{H}^T\ \underline{z}_i' = \underline{H}^T\ \underline{T}\ \underline{z}_i' = \underline{H}^T\ \underline{T}(\underline{H}\ \underline{H}^T)\underline{z}_i' = \underline{A}(\underline{H}^T\underline{z}_i') = \underline{A}\ \underline{z}_i \qquad (168)$$

so that $\underline{z}_i = \underline{H}^T\ \underline{z}_i'$. It therefore suffices to calculate (efficiently and in parallel) the matrix $\underline{H}^T$. As shown earlier

$$\underline{H}^T = \underline{H}_1^T\ \underline{H}_2^T \ldots \underline{H}_{n-1}^T \qquad (169)$$

and assuming (n-1) to be 2^k for some k, each product $\underline{H}^T_{2m-1}\ \underline{H}^T_{2m}$, $m=1,2,\ldots,2^{k-1}$ can be done at the same time, then two such products multiplied etc. For the price of the Haydn factor $\chi=\log_2 k_1$, parallelization would be achieved.

In this case, this price does not have to be paid. Since $\underline{z}_i'$, $i=1,\ldots,p$ are computed, each slave can go on to compute $\underline{z}_i$ by the above algorithm on its own: this part of the algorithm is inherently parallel.

It may be concluded that the ratio ρ of the complete problem, starting from the tridiagonal matrix will be rather close to being optimal indeed.

10. THE CASE STUDY-EPOC

INTRODUCTION

Electric Power Control was mentioned and its programs were shortly described in chapter 1. In the present chapter the solution of these problems on an ASP-system will be discussed.

We discuss the load-flow (LOAF), the state-estimation (STEP), the contingency analysis (CAP) and the economic dispatch (EDIP) programs. Monitoring and display is not mentioned because it is an inherently parallel problem.

In each case, the problem is first defined in short mathematically. Students of electrical and specifically power system engineering will have no trouble filling in the details; others may (if they so want) start from a "basic equation" defined in each case.

The methods of chapters 6 to 9 may be used to solve each of the four problems. As a matter of fact all four are usually solved by the Newton-Raphson method which leads to repeated solution of linear sets. Since these sets are extremely sparse, direct methods are usually advocated and we suggest the use of the poof-algorithm followed by block-elimination. Other methods of chapters 6 to 9 could also be used, especially orthogonalization. The chapter includes an estimate of the (time) load on the ASP-system and some conclusions.

10.1 LOAD-FLOW, LOAF

Aims: To define mathematically LOAF as a set of nonlinear, algebraic equations. To review the Newton-Raphson and Shamanski methods of solving them. To develop a method based on an algorithm by Hotelling and Bodewig (hence "Hobo"). To indicate ASP-implementation in each of the above cases.

Given an electric power network with buses numbered 0,1,...,m, LOAF may be defined as seeking the solution (column) vectors

$$\underline{v} = [v_0, v_1, \dots, v_m]^T; \quad \underline{w} = [w_0, w_1, \dots, w_m]^T \tag{1}$$

to the set of Kirchoff's equations:

$$\frac{p_k - jq_k}{v_k^2 + w_k^2}(v_k + jw_k) = \sum_{i=1}^{n} (g_{ki} + jb_{ki})(v_k + jw_k); \; k = 0,1,\dots,m \tag{2}$$

where $(p_k + jq_k)$ is the injected power, $(v_k + jw_k)$ is the bus or node voltage of bus k, $(g_{ki} + jb_{ki})$ is the admittance between buses k and i and $j = \sqrt{-1}$.

Node zero is the so-called "slack bus" and its voltage is constant, usually assumed to be 1+j0. Thus, through separation of the real and imaginary parts, (2) is equivalent to the following basic LOAF equations

$$\left.\begin{aligned} (p_k v_k + q_k w_k)/x_k^2 &= \Sigma(v_i g_{ki} - w_i b_{ki}); \; i\Sigma = 0,\dots,m \\ (p_k w_k - q_k v_k)/x_k^2 &= \Sigma(w_i g_{ki} + v_i b_{ki}); \; i\Sigma = 0,\dots,m \end{aligned}\right\} k = 1,2,\dots,m \tag{3}$$

$$\text{with } x_k^2 = v_k^2 + w_k^2, \; \underline{x} \equiv [v_1, w_1, v_2, w_2, \dots, v_n, w_n]^T \tag{4}$$

We will discuss the case that every generation and load bus has its p and q specified. This type of problem appears, for example in solving for transient stability and in static contingency analysis, which seeks to foresee the results of a change in a network structure. If it can be assumed that as a result of this change the outputs of the generators and the loads change very little, then the problem of determining the voltages after the change, given the powers before the change, reduces to loaf as defined above.

Apart from its usefulness in many applications, loaf exhibits symmetry (all buses but the slack bus are of the same type). Furthermore, it turns out that the system of equations corresponding to loaf is well-posed if the two equations - one of the p-type and another of the q-type of the slack-bus are deleted. The reason why two equations have to be deleted rather than one is that the law of conservation of energy applies to reactive as well as to real power. For both, a degree of freedom must be left to balance the generated, consumed and lost powers.

Loaf equations (3) may be written in the general form

$$\underline{r}\,(\underline{x}) = \underline{0} \qquad (5)$$

where $\underline{x}$ is the n-vector of voltages and $\underline{r}$ is a function-vector of n components.

Loaf equations (5) are nonlinear because they include the squares of the (unknown) voltages and they are algebraic rather than differential because they describe the steady-state and not the transient behaviour of the network. Their coefficients (admittances) are constant.

The right side of (2) is a linear set and one way of solving loaf is to use the "trick" of assuming the left side $(\underline{z})$ to be constant, solving the linear set, recalculating $\underline{z}$, solving it again and so on. Since each new set differs only slightly from the previous, iterative methods such as SOR, JA, SJ or SSOR can be used both on a monocomputer and on ASP. In one particular case, this approach is rather efficient namely for transient stability calculation since loaf has then to be solved repreatedly with only slightly changed p_k, q_k-powers. The initial vector $\underline{z}$ is then chosen on the basis of the previously computed values and the iterations start from a good approximation (had it been exact, no additional iterations would at all be required). Since, additionally, in this case a relatively low accuracy is required, only a few iterations may be required and the method should be rather efficient.

Loaf equations (5) may also be solved by the Newton-Raphson method, iterating

$$\underline{x}^{(n+1)} = \underline{x}^{(n)} - \underline{J}^{-1}\,(\underline{x}^{(n)})\cdot\underline{r}\,(\underline{x}^{(n)}) \qquad (6)$$

where $\underline{J}(\underline{x}_n)$ denotes the Jacobian of the vector function $\underline{r}(\underline{x})$ evaluated at $\underline{x}_n$. For brevity, we shall denote $\underline{J}(\underline{x}_n)$ by $\underline{J}_n$ and $\underline{r}(\underline{x}_n)$ by $\underline{r}_n$. The definition of $\underline{J}$ is:

$$J_{ik} = \partial r_j/\partial x_k \qquad (7)$$

the Jacobian has the following elements [Wa68]:

$$\partial p_k/\partial v_k = g_{kk} + (2q_k v_k w_k - p_k(v_k^2 - w_k^2))/|x_k|^4 \qquad (8)$$

$$\partial p_k/\partial w_k = -b_{kk} + (2p_k v_k w_k - q_k(v_k^2 - w_k^2))/|x_k|^4 \qquad (9)$$

$$\partial q_k/\partial v_k = b_{kk} + (2q_k v_k w_k - p_k(v_k^2 - w_k^2))/|x_k|^4 \tag{10}$$

$$\partial q_k/\partial w_k = g_{kk} - (2q_k v_k w_k + p_k(v_k^2 - w_k^2))/|x_k|^4 \tag{11}$$

For $r \neq k$ we have for the off-diagonal elements

$$\partial p_k/\partial v_r = v_k g_{kr} + w_k b_{kr};\ \partial q_k/\partial v_r = w_k g_{kr} - v_k b_{kr} = p_k/w_r \tag{12}$$

$$\partial p_k/\partial w_r = -v_k b_{kr} + w_k g_{kr};\ \partial q_k/\partial w_r = -w_r b_{kr} - v_k g_{kr} = p_k/v_r \tag{13}$$

As already mentioned, LOAF equations are often solved by the method of Newton-Raphson: Starting with an approximate solution $\underline{x}_0$ a sequence $\underline{x}_n$ of approximations to the solution $\underline{x}$ of (5) is formed through the repeated, iterative application of (6) or by any direct method e.g. Gaussian elimination. In that case, (6) is re-written as:

$$\underline{J}_k \cdot \underline{\Delta x}_{k+1} = \underline{-r}_k \text{ with } \underline{\Delta x}_{k+1} = \underline{x}_{k+1} - \underline{x}_k \tag{14}$$

which is regarded as a set of n linear equations in the unknowns $\underline{\Delta x}$. Solving (14) is more efficient than using (6), because solution by elimination usually requires less storage and less operations than matrix inversion (in the case of full matrices, the ratio is 1:3).

The basic Newton-Raphson (NR) algorithm proceeds therefore as follows: Given an initial approximation $\underline{x}_0$ and a convergence factor ε, do the following:

(A) Compute the vector of residuals of $\underline{r}$ using the current value of $\underline{x}$.

(B) If the largest component of this vector is smaller in absolute value than ε, stop. Otherwise, proceed.

(C) Form the elements of the Jacobian.

(D) Solve (14) for $\underline{\Delta x}$.

(E) Compute the new vector of unknowns $\underline{x}$ through $\underline{x} = \underline{x} + \underline{\Delta x}$.

(F) Return to step (A).

Under very general conditions ([OR70], Chapter 10), convergence of the Newton-Raphson (N-R) method is quadratic, rather than linear as in the case of Gauss-Seidel or other iterative methods. Practice indicates indeed, that the NR algorithm, when applied to non-linear, algebraic equations converges in fewer iterations (by an iteration we mean a pass through the steps (A) - (F)) than does a non-linear Gauss-Seidel version. This however does not necessarily mean that the time required for attaining convergence will be shorter. This is due to the fact that each iteration of the N-R algorithm entails elimination, a process which for full matrices requires $\Omega = n^3$ arithmetical operations as opposed to $\Omega = n^2$ for an iteration of G-S. Another disadvantage lies in the storage requirements of N-R. Whereas G-S requires only about as much space as is necessary for storing the usually sparse admittance matrix, N-R requires storage for $\underline{J}^{-1}$ or $\underline{L},\underline{R}$ which may not be sparse at all. Even if an ordered factorization is used, the phenomenon of fill-in (described in Chapter 6) requires excessive memory space. To alleviate these difficulties, it is possible to modify the NR-procedure so that fewer matrix inversions or factorizations are needed. One such modification of N-R, due to Shamanski ([OR70], p. 316) has proved effective in reducing the number of inversions, while retaining fast convergence. The main idea is to invert the Jacobian only once every m iterations. The method may be summarized as follows with $\underline{x}_{k,0} = \underline{x}_k$

$$\underline{x}_{k,i} = \underline{x}_{k,i-1} - \underline{J}^{-1}_{}(\underline{x}_k) \cdot \underline{r}(\underline{x}_{k,i-1}),\ i=1,2,\ldots,m \quad (15)$$

It can be seen that $\underline{J}_k^{-1}$ is used m times without updating. The following description of the algorithm of Shamanski uses a counter c to count these m "subiterations". At the beginning of operation, c is set to zero and $\underline{J}$ factored into $\underline{L}\cdot\underline{R}$.

(A) Compute vector of residuals $\underline{r}$;

(B) If $\max|r_i|<\varepsilon$, stop. Otherwise, proceed.

(C) Increment inner loop counter c. If c<m+1, go to (D); else

(C1) set c=0;

(C2) form $\underline{J}$ (x)

(C3) compute $\underline{J}^{-1}$(x) or rather $\underline{J}=\underline{L}\cdot\underline{R}$.

(D) Solve $\underline{r}(\underline{x}) = 0$ through $\Delta\underline{x} = -\underline{J}^{-1} \cdot \underline{r}(\underline{x})$ or $(\underline{L}\cdot\underline{R}) \cdot \Delta\underline{x} = -r(x)$

(E) Compute the new $\underline{x}$ through

$\underline{x} = \underline{x} + \Delta\underline{x}$

(F) Return to (A)

The most time-consuming part is (C3). If done by the Poof-algorithm, it will eliminate about half of the matrix $\underline{J}$ in say c steps (PS), each one using

$$\Omega_1 = 2m^2\omega/(pk) \quad (16)$$

operations, with k accounting for sparsity and m being the size of $\underline{J}$. The remaining full matrix is best solved by "block-elimination" which requires about

$$\Omega_2 \cong m^2\omega/(16p) \quad (17)$$

For each factorization, approximately c "back substitutions" are needed to complete a solution. Each of them requires:

$$\Omega_3 = m\omega/(kp)\ \mu\text{sec} \quad (18)$$

For large m, with $m \ll m^2$, this time may be neglected if compared to Ω_1 and Ω_2. Thus, the total time of a single "solution" is

$$\Omega \cong 2c\omega m^2/(kp) + m^2\omega/(16p) \cong (1/16 + 10/k)m^2\omega/p\ \mu\text{sec} \quad (19)$$

This Ω was used in chapter 4 to evaluate the loading of ASP if used to solve LOAF. If there is any fear that solving $\underline{J}\ \Delta\underline{x}=\underline{r}$ may need pivoting, the method of solving it by Given's rotations may be preferable.

For more adventurous souls we suggest a new method based on the formula by Hoteling & Bodewig (hence, the Hobo method). It may be derived as follows.

An approximation to the inverse of $(\underline{U} - \underline{A})$ may be obtained from the matrix identiy:

$$(\underline{U} - \underline{A})\ (\underline{U} + \underline{A} + \underline{A}^2 + \ldots + \underline{A}^m) = \underline{U} - \underline{A}^{m+1} \quad (20)$$

Indeed, if the spectral radius of $\underline{A}$, $r(\underline{A})<1$ then $\lim(\underline{A}^m)\to 0$ for $m\to\infty$. Hence, for large m, (20) yields

$$(\underline{U} - \underline{A})*(\underline{U} + \underline{A} + \underline{A}^2 + \ldots + \underline{A}^m) \cong \underline{U} \quad (21)$$

$$(\underline{U} - \underline{A})^{-1} \cong \underline{U} + \underline{A} + \underline{A}^2 + \ldots \underline{A}^m. \quad (22)$$

Suppose the inverse $\underline{J}_0^{-1}$ of a Jacobian $\underline{J}_0$ is known and the inverse of

$$\underline{J} = \underline{J}_0 - \underline{E} = (\underline{U} - \underline{E}\underline{J}_0^{-1})\underline{J}_0; \quad \underline{E} = \underline{J}_0 \cdot \underline{J}. \tag{23}$$

is required, where $\underline{E}$ is the (small) difference between $\underline{J}$ and $\underline{J}_0$. If $(E \cdot \underline{J}_0^{-1})$ is substituted for $\underline{A}$ in (22), then with $r(\underline{E}\,\underline{J}_0^{-1})<1$, we have:

$$\underline{J}^{-1} \cong \underline{J}_0^{-1}\,(\underline{U}-\underline{E}\cdot\underline{J}_0^{-1}) \cong \underline{J}_0^{-1}\,[\underline{U} + (\underline{E}\cdot\underline{J}_0^{-1}) + (\underline{E}\cdot\underline{J}_0^{-1})^2 + \ldots + (\underline{E}\underline{J}_0^{-1})^m] \tag{24}$$

This formula may be related to what is known as the Hotelling-Bodewig method of correcting the inverse. If $m=2^t-1$, then (20) can be rewritten as

$$(\underline{U} - \underline{A})\,((\underline{U} + \underline{A})\,(\underline{U} + \underline{A}^2)\,\ldots\,(\underline{U} + \underline{A}^{2t-1})) = \underline{U} - \underline{A}^{2t} \tag{25}$$

The product $(\underline{U} + \underline{A}) * (\underline{U} + \underline{A}^2) \ldots (\underline{U} + \underline{A}^{2t-1})$, which is an approximation to $(\underline{U} - \underline{A})^{-1}$ may be evaluated recursively in m steps, in either of two ways.

(1) Set $\underline{X}_0 = \underline{U}$ (unit matrix) and define

$$\underline{X}_{n+1} = \underline{X}_n(2\underline{U} - \underline{A}\cdot\underline{X}_n), \quad n=0,1,\ldots,m \tag{26}$$

(2) Set $\underline{X}_0 = \underline{U}$, $\underline{Y}_0 = \underline{A}$ and define

$$\left.\begin{aligned} \underline{X}_{n+1} &= \underline{X}_n\ (\underline{U} + \underline{Y}_n) \\ \underline{Y}_{n+1} &= \underline{Y}_n^2, \end{aligned}\right\} n=0,1,\ldots,m-1 \tag{27}$$

It can be shown that since in every iteration the highest power of $\underline{A}$ which appears in $\underline{X}_n$ is doubled, the method has quadratic convergence.

If $\underline{J}_0^{-1}$ of (24) is inserted into (14) and $\underline{A}$ substituted for $\underline{E}\cdot\underline{J}_0^{-1}$, the following results:

$$\underline{J}_0 \cdot \Delta\underline{x} = -\,(\underline{A}^m + \underline{A}^{m-1} + \underline{A}^{m-2} + \ldots + \underline{A}^2 + \underline{A} + \underline{U})\underline{r}. \tag{28}$$

If all terms in the parenthesis, except the unit matrix $\underline{U}$ are neglected, the Shamanski method results. It differs from the Newton-Raphson method in that $\underline{J}_0$ is kept for k iterations and only then (and not every single iteration) recomputed and inverted (or factored). This is the method normally used. The suggested Hobo-method will invert $\underline{J}_0$ once and then use m terms (m>1) of the series expansion instead of inverting $\underline{J}$ repeatedly. If may be formulated as follows:

(a) Compute $\underline{J}_0$ and invert (or factor) it.

(b) Compute vector of residuals $\underline{r}$.

(c) If max $|r_i|<\varepsilon$ for $1<i<n$, then stop.

(d) Form the variation $\underline{E}$ of $\underline{J}$ and $\underline{A} = \underline{E}\cdot\underline{J}_0^{-1}$

(e) Compute $\Delta\,\underline{x}$ from (28) using m terms of the series.

(f) Correct $\underline{x}$ through $\underline{x} = \underline{x} + \Delta\,\underline{x}$.

(g) Return to step (b).

If step (d) precedes (b), then $\underline{E}$, $\underline{A}$ and the sum are only computed once every k iterations - it is a mixture of Hobo with the Shamanski method.

Hobo raises a number of questions which will be answered in turn.

1. The algorithm requires the computation of powers of $\underline{A}$, which would consume too much time. It can be reduced considerably if (28) is rewritten in a Horner-like fashion:

$$\Delta\,\underline{x} = \underline{J}_0^{-1}\,(\underline{A}\,\ldots\,(\underline{A}(\underline{A}(\underline{A}\underline{r} + \underline{r}) + \underline{r}) + \ldots + \underline{r}) \tag{29}$$

This requires only m + 1 matrix-vector multiplications and m vector additions.

2. Computing $\underline{A} = \underline{E} \cdot \underline{J}_0^{-1}$ calls for a matrix multiplication which is a very time-consuming operation. This time may be reduced if (29) is used so that the repeated multiplication $\underline{A} \cdot \underline{r}$ is replaced by $\underline{E}\,(\underline{J}_0^{-1})\underline{r}$. This however raises the number of matrix-vector multiplications by a factor of two. For special cases this may be reduced. For instance, in the load-flow problem as defined earlier all elements of the Jacobian are constant, except the "diagonal" elements $\partial p_i/\partial v_i$, $\partial q_i/\partial v_i$, $\partial p_i/\partial w_i$ and $\partial q_i/\partial w_i$. Hence $\underline{E}$, being the difference of two Jacobians, consists only of n diagonal quads which are nonzero, or 4n nonzero elements, i.e.

$$\underline{J} = \underline{Y} + \underline{D} \tag{30}$$

Its elements are quads such that with y' the real, y" the imaginary part:

$$\bar{y}_{ik} = \begin{bmatrix} y'_{ik} & -y''_{ik} \\ y''_{ik} & y'_{ik} \end{bmatrix}; \quad D_{kk} = \begin{bmatrix} d'_k & d''_k \\ d''_k & d'_k \end{bmatrix} \tag{31}$$

$$d'_k = (2q_k v_k w_k + p_k(w_k^2 - v_k^2))/|u_k|^4;$$

$$d''_k = (2p_k v_k w_k - q_k(w_k^2 - v_k^2))/|v_k|^4$$

Next we redefine the initial "error" matrix as

$$\underline{E}_0 = \underline{I} - \underline{J}*\underline{J}_0^{-1} \tag{32}$$

and then iteratively calculate

$$\underline{J}_{i+1}^{-1} = \underline{J}_i^{-1} + \underline{J}_i^{-1} * \underline{E}_i; \quad \underline{E}_{i+1} = \underline{U} - \underline{J}*\underline{J}_{i+1}^{-1} \qquad j = 1,2,\ldots, \tag{33}$$

for as long as the norm of $\underline{E}_{i+1}$ is too large.

In the general case this process has quadratic convergence and requires a very large number of calculations. In the case of load-flow a simpler procedure is now suggested.

Insertion of $\underline{J}_0 = \underline{Y}$ into (32) yields:

$$\underline{E}_0 = -\underline{D}\,\underline{Y}^{-1} \tag{34}$$

The first approximation to $\underline{J}^{-1}$ is therefore

$$\underline{J}^{-1} = \underline{Y}^{-1} - \underline{Y}^{-1}\,\underline{D}\,\underline{Y}^{-1} \tag{35}$$

and solving $\underline{J}\,\Delta\,\underline{x} = -\underline{r}$ amounts to:

$$\Delta\underline{x} = \underline{Y}^{-1}\,\underline{D}\,\Delta\,\underline{y}; \quad \Delta\,\underline{y} = \underline{Y}^{-1} * \underline{r} \tag{36}$$

The modified algorithm is based on this scheme and on the fact that $\underline{Y}$ and consequently also $\underline{Y}^{-1}$ are stored in factored form. It consists therefore of:

(a) Compute all d'_k, d''_k according to (8) to (11) and (31).

(b) Compute $\underline{r}$ and then $\Delta\,\underline{y}$ from (36).

(c) Find new $\underline{x}$ in (36) and if needed, return to step (a).

Since $\underline{Y}^{-1}$ is stored in factored form, it is easily multiplied. Similarly, matrix $\underline{D}$ may be decomposed into a lower, bidiagonal matrix $\underline{L}$ and an upper bidiagonal matrix $\underline{R}$ (whose $R_{ii} = 1$). Multiplication $\underline{L}*\underline{R}=\underline{D}$ yields for elements of $\underline{L}$ and $\underline{R}$:

$$\left.\begin{array}{ll} L_{i,i-1} = 0;\ L_{i,i} = d'_k;\ R_{i,j} = d''_k/d'_k;\ L_{j,i} = d''_k & ;\ i=2k-1 \\ L_{j,j} = -((d'_k)^2 + (d''_k)^2)/d'_k;\ R_{j,j+1} = 0 & ;\ j=2k \end{array}\right\} \quad k=1,2,\ldots \tag{37}$$

This would be a very fast algorithm, but since it can be used only for particular numbering of Loaf-equations, we return to the original formulation (and $\underline{E}\ \underline{J}_0^{-1} = \underline{A}$). Since $\underline{E}$ has only n nonzero, diagonal quads the amount of work for multiplying $\underline{E}$ by $\underline{J}_0^{-1}$ is greatly reduced anyway. In $\underline{A} = \underline{U} - \underline{\Delta D} \cdot \underline{J}_0^{-1}$ only the diagonal matrix $\underline{\Delta D}$ changes. Therefore, the number of operations is approximately equal to that required by a matrix-vector multiplication (to be denoted mv). Moreover the quads are of the F-type and - as shown earlier - these may be multiplied rather efficiently.

It is usually difficult to even assess the number of operations Ω of the Newton-Raphson or Shamanski methods because the calculation of an inverse of $\underline{J}$ is involved (or equivalently, its factorization). Not so in the case of Hobo. A single iteration, if it includes m Horner steps, requires.

(a) Computation of $\underline{r}$, which needs approximately as many operations as one mv.

(b) Computation of $\underline{E}\cdot\underline{J}_0^{-1}$, which also requires time of one mv.

(c) The Horner loop, which requires m times mv.

(d) $\underline{J}_0^{-1}\ \underline{r}$, which requires one mv.

Altogether, there are (m+3) mv's. Observe that an iteration of the method of Shamanski which evaluates $\underline{J}^{-1}$ every m corrections of $\underline{x}$, requires 2(m-1)mv's in addition to the time and effort needed to compute $\underline{J}^{-1}$ and that the Newton-Raphson method requires an inversion every single iteration. This should be kept in mind when comparing the efficiency of the methods.

3. The diagonal elements of $\underline{E}$ are such that if the system is very lightly loaded (small p_k, q_k), then the nonlinear part may be neglected and $\underline{J}^{-1}$ approximated by the inverse of the constant part which is composed entirely of $\bar{0}$-quads. In fact, it is isomorphic to the (complex) admittance matrix. Its inverse is therefore also composed of $\bar{F}$-quads. It follows that all arithmetic operations use only $\bar{0}$ and $\bar{F}$-quads, which - as shown - leads to significant reduction in arithmetic work.

Having calculated the computational effort required for a single iteration, let us see next how many iterations are required for Hobo, i.e. let us discuss its convergence. The theorem which defines the convergence will also prove the following point:

As $\underline{x}^{(i)}$ approaches the limit, it is intuitively obvious that the precision of evaluating $\underline{J}^{-1}$ (x) and $\underline{\Delta\ x}$ by means of (29) must increase. Stated differently, the number of terms in the sum (24) must be increased to "keep pace" with the approximation in order to preserve superliner convergence.

The "generalized Ostrowski theorem" [OR70] although used for quite different purpose, may be adapted (with slight changes) to the Hobo method as follows.

<u>Theorem</u>: Let $G:D \subset R^n \to R^n$ be differentiable on an open neighbourhood $S_0 \subset D$ of a point $\bar{x} \in D$ at which G' is continuous and $G(\bar{x}) = 0$.

Suppose that $G'(x) = B(x) - C(x)$, (38)

where B and C are linear operators on R^n and the map $x \to B(\bar{x})$ is continuous on S_0,

$B(\bar{x})$ is nonsingular and $r(H(\bar{x}))<1$ with

$$H(\bar{x}) = B(x)^{-1}.\ C(x), \tag{39}$$

Then there exists an open neighborhood N of $\bar{x}$ such that for any $x^0 \in N$ and any sequence of positive integers $\ell_k, k = 0,1,\ldots$ the iterates x^k given by

$$x^{(k+1)} = x^{(k)} - B^{-1}\,(x^{(k)}\,(1 + H(x^{(k)}) + \ldots + H(x^{(k)})^{\ell_k - 1})\ G(x) \tag{40}$$

are well defined and converge to $\bar{x}$. If $\ell\to\infty$, the convergence is superlinear. If ℓ = constant, convergence is linear with the convergence factor less than $r(H(\bar{x}^{(k)}))'$.

The conditions of this theorem may be made to match the Hobo method perfectly if we substitute the load-flow equations for $G(x) = 0$. In that case $G'(x)$ becomes the Jacobian $\underline{J}(x)$. Substituting $\underline{J}_0$ for $B(x)$ and $\underline{E}$ for $C(x)$, we have a theorem which relates directly to the Hobo algorithm.

The theoretical results regarding the rate of convergence must be approached cautiously when dealing with a particular case like the practical load-flow. It must be kept in mind that these results are all dealing with asymptotic convergence, and the convergence properties are revealed only when very close to the solution; whereas in solving the load-flow problem we usually stop after a few iterations. There are virtually no theoretical results governing the behaviour of algorithms in their initial stages. Therefore the practical solution of non-linear equations, such as those of load-flow, depends on the intuition and experience of the solver, with only general guidance provided by theory. Experience indicates that in many cases the Hobo method gives excellent results with a very small number of iteration m.

To give some idea of the results to be expected, the methods of Newton-Raphson and Hobo were applied to the five-bus power system discussed in [SE68]. At the end of each iteration, the value

$$\delta = \sqrt{\Sigma\, r_i^2;}\quad i\ \Sigma = 1,\ldots,n \tag{41}$$

was computed and served as a measure of convergence. The results appear in the Table below. The DNR column gives the results for Newton-Raphson. Its quadratic convergence is evident. In the following columns, the corresponding Hobo results appear. For m fixed, this method has linear convergence, and yet it can be seen that if precision of 10^{-8} or less is required, the method requires as many iterations as DNR, but each iteration requires less arithmetical operations.

Main iteration	DNR	$\delta(m=2)$	$\delta(m=4)$
1	7.81×10^{-1}	7.81×10^{-1}	7.81×10^{-1}
2	7.63×10^{-3}	7.84×10^{-3}	7.66×10^{-3}
3	8.08×10^{-7}	9.79×10^{-6}	8.18×10^{-7}
4	1.38×10^{-11}	1.18×10^{-8}	1.11×10^{-11}

Hobo, as defined above uses Horner's scheme which is optimal. Each application of (29) amounts to one matrix-by-vector multiplication and one vector addition. The first was programmed in chapter 6 and for the specific case of (29) note that we may keep the same horizontal slice of $\underline{A}$ throughout and exchange only the vectors $\underline{y}_{i+1} = \underline{A}\ \underline{r} + y_i$. The speedup should approach the optimal.

We have discussed iterative, Newton-Raphson and the Hobo methods. In which cases of loaf should they be used?

In most cases, the Shamanski method will still be used, being fast, proven and amenable to ASP. The computational effort required in this case, with elimination and poof being used, was calculated and justifies its use. It is my personal view that as more results are being accumulated, the Hobo method will prove superior for loaf and will replace the method by Shamanski. Especially advocated is the mixture of Hobo and Shamanski's method, as well as the use of (30).

These methods are suitable for steady-state calculations, as required in STEP, CAP and EDIP. For dynamic simulations and stability calculations (not discussed in this book), iterative methods should prove faster.

10.2 STATE-ESTIMATION PROBLEM, STEP

Aims: To define the basic equations of STEP. To improve the solution of "normal" equations. To solve them by the conjugate gradient method sequentially and on ASP. To develop a new method based on "tearing" and prove that its ratio is optimal.

It is of interest to monitor voltages (v_i,w_i), power injections (p_i,q_i) at nodes $i=0,\ldots,n-1$ or power-flows p_{km},q_{km} over lines $1,\ldots,\ell$. Some of these quantities will be measured, others have to be calculated because:

- It is not possible to measure some quantities e.g. angles between bus voltages
- Metering and communication equipment is costly and money can be saved
- A lost measurement may be simulated by calculating it

As the "state vector" $\underline{x}$, that set of variables should be chosen which is sufficient to define uniquely the state of the network (e.g. v_i, w_i for $i=1,2,\ldots,n$) and moreover, from which all other values may be explicitly calculated. Since the phase-angle of the slack bus (numbered 0) is set to zero, the dimension of the state vector is $\dim(x) = 2*n - 1$ and the vector itself

$$\underline{x}^T = (v_0,v_1,\ldots,v_{n-1},w_1,\ldots,w_{n-1}) = (x_1,x_2,\ldots,x_{2n-1}) \qquad (42)$$

Knowing $\underline{x}$ and the network parameters, it is possible to evaluate and monitor all other quantities of the power system such as currents, injected powers or line-flows. The equations relating injections p_i, q_i to v_i, w_i are those of LOAF and line power-flows are:

$$p_{ki} = -(v_k(v_k-v_i) + w_k(w_k-w_i))g_{ki} + (v_k(w_k-w_i) - w_k(v_k-v_i))b_{ki} \qquad (43)$$

$$q_{ki} = (v_k(v_k-v_i) + w_k(w_k-w_i))b_{ki} + (v_k(w_k-w_i) - w_k(v_k-v_i))g_{ki} - (v_k^2+w_k^2)y_c \qquad (44)$$

All these equations are non-linear and relate $\underline{x}$ to the m-dimensional measurement vector $\underline{z}$ through

$$\underline{z} = \underline{f}(\underline{x}) \qquad (45)$$

Since measurements include errors, this equation must be replaced by

$$\underline{z} = \underline{f}(\underline{x}) + \underline{u} \qquad (46)$$

where $\underline{u}$ is an m-dimensional error vector (or vector of residuals).

From (46) it follows that

$$\underline{u} = \underline{z} - \underline{f}(\underline{x}) \qquad (47)$$

and it is the aim of the algorithm to calculate $\underline{x}$ such that the norm of $\underline{u}$ should be minimal. If this norm is Euclidian, then

$$e = \underline{u}^T * \underline{u} = \Sigma\ (z_i - f_i(x))^2;\ i\ \Sigma = 1,\ldots,m \qquad (48)$$

should be minimized. This process is known as "least squares minimization".

Suppose we linearize $\underline{f}(\underline{x}) = f(\underline{x}_0) - \underline{J}\ \underline{\Delta x}$ where $\underline{J}$ is the Jacobian matrix such that $J_{ij} = \partial f_i / \partial x_j$. Then, the vector of residuals $\underline{u}$ is

$$\underline{u} = \underline{J} \cdot \underline{\Delta x} + \underline{c};\ \underline{c} = \underline{z} - \underline{f}(\underline{x}_0) \qquad (49)$$

$\underline{u}$ should be identically zero, but is not, so that (45) is solved by minimizing the square of the "error", the scalar

$$e = \underline{u}^T\underline{u} = \underline{\Delta x}^T\ \underline{J}^T\underline{J}\ \underline{\Delta x} + \underline{\Delta x}^T\ \underline{J}^T\underline{c} + \underline{c}^T\ \underline{J}\ \underline{\Delta x} + \underline{c}^T\underline{c} \qquad (50)$$

Since $\underline{c}^T\underline{c}$ is constant, its derivative is zero. The second and third terms of $\underline{u}^T\underline{u}$ are identical since the transpose of any scalar (here $\underline{\Delta x}^T\ \underline{J}^T\ \underline{c}$) is the scalar itself. Thus $\underline{\Delta x}^T\ (\underline{J}^T\underline{J})\ \underline{\Delta x} + 2 \cdot \underline{\Delta x}^T\ (\underline{J}^T\ \underline{c})$ is to be minimized.

Define the "normal" matrix $\underline{A}$ and "right hand" vector $\underline{b}$ through

$$\underline{A} = \underline{J}^T \cdot \underline{J};\quad \underline{b} = -\underline{J}^T\ \underline{c} \qquad (51)$$

$\underline{A}$ is obviously symmetric, the quadratic form $(\underline{A}\ \underline{\Delta x})^T\ \underline{\Delta x} = (\underline{J}\ \underline{\Delta x})^T\ (\underline{J}\ \underline{\Delta x})$ being a scalar product of $\underline{J}\ \underline{\Delta x}$ with itself is non-negative for any $\underline{\Delta x}$ and $\underline{J}\ \underline{\Delta x} = \underline{0}$ requires $\underline{\Delta x} = \underline{0}$. This proves that $\underline{A}$ is a symmetric, positive-definite matrix. For such matrices, the set $\underline{A}\ \underline{\Delta x} = \underline{b}$ has a solution vector which provides a single minimum for $0.5\ \underline{\Delta x}^T\ \underline{A}\ \underline{\Delta x} + \underline{\Delta x}^T\ \underline{b}$ which is half of the expression to be minimized. Therefore minimization of $\underline{u}^T\underline{u}$ is equivalent to solution of $\underline{A}\ \underline{\Delta x} = \underline{b}$ with $\underline{A}$, $\underline{b}$ as in (51). (The procedure is iterative so that $\underline{x}$ will occasionally substitute for $\underline{\Delta x}$. It is assumed that all measurements z_i have equal precision - otherwise a "weighting", diagonal matrix would postmultiply $\underline{J}^T$ in $\underline{A}$ and $\underline{b}$).

State-estimation programs start by assuming a state-vector $\underline{x}_0$ and proceed iteratively, with the steps:

(a) Compute $\underline{J}$ (a function of $\underline{x}$), the normal matrix $\underline{A} = \underline{J}^T\ \underline{J}$ and vector $\underline{b}$.

(b) Solve $\underline{A} \cdot \underline{\Delta x} = \underline{b}$ a fixed, say ν number of times with the same $\underline{A}$ and $\underline{J}$ but updated $\underline{c} = \underline{z} - \underline{f}(\underline{x})$ and $\underline{x}$ corrected through $\underline{x} = \underline{x} + \underline{\Delta x}$.

(c) If $\underline{u}^T\underline{u} < \varepsilon$ stop; otherwise restart at (a) with the new $\underline{x}$.

The solution of $\underline{A}\ \underline{\Delta x} = \underline{b}$ requires $n^3/3$ operations and to save time is done by factorization i.e., $\underline{A} = \underline{L}\ \underline{U}$ done once and reused ν times in step (b). An additional way to save time is suggested below.

$\underline{A}$ was proven to be a symmetric, positive-definite matrix. As such it may be factored into $\underline{L}\ \underline{D}\ \underline{L}^T$ with $\underline{L}$, a lower, unit triangular and $\underline{D}$ a diagonal matrix. There is no reason why $\underline{A}$ has to be calculated first and then factored; $\underline{L}$ and $\underline{D}$ of

$$\underline{J}^T\ \underline{J} = \underline{L}\ \underline{D}\ \underline{L}^T \tag{52}$$

can be calculated directly for i=1,2,...,n through:

$$d_{ii} = \underline{J}_{\cdot i}\ \underline{J}_{\cdot i} - \Sigma \ell_{ij}\ e_{ij};\ j\Sigma=1,\dots,i-1 \tag{53}$$

$$e_{ij} = \underline{J}_{\cdot i}\ \underline{J}_{\cdot i} - \Sigma \ell_{jk}\ e_{ik};\ \ell_{ji}=e_{ji}/d_{ii};\ k\Sigma=1,\dots,i-1;\ j=i+1,i+2,\dots n \tag{54}$$

The only operations involving all n elements are the $[1+2+\dots+(n-1)]n$ scalar products $\underline{J}_{\cdot i}\ \underline{J}_{\cdot i}$ and $\underline{J}_{\cdot j}\ J_{\cdot i}$ with $\underline{J}_{\cdot k}$ denoting the k-th column of $\underline{J}$. Altogether, the number of operations is

$$\Omega_{52} \cong 0.5n(n+1)n\omega \cong 0.5n^3\omega \tag{55}$$

The solution of $\underline{L}\ \underline{D}\ \underline{L}^T\ \underline{\Delta x} = \underline{-J}^T\ \underline{c}$ requires only $\Omega=n^2\omega$ and may be disregarded, since $n^2 << n^3$. Normally, $n^3\omega$ is needed for $\underline{A} = \underline{J}^T\ \underline{J}$ and $(n^3/6)$ for $\underline{A} = \underline{L}\ \underline{R}$. Direct factorization has saved $(2n^3/3)\omega$ and storage space, since $\underline{A}$ is not stored at all. (Storage of $\underline{J}$, $\underline{L}$ and $\underline{D}$ requires $\cong 2*0.5n^2=n^2$ locations.) Sparsity can be used in both cases.

One method of solving $\underline{A}\ \underline{x} = \underline{b}$ would be by the conjugate gradients algorithm (see 7.1.4). It would consist of initialization

$$\underline{r}^{(0)} = \underline{b} - \underline{A}\ \underline{x}^{(0)};\ e_{-1} = 0 \tag{56}$$

and the iterations (i=0,1,2,...) below until $r^{(k)}*r^{(k)}<\varepsilon$.

Let us first copy a less known version of it [Ru76], developed by Rutishauser (in which $\underline{s} = \underline{A}\ \underline{r}$). Dispensing with initialization, it could be summarized as starting with values of $d_{i-1}, e_{i-1}, \underline{r}$; and doing for i=2,3,..:

$$q_i = (\underline{r}_i^T \cdot \underline{s}_i)/d_{i-1} - e_{i-1} \tag{57}$$

$$\underline{\Delta r}_{i+1} = [e_{i-1}\ \underline{\Delta r}_i - \underline{s}_i]/q_i;\ \underline{r}_{i+1} = \underline{r}_i + \underline{\Delta r}_{i+1};\ \underline{s}_{i+1} = \underline{A}\ \underline{r}_{i+1} \tag{58}$$

$$d_i = \underline{r}_{i+1}^T\ \underline{r}_{i+1};\ e_i = q_i(d_i/d_{i-1}) \tag{59}$$

$$\underline{s} = \underline{A}\ \underline{R}_i;\ \underline{\Delta x}_{i+1} = (\underline{r}_i - e_{i-1}\ \underline{\Delta x}_i)/q_i;\ \underline{x}_{i+1} = \underline{x}_i + \underline{\Delta x}_{i+1} \tag{60}$$

We will introduce next some simplification which results from the fact that $\underline{A} = \underline{J}^T\ \underline{J}$. Inserting it yields

$$\underline{r}_i^T\ \underline{s}_i = \underline{r}_i^T \cdot \underline{A}\ \underline{r}_i = \underline{r}_i^T\ \underline{J}^T\ \underline{J}\ \underline{r}_i =$$

$$(\underline{J}\ \underline{r}_i)^T(\underline{J}\ \underline{r}_i) = \underline{w}_i^T\underline{w}_i;\ \underline{w}=\underline{Jr} \tag{61}$$

The algorithm is therefore as follows: $(\underline{s} = \underline{J}^T\underline{J}\underline{r}_i = \underline{J}^T\underline{w})$:

$$\underline{s}_i = \underline{J}^T\underline{w}_i;\ q_i = (\underline{w}_i^T \cdot \underline{w}_i)/d_{i-1} - e_{i-1} \tag{62}$$

$$\underline{r}_{i+1} = \underline{r}_i + [e_{i-1}(\underline{r}_i - \underline{r}_{i-1}) - \underline{s}_i]/q_i;$$

$$\underline{w}_{i+1} = \underline{w}_i + [e_{i-1}(\underline{w}_i - \underline{w}_{i-1})\underline{Js}_i]/q_i \tag{63}$$

$$d_i = r_{i+1}^T\underline{r}_{i+1};\ e_i = q_i(d_i/d_{i-1}); \tag{64}$$

and start it by computing the new $\underline{x}_{i+1}$.

We have now two matrix-vector multiplications, $\underline{J}^T\underline{w}$ and $\underline{Js}$ instead of one, and need thus $2mn\omega$, but we do not need $mn^2\omega$ for $\underline{A} = \underline{J}^T\underline{J}$ as needed normally. Additionally, if $\underline{J}$ is sparse (which it very much is), say has d per-unit non-zero entries, then the algorithm requires only $2dnm\omega$. We should compare this time $(mn^2+dnm^2)\omega$ for using the conjugate gradient method on $\underline{A}\ \underline{x} = \underline{b}$ with $n^3\omega$ for the normal solution. In each case, CG as defined above requires fewer operations and quite obviously less storage (since $\underline{A}$ is not stored at all). Also, the round-off errors inherent in the calculation of normal equations can be avoided.

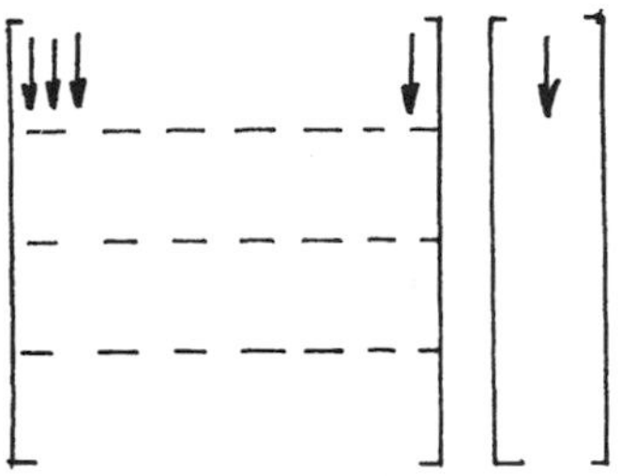

Fig. 1: Calculation of $\underline{J}^T \underline{w}$

The data outlay for ASP is that $\underline{J}$ is stored in slices, vectors $\underline{s}$, $\underline{r}$ and $\underline{w}$ as well as scalars d,e and q are stored in all local and in the main memory. As a matter of fact, two values d_i, d_{i-1} and two values $\underline{w}_i^T * \underline{w}_i$, $\underline{w}_{i-1}^T * \underline{w}_{i-1}$ are kept in storage to make the calculation of q_i and e_i more efficient. Our problem is that we need both $\underline{J}*\underline{s}$ and $\underline{J}^T * \underline{w}$ and do not want to store both horizontal and vertical slices of $\underline{J}$. Fig. 1 shows that we do not have to. If $\underline{J}$ is stored by horizontal slices, $\underline{J}*\underline{s}$ is done as discussed in chapter 4 and $\underline{J}^T * \underline{w}$ as shown in Fig. 1. Here every slave q would compute:

$$s_i^{(q)} = \Sigma J_{ki} w_k; \quad k \Sigma = (q-1)h+1; \quad i=1,\ldots,n \tag{65}$$

The resulting $\underline{s}$ must be summed by the master which involves $2n\tau p$.

The ASP-program could be as follows:

P(1): Calculate $\underline{s} = \underline{J}^T * \underline{w}$ as above.

S(1): Transfer pn s-values to the master. Compute there $\underline{s}_i$ and q_i. Transfer them to all p slaves

P(2): Each slave calculates its horizontal slice of $\underline{r}$, $\underline{J}*\underline{s}$ and $\underline{w}$.

S(2): These are sent to the master which computes $\underline{w}^T * \underline{w}$, $\underline{r}^T * \underline{r}$ and e_i.

In addition to the two bus synchronizations, $\Omega_{p(1)} = nh\omega$, $\Omega_{S(1)} = 2pn\tau + n\alpha + \mu + \alpha$, $\Omega_{p(2)} = hn\omega + 5h\mu + 6h\alpha$, $\Omega_{s(2)} = 2n\omega + 2\mu$. All except matrix-times-vector multiplications may be neglected so that

$$\rho \cong [2nh\omega + (2pn + 3h)\tau + 2\beta]/(2n^2\omega) \cong 1/p + p\tau'/n + \beta'/n^2 \tag{66}$$

As seen, the speedup is close to being optimal. We can make it even higher if we use the "tearing" approach.

Let us start with a preliminary but basic remark. Least square estimation [SH74] is defined so that under certain conditions (to be discussed), the network may be divided into p subnetworks. Each slave may then be assigned a single subnetwork which it estimates by applying the customary least-square technique. The results obtained by the p slaves are then transferred to the master which coordinates them. The conditions mentioned are:

(1) The "subnetworks" result from a fictitious cutting of lines. Only lines on whose two ends both active and reactive powers are measured, may be cut.

(2) Every partial network must obey the "observability principle" which, in a simplified form may be stated as follows: In order to estimate a network, its Jacobian matrix $\underline{J}$ must not have linearly dependent columns. Normally this is found out by elimination. At each step, as zeros replace the elements below the diagonal, the upper triangle is checked. If the value of its elements are so small as to be

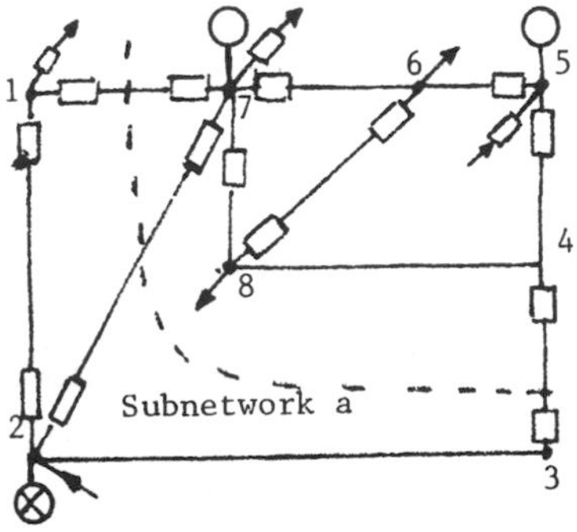

Fig. 2: Network example

considered zero, there exist dependent columns. It is shown in [Bo79] that the independency can be ascertained by constructing two network trees: one based on active-power measurements, the other on both reactive-power and voltage measurements. The existence of these two trees is a sufficient condition for estimating the network-state, given the measurements.

To explain it, we show in Fig. 2 an 8-bus network with a measurement system. It will be assumed that both active and reactive powers are measured (▭ denotes power measurement, ⊗ voltage measurement).

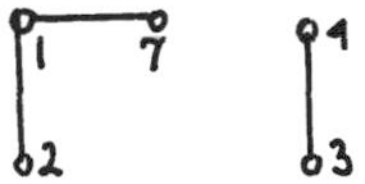

Fig. 3: Tree

Suppose, we fictitiously cut this, obviously "observable" network, along the dashed line. Subnetwork "a" includes nodes 1,2,3,4 and 7. It is important to note the following: Since each subnetwork has another slack-bus, but the original network had only a single such bus, the relative angles of the subnetworks will differ. Simulation showed that the angle-difference is constant and can be adjusted if we know it at least in one bus. This angle-difference is found at a bus to which a torn line is connected - provided we include the power flow of the cut line and no other measurements at this bus. Thus power-flows 2-7 and 1-7 are included in subnetwork "a" of Fig. 2, but not the measurements taken at bus 7. Since there were no measurements taken in line 2-3, not all buses of subnetwork "a" are connected by either tree. Therefore subnetwork "a" cannot be estimated since it does not obey the observability criterion.

The justification of subdividing the network (see Fig. 4) is as follows. The solution for subnetwork "b" of Fig. 5 is completely equivalent to that of Fig. 4. We have treated each line through which power flows out of subnetwork "b" as a load-node and each node through which it flows into "b" as a generator node. Because of condition (1) we may do this in every line which was cut and because of condition (2) we may be assured that enough measurements were taken so that all subnetworks can be estimated. Basically, a subnetwork such as "b" of Fig. 5 "does not know" that it is a part of a larger network. The measured values for the additional fictitious load and generator nodes are in no way different from its internal nodes. All show errors to be levelled out by the stationary state estimation algorithm. The algorithm consists of the S(1) and S(2) steps done by the master and the P(1) step done by all p slaves.

S(1): The master "divides" the network data among the p slaves, checking first that both conditions are obeyed. Other data e.g. that needed to compute $\underline{f}(\underline{x})$ for $\underline{A}\ \underline{\Delta x} = \underline{b}$ are also transferred. If the sum-total of values to be sent through the bus is m, we need the "time" $m\tau$ for it (We assume that state estimation programs are stored in the local memories, prior to activating step S(1).

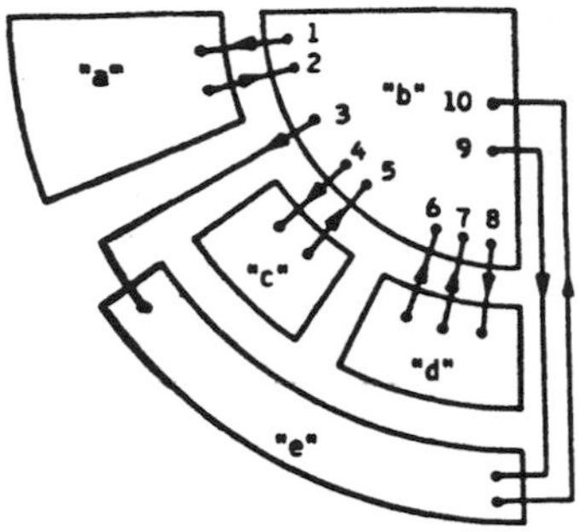

Fig. 4: Fictitiously cut network

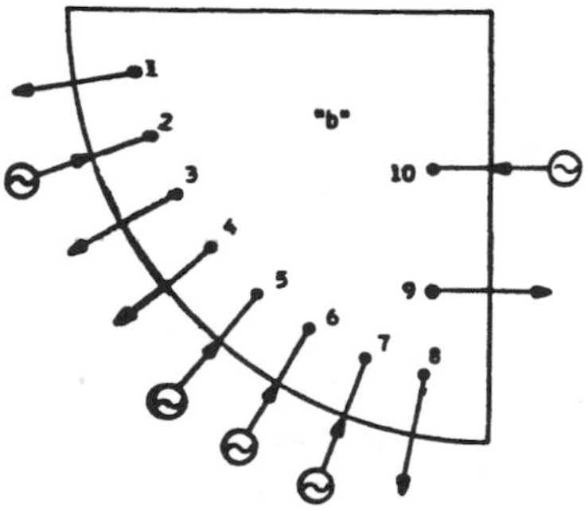

Fig. 5: Subnetwork b of Fig. 4

P(1): Assuming an even distribution of $h=m/p$ data per slave i.e. matrices of order hxh, the required "time" i.e. number of operations is

$$t_1 = 3h^3\omega/3 = h^3\omega = m^3\omega/p^3 \qquad (67)$$

Since back-substitution is proportional to m^2, computing $\underline{f}(\underline{x})$ to m and m is assumed large even for the subnetworks, these times may be neglected compared to t_1.

S(2): The master collects the data for which it needs the time $t_2=m\beta$.

Next we calculate the time needed by a single computer. In order not to get too good results, we will assume that in this case all data movement may be neglected, so that the time for estimating the (uncut) network is

$$t_s = (3m^3/3)\omega = m^3\omega \qquad (68)$$

The time reduction ratio is therefore

$$\rho = \frac{m^3\omega/p^3 + 2m\tau + \beta}{m^3\,\omega} = \frac{1}{p^3} + \frac{2\tau'}{m^2} + \frac{\beta'}{m^3} \qquad (69)$$

where β is the synchronization time needed ahead of S(2). Since we consider only large networks, we may safely neglect the terms with β' and τ', and get $\rho \cong 1/p^3$ (70)

This ratio is too high and should be explained. The reasons for it are: (a) Each slave works most of the time independently of and concurrently with other slaves. It inverts the matrix and computes i times $\underline{A}\ \underline{\Delta x} = \underline{b}$. During this entire time, it works completely autonomously; it has no connection with other computers and needs none. (b) The data to be transferred initially by the master and gathered by it at the end of computation, is transferred by blocks, hence rather fast. (c) Only one

Bus	V_o	Case 0		Case 1		Case 2		Case 3	
		V_a	V_b	V_a	V_b	V_a	V_b	V_a	V_b
1	1.061	1.065	1.061	1.061	1.059	1.059	1.059	1.060	-
2	1.046	1.050	1.046	1.046	1.045	1.044	1.046	1.045	1.049
3	1.011	-	1.010	-	1.011	-	1.012	1.010	1.014
4	1.019	1.020	1.017	1.018	1.019	1.021	1.020	1.017	1.020
5	1.020	1.023	1.019	1.020	1.021	1.021	1.022	1.020	1.022
6	1.070	1.070	-	1.070	-	1.071	-	1.069	1.070
7	1.059	-	1.062	-	1.064	-	1.065	-	1.061
8	1.091	-	1.092	-	1.088	-	1.091	-	1.090
9	1.055	-	1.056	1.053	1.057	1.058	1.060	-	1.055
10	1.050	1.052	1.052	1.048	1.053	1.052	1.056	-	1.051
11	1.056	1.056	1.058	1.057	1.061	1.058	-	-	1.056
12	1.055	1.055	-	1.056	-	1.056	-	-	1.056
13	1.048	1.050	1.050	1.051	-	1.049	-	-	1.052
14	1.035	1.038	1.038	1.035	1.035	1.036	1.044	-	1.035

Table 2: Comparison of estimated voltages V_a, V_b, in subnetworks a and b to V_o of the uncut network (Voltages V_o, V_a, V_b in p.u.-values)

Line from-to	P_o (uncut net)	Case 0 P_a	Case 0 P_b	Case 1 P_a	Case 1 P_b	Case 2 P_a	Case 2 P_b	Case 3 P_a	Case 3 P_b
1-2	156.5	156.7	156.3	157.1	156.3	159.7	155.2	155.1	-
1-5	75.8	75.9	-	74.8	-	74.4	-	75.1	-
2-3	72.9	-	72.3	-	72.2	-	71.7	72.9	-
2-4	56.4	-	56.4	-	55.9	-	55.5	56.5	54.9
2-5	42.0	42.3	41.9	40.5	41.5	39.0	41.3	41.7	-
3-4	-22.7	-	-22.1	-	-22.5	-	-22.4	-22.5	-23.6
4-5	-60.5	-66.6	-60.7	-62.9	-60.3	-61.8	-59.6	-62.2	-59.8
4-7	29.4	-	29.3	-	29.4	-	28.6	-	26.1
4-9	16.6	-	16.2	-	16.0	-	16.0	-	15.6
5-6	44.9	42.6	-	43.7	-	43.6	-	44.2	43.4
6-11	8.6	7.3	-.	9.0	-	7.6	-	-	6.6
6-12	8.4	7.7	-	7.6	-	7.3	-	-	8.4
6-13	20.4	17.4	-	17.5	-	18.4	-	-	19.4
7-8	-1.5	-	-2.9	-	-1.8	-	-0.7	-	-0.4
7-9	28.1	-	26.6	-	25.0	-	26.6	-	29.2
9-10	5.8	-	4.6	-	4.8	3.6	1.7	-	5.3
9-14	10.2	-	9.0	8.6	8.5	9.3	13.3	-	10.9
10-11	-3.3	-5.5	-3.1	-7.4	-3.7	-3.6	-	-	-4.0
12-13	2.6	1.6	-	1.7	-	2.5	-	-	1.8
13-14	5.5	7.0	4.7	6.6	-	5.7	-	-	5.8

Table 3: The estimated real-power flows in the uncut (P_o) and divided networks (P_a, P_b) - always per MW

Line from-to	Q_o (uncut net)	Case 0 Q_a	Case 0 Q_b	Case 1 Q_a	Case 1 Q_b	Case 2 Q_a	Case 2 Q_b	Case 3 Q_a	Case 3 Q_b
1-2	-20.1	-21.1	-19.8	-19.9	-22.3	-21.1	-23.6	-20.6	-
1-5	3.9	4.7	-	4.0	-	2.7	-	4.1	-
2-3	3.4	-	4.2	-	3.3	-	3.2	3.6	-
2-4	-2.1	-	-1.2	-	-2.5	-	-2.8	-1.2	-0.4
2-5	1.1	2.4	1.8	1.4	-0.1	0.2	0.5	1.6	-
3-4	3.0	-	2.8	-	2.6	-	2.3	3.7	3.9
4-5	16.2	14.6	15.0	15.9	13.2	19.5	16.3	14.7	14.7
4-7	-7.9	-	-10.3	-	-10.1	-	-10.3	-	-8.1
4-9	0.1	-	-0.5	-	-0.5	-	-0.6	-	0.2
5-6	13.0	14.0	-	12.8	-	12.8	-	12.8	13.5
6-11	3.6	3.8	-	2.8	-	3.2	-	-	4.4
6-12	2.3	2.3	-	2.2	-	2.7	-	-	2.0
6-13	8.4	7.1	-	6.7	-	8.7	-	-	5.8
7-8	-18.9	-	-17.6	-	-14.8	-	-15.7	-	-17.7
7-9	4.6	-	6.5	-	6.6	-	5.9	-	5.6
9-10	4.7	-	3.8	-	3.8	5.4	4.3	-	4.2
9-14	3.1	-	2.7	3.1	4.9	4.2	0.2	-	3.2
10-11	-2.0	0.1	-2.3	-1.7	-2.9	-1.7	-	-	-1.6
12-13	1.2	0.9	-	0.8	-	0.9	-	-	0.4
13-14	1.0	0.5	1.4	1.7	-	1.2	-	-	2.3

Table 4: The estimated reactive-power flows in the uncut (Q_0) and divided networks, (Q_a-Q_b) - always per MVAR

synchronization is needed. We thus obey the "parallelization principle". (d) We will show that convergence is the same as for the uncut network. If this network was divided evenly, no reduction of speedup is due to asymmetry of tasks.

We assumed that 1/p is the optimum ratio. It stands to reason that with, say p=10 slaves, we cannot compute faster than 10 times that of a single computer. In our case though, (70) would yield a speedup of 1000. The explanation is that in our case practically all the time is taken by elimination which is proportional to n^3 of the matrix. Thus a network of order n/p needs only n^3/p^3 operations.

In actual practice, the ratio will not be so good, because of the following factors: (a) The matrices are very sparse, so that their factorization is proportional to n or n^2 rather than to n^3. The ratio is thus between $1/p$ and $1/p^2$.

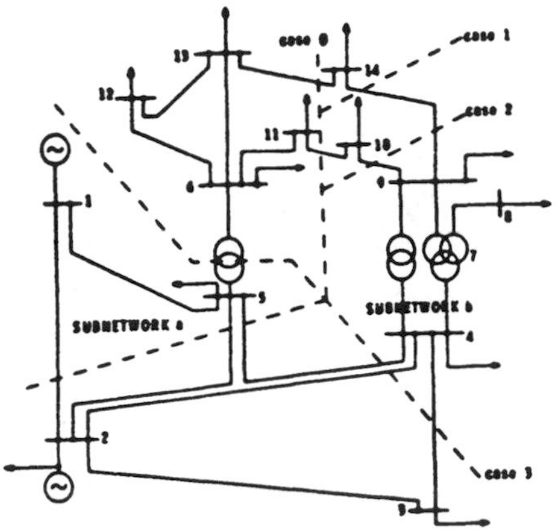

Fig. 6: IEEE 14-bus network

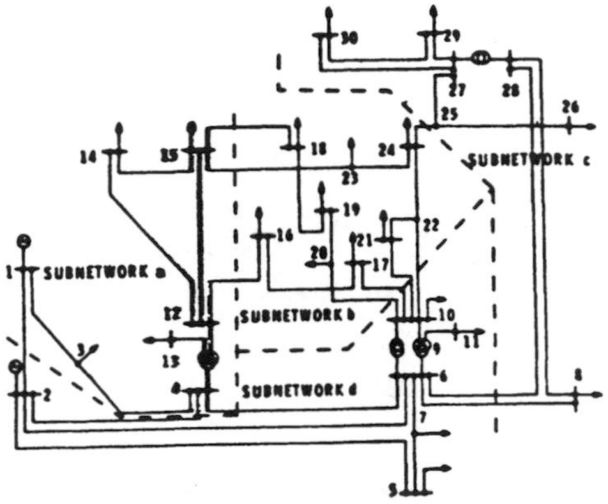

Fig. 7: IEEE 30-bus network

(b) It might be argued that since we have (p+1) computers (p slaves and a master), the optimum ratio should be $1/(p+1)$ instead of $1/p$.

The time required for completion is directly proportional to convergence. Should we need more iterations for any of the subnetworks, this would decrease speedup. The examples below show that this is not the case.

In order to prove the merits of the method, the IEEE 14- and 30-bus standard networks were simulated. The 14-bus system (Fig. 6) was cut into two subnetworks in a number of ways denoted as cases 0,1,2, and 3. In each case the solution started from a "flat start" and needed three iterations of the Newton-Raphson procedure in order to converge. The results obtained for the uncut as well as for the two subnetworks in each of the 4 cases are shown in Tables 2, 3, and 4. Compared to the uncut networks, these show a remarkable closeness of estimated values.

It is customary to judge the closeness of solution by the sum of squares of errors mostly normalized in order for the results to be independent of the number of measurements and unknowns. For our four cases, e is shown in Table 5. All values are so small that we may reach the conclusion: We may cut the networks in any way we deem best, provided all subnetworks obey the two conditions stated.

The next question is whether a network can be split in more than two networks. To this effect, the 30-bus network (Fig. 7) was divided into four subnetworks and the partial solutions compared to the overall (convergence was again obtained in three iterations, in all cases). The values of e as they appear in Table 5 are so small that we may draw the conclusion: The network may be cut into $p > 2$ subnetworks thus providing work for all p slaves.

Whether bad data can be detected by the measurement system of a subnetwork, depends mainly on the local redundancy defined for each bus j through m_j/n_j. m_j comprises the number of measurements at bus j and at all its direct neighbours; n_j is the corresponding number of unknown state-variables. A local redundancy of 2 is considered to be optimal for a sufficient detection probability of bad data.

In case of Fig. 6 we have reversed the power flow of line 1-2 (made it -156.7). The result was that (a) Subnetwork "a" had a very large e. (b) The normalized residual for flow in line 1-2 was unusually large. The first shows that detection, the second shows that identification of bad data was achieved.

We cannot "tear" the networks into a too large number k. Thus, subnetwork "a" of the 14-bus IEEE-network (Fig. 6) has for case 0 nodes 2,4,10,14 in addition to 1,5,6,11,12,13 and subnetwork "b" has nodes 1,5,11,13 in addition to nodes 2,3,4,7, 8,9,10,14. For the original network n was 14. For subnetwork a: n=10; and for subnetwork b: n=12. Thus, the "time" would be $10^3 + 12^3 = 2728$ instead of 2744 i.e. there is practically no computational gain whatsoever. It should be noted that this resulted from the network chosen being very small and highly interconnected. However for practical, large networks the theoretical gain of k^2 will only insubstantially be reduced by the inclusion of the additional nodes.

	Normalized $\mathcal{E}(\hat{x})$ Net a	Net b
Uncut Network	-1.17	
Case 0	-0.99	-0.18
Case 1	0.16	0.08
Case 2	-1.03	-0.76
Case 3	0.50	-0.25

Table 5: Normalized $\mathcal{E}(\hat{x})$

	Normalized $\mathcal{E}(\hat{x})$
Uncut Network	-0.03
Net a	-0.73
Net b	-1.03
Net c	0.66
Net d	0.36

Table 6: Normalized $\mathcal{E}(\hat{x})$

10.3 CONTINGENCY ANALYSIS PROGRAM-CAP

Aims: To define the problem and review how it can be solved by repeated application of LOAF. To develop a method for setting-up and using the Z-matrix for CAP. Both parts of this new method are based on material of Chapter 5.

In its simplest form the problem may be defined as follows. Starting from a given state calculated either by LOAF or STEP, changes are made in the network and their influence noted. In particular the question of whether connecting and disconnecting lines will lead to overload on other lines has to be answered. The basic equations are therefore those of LOAF and the most common way to solve CAP is by repeated solution of LOAF. Here, we go another way.

In Chapter 5 we have developed a general formula

$$(\underline{U} - \delta\, \underline{w}\, \underline{v}^T)^{-1} = \underline{U} - \gamma\, \underline{w}\, \underline{v}^T;\ \gamma = \delta/(\delta\, \underline{v}^T\, \underline{w} - 1) \tag{71}$$

This formula can be used to calculate an inverse for a matrix $\underline{B}$ different from a given $\underline{A}$ by either a single element (Sherman-Morrison method) or by four symmetric changes. This last case is especially valuable for CAP. We simply say that connecting or disconnecting a line i-j changes the admitances y_{ii}, y_{jj} by some Δ and y_{ij}, y_{ji} by $(-\Delta)$. For that case, it was shown in Chapter 5, that the inverse $\underline{Z}$ of the admittance matrix $\underline{Y}$ can be written as:

$$\underline{Z}' = \underline{Z} + \psi\, \underline{w}\, \underline{w}^T;\ \psi = \Delta/(\Delta(2\,Z_{ij} - Z_{ii} - Z_{jj}) + 1) \qquad (72)$$

and any element w_k can be computed as $w_k = Z_{ki} - Z_{kj}$.

Normally the $\underline{Z}$ matrix is collected by Kron's method (Chapter 5 again).

The main objection to the use of $\underline{Z}$-methods is that $\underline{Z}$ being a dense matrix, requires n^2 storage locations. Let us observe that the storage needed in any ASP-version will not be larger than those in a single computer if each memory holds only a "slice" (Fig. 8) of $\underline{Z}$. Secondly, the prices of memories especially of chips as used for slave-memories, decrease steadily. Thus, <u>if</u> we can divide the elements of $\underline{Z}$ evenly among the (slave) memories, the methods are workable.

	1	2	3	4	5	6	7	8	9	10	11	12
1	X	X	X	X	X	X	X	X	X	X	X	X
2		X	X	X	X	X	X	X	X	X	X	X
3	#1		X	X	X	X	X	X	X	X	X	X
4				X	X	X	X	X	X	X	X	X
5	#2				X	X	X	X	X	X	X	X
6						X	X	X	X	X	X	X
7							X	X	X	X	X	X
8								X	X	X	X	X
9									X	X	X	X
10	#3-slice									X	X	X
11											X	X
12												X

Fig. 8: Slice of $\underline{Z}$ for n=12 and with p=3

Such division (e.g., Fig. 8) is hardly possible while using Kron's reduction. Moreover, it requires both $Z_{i,n}$ and $Z_{n,j}$. Thus we either store a full matrix or use an appropriate IF-statement, but this is rather complicated since $Z_{j,k}$ may be in one slice while $Z_{k,j}$ in another. Thus, movement of data would be involved and this could severely increase the time-ratio.

If (72) is used instead then the ASP-program might be:

<u>S(0)</u>: Let the master divide the network into p trees, each starting on ground. This should not be difficult, since it really means that each should include at least one generator. The master then transfers program and data to the slaves.

<u>P(1)</u>: Each slave collects $\underline{Z}$ of its tree. This requires to build it step-by-step as follows:

(a) If the line connects to ground (through a generator) row and column k of zeros is added to the existing (k-1)*(k-1) matrix $\underline{Z}$. Then $Z_{k,k}$ is made Z_ℓ (the impedance of the added line).

(b) If line p-q starts in node p already included in $\underline{Z}$, a column and row k are added such that their elements are:

$$Z_{iq} = Z_{ip} \text{ for } i=1,\ldots,k;\ Z_{kk} = Z_{pp} + Z_\ell;\ \text{and } Z_{ji} = Z_{ij} \qquad (73)$$

Actually, if there are links internal to the trees, they can be included in the

$\underline{Z}$'s of the subnetworks. The result would be a block-diagonal matrix (Fig. 9) with the blocks representing the subnetworks and thus being symmetrical.

$$\begin{bmatrix} \underline{Z}_a & & & & 0 \\ & \underline{Z}_b & & & \\ & & \cdot & & \\ & & & \cdot & \\ 0 & & & & \underline{Z}_p \end{bmatrix}$$

Fig. 9: $\underline{Z}$ for the subnetworks

S(1): The master redistributes part of the data, so that each slave will hold approximately the same amount of data even after the addition of the intertree links (e.g., Fig. 8).

The number of P(i), S(i) and P(ii) steps to follow is ℓ, the number of intertree links. For each:

P(i): Compute a slice of $\underline{w}$. This requires $h\alpha$ where h is considered an integer.

S(i): The master collects the slices of $\underline{w}$, computes ψ and then broadcasts both to all p slaves.

P(ii): Each slave executes (72) on its part of $\underline{Z}$.

Since the next step P(i) is also parallel, they can be combined, if the first P(2) is "faked" and S(2) is done right after S(1).

For each link, one synchronization β and $2n\tau$ transfers are required in S(i), where the time to compute ψ, namely $3\alpha+2\mu$ was neglected. In each combined P(i) - P(ii), each slave needs time of $h(\alpha+2\mu)$. In normal execution addition of a link would require $n(\alpha+2\mu)$. Thus

$$\rho = 1/p + (2n\tau + \beta)/(n^3(\alpha + 2\mu)$$

This is practically an ideal ratio, but since $\underline{Z}$ starts to fill-in, the matrix (e.g., Fig. 8) will need a lot of memory space. If this is not available in the memories of the slaves, shifting of data to secondary memories would be necessary. This would increase ρ considerably.

If we have computed $\underline{Z}$, we calculate the voltages applying a single matrix-vector operation $\underline{v} = \underline{Z}\ \underline{i}$. We could therefore use (72) again and again, updating $\underline{Z}$ for each of the CAP-cases.

It was noted that $\underline{Y}$ is sparse, $\underline{Z}$ is dense and this leads to another method. Suppose, the original $\underline{Y}$ is factored into

$$\underline{Y} = \underline{L}\ \underline{D}\ \underline{L}^T \qquad (75)$$

This can be done since the admittance matrix $\underline{Y}$ is symmetric and if an ordering policy is applied, the lower triangular matrix $\underline{L}$ will retain some sparsity.

The basic idea is that a change in a single impedance which changes an entire row and column j (abbreviated rowcol-j), will be solved by first removing rowcol-j from $\underline{L}$, $\underline{D}$ and then adding a new rowcol.

Since the calculation of the $\underline{L}$, $\underline{D}$-factors proceeds as $i=1,2,\ldots,j,j+1,\ldots n$, removal of row and column j can only change $\underline{L}_2$, $\underline{D}_2$ of Fig. 10 (they will be called $\underline{L}_2'$, $\underline{D}_2'$) but not other submatrices. By multiplication:

$$\underline{L}_2'\ \underline{D}_2'(\underline{L}_2')^T = \underline{L}_2\ \underline{D}_2\ \underline{L}_2^T + d_j\ \underline{u}\ \underline{u}^T \qquad (77)$$

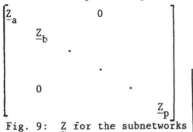

where $\underline{u}$ is the removed column j of $\underline{L}$. A method based on (70) could again be used, but since (77) is known as "rank-1 modification", the Cl-algorithm [GGMS 74] can be applied directly: α_1 and $w^{(1)}$ are first defined, and then (78)-(80) computed for $j = 1,\ldots, m = n - j$:

$$\alpha_1 = d_j;\ \underline{w}^{(1)} = \underline{u};\ p_j = w_j^{(j)};\ d_j' = d_j + \alpha_j p_j^2 \tag{78}$$

$$\beta_j = p_j\alpha_j/d_j';\ \alpha_{j+1} = d_j\alpha_j/d_j' \tag{79}$$

$$\left.\begin{aligned} w_r^{(j+1)} &= w_r^{(j)} - p_j L_{r,j} \\ L'_{r,j} &= L_{r,j} + \beta_j w_r^{(j+1)} \end{aligned}\right\} r = j+1,\ldots,m \tag{80}$$

Since nearly all operations occur in the loop on r, their total number is approximately $2m^2\omega$.

The new row-col is added as rowcol-n since there is no reason to insert it where it was. If we assume that the new matrices are written as (81) then by equating submatrices in the product $(\underline{L}\ \underline{D}\ \underline{L}^T)$ of (82):

$$L' = \begin{bmatrix} \underline{L} & \underline{0} \\ \underline{u}^T & 1 \end{bmatrix};\quad D' = \begin{bmatrix} \underline{D} & \underline{0} \\ \underline{0} & d \end{bmatrix} \qquad \begin{bmatrix} \underline{L} & \underline{0} \\ \underline{u}^T & 1 \end{bmatrix}\begin{bmatrix} \underline{D} & \underline{0} \\ \underline{0} & d \end{bmatrix}\begin{bmatrix} \underline{L}^T & \underline{u} \\ \underline{0} & 1 \end{bmatrix} = \begin{bmatrix} \underline{Y} & \underline{y} \\ \underline{y}^T & \theta \end{bmatrix} \tag{81)(82}$$

we obtain the two unknowns $\underline{u}$ and d from:

$$(\underline{LD})\underline{u} = \underline{y};\ d = \theta - \underline{u}^T\ \underline{D}\ \underline{u} \tag{83}$$

The operations count here is approximately $m^2\omega/2$ so that together with the removal of rowcol-j, only $5m^2\omega/2$ are needed (instead of $n^3\omega/3$).

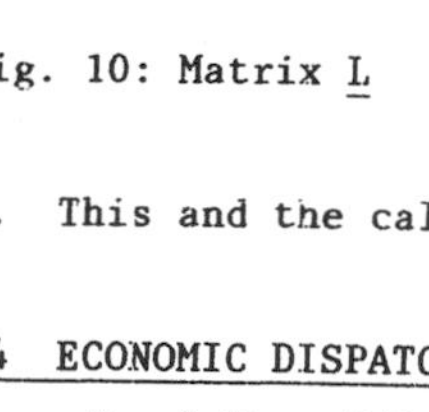

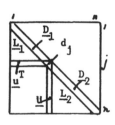

Fig. 10: Matrix $\underline{L}$

Scheduling of factorization proceeds according to sparsity considerations i.e. randomly. The rowcol to be changed must therefore be assumed at $j \cong n/2$ and the number of operations is reduced from $n^3/3$ to $5n^2/8$ i.e., $8n/15 \cong 0.5n$-fold. This is an order-of-magnitude reduction.

The above algorithm can obviously be programmed for ASP. This and the calculation of the speedup are left as an exercise.

10.4 ECONOMIC DISPATCH PROGRAMS, EDIP

Aims: To define Edip mathematically. To review the B-matrix method. To extend the gradient method and in particular the parallel search method which is part of it. To show that there are two approaches for formulating Edip as a sequence of linear programming problems, the x-approach being "better".

10.4.1 The B-matrix method

The power system is supplied by generated and tie-line powers p_i, $i=1,\ldots,n_g$ and p_j, $j=1,\ldots,n_t$ resp. It supplies p_ℓ, $\ell=1,\ldots,n_\ell$ loads and has losses which total p_e. The energy conservation law may be stated as:

$$\phi = \Sigma p_i + \Sigma p_j - \Sigma p_\ell - p_e = 0, \; i\,\Sigma=1,\ldots,n_g, \; j\Sigma 1,\ldots,n_t, \; \ell\Sigma=1,\ldots,n_\ell \quad (84)$$

The cost of generation depends only on p_i so that

$$c = \Sigma c_i(p_i), \; i\,\Sigma = 1,\ldots,n_g \quad (85)$$

The problem of supplying all loads with the minimum cost can be solved by the method of Lagrange. Define a function

$$f(p,\lambda) = c + \lambda\phi \quad (86)$$

differentiate it and set the derivatives to zero. In the present case $\partial f/\partial\lambda = \phi = 0$ is again (84). Differentiating with respect to p_i of every generator:

$$\partial f/\partial p_i = \partial c_i/\partial p_i + \lambda - \lambda\partial p_e/\partial p_i = 0 \quad (87)$$

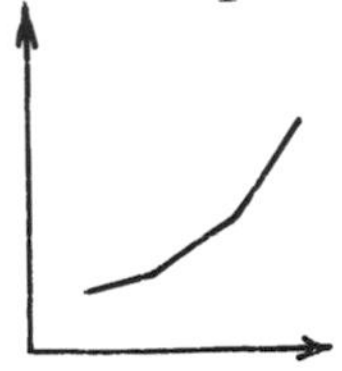

Fig. 11: Costs

The incremental costs $\partial c_i/\partial p_i$ can normally be represented as a quadratic function and approximated by a broken line (Fig. 11). The losses can be represented by an nxn matrix $\underline{B}$ so that

$$p_e = \Sigma\Sigma\, p_i B_{ij} p_j; \; i\,\Sigma = j\,\Sigma = 1,\ldots,(n_g+n_t) \quad (88)$$

It is at this point immaterial how $\underline{B}$ is computed, since this is done anyway offline and stored in memory. The use of $\underline{B}$ will be exemplified by a system with two generators and no tie lines. For this case (88) yields:

$$\partial p_e/\partial p_i = \Sigma\, 2\, B_{ij} p_j, \; j=1,\ldots,n_g \quad (89)$$

so that the 3 unknowns (λ, p_1, p_2) can be calculated from:

$$\partial c_1/\partial p_1 - 2\lambda B_{21} p_1 = -\lambda; \; \partial c_2/\partial p_2 - 2\lambda B_{12} p_2 = -\lambda; \; p_1+p_2+p_e = p_{known} \quad (90)$$

in which $\partial c_1/\partial p_1 = k_1 p_1$ and $\partial c_2/\partial p_2 = k_2 p_2$ from graphs exemplified in Fig. 11 is thus a set of linear equations which can be solved easily. The flaw here is that no contraints were observed; this is done in the next method.

10.4.2 The gradient method

This is the most widely used method [DT68]. To review it, write first loaf as:

$$\underline{r}\,(\underline{a}, \underline{u}, \underline{x}) = \underline{0} \quad (91)$$

where the vectors are: $\underline{a}$ = a'priori known quantities (e.g. admittances), $\underline{u}$ = control variables (e.g. generated powers), $\underline{x}$ = state variables (e.g. voltages) and $\underline{r}$ = residuals. The vectors $\underline{a}$, $\underline{u}$, $\underline{x}$ are also bound by some constraints e.g. bounds for voltages or powers, so that we must also obey

$$\underline{s}\,(\underline{a}, \underline{u}, \underline{x}) \geqq 0 \quad (92)$$

There are two formulations for economic dispatch. In the "minimum cost" formulation, a minimum cost (85) is sought such that both (91) and (92) are satisfied; in the "minimum loss" formulation p_e instead of c is to be minimized. In both cases, the result is a $\underline{u}$ - vector.

To define the method proceed as follows. If the Lagrangian:

$$\ell = c + \underline{\lambda}^T \cdot \underline{r} \quad (93)$$

is differentiated with respect to $\underline{\lambda}$, load-flow equations result. A parallel version of the Newton-Raphson method for solving them exists. It calculates $\underline{x}^{(v)}$ for given $\underline{u}^{(v)}$, and leaves the Jacobian:

$$\underline{J} = \partial \underline{r}/\partial \underline{x} \tag{94}$$

in the private memories in factored form. Then

$$\partial \ell/\partial \underline{x} = \partial c/\partial \underline{x} + (\partial \underline{r}/\partial \underline{x})^T \cdot \underline{\lambda} = \partial c/\partial \underline{x} + \underline{J}^T \cdot \underline{\lambda} = 0 \tag{95}$$

is used in order to calculate $\underline{\lambda}$. Since $\underline{J}^T$ is known, this amounts to back-substitution, and may also be done in parallel. Finally, the gradient vector

$$\underline{g} \triangleq \partial \ell/\partial \underline{u} = \partial c/\partial \underline{u} + (\partial \underline{r}/\partial \underline{u})^T \cdot \underline{\lambda} \tag{96}$$

is computed, and if its norm is $||g|| < \varepsilon$ the computation is complete. Otherwise, the control variables are updated according to

$$\underline{u}^{(v+1)} = \underline{u}^{(v)} - k * \underline{g} \tag{97}$$

and the process restarted from a new solution of load-flow.

The parallel evaluation of $\underline{g}$ is trivial, since its components g_i are independent. Therefore, each slave calculates h=n/p of them and the master then broadcasts the entire vector $\underline{g}$ to all p slaves. The parallel calculation of the constant k is more complicated. In most cases, it is best calculated by a unidimensional search.

There exists a parallel minimax method [KM68] based on the Fibonacci sequence. Normally, such search methods are sequential, i.e. the next Fibonacci number F_i is chosen between two values, the function whose minimum is sought is evaluated and based on a comparison with the previous values a new F_i is chosen. The parallel version considers policies in which a sequence of k-tuples of function values is determined, with the next k-tuple of points to be computed dependent on the results of all previous evaluations.

The algorithm can be looked-up in [KM68]. We will next introduce a much simpler method, "program" both for ASP and show that the simpler method has some advantages.

Suppose, that the parallel-processor system has (p=5) five slaves. Then (with k=p, $\theta \cong 1$) the forming equation according to [KM 68] is

$$G_r = 3(G_{r-1} + G_{r-2}) \tag{98}$$

The "distances" are thus: 1, 3, 12, 45, 171, 648, 2457. Thus, if the initial "interval of uncertainty" is 0 to 2457, and assuming that the optimum lies around 1413, the five steps of the algorithm would be as per the table below.

Step	$f(x_1)$ computed at x_i = x_1	x_2	x_3	x_4	x_5	$f(x_i)$ known at x_i	Bracketed by x_{low}	x_{high}	G_1	G_2
1	171	819	990	1638	1809		990	1809	171	648
2	1161	1206	1377	1422	1593	1638	1206	1422	45	171
3	1251	1263	1308	1320	1365	1377	1365	1422	12	45
4	1380	1392	1395	1407	1410	1377	1407	1422	3	12
5	1411	1414	1415	1418	1419	1410	1410	1414	1	3

The "simple search" algorithm is defined separately for p even and odd, as was that of [KM68].

For even p, the initial distance L is divided by (p+1) and q computed through

$G_i = L/(p+1); \; q = (p/2)+1$ (99)

The algorithm proceeds computing $f(x_i)$ at x_i separated by

$$G_i = G_{i+1}/q. \quad (100)$$

For an odd p, the first step is the same as above, but in the following steps each "half" of the remaining distance is divided by

$q_1 = (p/2) - 1; \; q_2 = q_1 - 1.$ (101)

The table below summarizes the first five steps of this algorithm for p=5 and for an initial "interval of uncertainty" of $0 \geqq L \geqq 2400$. (Some of the x_i's are rounded).

Step	$f(x_i)$ computed at x_i = x_1	x_2	x_3	x_4	x_5	$f(x_i)$ known at x_i	Bracketed by x_{low}	x_{high}	G_1	G_2
1	400	800	1200	1600	2000		800	1600	400	400
2	933	1067	1300	1400	1500	1200	1300	1500	400/3	100
3	1333	1367	1425	1450	1475	1400	1400	1450	100/3	25
4	1408	1417	1431	1437	1444	1425	1400	1417	25/3	25/4
5	1403	1406	1410	1412	1415	1408	1406	1410	25/9	25/12

We may compare the two methods in two ways. In the Fibonacci method, the interval of uncertainty was reduced 2457/4 = 614.25-fold in time 5T, where T is the average time it takes a slave to evaluate the function $f(x_i)$. In the method proposed here it was reduced 2400/4.85 ≅ 497 fold in the same time. The ratio of about 1.2 is more than paid for by the simpler program. Moreover, the values x_i are computed by the master and reducing the sequential step improves efficiency. Comparing the two methods another way leads to the statement, that the new method requires at most one additional T to get the same final interval of uncertainty as the minimax, Fibonacci search method.

10.4.3 <u>Methods based on linear programming</u>

The problem of optimizing power dispatch may [NF73] also be formulated as that of minimizing

$$c = c_c + \underline{c}_\ell^T \underline{p}_g + \underline{p}_g^T \underline{C} \, \underline{p}_g \quad (102)$$

for the so-called "minimum-cost", or

$$c = \Sigma \; (p_g)_i ; \; i \; \Sigma = 1,\ldots,n_g \quad (103)$$

for the "minimum-loss" problem. Here, c is cost, subscript g denotes generator, ℓ load, superscript T is transposition and ng, nℓ, nn the number of generators, load points and total number of nodes respectively.

In both cases, load-flow equations (91) and the inequalities (92) have to be satisfied.

The problem is seen to be one of non-linear, constrained minimization. The solution we suggest is based on linearizing any nonlinear part of it.

Let $\underline{a}$, $\underline{u}_0$, $\underline{x}_0$ be a steady-state point. If $\underline{u}_0$ is changed to $\underline{u}_0 + \Delta\, \underline{u}$, the next equilibrium point will be described by:

$$\underline{r}(\underline{a},\ \underline{u}_0 + \Delta\, \underline{u},\ \underline{x}_0 + \Delta\, \underline{x}) = \underline{0} \qquad (104)$$

With a Taylor expansion applied to $\underline{r}$, the nonlinear term neglected and the initial equation

$$\underline{r}\ (\underline{a},\ \underline{u}_0,\ \underline{x}_0) = \underline{0} \qquad (105)$$

subtracted, we have

$$(\partial\underline{r}/\partial\underline{x}) * \Delta\, \underline{r} = -(\partial\underline{r}/\partial\underline{u}) * \Delta\, \underline{r} \qquad (106)$$

Since $\partial\underline{r}/\partial\underline{x} = \underline{J}_x$ is the Jacobian of load-flow, and $\partial\underline{r}/\partial\underline{u} = \underline{J}_u$ that of the control functions, (106) may be rewritten as:

$$\Delta\, \underline{x}/\Delta\, \underline{u} = -\underline{J}_x^{-1} * \underline{J}_u = \underline{S} \qquad (107)$$

where $\underline{S}$ is the (nx*nu) sensitivity matrix (nx is dimension of x, nu of u).

If we treat any other function (e.g. cost)

$$\underline{f} = \underline{f}(\underline{a},\ \underline{u},\ \underline{x}) \qquad (108)$$

in the same way, then for a change Δu_j:

$$\Delta f = (\partial f/\partial u_j)\Delta u_j + \Sigma\ (\partial f/\partial x_i)(\partial x_i/\partial u_j)\Sigma u_j;\ j\Sigma=1,\ldots,nx \qquad (109)$$

$$\Delta f/\Delta u_j = \partial f/\partial u_j + \Sigma\ (\partial f/\partial x_i)(\partial x_i/\partial u_j);\ i\Sigma=1,\ldots,nx \qquad (110)$$

Both the state (x_j) and functional (f) variables have to satisfy:

$$x_i^m \leqq x_i \leqq x_i^M \qquad (111)$$

This inequality may be separated into two parts as follows:

$$x_i^0 + \Delta x_i \leqq x_i^M;\ x_i^0 + \Delta x_i \geqq x_i^m, \qquad (112)$$

where x_i^0 is the stationary point. If Δx_i is expanded, this leads to

$$x_i^m - x_i^0 \leqq \Sigma\ (\partial x_i/\partial u_k)\ \Delta u_k \leqq x_i^M - x_i^0;\ k\Sigma=1,\ldots,nu \qquad (113)$$

which is a linear inequality.

For the minimum-cost problem a perturbation may be applied to (102) to yield:

$$c + \Delta c = c_c + \underline{c}_\ell^T(\underline{p}_g+\underline{\Delta p}_g) + (\underline{p}_g+\underline{\Delta p}_g)^T\ \underline{C}(\underline{p}_g+\underline{\Delta p}_g). \qquad (114)$$

Subtracting c as per (102), we obtain

$$\Delta c = c_\ell^T\ \underline{\Delta p}_g + \underline{p}_g^T\ \underline{C}\ \underline{\Delta p}_g + \underline{\Delta p}_g\ \underline{C}\ \underline{p}_g + \underline{\Delta p}_g\ \underline{C}\ \underline{\Delta p}_g \qquad (115)$$

The transpose of any scalar a is a itself, so that the second and third terms of (115) are the same. If in addition the "power sensitivity matrix" $\underline{S}_p$ is introduced:

$$\underline{\Delta p}_g = \underline{S}_p * \Delta\, \underline{u} \qquad (116)$$

then (115) and (116) yield

$$\Delta c = (\underline{c}_\ell^T + 2\underline{p}_g^T\underline{C})\ \underline{S}_p\underline{\Delta u} + \underline{\Delta u}^T\ \underline{S}_p^T\ \underline{C}\ \underline{S}_p\underline{\Delta u} \qquad (117)$$

Since we start with a given cost c, its minimization is equivalent to minimizing Δc. We have thus linearized the constraints but the object function c is still quadratic (117). For minimum loss (103) may be expanded, and if $\underline{S}_p$ is used, the object function becomes $\underline{\Delta c}$ i.e. linear:

$$\underline{\Delta c} = \Sigma\ (\partial p_{gi}/\partial u_k)\ \Delta u_k = \underline{S} * \underline{\Delta u};\ k\Sigma=1,\ldots,ng \qquad (118)$$

Since the method relies on varying the control vector $\underline{u}$, it will be called the "u-method". It may be summarized thus:

(a) Solve $\underline{r}(\underline{a},\underline{u}_0,\underline{x}_0)=\underline{0}$ to yield $\underline{u}_0$, $\underline{x}_0$.

(b) Calculate sensitivity matrices.

(c) If $\Delta c<\varepsilon$ and the variables obey the constraints - stop. Otherwise:

(d) Solve the linear (Lp) or quadratic (Qp) programming problem.

(e) Update u_0 to be $u_0+\Delta u$ and return to (a).

Note that for minimum cost a quadratic programming "package" must be "called". It was pointed out in [NF73] that linearization would in this case lead to divergence.

The load flow equations may be written as:

$$\underline{r} = \underline{d}(\underline{a},\ \underline{u},\ x) - \underline{f} = \underline{0} \tag{119}$$

where $\underline{x}$ is again the state vector of voltages and $\underline{f}$ of (active and reactive) powers. When (119) is differentiated, the result is

$$\underline{\Delta r} = (\partial\underline{r}/\partial\underline{x})\underline{\Delta x} + (\partial\underline{r}/\partial\underline{f})\underline{\Delta f} = \underline{0} \tag{120}$$

$(\partial\underline{r}/\partial\underline{f})$ is a (2nn*2nn) negative unit matrix, $(\partial\underline{r}/\partial\underline{x})$ is the load-flow Jacobian,

$$\underline{\Delta f} = \underline{J}_x\ \underline{\Delta x} \tag{121}$$

$\underline{J}_x$ serves here as a sensitivity matrix and its calculation is equivalent to substitution, ergo is trivial. For other functions:

$$\underline{e} = \underline{e}(\underline{x},\ \underline{f}) \tag{122}$$

the sensitivity of $\underline{e}$ to a change in $\underline{\Delta x}$, will be given by (110) with the following substitutions: f→e, u→f and nx→2*nn.

It is now simple to keep the voltages bounded. As for the powers $\underline{f}$, or the function $\underline{e}_i$, limiting them leads to (113) with the substitutions (x->f, u->x) and (x->e, u->x), respectively. Summation is from 1 to 2*nn. For the minimum-cost problem, (117) with (u->x) and for the minimum-loss, (118) with (u->x) hold. The minimum-cost sensitivities form an ngxng matrix

$$\underline{S} = (\partial p_{gi}/\partial x_i) \tag{123}$$

Since it is now the state-vector $\underline{x}$ which is being varied, the method is called the "x-method". Its (a) and (b) steps are the same as in the u-method (although the sensitivities are different). The other steps are:

(c) Solve the Lp problem.

(d) Update the state-vector $\underline{x}$ to be $\underline{x} + \underline{\Delta x}$.

(e) If $\underline{\Delta c} < \varepsilon$ then stop. Else return to (b) - and not to (a).

Two differences are noticeable here. In the x-method, load-flow is automatically accounted for in step (c), so that there is no need to return to (a) and solve it again. Also, in (c) the cost-function is linearized - and the results will prove that unlike the u-method, convergence is not reduced.

A rather superficial comparison of required storage space can be carried out as follows. In the u-method, there are 2*ng unknowns (powers) and 4(ng+nn) constraints in Lp (as load-nodes are not included). In the x-method, there are 2*nn unknowns (voltages) and 4(ng+nn)+2*nℓ constraints. Assuming ng=0.1*nn and nℓ=0.9*nn, the required storage ratio of the u and x-methods

$$\frac{M_u}{M_x} = \frac{2ng(4ng+4nn)}{2nn(4ng+4nn+2n\ell)} \cong \frac{0.2nn(0.4nn+4nn)}{2nn(0.4nn+4nn+1.8nn)} \cong 0.07 \qquad (124)$$

At first glance, the memory M_u required in the u-method is much smaller than M_x. We shall disprove this with the aid of a more detailed count and with the Lp-program itself included in the considerations.

Let us define a vector $\underline{h}$ of powers through $h_{2i} = q_i$; $h_{2i-1} = p_i$ and of voltages (v_i+jw_i) through $x_{2i-1} = v_i$; $x_{2i} = w_i$.

In the u-method, the control variables (p_i, q_i) must obey:

$$h_i^m - h_i^0 \leqq \Delta h_i \leqq h_i^M - h_i^0;\ i = 1,\ldots,2{*}ng,\ h_i = h_i^0 + \Delta h_i \qquad (125)$$

Since some of the Δh_i may be negative and Lp can only operate on nonnegative variables, new (primed) variables are introduced through:

$$\Delta h_i' = \Delta h_i - (h_i^m - h_i^0);\ i = 1,\ldots,2{*}ng \qquad (126)$$

so that the conditions of (125) reduce to

$$0 \leqq \Delta h_i' \leqq h_i^M - h_i^m \qquad (127)$$

The Simplex Method accounts automatically for unequalities on the left. For those on the right, note that the variables of Lp are bounded through

$$x_i \leqq d_i \qquad (128)$$

Suppose that the simplex method provides a feasible basis solution for which

$$x_i = b_i \text{ for } i = 1,..,m \text{ and } x_i = 0 \text{ for } i = m+1,..,n \qquad (129)$$

For the next step, a non basic variable x_s is increased from zero to a positive value. For the basic variables

$$x_i = b_i - a_{is}x_s;\ i = 1,\ldots,m \qquad (130)$$

holds, with non negatively secured, in the simplex method by removing from the basis an x_r for which

$$b_r/a_{rs} = \min(b_i/a_{is}) \text{ for all } a_{is} > 0 \qquad (131)$$

In the same way, we may secure that the basic variables should satisfy (128). Since $x_i = d_i$ only if $a_{is} < 0$, the first basic variable to achieve maximum, x_{r1} is calculated from:

$$\frac{b_{r_1} - d_{r_1}}{a_{r_1,s}} = \min_{a_{is}<0} \frac{b_i - d_i}{a_{is}};\ i = 1,\ldots,m \qquad (132)$$

As regards the variable x_r to be removed from the basis, the choice should fall on the first to vanish or achieve maximum - i.e. if

$$(b_r/a_{rs}) < (b_{r_1} - d_{r_1})/(a_{r_1,s}) \qquad (133)$$

If x_{r_1} is chosen, a change of variables is required since $x_{r_1} = d_{r_1}$ and the value of all non basic variables must be zero. x_{r_1} is therefore replaced by y_{r_1} such that

$$y_{r_1} + x_{r_1} = d_{r_1};\ y_{r_1} \geqq 0 \qquad (134)$$

This is effected by changing r_1 from

$$\Sigma \; a_{r_1 j} x_j + x_{r_1} = b_{r_1} \; ; \; j = 1,\dots,n; j \neq r_1 \tag{135}$$

into $\Sigma \; a_{r_1 j} x_j - y_{r_1} - d_{r_1}$ (136)

y_{r_1} will now be zero and the process may continue.

As is seen, inequalities (128) call for treatment only insofar as choice of variables is concerned, which does not entail additional storage (or an appreciable number of operations). If (128) is added to the constraints, additional storage space would be required.

There still are 4*nn constraints on the voltages

$$x_i^m \leqq x_i \leqq x_i^M, \tag{137}$$

which may be rewritten as (139) and analog for primed variables.

$$x_i^m - x_i^0 \leqq \Sigma \quad ((\partial x_i/\partial h_j)\Delta h_j) \leqq x_i^M - x_i^0 \; ; \; j \; \Sigma = 1,\dots,2ng \tag{138}$$

$$x_i^m - x_i^0 + \Sigma \; \frac{\partial x_i}{\partial h}(h_j^m - h_j^0) \leqq \Sigma \; \frac{\partial x_i}{\partial h} \Delta h_j' \leqq x_i^M$$

$$- x_i^0 + \Sigma \; \frac{\partial x_i}{\partial h_j}(h_j^m - h_j^0) \; ; \; j\Sigma=1,\dots,2n_g \tag{139}$$

In the simplex method a "slack variable" t is added to each constraint

$$g(y) \leqq a \tag{140}$$

transforming it into $\quad g(y) + t = a; \; t \geqq 0$ (141)

Note that if a<0, then t cannot be used as a basic variable. This will in fact increase the number of non-basic variables and thereby the size of the required storage space. Hence, each time the left member of (140) is positive or the right one negative, a non-basic variable has to be added. The number nt of these variables will lie between 0 and 4*nn. Altogether, the u-method has 4*nn constraints and (2*ng+nt) non-basic variables (with 0≦nt≦4*nn).

The partial derivatives in (140) are elements of $\underline{S}$, but since load-flow may be written as in (119) with $\underline{f}$ the node powers (control variables), it follows that

$$\underline{J}_u = -(\underline{U},\underline{0}) \tag{142}$$

where $\underline{U}$ is a (2*ng)*(2*ng) unit, and $\underline{0}$ an (2*ng)*(2*nn-2*ng) zero matrix. Matrix $\underline{J}_x$ of (107) is sparse, since each node is connected with a rather limited number (say d) of the nodes, while $\underline{J}_x^{-1}$ and sensitivity matrix $\underline{S}$ are dense.

The x-method involves voltage constraints

$$x_i^m - x_i^0 \leqq \Delta x_i \leqq x_i^M - x_i^0 ; \; i = 1,\dots,nn \tag{143}$$

Changing x in the same way as h in (27), we have

$$0 \leqq \Delta x_i' \leqq x_i^M - x_i^m \tag{144}$$

Again, neither the left nor the right members add to the required storage space. The constraints which remain to be treated are:

$$h_i^m \leq h_i \leq h_i^M;\; i = 1,\dots,2{*}ng \tag{145}$$

Transformation of Δx into $\Delta x'$ for these inequalities leads to

$$h_i^m - h_i^0 + \sum_{j=1}^{2*nn} \frac{\partial h_i}{\partial x_j}(x_j^m - x_j^0) \leq \sum_{j=1}^{2*nn} \frac{\partial h_i}{\partial x_j}\Delta x_j'$$

$$\leq h_i^M - h_i^0 + \sum_{j-1}^{2*nn} \frac{\partial h_i}{\partial x_j}(x_j^m - x_j^0) \tag{146}$$

For each positive left or negative right member, a non-basic variable must be added. Hence their number $0 \leq nt_1 \leq 4{*}ng$. (147)

The load-flow equations for the x-method may be written as

$$h_i = h_i^L;\quad i = 2{*}ng+1,\dots,2{*}nn \tag{148}$$

and regarded as additional equality constraints. Transformed, they read

$$\sum_{j=1}^{2*nn} \frac{\partial h_i}{\partial x_j}\Delta x_j' = h_i^L - h_i^0 + \sum_{j=1}^{2*nn} \frac{\partial h_i}{\partial x_j}(x_i^m - x_i^0) \quad i = 2{*}ng+1,\dots,2nn \tag{149}$$

If the load-flow equations are solved in each iteration, then $h_i^L - h_i^0 = 0$, or (149) constitutes the correction to the linear set (as against the original non-linear set). Altogether, there are $4{*}ng$ generation constraints (146) and $2{*}n\ell$ load constraints. The number of non-basic variables is $2{*}nn+nt_1$ where $0 \leq nt_1 \leq 4{*}ng$.

Summing up, the storage requirements are in a ratio

$$\frac{M_u}{M_x} = \frac{4{*}nn * (2{*}ng+nt)}{(2{*}n\ell+4{*}ng) * (2{*}nn+nt_1)} \cong \frac{20{*}nn + 100{*}nt}{132{*}nn} \tag{150}$$

even if the worst case, $nt_1 = 4{*}ng$, is assumed for the x-method. Thus, if $nt > 1.12{*}nn$, then $M_x \leq M_u$. Since $0 < nt < 4{*}nn$, in about 3/4 of the cases, this should be true. Moreover, the sensitivity matrix $\underline{S} = \underline{J}_x$ (as per (140)) is very sparse. We thus arrive at the conclusion that in most cases the x-method requires less storage space and operates with a sparse matrix.

We will now compare the computational effort required by the two methods.

Since in the x-method the load-flow equations are included in the constraints, there is no need to solve them separately. Calculation of $\underline{S}$ by the u-method entails a large amount of back-substitutions as against the trivial insertion of x in the equations defining J_x by the x-method. The latter is also the case in checking convergence (calculation of powers).

The methods should be parallelized. For the u-method, this entails parallel solution of load-flow, of the Lp-problem and calculation of $\underline{S}$, including the necessary back-substitutions. In the x-method, load-flow is solved only once, $\underline{S}$ is calculated by trivially parallelizable insertion and a more efficient program is available for the Lp-problem, since the $\underline{S}$-matrix is very sparse.

Both methods discussed above are iterative, with the nonlinear constraints linearized at the start of each Lp-process. For the Lp not to yield results incompatible with the constraints, the linearization must be confined to a small area about the preceeding optimum. A step thus occurs around a local minimum known from the preceding step. Such processes are known as "boxstep" methods [MHB75] and it has been proved [GS61] that if the objective function is concave and the set of constraints convex, the process converges. It should be noted that the voltages x_i are normally constrained to lie in a narrow band ($|\Delta x| \leq 0.1$), whereas the powers p_i lie in a much broader one. Therefore, the constraint on the linearization is less stringent in the x-method.

The crux of the methods is the choice of the box-size ε. If it is chosen too small, convergence is slow whereas too large ε may result in divergence as linearization is unfeasible. The cost function for the 14-bus network of [NF73], with constraints as in Table 5 and with the minimum loss problem solved by the x-method is shown in Table 6. It can be seen that for $\varepsilon = 4*10^{-2}$ there is initial rapid convergence, but oscillation sets in beginning with step 3. (The cost at step 1 is the same as that arrived at in [NF73]).

Choice of a suitable ε is normally very difficult In power systems and for the x-method, it will be shown that the box size should be governed by

$$E(q_i) = E(p_i) \leq 2 \ \Sigma \ (|g_{ij}| + |b_{ij}|) * \varepsilon^2 = K_i \varepsilon^2 \ ; \ j\Sigma 1,\ldots,nn \tag{151}$$

Load-flow equations may be written as follows:

$$r_{2k-1} = v_k * \alpha_k + w_k * \beta_k - p_i = 0 \tag{152}$$

$$r_{2k} = w_k * \alpha_k - v_k * \beta_k - q_i = 0 \tag{153}$$

where by definition

$$\alpha_k = \Sigma \ (g_{kh} v_h - b_{kh} w_h); \quad \beta_k = \Sigma \ (b_{kh} v_h + g_{kh} w_h); \ h\Sigma = 1,\ldots,n \quad (154)(155)$$

For a change of voltages

$$v_i = v_i^0 + \Delta v_i; \ w_i = w_i^0 + \Delta w_i \tag{156}$$

the powers will be:

$$p_k^0 + \Delta p_k = v_k * \alpha_k + w_k * \beta_k \ ; \quad q_k^0 + q_k = w_k * \alpha_k - v_k * \beta_k \tag{157}$$

From these and (152,153), we have

$$\Delta p_i = \sum_{h=1}^{n} \frac{\partial r_{2i}}{\partial v_h} \Delta v_h + \frac{\partial r_{2i}}{\partial w_h} \Delta w_h \quad + \Delta v_i * \alpha_i' + \Delta w_i * \beta_i \tag{158}$$

$$\Delta q_i = \sum_{h=1}^{n} \frac{\partial r_{2i-1}}{\partial v_h} \Delta v_h + \frac{\partial r_{2i-1}}{\partial w_h} \Delta w_h \quad + \Delta w_i * \alpha_i' + \Delta v_i * \beta_i' \tag{159}$$

$$\alpha_k' = \Sigma \ (g_{kh} \Delta v_h - b_{kh} \Delta w_h); \ \beta_k' = \Sigma \ (b_{kh} \Delta v_h + g_{kh} \Delta w_h); \ h\Sigma = 1,\ldots,n \tag{160}$$

The two last terms of (158) and (159) are neglected during linearization, so that the <u>error</u> introduced through linearization is

$$E(p_i) = \Delta v_i * \alpha_i' + \Delta w_i * \beta_i'; \quad E(q_i) = \Delta w_i * \alpha_i' + \Delta v_i * \beta_i' \tag{161}$$

Addition of the constraints

$$\Delta v_i \leq \varepsilon; \quad \Delta w_i \leq \varepsilon \tag{162}$$

leads directly to (151).

In most power systems, a node is connected only to d ($d \leq 3$) other nodes, so that the sum ranges only over d indices j. The constants

$$K = \max K_i ; \quad \text{all } i,$$

for networks A and B of [NF73] are given in Table 7. Assuming that the admittance values and d are independent of network size, these K give a good indication as to the choice of a proper ε.

Table 6 leads to another conclusion, namely that ε should not be constant. Whenever, in the iterative process the cost increases, the process should backtrack one step and start with a smaller ε.

i	1	2	3	4	5	6	7	8	9	10	11	12	13	14
$-p_L$	0	.217	.992	.478	.076	-.488	0	0	-.305	.090	.035	.007	.135	.149
$-q_L$	0	.127	.192	-.039	.016	.075	0	0	.165	.058	.018	.016	.058	.050

Generator, node	p^m	p^M	q^m	q^M
1	.50	2.0	-.20	1.0
2	-.017	.783	-.40	.50
6	.088	.888	-.06	.45
0	-.095	.705	-.06	.45

All real voltages 0.9 to 1.1; All imaginary parts -0.2 to 0.2

Table 5: Constraints

Iteration No.	1	2	3	4	5	6	7	8	9	10	11
$\varepsilon = 10^{-2}$	.081	.081	.074	.064	.057	.051	.047	.044	.042	.041	.039
$\varepsilon = 4 \cdot 10^{-2}$	.081	.054	.046	.040	.045	.041	.042	.041	.041	.041	.041
Varying ε	.081	.054	.046	.040	.040	.039	.038	.038	.038	.038	.038

Table 6: Cost for x-Method with different ε

	Number of Nodes	K
Network A	14	97.7
Network B	23	499.0

Table 7: Constant K

Conclusions

Two methods, "x" and "u" were discussed. Both of them, and expecially the x-method, are based on linearization.

It was shown that in most cases, appearances notwithstanding, the x-method requires less storage space. Moreover, its sensitivity matrix is very sparse and less operations per iteration are required.

With ε chosen properly, the number of iterations (convergence) of the two methods is similar. Choice is dictated by a constant estimated for power systems as in Table 7. The best approach is to vary ε adapting it to the ever narrowing box-size.

REFERENCES

[AHU 76] Aho, Hopcroft, Ullmann: "The design and analysis of computer algorithms," Addison-Wesley, 1976.

[Al 76] Alvarado: Computational complexity in power systems," Trans. IEEE, Vol. PAS-95, No. 4, 1976, pp. 1028-1037.

[An 66] Anderson: "Program structures for parallel processing," Comm. ACM, Vol. 8, No. 12, 1965, pp. 786-788. (A note on it appeared in a letter by N. Wirth in Comm. ACM, Vol. 9, No. 5, 1966, pp. 320-321).

[Ba 72] Baskin, et al.: "PRIME-a modular architecture for terminal-oriented systems," SJCC, Vol. 40, 1972, pp. 431-437.

[Ba 73] Batcher: "Staran/Radcap hardware architecture," Sagamore Conf., pp. 147-152, "The Flip Network in Staran," Sagamore Conf., pp. 65-71.

[BAH 76] Brammeler, Allan, Hamman: "Sparsity," Pittman (London).

[BBK 68] Barnes et al.: "The Illiac-IV Computer," Trans. IEEE, Vol. C-17, No. 8, pp. 746-760.

[Be 66] Berezin, Zhidkov: "Computing methods," Fizmatgiz, Moscow, 1966 (An English translation of a previous edition appeared in London by Pergammon Press and Addison-Wesley, 1965).

[Be 65] Benes: "Mathematical Theory of Connecting Networks," Academic Press (NY).

[BL 80] Baqai, Lang: "Reliability aspects of the Illiac-IV Computer," Conference paper and NSF-Grant MC72-03633 A04.

[BM 75] Borodin, Munro: "The computational complexity of algebraic and numerical problems," American Elsevier, 1975.

[Bo 79] Bongers: "Doctoral Thesis, University of Dortmund, W. Germany.

[Br 73] Brinch-Hansen: "Operating system principles," Prentice-Hall, 1973.

[Br 74] Brent: "The parallel evaluation of general arithmetic expressions," Journ. ACM, Vol. 21, No. 2, 1974, pp. 201-206.

[BR 75] Brown: "Solution of large networks by matrix methods," J. Wiley, Inc.

[BS 76] Bell, Strecker: "Computer Structures: What have we learned from the PDP11?", IEEE Computer Society, The III annual symposium on computer architecture, Jan. 19-21, 1976, pp. 1-14.

[BW 75] Brandsma, Waumans: "A common bus switch," Internal report of the Phillips Research Laboraties, Eindhoven, 1975.

[CJ 70] Clint, Jennings: "The evaluation of eigenvalues...," The Computer Journal, Vol. 13, 1970, pp. 76-80.

[CK 75] Chen, Kuck: "Time and parallel processor bounds for linear recurrence systems," Trans. IEEE, Vol. C-24, No. 7, 1975, pp. 701-717.

[Co 63] Corbato: "On the coding of Jacobi's method," Journal ACM, Vol. 10, pp. 123-125.

[Co 72] Cornell: "Parallel processing of ballistic missile defense radar data with PEPE," COMPCON 72.

[Co 74] Comtre (Enslow Jr. Ed.): "Multiprocessors and parallel processing," J. Wiley Inc., 1974 (appears also [EN 74]).

[Co 76] Cornell: "Parallel Element Processing Ensemble," in (Wh 76), pp. 173-190.

[Co 63] Conway: "A multiprocessor system design," FJCC, Vol. 24, pp. 139-146.

[Cs 75] Csanky: "Fast parallel matrix inversion algorithms," 16 Annual Symposium on foundations of computer science (SWAT), Berkeley, 1975.

[CW 77c] Conrad, Wallach: "A faster SSOR algorithm," Num. Math., Vol. 27, 1977, pp. 371-372.

[CW 77a] Conrad, Wallach: "Iterative solution of linear equations on a parallel processing system," Trans. IEEE, Vol. C-26, No. 2, pp. 838-847.

[CW 77b] Conrad, Wallach: "Parallel, optimally ordered factorization, PICA-Conference (IEEE), May 1977, pp. 302-306.

[CW 79] Conrad, Wallach: "Alternating methods for sets of linear equations," Num. Math. Vol. 32, No. 1, 1979, pp. 105-108.

[CW 80] Conrad, Wallach: "On block-parallel methods for solving linear equations," Trans. IEEE, Vol. C-29, No. 5, pp. 354-359.

[Da 63] Dantzig: "Linear programming and extensions," Princeton Un. Press, 1963.

[Da 69] Davis: "The Illiac IV Processing Element," Trans. IEEE, Vol. C-18, No. 9, pp. 800-816.

[DB 74] Dahlquist, Bjorck: "Numerical Methods," Prentice-Hall.

[De 73] Denning: "Third generation computer systems," Computing Surveys, Vol. 3, No. 4, 1973, pp. 175-216.

[Di 68] Dijkstra: "Cooperating sequential processes," in F. Genuys (Ed.) "Programming Languages," Academic Press, 1968.

[Di 73] Digital Equipment Co.: "PDP11/45 Processor Handbook" and "Peripherals Handbook PDP11," Maynard, Mass., 1973.

[DL 74] DyLiacco: "Real-time computer-control of power systems," Proc. IEEE, Vol. 62, No. 7, 1974, pp. 884-891.

[DT 68] Dommel, Tinney: "Optimal Power Flow Solutions," Trans. IEEE, Vol. PAS-87, pp. 1866-1876.

[Du 77] Duff: "A survey of sparse matrix research," Proc. IEEE, Vol. 65, 1977, pp. 500-535.

[En 77] Enslow: "Multiprocessors - a survey," Computer Surveys, ACM, Vol. 9, No. 1, 1977, pp.

[EP 77] EPRI: "Exploring applications of parallel processing to power systems analysis problems," EPRI EL-566-Special Report, October 1977.

[EP 80] EPRI Workshop, Dallas, 1980.

[Er 77] Erisman: "Decomposition and sparsity with application to distributed computing," in (EP 77).

[ET 73] Evensen, Troy: "Introduction to the architecture of a 288-element PEPE," 1973 Sagamore Computer Conference on Parallel Processing, pp. 162-169.

[Fa 59] Fadeeva: "Computational methods of linear algebra," Dover, 1959.

[Fe 72] Feng: "Some characteristics of associative/parallel processing," Proc. of Sagamore Comp. Conf., 5-16.

[FH 78] Fuller, Harbison: "The C.mmp Multiprocessor," CMU-CS-78-148, Report CMU, Pittsburgh.

[Fl 72] Flynn: "Some computer-organizations and their effectiveness," Trans. IEEE, Vol. C-21, 1972, pp. 948-960.

[Fo 64] Fox: "An introduction to numerical algebra," Oxford Clarendon Press, 1964.

[Fo 76] Foster: "Context addressable, parallel processors," Van Nostrand.

[Fu 76] Fuller: "Price/performance comparison of C.mmp and the PDP-10," in (BS 76), pp. 195-202.

[FSS 76a] Fuller, Swan, Sieworek: "The design of multimicro-computer systems," Third Symposium on Computer Architecture, Jan. 1976, pp. 123-128.

[Ga 66] Gastinel: "Analyse numerique lineaire," Herman Press, Paris 1966 (An English translation exists).

[Ge 68] Gentleman: "Least squares computations by Given's transformation without square roots," J. Inst. Maths. Applics, Vol. 12, pp. 329-336.

[GG 76] Gentleman, George: "Sparse matrix software (in "Sparse Matrix Computations," edited by J.R. Bunch and D.J. Rose, Academic Press, 1876).

[GGMS 74] Gill, Golomb, Murry, Saunders: "Methods for modifying matrix factorizations," Math. Comput., Vol. 28, pp. 505-535.

[Gi 74] Gilmore: "Matrix computations on an associative processor," Proc. Sagamore Conf. pp. 272-290.

[GL 81] George, Liu: "Computer solution of large sparse systems," Prentice-Hall.

[Go 66] Gosden: "Explicit parallel processing description," FJCC, 1966, pp. 651-660.

[Gr 76] Granberg: "APZ 150: "A multiprocessor system or the control of telephone exchanges," in (Wh 76), pp. 289-306.

[GS 61] Griffith, Stewart: "A nonlinear programming technique," Management Science, Vol. 7, 1961, pp. 379-392.

[Gu 78] Gustavson: "Two fast algorithms for sparse matrices: multiplication and transposition," ACM Trans. on Math. Software, Vol. 4, No. 3, pp. 250-269.

[GW 73] Gourlay, Watson: "Computational methods for matrix eigenproblems," J. Wiley, 1973.

[Ha 63] Hadley: "Linear programming," Addison-Wesley, 1963.

[Ha 72] Handschin (Ed.): "Real-time control of electric power systems,"

[Ha 74] Hammarling: "A note on modification to the Given's plane rotation," J. Inst. Maths. Applics, Vol. 13, pp. 245-258.

[Ha 77] Handler: "The impact of classification schemes on computer architectures," Proc. of the International Conf. on Parallel Processing, pp. 7-15.

[He 64] Henrici: "Elements of numerical analysis." J. Wiley, 1964.

[He 73] Heart et al.: "A new minicomputer/multiprocessor for the ARPA network," Nat. Comp. Conf., 1973, pp. 529-537.

[He 76] Heller: "A survey of parallel algorithms in numerical linear algebra," Carnegie-Mellon University, February 1976.

[HS 52] Hestenes, Stiefel: "Method of conjugate gradients for solving linear systems," Journ. Res. NBS, Vol. 49, pp. 409-436.

[IBM 72] IBM: "SIMPL/1 program reference manual," Program product, 5734-XXB, 1972.

[IE 74] IEEE: Special issue on "Computers in the power industry," Proc. IEEE, Vol. 22, No. 7. 1974.

[KK 79] Kober, Kuznia: "SMS - a multiprocessor architecture for high speed numerical calculations," Euromicro Journal, Vol. 5, No. 1, 1979, pp. 48-52.

[KKK 76] Kober, Kopp, Kuznia: "SMS 101...," Euromicro Journ., 1976, pp. 56-64.

[KLS 77] Kuck, Lawrie, Sameh: "High Speed Computer and Algorithm Organization," Academic Press.

[KM 68] Karp, Miranker: "Parallel Minimax search for a maximum," Journal of Combinatorial Theory, Vol. 4, pp. 19-35.

[Ko 74] Korn: "Back to parallel computation...," Simulation, August 1974, Vol. 19, No. 2, pp. 37-45.

[Ko 76] Kober: "A fast communication processor for the SMS multimicroprocessor system," Euromicro Journal, 1976, pp. 183-189.

[Ko 77] Kober: "The multiprocessor system SMS 201 - Combining 128 microprocessors to a powerful computer," COMPCON 77, Fall, pp. 225-230.

[Kop 77] Kopp: "Numerical weather forecast with the SMS 201," Proc. IMACS-GI-Symposium on parallel computers and mathematics, Munich, March 1977, pp. 265-268.

[KS 72] Kuck, Sameh: "Parallel computations of eigenvalues of real matrices," Information Processing 71, North Holland Co., pp. 1266-1272.

[Ku 68] Kuck: "Illiac-IV software and application programming," Trans. IEEE, Vol. C-17, pp. 758-770.

[Ku 77] Kuznia: "Parallelrechner mit Mikroprozessoren," Carl Hanser Verlag, München, pp. 63-68.

[Ku 78] Kuck: "A survey of parallel machine organization and programming," Computing Surveys, ACM, Vol. 9, pp. 29-50.

[La 75] Lawrie et al.: "Glypnir - a programming language for Illiac-IV," Comm. ACM, Vol. 18, pp. 170-178.

[LWC 79] Leven, Wallach, Conrad: "Mathematical programming methods for power dispatch," PICA-Conference (IEEE, CH 1317-3/79) pp. 137-141.

[Ma 73] Martin, Dingledine, Patterson: "Operating system and support software for PEPE," 1973 Sagamore conference on parallel processing, pp. 170-178.

[Ma 74] Mayer: "Zuverlässigkeit von Systemen," Technische Rundschau, Bern, 5.2, 1974.

[Mc 70] McIntire: "An introduction to the Illiac-IV computer," Datamation, April, pp. 60-67.

[MHB 75] Marsten, Hogan, Blankenship: "The boxstep method for large scale optimization," Operations Research, Vol. 23, 1975, pp. 389-405.

[Mi 71] Miranker: "A survey of parallelism in numerical analysis," SIAM Review, Vol. 15, 1972, pp. 524-547.

[MM 61] Morrison, Morrison: "Charles Babbage and his calculating engines," Dover Inc., NY.

[MN 71] McNamee: "Algorithm 408," Comm. ACM, Vol. 14, No. 4, 265-273.

[Mo 78] Morven-Gentleman: "Some complexity results for matrix computations," Journ. ACM, Vol. 25, 1978, pp. 112-115.

[Na 79] Nagel: "Solving linear equations with the SMS 201," Euromicro Journal, Vol. 5, No. 1, 1979, pp. 53-54.

[NF 73] Nabona, Freris: "Optimization of economic dispatch through quadratic and linear programming, Proc. IEE (London) Vol. 120, No. 5, pp. 574-580.

[No 69] Noble: "Applied Linear Algebra," Prentice-Hall 1969.

[Or 67] Ortega: "The Givens-Householder method for symmetric matrices," in (Ra 67), pp. 94-115.

[OR 70] Ortega and Rheinboldt: "Iterative solutions of nonlinear equations in several variables," Academic Press 1970.

[Pe 67] Pease: "Matrix inversion using parallel processing," Journ. ACM, Vol. 14, No. 4, 1967, pp. 757-764.

[Pe 69] Pease: "Inversion of matrices by partitioning," Journ. ACM, Vol. 16, pp. 302-314.

[Rb 70] Robert: "Méthodes itératives "serie parallèle," C.R. Acad.Sc. Paris, 271.

[Re 74] Reyling: "Performance and control of multiple microprocessor systems," Computer Design, 1974, pp. 81-86.

[Re 71] Reid: "Large, sparse sets of linear equations," Academic press, 1971.

[RH 73] Reid, Hasdorff: "Economic dispatch using quadratic programming," Trans. IEEE, Vol. PAS-92, 1973, pp. 2015-2023.

[RLT 78] Randell, Lee, Treleaven: "Reliability issues in computing system design," Computing Surveys, ACM, Vol. 10, No. 2, pp. 123-165.

[Ro 76] Rose, Tarjan, Luecker: Algorithmic Aspects of vertex elimination on graphs. SIAM J. Comput., Vol. 5, No. 2, June 1876.

[Ros 70] Rose: "Triangulated graphs and the elimination process," J. Math. Anal. Appl. 32 (1970), pp. 597-609.

[RR 78] Ralston, Rabinowitz: "A first course in numerical analysis," McGraw-Hill.

[Ru 76] Rutishauser: "Vorlesungen uber numerische Mathematik," Birkhauser Co.

[Ru 77] Russo: "Interprocessor communication for multimicrocomputer system," Computer, April 1977, pp. 67-76.

[RW 60] Ralston, Wilf: "Mathematical methods for digital computers.

[RW 67] Second part of [RW 60]. Both J. Wiley.

[RW 81] Richter, Wallach: "Remarks on real-time, master-slaves operating system," Microprocessing and Microprogramming.

[Sa 77] Sameh: "Numerical Parallel Algorithims, a Survey," in (KLS 77), pp. 207-228.

[SB] Stoer, Bulirsch: "Introduction to numerical analysis," Springer Verlag, 1980.

[SBM 62] Slotnick, Borck, McReynolds: "The SOLOMON computer," FJCC, Vol. 22, pp. 97-107.

[SB 77] Sameh, Brent: "Solving triangular systems on a parallel computer," SIAM Journ. Num. Analysis, Vol. 14, No. 6, pp. 1101-1113.

[Sch 75] Schomberg: "A special purpose computer for partial differentil equations," AICA Conference, pp. 187-191.

[SE 68] Stagg, El-Abiad: "Computer methods in power system analysis," McGraw-Hill.

[SFS 76] Swan, Fuller, Sieworek: "Structure and architecture of Cm*: a modular multimicroprocessor," Comp. Science Research Review, CMU, 1975-1976.

[Sh 55] Sheldon: "On the numerical solution of elliptic difference equations," Math. Tables Aids Comput., 9, pp. 101-112 (1965).

[SH 74] Schweppe, Handschin: "Static state estimation in power systems," Proc. IEEE, Vol. 62, No. 7, pp. 972-982, July 1974.

[SRS 73] Schwarz, Rutishauser, Stiefel: "Numerical Analysis of Symmetric Matrices," Prentice-Hall, 1973.

[St 69] Strassen: "Gaussian elimination is not optimal," Numerische Mathematik, 13, pp. 354-356, 1969.

[St 73] Stone: "Problems of parallel computation (in Complexity of Sequential and Parallel Numerical Algorithms," in (Tr 73).

[SW 78] Shimor, Wallach: "A multibus-oriented parallel processor system - Mopps," Trans. IEEE, Vol. IECI-25, No. 2, pp. 137-142.

[Ta 72] Tarjan: "Depth-first search and linear graph algorithms," SIAM J. Compt., 1, pp. 146-169, 1972.

[TH 67] Tinney, Hart: "Power-flow solution by Newton's method," Trans. IEEE, Vol. PAS-86, No. 11, pp. 1449-1460.

[Thu 72] Thurber, et al.: "A systematic approach to the design of digital bussing structures," FJCC, 1972, pp. 719-740.

[Thu 76] Thurber: "Large scale computer architecture," Hayden Co., 1976.

[TL 80] Tomann, Liedl: "Reliability in microcomputer arrays," Microprocessing and Microprogramming, Vol. 7, No. 3, pp. 185-190.

[TP 73] Thurber, Patton: "The future of parallel processing," Trans. IEEE, Vol. C-15, pp. 1140-1143,

[Tr 73] Traub (Ed.): Symposium on Complexity of Sequential and Parallel Numerical Algorithms, Academic Press, 1973.

[TW 75] Thurber, Wald: "Associative and parallel processors," Comp. Surveys, Vol. 7, No. 4, pp. 215-255.

[TW 67] Tinney, Walker: "Direct solution of sparse network equations by optimally ordered triangular factorization," Proc. IEEE.

[TW 78] Tolub, Wallach: "Sorting on a MIMD-type parallel processing system," Euromicro-Journal, No. 4, 1978, pp. 155-161.

[Va 62] Varga: "Matrix iterative analysis," Prentice-Hall, 1962.

[Wa 68] Wallach: "Gradient methods for load-flow problems," Trans. IEEE, Vol. PAS-87, No. 5, 1968, pp. 1314-1318.

[Wa 74] Wallach: "Parallel processor systems in power-dispatch," IEEE, Summer Power Meeting, July 1974, Papers (74334-9 and C74335-6).

[Wa 75] Wallach: "On the use of rectangular coordinates in load-flow problems," Israel Journ. of Techn., (in English), Vol. 13, No. 6, pp. 377-385.

[Wa 77a] Wallach: "Scheduling of algorithms for concurrent execution," The Comp. Journ., Vol. 28, No. 2, 1977, pp. 132-136.

[Wa 77b] Wallach: "MIMD-type parallel processing in electric power control in (EP 77), pp. 287-308.

[Wa 78] Wallach: "Remarks on parallelization of economic dispatch calculations," VI Power Systems Computation Conference, 1978, pp.

[Wa 81] Wallach: "Alternating sequential/parallel processing," Trans. IEEE, Vol. PAS-101, pp.

[Wa 81b] Wallach: "Alternating Sequential/Parallel methods of calculating eigenvalues of symmetric matrices," to appear in Computing.

[WB 69] Wallach, Bar-Levi: "On the direct solution of Dirichlets problem in two dimensions," Computing, Vol. 5, No. 3, pp. 45-56.

[WB 72] Wulf, Bell: "C.mmp - a multi-miniprocessor," F.J.C.C., Vol. 98, pp. 765-777, 1972.

[WC 76] Wallach, Conrad: "Parallel solutions of load-flow problems," Archiv für Elektrotechnik, Vol. 57, 1976, pp. 345-354.

[WC 77] Wallach, Conrad: "Fast algorithms for load-flow problems," Archiv für Elektrotechnik, 1977, Vol. 59, No. 1, pp. 61-68.

[WC 79a] Wallach, Conrad: "Fast methods of state estimation," IEEE, Winter Power Meeting, 1979, paper A79034-0.

[WC 79b] Wallach, Conrad: "On efficient solutions of load-flow problems," Archiv für Elektr. (in English), Vol. 61, No. 1, 1979, pp. 1-6.

[WE 67] Wallach, Even: "Application of Newtons method to load-flow calculations," Proc. IEE (London), Vol. 114, No. 2, 1967, pp. 372-374.

[We 68] Westlake: "A handbook of numerical matrix inversion and solution of linear equations," John Wiley, 1968.

[We 80] Weitzman: "Distributed micro/minicomputer systems," Prentice-Hall.

[WEY 71] Wallach, Even, Yavin: "Improved methods for load-flow calculations," Trans. IEEE, Vol. PAS-90, No. 1, 1971, pp. 116-122.

[Wh 76] White (ed.): "Multiprocessor systems," Infotech Report VII, 1976, Infotech Limited, Nicholson House, Maidenhead, Berks, England, SL6 ILD.

[WH 77] Wing, Huang: "A parallel triangularization process of sparse matrices," Proc. International Conf. on Parallel Processing (IEEE, 77CH 1253-4C) August 1977, pp. 207-214.

[WHB 81] Wallach, Handschin, Bongers: "An efficient parallel processing method for power system state estimation," Trans. IEEE, Vol. PAS-101, pp.

[Wi 65] Wilkinson: "The Algebraic Eigenvalue Problem," Clarendon Press, 1965.

[Wi 68] Winograd: "A new algorithm for inner product," IEEE Trans. on Computers, Vol. C-17, No. 7, pp. 693-694, July 1968.

[WL 80] Wallach, Leven: "Alternating sequential/Parallel versions of the Simplex Algorithm," Euromicro Journal, Vol. 6, pp. 237-242.

[WS 80] Wallach, Shimor: "Alternating Sequential/Parallel methods for FFT," Trans. IEEE, ASSP-28, No. 2, pp. 236-242.

[YF 77] Yau, Fung: "Associative Processor Architecture - A Survey," Computing Surveys, Vol. 9, pp. 3-28.

[YG] Young, Gregory: "A survey of numerical mathematics," Addison-Wesley, 1973.

[Yo] Young: "Iterative Solution of large linear systems," Academic Press.

[Yo 70] Young: "Convergence properties of the symmetric and unsymmetric successive overrelaxation methods and related methods," Mathematics of computation, Vol. 24, No. 112, October 1970.

[Zo 71] Zollenkopf: "Bi-Factorization," pp. 75-96 of (Re 71).

INDEX

Vol. 77: G. V. Bochmann, Architecture of Distributed Computer Systems. VIII, 238 pages. 1979.

Vol. 78: M. Gordon, R. Milner and C. Wadsworth, Edinburgh LCF. VIII, 159 pages. 1979.

Vol. 79: Language Design and Programming Methodology. Proceedings, 1979. Edited by J. Tobias. IX, 255 pages. 1980.

Vol. 80: Pictorial Information Systems. Edited by S. K. Chang and K. S. Fu. IX, 445 pages. 1980.

Vol. 81: Data Base Techniques for Pictorial Applications. Proceedings, 1979. Edited by A. Blaser. XI, 599 pages. 1980.

Vol. 82: J. G. Sanderson, A Relational Theory of Computing. VI, 147 pages. 1980.

Vol. 83: International Symposium Programming. Proceedings, 1980. Edited by B. Robinet. VII, 341 pages. 1980.

Vol. 84: Net Theory and Applications. Proceedings, 1979. Edited by W. Brauer. XIII, 537 Seiten. 1980.

Vol. 85: Automata, Languages and Programming. Proceedings, 1980. Edited by J. de Bakker and J. van Leeuwen. VIII, 671 pages. 1980.

Vol. 86: Abstract Software Specifications. Proceedings, 1979. Edited by D. Bjørner. XIII, 567 pages. 1980

Vol. 87: 5th Conference on Automated Deduction. Proceedings, 1980. Edited by W. Bibel and R. Kowalski. VII, 385 pages. 1980.

Vol. 88: Mathematical Foundations of Computer Science 1980. Proceedings, 1980. Edited by P. Dembiński. VIII, 723 pages. 1980.

Vol. 89: Computer Aided Design - Modelling, Systems Engineering, CAD-Systems. Proceedings, 1980. Edited by J. Encarnacao. XIV, 461 pages. 1980.

Vol. 90: D. M. Sandford, Using Sophisticated Models in Resolution Theorem Proving.
XI, 239 pages. 1980

Vol. 91: D. Wood, Grammar and L Forms: An Introduction. IX, 314 pages. 1980.

Vol. 92: R. Milner, A Calculus of Communication Systems. VI, 171 pages. 1980.

Vol. 93: A. Nijholt, Context-Free Grammars: Covers, Normal Forms, and Parsing. VII, 253 pages. 1980.

Vol. 94: Semantics-Directed Compiler Generation. Proceedings, 1980. Edited by N. D. Jones. V, 489 pages. 1980.

Vol. 95: Ch. D. Marlin, Coroutines. XII, 246 pages. 1980.

Vol. 96: J. L. Peterson, Computer Programs for Spelling Correction: VI, 213 pages. 1980.

Vol. 97: S. Osaki and T. Nishio, Reliability Evaluation of Some Fault-Tolerant Computer Architectures. VI, 129 pages. 1980.

Vol. 98: Towards a Formal Description of Ada. Edited by D. Bjørner and O. N. Oest. XIV, 630 pages. 1980.

Vol. 99: I. Guessarian, Algebraic Semantics. XI, 158 pages. 1981.

Vol. 100: Graphtheoretic Concepts in Computer Science. Edited by H. Noltemeier. X, 403 pages. 1981.

Vol. 101: A. Thayse, Boolean Calculus of Differences. VII, 144 pages. 1981.

Vol. 102: J. H. Davenport, On the Integration of Algebraic Functions. 1–197 pages. 1981.

Vol. 103: H. Ledgard, A. Singer, J. Whiteside, Directions in Human Factors of Interactive Systems. VI, 190 pages. 1981.

Vol. 104: Theoretical Computer Science. Ed. by P. Deussen. VII, 261 pages. 1981.

Vol. 105: B. W. Lampson, M. Paul, H. J. Siegert, Distributed Systems – Architecture and Implementation. XIII, 510 pages. 1981.

Vol. 106: The Programming Language Ada. Reference Manual. X, 243 pages. 1981.

Vol. 107: International Colloquium on Formalization of Programming Concepts. Proceedings. Edited by J. Diaz and I. Ramos. VII, 478 pages. 1981.

Vol. 108: Graph Theory and Algorithms. Edited by N. Saito and T. Nishizeki. VI, 216 pages. 1981.

Vol. 109: Digital Image Processing Systems. Edited by L. Bolc and Zenon Kulpa. V, 353 pages. 1981.

Vol. 110: W. Dehning, H. Essig, S. Maass, The Adaptation of Virtual Man-Computer Interfaces to User Requirements in Dialogs. X, 142 pages. 1981.

Vol. 111: CONPAR 81. Edited by W. Händler. XI, 508 pages. 1981.

Vol. 112: CAAP '81. Proceedings. Edited by G. Astesiano and C. Böhm. VI, 364 pages. 1981.

Vol. 113: E.-E. Doberkat, Stochastic Automata: Stability, Nondeterminism, and Prediction. IX, 135 pages. 1981.

Vol. 114: B. Liskov, CLU, Reference Manual. VIII, 190 pages. 1981.

Vol. 115: Automata, Languages and Programming. Edited by S. Even and O. Kariv. VIII, 552 pages. 1981.

Vol. 116: M. A. Casanova, The Concurrency Control Problem for Database Systems. VII, 175 pages. 1981.

Vol. 117: Fundamentals of Computation Theory. Proceedings, 1981. Edited by F. Gécseg. XI, 471 pages. 1981.

Vol. 118: Mathematical Foundations of Computer Science 1981. Proceedings, 1981. Edited by J. Gruska and M. Chytil. XI, 589 pages. 1981.

Vol. 119: G. Hirst, Anaphora in Natural Language Understanding: A Survey. XIII, 128 pages. 1981.

Vol. 120: L. B. Rall, Automatic Differentiation: Techniques and Applications. VIII, 165 pages. 1981.

Vol. 121: Z. Zlatev, J. Wasniewski, and K. Schaumburg, Y12M Solution of Large and Sparse Systems of Linear Algebraic Equations. IX, 128 pages. 1981.

Vol. 122: Algorithms in Modern Mathematics and Computer Science. Proceedings, 1979. Edited by A. P. Ershov and D. E. Knuth. XI, 487 pages. 1981.

Vol. 123: Trends in Information Processing Systems. Proceedings, 1981. Edited by A. J. W. Duijvestijn and P. C. Lockemann. XI, 349 pages. 1981.

Vol. 124: W. Polak, Compiler Specification and Verification. XIII, 269 pages. 1981.

Vol. 125: Logic of Programs. Proceedings, 1979. Edited by E. Engeler. V, 245 pages. 1981.

Vol. 126: Microcomputer System Design. Proceedings, 1981. Edited by M. J. Flynn, N. R. Harris, and D. P. McCarthy. VII, 397 pages. 1982.

Voll. 127: Y.Wallach, Alternating Sequential/Parallel Processing. X, 329 pages. 1982.

This series reports new developments in computer science research an teaching – quickly, informally and at a high level. The type of materi considered for publication includes:

1. Preliminary drafts of original papers and monographs
2. Lectures on a new field or presentations of a new angle in a classic field
3. Seminar work-outs
4. Reports of meetings, provided they are
   a) of exceptional interest and
   b) devoted to a single topic.

Texts which are out of print but still in demand may also be considere if they fall within these categories.

The timeliness of a manuscript is more important than its form, whic may be unfinished or tentative. Thus, in some instances, proofs may b merely outlined and results presented which have been or will late be published elsewhere. If possible, a subject index should be include Publication of Lecture Notes is intended as a service to the internationa computer science community, in that a commercial publisher, Springer Verlag, can offer a wide distribution of documents which would othe wise have a restricted readership. Once published and copyrighte they can be documented in the scientific literature.

Manuscripts

Manuscripts should be no less than 100 and preferably no more than 500 pages in length.
They are reproduced by a photographic process and therefore must be typed with extreme care. Symbo not on the typewriter should be inserted by hand in indelible black ink. Corrections to the typescri should be made by pasting in the new text or painting out errors with white correction fluid. Authors recei 75 free copies and are free to use the material in other publications. The typescript is reduced slightly size during reproduction; best results will not be obtained unless the text on any one page is kept with the overall limit of 18 x 26.5 cm (7 x 10½ inches). On request, the publisher will supply special paper w the typing area outlined.
Manuscripts should be sent to Prof. G. Goos, Institut für Informatik, Universität Karlsruhe, Zirkel 2, 7500 Karl ruhe/Germany, Prof. J. Hartmanis, Cornell University, Dept. of Computer-Science, Ithaca, NY/USA 1485 or directly to Springer-Verlag Heidelberg.

Springer-Verlag, Heidelberger Platz 3, D-1000 Berlin 33
Springer-Verlag, Neuenheimer Landstraße 28–30, D-6900 Heidelberg 1
Springer-Verlag, 175 Fifth Avenue, New York, NY 10010/USA

ISBN 3-540-11194-8
ISBN 0-387-11194-8